EUROPEAN AND INTERNATIONAL MEDIA LAW

European and International Media Law

Liberal Democracy, Trade, and the New Media

PERRY KELLER

OXFORD
UNIVERSITY PRESS

OXFORD

UNIVERSITY PRESS

Great Clarendon Street, Oxford OX2 6DP

Oxford University Press is a department of the University of Oxford.
It furthers the University's objective of excellence in research, scholarship,
and education by publishing worldwide in

Oxford New York

Auckland Cape Town Dar es Salaam Hong Kong Karachi
Kuala Lumpur Madrid Melbourne Mexico City Nairobi
New Delhi Shanghai Taipei Toronto

With offices in

Argentina Austria Brazil Chile Czech Republic France Greece
Guatemala Hungary Italy Japan Poland Portugal Singapore
South Korea Switzerland Thailand Turkey Ukraine Vietnam

Oxford is a registered trade mark of Oxford University Press
in the UK and in certain other countries

Published in the United States
by Oxford University Press Inc., New York

© P. Keller 2011

The moral rights of the author have been asserted
Database right Oxford University Press (maker)

Crown copyright material is reproduced under Class Licence
Number C01P0000148 with the permission of OPSI
and the Queen's Printer for Scotland

First published 2011

British Library Cataloguing in Publication Data
Data available

Library of Congress Cataloging in Publication Data
Library of Congress Control Number: 2011923114

Typeset by SPI Publisher Services, Pondicherry, India
Printed in Great Britain
on acid-free paper by
CPI Antony Rowe, Chippenham, Wiltshire

ISBN 978–0–19–826855–0

1 3 5 7 9 10 8 6 4 2

Contents

List of Abbreviations

ACLU	American Civil Liberties Union
ACT	Association of Commercial Television in Europe
AER	European Radio Association
AOL	America On Line
AVMS	Audiovisual Media Services
CE	Council of Europe
CERD	Convention on the Elimination of All Forms of Racial Discrimination
CODEXTER	Committee of Experts on Terrorism
CPC	Central Product Classification
CRIS	Communication Rights in the Information Society
DSU	Understanding on Rules and Procedures governing the Settlement of Disputes
EBU	European Broadcasting Union
ECE	United Nations Economic Commission for Europe (see UNECE)
ECHR	European Convention on Human Rights
ECJ	European Court of Justice
EEC	European Economic Community
EFTA	European Free Trade Association
ENPA	European Newspaper Publishers' Association
EPC	European Publishers Council
EU	European Union
EWCA	England and Wales Court of Appeal
FOIA	Freedom of Information Act
FYROM	Former Yugoslav Republic of Macedonia
GATS	General Agreement on Trade in Services
GATT	General Agreement on Tariffs and Trade
GTI	Global Transparency Initiative
ICANN	Internet Corporation for Assigned Names And Numbers
ICCPR	International Covenant on Civil and Political Rights
ICESCR	International Covenant on Economic, Social and Cultural Rights
IFIs	International Financial Institutions
IGF	Internet Governance Forum
IRA	Irish Republican Army
ISO	International Organization for Standardization
ISP	Internet service provider
ITU	International Telecommunication Union
MAI	Multilateral Agreement on Investment
MFN	most favoured nation
NAFTA	North American Free Trade Agreement
NATO	North Atlantic Treaty Organization
NWICO	New World Information and Communication Order
OAS	Organization of African States
OECD	Organisation for Economic Co-operation and Development

OFCOM	Office of Communications
OSCE	Organization for Security and Co-operation in Europe
PEGI	Pan European Game Information
PTAs	Preferential Trade Agreements
SCM	Agreement on Subsidies and Countervailing Measures
SGEI	services of general economic interest
SPS	Sanitary and Phytosanitary Measure
SSCL	Services Sectoral Classification List
TBT	(Agreement on) Technical Barriers to Trade
TEU	Treaty on European Union
TFEU	Treaty on the Functioning of the European Union
TRIMS	Agreement on Trade-Related Investment Measures
TRIPS	Trade-Related Aspects of Intellectual Property Rights
UDHR	Universal Declaration of Human Rights
UN	United Nations
UNECE	United Nations Economic Commission for Europe (see ECE)
UNESCO	United Nations Educational, Scientific and Cultural Organization
VPRT	The German Association of Commercial Radio and Telecommunications Providers
WGIG	World Group on Internet Governance
WSIS	World Summit on the Information Society
WTO	World Trade Organization

Table of Cases

EUROPEAN UNION (GENERAL COURT)

EUROPEAN ECONOMIC AREA (EFTA COURT)

COUNCIL OF EUROPE (EUROPEAN COURT OF HUMAN RIGHTS)

COUNCIL OF EUROPE (EUROPEAN COMMISSION OF HUMAN RIGHTS)

INTERNATIONAL CENTRE ON SETTLEMENT
OF INVESTMENT DISPUTES

PERMANENT COURT OF INTERNATIONAL JUSTICE

INTERNATIONAL COURT OF JUSTICE

INTERNATIONAL CRIMINAL TRIBUNAL
FOR THE FORMER YUGOSLAVIA

NATIONAL CASES (AUSTRALIA)

NATIONAL CASES (FRANCE)

NATIONAL CASES (UNITED KINGDOM)

NATIONAL CASES (UNITED STATES)

Table of Treaties

Table of Legislation

EUROPEAN UNION (JOINT ACTIONS AND FRAMEWORK DECISIONS)

EUROPEAN UNION (DECISIONS)

Commission

Table of Declarations, Resolutions, and Other Non-Binding Instruments

EUROPE (EUROPEAN UNION)

Declarations

Recommendations

Resolutions

Communications

EUROPE (COUNCIL OF EUROPE)

Declarations

Recommendations

INTERNATIONAL (UNITED NATIONS)

Resolutions

Other

INTERNATIONAL (WORLD TRADE ORGANIZATION)

Declarations

Communications

Introduction

This book explains contemporary European and international media law from a liberal democratic perspective. To accomplish this broad objective, it describes domestic media law as, very simply, the set of rules that the state uses to define its relationship with the media and to manage, as best it can, the public information environment in which it exists. Control of that relationship has been essential to the security, authority, and legitimacy of the state since the first appearance of the print media in the pamphlets and posters of the 1600s. Aside from the media's potential to incite public disaffection or even violence towards the state and to disclose its secrets, media publications threaten intrusion into the privacy of individuals and the ruin of their reputations as well as exposure of households and communities to grossly offensive images and comment. The state that cannot contain those threats to itself and the public will struggle to survive.

Yet, for all that, the flow of information and ideas is also indispensable to many governmental aims, whether democratic or authoritarian in nature. Without a sufficient flow of accurate information, commerce cannot flourish and the public is often left confused and apprehensive and, moreover, unable to participate effectively in democratic life. States have consequently been compelled to balance their many reasons for restricting publication with sufficient laxity to obtain the benefits of an active media. Indeed, the state often intervenes to promote its public policy goals by encouraging media publication or even taking charge of that process itself.

The relationship between the media and the state has nonetheless always been in flux and is rarely under the complete control of any state. For centuries, the publication of media content has been driven forward by the pursuit of revenue and profit harnessed to an unquenchable consumer demand for news and entertainment. The speed and reach of media publication has also steadily increased as commercial forces, sometimes aided or supplanted by the state, have exploited new communication technologies. In the media state relationship, the state is therefore usually on the back foot, adapting its legal and administrative powers to an ever enlarging sphere of public communication. However, in that process, the state has enjoyed the ultimate advantage of coercive power, which it can deploy against the vulnerable processes of content production and distribution, including editors and journalists as well as printers, book sellers, and broadcasting managers. The rise of the internet has however threatened to overturn that long standing advantage.

Even in countries as dedicated to close control over media content as China, the current communications revolution, in which mass and personal as well as foreign and domestic communication have merged, has created new forms of media that severely challenge the state's capacity to set the boundaries of public information. As China has demonstrated, it is only with resources and ingenuity that the state can make its territorial boundaries felt in the contemporary global flow of information and ideas.

Beyond commerce and technology, the relationship between the media and the state has developed under political and social pressures that fostered markedly different ideas about the purposes and limits of the state. It is here that liberalism has made its special mark on media law and policy, providing a rich store of ideas and arguments favouring an expansive sphere of speech and publication that is comparatively free from interference by others. Liberalism's emphasis on media freedom is grounded in its fundamental concern for personal liberty, which is often bound to a deep suspicion of the motives and methods of the state. Yet the broad tradition of liberal thought also carries other concerns about personal autonomy that emphasize the dignity and well being of the individual and severely complicate rights to speak and publish freely where expression causes harm.

This awkward balancing of liberty and restraint has been a central issue in liberal thought since the Enlightenment and the elevation of individual freedom and well being to the first rank of moral and political concerns. Consequently, the argument that the liberty to publish is essential to democratic forms of government, enabling an informed citizenry, has played a pivotal role in curbing legitimate claims for restraint and protection from harmful and offensive publications. Accordingly, where there is a public interest in wider access to information, the protection of collective and individual security and well being should yield to the needs of democracy and the open scrutiny of public authorities and affairs. These consequential aims are also profoundly liberal democratic, embracing the accountability of democratic government and the pursuit of effectiveness and integrity in public administration. When coupled with economic arguments for efficiency and consumer choice through the liberalization of markets for media goods and services, this consequentialism gives liberal democracy a generally coherent and stable approach to problems of freedom of expression. In the internet era, this has moreover provided a basic point of reference for the development of law and policy in a fast changing public information environment.

This critically important relationship between the media and the liberal democratic state is at the heart of this book. However, its focus is not on the problems of particular liberal democracies in maintaining effective control over public information in the midst of a communications revolution. As much as the media state relationship is defined by the territorial state, it has never been easily contained within those boundaries. Information and ideas, whether in printed form or transmitted by wireless or wired means, have always flowed or seeped across borders. Maintaining state control over the domestic public information environment has therefore involved constant tending of the state's defences against unwanted foreign sourced content. In addition to unilateral measures, governments have also looked to like minded, neighbouring states for assistance in combatting illicit publications and transmissions. Indeed, as cross border communications have grown in scale and complexity so too have efforts to cooperate regionally and internationally in areas of mutual concern. The focus of this book is therefore on the comparatively successful effort to entrench liberal economic and political principles into the laws and institutions of European public order, which has had profound consequences for domestic media law and policy across Europe. It is also on equally long running efforts to entrench those same principles into international public order.

Since World War II, cooperation between states on media content standards and communications infrastructures has been gradually subsumed into the fabric of newly constructed regional and international legal regimes. In Europe, the world's pre-eminent regional order, domestic media law is now enmeshed in thickly layered rules broadly founded on market based economic relations and political liberalism. In the international sphere, parallel efforts to entrench liberal economic and political values in the institutions and agreements that support a nascent global public order have been markedly less successful. Undoubtedly, in establishing the WTO, the United States and its allies seized a critical moment with the collapse of the Soviet Union to secure the foundations of a market based, global economic order. However, despite a near decade of multilateral negotiations in the Doha Round, the aspirations of the WTO treaties have yet to be fulfilled. The bold assumption that the post Cold War era would see a worldwide triumph of political liberalism has moreover proven even less credible. On the contrary, it appears that the global entrenchment of liberal economic relations has left behind the liberal democratic political project, accepting participation by any form of government provided it trades on a market basis.

Despite their profound differences, the European regional order and the international patchwork of regimes share common features that are immensely important to the future of domestic media law. In both spheres, the core treaties embrace the idea that the legitimacy of state conduct, both internal and external, should be determined according to supranational, objective legal standards. As a result, European and international law claim to set out the boundaries for legitimate state conduct generally and, more specifically, the proper conduct of the state in relation to the media.

Structural similarities in European and international law have also caused them to share two fundamental weaknesses. The first of these stems from the awkward relationship between supranational obligations and national sovereignty. In European and international legal regimes, the limits of national sovereignty are defined by the scope of member state obligations and any permitted exceptions or rights of derogation. The gradual deepening of European and international obligations has however kept these boundaries between national and supranational authority in constant flux, causing perpetual uncertainty in domestic law. Secondly, efforts to establish European and global public order have been built on a clear, formal separation between the fields of economic and human rights law. This separation had many advantages, not the least ensuring that each regime could develop with distinct, manageable goals. Nonetheless, it also created a deep fault line that has not only created enormous problems for the coherence and consistency of European and international law, but has also severely complicated the relationship of supranational and domestic law.

In the media sector, where commercial, social, and political issues are often inseparable, the distinction between supranational economic and human rights obligations has rendered domestic law more opaque and unpredictable. A media claim, for example, that the state should not interfere with the publication of a particular piece of information can be pursued as an economic rights claim or as a human rights claim. While that is perhaps a useful conceptual distinction at the domestic level, it is not useful that those claims are oriented towards different fields of European and international law. Even worse, in supranational economic law, there have historically been virtually no substantive obligations that protect collective or individual interests from harmful media publications. While these are often covered through various exceptions to trade and market access obligations, it is only in the human rights field that they have received positive protection from the outset. Supranational economic law has therefore always held certain advantages for an argument for greater liberty to publish and distribute media content, attracting forum shopping by claimants and forum shifting by negotiating governments.

Constitutionalism has been the most obvious solution to the deep structural problems of European and international law. A constitutional framework of common values and principles offers a basis on which the ambiguous interface between national autonomy and supranational obligations as well as the equally difficult one between supranational economic and human rights law can be resolved. Europe moreover has moved a long way in this direction. Most recently, the member states have adopted the Treaty of Lisbon, which not only made the Charter of Fundamental Rights legally binding for most member states and paved the way for the EU to become a party to the European Convention on Human Rights, but also strengthened the basis for non-market public policy measures in EU Law. In contrast, the international sphere remains fragmented. Many questions about the limits of national autonomy and the relationship between different regimes are far from resolution. The interface between international economic and human rights law is especially weak, to the extent that human rights issues are more likely to arise in the WTO as a matter of domestic public policy than through any articulation of principle by UN human rights bodies.

From a liberal democratic perspective, constitutionalism offers several notable benefits for the development of European and international media law. Doctrinal coherence, based on liberal economic and political values, that closes the gap between economic and human rights law is essential in creating a more stable relationship between supranational and domestic media law. In addition, constitutionalist methods bring greater uniformity to domestic law, which is also plainly beneficial in an era of instantaneous cross border communication and media globalization. There are nonetheless many objections to supranational constitutionalism, some of which are particularly significant for the media state relationship. Media law is intensely local. It is always uniquely important to its place, reflecting differences in languages, religious faiths, popular beliefs and traditions, political preferences, and even the consequences of local geography. Equally important, the media state relationship is always changing, even while enmeshed in local circumstances. This not only involves change through the developments of communication technologies or media services referred to above, but also through the evolution of the state itself. The contemporary liberal democratic state, highly porous and interlinked with non-state institutions and networks, has broadened its methods of law and administration. In the media sector, many governments have, for example, turned to methods of co and self regulation to maintain more effective and responsive control over new media services.

The aims of supranational constitutionalism, including coherence and consistency across boundaries, are often at odds with this diversity in local circumstances and methods of law and regulation. European and international rule making and adjudication are clearly designed to allow member states sufficient leeway to implement their obligations in ways that suit national circumstances. Nonetheless, the logic of common obligations means that that margin of discretion should not be so wide that participating states are able to avoid the central purposes of those obligations. In Europe, the incorporation of many new member states has moreover depended on the rigour and integrity of regional economic and human rights rules, especially considering that new member states are often in transition from a non-democratic past.

There is however no bright line that separates illiberal and liberal practices. A common rule for member states, even when flexible, will also eliminate public policy choices and measures that are plainly justifiable on liberal democratic grounds. It is, as a result, impossible in European law to fully accommodate American constitutional principles on freedom of expression. The structure of the European Convention on Human Rights and an irreversible commitment to proportionality analysis have frequently placed American preferences for greater liberty to speak and publish outside the bounds of European law.

In the international sphere, differences in national media law and policy are less often confined by common obligations. More often, these differences have proven to be a roadblock to agreement. In the international human rights field, the implications of the right to freedom of expression remain contentious. There is certainly no universal or even general consensus that this right bears an exclusively liberal democratic meaning and, as influence over global affairs shifts away from the western democracies, that goal will not be achieved in the foreseeable future. Even in the field of trade relations, where the principle of market based trade is widely accepted, many governments, including major liberal democracies, have rejected the application of that principle to trade in media goods and services, demanding strong protections for their non-market public policies.

Constitutionalist objectives in the international sphere, especially in relation to media law and policy, are therefore highly problematic. On one hand, a constitutionalist vision of global public order, in some form, is probably an unavoidable necessity. Liberal democracy is also likely to remain at the heart of that vision. Although its reputation has waned considerably since the end of the Cold War, no significant competing intellectual framework has emerged to provide an alternative understanding of the role of the state or the structure of international order. Authoritarian capitalism is, so far, an exception to the liberal democratic project rather than an alternative vision of world order.

On the other hand, the communications revolution has ruptured the traditional media state relationship. The increasing globalization of media services has over-turned once effective methods of state control, including methods of cooperation between states to manage content standards. Consequently, while public exposure to new ideas, images, and information has broadened exponentially, governments have needed to reconsider their basic goals for media content and look for ways to achieve them. The media state relationship has therefore become volatile and unpredictable. Given how widely states range in their politics and capacities, it is thus not surprising that international human rights and trade law have failed to provide a common understanding of the nature of the media state relationship or how it should be encompassed within any notion of global public order.

It is not obvious that the resolution of that problem lies in liberal democratic constitutionalism. Ultimately, this is a test of liberalism's claim to universality and its argument that legitimate differences can be accommodated through mutual tolerance. In the internet era, however, the clash of different ideas and beliefs has gone well beyond the scope of liberal tolerance. The liberal democratic model, whether in a European or other form, is unacceptable in the wider international sphere, at least not before a radical dilution of its liberalism. From this perspective, the concept of legal pluralism seems to provide a better description of the present conflict of radically different views on the future of the media state relationship.

Part I of *European and International Media Law* looks first at the changing relationship between the media and the state from an internal perspective, focusing on the effects of new technologies and services as well as the liberal and democratic context for those changes. It then expands the focus to European and international law, explaining how domestic media law fits within supranational economic and human rights frameworks. Part II of this book then examines the principal obliga-tions, exceptions, and rights of derogation in European and international law that bear on the domestic media state relationship. It does not however address copy-right, which is largely beyond scope of this work. In Part III, the book covers state measures that generally have a restrictive effect on the liberty to publish. These include measures that restrict expression that directly affects the state, such as criticism of public authorities and incitement to violence, as well as measures that protect the well being of others and also preserve the authority and legitimacy of the state, including measures concerning pornography and incitement to hatred. The book concludes with Part IV, which concerns positive intervention in media markets to achieve political, social, and cultural policy goals.

PART I

MEDIA LAW AND LIBERAL DEMOCRACY

1

The New Media and the New State

Among the key relationships that define the modern state, few are more important than the extraordinary bond that exists between the media and the state. This relationship has its distant origins in the invention of the written word, which not only quickened the spread of information and ideas, but also fed the rise of government and commerce. Yet it was only with the appearance of the early mass media, in the form of printed pamphlets and newsletters, that the media state relationship truly began to emerge.[1] As printing advanced, the new vernacular press gave rise to a national public information environment that became increasingly important to the goals and health of the state.

The practice of statecraft thus became both enriched and more difficult as it became necessary for the developing modern state to maintain control over this fertile and also threatening public information environment. If the state could not achieve reasonably effective control over publishers and distributors, it risked chronic instability and loss of autonomy. In short, a state could not survive over the long term if its media operated in ways that were hostile or inconsistent with its basic claims to legitimacy and authority. Without the power to determine the boundaries of acceptable public information and entertainment, the state could not maintain its security and identity.[2] From its earliest beginnings, the media has therefore been locked in a close embrace with the state, each re-creating the other in its image.[3] While the state attempts to restrain or foster different kinds of media content to maintain its security, authority, and legitimacy, it is also being moulded by commercial and popular innovations in public communication. The struggle to define the proper limits of state control over public speech is thus one of the most potent narratives in the history of liberalism and democratic politics. Equally significant, the media state relationship was also essential to the successes of European colonization and cultural dominance. Without books, newspapers, and other printed works, Europe's colonial regimes could not have taken root and created the social and cultural foundations for contemporary globalization.

[1] Briggs, A and Burke, P., *A Social History of the Media From Gutenberg to the Internet*, 2nd edn (Polity Press, 2005), ch 3; Starr, P., *The Creation of the Media* (Basic Books, 2004), 30–33.
[2] On the relative importance of law and regulation as compared to other influences on the media, see Schauer, F., 'On the Relationship Between Press Law and Press Content,' in Cook, T. (ed.), *Freeing the Presses: The First Amendment in Action* (Louisiana State University Press, 2005).
[3] Starr, P., n. 1 above 23–46.

Over centuries, the media state relationship in Europe and elsewhere developed several common features. The first of these is that media policy and law are in constant contention with the formidable forces that drive the daily production and distribution of information and entertainment content. While these forces are rooted in the pursuit of profit and the desire for power, it is the close connection between these goals that gives the media much of its special complexity. The media is a focus for commercial investment and endeavour, but is also frequently subsidized or directed for political, religious, or social ends. Secondly, government media policies and laws are founded on multiple compromises between the prevention of harm and the promotion of benefit. In the former category, states maintain permanent legal and other defences and remedies against two, closely related, types of potential harm. The more immediate is the harm that the media may cause to the security or effectiveness of the state through threats to national security or public order, including disclosure of state secrets or incitement to violence against public authorities. This may take the form of a broad assault on the territorial or institutional integrity of the state or a narrower one that targets members of the governing elite.

The other type of harm arises where media publications threaten the well being of individuals or society generally. This may occur through incitement of religious hatred, exposure of children to violent pornography, or unauthorized publication of private information. These forms of harm challenge common social and cultural values, which are often directly or indirectly related to the state's own claims to authority and legitimacy. Incitement of ethnic hatred against indigenous and immigrant communities can, for example, also be an attack on the laws and policies that protect those communities. Consequently, in its efforts to determine and enforce the boundaries of legitimate expression, the state must, within that sphere, also decide the rules for the co-existence of incompatible beliefs and ways of life. For this reason, the media state relationship is famously rife with the intractable problems of moral pluralism.[4]

Yet, when it restricts the publication or distribution of media content, the state faces an often sharp dilemma. Restrictions on the media also threaten the benefits of convenient public access to information and entertainment content. These notably include the constant flow of information necessary for profitable commerce and effective participation in public affairs. Consequently, even states that maintain highly restrictive media content laws will typically permit specialist publications aimed at strategically important economic sectors or areas of state administration.[5] In addition, most states directly or indirectly support the production and distribution of information and entertainment content to achieve their various public policy goals. In the European liberal democratic model, this has taken the form of public service media, which are in principle charged with the provision of a

---

[4] For an overview of moral or value pluralism, see Mason, E., 'Value Pluralism', *Stanford Encyclopedia of Philosophy* (2006), (<http://plato.stanford.edu>).

[5] In China, for example, Reference News (*Cankao Xiaoxi*), a digest of news stories taken from the foreign press, was for many years restricted to Party cadres of an approved rank.

diverse range of content.[6] In contrast, in illiberal democracies or non-democratic countries, a state or quasi state agency will typically guide the media to achieve the political and social content goals of that state.[7]

Thirdly, media law is structured around the physical vulnerabilities of the media to the state's potential use of coercive force. That blunt fact certainly does not ignore the complexity of the media state relationship, which is a dynamic mix of public policy, criminal and civil law, as well as regulatory and other measures, which are nested in dense political, governmental, professional, and commercial networks. The state's management of its domestic media realm is, moreover, under relentless pressure from the inward flow of foreign produced information and entertainment content.[8] However, the state's management of this complex regime ultimately rests on its ability to use effective coercive measures. Indeed, without the capacity to act against the key individuals and facilities that are essential to the operation of the media, a state cannot hope to maintain control over its public information environment.

The major problem for the state in maintaining this grip on the media has always been that the specific vulnerabilities of the media are continually evolving. Even when a state has secured an extraordinary degree of control over the individuals and facilities within its reach and has also managed to secure its borders against foreign sources, new technologies or methods of communication have inevitably opened a breach. States are therefore permanently in pursuit of an evolving communications and media sector. That pursuit, moreover, is hampered by the state's need to maintain the flow of information and ideas important to its public policy goals and, in many cases, the need to abide by constitutional obligations that preserve freedom of expression.

While the history of the media state relationship is thus one of constant change and instability, it can nonetheless be usefully described for purposes of media law and policy in terms of three, overlapping eras; each dominated by particular sets of communications technologies. These began with the long era of print based media, which abruptly ended less than a century ago with the rapid rise of radio broadcasting. In the following decades, the new broadcast media grew dramatically in scale and power and utterly transformed the nature of public access to information and ideas. Yet the broadcast era was paradoxically short and has already given way to a third era, which is characterized by internet based communication. Plainly, broadcasting remains one of the most influential forms of media throughout much of the world and, despite devastating declines in readership in many countries, print publication is also still a significant media platform.[9] Moreover, print and broadcast

---

[6] Smith, A., 'Television as a Public Service Medium', in Smith, A. (ed), *Television: An International History* (Oxford University Press, 1995), ch 3; Nissen, C., *Public Service Media in the Information Society* (Media Division, Directorate General of Human Rights, Council of Europe, 2006).

[7] Brady, A.M., *Marketing Dictatorship: Propaganda and Thought Work in Contemporary China* (Rowman & Littlefield, 2008), ch 2: 'Guiding Hand: The Role of the Propaganda System'.

[8] See, generally, Briggs, A. and Burke, P., n. 1 above.

[9] See, for example, *State of the News Media 2010*, Pew Research Center Publications, (15 March 2010), <http://pewresearch.org>.

media companies produce much of the premium content that is distributed, with or without the owner's consent, through the internet. Nonetheless, the current revolution in communications technologies and services has not only transformed the media sector generally, introducing a plethora of new kinds of media, it has also radically changed the nature of broadcasting and print publication. Unlike the preceding broadcast media, which became a new, separate media realm, the internet has become the platform on which all media forms can merge.

In each of these eras, the character of media law has shifted according to the changing technologies and methods of media content production and delivery. Mass print publication was particularly vulnerable to the coercive power of the state. It required large, expensive machinery that was noisy even when operating on a small scale. As well, the weight of a paper publication of any size meant that transport in bulk over distances was difficult and distribution to consumers was labour intensive. Consequently, the individuals responsible for production and distribution typically needed to be present to manage these processes efficiently. The combination of these vulnerabilities made it possible for reasonably successful states to attempt to control domestic mass publication.[10] Where its customs and border controls were equally effective, no major distribution of foreign sourced, printed material could occur without the permission of the state.

Cinema films, the first genuine competitor to the print media, enjoyed several advantages over paper based publication. They did not require literacy and could be consumed simultaneously by large groups of people, thus introducing the public to the extraordinary power of entertainment and news delivered in the form of moving images. And while individual films were bulky and fragile, they could be screened many times to reach a significant audience. Indeed, the profits gained through the repeated screening of a single film were essential to the establishment of a major international trade in cinema films, which was soon centred on Hollywood in the United States.[11] Yet, to reach a significant audience, films had to be screened in publicly accessible places, typically requiring large projection equipment. This highly conspicuous public process made it relatively easy for the state to identify the individuals and facilities essential to the production and screening of cinema films. As a result, the censorship and classification of films as well as the licensing of cinemas quickly became standard government measures.[12] In addition, those governments alarmed by the social or political influence of foreign films were able to curb their domestic distribution through selective import approvals and screen quotas.[13]

---

[10] Briggs, A. and Burke, ch 3: 'The Media and the Public Sphere in Early Modern Europe', n. 1 above.

[11] Vasey, R., 'The World Wide Spread of Cinema', in Nowell-Smith, G. (ed.), *The Oxford History of World Cinema*, (Oxford University Press, 1999), 80.

[12] Maltby, R., 'Censorship and Self Regulation', in Nowell-Smith, G. (ed.), *The Oxford History of World Cinema*, (Oxford University Press, 1999), 235.

[13] See, for example, the United Kingdom's Cinematograph Films Act 1927, which introduced domestic film quotas for distributors and cinemas.

Despite the established popularity of the cinema, radio broadcasting emerged in the late 1920s to become a much more powerful form of media.[14] This occurred despite the significant disadvantage of being restricted to sound transmission, unlike the newly developed audiovisual cinema films. At the same time, like the cinemas, radio broadcasting lacked a return path for direct communication from listeners to providers, which was very unlike the nascent, fully interactive telephone services of the same period.[15] Yet radio broadcasting had particular strengths that made it a focus for acute governmental concern and excitement. As with cinema audiences, its listeners did not need to be literate, but more importantly they could receive its broadcasts in any home or other place equipped with a receiver. This gave radio broadcasting an unprecedented potential to reach and influence national audiences.

From the outset, broadcasting to the public had posed an immediate threat to a vital security interest of the state. Radio transmission was already a well developed form of military communication. Governments were therefore anxious to ensure that these communications were not disrupted by broadcasts using the same or adjacent frequencies.[16] Radio broadcasting, which itself needed a substantial share of the usable radiospectrum, was therefore soon confined to allocated frequencies and subject to licensing or direct state control.[17] As well, radio's unprecedented influence over domestic audiences provided an additional justification for governments not only to limit the number of providers, but to also to regulate their programme and advertising content.[18]

In non-democratic countries, including most colonial possessions, the advent of radio broadcasting complicated government control of the media, requiring new prohibitions, licensing controls, and content rules to ensure that domestic broadcasting, like the print media, operated in a compliant manner.[19] Certainly, the specific features of any system of media control, whether liberal democratic or otherwise, have historically varied hugely according to local circumstances. Rigorous enforcement of licensing rules may, for example, be unnecessary where

---

[14] Starr, P., n. 1 above, 327.

[15] Based on circuit switched networks and analogue transmission technology, telecommunications delivered simple voice and data services. In most cases, the high costs of establishing competing networks created natural monopolies, which were typically subject to state ownership or close regulation.

[16] Winston, B., *Media Technology and Society: A History from the Printing Press to the Superhighway* (Routledge, 1998), 70.

[17] On the history of broadcast licensing, see Horvitz, R.J., 'Media Licensing, Convergence and Globalization', 1 *EastBound* (2006) March 13.

[18] Crisell, A., *An Introductory History of British Broadcasting*, 2nd edn (Routledge, 2002).

[19] In China, for example, under the Communist Party the methods of media regulation and control in the broadcasting and print sectors have always been roughly equivalent, depending on Party membership and disciplinary systems for key editorial staff in combination with state ownership or supervision of media outlets as well as licence restrictions. On the development of the Chinese media system since the Cultural Revolution, see Zhao, Y., *Media, Market, And Democracy in China: Between the Party Line and the Bottom*, (University of Illinois, 1998), and Scotton, J. and Hachten, W., *New Media for a New China* (Wiley-Blackwell, 2010).

would-be publishers or broadcasters lack financial resources and access to essential technologies or the general population is illiterate and impoverished. Nonetheless, the logic of media control means that each new form of media must, by some means, be brought under existing content standards.

In the comparatively small number of liberal states, the new systems introduced to control broadcasting were a marked departure from a history of gradual withdrawal of the state from direct regulation of the press.[20] There were two related justifications for this policy reversal. First, the scarcity of available radiospectrum frequencies limited the number of broadcasters able to operate in any area. Secondly, the new medium had an extraordinary reach and influence over the public. The liberal democratic media model, consequently, became marked by a distinctive dichotomy in the treatment of the print and broadcast media. In the post World War II period and later in the post Cold War period, this dichotomy was replicated as liberal democracy spread more widely. The rapid growth of television in the 1950s and the subsequent development of new forms of radio and television delivery, most importantly cable, did little to disturb the reasonably effective control that many national governments enjoyed over their media sectors. Given its ultimate control over the physical processes of production and distribution, including printing presses, broadcast transmitters, telephone wires, and cable networks, the state usually held a decisive leverage over an increasingly diverse media realm. In addition, barriers to market entry, including high printing costs and spectrum scarcity, helped to ensure that only a handful of major media companies dominated national markets. While these were very often commercially and politically powerful institutions, they were also locally based and potentially vulnerable to the state.

Effective control over the national media sector was by no means universal. For countries that shared a common language with a more populous and wealthy neighbouring state, national autonomy in media matters began to decline sharply with the development of powerful terrestrial broadcast transmitters. In Canada, for example, where the majority of the population lived within reception range of well resourced, American television providers, the domestic public information environment became a cross border hybrid, especially for English speakers.[21] For non-democratic states concerned about domestic reception of foreign broadcasts, a range of measures could be taken to make access more difficult, including prohibitions on the reception of foreign broadcasts by households or local cable networks or the jamming of broadcast signals.[22] In liberal democracies, draconian measures indiscriminately blocking access to foreign content were politically unjustifiable and often unconstitutional. These governments chose instead to obstruct foreign

---

[20] Starr, P., n. 1 above, 339–346.

[21] Raboy, M., 'Canada' in Smith, A. (ed.), *Television: An International History*, 2nd edn (Oxford University Press, 1998), 162.

[22] See, for example, Yan, M., 'China and the Prior Consent Requirement: A Decade of Invasion and Counter-Invasion by Transfrontier Satellite Television', 25 *Hastings Communication & Entertainment Law Journal* (2002–2003) 265.

broadcasters with more selective measures and to subsidize domestic television programme production and distribution.[23]

In the 1980s, the Canadian predicament over cross border broadcasting soon became universal with the development of direct-to-home reception for satellite television. The wide area of reception for satellite signals, often simultaneously covering dozens of countries, created an extraordinary opportunity for commercial broadcasters. In the right circumstances, a commercial satellite television service, based in a state with a hospitable regulatory regime, could draw substantial advertising and subscription revenue out of targeted countries of reception.[24] There were nonetheless critical weaknesses in the operation of a satellite broadcasting venture. The high cost of sports, films, and other popular content as well as satellite fees, marketing services, and subscription systems formed a substantial collective barrier to market entry. Only a few, major firms could therefore operate successfully in these conditions and their revenue streams from major markets were still vulnerable to state action.[25]

Satellite broadcasters were merely remote and certainly not free from state control, although that control was comparatively relaxed in some places.[26] Under the rules of the International Telecommunication Union, a UN agency, satellite orbits and operations must be registered by a sponsoring government authority.[27] Satellite broadcasters are therefore ultimately beholden to a national government when operating a satellite or, more typically, leasing capacity.[28] In Europe, member states have therefore been able to use their collective grip on satellite facilities to establish regional standards for television content through both the European Union and the Council of Europe.[29] European coordination of content standards is, however, exceptional and reflects the continent's high levels of economic and political integration.

As the Cold War era faded, the development of satellite broadcasting coincided with a broad surge in global economic and cultural exchange.[30] These changes soon

---

[23] See, for example, United Kingdom, Marine Broadcasting Offences Act 1967 and the Council of Europe, European Agreement for the Prevention of Broadcasts transmitted from Stations outside National Territories, (CETS No.: 053).

[24] In Sweden, for example, the Swedish company Kinnevik launched a Swedish language satellite television TV3 in London in 1987 to break the monopoly of the Swedish public service broadcasting system.

[25] Collins, R., *Satellite Television in Western Europe* (Libbey, 1992).

[26] See, for example, Dyson, K., 'Luxembourg: Changing Anatomy of an International Broadcasting Power', in Dyson, K., and Humphreys, P. (eds), *The Political Economy of Communications: International and European Dimensions* (Routledge, 1990).

[27] On the international law background to satellite broadcasting in the 1980s, see Fletcher L. *The United States and the Direct Broadcast Satellite: the Politics of International Broadcasting in Space* (Oxford University Press, 1988), ch 4.

[28] See, for example, the vulnerability of Al Manar, a satellite broadcaster owned by the Lebanese political party Hezbollah, to European broadcasting authorities, despite not being established in a member state, *EU Rules and Principles on Hate Broadcasts: Frequently Asked Questions*, MEMO/05/98, (17 March 2005).

[29] See Chapter 4.

[30] On globalization, see James, H., *The End of Globalization: Lessons from the Great Depression* (Harvard University Press, 2001). See also Osterhammel, J., Petersson, N., and Geyer, D., *Globalization:*

became associated with the term 'globalization', which, at its simplest, describes the diverse ways that individuals and communities have become more closely connected across great distances. The economic dimensions of globalization have often been used to describe the essence of this process. 'Fundamentally, [globalization] is the closer integration of the countries and peoples of the world which has been brought about by the enormous reduction of costs of transportation and communication, and the breaking down of artificial barriers to the flows of goods, services, capital, knowledge, and (to a lesser extent) people across borders.'[31] Yet, as Anthony Giddens has commented, 'Globalisation is not solely, or even primarily, brought about by the integration of the world marketplace. It is driven, above all, by the advance of communications, which is creating a world where "no one is outside".'[32]

The idea that communications technologies and services are at the heart of globalization is important both as a claim of fact and as a public policy intuition. As a functional matter, there is considerable truth in the observation that communications and media services have been essential to the process of globalization. Without convenient, reliable communication systems, the torrent of cross border information flows that have made globalization possible would not exist. However, the symbolic importance of the communications and media sectors to cultural and social concerns has often loomed even larger in the public policy sphere, sometimes well beyond their measurable impact. For a brief period, satellite television broadcasting became identified as a primary vehicle for the flow of information and ideas across borders and the resulting economic and social opportunities and dislocation. Satellite broadcasting therefore became a focus for public policy work, which led to major developments in national legislation and regulation.[33] It also had a significant impact on European and international law and policy making and led to the adoption of important instruments setting out common principles for the treatment of foreign satellite services.[34] The sensitivity of these issues for many states however just as often frustrated agreement or resulted in awkward, unresolved compromises.[35] Increasingly, the clash of different national media policies, frequently grounded in deeply held political and social beliefs, was becoming an inescapable feature of domestic media law and policy.

A Short History (Princeton University Press, 2005); Robertson, R., *Globalization: Social Theory and Global Culture* (Sage, 1992).

[31] Stiglitz, J.E., *Globalization and its Discontents* (Penguin Books, 2006), 9, see also 22.

[32] Giddens, A., 'Talking to the Planet' *The Guardian* (16 December 2002), Media, 7.

[33] See, for example, the special provisions introduced into the United Kingdom Broadcasting Act 1990, which protected domestic satellite broadcasters not only from public service obligations, but also from European content quotas. See also Case C-222/94, *Commission v. United Kingdom* [1996] ECR I-4025.

[34] See Chapters 4, 5, and 6.

[35] On the attempted negotiation of a liberalization of audiovisual services during the Uruguay Round trade negotiations, see Chapter 5.

Technologies of liberty and equality

Satellite television broadcasting gave many governments a foretaste of the confrontation of ideas and ways of life that has now become synonymous with the internet revolution. Like broadcasting, the internet emerged through a critical combination of technological and institutional developments that transformed the ways in which people access and experience information and entertainment media. The internet however has not followed broadcasting to become yet another distinct communications and media platform following its own separate trajectory of development. The internet is part of a wider communications revolution that, in much of the world, has made the idea of separate forms of media obsolete.[36] The internet era is the era of convergence: the merger of media, telecommunications and information technologies, infrastructures, and services.[37] These changes have shaken apart distinctions accumulated through a century of developments in technologies and services. In that now vanishing world, each electronic communications and media service was characterized by the dedicated domestic appliance needed to receive it: telephones provided voice telecommunication services and televisions provided linear audiovisual services. With convergence, the same service could be delivered to the consumer over a variety of communications platforms.[38] Audiovisual programmes, once exclusive to broadcast networks, could therefore be streamed through the internet or broadcast over mobile phone networks. Equally, a single platform could deliver a variety of previously separated services. The traditional twisted-pair copper wiring once devoted to voice telephone calls could, for example, be adapted to provide broadband access to the internet.

Of the many technological achievements that lie behind this communications revolution, the most pervasive was certainly digitization. The boundaries separating different forms of media were based on technological barriers that prevented the convenient, cost effective transfer of content from one form to another. Indeed, national media laws and regulation were shaped by the presumption that each form of media was readily distinguishable according to the nature of its content and the means of its delivery. With digitization, media providers were able to record and transmit text, sound, and images (both still and moving) in common digital

---

[36] Winston, B., n. 16 above, 134.

[37] For discussions of convergence and its effects on the media see OFCOM, *What is Convergence? A Submission to the Convergence Think Tank* (7 February 2008); Joan Shorenstein Center on the Press, Politics and Public Policy, *Creative Destruction: An Exploratory Look at News on the Internet* (John F. Kennedy School of Government, Harvard University, 2007); Nissen, C., *Public Service Media in the Information Society* (Media Division, Directorate General of Human Rights, Council of Europe, 2006).

[38] European Commission, *Green Paper on the Convergence of the Telecommunications, Media and Information Technology Sectors, and the Implications for Regulation. Towards an Information Society Approach*, COM (97) 623, 1. See also Standage, T. 'Your Television is Ringing' *The Economist* (12 October 2006).

formats, thus effectively collapsing these long standing barriers.[39] These new capabilities were moreover not limited to major content providers and rapidly became available to individual users. Even the single blogger operating at home could instantly store or transmit digitized content, from text to audiovisual, in unprecedented volumes through different communications channels, regardless of geographical distance.[40] On the other hand, it took nearly two decades for the promises of convergence to become a significant reality for middle class households. Moreover, for many others who lack access to advanced communications infrastructures and services, full participation in the era of convergence has yet to occur. Conversion to digital broadcast signals, for example, has taken years of planning and in many countries is far from complete.[41] The current communications revolution has also been costly, featuring spectacular investment bubbles that have exploded into public and private losses.[42]

Each of the three sectors central to convergence—media, telecommunications, and information technology—brought its own conceptual and regulatory history to the internet era. Of these three, the policy environment of the information technology sector was particularly important in forming early regulatory assumptions about the internet. Unlike the broadcasting and telecommunications sectors, information technology services were largely unregulated. These services were typically provided by stand alone, or minimally networked, computers that depended on the transfer of data through a simple physical carrier medium, such as a diskette. There were apparently no natural monopolies in the supply of hardware or software and few economic justifications for sector specific regulation. In the United States, the unregulated, market driven information technology sector provided the birth place for the internet.[43] Not surprisingly, this environment encouraged a vibrant celebration of the liberty enhancing potential for internet based communication. Excitement about the inherent freedom enhancing qualities of the internet was matched by a deep hostility towards government regulatory intervention. To many, it seemed that, in the new world of 'cyberspace', individuals

---

[39] McKinsey & Company, *Comparative Review of Content Regulation*, Report for the Independent Television Commission (1 May 2002).

[40] Andersen, A., *Outlook of the Development of Technologies and Markets for the European Audiovisual Sector up to 2010*, (Directorate General for Education and Culture, European Commission, 2002), 136–137.

[41] Dwivedi, Y.K ., Papazafeiropoulou, A., and Choudrie, J. (eds), *Handbook of Research in Global Diffusion of Broadband Data Transmission* (IGI Global, 2008). On the financial and social costs of conversion of national television infrastructures to digital carriage, see, for example, Analysys Limited, *Public Policy Treatment of Digital Terrestrial Television (DTT) in Communications Markets, Final Report for the European Commission* (2005).

[42] Honan, M. and Leckart, S., '10 Years After: A Look Back at the Dotcom Boom and Bust', *Wired* (March 2010).

[43] 'The Internet is more closely associated with IT and software industries than with telecommunications whose infrastructure it uses. Whilst the network over which much of the Internet traffic flows is subject to detailed regulation; the organisation, management and allocation of resources within the Internet has been largely industry and user led.' European Commission, *Green Paper on the Convergence of the Telecommunications, Media and Information Technology Sectors, and the Implications for Regulation. Towards an Information Society Approach* COM (97) 623, 38.

and communities could find market based or consensual answers to their problems, free from the clumsy hands of the state.[44]

The development of the internet was in many ways radically different than the advent of any previous sets of innovative communications technologies, including the printing press. Certainly, the internet was similar in simply making it much easier than before to express and communicate information and ideas to others. It also however brought new features that not only broke down a host of boundaries between forms of personal and mass communication, but also overturned a mass media model that had endured for centuries. Until the internet, publishers and broadcasters packaged and delivered information and entertainment content to readers, listeners, and viewers who were, by force of circumstances, largely passive recipients. Through digitization, specific kinds of content were freed from particular methods of delivery. The audiovisual programme, for example, was no longer tied to scheduled delivery into the home through traditional linear television, gradually becoming available on a range of electronic platforms, including digital linear television, video on demand, internet streamed video, and mobile network video. Consumers therefore began to view discrete segments of content, such as audiovisual programmes, as products in themselves that were entirely separate from whatever means used to view them.[45] In the same way, printed newspapers became no more than a convenient 'wrapper' for content that could easily be found online or through broadcast services.

Equally, if not more important, the current communications revolution gave content recipients the opportunity to be their own content producers. From simple beginnings, such as the ability to post text or images on personal webpages, user generated content has become an extraordinary global flood of mixed original and re-used content that appears in a multitude of forms and manners.[46] These now notably include video posting, social networking, blogging, tweeting, and participation in virtual game worlds. The leading providers that support these kinds of third party content are often commercially operated companies, which have pursued business models involving substantial openness and accessibility for internet users.[47]

Beyond these new ways for individuals to make information and ideas available, the internet era also brought the interactivity of personal communication into the mass media sector. Indeed, interactivity quickly became one of the essential features used to distinguish new from old media services, although that distinction also quickly became obsolete. Established media organizations began not only to make

---

[44] Johnson, D. and Post, D., 'Law and Borders—The Rise of Law in Cyberspace', 48 *Stanford Law Review* (1996), 1367.

[45] For a discussion of this trend, see McKinsey & Company, n. 39 above.

[46] For different views over the past decade regarding the development of new media services, see Andersen, A., n. 40 above; OECD, *Participative Web and User Produced Content: Web 2.0, Wikis and Social Networking* (OECD Publishing, 2007); 'A World of Connections: A Special Report on Social Networking', *The Economist* (January 2010).

[47] Facebook is currently the most notable example of this business model. On information openness and privacy concerns regarding Facebook, see Grimmelmann, J., 'Saving Facebook', 94 *Iowa Law Review* (2009), 1137.

their own content available through branded websites, but also to create interactive elements that permitted users to comment and otherwise contribute to these websites. In parallel, the digitization of broadcast services opened the way for interactive listener and viewer participation, famously including the global phenomenon of voting in popular entertainment contests.

The internet era has therefore brought a wealth of new possibilities for individual communication and media participation, which in turn has greatly expanded the possibilities for personal autonomy.[48] That has undoubtedly been the experience of many active participants. Even for those individuals who do not actively participate, their sense of autonomy is often increased simply through access to information made available by others. This is most obviously the case where individuals become better informed consumers of goods and services. This relationship of increased information flows and more informed consumption choices has been idealized as the essence of the internet era. 'Ubiquitous connectivity means fundamentally that the individual becomes the agent of everything. Moving, frictionless, from one community to another, consuming, freely, from a wide universe of sources; publishing, from each individual to any number and size of audience—this is the consumer of the age we live in.'[49]

The convergence revolution has also transformed the political sphere, widening the opportunities for participation and promising more effective forms of democracy.[50] Collective participation opened the way for new sources of aggregate knowledge as well as online networks and communities in which people can interact for political purposes.[51] These are widely seen as elements of a networked public sphere that will generate innovative solutions to social and political problems.[52] Online participation has plainly transformed the nature of public debate,

---

[48] 'The second major implication of the networked information economy is the shift it enables from the mass-mediated public sphere to a networked public sphere. This shift is also based on the increasing freedom individuals enjoy to participate in creating information and knowledge, and the possibilities it presents for a new public sphere to emerge alongside the commercial, mass-media markets.' Benkler, Y., *The Wealth of Networks: How Social Production Transforms Markets and Freedom* (Yale University Press, 2006), 10; 'My argument is that these new forms of mass, creative collaboration announce the arrival of a society in which participation will be the key organising idea rather than consumption and work. People want to be players not just spectators, part of the action, not on the sidelines.' Leadbeater, C., *We-think: the Power of Mass Creativity* (Profile Books, 2008); Zittrain, J., 'The Generative Internet' 119(7) *Harvard Law Review* (2006), 1974–2040.

[49] Murdoch, J. (Chairman and Chief Executive, News Corporation, Europe and Asia and Non-Executive Chairman, BSkyB), *Your Compass in a Changing World*, The Marketing Society Annual Lecture, (24 April 2008).

[50] Gillmor, D., *We the Media: Grassroots Journalism, By the People, For the People* (O'Reilly Media, 2004); Kluth, A., 'Among the Audience' *The Economist* (20 April 2006).

[51] See, generally, Sunstein, C., *Republic.com 2.0*, (Princeton University Press, 2007).

[52] Habermas, J., *The Structural Transformation of the Public Sphere* (Polity Press, 1989); Benkler, Y., n. 48 above 10; Sunstein, C., *Infotopia: How Many Minds Produce Knowledge* (Oxford University Press, 2006); Castells, M., Fernandez-Ardevol, M., Linchuan Qiu, J., and Sey, A., *Mobile Communication and Society: A Global Perspective* (MIT Press, 2006); Castells, M., 'Communication, Power and Counter-power in the Networked Society' 1 *International Journal of Communication* (2007), 238–266; Leadbeater, C., n. 48 above; Anderson, C., *The Long Tail: How Endless Choice is Creating Unlimited Demand* (Random House Business Books, 2006).

even in countries where the media operates under close government control.[53] On this view:

[T]he Internet is redistributing political influence; it is broadening the public sphere, increasing political participation, involving citizens in political activities that were previously closed to them, and challenging the monopoly of traditional elites. This . . . definition of democratization presumes first and foremost that the technology will amplify the political voice of ordinary citizens.[54]

For many households and businesses, the internet era has fulfilled much of its promise as a technology of freedom of expression. It has witnessed new forms of communication that have exponentially increased access to information and entertainment content and brought the power of mass communication to the ordinary individual.[55] The boundaries that once clearly separated the distinctive category of freedom of the press from the wider sphere of freedom of speech have also largely disappeared. The internet era has therefore offered unprecedented opportunities to put to the test long standing questions about the value and utility of personal freedom.[56] Will individuals and communities, for example, become less tolerant of state imposed restraints as they become accustomed to more content choices and more avenues for communication and participation? More generally, will convergent media services ultimately overcome the obstacles that have thwarted a half century of efforts to make a liberal vision of freedom of expression into a universal norm? Among other things, these questions hinge on assumptions about the connection between consumer choice or market freedom and citizen choice or political freedom. In short, they ask whether open, tolerant societies are the natural political twin of efficient, competitive markets.

Technologies of harm and inequality

While the internet is rightly celebrated as a technology of liberty, it is just as often associated with increased threats to security, order, and well being. In this respect at least, the internet is much like earlier communication technologies. Just as audible speech has always carried the risk of harm to others, any method that makes communication easier brings a risk of amplifying that harm. Arguments about restrictions on freedom of expression in the internet era therefore merely carry forward ancient concerns about the damage that speech may cause to state, public, and private interests. For the state, these concerns are the familiar ones of unauthorized disclosure of secret

---

[53] On the impact of new technologies and other influences on contemporary journalism in China, see Polumbaum, J., *China Ink: The Changing Face of Chinese Journalism* (Rowman & Littlefield, 2008).

[54] Hindman, M., *The Myth of Digital Democracy* (Princeton University Press, 2008), 6.

[55] 1st Council of Europe Conference of Ministers Responsible for Media and New Communication Services, *A New Notion of Media?* (2009); United Kingdom Department for Culture, Media and Sport, *The Digital Britain Final Report* (2009), ch 2: 'Being Digital'.

[56] On liberalism and freedom of expression, see Chapter 2.

information as well as seditious criticism and incitement of violence directed towards its institutions, leaders, and personnel. The concerns of private individuals, associations, and businesses are also familiar: the unauthorized disclosure of personal or confidential information, defamatory criticism, incitement to hatred, and exposure to pornography and other harmful or unwanted content.

Nonetheless, the current communications revolution has exponentially increased the risk of these historic harms.[57] Improvements in the storage and transmission of data achieved through digitization have meant that information is no longer as transient, obscure, or distant as it once was. The harms as well as the benefits brought by the internet consequently penetrate further and persist longer. Inter-activity, moreover, by breaking down distinctions between mass and personal communication has weakened control over content, making it harder to know who has access to particular content or how far it may spread.

The internet era has therefore also become an age of heightened anxiety. Intrusion and exposure of personal life have weakened the accustomed anonymity of modern life. Through social networking and other new ways of communication many have found themselves abruptly thrown back into the transparency of the Victorian village. New technologies have also made it possible to track lives and businesses for intrusive purposes, both lawful and unlawful, while unsolicited offensive content spills into households through multiple communication plat-forms and services, often exposing families to ways of life they find repugnant or assault their identity and values. At the same time, the isolation that once protected endangered languages and cultures is rapidly disappearing. And not least, criminal and terrorist organizations have flourished through new communications services: recruiting and training members, managing their funds, planning operations, and publicizing their successes.[58] Consequently, anxieties about these potential harms, real as well as exaggerated, are as important to communications and media policies as the confidence and enthusiasm just as often expressed about the benefits of the communications revolution.

Beyond this intensification of well known harms, the internet era has also seen the rise of other challenges that are more specific to the effects of digitization and convergence. Chief among these is the hollowing out of many broadcast and print media companies, leaving them unable to fund the high costs of investigative reporting of domestic and foreign news. Over the past decade, information and entertainment media markets have fragmented, while new media and other services have gained public attention, causing these bastions of the old media to lose advertising and subscription revenue. In Europe, '[t]he audience share of the "primary" channels has decreased, and a shrinking number of channels are able to attract a significant audience share. The major national markets, such as Germany, France, Italy and the UK, are the first to be affected by this ever-increasing

---

[57] See Solove, D., 'Speech, Privacy, and Reputation on the Internet', in Nussbaum, M. and Levmore, S., (eds), *The Offensive Internet: Speech, Privacy and Reputation* (Harvard University Press, 2011), 15.

[58] Rid, T., 'Web Special: War 2.0' *Hoover Institute Policy Review* (Stanford University, 2007).

fragmentation.'[59] The print media sector in much of the world has suffered even greater losses, leaving the future of the privately held, printed newspaper in doubt.[60] As a result, some of the longest established sources of daily news and current affairs are now less able to supply the broad range of diverse information they once delivered.[61] Their role as accessible, omnibus sources of information essential to personal and commercial pursuits as well as participation in political affairs is in decline. For liberal democracies, this has become a worrying threat to the health of democratic life.

In the face of this decline, the public policy question has become whether thriving new interactive media services, inside and outside the traditional core media companies, will more than fill this gap. Interactivity and accessibility have not only opened doors to a wealth of new information sources, but have also given rise to critical networks and communities that bring overlooked information to public attention and also expose error and deception in public affairs. While the internet may be helping to destroy old media bastions, it is also apparently creating alternative forums for robust, well informed public discussion.

There is, however, a significant downside to these changes. The existence of a daily cornucopia of online information and comment is undeniable. Yet, the important question is whether the public has access to well researched, informative, and useful content that is clearly presented in convenient, accessible forms and places. In previous eras, that was the great democratic public purpose of newspapers and broadcasters. Governments could moreover easily intervene to support that function through subsidies and programme mandates. They could also require domestic broadcasters, particularly the main television services, to provide their viewers with news and current affairs information during prime time viewing periods.

With the fragmentation of media markets, newspapers and broadcasters have lost much of their dominance. They now share their role as the gates and gatekeepers of public knowledge with search engines, portal web sites, and other new services. On one view, the internet era has thus only brought changes in the major controllers of public knowledge, who determine what information is easily accessible, rather than introducing a radically different media sphere in which individual users genuinely control information choice and access. If the old media models dominated through the selective production of information for public consumption, the new typically do so through the selective filtering of content before delivery to users. The selection or exclusion of socially and politically important information and analysis has therefore shifted from content production towards content filtering.[62] As

---

[59] European Commission (2008), Eighth Communication on the application of Articles 4 and 5 of Directive 89/552/EEC 'Television without Frontiers', as amended by Directive 97/36/EC, for the period 2005–2006 [SEC (2008) 2310].

[60] Alterman, E., 'Out of Print: The Death and Life of the American Newspaper' *The New Yorker* (New York, 31 March 2008).

[61] Lee Bollinger, 'Journalism Needs Government Help', *Wall Street Journal* (14 July 2010).

[62] Hindman, M., *The Myth of Digital Democracy* (Princeton University Press, 2008), 13.

Matthew Hindman has commented, '[W]hen considering political speech online, we must be mindful of the difference between speaking and being heard.'[63]

There are, furthermore, concerns that these plentiful new media sources often lack the financial and human resources needed to fund in-depth, authoritative reporting.[64] 'Whereas a newspaper tends to stand by its story on the basis of an editorial process in which professional reporters and editors attempt to vet their sources and check their accuracy before publishing, the blogosphere relies on its readership—its community—for quality control.'[65] The public is therefore at greater risk of inaccurate or distorted information, which easily spreads in a viral fashion through communication networks. In the worst circumstances, such as the Danish cartoons crisis, those networks can carry a blend of fact and fantasy instantly across borders, surprising and outrunning public authorities.[66]

One of the chief difficulties in managing the problem of public access to a broad spectrum of accurate information lies in the nature of news consumption. In many circumstances, accurate information is indistinguishable from false information. As much as we may wish to be well informed, we often do not know enough to be able to judge the quality of the information we possess. Moreover, the 'facts' that fit most closely with personal convictions are frequently the most believable. News information is therefore a type of merit good, where the collective consequences of individual consumer choices do not necessarily lead to the production and distribution of the goods and services most useful to consumers.

It is therefore also possible that new media services will just as often provoke immediate response and direct action, as they will the consensus building and deliberative decision making that is often expected from the electronic public sphere of the internet era.[67] It is even questionable whether the experience of choice, control, and participation in information and entertainment services contributes to the civic virtues needed for democratic decision making.[68] It may, on the contrary, be that the internet based explosion in consumer choice and participation is at best only loosely connected to democratic political choice and participation.

The internet era has also given rise to related concerns about inequalities of access to internet news and information services and the consequent worsening of social and educational exclusion. Many internet based information resources are entirely beyond the reach of households that lack broadband internet access and, in some cases, the ability to purchase specific content. The latter problem may well increase as content becomes further commodified and globally marketed through business models that more effectively exploit the revenue potential of information,

---

[63] Ibid.
[64] Alterman, E., n. 60 above; Leetaru, K., 'New Media vs. Old Media: A Portrait of the Drudge Report 2002–2008' 14(7) *First Monday* (2009). See also Jones, R., 'Litigation, Legislation and Democracy in a Post-Newspaper America', *Washington and Lee Law Review*, (forthcoming), <http://ssrn.com/abstract=1710910>. For a different view, see Massing, M., 'The News about the Internet' 56 (13) *New York Review of Books* (13 August 2009).
[65] Alterman, E., n. 60 above.
[66] 'The Limits to Free Speech—Cartoon Wars', *The Economist* (9 February 2006).
[67] See, for example, Downey, T., 'China's Cyberposse', *New York Times* (3 March 2010).
[68] Sunstein, C., n. 51 above.

images, and ideas.[69] In short, much of the premium content that is currently available for free may well be locked behind payment walls in the future. There is as well a substantial educational barrier to universal access to the diverse and complex resources of the new media.[70] The communications revolution may therefore sustain or even extend inequalities between communities as well as households.

Public policy concerns about public access to news and information in the internet era are not directly applicable to the entertainment media. Compared to information content, entertainment content tends to have fewer merit qualities. Ostensibly, the primary object of dramatic films, programmes, and other entertainment content is to satisfy the desires of the individual consumer, who is normally capable of autonomously deciding whether those desires have been satisfied by that content. On that basis, market driven, new media services are well suited to supply content that satisfies consumer demands in different genres. Nonetheless, the entertainment media are also valued for their contribution to the social and cultural needs of individuals, communities, and societies. The fragmentation of media markets and spread of digital piracy, which has made it harder to recover production and distribution costs of large scale, high quality works, has consequently made that relationship more complex and precarious. These changes particularly disadvantage smaller linguistic or cultural populations, which do not naturally form markets large enough to support an entertainment media capable of competing effectively with imports in both price and quality.[71]

As the consumption of information and entertainment content has fragmented, households are also no longer tied to the major national television channels as they once were. In many countries, these channels have provided important vehicles for the delivery of subsidized national and local content, which fostered social and cultural solidarity through shared mass viewing. Changes in media consumption inevitably raise important questions about the durability and importance of those bonds and whether they can be sustained. Finally, public policy concerns about the quality and sufficiency of public access to information and entertainment content have a common thread. Regardless of the radical changes brought by the communications revolution, the challenge for market based economic policy remains to balance the need for large media companies, which have the scale and scope to maintain high quality content production and distribution, with the need to ensure that there is a sufficient plurality of producers and distributors and none enjoys excessive dominance.

---

[69] See Balkin, J., 'The Future of Free Expression in a Digital Age' 36 *Pepperdine Law Review* (2008), 427–444.

[70] International Telecommunications Union, *World Telecommunication/ICT Development Report*, 9th edn (ITU, 2010).

[71] Tongue, C., 'Why a UNESCO Convention on Cultural Diversity of Expression?', in Pauwels, C., Kalimo, H., Donders, K., and Van Rompuy, B. (eds), *Rethinking European Media and Communications Policy* (Institute for European Studies, 2010), 241. But also consider the arguments for potentially thriving niche markets, Anderson, C., *The Long Tail: Why the Future of Business Is Selling Less of More* (Hyperion, 2006).

Digitization and convergence have broken down many long established barriers to market entry. This has created openings for a remarkable number of new information and entertainment products and services, which collectively have changed the nature of work and personal life for many. Yet, despite this destruction of market barriers, convergence has not necessarily led to increased competition in media markets.[72] Some of the old market gates or bottlenecks have remained and new ones have developed, including strategic commercial control over premium content, electronic networks, and specialized services, such as search engines or social networks.

Since the beginnings of the internet boom of the 1990s, media and communications companies have looked for economies of scale and scope to take advantage of the convergence process. Without these, they would not be able to fund the costs of producing major films or acquiring key sports rights and distributing them to mass audiences at a profit.[73] One of the leading strategies was therefore to operate internationally over major delivery platforms and in major content forms.[74] This meant increasing vertical integration, in which companies attempted to grow along the content value chain, from production through aggregation to distribution. This brought the control of electronic networks, including broadcast, internet, and mobile networks, together with the control of content rights.

Initially, the most successful companies appeared to be those that held a strong position in the print, film, and broadcast media. Newly created giants, like AOL Time Warner and Vivendi Universal, joined Disney, Bertelsmann, Viacom, News, and Sony corporations on the commanding heights of a global media sphere. This gave rise to strong anxieties about the economic, social, and cultural consequences of global dominance by an oligopoly of convergent media and communications behemoths.[75] Yet, these companies did not find it easy to exploit the unpredictable opportunities of the internet and other new media platforms. The merger of AOL and Time Warner, for example, famously failed to deliver the benefits of convergence out of its disparate parts, and Vivendi later shed many of its media assets.[76]

In the communications revolution, market dominance has turned out to be a potent threat to diversity and choice, while also very difficult to assess in any specific instance. In a rapidly changing technological and commercial environment, dominance can often be transitory and regulatory interference unnecessary. At the same time, the extraordinary position of companies such as Microsoft, Google, and Facebook make clear that powerful dominance, which allows a company to leverage its way into each new phase of the internet era, is also a reality that may require a

---

[72] OECD, *Media Mergers* (2003) DAFFE/COMP 16, 26.

[73] European Institute for the Media, Final Report to the European Parliament, *Study on the information of the citizen in the EU: obligations for the media and the Institutions concerning the citizen's right to be fully and objectively informed* (31 August 2004).

[74] Andersen, A., n. 40 above, 9.

[75] 'A Global Oligopoly', *The Economist* (21 November 1998), Technology and Entertainment, 4.

[76] 'Vivendi mulls its future; Adieu, Hollywood', *The Economist* (5 December 2009). See also Peltier, S., 'Mergers and Acquisitions in the Media Industries: Were Failures Really Unforeseeable?' *Journal of Media Economics* (17 April 2004), 261.

concerted state response. Although even the extraordinary market power of these media enterprises could wane rapidly in the face of new technologies and services.[77]

Technologies of surveillance and control

Historically, even the most restrictive government often tolerated the circulation of some content that was formally proscribed or restricted.[78] The financial and administrative costs of absolute enforcement were not only too high, but they also restricted the flow of information important to commerce, education, and other interests the state wished to advance. A state could only hope to control the major organized sources and channels of information and entertainment. The circulation of illicit information and opinions could potentially be kept to a minor irritant, provided the state ensured that it is not repeated on any credible platform.

Yet the arrival of the internet appeared to sound the death knell for this strategy of control over the high ground of mass media and the tolerance of private gossip and rumour mongering. The internet had caused two related changes that promised eventually, if not immediately, to break the capacity of the state to maintain control not only over the media, but over the wider communications sector. First, the breakdown of the distinction between mass and personal communication had sparked an exponential rise in the numbers of content providers. New internet developments, such as the invention of hypertext and the introduction of the Mosaic web browser, stoked this process, leading to personal webpages, weblogs, and other new forms of media. Sheer numbers have threatened to overwhelm the state's ability to comprehend its national information environment, let alone maintain control over millions of participating users as well as a sprawling commercial information and entertainment sector.[79] Secondly, the internet appeared to make national boundaries an irrelevance in the world of online communication. In the early architecture of the internet, unlike satellite broadcasting, the geographical location of the content provider and the recipient had no particular significance. As a result, foreign based content sources threatened to merge seamlessly with the domestic media sphere, breaking down the external walls that are essential to the media state relationship.

The response of the state to these challenges was initially cautious and experimental. Few governments could claim to understand the implications of digitization and internet communication and know which measures would be most

[77] On the potential effects of the shift to content consumption through 'apps', see Anderson, C. and Wolff, M., 'The Web Is Dead. Long Live the Internet', *Wired* (September 2010). On the changing architecture of the internet, see van Schewick, B., *Internet Architecture and Innovation* (MIT Press, 2010).

[78] For an example of the weaknesses in the Chinese government's control system, see Pan, P., 'The Click That Broke a Government's Grip', *Washington Post* (19 February 2006).

[79] Castells, M., 'Communication, Power and Counter-power in the Networked Society' 1 *International Journal of Communication* (2007), 238.

effective, given their particular technical, financial, and political constraints. In democratic states, the latter was often one of the most important limitations. During the formative years of internet policy making, the public policy environment in the western democracies was powerfully opposed to the use of licensing and other broadcast media regulatory methods.[80] In the United States in particular, initial government attempts to find the vulnerabilities of the internet and regulate internet content aroused intense debate and opposition.[81] The libertarianism of the first decade of public internet access certainly had no necessary connection with the internet; these ideas of liberty from the state applied as much to laws restricting the hand printing of pamphlets as they did to regulations limiting internet content. Yet libertarian arguments focused attention on the crucial question of whether the new internet medium should be kept beyond the control of the state.[82] Nonetheless, the essential objectives of the state in matters of information and entertainment content remained the same. To safeguard its security, authority, and legitimacy and thus protect its long term survival, the state needed to limit the potential harms and foster the benefits of these new communications technologies and media services.

On one level, governments began to reconsider the conceptual foundations of their communications and media regimes. It was clear that some key assumptions underpinning these regimes would ultimately fail, most notably the assumption that free-to-air, linear television has a uniquely powerful impact on the public. According to the principles of convergence, audiovisual content would eventually become equally accessible in the home on other platforms. It would therefore become increasingly impractical to continue to apply laws or regulations that segregated the media according to the specific characteristics of each delivery method.[83] The effective protection of children from exposure to harmful or offensive audiovisual programmes in the home, for example, would have to broaden to take account of new audiovisual services, in particular those available through broadband internet and mobile networks.

As a result, communications and media policy in many countries began to shift towards a simpler, fundamental division between infrastructure services and content services. Infrastructure broadly includes electronic networks, such as those carried on wire, cable or radio waves, and devices, such as radios, televisions, games consoles, personal computers, mobile phones, and MP3 players. Content simply means any form of recorded or live analogue or digital content capable of being delivered through those platforms and devices. While this radically new understanding of the communications and media law and regulation had a refreshing simplicity, the reality in domestic and cross border media markets was far more complicated. While free-to-air linear television viewing was set to decline, it still

---

[80] See Chapter 3.

[81] Reno, *Attorney General of the United States, et al. v. American Civil Liberties Union et al.* (1997), 521 U.S. 844.

[82] See, for example, Murray, A., *The Regulation of Cyberspace* (Routledge-Cavendish, 2006), 227–229.

[83] McGonagle, T., 'Co-Regulation of the Media in Europe: The Potential for Practice of an Intangible Idea', *IRIS Plus*, 2002–10.

retained a powerful place in many households. Governments therefore needed to put in place new legal and regulatory frameworks to support the process of convergence, while also maintaining established regimes for their print and broadcast media.

These changes in regulatory concepts and frameworks did not alter the basic mechanics of state control over the media. In considering how internet based services should be brought under national control, governments drew on centuries of experience and looked for the individuals and facilities essential to online content production and distribution. For many, internet service providers (ISPs), who provide local internet access for most households and businesses, were the obvious first target. While many small ISPs had sprung into operation, their numbers were not unmanageable, and, regardless of ownership, they needed to operate locally. ISPs therefore provided an easily identifiable, locally based party who could bear liability for the offensive and harmful content travelling through their access networks.[84]

In other respects, internet service providers were not well suited to this role. ISPs very often functioned as simple conduits between users and the wider internet, having no prior knowledge of the third party content accessed through their networks. To this extent they resembled telecommunications operators, who historically did not bear responsibility for the content they carried, unlike broadcasters, who were usually held responsible for all the content they broadcast, whether original or third party. Nonetheless, ISPs do have the capacity to prevent their subscribers from accessing some prohibited content, which made a simple application of the existing telecommunications regulatory model to ISPs inappropriate. Yet their very limited ability to control access to third party content made the broadcasting model equally inapplicable. In the face of this technical uncertainty, government decisions on ISP liability tended to follow underlying policy preferences regarding the balance between the potential benefits of greater liberty to publish and the potential harms to the state and others that unconstrained expression may cause. In Europe, ISPs receive conditional protection from liability, while in the United States it is often unconditional.[85]

Beyond the initial question of ISP liability, government efforts to find the vulnerabilities of original content providers moved from hesitancy to increasing confidence as the dynamics of the new technologies and services became more apparent. This was certainly an awkward process, as they sought workable compromises between their growing determination to curb internet based harms and their desire to foster the benefits of public internet access. This was no small task, given that the complexity of the convergent communications and media sphere ensured that any measures taken to regulate content were likely to be blunt and carry unintended side effects.[86]

[84] Timofeeva, Y., 'Establishing Legal Order in the Digital World: Local Laws and Internet Content Regulation', 1(1) *Journal of International Commercial Law and Technology* (2006), 41–51.

[85] See Chapter 4.

[86] Murray, A., n. 82 above.

The rapid commercialization of the internet undoubtedly favoured greater, if not fully effective, state control. The special vulnerability of commercial content service providers, even when not directly present in a particular state, is that they must find some way to market their services to its residents and generate a corresponding income stream, typically through advertising or subscription fees. They are consequently exposed to the coercive powers of the state through their reliance on local intermediaries and revenue sources. This vulnerability, however, depends largely on the size of the particular services provider. Peter Swire has described this question of vulnerability as a distinction between the 'elephants' and the 'mice' of the internet. 'Elephants are large companies or other organizations that have major operations in a country. Elephants are powerful and have a thick skin, but are impossible to hide. They are undoubtedly subject to a country's jurisdiction. Once laws are enacted, they likely will have to comply.'[87]

Increasingly, democratic as well as non-democratic states have found ways to impose liability on foreign content providers.[88] For their part, many internet based content providers have opted to impose their own rules on third party users to avoid legal liability in the jurisdictions where they are commercially most active.[89] Even when based in countries offering relatively relaxed content rules, they have had little choice but to become more attuned to the laws of foreign states and the expectations of foreign consumers.[90] In contrast, small content providers are, in Swire's terms, the 'mice' of the internet who can often evade and ignore domestic as well as foreign laws and sensitivities. 'By contrast, mice are small and mobile actors, such as pornography sites or copyright violators, who can reopen immediately after being kicked off of a server or can move offshore. Mice breed annoyingly quickly—new sites can open at any time. Where harm over the Internet is caused by mice, hidden in crannies in the network, traditional legal enforcement is more difficult.'[91] Of course, there are also many points on the spectrum between the internet's vulnerable elephants and its invisible mice.

The intricacies of this expanding new media sphere also prompted many governments to look beyond direct state intervention to other methods that seem more suited to their diverse public policy purposes. Most notably, this has involved greater use of co and self regulation as well as increased reliance on consumer self responsibility. While this has been a radical change of emphasis for many states, the underlying idea that content producers, distributors, and consumers should police themselves is a basic element not only of media law but of law itself. It is however a highly sensitive issue for liberal democracies as the degree to which the media becomes responsible for maintaining the state's content rules also raises the question of how far the media is co-opted by the state. British contempt of court rules,

---

[87] Swire, P.P., 'Elephants and Mice Revisited: Law and Choice of Law on the Internet' 153(6) *University of Pennsylvania Law Review* (2005), 1975–2002.

[88] See, for example, *Dow Jones and Company Inc v. Gutnick* (2002) HCA 56.

[89] See, for example, YouTube Community Guidelines, (<http://www.youtube.com/t/community_guidelines>).

[90] 'New York Times blocks UK access to terror suspect story' *Press Gazette* (1 September 2006).

[91] Swire, P.P., n. 87 above.

for example, impose strict liability for publications that potentially prejudice judicial proceedings.[92] The media, as a result, carries most of the burden of protecting juries and witnesses from prejudicial information, in sharp contrast to the United States, where that is the responsibility of the courts.[93]

Compelling internet based and other new media companies to take partial or full responsibility for rule making and enforcement has a number of obvious advantages for the state. In a rapidly changing technological and commercial environment, it is frequently more effective to rely on the expertise of the companies most closely involved in those changes. Co and self regulation also allow the state to transfer enforcement costs, while distancing itself from the censorship tasks involved. Greater reliance on consumer responsibility can yield similar benefits. Individuals and households retain a sense of autonomy and also relieve the state of some of the burden of protecting the public from harmful and offensive content. The risks for the state in these strategies are equally well known. It has distanced itself from its coercive leverage over the public information environment and must rely on indirect methods to ensure accountability and reliability.

In the internet era, government attention has also turned to the basic architecture and software applications that support new media services. This again is not new to media law and regulation, which has always been anchored in the specific vulnerabilities of communications technologies and facilities. However, the technological complexity of convergence has made the control and manipulation of the communications architecture and major applications a separate field for the pursuit of both state and commercial interests. It is, for example, now widely recognized that software code can be an important alternative, or at least supplement, to legal methods of managing public access to information and entertainment content.[94]

While the evolution and control of communications technologies has often been a focus for the debate over media law and regulation in the internet era. The fate of the media state relationship plainly does not hang solely on the twists and turns of technological change.[95] The frequent wrong turnings and dead ends of the current communications revolution are often quickly forgotten, hidden in the debris of recent history.[96] In the late 1990s satellite mobile phones, for example, were

---

[92] United Kingdom, Contempt of Court Act 1982, s. 2.
[93] *Nebraska Press Association v. Stuart*, 427 U.S. 539 (1976).
[94] Lessig, L., *Code: And Other Laws of Cyberspace*, 2nd edn (Basic Books, 2006). See also Reidenberg, J.R., 'Lex Informatica: The Formulation of Information Policy Rules through Technology', 76(3) *Texas Law Review* (1998), 553–594; Engel, C., 'The Role of Law in the Governance of the Internet' *Max Planck Institute for Research on Collective Goods* [2002] No. 2002/13; Murray, A. and Scott, C., 'Controlling the New Media: Hybrid Responses to New Forms of Power' 65(4) *Modern Law Review* (2002), 491–516; Samuelson, P., 'Mapping the Digital Public Domain: Threats and Opportunities' 66(1/2) *Law & Contemporary Problems* (2003), 147–171; Birnhack, M. and Elkin-Koren, N., 'The Invisible Handshake: the Re-emergence of the State in the Digital Environment', 8(6) *Virginia Journal of Law & Technology* (2003); Reidenberg, J.R., 'States and Internet Enforcement', 1 *University of Ottawa Law and Technology Journal* (2004), 213–230; Zittrain, J., 'A History of Online Gatekeeping', 19(2) *Harvard Journal of Law and Technology* (2006), 253–298.
[95] On the recurrence of technological determinism in the communications and media field, see Webster, F., *Theories of the Information Society* (Routledge, 1995).
[96] See, for example, 'Survey: Technology and Entertainment', *The Economist* (21 November 1998).

thought to be one of the winning technologies of the day. As the costs and size of receiving equipment fell and the geographical coverage of satellites increased, satellite phone ventures, such as Globalstar and Iridium, received billions of dollars of investment. In 1998, the *Financial Times* cited the superb technical factors favouring these services:

[T]he increased use of satellite for domestic television signals has spread start up costs; the ease and speed of installation compared to land based telecoms; and the growth of competition amongst satellite service providers. But the two most important factors are the high bandwidth offered by satellite and the ability to use the technology for compressed digital signals.[97]

Nonetheless, these companies soon went into bankruptcy protection, leaving investors with enormous losses.[98] Other phone technologies turned out to be better suited to the market conditions of the time.

Communications technologies are therefore crucial to any understanding of the media state relationship. But their role needs to be seen in the dense context of that relationship, which has evolved over centuries and is subject to a diverse array of influences, any of which can be more important than the communication technologies of the day. As Yochai Benkler comments,

The technical platforms of ink and rag paper, hand-presses, and the idea of a postal service were equally present in the early American Republic, Britain, and France of the late eighteenth and early nineteenth centuries. However, the degree of literacy, the social practices of newspaper reading, the relative social egalitarianism as opposed to elitism, the practices of political suppression or subsidy, and the extent of the postal system led to a more egalitarian, open public sphere, shaped as a network of smaller-scale local clusters in the United States, as opposed to the more tightly regulated and elitist national and metropolis-centered public spheres of France and Britain.[99]

In many circumstances, it is the support or opposition of the state that is critically important in determining the technological architecture of communications and media services. Very often, technological change has gone hand in hand with legal and regulatory changes that facilitate and mould its development. In the 1920s the advent of terrestrial radio broadcasting quickly led to new agencies of the state and concepts of regulation. These prominently included the Federal Communications Commission in the United States and the British Broadcasting Corporation in Britain.[100] Subsequent new methods of radio and television delivery, such as cable and satellite, brought new regulatory distinctions and requirements.

---

[97] 'Fresh Business Opportunities', *Financial Times IT Supplement* (6 May 1998), v.

[98] The Iridium and Globalstar businesses successfully relaunched after the companies emerged from bankruptcy proceedings.

[99] Benkler, Y., n. 48 above, ch 6, 178.

[100] The Federal Communications Commission, created by the 1934 Communications Act, replaced the Federal Radio Commission. The British Broadcasting Corporation was created by Royal Charter in 1927, replacing the British Broadcasting Company. Starr, P., n. 1 above; Crissell, A., *An Introductory History of British Broadcasting* (Routledge, 1997); Smith, A. and Paterson, R. (eds), *Television: An International History*, 2nd edn (Oxford University Press, 1998).

Quite often, governments have supported a specific method of delivery as the preferred national platform for radio and television in order to protect these services and their capacity to carry out public service obligations. When radio-spectrum was awarded at little or no cost to broadcasters, the resulting public subsidy favoured the further development and protection of terrestrial broadcasting networks.[101] Where terrestrial broadcasting was unsuitable, other countries made similar commitments to the development of cable networks as the primary national platform for radio and television.[102] Once governments were committed to particular platforms, they often fiercely resisted the introduction of new platforms that threatened their established delivery system.[103] In short, since long before the manipulation of internet software, the state has been guiding and shaping the principal technologies used to operate communication and media services.

The internet is, to some extent, no more than the latest emblematic technology to arrive in the rich history of communications and media regulation. The difference is that, unlike in previous generations of communications technologies, the internet is far more integrated internationally and much of its vital infrastructure has been under American control.[104] This global unity, which underpins its apparent borderless character, is by no means necessary, yet so far no state has established a wholly separate national internet.[105] Instead, governments have worked assiduously to understand the internet's technologies and commercial practices and discover where it is most vulnerable to local control. This has meant increasingly sophisticated content blocking and filtering to limit public access as well as the targeting of those providers whose revenue streams or other local connections lay them open to state action.[106] For those states, such as China,

---

[101] For example, terrestrial, free-to-air broadcasting in Britain.

[102] These included Belgium, the Netherlands, and Luxembourg; Brants, K. and Jankowski, N., 'Cable television in the Low Countries', in Negrine, R., (ed), *Cable Television and the Future of Broadcasting* (Croom Helm, 1985).

[103] See, for example, the imposition of special taxes to discourage the installation of satellite dishes in Belgium: Case C-17/00, *François De Coster v. Collège des bourgmestre et échevins de Watermael-Boitsfort* [2001] ECR I-9445.

[104] The United States has gradually relinquished elements of exclusive control over the internet, while retaining control of key functional elements. It has, for example, made provision for greater international accountability for the Internet Corporation for Assigned Names And Numbers (ICANN) under the 2009 Affirmation of Commitments made between the United States Department of Commerce and ICANN, which is an independent, non-profit-making private corporation established and operated under the laws of California and entrusted with the coordination of technical administration of the global internet. See 'ICANN be Independent: Regulating the Internet', *The Economist* (25 September 2009).

[105] See, for example, China, where web users were rerouted to alternative search engines while seeking Google. Reuters, 'Blocked Web Surfers in China get Detour' (9 September 2002).

[106] See, for example, convictions of Google executives for violation of Italian privacy laws, Donadio, R., 'Larger Threat is Seen in Google Case', *New York Times* (24 February 2010); Povoledo, E., 'Italian Judge Cites Profit as Justifying a Google Conviction', *New York Times* (12 April 2010).

that are willing to engage in more intensive methods of surveillance and enforcement, individual users can also be monitored and sanctioned.[107]

Despite its potential influence over the development of communications technologies, the state is in competition with other forces that can be just as influential. In market economies, investment has flowed primarily into the communications technologies that seem most likely to deliver revenue and profits.[108] This is also true for many state media, who may depend wholly or partly on commercial revenues or may require a significant share of the viewer market to justify public subsidies. Consequently, the effectiveness of a set of technologies is only one of the commercially relevant factors important to investment. The security of intellectual property rights or other barriers to market entry can be just as decisive. The ferocious international legal offensive waged by major rights holders to suppress unauthorized copying and use has, if anything, demonstrated the influence of commerce over communication technologies.[109]

The collective influence of consumer choice has also figured decisively in the growth of new media services. Even in the heady atmosphere of the 1990s internet bubble, it was clear that convergent services could not succeed unless they were affordable and convenient for individuals and communities.[110] The collapse of that speculative bubble occurred, in part, because many promised services were not available or effective at a reasonable price.[111] In this decade, consumers have drawn advertising revenue in their wake as they turned to new online services, forcing the traditional media to follow.[112] Yet despite the obvious impact of consumer choice on the evolving character of the media in the internet era, the social and political consequences are more contentious. On one view, market demand is the wellspring of innovation and diversity. Accordingly, consumer demand creates opportunities for a myriad of content sources that could have never reached the public in previous eras.[113] This is a compelling argument and it has a place in any attempt to understand the contemporary media and its relationship with the state. There are however more critical perspectives on the consequences of consumer demand in an era of extraordinary content availability and technological complexity. As Jonathan Zittrain has argued, public demand for convenient, intelligible choices

---

[107] Zittrain, J. and Edelman, B., 'Internet Filtering in China', 7(2) *IEEE Internet Computing* (2003). 70–77.

[108] On the influence of neo-classical economic ideas on communications policies in the 1990s, see Flichy, P., *Dynamics of Modern Communication* (Sage, 1995).

[109] In Britain, see, for example, Department for Culture, Media and Sport and Department for Business, Innovation and Skills, ch 4, 'Creative Industries in the Digital World', in *Digital Britain* (Final Report), (June 2009). See also 'Online Infringement of Copyright', ss. 3–18, Digital Economy Act 2010.

[110] Department of Culture, Media and Sport and the Department of Trade and Industry, *Regulating Communications: Approaching Convergence in the Information Age* (1998) CM4022 (July), 11.

[111] 'The high costs of new networks and services have (at least temporarily) outstripped consumer willingness to pay, leading to a slowdown in take-up and some prominent business failures' McKinsey & Company, n. 39 above, 10.

[112] Van Duyn, A., 'Media Groups are Grappling with a Drift of Revenue to the Web' *The Financial Times* (London, 1 January 2007).

[113] For example, Anderson, C., n. 52 above; Benkler, Y., n. 48 above, 8.

has combined with imaginative commercial strategies to produce services that are increasingly closed to user experimentation, destroying one of the fundamental sources of innovation behind the communications revolution.[114] In addition, that strong consumer desire for convenience and intelligibility goes hand in hand with other demands for protection against harmful or offensive content. These concerns have helped to drive new media services to incorporate inbuilt personal censorship facilities which often achieve their objectives through broad brush content exclusions.

The communications revolution has brought about a global experiment in the social, political, and economic consequences of vastly improved capacities to publish and access information and entertainment content. This openness to participation has produced an unprecedented diversity in the sources and nature of media content. Innovation and creativity have, as a result, flourished in all aspects of individual and collective life. These developments have also stimulated debate about a renewed emancipation of the individual achieved spontaneously through technology rather than the more arduous and precarious reform of social and political traditions and practices.

That vision however faces two major challenges. The first stems from the deepening commercialization of the convergent communications and media sphere. While this sphere is still undergoing radical change and dislocation, commercial goals remain the same: increasing market share, revenue, and profits. There is therefore a global competition to build successful services that satisfy consumer demand for bundled interactive features and conveniently accessible content. These services however also inevitably have a major role in setting the boundaries and nature of the public information environment, often in ways hardly noticeable to consumers.

At the same time, the interest of states in asserting control over the public information environment remains similarly unchanged: protecting the security, authority, and legitimacy of the state. Governments have therefore made determined efforts to overcome the difficulties of content control in the internet era. They have not only forced major information and entertainment services to comply with local laws through their financial vulnerabilities, but have also pushed the development of technical means to block and filter illicit content. In the process, they have changed the nature of the media state relationship, shifting the focus of state control away from the public realm of law and regulation towards the more opaque realm of commercial self regulation and technical fixes.[115]

Any account of the media in the internet era must therefore take into account the influence of commercial and state power over the possibilities for personal emancipation through new communication technologies. Nonetheless, that

---

[114] Zittrain, J., 'The Generative Internet', 119(7) *Harvard Law Review* (2006), 1974–2040; Zittrain, J., *The Future of the Internet: And How to Stop It* (Allen Lane, 2008).

[115] On hidden internet censorship, see Deibert, R., and Rohozinski, R., 'Beyond Denial: Introducing Next-Generation Information Access Controls', in Deibert, R., Palfrey, J., Rohozinski, R., and Zittrain, J. (eds), *Access Controlled: The Shaping of Power, Rights, and Rule In Cyberspace* (MIT Press, 2010).

understanding can also be misleading. From the very beginnings of the mass media, states have rarely exerted complete control over their domestic media for any lengthy period and complete commercial dominance is even less common. Even the most effective state has had to accept that, without draconian measures, there will always be small scale illicit media content seeping through its legal and other defences. The communications revolution has undoubtedly enlarged the possibilities for the publication and distribution of restricted or prohibited information or entertainment content. Despite improving technologies of surveillance and filtering, the state cannot hope to maintain its previous standards of close control over the current multitudes of domestic and foreign content sources accessible within its boundaries.[116] In many countries, the state has been forced to cede a large measure of responsibility for content choices to individuals and households. This is certainly an unprecedented loosening of the historic grip of the territorial state not only on the media but also on its population.

[116] In China, for example, online discussion has become a powerful element in national and local politics. See, for example, Branigan, T., 'Chinese Woman who Killed Official Bailed after Online Outcry', *The Guardian* (27 May 2009).

2

The Media and the Liberal Democratic State

The internet era has seen a sharp rise in the powerful tensions that exist between the media and the state. New communications and media services have brought an extraordinary expansion in the human capacity to communicate information and ideas, while also expanding the capacity to do harm. These technologies have also given the state greater potential powers to shape and restrict the flow of public and private communication. These changes have focused attention on two pressing questions at the heart of contemporary liberal democratic media public policy: when and how should the state protect or actively foster advances in the capacity to communicate or access information; and, when and how should the state limit potential or actual harm arising out of these new technologies and services? While these questions primarily concern communications and media services, they also raise underlying concerns about the legitimacy of the state and how its ambitions and fallibilities should be limited and managed.

This array of complex questions and concerns about the evolving media state relationship can be looked at from three different perspectives. These are the liberty to publish and distribute content, the protection of the security and authority of the state, and the protection of the well being of individuals, communities, and society in general. These aspects offer three different perspectives on the legal and other measures that restrain the production and distribution of content as well as the legal rights, remedies, and other measures that protect or promote capacities or opportunities to publish. Note that the words 'publish' and 'publication' are used here to refer to all forms of the initial communication of content to the general public, including printing, broadcasting, and other electronic transmission.

The liberty to publish principally concerns the interests of the media, however broadly defined, in publishing information or entertainment content free from restriction by the state. This is consequently the freedom to publish according to the needs and preferences of the publisher, whether those are commercially, socially, or politically motivated. In most countries, however, it is the commercial pursuit of revenue and profit that normally powers and shapes the daily outflow of information, images, and ideas through the media's distribution channels. That is not to overlook the considerable interest of the state, as well as the wider public interest, in convenient public access to abundant information and entertainment content. The essence of the liberty to publish may be freedom from the state, but that does not mean the state will necessarily seek to constrain that liberty.

The second perspective concerns the protection of the state's security and public order interests from the harmful effects of media publication. This aspect also runs both ways between the media and the state. It primarily concerns the state's interest in self preservation from threats to its security and authority arising out of media publications. But just as the state will always have a compelling, if sometimes limited, interest in protecting the public flow of information and ideas, the media has a vital interest in the preservation of the territorial state, which historically has provided the public order and property rights essential to a flourishing media sector.

The third perspective on the media state relationship concerns the protection of individuals, communities, and society at large from the harmful effects of media publication. These interests are extraordinarily diverse. They include protection from media publications that disclose personal information without consent, injure reputations, express hatred towards ethnic communities, religious beliefs or sexual orientation, or expose people to pornographic or violent words and images. At the same time, the well being of individuals and groups encompasses the promotion of beneficial information and entertainment content, such as access to information necessary for participation in public affairs or access to culturally important entertainment content. The idea of 'well being' therefore inevitably includes the liberty to publish as well as its constraint. Here, however, the concept of well being is expressed as a demand that the state provide effective protection from or access to specific kinds of information or entertainment content.

These ostensibly non-state interests are nonetheless thoroughly enmeshed in the media state relationship. The state's claims to authority and legitimacy depend significantly on its ability to protect these interests effectively from harmful publications and also to ensure public access to beneficial or desirable content. It is moreover the state that ultimately arbitrates between the conflicting demands for greater liberty to publish and greater protection for individuals and society and expresses its decisions through media law and regulation.

These three perspectives on the media state relationship help to illuminate its various tensions and also take it beyond the simple dichotomy of the oppressive state and the freedom seeking media. On the other hand, this generic framework must be placed in the local context that makes every national media regime distinctive. Beyond the contemporary mix of political structures and parties, religious and ethnic differences, and the geographical circumstances of the state, these contexts are also historical. The laws and institutions developed in the print and broadcasting eras endure and provide the foundations for legal and regulatory decisions in the internet era. Media law and policy is therefore profoundly local.

Liberalism and expression

In the media state relationship, moral and political arguments also lie close to the surface. The publication of information and ideas is beset with conflicts that lead directly to questions about the legitimate expectations of individuals, the proper basis for relations within and between communities, and the legitimate needs of the state. Moral and political philosophy therefore provides, if not clear answers to these questions, at least a body of concepts and ideas that helps to orientate thinking and guide the problem solving process in the media field. These branches of philosophy are of course not alone in influencing media law and public policy; religious doctrine as well as cultural and social traditions are often equally or more influential.

Aside from its obvious importance to the intellectual foundations of liberal democracy, liberal moral and political theory offers a rich resource for understanding the media state relationship's many tensions and disputes. Liberalism, with its deep concern for individual liberty, is intimately connected with the history of press censorship and freedom. It offers, if anything, an overabundance of arguments about the right to freedom of speech and publication and its many opposing rights and interests. Indeed, liberalism is unrivalled in making the protection of freedom of expression an essential test for the legitimacy of the state.

As a loose family of ideas within the Enlightenment heritage, liberalism has no common doctrine and is broad enough to encompass the ideas of theorists as radically different as Hayek and Raz.[1] Nonetheless, liberal thought is marked by a commitment to the ideal that each individual is entitled to choose and pursue his or her personal goals or way of life.[2] This ideal, moreover, is not only directed at the individual as a political or social being, but also as an economic one. Liberalism therefore envisions, to a greater or lesser degree, an individual free to pursue self interest by holding property and engaging in commerce and material consumption. Yet despite this common commitment to the value of personal liberty, liberalism is also notoriously divided over its importance in relation to other human needs or the nature of any specific rights to liberty. Nor is the ideal of personal freedom exclusively liberal, as it occurs, strongly or weakly, in liberalism's near and distant cousins, including libertarianism, republicanism, social liberalism, and communitarianism.

In the relationship between the media and the state, liberalism's great innovation was to use freedom of expression to open a space in the centre of the public information environment where the state is not permitted to interfere without adequate justification. This powerful presumption in favour of the liberty to speak and publish free from external coercion is rooted in Enlightenment ideas about the nature of the state and its relationship with the pre-political rights of its citizens.[3] It

---

[1] On the breadth of the liberal intellectual tradition, see John Gray, 'Back to Mill' 17 *The New Statesman*, No. 833 (2004).
[2] Schauer, F., *Free Speech: A Philosophical Enquiry,* (Cambridge University Press, 1982), 60. On the formation of the liberal tradition and its contemporary concerns, see Galston, W., 'Two Concepts of Liberalism', 105(3) *Ethics* (1995), 516, and Galston, W., *Liberal Pluralism: the Implications of Value Pluralism for Political Theory and Practice* (Cambridge University Press, 2002).
[3] In the liberal tradition, Locke is one of the most well known exponents of the pre-political freedom of the individual, although Hobbes, while no liberal, had already done much to place the individual at the heart of political theory. See Dupre, L., *The Enlightenment and the Intellectual Foundations of Modern Culture* (Yale University Press, 2005), 159–162.

remains a highly potent, if controversial, strand of liberal thought. As William Galston has written,

> Liberalism requires a robust though rebuttable presumption in favor of individuals and groups leading their lives as they see fit, within a broad range of legitimate variation, in accordance with their own understanding of what gives life meaning and value. I call this presumption the principle of *expressive liberty*. This principle implies a corresponding presumption (also rebuttable) against external interference with individual and group endeavors.[4]

Such a presumption demands at the very least that freedom of expression is weighted heavily in any balancing of rights or interests, or more aggressively, that no balancing exercise is possible in the face of that presumption.[5]

    This aggressive argument for minimal state intervention featured prominently in the libertarian influenced, intellectual atmosphere of the early internet years.[6] Since then, even in the United States, public policy debates have become somewhat less hostile to government restrictions on internet based activities, yet the argument for a comparatively unrestricted right to speak and publish is still highly influential in many liberal democracies.[7] On this view, there are few circumstances in which the state may legitimately restrict that fundamental right and the protection of the feelings of others will rarely be one.[8] In the media sphere, it supports the argument that freedom of the press cannot be fully protected without accepting a large measure of offensive, irreverent, and unruly expression.[9]

Harm and robust tolerance

Arguments for minimal restraints on the liberty to publish draw heavily on the legacy of classical liberalism, including J.S. Mill's expansive defence of personal freedom, which he famously underpinned with the harm principle.[10] According to Mill, 'the only purpose for which power can be rightfully exercised over any member of a civilised community, against his will, is to prevent harm to others'.[11] Plainly, Mill was not arguing that offensive publications, which do not cause actual harm, should circulate freely. He was asserting that the state should not use its coercive powers against their publishers, who nonetheless remain open to the

[4] Galston, W., *Liberal Pluralism* n. 2 above, 3.
[5] On balancing, see below under 'Proportionality analysis'.
[6] See, for example, Johnson, D. and Post, D., 'Law and Borders—The Rise of Law in Cyberspace', 48 *Stanford Law Review* (1996), 1367.
[7] See, for example, Wilson, B., *What Price Liberty?* (Faber and Faber, 2009), ch 17.
[8] '[A]s a purely formal matter, the state only respects people's autonomy if it allows people in their speech to express their own values—no matter what these values are and irrespective of how this expressive content harms other people or makes government processes or achieving governmental aims difficult', Baker, E., 'Hate Speech' in Hare, I. and Weinstein, J. (eds), *Extreme Speech And Democracy* (Oxford University Press, 2009).
[9] See Schudson, M., *Why Democracies Need an Unlovable Press* (Polity Press, 2008), 50–62.
[10] John Stuart Mill, *On Liberty* (Routledge, 1991), 17.
[11] Ibid.

possibility of constraint through arguments of reason or the rules of social custom or courtesy. It should also be possible for individuals to avoid publications likely to cause them offence.

While the harm principle has its well known problems, its apparent simplicity and clarity is still attractive in defending a broad view of the liberty to publish.[12] By protecting all speech and publication that does not cause harm, the principle draws on an important variant of the liberal concept of tolerance. It demands that the coercive powers of the state should not be used to restrain expression, even when distasteful or repugnant to others. To act otherwise would be intolerant of harmless differences and thus breach the essential compact that underpins co-existence between individuals and communities having diverse aims and preferences. It is also a view of tolerance that is directly rooted in the origins of liberalism in Europe's devastating religious wars, which demonstrated the bloody consequences of refusing to tolerate differences of faith. The harm principle therefore demands a certain robustness of character in the face of offensive expression. This reflects the harm principle's focus on the relative importance of a specific harm in relation to personal and collective liberty, rather than evaluating the harm as such.

The scope of that demand for tolerance and robustness is however unclear. Harm and the causation of harm come in many forms. Most often, speech and publication cause harm consequentially rather than directly as the harm only arises after the information or ideas pass through the minds of others, who are capable of disregarding their harmful intent or implications. As a result, the question of when expression engages the harm principle almost inevitably involves a judgement about the probabilities of a specific harm occurring in a given situation. In some circumstances, the risk and nature of the harm is so great that the expression can reasonably be prohibited outright. More often, the connection between the published information or ideas and any potentially harmful consequences is uncertain, leaving the question of liability open to debate. Furthermore, the range of expression protected by the harm principle is remarkably broad if the harm must involve physical damage or material loss. Yet some of the most difficult questions in the field of media law arise where demeaning or offensive expression causes psychological distress. At what point should tolerance of offence, and its expectation of a robustness of character, yield to concerns for the well being of the distressed individual?

Universality and value pluralism

Questions about the meaning of harm and its relationship with freedom bring to the surface some of liberalism's most intractable problems. Liberalism's claim to provide a universal framework for the co-existence of ways of life based on a respect for individual freedom necessarily rests on a particular view of the nature of the

---

[12] See, for example, Feinberg, J., *Harm to Others* (Oxford University Press, 1984).

person and his or her entitlements. In short, the proper limits of freedom and the meaning of harm cannot be resolved without a conclusive view on the essential needs of human beings. Classical liberalism presumed that individuals, when relying on reason rather than emotion or unexamined belief, would ineluctably arrive at a common understanding of the prerequisites for civilised society. Rather often, these were also presumed to be exemplified by the ideals of European high culture. Consequently, liberalism was only universal to the extent it assumed the gradual adoption of these values.

Contemporary liberalism has made significant efforts to establish universal principles that also genuinely accommodate social and cultural diversity. In that process, liberalism has moved painfully and often hesitantly towards a recognition of the naivety or hubris of imagining a convergence of values on a European derived norm. This reinvigoration of the problem of universality and diversity was a major element in the work of Isaiah Berlin, whose view of liberal universality was based on an acceptance of irreconcilable diversity.[13] Value pluralism, the idea that there are incommensurable beliefs about what is good and how life ought to be lived, is now broadly accepted amongst liberal theorists.[14] As a result, contemporary liberalism frequently makes a critical distinction between the fundamental rules that enable individuals to choose their preferred ways of life and the rules inherent to those ways of life.

The fact of value pluralism gives rise to an immediate difficulty. It is plain that a society that respects personal freedom must tolerate incommensurable beliefs and ways of life and, therefore, the liberal state must strive to be neutral between particular conceptions of the good.[15] The difficulty lies in determining the nature and limits of that tolerance. The robust tolerance described above insists that the state should not intervene to limit acts or expression that do not cause harm. On that view, peaceful co-existence in a society of increasing value pluralism demands patience and resilience in the face of offence. Accordingly, the liberty to speak and publish with minimal constraints remains a paramount principle and no cultural, social, or religious beliefs or preferences should be protected from rigorous inquiry and even derisory criticism.

Despite its attractiveness as an argument for freedom from state coercion, robust tolerance is not easily reconciled with a concern for personal well being, which is also a prominent value in liberal thought. The publication of demeaning, offensive, or embarrassing expression can easily have negative consequences for others, even when it falls short of a strict harm standard. Constant racist or homophobic abuse,

---

[13] Berlin, I., 'Two Concepts of Liberty' in *Four Essays on Liberty* (Oxford University Press, 1969).
[14] Value pluralism is a theory of 'the moral universe we inhabit', Galston, W., *Liberal Pluralism: The Implications of Value Pluralism for Political Theory and Practice* (Cambridge University Press, 2002), p. 30; '[T]here are many kinds of human flourishing, some of which cannot be compared in value', Gray, J., *The Two Faces of Liberalism* (Polity Press, 2000) 6; and '[T]here is an irreducible plurality of reasonable values and reasonable conceptions of the good', Kekes, J., *Against Liberalism* (Cornell University Press, 1997), 6.
[15] Rawls, J., *A Theory of Justice* (Harvard University Press, 1971).

for example, can have a blighting effect on the recipients' lives. The internet has moreover intensified these issues by giving global scope to abusive expression that was once confined to verbal exchanges in schools or workplaces. The reconciliation of competing claims to liberty and well being has therefore become one of contemporary liberalism's major challenges.

Autonomy and sensitive tolerance

Much of the theoretical work in this area has centred on the deontological concept of autonomy, which potentially provides the basis for a holistic vision of the rights of the person in a liberal society.[16] Autonomy broadly refers to the capacity of an individual to live according to reasons and goals that are his or her own and not significantly affected by external coercion, pressure, or manipulation.[17] The autonomous person thus enjoys internal self-realization and self-government in relation to others. Consequently, even in circumstances where the enjoyment of personal freedom serves no functional purpose for anyone else, it remains indispensable to the autonomy of the person concerned. Autonomy therefore has a particularly important role in the defence of artistic expression, where consequential arguments for freedom of speech discussed below often have limited force.

Expression, in all its variety, is undoubtedly at the core of autonomy. Without freedom of speech and publication, individuals cannot fully express their preferences or engage collectively in chosen ways of life. The value of autonomy, however, is that it places the individual's need for freedom of expression in a rich context, which notably includes physical and mental well being.[18] The concept of autonomy can therefore be used to support the argument that individuals are entitled to various positive benefits necessary to liberty and well being, including reasonable access to food, housing, healthcare and education, to achieve a level of well being sufficient to enable adequate personal freedom. Individuals may similarly be entitled to protection or assistance to maintain their psychological well being, which could include a sufficient sphere of privacy as well as a secure social and cultural identity.

Autonomy grounded arguments for the protection of well being also draw support from the concept of human dignity, which has become an increasingly

---

[16] Christman, J. and Anderson, J. (eds), *Autonomy and the Challenges to Liberalism: New Essays* (Cambridge University Press, 2005).

[17] 'James Griffin's human right to liberty is not the right to do whatever one wants; it is a right to the liberty that is necessary for normative agency', Griffin, J., *On Human Rights* (Oxford University Press, 2008), 167–168.

[18] Famously, Rawls, J., *Political Liberalism* (Columbia University Press, 1993) and Raz, J., *The Morality of Freedom* (Clarendon Press, 1986). More recently, for example, Martha Nussbaum's ten Central Human Capabilities necessary to living a fully human life in Nussbaum, M., *Women and Human Development* (Cambridge University Press, 2000); Griffin's argument that normative agency requires the exercise of autonomy, which requires both liberty rights and welfare rights, in Griffin, J. n. 17 above, 182.

familiar point of reference in European and international human rights law.[19] Human dignity has its own long association with liberal moral and political theory, notably in Kant's assertion that the dignity of each human being should be given equal respect, regardless of any claims to respect based on merit.[20] That entitlement to equality and respect continues to be a prominent element in contemporary accounts of human dignity.[21] Where the exercise of personal freedom impinges on the well being of others, respect for human dignity can be a supplement to the harm principle, justifying tighter limits on liberty.[22] It is also, however, possible to draw on the ambiguous concept of human dignity to support arguments for freedom from constraint.[23]

The argument that a person's choices should not disproportionately impair the ability of others to make their own choices has obvious implications for the media state relationship. In the three perspectives on that relationship discussed above, this argument shifts the balance away from the liberty to publish towards the protection of personal and collective well being. Moreover, it requires that the notion of harm be defined expansively to include psychological injury as well as injuries that result in physical or material loss. Indeed, it will sometimes permit restrictions on the liberty to publish where the content has not caused harm, but nonetheless deeply offends the dignity of those affected.

That idea has received serious theoretical attention, particularly in Joel Feinberg's work on freedom of expression and offence, in which he advocated that the state may legitimately restrict expression that causes profound offence.[24] Feinberg however imposed firm limits on this principle. In his view, the justification for restricting offensive expression rests on several important factors, including the intent of the speaker, the degree of offence, and the social or political importance of the expression.[25] He also argued that 'no one has a right to protection from the state against offensive experiences if he can easily and effectively avoid them without unreasonable effort or inconvenience'.[26]

---

[19] Steven Heyman, for example, has asserted that the liberal right to freedom of expression is founded on respect for the autonomy and dignity of human beings, Heyman, S.J., *Free Speech and Human Dignity* (Yale University Press, 2008), 2. On the concept of human dignity more generally, see McCrudden, C., 'Human Dignity and Judicial Interpretation of Human Rights', 19(4) *European Journal of International Law* (2008), 655.

[20] Sensen, O., 'Kant's Conception of Human Dignity', 100(3) *Kant-Studien* (2009), 309–331; and 'Human Dignity in Historical Perspective: The Contemporary and Traditional Paradigms' in *European Journal of Political Theory* (forthcoming).

[21] Feldman, D., 'Human Dignity as a Legal Value—Part I' *Public Law* (1999), 682–702; Feldman, D., 'Human Dignity as a Legal Value—Part II' *Public Law* (2000), 61–76.

[22] Heyman, S.J., *Free Speech and Human Dignity* (Yale University Press, 2008), 2. Also, Carmi, G. E., 'Dignity Versus Liberty: The Two Western Cultures Of Free Speech', 26 *Boston University International Law Journal* (2008), 277–374.

[23] Schauer, F., n. 2 above, 61–66.

[24] Feinberg, J., *Offense to Others* (Oxford University Press, 1985). See also Raz, J., n.18 above, 420: Beyond the Harm Principle.

[25] Feinberg, J., n. 24 above.

[26] Ibid., at 32. See also Raz, J., n. 18 above, 'Coercion can be used to prevent extreme cases where severely offending or hurting another's feelings interferes with or diminishes that person's ability to lead

In the internet era, Feinberg's offence principle may become more appealing in liberal societies, but at the same time more difficult to apply. Personal communication often contains highly offensive content of the sort that major media outlets routinely refuse to publish under their own editorial rules. Historically, those personal thoughts usually stayed within small groups of recipients and those individuals most likely to be offended were often ignorant of the specific content. Digitization, interactivity, and new communications services, not least the internet, have however made personal communication of this kind a staple of the public information and entertainment sphere. While major hosting services, such as YouTube, have guidelines to limit the amount of offensive content that third party users make available on their sites, supervision of these rules frequently relies on user complaints systems. In these circumstances, the factors that determine whether offensive expression should be restricted tend to be viewed differently. Offence that was once locally contained is electronically available to a far wider audience and those most offended can less easily avoid exposure.

A turn towards greater protection for the well being of others brings with it a different view of the liberal demand for tolerance. From this perspective, the argument that the powers of the state should rarely, if ever, be used to prevent or sanction demeaning or offensive expression ignores the liberal state's responsibilities for the autonomy and dignity of those negatively affected. To require that individuals exhibit a robust tolerance towards expression that demeans or offends them is effectively the grant of a general licence to insult and offend, the worst consequences of which are typically borne by vulnerable minorities.[27]

The alternative form of tolerance is one that is based on mutual respect and the recognition of the sensitivities of others. Accordingly, the state is justified in restricting speech and publication where they seriously impinge on the mental and physical well being of others, interfering with their rights to autonomy and dignity. Yet this more sensitive approach to tolerance has its own problems in reconciling the competing principles of liberalism. Its implications for personal freedom, a value often thought to be the essence of liberalism, are plainly repressive. Sensitive tolerance cannot, for example, rest on a distinction between an obligation of utmost respect for the self regarding activities of others and more limited respect for their other regarding activities. Aside from the difficulties in maintaining that dichotomy, it is often the self regarding activities of others, such as the voluntary wearing of the hijab or the expression of homosexual love, that draw the most vehement criticism, frequently stemming from deeply held, moral principles. The demand that these actions be respected, under the principle of tolerance, imposes a contentious burden of censorship, especially where this demand is enforced by the state.

---

a normal autonomous life in the community. But offence as such should be restrained and controlled by other means, ones which do not invade freedom', 421.

[27] On toleration as demanding a repression of the self, see Brown, W., *Regulating Aversion: Tolerance in the Age of Identity and Empire* (Princeton University Press, 2008).

The consequences can be as stifling to conservative non-liberals as they are to libertarians where sensitive tolerance requires outward respect for ways of life they find intolerable. For individuals whose religious faith asserts an exclusive understanding of truth, the conflict between the demands of liberal tolerance and belief can be extreme. Sensitive tolerance and mutual respect is thus often incompatible with the realization of a non-liberal way of life. It is also an irony of autonomy's internal tensions that, quite apart from sensitive tolerance, the ideas of individual or collective well being are readily adapted to other arguments for the restriction of liberty. Indeed, in some circumstances, these ideas open the door to restrictions that breach long standing liberal objections to paternalism and moralism. In terms of media content, paternalism describes restrictions on content that apply regardless of the fact that access to the content in question causes harm to no one, except possibly the adults who choose to view it.[28] More commonly, however, in relation to freedom of expression, the concern is with moralism. This occurs where speech and publication is restricted because it is thought to undermine a society's public moral standards.[29] Liberalism is traditionally hostile to moralism, which seeks to transpose perfectionist ideals of human conduct into obligatory rules of general behaviour, regardless of whether any demonstrable harm arises from their breach.

Problems of moralism are a recurring feature of liberal democratic politics. Public policy decisions often reflect the preferences of democratic majorities for the ordering of public and even private life according to popular beliefs about the good. In this context, the moral strictures of religious faiths or ethical traditions are especially important as they often provide the rules of conduct used to articulate those majority preferences.[30] Religious or ethical doctrine can therefore have a prominent role in episodes of majoritarian moralism. H.L.A. Hart famously set out his Millian opposition to the moralist imposition of rules of general conduct when writing in favour of the decriminalization of homosexual relations.[31] He argued that coercive enforcement of the moral preferences of majorities was intellectually flawed, not least because these preferences were apt to change significantly over time.[32] However, the problem Hart did not fully overcome is the objection that communities are held together by their shared beliefs. To reject the enforcement of those communal standards by the state because they violate principles of liberty risks the erosion of communal bonds and the collective well being they embody.

---

[28] See, for example, the Obscene Publications Act 1959, where content was deemed illegal where it would 'deprave and corrupt' the viewer.

[29] H.L.A. Hart skilfully restated Mill's argument against moralism in his well known exchange with Patrick Devlin over the issue of decriminalization of homosexuality in Britain: Hart, H.L.A., 'The Preservation of Morality and Moral Conservatism' and 'Moral Populism and Democracy' in *Law, Liberty and Morality* (Stanford University Press, 1963). In response, see Devlin, P., *The Enforcement of Morals* (Oxford University Press, 1965).

[30] Islam, Judaism, and Christianity are all important to the fusion of faith and politics. In East Asia similar issues arise in the renewal of the Confucian ethical tradition. See Bell, D.A., *Beyond Liberal Democracy: Political Thinking for an East Asian Context* (Princeton University Press, 2006).

[31] Hart, H.L.A., n. 29 above.

[32] Ibid., 69.

Individual and collective efforts to live in accordance with a particular understanding of the good depend heavily on the stability and protection offered by strong religious, social, and cultural bonds. While Hart's insistence on a broad interpretation of personal liberty is crucially important to beleaguered minorities, it also makes liberal democracy unattractive to many non-liberals.

Hart's position rests on familiar liberal ground. The ultimate value of moral beliefs, in relation to personal autonomy, lies in their capacity to provide fulfilling choices for individuals that also do not unreasonably limit the opportunities for others to live autonomous lives. In matters of public morality, the responsibility of the liberal state is therefore to ensure that collective choices do not impair the capacity of individuals to make moral choices that do not harm others or themselves. These arguments rest on liberalism's claim to universality, which contends that individual freedom to pursue a personal notion of happiness is a universal point of reference to judge the imposition of rules of conduct. On this basis, a wide range of ideas about the good can co-exist through a common respect for personal liberty and well being. The soundness of that universal point of reference is however one of liberalism's great contentious questions. Instead, the pivotal role of freedom of choice in liberal thought may simply be yet another culturally and historically specific understanding of human happiness and fulfilment. It is therefore no more universal than the perfectionist beliefs and traditions it seeks to bring under its control. On that view, a liberal political order is uniquely legitimate only for those who share its premises.

Positive and negative liberty

Autonomy has also broadened the debate over the nature of liberty, including the right to freedom of expression. Historically, one of the hallmarks of liberalism has been its implacable opposition to arbitrary or unjustifiable restraints on expression. This began with the great intellectual struggle against the powers of the monarchical state and has continued undiminished in liberalism's resistance to the majoritarian excesses of the democratic state. Even the complex claims of well being and dignity against liberty have merely renewed this debate over the justifications for restricting speech and publication. Where the state, for example, has acted in defence of individual and collective well being to counter incitement to hatred, it has employed negative restrictions.

In contrast, other autonomy based arguments for personal freedom call for the state to take positive measures to secure sufficient opportunities for personal freedom, including freedom of expression. These arguments belong to a development in liberalism that, in Britain, goes back well over a century to the 'new liberalism' of Green and Hobhouse.[33] Isaiah Berlin later described this as positive liberty, which supports or augments the personal capacities and external circumstances that are

[33] Nettleship, R.L. and Nicholson, P.P. (eds), *Collected Works of T.H. Green*, 5 vols (Thoemmes, 1997); Hobhouse, L.T., *Liberalism* (Williams and Norgate, 1911).

thought necessary for adequate freedom.[34] In the language of liberal autonomy, these are the conditions necessary for individuals to have a sufficient opportunity to realize their own chosen purposes in life. Negative liberty, on the other hand, refers to each person's enjoyment of his or her human faculties free from unwarranted external constraints.[35]

The distinction between positive and negative liberty is a well known oversimplification and has been subject to significant revision by other liberal theorists.[36] Yet it does very effectively describe the strong division between classical liberalism, which is not particularly concerned with the innate or circumstantial inequalities between individuals, and the development of an alternative liberalism, which sees personal freedom not only as an absence of constraint, but also as access to the material and intellectual conditions that make the fulfilment of autonomy possible.[37] In this vein, Conor Gearty has described the idea of human rights as two dimensional.

The two are linked in that each flows from a commitment to human dignity, which is in turn manifested in acts of compassion towards the other. In its prohibitory form, this demands that we do not degrade our fellow humans by depersonalizing them. The positive side, stressing growth and personal success, sees human rights as radically pluralist in the hospitality towards others—rather than mere tolerance of them—that its underlying ethic demands. Viewed as a whole, therefore, human rights is an idea that both protects us as persons and enables us to grow at the same time.[38]

Consequently, negative and positive liberty can be seen as two necessary and interlinked aspects of personal autonomy. Yet, as Berlin argued, they also describe different understandings of the liberal commitment to moral equality. The concept of positive liberty has tended to generate obligations on the state to assist those who are disadvantaged in abilities or circumstances.[39] In the media sphere, this has worked in two directions. Liberal democratic governments have intervened in various ways to ensure the quality and diversity of media content; they have also taken other measures to reduce the financial and other barriers to basic media services.[40] These interventionist media and communications policies also reflect positive liberty's typically sceptical view of the capacity of markets to achieve a fair

---

[34] On the distinction between negative and positive liberty, see Berlin, I., 'Two Concepts of Liberty' in *Four Essays on Liberty* (Oxford University Press, 1969).

[35] Feinberg, J., 'Freedom and Liberty' in Craig, E. (ed.), *Routledge Encyclopedia of Philosophy* (Routledge, 1998).

[36] See, for example, MacCallum, G.C. Jr, 'Negative and Positive Freedom', 7(3) *Philosophical Review* (1967), 312–334.

[37] On liberal procedural formalism, see Nussbaum, M., n. 18 above.

[38] Gearty, C., *Can Human Rights Survive?* (Cambridge University Press, 2006), 140–141.

[39] On differences between classic and social justice liberalism, see Gaus, G., 'On Justifying the Liberties of the Moderns: A Case of Old Wine in New Bottles', in Paul, E., Miller, F., and Paul, J. (eds), *Liberalism: Old and New*, (Cambridge University Press, 2007), 84.

[40] Nissen, C., Part 5, 'Objectives and Obligations of Public Service Media', *Public Service Media in the Information Society*, Report prepared for the Council of Europe's Group of Specialists on Public Service Broadcasting in the Information Society (MC - S - PSB); Media Division, Directorate General of Human Rights, Council of Europe (2006).

distribution of goods and services and its optimistic view of the state's capacity to act benignly and effectively. From this perspective, the world's thriving commercial media are therefore something of a mixed blessing. While they yield an exciting cornucopia of information and entertainment content, they will often neglect unprofitable social and cultural needs.

Negative forms of liberty are not necessarily indifferent to the imbalances of power, resources, and knowledge that expand or cramp the possibilities for personal autonomy. The chief argument from this side is that the state should not be trusted to remedy these ills and misfortunes. Even the well intentioned state is unlikely to perceive its biases or to act more competently than individuals or groups pursuing their self chosen best interests. State intervention in the media is therefore likely to be less effective than market based solutions and will inevitably distort fair market competition. The satisfaction of human needs is thus best determined by the collective outcomes of individual choices rather than through the paternalist assumptions of the state.[41] In normal circumstances, the production and distribution of media content should therefore be wholly, or at least primarily, a response to market demand. Moreover, on this view, where the state intervenes in media markets its usual shortcomings are compounded by the serious risk of increased state censorship.[42] It is the nature of the state to seek greater control over its public information environment and consequently, even where it acts for ostensibly good purposes, direct state involvement in the media sector is too easily turned to other purposes. The pursuit of equality through the state, in short, endangers personal liberty and freedom of speech.[43]

Freedom of expression and consequential reasoning

Autonomy's extraordinary breadth has made it as much an intellectual quagmire as a resource for liberal democratic public policy. The deontological nature of autonomy gives it an omnipresent importance to liberalism's fundamental claims about the moral dimensions of human life and consequently the proper foundations of social and political relations. Autonomy is therefore present in all aspects of the media state relationship, enriching and illuminating its many tensions and conflicts. Yet that wealth of ideas also gives autonomy a remarkable ability to sustain a wide array of opposing contentions. Liberalism's seminal argument for the liberty to speak and publish free from external coercion is thus entangled in the various claims of individuals and groups to well being and arguments about the role of the state in liberal democratic media markets.

[41] Hayek, F., *The Constitution of Liberty* (University of Chicago Press, 1978); Friedman, M., *Capitalism and Freedom* (University of Chicago Press, 1962) (re-print in 2002); Nozick, R., *Anarchy, State and Utopia* (Basil Blackwell, 1974).
[42] Schauer, F., n. 2 above, 86.
[43] Wilson, B., *What Price Liberty?* (Faber and Faber, 2009), ch 8.

As a result, consequential arguments in favour of freedom of speech and publication have come to enjoy an inordinate influence in liberal democratic media law and policy.[44] In the face of opposing positions equally, if contentiously, grounded in autonomy, media law and policy often turns to consequential reasoning to decide which should be preferred.[45] The two best known consequential arguments are that, first, freedom of expression is necessary for effective democracy,[46] and, second, that is necessary for the discovery of truth.[47] These arguments, while often used independently, overlap in their justifications for the closer scrutiny of governmental and other public bodies, politicians, and other public figures as well as incidents or issues of public importance. Both therefore can be critically important in determining when the liberty to publish should outweigh personal or collective claims to well being. While, for example, liberal concern for the autonomy and dignity of the person will normally justify the individual's right to control the disclosure of personal medical information, that right may be overridden where it obstructs legitimate interests in the disclosure of truth or in democratic accountability. The intervention of these consequential considerations helps to ensure that the deontological protection of well being does not become a ready pretext for the concealment of wrongdoing.

These consequential arguments are also useful in softening, if not resolving, the liberal dilemma of the state. While liberalism is sceptical of the state's claims to authority and wary of its use of coercive force, liberal democracy has not transcended the Hobbesian fact of the territorial state and must rely on its protective powers. Consequential arguments for democracy and openness, however, can be used to force the state to justify its restrictions and secrecy. Admittedly, these arguments are less useful when applied to the problem of legitimate state intervention in media markets for public policy purposes. In debates over state intervention to achieve greater diversity in the supply of media content or equality in public access to content, consequential arguments for freedom of expression are readily marshalled on either side.[48]

The arguments for democracy and truth are directed unequivocally towards greater personal and collective liberty to speak and publish. Within their scope,

---

[44] See, for example, the role of 'public interest' and 'public figure' principles in European and American privacy and defamation law, as discussed in Chapter 10.

[45] Indeed, in European human rights law, this preference for consequential reasoning is almost to the exclusion of any other principle supporting freedom of expression. See Chapter 6.

[46] The democratic argument for freedom of expression. Best known and most widely used by judges in interpreting constitutional rights to freedom of expression in liberal democracies, for example ECHR, USSC. Meiklejohn, A., *Free Speech and Its Relation to Self-Government* (Harper Brothers, 1948); Raz, J., 'Free Expression and Personal Identification' 11(3) *Oxford Journal of Legal Studies* (1991), 303–324; Post, R., *Constitutional Domains: Democracy, Community, Management* (Harvard University Press, 1995). Significant connections with republicanism, see Honohan, I., *Civic Republicanism* (Routledge, 2002), Petit, P., *Republicanism: A Theory of Freedom and Government* (Oxford University Press, 1999).

[47] In Britain, argued by John Milton in his 1664 *Areopagitica* speech to Parliament, a polemic against the Licensing Order of 1643. Much later developed by Mill, J.S., n. 11 above, owing more to Mill's utilitarianism than the Kantian legacy that has deeply influenced the concept of autonomy.

[48] For example, curtailing media ownership to protect pluralism. See Chapter 14.

they can exert an overwhelming intellectual force against restraints on the flow of information and ideas. However, as consequential rather than deontological arguments, they are more vulnerable to empirical scrutiny. Behind the powerful rhetoric of democracy and truth, their persuasiveness is strongest where the claim that greater liberty to speak and to publish demonstrably leads to better democracy and more accurate or well reasoned decision making. The countervailing forces in the media state relationship, including the state's security interests or the public interest in protection from harmful or offensive expression, can moreover be expected to push the consequential arguments for liberty onto this narrower ground.

Ostensibly, the scope of the democratic argument for freedom of expression is enormous, covering any expression that is significant to participation in democratic politics or the formulation of law, regulation, or public policy more generally. However, this scope depends very much on the sort of democracy envisioned. Deliberative democracy, for example, with its emphasis on continual, direct participation by citizens in public affairs, requires much more extensive public access to knowledge than is necessary for effective representative democracy.[49] More limited forms of democracy therefore sustain more limited consequential arguments for freedom of expression. In addition, developments in communications technologies and media services change the practical implications of these different democratic arguments. Broadband access to the internet has, in this way, dramatically shifted the debate over public access to information and participation in political decision making, raising hopes and misgivings about the spontaneous growth of internet based deliberative democracy.[50]

The consequential argument for freedom of expression based on truth has its own apparent breadth and empirical limitations. It rests on the sweeping proposition that truth, or justified belief, is best revealed through open debate, in which claims and criticisms are unimpeded by fear of coercion or retribution.[51] Accordingly, as J.S. Mill argued, even self-evidently harmful or false ideas deserve protection as they challenge and thereby renew public understanding of truth through its defence.[52] In Joel Feinberg's more recent formulation,

There is a social gain then from constantly re-examining public policies, probing for difficulties and soft spots, bringing to light new and relevant facts, and subjecting to doubt hitherto unquestioned first premises. Without these challenges, nations have a natural tendency to drift complacently into dead ends and quagmires. For that reason, no amount of

---

[49] Dryzek, J., *Deliberative Democracy and Beyond* (Oxford University Press, 2000); Gutmann, A. and Thompson, D.F., *Why Deliberative Democracy?* (Princeton University Press, 2004); Posner, R.A., *Law, Pragmatism and Democracy* (Harvard University Press, 2003).

[50] Sunstein, C., *Republic.com 2.0* (Princeton University Press, 2007); Hindman, M., *The Myth of Digital Democracy* (Princeton University Press, 2008), and Castells, M., *Communication Power* (Oxford University Press, 2009).

[51] Campbell, T., *Rights: A Critical Introduction* (Routledge, 2006), ch 8.

[52] For J.S. Mill's various defences of the liberty to express self evidently false ideas, Mill, J.S., n. 10 above, ch 2.

offensiveness in an expressed opinion can counterbalance the vital social value of allowing unfettered personal expression.[53]

This argument has an obvious application to the operation of markets for goods and services. An unrestricted flow of information helps producers and distributors to become more efficient and helps consumers to choose the products best suited to their needs. The idea of markets, however, has a different, but also powerful, association with the argument for truth. This is the claim that, just as competitive markets can produce the goods and services consumers desire at optimal prices, open competition in the 'marketplace of ideas' will similarly yield the most useful information and ideas. This also strongly suggests that liberty of speech and publication is not only primarily a question of freedom from the state, but also that the most important information and ideas are those most sought after in a competitive market. This concept of a market place of ideas has its most famous origins in American constitutional jurisprudence, where the ideal of the minimal state is famously influential.[54]

The argument from truth has encouraged a sceptical view not just of the state, but of all institutions capable of restricting freedom of speech. On this view, all authority should be open to correction and all principles should be open to revision. It argues that regardless of benign intent, decision makers are fallible and institutions tend towards secrecy and self-justification and therefore liberty is always precarious and vulnerable.[55] The remedy is therefore extensive openness to public scrutiny and a broad acceptance of public criticism.

It is, nonetheless, also clear that unrestricted debate does not necessarily yield comprehensive discussion or well reasoned decision making.[56] Much depends on the conditions of debate, including the key question of who is able to contribute and be heard. Moreover, even where opinion from all sides of an issue is reasonably well represented, this may not compensate for the skewing effects of other factors, including audience bias, poor communication, or the complexity of the issues.[57] In short, open debate is much like open markets, useful for certain purposes but prone to various kinds of market failure.[58] As a result, the argument for truth has a core of demonstrable effectiveness in situations where its deficiencies are absent or controlled. Robust, open debate is therefore most effective as a path to decision making in closed processes that focus attention on relevant issues and exclude distracting or

[53] Feinberg, J., n. 24 above, 38–39.
[54] Justice Oliver Wendell Holmes's dissenting opinion in *Abrams v. U S*, 250 U.S. 616 (1919): '. . . the best test of truth is the power of the thought to get itself accepted in the competition of the market, and that truth is the only ground upon which their wishes safely can be carried out'.
[55] Milton, J. (1644), *Areopagitica: Speech to the Parliament of England*: 'This I know, that errors in a good government and in a bad are equally almost incident; for what magistrate may not be misinformed, and much the sooner, if liberty of printing be reduced into the power of a few?' For the contemporary polemical argument that liberty is always at risk, see Wilson, B., n. 43 above.
[56] Sunstein, C., n. 50 above, ch 3.
[57] Barendt, E., *Freedom of Speech* (Oxford University Press, 2005); Campbell, T., *Rights: A Critical Introduction* (Routledge, 2006).
[58] On market failure in the traditional broadcast sector, see Graham, A. and Davies, G., *Broadcasting, Society and Policy in the Multimedia Age* (University of Luton Press, 1997).

malign contributions. Its effectiveness in the contemporary public sphere, with its multitude of information sources and distribution channels, is mixed. The rough and tumble of public debate through the traditional and new media has undoubted advantages in disclosing significant information and encouraging participation, but it is also beset with problems of media inaccuracy and distortion and public prejudice and panic.[59]

Consequential arguments are therefore most influential when operating in the right circumstances. In the media state relationship, their impact is frequently decisive in securing greater liberty to publish where underlying claims based on autonomy are deadlocked or simply confused. Yet, their deficiencies open them to powerful counter arguments. Where the information and entertainment media seriously harm individual or collective well being or demonstrably undermine the security of the state, consequential arguments for freedom of expression can quickly lose their intellectual force. Liberal democratic differences over freedom of speech are therefore most pronounced where consequential arguments lead to risks of substantial harm. European and American rules governing the media thus often split precisely on the question of what risks or actual harm the state or other parties must bear in order to protect the benefits of a greater liberty to publish. These arguments are most acute where the state uses criminal sanctions to restrict expression.

Heavy reliance on consequential arguments has also created a different problem for the evolution of liberal democratic media law and policy. While the arguments for democracy and truth are often linked to liberalism's deeper interests in the autonomous self, as consequential arguments they have no necessary connection with liberal deontology. As discussed above, the nature of the democratic argument depends on the form of the democracy advanced, which can be non-liberal as well as liberal.[60] The argument for truth has the least necessary connection with liberal autonomy, despite J.S. Mill's pairing of the two concepts. The argument that open debate exposes deceit and error is an intuitive idea in the long tradition of sceptical inquiry, which is plainly not exclusive to liberal democracy.

Consequently, the openness of these arguments to non-liberal moral and political theory risks further obscuring the boundaries between liberal democracy and its competitors. As governments seek common ground for regional and global cooperation, the principles of democracy and open debate possess an attractive universality. Yet ironically the more they become entrenched in the fabric of international public order, the more these principles are likely to lose their close association with liberalism. The danger for liberal democracies is thus that, instead of projecting liberal democratic values outward, these principles will become a portal for non-liberal interpretations to flow back into domestic public policy and even constitutional adjudication.

---

[59] Lloyd, J., *What the Media are Doing to our Politics* (Constable, 2004), ch 3.
[60] Zakaria, F., 'The Rise of Illiberal Democracy', 76(6) *Foreign Affairs* (1997); Zakaria, F., *The Future of Freedom* (W. W. Norton & Company, 2004).

Liberalism, democracy, locality, and the media

Liberalism is the great intellectual resource of liberal democracy. While it may lack a common doctrine, its plentiful ideas feed the development of law and policy throughout the liberal democratic world. Yet liberal democratic politics are also something of a shotgun marriage between democracy's majoritarian consequences and liberal principles of personal autonomy.[61] There is undoubtedly a degree of mutual compatibility between democracy and liberalism. The idea of autonomy as self government, for instance, adds an important dimension to democratic ideas about participation in decision making in the public realm. Democratic majorities are however prone to illiberal responses and preferences, suppressing the liberty and harming the well being of individuals and groups in the process.

Consequently, the combination of liberalism and democracy is only workable where liberal principles fetter the choices of democratic majorities.[62] As William Galston has argued,

> To create a secure space within which individuals and groups may lead their lives, public institutions are needed. Liberal public institutions may restrict the activities of individuals and groups for four kinds of reasons: first, to reduce coordination problems and conflict among diverse legitimate activities and to adjudicate such conflict when it cannot be avoided; second, to prevent and when necessary punish transgressions individuals may commit against one another; third, to guard the boundary separating legitimate from illegitimate variations among ways of life; and finally, to secure the conditions—including cultural and civic conditions—needed to sustain public institutions over time.[63]

Plainly, the media state relationship is a major focus for the tensions that run between democracy and liberalism. Democratic majorities may support the liberty to speak and publish, even when that entails serious incitements to racial hatred against minority groups. Majorities may also give fulsome support to state security or public order measures that curb dissenting expression. Conversely, liberal principles of autonomy and equality, often entrenched in law and public policy, provide an important resource for efforts to counter majority preferences.

While the complex interplay of democratic and liberal principles is a prominent feature of media law in most liberal democracies, national media regimes are nonetheless unique. Each one is shaped by the extraordinary mix of language, culture, religion, geography, and much else that is distinctive to each locality. As a result, liberal democracies are exceptionally diverse in the ways they manage the tensions between democracy and liberalism in media law, regulation, and policy.

---

[61] Fareed Zakaria has argued that 'constitutional liberalism', which includes the rule of law, a separation of powers, and the protection of basic liberties of speech, assembly, religion, and property, is theoretically different and historically distinct from democracy. 'The Rise of Illiberal Democracy', n. 60 above.

[62] This is reflected in the unresolved question of whether democratic rights are liberal human rights. See Griffin, J., *On Human Rights* (Oxford University Press, 2008), 248–249.

[63] Galston, W., *Liberal Pluralism: The Implications of Value Pluralism for Political Theory and Practice* (Cambridge University Press, 2002), 3.

Yet in spite of this diversity, the past half century has seen a remarkable convergence in the structures, methods, and principles of media law. The reasons for this convergence are not however hard to find. Domestic media law, whether liberal democratic or not, has many underlying common features. As discussed in Chapter 1, coercive state control over the media is targeted at the key individuals and facilities essential to the production and distribution of media content. This has provided a deep template for the reception of legal and regulatory rules and practices. Furthermore, this receptivity is often enhanced by the enduring effects of European colonial regimes, which frequently involved the wholesale transfer of legal and administrative systems. Throughout the world, even in states not colonized directly, legal principles and methods are therefore typically structured on European civil or common law models and remain open to further exchange.

For many governments, there are also good contemporary reasons to adopt foreign legal models. Similarities in legal structures and principles make economic or political cooperation with leading states more effective. They can also strengthen the internal and external authority of the state by demonstrating its conformity to global expectations about the necessary institutions and processes of a legitimate state. Isomorphism of this kind has been particularly important to the spread of liberal democratic constitutional and legal structures important to the media, in particular the adoption of bills of rights.[64] There is of course a great difference between the adoption of foreign models and actual legal and administrative practice, which may continue to follow indigenous methods regardless of formal law and institutions.[65] The export of legal principles and regulatory regimes is moreover long associated with the global dominance of Europe and latterly America. The use of law to structure global relations may fade with the decline of western influence on world affairs.

Constitutionalism

This widespread convergence in the formal structures of law and government is often described as a process of constitutionalization. Its basic features include the adoption of constitutional texts that declare the foundational principles of the state and the allocation of powers to the major units of government. They invariably also include the entrenchment of selected individual rights in some form of supreme law.[66] The nature of those constitutionalized rights is however by no means

---

[64] Isomorphism means the tendency for organizational forms and purposes to become more alike. See Goodman, R. and Jinks, D., 'Toward an Institutional Theory of Sovereignty' 55(5) *Stanford Law Review* (2003), 1749–1788. The concept of isomorphism has developed out of the work of Walter Powell and Paul DiMaggio, see Powell, W. and DiMaggio, P., 'The Iron Cage Revisited: Institutional Isomorphism and Collective Rationality in Organizational Fields', 48(2) *American Sociological Review* (1983), 147–160.

[65] Goodman, R. and Jinks, D., n. 64 above, 1752.

[66] Gardbaum, S., 'A Democratic Defense of Constitutional Balancing', 4(1) *Law & Ethics of Human Rights* (2009), 1045.

consistent, even though many are drawn from the canon of rights celebrated in the 1948 Universal Declaration of Human Rights.[67] In liberal democracies, civil and political rights have historically been more prominent, although economic and social rights also come to enjoy constitutional entrenchment in some places.[68]

The structure of constitutionalized rights also varies considerably. Their relationship, for example, may be one of equality or hierarchy. The latter moreover may occur not only between the categories of civil and political rights as compared to economic and social rights, but also within either of those categories. The right to freedom of expression therefore may have the same weight as the right to privacy or may take priority over it. Finally, modes of interpretation and application differ according to the common or civil law origins of the national legal system as well as its particular doctrines of constitutional and general law. A focus on textual meaning, possibly including original intent, may well lead to very different conclusions than one that views the text as a dynamic instrument.

One of the most distinctive features of contemporary constitutionalism is the direct application of protected rights in the adjudication of disputes. In most cases, this means that exclusive or primary powers of interpretation have been vested in the courts and can be invoked through processes of judicial or constitutional review.[69] For many states, this has also involved an often controversial shift of power from their legislative and executive bodies to their judiciaries.[70]

National high courts and supranational tribunals have become increasingly important, even crucial, policy-making bodies. To paraphrase Alexis de Tocqueville's observation regarding the United States, there is now hardly any moral, political, or public policy controversy in the new constitutionalist world that does not sooner or later become a judicial one.[71]

The most obvious effect of the constitutional entrenchment of rights in liberal democracies is to formalize the relationship between law and liberalism. Law making and executing bodies are expected to ensure that they act consistently with the requirements of entrenched rights, as interpreted by the courts. For the courts, those requirements in turn need to be interpreted consistently with the fundamental values of liberalism. Given the great breadth and many uncertainties

[67] For example, Article 1(2) of the Basic Law of the Federal German Republic (1949) states that inviolable and inalienable human rights are the basis of every community and of peace and justice in the world.

[68] Note that the European Union Charter of Fundamental Rights contains civil and political as well as economic and social rights. Note also that Britain, Poland, and the Czech Republic, which are state parties to the European Convention on Human Rights—a treaty largely dedicated to civil and political rights—have refused to accept the Charter as a legally binding instrument under the terms of the Treaty of Lisbon. See Protocol on the Application of the Charter of Fundamental Rights of the European Union to Poland and to the United Kingdom.

[69] See, generally, Beatty, D. (ed.), *Human Rights and Judicial Review: A Comparative Perspective*, (Brill, 1994).

[70] Waldron, J., 'The Core of the Case against Judicial Review', 115(6) *Yale Law Journal* (2006), 1346–1406.

[71] Hirschl, R., 'The Political Origins of the New Constitutionalism', 11(1) *Indiana Journal of Global Legal Studies* (2004), 71–108.

of liberal theory, that gives the judiciary wide leeway in crafting constitutional doctrine, leaving the door open to ideas that are more republican, libertarian, communitarian, or even socialist than mainstream liberal. Nonetheless, liberal democratic constitutional law as such invariably rests on a commitment to liberalism's cores principles of moral autonomy and moral equality.

While the courts are obliged to ground constitutional rights in liberal moral and political theory, as a matter of principle or pragmatics they must also ensure that their actions respect, but are not overwhelmed by, the demands of the state and democratic majorities. This judicial balancing illustrates a critical distinction between liberalism and liberal democracy. On a pragmatic view, a successful liberal democratic state is one that is strongly oriented towards liberalism's commitment to individual freedom, but is also able to accommodate illiberal measures where necessary. These will go beyond liberalism's awkward compromises between liberty and well being and embrace majority illiberal beliefs and prejudices as well as the state's anxious concerns about its security and effectiveness. The courts and other public institutions and mechanisms in these successful states provide the forums and procedures in which the recurring conflicts between liberal principles and illiberal preferences are worked out.

Constitutionalism thus powerfully reworks the liberal democratic media state relationship, strengthening its law based character. The tensions and conflicts arising between the liberty to publish, the security and authority of the state, and the protection of individual and collective well being are therefore expressed in terms of constitutional principles, rights, and interests. This means that the right to freedom of expression will play a pivotal role in deciding whether the liberty to publish should be protected, fostered, or restricted. Its close relationship with the concept of autonomy will be worked and reworked in efforts to produce consistent reasoning to explain those decisions.

The First Amendment model

No country has exerted greater influence than the United States on the global development of liberal democratic constitutional rights in relation to the media state relationship. This pervasive influence arose in part from the advantages gained from the early American start as an avowedly liberal democratic republic. Even though US constitutional doctrine concerning the media did not begin to develop in earnest until the beginning of the twentieth century, the United States was the first to do so amongst the western democracies.[72] As a result, all other liberal democratic courts and legislators have worked downstream from events in the United States in their own constitutional decisions concerning the media. The principles and ideas developed in the application of the First Amendment have

---

[72] Rabban, D.M., 'The Emergence of Modern First Amendment Doctrine', 50(4) *University of Chicago Law Review* (1983), 1205–1355.

consequently become fused into the common knowledge of liberal democratic constitutional law.[73]

Ironically, the First Amendment's influence abroad is also limited by its pre-eminent place in American constitutional law and government. This can be attributed partly to the way in which the courts interpret and apply the text of the federal Constitution, which is treated as an authoritative statement of the nation's fundamental principles of government. The judicial focus is therefore necessarily on its correct interpretation, which tends to be highly interpretivist, often respecting origins and producing predictable rules limiting judicial discretion.[74] The First Amendment is thus embedded in a document that remains highly attuned to American history and precedent.

The words of the First Amendment are, moreover, famously unconditional.[75] Judicial interpretation has given this simple assertion of the right to speak and publish freely a sweeping breadth, expressing a robust faith in the curative powers of expression to reverse or mitigate the harm it may have caused.[76] American constitutional doctrine therefore remains committed to Justice Holmes's vision of the market place of ideas.[77] It is also sceptical of positive state intervention to assist individuals or communities that have limited access to the media or restrictive measures intended to foster diversity through controls on media ownership.[78] At the same time, the exceptional strength of First Amendment principles has meant that its application can be narrower than equivalent constitutional rights to expression in other countries.[79]

The American media state relationship is therefore decisively tipped towards the liberty to publish. First Amendment doctrine is fundamentally sceptical of any claim that restrictions on the media are necessary to protect the state's security or effectiveness. For a restriction of this kind to be upheld, the state must demonstrate clear proof of the legitimacy of its intentions and the efficacy of its methods.[80] It is,

---

[73] For example, the 'public figure' principle developed under *New York Times v. Sullivan* (1964) 376 U.S. 254 and its US appellate court progeny. See Chapter 10.

[74] This approach to constitutional review is especially important in American constitutional theory. See, notably, Dworkin, R., *Taking Rights Seriously* (Harvard University Press, 1977).

[75] 'Congress shall make no law respecting an establishment of religion, or prohibiting the free exercise thereof; or abridging the freedom of speech, or of the press; or the right of the people peaceably to assemble, and to petition the Government for a redress of grievances', United States Constitution, First Amendment, 1791.

[76] See Carmi, G.E., 'Dignity Versus Liberty: The Two Western Cultures of Free Speech', 26 *Boston University International Law Journal* (2008), 277–374, which contrasts the American constitutional model, characterized as liberty-based, with a dignity-based German model.

[77] See, for example, *Citizens United v. Federal Election Commission*, 558 U.S. 50 (2010).

[78] Stein, L., 'Understanding Speech Rights: Defensive and Empowering Approaches to the First Amendment', 26(1) *Media, Culture & Society* (2004), 102–120.

[79] Kumm, M., 'Democracy is Not Enough: Rights, Proportionality and the Point of Judicial Review' in Klatt, M. (ed.), *The Legal Philosophy of Robert Alexy* (Oxford University Press, 2009), 8. Schauer, F., 'Freedom of Expression Adjudication in Europe and America: A Case Study in Comparative Constitutional Architecture' in Nolte, G. (ed.), *European and U.S. Constitutionalism,* (Cambridge University Press, 2005), and Fried, C., *Right and Wrong* (Harvard University Press, 1978).

[80] For example, the Pentagon papers case, *New York Times Co. v. United States,* (1971) 403 U.S. 713.

in particular, rarely legitimate for the state to make distinctions between protected forms of expression based on whether their content has harmful or beneficial effects.[81] In short, the state cannot restrict expression simply because it disapproves of its content or viewpoint.

In addition, the federal Constitution's Bill of Rights does not explicitly recognize a right to many forms of physical or mental well being, except those narrowly focused on protection of the individual from coercion by the state.[82] As a result, the liberty to publish normally takes precedence in American law over the protection of individuals and communities from harmful expression. Those concerns, including protection from incitement to hatred, are merely legitimate, but secondary, public policy purposes.[83] The Bill of Rights is not unusual in its lack of express rights to well being, which also occurs in many other liberal democratic constitutional human rights instruments. However, the absence of an explicit constitutional right to privacy has become a key factor in the growing divide between American and European human rights law. In the latter, the right to privacy has become the basis for an expanding concept of private personality and life importing several aspects of well being.[84]

The pre-eminent status of freedom of expression in the United States is one of the chief reasons for the celebrated 'exceptionalism' of American constitutional law.[85] Yet these exceptional features, including the profoundly domestic orientation of First Amendment doctrine, have hampered efforts to export American principles of free speech internationally. Where other liberal democracies encounter problems in media law already considered in First Amendment jurisprudence, American law can be influential.[86] Yet, in many instances, the courts in these countries have rejected American examples, which are often highly prescriptive and rooted in textual analysis.[87]

---

[81] Content and viewpoint neutrality. On the importance of 'excluded reasons' to American constitutional law, see Halberstam, D., 'Desperately Seeking Europe: On Comparative Methodology and the Conception of Rights', 5(1) *International Journal of Constitutional Law* (2007), 166–182.

[82] For example, the Fourth Amendment, protection from unreasonable search and seizure, and the Eighth Amendment, prohibition of excessive bail and cruel and unusual punishment.

[83] Incitement to hatred, see Chapter 13. See Heymann, S.J., 'Hate Speech, Public Discourse, and the First Amendment' in Hare, I. and Weinstein, J., *Extreme Speech and Democracy* (Oxford University Press, 2009) on 'social interests'.

[84] See Chapter 10.

[85] Schauer, F., 'The Exceptional First Amendment' in Ignatieff, M. (ed.), *American Exceptionalism and Human Rights* (Princeton University Press, 2005), 29–56 and Schauer, F., 'Freedom of Expression Adjudication in Europe and America: A Case Study in Comparative Constitutional Architecture' in Nolte, G. (ed.), *European and U.S. Constitutionalism* (Cambridge University Press, 2005).

[86] For example, *Lingens v. Austria* (Application No. 9815/82, 8 July 1986), (ECHR); *Reynolds v. Times Newspapers* (2001) 2 AC 12; and *Lange v. Australian Broadcasting Corporation* (1997) 189 CLR 520.

[87] Ibid.

Proportionality analysis

In contrast to American constitutional methods, other approaches to the adjudication of constitutionalized rights allow greater leeway for local preferences, including a more expansive role for the state as well as greater legal protection for aspects of well being. Many of these alternatives are forms of proportionality analysis, which is undoubtedly the method of constitutional adjudication most often associated with the rift in liberal democratic constitutionalism.[88] Its widespread embrace has opened the way to domestic and supranational judicial decisions that are plainly inconsistent with First Amendment principles, effectively foreclosing potential transatlantic and wider alignment on many media related issues.[89]

Proportionality analysis is sometimes used to describe what is no more than simple balancing, in which opposing interests are considered on their own merit. In its fully developed form, however, proportionality goes well beyond simple balancing in an effort to find the best compromise between opposing rights or, in other cases, opposing rights and interests. This sophisticated form of proportionality analysis was first developed by the German Constitutional Court, which uses a four step process to determine whether a measure is an unconstitutional violation of a protected right.[90] The first step is to decide whether the contested measure is directed towards a legitimate public policy purpose. It that test is satisfied, it is then necessary to decide whether the measure is 'suitable' (rationally related to that purpose) and 'necessary' (no more restrictive of the right concerned than necessary to achieve that purpose). If the measure also passes these tests, the final step is to decide whether it is proportionate 'in the narrow sense' (*proportionality stricto sensu*). This means that the decision maker must weigh the benefits of the measure against its negative effects on the right concerned, considering relevant factors. While other courts have developed different processes of proportionality analysis, the German model is arguably its classic form.[91]

Necessity, or means-ends analysis, as well as balancing are certainly well known in American constitutional jurisprudence.[92] However, they do not form part of any single test and can be used selectively depending on the issue and the application of presumptions and other rules of constitutional analysis.[93] These include the categorization of speech or publication to determine the degree of protection any instance of expression ought to receive under the First Amendment. Direct incitement to immediate violence, for example, is a largely unprotected category of

---

[88] Weinrib, L., 'The Postwar Paradigm and American Exceptionalism' in Choudhry, S. (ed.), *The Migration of Constitutional Ideals* (Cambridge University Press, 2006), 84.

[89] See Chapter 10.

[90] Stone Sweet, A. and Mathews, J., 'Proportionality Balancing and Global Constitutionalism', 47(1) *Columbia Journal of Transnational Law* (2008), 73–165.

[91] For example, Canada.

[92] Stone Sweet, A. and Mathews, J., n. 90 above.

[93] Gardbaum, S., 'A Democratic Defense of Constitutional Balancing', 4(1) *Law & Ethics of Human Rights* (2009) (UCLA School of Law Research Paper No. 09–09).

expression and consequently balancing analysis is unnecessary to determine the validity of its legal prohibition.[94] Balancing is moreover controversial amongst American judges and legal scholars and is not applied in the wide ranging manner of full blown proportionality analysis.[95]

One of the main advantages claimed for proportionality analysis is that it gives judges an argumentation framework that does not pre-determine outcomes.[96] Instead, it is intended to ensure that constitutionally protected rights are realized to the greatest extent possible in the circumstances given countervailing rights and interests.[97] This purpose is particularly well suited to the resolution of disputes arising in the media state relationship. Given the complex array of competing rights and interests present in the liberal democratic media sphere, proportionality analysis allows judges to consider the application of the right to freedom of expression in its full context without prejudging the outcome. In this process, the state is forced to make reasoned arguments for restricting the liberty to publish or, in other situations, make arguments for allowing expression which harms or offends others.[98]

Proportionality analysis, as a generic argumentation framework, has helped to develop consistency in the treatment of media issues across liberal democracies committed to the ideal of universal human rights. Nonetheless, critics have argued that, because of its inbuilt flexibility, proportionality analysis threatens the vital connection between constitutional law and the distinctive nature of the democratic polity concerned.[99] On this view, constitutional adjudication in a self-governing community requires an interpretive approach that is anchored in the particular decisions and institutions of that polity.[100] Constitutional texts approached in this manner provide a degree of external constraint on legal decision making that cannot be provided by open-ended principles.[101] As Frederick Schauer argues,

[T]he typical subsumption inquiry is largely constrained, largely textually interpretive, and largely characterized by the way in which the constraints of a moderately clear text, when one exists, exclude numerous factors and considerations that would not only otherwise be

---

[94] *Brandenburg v. Ohio*, (1969) 395 U.S. 444.

[95] On balancing in US law, see early arguments in Pildes, R.H., 'Avoiding Balancing: The Role of Exclusionary Reasons in Constitutional Law' 45(4) *Hastings Law Journal* (1994), 711–752. More recent discussion in Baker, E., 'Hate Speech' in Hare, I. and Weinstein, J. (eds), *Extreme Speech and Democracy* (Oxford University Press, 2009).

[96] Stone Sweet, A. and Mathews, J., n. 90 above, 76 and 89.

[97] On fundamental rights as 'optimising requirements', see Robert Alexy, for example: Alexy, R., *A Theory of Constitutional Rights,* 2nd edn (Oxford University Press, 2002).

[98] Kumm, M., n. 79 above.

[99] Jackson, V.C., 'Being Proportional about Proportionality' 21 *Constitutional Commentary* (2004), 803 and 821.

[100] Ibid.

[101] Schauer, F., 'Balancing, Subsumption and the Constraining Role of Legal Text', in Klatt, M. (ed.), *Institutional Reason: The Legal Philosophy of Robert Alexy* (Oxford University Press, forthcoming 2011).

relevant, but would also, typically, be relevant were the methodology to be one of balancing or proportionality rather than subsumption.[102]

Proportionality analysis is also criticized for presenting a misleading impression of neutrality. Determining the proper scope of fundamental rights, such as the right to freedom of expression, involves qualitative decision making, which cannot be avoided by balancing methods. In proportionality analysis, a court must select which factors are relevant and how much weight each should be given. Even where precedent dictates the rights, interests, and other factors that need to be considered, the weight attached to any factor will vary considerably in the complex circumstances of the dispute. At worst, the process becomes a mechanistic weighing of incommensurable values and principles.[103] This lays proportionality analysis open to the further objection that it does not require courts to take a strong moral position on fundamental liberal principles. As Kai Möller puts it, '[W]e should not expect to be able to defend morally controversial positions about constitutional rights on the basis of an approach that takes no side in moral debates.'[104] Proportionality analysis is thus an essentially consequentialist form of reasoning and is not properly grounded in the deontological principles at the heart of liberalism.[105]

Constitutional rights

Plainly, judges are more likely to work from within a settled moral framework when they are required to interpret and apply constitutional texts. On this basis, they are also arguably better able to identify the vital social or moral issues at the heart of the dispute, rather than engage in a balancing exercise that glides over those underlying issues. This is not to argue that proportionality analysis prevents judges from adopting a moral perspective on the dispute. It is hardly possible to determine the proper scope of the right to freedom of expression without recourse to some fundamental moral understanding.[106] Yet, where judges are guided by the meaning of a constitutional text, the necessary moral understanding of the issues at hand will probably be clearer and more prescriptive.

---

[102] 'Subsumption' meaning the outcome is subsumed under the relevant and authoritative legal language. Ibid.
[103] Tsakyrakis, S., 'Proportionality: An Assault on Human Rights?' Jean Monnet Working Paper (2008) 09/08.
[104] Möller, K., 'Balancing and the Structure of Constitutional Rights' 5(3) *International Journal of Constitutional Law* (2007), 453–468.
[105] Kumm, M., 'Political Liberalism and the Structure of Rights: On the Place and Limits of the Proportionality Requirement' in Pavlakos, G. (ed.), *Law, Rights, Discourse: The Legal Philosophy of Robert Alexy* (Hart Publishing, 2007), 153.
[106] Ibid., 148–149 and Jackson, V.C., 'Being Proportional about Proportionality', 21(3) *Constitutional Commentary* (2004), 803–860. Andenas and Zleptnig have argued that the basic idea underlying proportionality is that citizens should have their freedom of action limited only so far as necessary in the public interest. See Andenas, M. and Zleptnig, S., 'Surveillance and Data Protection: Regulatory Approaches in the EU and Member States', 14(6) *European Business Law Review* (2003), 765–813.

Aside from simple interpretivism, rights based analysis is the leading alternative to proportionality analysis in methods of constitutional adjudication. It rests on the argument that certain core rights embody the basic moral prerogatives of liberal democracy and therefore enjoy a higher status when confronting opposing interests.[107] Ronald Dworkin expressed this idea by describing rights as 'trumps' that prevail over ultilitarian or other relevant considerations.[108] In a similar vein, Jürgen Habermas described rights as firewalls, arguing that the purpose of making a principle into a fundamental right is to insulate it from the effects of legitimate public policy.[109] Rights therefore cannot be reduced to the principles they embody. They are peremptory claims on others justified by the interests of the right holder, either personally or as a representative of broader social interests, and should prevail to the maximum possible extent.[110] On that basis, by effectively downgrading rights to the status of mere principles, proportionality analysis fails to acknowledge one of the major purposes of constitutionalism: the institutionalization of the core beliefs of a liberal democratic society.[111]

Consequently, rights based analysis addresses the problems and tensions of the media state relationship in a very different manner. The liberty to speak and publish sits at the heart of the constitutional right to freedom of expression and is thus presumed to prevail over any opposing interests of the state. Nonetheless, the effect of the presumption is not to deny the legitimacy of state interests or prevent their legal enforcement. Like any other theory concerning the liberal democratic state, rights based analysis cannot avoid the fact that a secure and effective territorial state is necessary for the success of political liberalism. As a result, the presumption that rights prevail against state interests is, in effect, a set of rules about the legitimate purposes of the state and its burden of proof when seeking to restrict freedom of expression. In comparison, proportionality analysis is likely to be more generous in defining the legitimate purposes of the liberal democratic state and less demanding in the justifications it requires for restrictive measures.

Rights based analysis is moreover not concerned with rights per se, but with the protection of selected rights that embody the fundamental principles of a society and its state. It is only these constitutionalized rights that should never be subject to balancing in relation to state or other interests.[112] They should therefore be well defined and not go beyond their core concerns and new rights should be resisted as

---

[107] See Kumm, M., n. 105 above, 134.

[108] Dworkin, R., *Taking Rights Seriously* (Harvard University Press, 1977), xi. On rights as trumps in constitutional adjudication, see Jackson, V.C., n. 106 above, 818–819. See also Rawls's principles of right, the 'priority of the right over the good' in Rawls, J., *A Theory of Justice* (Harvard University Press, 1971).

[109] Habermas, J., *Between Facts and Norms: Contributions to a Discourse Theory of Law and Democracy* (MIT Press, 1996), 258–259. See also Baynes, K., 'Democracy and the Rechsstaat' in White, S. (ed.), *The Cambridge Companion to Habermas* (Cambridge University Press, 1995).

[110] Kumm, M., 'What Do You Have in Virtue of Having a Constitutional Right? On the Place and Limits of the Proportionality Requirement' New York University Law School (2006), (Public Law Research Paper No. 06-41).

[111] See Kumm, M., n. 105 above, 139–140.

[112] Ibid., 142.

they are likely to obscure and conflict with the primary ones.[113] In contrast, proportionality analysis is not only less strict in defining the boundaries of rights, but also recognizes a greater range of rights, given that any relevant right or interest needs to be considered in the determination of proportionality. The protection of children from violent pornography, for example, may be brought within the scope of a right or treated as a legitimate interest to the same effect.

Despite the international influence of rights based analysis, proportionality analysis has become the leading method of constitutional adjudication in the liberal democratic world. Different versions have not only spread to regional and international regimes, but have also taken root in many domestic legal systems.[114] This popularity is due in part to the great adaptability of proportionality analysis to different sets of rights and interests and its flexibility in outcomes, which can allow a significant role for local circumstances in adjudication. That is also one of its chief faults. Although grounded in liberal democratic principles, proportionality analysis has difficulty maintaining a clear boundary between liberal democracy and its alternatives. It is best suited to consequential arguments—whose limits are not necessarily contiguous with liberalism—and resists deeply held moral positions.

The United States therefore retains considerable influence over the development of liberal democratic media law throughout the world. It is certainly difficult for other countries to embrace the intensely domestic and highly prescriptive American approach to the constitutional adjudication of the right to freedom of expression. Yet American exceptionalism has given the United States a distinctive voice favouring the liberty to publish in debates over the proper relationship between the media and the liberal democratic state.[115] It is also a haven for the development of alternatives to proportionality analysis in constitutional law.

Legal and regulatory convergence in the internet era

Constitutional law is enormously important to the development of liberal democratic media law and policy. It is a primary source of the principles and methods of analysis that are crucial to the resolution of disputes and tensions in the domestic media state relationship. Without them, the foundations of the contemporary liberal democratic state would be at risk, rudderless in a complex, rapidly changing political and economic environment. Externally, constitutional law has also become one of the principal fields for debate and common understanding in the liberal democratic world. It therefore provides a shared conceptual language that not only

---

[113] Möller, K., 'Balancing and the Structure of Constitutional Rights', 5(3) *International Journal of Constitutional Law* (2007), 453–468.

[114] These include European human rights law, European Union law, World Trade Organization law, as well as domestic legal systems in not only civil but also common law traditions, such as Britain, Canada, and New Zealand.

[115] Carmi describes this exceptionalism as liberty oriented compared to other liberal democracies, which are predominantly dignity oriented. Carmi, G.E., 'Dignity Versus Liberty: The Two Western Cultures Of Free Speech', 26 *Boston University International Law Journal* (2008), 277–374.

enables closer cooperation, but also allows governments and other parties to disagree in a shared conceptual language, making the future resolution of these disagreements more likely.

Yet, as vitally important as constitutional law has now become, it is not a driving force in the media state relationship. It comes into play in response to public or private acts. This is plainly the case in adjudication, but it is also true where constitutional principles are used to assess the legality of regulatory decisions or policy proposals. The driving force within the media state relationship comes instead from the economic and political interests and projects of the moment.[116] They guide the deployment of new communications technologies and shape the supply of media services.

In the internet era, the torrent of new communication technologies has captured the public eye. For the wealthier segments of the world's population, these have brought an extraordinary access to information and entertainment content that is readily available, almost anywhere, through wired or wireless devices. Less noticeable, but often more important, are the radical changes that have occurred not just in commercial strategies and practices, but also in government communications and media policies.

In the formative years of the internet era, many governments were seized by the urgent need to grasp the potential benefits of the unfolding communications revolution.[117] For some, putting the country at the forefront of the new information led global economy became an absolute priority.[118] At this point, however, the rise of the internet as a public communications platform was also coinciding with a major change in the transatlantic public policy environment. The resurgence of classical liberal economic policies, which had begun in the United States and Britain, was sweeping outwards to influence, if not transform, public policy in much of the rest of the world. These policies found a seemingly perfect vehicle in the internet, which promised to break down the thicket of legal, regulatory, and other barriers obstructing the free flow of information and entertainment content, thereby achieving a dual *telos* of economic liberalization and political democratization. For some, it seemed possible that the media might finally escape its bondage to the state and exist in 'cyberspace', free from legal and regulatory control.[119] In this atmosphere, governments were widely advised against incorporating the new media into their existing broadcasting regulatory regimes.[120] Instead, they were urged to allow these new services the freedom to grow without intrusive state intervention, rather than risk chilling economic growth and political emancipation.

---

[116] 'To think politically is to think about agency, power, and interests, and the relations among these', Geuss, R., *Philosophy and Real Politics* (Princeton University Press, 2008), 25.

[117] See Chapter 1.

[118] See, for example, the response of the British government to the effects of convergence on the media sector, *Regulating Communications: Approaching Convergence in the Information Age*, Cm 4022, (July 1998).

[119] For the internet separatist position see Johnson, D.R. and Post, D.G., 'Law And Borders: The Rise of Law in Cyberspace', 48(5) *Stanford Law Review* (1996), 1367–1402.

[120] See Chapter 4.

Consequently, the reaction of most liberal democracies to the advent of the internet has been decidedly different than their assertion of control over broadcast services many decades before. Without doubt, their efforts have been unmistakably directed towards the centuries old necessity of securing control over the national public information environment. They have therefore looked for the vulnerabilities of the new communications technologies and the services that rely on them and, where possible, have attempted to bring them within the coercive grip of the state.

In the internet era, the state has faced two intermeshed challenges: the swelling numbers of content providers and the collapse of clear boundaries between foreign and domestic based content. Media regimes have in short been threatened by uncontrollable diversity and the failure of distance. Traditionally, achieving genuine mass distribution of media content required, at the very least, the funds needed to pay for expensive production and distribution facilities. This barrier maintained the critical distinction between mass and personal communication and also severely restricted the numbers of mass media companies and outlets. It was next to impossible for the state to control the passive consumers of media content, but most producers and distributors were too large to escape notice. As described in Chapter 1, digitization has now destroyed these well worn distinctions. While individual internet users and content creators remain infinitely small compared to old and new media businesses, their collective output is overwhelming. They have also brought the relative anonymity of personal communications to the new mass media.

This revolution in technologies and services also overtook the established barriers that controlled the entry of foreign media content. The internet appeared to create a seamless global network of networks that allowed content to flow uncontrolled across borders, effectively destroying the distinctions between foreign and domestic media. More than the uncontrollable diversity of content sources, the threat to the boundaries of the national public information sphere was a direct challenge to the security of the state and its control over public order, morals, and culture.

All states consequently needed to make far reaching changes to their communications and media laws and regulations. This has involved considerable trial and error as governments have sought to apply basic principles of responsibility and liability to the distribution of content through new media services. The idea that the deliberate originator of content should bear primary responsibility is a universal principle for criminal culpability and civil liability for unlawful content. Logically, pre-existing rules based on this principle must apply to individuals who intentionally make unlawful content available on the internet. Many liberal democracies have however moved cautiously and hesitantly in that direction, reluctant to accept the administrative and financial burden of a task that could easily spark public opposition to an apparently draconian intrusion into private life.[121]

---

[121] See, for example, opposition in Britain to the provisions of the Digital Economy Act 2010 concerning online infringement of copyright, which include limiting internet access. Killock, J., 'Digital Economy Bill is disaster for digital economy', *New Scientist* (12 March 2010).

From broadcast to internet regulation

Inevitably, the scale of unlawful activity or instances of gross unlawfulness have forced even reluctant liberal democratic governments to find or provide ways to detect and sanction individual content originators.[122] Yet, many have preferred to pursue the commercial providers and operators that make mass individual participation possible. As the commercialization of the internet gathered pace, individual content origination began to be channelled through services that provided convenient ways for individuals to post content. There was, however, no clear consensus on the extent to which these services should be held responsible for the third party content they were hosting.

Historically, responsibility for the distribution of prohibited or restricted content was based on degrees of knowledge and control that depended on the nature of the communications technologies and services concerned. The two obvious precedents for internet hosting were broadcasting and telecommunications. Broadcasters were usually held responsible for all the content they broadcast because they held ultimate control over the broadcasting process. Even where they broadcast live, they were able to choose the circumstances and put protections in place to minimize the risk of broadcasting unlawful content.[123] In comparison, telecommunications operators normally had no content responsibility as they could not reasonably monitor the huge volume of voice and data passing instantaneously through their networks.[124]

The emerging business model for third party content hosting, in which individuals were able to post content without the prior knowledge or approval of the service provider, plainly did not fit the rules for broadcasting pre-recorded content. Yet content hosting was also unlike telecommunications. By its nature, the content was not transient and, once given notice, the host service provider could easily remove objectionable content. Indeed, it was apparent that the regulatory standard of reasonable prudence for live broadcasting could be adapted to the circumstances of hosting. In the United States, however, concerns about the chilling effect of state intervention in internet services led to legislation exempting providers from liability from a variety of content prohibitions, including defamation and obscenity laws.[125] European legislation, on the other hand, settled that throughout the EU content

---

[122] For example, *Liskula Cohen v. Google* (2009) Index No. 100012/09 (N.Y. Co. August 17, 2009).

[123] This is still often the case for traditional broadcasters. See, for example, the United Kingdom, Office of Communications (OFCOM) Broadcasting Code for licensed services.

[124] See, for example, the English case, *Bunt v. Tilley and others* [2006] EWHC 407 (QB), in which the court found no liability at common law for telecommunications companies that carry defamatory content, where they 'fulfil no more than the role of a passive medium for communication', (para. 37).

[125] Section 230, Communications Decency Act 1996, (47 U.S.C. s. 230).

hosting services must take reasonable action when given notice to avoid legal liability for hosted third party content.[126]

The debate over other internet intermediaries, in particular internet service providers (ISPs) who connect local customers to the internet, has followed a similar path. In one respect, the operator of an internet connection service is much like a telecommunications services operator, as it does not have any reasonable way of monitoring the flow of information and entertainment content subscribers access through its network. Nonetheless, ISPs are able to prevent their users from gaining access to specific websites and this has provided the basis for limited legal and regulatory responsibility. Yet this blocking capacity is far from genuine editorial control and there is little agreement on how much of the burden of content control should be placed on ISPs.[127]

As their populations gained unprecedented access to foreign based media through the internet, governments were also forced to reconsider the jurisdictional scope of their liability rules for content publication. There was certainly no clear answer to the question of when a state could reasonably claim the right to enforce its laws against content providers who had done nothing more than make their content available on the internet from a foreign place. The alternatives were also starkly opposed. The United States championed the principle of no jurisdiction for mere availability, which was consistent with its domestic rules of jurisdiction and its policy of limited state interference in internet based markets.[128] Moreover, as many major content providers and distributors argued, a broader jurisdictional rule would require that they know the laws of all countries and ensure their content complied with the most restrictive.[129]

Other states, even when sympathetic, were reluctant to accept this position. If a state were to renounce the right to assert jurisdiction on the basis of mere availability on the internet, it would effectively abandon any hope of maintaining the centuries old division between domestic and foreign information spheres. Consequently, many governments have chosen to exercise legislative jurisdiction when online content can be accessed from within their territories, regardless of the location of the principal computer on which it is hosted. Major content providers have therefore had to accept that they are potentially vulnerable to legal and regulatory sanctions in the distant places where their content is consumed.[130] As discussed in Chapter 1, their commercial interests force them to consider the

[126] Articles 12–15, Electronic Commerce Directive (Directive 2000/31/EC of the European Parliament and of the Council of 8 June 2000 on certain legal aspects of information society services, in particular electronic commerce, in the Internal Market). See also Chapter 8.
[127] See, for example, Davies, C., 'The Hidden Censors of the Internet' *Wired Magazine* (20 May 2009).
[128] See Chapter 7.
[129] *Dow Jones and Company Inc. v. Gutnick* (2002) HCA 56.
[130] Goldsmith, J., 'Regulation of the Internet: Three Persistent Fallacies', 73(4) *Chicago Kent Law Review* (1999), 1119–1131; Goldsmith, J. and Wu, T., *Who Controls the Internet? Illusions of a Borderless World* (Oxford University Press, 2006); Reidenberg, J., 'States and Internet Enforcement', 1 *University of Ottawa Law and Technology Journal* (2003), 213–230; Thompson, C., 'Google's China Problem (and China's Google Problem)', *New York Times Magazine* (23 April 2006).

domestic rules that govern their major markets.[131] Increasingly aggressive claims of national jurisdiction, however, have also created disputes with other states, which have not welcomed foreign controls on lawful domestic activities.[132]

Platform neutrality

The policy argument against state intervention in internet based services and markets not only influenced the development of liability and jurisdictional rules, but also had a powerful effect on regulatory theory. This included the adoption, fully or partially, of a radically new view of the overlapping communications and media sectors. Instead of segmenting each communications or media service into its own vertical category, binding together specific delivery technologies with specific content forms (for example, transmission over switched circuit networks with voice telephony services and broadcasting over the radiospectrum with radio and television services), governments were urged to implement a simple, horizontal distinction between communications infrastructures and information and entertainment content.[133] This would better reflect the realities of a convergent communications and media sphere, in which any content could be delivered over through any infrastructure or 'platform'. They were also urged to overhaul their legal and regulatory regimes to implement this vision as soon as possible, to remove obstacles to convergence.

One of the principal benefits in adopting this much simplified structure was that it became easier for governments to achieve regulatory neutrality. The idea that governments ought to apply regulatory rules in a neutral way to all communications and media services competing in the same market expressed one of the major aims of neoclassical economic policy: that necessary state intervention should neither advantage nor disadvantage particular market competitors. Infrastructure regulation, once separated from content concerns, could thus be aimed primarily at the achievement of equality of competitive opportunities across communications platforms. The scope of regulatory rules would therefore be defined by the boundaries of the relevant market rather than technical differences in the delivery infrastructure. Mobile phone networks, for example, would not be disadvantaged by regulation when developing audiovisual services to compete with broadcast television and internet networks. Similarly, content regulation would be applied in a neutral way to information and entertainment content, regardless of the provider.

---

[131] See Weinrib, L., n. 88 above.

[132] See Chapter 7.

[133] The European Union Framework for Electronic Communications, adopted in 2002, formalized a division between the regulation of infrastructure and content services that hinges on the principle of platform neutrality. Van Eijk, N., 'New European Rules for the Communications Sector' *IRIS Plus*, 2003–2. The European Union introduced reforms to this regulatory framework in 2009. European Commission, *EU Telecoms Reform: 12 reforms to pave way for stronger consumer rights, an open internet, a single European telecoms market and high-speed internet connections for all citizens*, MEMO/09/513, (Brussels, 20 November 2009).

Genuine regulatory neutrality was clearly impossible. Entrenched providers and operators dominated the communications and media sectors, often blocking market entry while also serving as vehicles for important public policies.[134] Neutrality was therefore less a policy prescription than a general policy orientation, which was to be achieved through equivalent measures depending on prevailing circumstances.[135] This was especially true of content regulation. Before mass broadband access to the internet, traditional linear television, whether delivered through terrestrial relay, cable, or satellite, remained the dominant form of audiovisual media in the developed world. In many liberal democracies, this sector was also typically at one end of a spectrum of graduated content regulation that moved abruptly to a loosely or entirely unregulated print media sector at the other end.[136] Within the television sector, further distinctions between modes of delivery tended to set free-to-air broadcast television apart as the most intensely regulated form of media.[137] In principle, these structures should have been dismantled as convergence brought old and new forms of audiovisual media into direct competition. This, however, has yet to occur in many highly advanced national media markets.

Convergence has turned out to be an unpredictable process, sometimes moving hesitantly and at others with unexpected speed. It certainly began well before the invention of the internet and still has some way to run before modes of content delivery are entirely indistinguishable and irrelevant to consumers. Despite competing in overlapping markets, the most popular audiovisual services can still be distinguished by ease of access, user control over content, and editorial responsibility for content. While the experience of free-to-air, linear television has changed dramatically through digitization, it is still not the same as a video on demand service and is a world away from internet based video hosting services.

As a result, instead of a simplification of content regulation, in many liberal democracies the communications revolution has brought regulatory complexity and confusion.[138] In a public policy environment that encouraged market based solutions, governments attempted, to a greater or lesser extent, to assimilate internet based services into the more lightly regulated end of the content regulation

---

[134] See, for example, BBC and ITV dominance of the British television market before the advent of satellite television. Crissell, A., *An Introductory History of British Broadcasting* (Routledge, 1997), chs 5, 6, and 10.

[135] Van Eijk, N., 'Regulating Old Values in the Digital Age' *Conference on Guaranteeing Media Freedom on the Internet* (OSCE, 2004).

[136] Compare, for example, the absence of government regulatory authorities for the print media in Britain and the United States with the long established presence of state authorities empowered to sanction licensed broadcasters for breaches of legally binding programme content rules.

[137] See, for example, the United Kingdom, Broadcasting Act 1990, under which the terrestrial free-to-air television broadcasters (Channels 3, 4, and 5) were subject to positive programme obligations not imposed on cable or satellite television broadcasters.

[138] See, for example, the confusion of regulatory responsibilities that contributed to the 'premium rate scandal' in Britain. See United Kingdom, Office of Communications (OFCOM), *Report of an Inquiry into Television Broadcasters' use of Premium Rate Telephone Services in Programmes* (The Richard Ayre Report), (18 July 2007).

spectrum.[139] However concerns about public exposure to a deluge of unlawful or offensive content also meant that these services were rarely left entirely to market forces and general law. Instead, they were often brought under a variety of new regulatory bodies, rules, and methods.[140] In these increasingly complex regulatory systems, pre-existing regimes for traditional broadcasting have tended to survive, while innovative elements involving co and self regulation and greater consumer responsibility have also been developed to govern new media services.[141]

The result is often a cascade of variable responsibility for prohibited or restricted media content running from providers and intermediaries to the ultimate consumers. In each media service, the burden of responsibility can be differently assigned according to the nature of the content and the relationship between the service and content providers and the consumer. In addition, the state may also establish a co or self regulatory regime for a particular market segment, such as internet service providers or video on demand providers.[142] Under these regimes, commercial operators take responsibility not only for limiting public access to illicit content, but also for maintaining and enforcing the relevant industry standards.[143] This shift towards industry led content control has been accompanied by a new emphasis on consumer responsibility for the use of media services available in the home.[144] Indeed, where the content selected by the user is the product of harm to others,

---

[139] See, for example, *Green Paper on the Protection of Minors and Human Dignity in Audiovisual and Information Services* COM (96) 483 final (16 October 1996). See also Chapter 12.

[140] Compare, for example, the regulation of television services under the Communications Act 2003 and OFCOM Broadcasting Code, on-demand audiovisual services under the Audiovisual Media Services Regulations 2009, and audiovisual hosting services, which are only subject to general law in Britain.

[141] Co-regulation, a term widely used in Europe, describes regulatory schemes in which self regulation is mixed with direct or indirect state participation. 'Co-regulation allows for the implementation of the objective defined by the Community by means of measures taken by the recognised stakeholder in a given area. The legislature decides to what extent the design and application of implementing measures may be entrusted to stakeholders on account of their recognised experience on the issue. Where this mechanism fails to produce the expected results, the legislature reserves the right to directly employ statutory measures', Commission of the European Communities, *Communication on the Future of European Regulatory Audiovisual Policy,* COM (2003) 784 final. See also Hans Bredow Institute and the Institute of European Media Law, *Study on Co-Regulatory Measures in the Media Sector for the European Commission* (2006).

[142] Endorsed by the Council of Europe Committee of Ministers, *Recommendation R (97)19 of the Committee of Ministers to Member States on the Portrayal of Violence in the Electronic Media*; European Ministerial Conference, Ministerial Declaration: 'Responsibility of the Actors' *Global Information Networks: Realising the Potential* (Bonn, July 1997); Commission of the European Communities, *Communication on Audiovisual Policy: Principles and Guidelines for the Community's Audiovisual Policy in the Digital Age* COM (1999) 657 final stressed the importance of co and self regulatory instruments.

[143] The line of responsibility from self regulating content providers to the state is long and unclear. See McGonagle, T., 'Co-Regulation of the Media in Europe: The Potential for Practice of an Intangible Idea' *IRIS Plus*, 2002–10.

[144] See, for example, the Council of the European Union, Recommendation 98/560/EC on the Development of the Competitiveness of the European Audiovisual and Information Services Industry by Promoting National Frameworks Aimed at Achieving a Comparable and Effective Level of Protection of Minors and Human Dignity (1998). On self regulation and viewer responsibility, see the European Union Commission, 'Digital Age: European Audiovisual Policy', Report from the High Level Group on Audiovisual Policy, Directorate General X, Chapter iii, 5, 26 October 1998.

such as indecent images of children, consumer responsibility may include criminal liability.[145]

In these circumstances, content law and regulation in many liberal democracies is in a state of flux. In principle, market competition and regulatory neutrality should ensure the efficient evolution of services through consistent regulation, despite the many differences that now exist between media services. While these differences plainly preclude identical treatment, neutrality typically means the equivalent application of common principles. In the protection of children from harmful content, for example, these principles will therefore vary according to the potential effects of types of media content on children of different ages. Equivalent application means that these substantive principles can be applied variably to services depending on their accessibility by unsupervised children and the degree to which parents have notice of the specific content and are able to control its availability in the home.[146]

That picture, however, does not take into account the constant evolution of media services in the midst of a communications revolution. Traditional linear television services are distinctively different from video on demand services, yet for many households with broadband internet access both are just as easily accessed by children, the only noticeable difference being the need to choose content from a schedule or a menu. For several years, these services were on either side of a clear regulatory divide between 'push' and 'pull' technologies. It was reasoned that providers of content that is pushed to the consumer, such as linear, free-to-air television channels, should bear primary responsibility for making their pro-grammes and advertising available in the home. Whereas providers of content that is pulled or selected individually by a consumer, such as a film downloaded on demand from an internet website, should bear a lighter burden of responsibility. That conceptually interesting reasoning however makes little sense if consumers do not experience a similar gulf when they access the services. Regulatory neutrality that hinges on questions of access and consumer choice must be constantly reassessed not only as technologies and commercial practices change, but also as habits of consumption change.

Market and state in media policy

This ongoing reassessment must also be put in the context of deep running debates over the relative importance of market and non-market public policy goals in the media sector. During the 1990s, neo classical economic arguments had a powerful influence on fledgling internet policy in many liberal democracies, especially when these were combined with liberal moral and political arguments for greater freedom

---

[145] See, for example, s. 160(1) of the Criminal Justice Act, 1988 in Britain, which makes it an offence to possess indecent photographs of children, which includes images stored on a computer.
[146] For example, in Britain, the OFCOM *Broadcasting Code*, Section 1.

of expression through restraint of the state.[147] In the midst of a communications revolution, this marked a decisive turn in public policy that left behind the assumptions and regulatory styles of the broadcast era. In the new era, states were advised to let internet services grow unencumbered by direct state regulation.[148]

This was an extraordinary change in direction for media law and policy. It was, in effect, a call to expand the liberty to publish in tandem with the expansion of the public information sphere through convergence. In this way, the powerful presumptions and guarantees favouring freedom of the press could be applied to the merging sphere of mass and personal communications. To the extent these aims were achieved, it was a historic re-weighting of the balance between the liberty to publish and the security and well being interests of state and society.

Over a decade later, while market based arguments remain a potent force in media public policy debates, other policy concerns have reined in the heady expectations of the early internet years. As more households gained broadband access, the internet truly became a cornucopia of all things. While now essential to every sector of public and commercial life in much of the world, the internet is also widely viewed as a global platform not only for the communication of harmful content, but also for intrusion and surveillance into commercial and personal life. Although liberal democracies have largely avoided a return to the regulatory regimes of the broadcast era, they have nonetheless worked to bring these threats to security and well being under effective control.[149] The expansion of the liberty to publish brought about by the communications revolution has consequently gone into reverse, shrunken by these efforts to curb the advocacy of terrorism, obscene pornography, incitement to hatred, and breaches of privacy.

As it turns out, the merger of mass and personal communication has worked in both ways. Liberal principles of freedom of the press have undoubtedly become more accessible to millions of individuals who participate in the dissemination of information and ideas through new media services. The major information and entertainment media, however, are also being drawn into a tightening array of laws, regulatory measures, and technologies intended to protect the state, the community, and the home from the excesses of the communications revolution. In this renewed confrontation between the liberty to publish and the protection of the state and the public from harm, constitutional adjudication has taken on a key role.[150] Once chiefly associated with American law, the constitutional adjudication of the media state relationship is now a common feature of liberal democratic media law and policy. Courts have consequently been forced to develop the conceptual tools necessary to establish doctrinal certainty on the loose ground of liberal moral

[147] See, for example, United States Government, *A Framework for Global Electronic Commerce* (The White House, 1997).
[148] See, for example, *Green Paper on the Protection of Minors and Human Dignity in Audiovisual and Information Services*, n. 139 above.
[149] See Chapter 12.
[150] At times decisive in changing the direction of law and policy making, for example in the United States Supreme Court, *Reno v. American Civil Liberties Union* (1997), 521 U.S. 844, and in the ECHR in *VgT Verein gegen Tierfabriken v. Switzerland* (Application No. 24699/94) (28 June 2001).

and political theory. In many instances, they have turned to some version of proportionality analysis, which can be highly effective in forcing the state to justify its conduct through reasoned arguments. This form of constitutional reasoning however is not as good at producing fundamental moral perspectives on the proper relationship between the liberty to publish and the prevention of harm. It is instead prone to rely on shallower consequential arguments to determine when liberty should prevail.

3

Liberal Democracy and the Media in European and International Law

As World War II drew to a close, the United States embarked on far reaching efforts to entrench liberal economic and political principles into the renewed foundations of international order.[1] While these policies were initially directed towards the reform of relations between states, their ultimate aim was to shape the character of the world that would emerge through the restoration of order in Europe and the dismantling of the European colonial empires.[2] This was, in short, an effort to universalize an economic and political heritage derived not just from western experience, but in particular from that of the United States.[3] It was, for example, strongly imbued with a faith in the beneficial consequences of freedom of speech for commerce as well as liberal democracy.[4] More generally, this initiative was also an ambitious application of liberalism's claim to universality: the idea that liberal values can be adopted in all societies, regardless of their economic, cultural or social history, or present circumstances. It was therefore a frontal assault on the foundations of non-democratic government, not least through the promotion of the liberty to speak and publish.

These efforts, often drawing western European support, led to the creation of two new and very separate fields of international law and policy: human rights and

[1] While the close of World War II marked the beginning of the American internationalist era, the inspiration to secure the principles of democratic government in Europe and beyond owed much to the earlier Wilsonian vision. See, for example, President Woodrow Wilson's 'Peace without Victory' speech of January 1917, in which he stated, 'These are American principles, American policies . . . And they are also the principles and policies of forward-looking men and women everywhere, of every modern nation, of every enlightened community. They are the principles of mankind and must prevail.' See also Ikenberry, G.J., 'Why Export Democracy?: The "Hidden Grand Strategy" of American Foreign Policy', 23(2) *The Wilson Quarterly* (1999), 56–65.

[2] While United States policy on decolonization was not consistent, the United States government did insist that the Wilsonian ideal of 'self determination' was formally incorporated into the founding instruments of the post war era, including the Atlantic Charter, the Declaration by United Nations, and the United Nations Charter, but not explicitly in the Universal Declaration of Human Rights.

[3] For general discussion, see Simmons, B.A., Dobbin, F., and Garrett, G., 'Introduction: The International Diffusion of Liberalism', in Simmons, B.A., Dobbin, F., and Garrett, G. (eds), *The Global Diffusion of Markets and Democracy* (Cambridge University Press, 2008), 1. See also Weinrib, L., 'The Postwar Paradigm and American Exceptionalism' in Choudhry, S. (ed.), *The Migration Of Constitutional Ideals* (Cambridge University Press, 2006).

[4] Franklin Roosevelt, when setting out his vision of a reformed world order in 1941, explicitly named 'freedom of speech and expression' as the first essential freedom. Roosevelt, F.D., 'Four Freedoms' *State of the Union Address to Congress*, (6 January 1941).

trade. The former was ushered in through the newly created United Nations, whose General Assembly approved the ground breaking Universal Declaration of Human Rights in 1948. Somewhat later, but equally significant, the United States and its market based trading partners improvised the basis for a multilateral trade regime out of the orphaned General Agreement on Trade and Tariffs (GATT).[5]

While the scope and methods of the United States were novel, there was nothing new in a dominant state attempting to determine the rules for political and economic relations between states.[6] This was arguably only the next chapter in the long Anglo-American struggle for authority over other major powers. The post war project was steeped in that joint history, carrying its pre-occupation with liberalism and its faint regard for alternatives. In the same period, Britain and France were competitively engaged in related efforts to guide the restoration of order in western Europe. Here as well, liberalism was a major inspiration, but often in ways distinctly at odds with the economic and political principles advanced by the United States. Yet the strategic aims were much the same. The British and French sought to secure an external order that closely reflected their domestic ones, with all the economic and political advantages that would potentially follow.

In close parallel with the emerging post war, international regime, the new western European order was also divided into two distinct fields: a developing European human rights field under the Council of Europe,[7] and the foundations of a European common market under the European Union.[8] British participation in the founding of the former, but not the latter, helped to keep the two organizations and fields of law clearly separate during these formative years. In the international sphere, a different split developed between the larger number of countries willing to accept, at least formally, UN human rights treaty obligations and the smaller number willing and able to accept market based, multilateral trade obligations of the GATT.

The emerging western European and international orders were also highly innovative in the creation of new forms of inter-state obligation and cooperation. Outwardly, their founding agreements conformed to well established assumptions about international law and relations, such as the pre-eminence of states and the role of treaties in structuring their relations. However, unlike more traditional treaties, these agreements not only concerned the mutual external relations of the state parties, but were also directed very specifically at their internal laws and policies.[9] This shift towards the regulation of internal affairs would eventually

---

[5] World Trade Organization, *The GATT years: from Havana to Marrakesh*, <http://www.wto.org>.
[6] On the role of dominant states in determining the global trading order, see Patterson, D. and Afilalo, A., 'Statecraft, Trade, and the Order of States', 6(2) *Chicago Journal of International Law* (2006), 725–760, and Patterson, D. and Afilalo, A., *The New Global Trading Order: The Evolving State and the Future of Trade* (Cambridge University Press, 2008).
[7] On European human rights law, see Chapter 6.
[8] In this book, the term European Union is used to refer to the current regional organization as well as its predecessors, except where a specific name is needed for clarity.
[9] Battini, S., 'The Globalization of Public Law', 18(1) *European Review of Public Law* (2006), 9–10.

have enormous consequences for the then comparatively isolated media regimes of the participating states.

The parallels between western European and international spheres were however frequently overshadowed by their differences. In Europe, the new human rights and economic obligations were set within strong institutional structures, including binding interpretation by supervisory bodies modelled on domestic superior courts. International human rights law, in contrast, was increasingly ambitious in scope but also institutionally feeble, leaving interpretation and application largely in the hands of the state parties. In contrast, the parties to the GATT were more cautious in their gradual expansion of trade law, which was just as well given its lightly supported, consensus driven processes.

Many factors played a part in the rapid development of regional law and institutions in western Europe in the post World War II decades. Yet, aside from the obvious need to rebuild after the devastation of the war and the rising sense of peril from the Soviet Union, few were more significant than the self consciously liberal democratic nature of the small group of participating states.[10] For the media in western Europe, this meant a legal and political environment that affirmed the importance of markets in the production and distribution of media content and that was also open to liberal moral and political arguments for greater freedom of expression. The European Court of Human Rights captured the spirit of this consensus in its oft repeated declaration that parties must ensure that their media laws and measures are consistent with the requirements of 'pluralism, tolerance and broadmindedness, without which there is no democratic society'.[11]

Attempts to entrench liberal values deep into the agencies and agreements of the United Nations, however, faced immediate opposition from the Soviet Union and its supporters. The promotion of trade liberalization through the GATT was also necessarily limited to only those states willing to accept the liberalization of trade in goods that was at least calculated on a market basis. Yet, despite these obstacles, American led efforts, sometimes described as liberal internationalism, achieved some remarkable results. For the market based liberal democracies, these multilateral agreements and organizations facilitated greater cooperation not only in international relations but also in the coordination of their domestic laws and policies. They were able to build a shared liberal democratic understanding of global human rights and to lay the foundations of the trade regime that would eventually became the World Trade Organization.

---

[10]   On the political and social aspiration of the new western European regional order, see the Statute of the Council of Europe (Treaty of London, 1949). On the founding of the European Union as a market based, regional order (albeit with considerable tolerance for state intervention), see the Treaty establishing the European Economic Community (Treaty of Rome, 1957). See also Szyszczak, E., *The Regulation of the State in Competitive Markets in the European Union* (Hart Publishing, 2007), 3–7.

[11]   *Handyside v. United Kingdom* [1979] 1 EHRR 737, para. 49. McGonagle, T., 'Safeguarding Human Dignity in the European Audiovisual Sector' *IRIS Plus*, 2007–6, describes these prerequisites as an example of the 'operative public values' of the European regional order (borrowing that concept from Bhikhu Parekh, see Parekh, B., *Rethinking Multiculturalism: Cultural Diversity and Political Theory* (Palgrave Macmillan, 2000).

Treaty obligations could however only contribute to these successes. To create effective multilateral regimes, the United States and its European allies needed to combine formal treaties with political arrangements that could effectively guide treaty interpretation, improve domestic implementation, and resolve disputes.[12] These forms of political cooperation, built on the strategic relationships of the major western democracies, gave them huge practical advantages in jointly managing their interdependence.[13] Government elites could operate as 'clubs' of negotiators, often technically trained, bargaining with one another within specified issue areas. The regimes smoothed the rough edges of policy by reducing the costs of making and enforcing agreements, but only as long as the fundamentals of policy, which were largely determined domestically, were cross nationally consistent.'[14]

Smooth cooperation between the western democracies also depended on a joint acceptance that their formal obligations to liberalize economic relations should respect the autonomy of each participating state in determining its own essential domestic policies.[15] This understanding was especially important for the preservation of national media regimes, which in many cases were thickets of protective social, cultural, and political measures. National autonomy in the media sector was consequently protected by the design of the foundational European and international trade agreements, which in principle attempted to balance liberalization with the autonomy of the sovereign state.

There was however an obvious conflict between the pursuit of a greater cross border flow of media content and the continuing national protection of the domestic media. This conflict was, moreover, present in the internal laws of most major liberal democracies as well as in their new European and international treaty obligations. These states had dominated the development and global spread of media goods and services for several centuries. Since overtaking China's early lead in mass printing technologies, the Europeans and Americans had led successive revolutions in the communications technologies and methods that helped to create the modern state. They were the first to develop industrialized printing as well as radio and television broadcasting and had used these extensively in controlling their overseas territories and carrying their influence throughout the world. Maintaining their dominance in the international flow of information and entertainment content therefore remained as vitally important to them as the pursuit of social, cultural, and other domestic media concerns.

[12] Picciotto, S., 'Networks in International Economic Integration: Fragmented States and the Dilemmas of Neo-Liberalism', 17(2/3) *Northwestern Journal of International Law and Business* (1996), 1014–1056, at 1029.
[13] Keohane, R. and Nye, J., 'The Club Model of Multilateral Cooperation and Problems of Democratic Legitimacy' in Porter, R. et al. (eds), *Efficiency, Equity, Legitimacy: The Multilateral Trading System at the Millennium* (Brookings Institution Press, 2001), 264–265.
[14] Ibid.
[15] Ruggie, J.G., 'International Regimes, Transactions and Change: Embedded Liberalism in the Postwar Economic Order', 36(2) *International Organization* (1982), 379–415.

A common treaty architecture

The basic economic and human rights treaties created in the early post war decades shared a common architecture, which was intended, among many other things, to balance the liberty to publish and distribute content with the power to impose legitimate restrictions. When looked at from a media perspective, these treaties are structured around primary obligations that protect the free flow of media content. These are stated in the form of obligations on state parties to protect various principles that secure non-discriminatory, liberalized market access for media goods and services or to protect freedom of expression[16] This was not the only way these treaties could have been structured to achieve their aims. As discussed in Chapter 2, the liberal democratic, media state relationship is necessarily a complex meshing of the liberty to publish and distribute content and protections for competing state and public interests. To create primary obligations that favoured the liberty to publish placed the recognized interests of the state and the public in a permanently defensive position.

Yet this drafting choice was not only arguably oriented towards the fundamental goals of liberalism, but equally importantly it reflected the pressing conditions and needs of the time. For many American and western European policy makers, their challenge was to recreate the conditions of openness that had prevailed before World War I and the subsequent economic and political crises of the 1920s and 1930s. This task was however immeasurably complicated by the Soviet Union's occupation of eastern Europe and its strengthening global influence. A fundamental commitment to economic and political liberty would begin to ease the flow of information and entertainment content between liberal democracies, which was then encumbered with domestic legal and other restraints as well as linguistic and cultural barriers. At the same time, this commitment was a powerful statement of liberal democratic values meant to challenge non-democratic and non-market based states.

While every participating government in these treaties had some reservations as to how far that easing should go, the acceptance of primary obligations favouring the 'free flow of information' was also palatable for other practical reasons.[17] Given the technological and commercial limits of the time, national media sectors were

[16] For Europe, see Article 10 (the right to freedom of expression) of the European Convention on Human Rights, as well as Articles 28–30, 34–37, 110 (goods), 56–57 (services), 49 (establishment), of the Treaty on the Functioning of the European Union. For international law, see Articles 19 of the Universal Declaration of Human rights and the International Covenant on Civil and Political Rights as well as Articles I and III of the General Agreement on Tariffs and Trade and Articles II and XVII of the General Agreement on Trade in Services.

[17] On the use of 'free flow of information' as a foreign policy statement, see Thussu, D.K., *International Communication: Continuity and Change*, 2nd edn (Hodder Arnold Publications, 2006), 55. Although most often associated with American foreign policy, western European governments and organizations have also adopted the phrase 'free flow of information' to describe their media policy positions. See, for example, the Council of Europe, Committee of Ministers Declaration on Freedom of Expression and Information 1982.

comparatively isolated and not particularly vulnerable to liberalized access for foreign media. In addition, the treaties themselves included broad provisions permitting restrictions on the media, including barriers to foreign content, where freedom to publish or broadcast would endanger legitimate domestic public policy purposes. The primary obligations to safeguard the economic and political freedom of the media were thus balanced in each treaty with express exceptions. These significantly included the right to use measures necessary for the protection of national security, public morals, or public order.[18]

While the architecture of the treaties, as they affect the media, is strikingly similar, they also contain equally important differences. The express exceptions contained in the human rights treaties, for example, may be linked to other primary obligations, such as the right to a private life, or alternatively may only refer to a legitimate interest, such as the protection of public order. This creates an apparent hierarchy in which some exceptions are, in principle, weighted more heavily than others.[19] In the economic field, European Union law has vastly outpaced international trade law in recognizing an open category of public policy exceptions that are implicit in the rules of free movement, which permit conditional derogation from primary obligations.[20]

Nonetheless, the fundamental architecture of the treaties determined that European and international media law would develop in the interfaces between primary treaty obligations and recognized exceptions. That logically accords with the nature of the media state relationship, which is characterized by dynamic tensions between liberty and restraint. The primary treaty obligations, which support the liberty to publish and distribute content, are therefore only one of the active forces built into the treaties. They cannot be properly understood unless they are viewed in their deep relationship with the conditions and exceptions that represent legitimate interests in the restraint of expression.

What is more, over the past half century these interfaces between liberty and restraint have grown dense with additional rules and provisos, especially in the European sphere. This has occurred not just through the adjudication of disputes, but also through the accumulation of supplementary agreements. These moreover not only carry forward the dichotomy of protected liberties and permitted restraints, but sometimes reverse the order of priority. Recent treaties and other instruments concerning terrorism, for example, oblige the state parties to restrict

---

[18] For Europe, see Article 10(2) of the European Convention on Human Rights, as well as Articles 30 and 52 of the Treaty on the Functioning of the European Union. For international law, see Article 29 of the Universal Declaration of Human Rights and Article 19(3) of the International Covenant on Civil and Political Rights as well as Articles XX and XXI of the General Agreement on Tariffs and Trade and Article XIV and XIV*bis* of the General Agreement on Trade in Services.

[19] See, for example, the greater weight given to the fundamental right to respect for private life (protected by Article 8 of the ECHR) as compared to the legitimate interest in preventing gross offence to religious belief (recognized under the 'rights of others' ground for exceptions under Article 10(2) of the ECHR).

[20] On exceptions and derogation from the rules of free movement, see Chapter 4.

some forms of expression, while also imposing protective conditions that are anchored in the primary obligations of the main treaties.[21]

Plainly, European economic and human rights are now hugely different from their international law counterparts. The relative coherence, reach, and breadth of the combined European regime has been ambitiously compared to that of a proto-state, while the international patchwork of assorted organizations and their associated legal regimes is more often seen as evidence of the ineffectiveness of global public order. European institutions and law also possess an incontrovertible liberal democratic character that the western democracies have failed to instil in the international sphere to any comparable degree. Nonetheless, European law has deep roots in public international law and still shares some of its basic assumptions about the nature and interpretation of rights and obligations between states. The main European and international economic and human rights treaties also, as discussed above, share a common foundational architecture. Consequently, media issues are frequently conceptualized and managed in broadly comparable ways.

The legitimate purposes and limits of the state

European and international media law are also both troubled by the problem of determining the proper limits of national autonomy when interpreting and developing the interfaces between the primary treaty obligations and permitted exceptions or derogations. While the conditions attached to these exceptions or derogations vary considerably, there are no circumstances in which a state party can claim an unfettered right to impose restrictions on the publication or distribution of media content.[22]

The foundational European and international treaties were therefore critically important in the transformation of sovereignty in the post World War II era. By setting conditions on the right of states to pursue non-conforming public policy goals, they were in effect defining the legitimate limits and purposes of the state. This of course was not a new concept. It was however a more refined and legalized basis for the historic idea that the legitimacy of a state depends upon its domestic conduct. That idea was essential to the centuries old distinction between the predominantly Christian and European 'civilized' states and other 'uncivilized' territorial authorities. In their post war efforts to entrench liberal political and economic values into the renovated foundations of European and international order, the American, British, and French governments attempted to create new non-religious or racial standards for the legitimacy of states. In Europe, those efforts were highly successful, yielding a regional regime in which liberal principles provide

---

[21] On European and international prescriptive rules concerning the criminalization of incitement to terrorism, see Chapter 8.

[22] On the question whether the security exceptions of the GATT and the GATS grant absolute discretion to state parties, see Chapter 8.

a litmus test for legitimate conduct. In the international legal order, the proper contours of the legitimate state remain fiercely contested.

The idea that the legitimacy of the state should be determined according to objective, external legal standards raised urgent questions about national autonomy. What, for example, are the appropriate limits for the domestic conduct of a state and how should those limits be established generally or applied in the individual case? These questions are particularly important to the evolution of European and international media law. Given that national control over the public information environment is one of the key factors that determines the basic character, and indeed the survival, of the state, national governments have widely resisted pressures to cede authority over media issues. In earlier decades, it was at least axiomatic that their treaty obligations would not unduly constrain national autonomy when pursuing public policy goals in the media sector.[23] As those assumptions gave way, it was a slight reassurance, even to liberal democracies, that one of the major purposes of entrenching liberal values into treaty obligations was to support the liberal democratic nature of domestic media regimes. That reassurance does not satisfy objections directed at the use of external standards and their methods of supervision. These will always potentially restrict or thwart the pursuit of legitimately liberal democratic media public policies, even when those standards are broadly consistent with those of the state itself. The media state relationship is too intensely local, involving interwoven political, social, and economic relationships and practices to be governed sensitively or effectively from a remote, external vantage point.[24]

Even in Europe, where external economic and human rights obligations are undeniably grounded in liberal democracy, the use of external standards has frustrated local choices that are not indisputably illiberal.[25] Liberalism is simply too varied a tradition to provide anything more than loosely framed principles to guide decisions concerning liberty and restraint in the media sector.[26] When European judges and other decision makers draw on those principles to decide specific cases or instances, they inevitably foreclose alternatives that are equally within the bounds of liberal democracy. It is this foreclosure of alternatives that is often seen as one of the chief faults of resort to external standards. Yet, where those standards, or their methods of application, are relaxed to permit wide variations to account for local circumstances, they easily fade into irrelevance. In the international sphere, it is relaxation to the point of irrelevance that is just as often the source of complaint.[27]

---

[23] This is an application of the concept of 'embedded liberalism', identified by Ruggie to the media sector: Ruggie, J.G., n. 15 above.

[24] On the problems of supranational adjudication of human rights law, see Hoffman, L., *The Universality of Human Rights*, Judicial Studies Board Annual Lecture 2009.

[25] See, for example, Chapter 10 on the incompatibility of the United States 'constitutional privilege' in the law of defamation with the requirements of European Human Rights law, in particular Article 8 of the ECHR.

[26] See Chapter 2.

[27] See, for example, Posner, E., 'Human Welfare, Not Human Rights', 108(7) *Columbia Law Review* (2008), 1758–1801.

The economic law and human rights law divide

In addition to the problem of national autonomy, European and international media law have also been encumbered with the difficult and often unresolved relationship between economic and human rights obligations. The creation of two separate fields of law, one intended to address the economic character of the liberal state and the other its political and social dimensions, has meant that domestic media law has had to answer to two overlapping, but distinct, sets of external standards. This occurs because the production and distribution of media content is a largely commercial economic activity as well as a focus for intense civil and political human rights concerns.

Initially, European and international law left the coordination of rights and obligations stemming from economic or human rights treaties to the state parties. In the circumstances, this was not altogether difficult. Given the liberal democratic inspiration of the main treaty drafters in both spheres, the provisions of the treaties on either side of the human rights and economic divide are reasonably complementary. Economic law generally assumes that compliance with its primary obligations will not compromise human rights and, where that might occur, offers exceptions or rights of derogation. Similarly, liberal democratic human rights law supports the freedom to own property and engage in commerce.[28]

There is moreover a striking synergy between the economic law based right of fair access to information and entertainment markets and the human rights based concept of freedom of expression.[29] The principles of market access and free speech can be used to sustain a complementary argument for equality of competitive opportunity in media content production and distribution. On the basis of this fused economic and political argument, foreign suppliers of content have a right of equal access to domestic consumers. This is why the Cold War foreign policy catchphrase 'free flow of information' has had such apparent innate power. As a dual economic and human rights demand for a laissez faire approach to the media, it has the considerable advantages of intuitive simplicity and broad coherence, tapping into the liberal economic arguments for efficient markets for information and entertainment content as well as its political and moral ones for freedom of speech.

There are however several reasons why this dual argument is frequently weak or ineffective, all of which stem from the Hobbesian observation that freedom is only possible within the bounds of the secure territorial state and the public order it can

---

[28] This notably includes the fundamental legal and political principle that intellectual property rights are compatible with the liberty to publish. Hugenholtz, P., 'Copyright and Freedom of Expression in Europe', in Rochelle Cooper Dreyfuss, R., First H., and Zimmerman, D. (eds), *Expanding the Boundaries of Intellectual Property* (Oxford University Press, 2001); Smith, G., 'Copyright and Freedom of Expression in the Online World', 5(2) *Journal of Intellectual Property Law & Practice* (2010), 88–95.

[29] Sykes, A.O., 'International Trade and Human Rights: An Economic Perspective' in Abbott, F.M., Breining-Kaufmann, C., and Cottier, T. (eds), *International Trade and Human Rights: Foundations And Conceptual Issues: World Trade Forum v.5* (University of Michigan Press, 2006), 69–92.

provide. Once the liberty to publish threatens serious injury to the state or to the well being of others, combined political, moral, and economic arguments for freedom begin to exhaust themselves. This balance between liberty and the power of the state is consequently built into European and international law in the form of competing rights and exceptions. The state may thus impose restrictions on the media to protect another recognized human right that is in direct tension with freedom of expression, such as the right to respect for privacy.[30] A state may also use the right to freedom of expression itself to support its intervention in media markets in ways that disadvantage domestic or foreign competitors. This is invariably the case, for example, where the state subsidizes public service media as a vehicle for the delivery of pluralist news and information, which helps to fulfil the public's right of access to information.

Finally, even where a state's reasons for imposing restrictions have no plausible basis in any protected human right, the dual free flow argument may still be blocked where a state can reasonably rely on permitted exceptions, such as national security and public order. It is true, as a matter of textual interpretation and doctrine, that these exceptions are secondary to the primary obligations. Yet that hierarchical relationship essentially concerns the manner in which a state must justify its use of an exception. There are many circumstances in which the state is plainly entitled, as a matter of economic or human rights law, to restrain the publication or distribution of media content. The treaties themselves presuppose the existence of effective states. Consequently, they implicitly accept the ultimate right of the state to protect its territorial and institutional existence and maintain order amongst its population.

While economic and human rights treaty obligations can operate in a powerful complementary manner, they are just as often pitted against each other in the complex issues that arise in the media state relationship. European and international media law, which rest equally in the economic and human rights fields, are therefore highly exposed to problems of incoherence at the interface between the two. In Europe, following the Lisbon Treaty, the progressive integration of these two fields has advanced considerably, although underlying divisions will undoubtedly remain problematic.[31] In comparison, the international sphere is an assembly of principles, rules, and guidance nested in a loose framework of instruments and practices. In this sphere, states remain, by default, largely responsible for managing the tensions that arise out of their human rights and trade obligations.

Multilateral renewal after the Cold War

Throughout the first decades of the Cold War, neither European nor international law had a significant impact on domestic media regimes. The struggle with the Soviet Union galvanized the efforts of western democracies to cooperate successfully, but

---

[30] See Chapter 10.
[31] See Chapters 4 and 6.

also frustrated their global policy ambitions and excused their support of repressive autocracies. These were the conditions in which the major economic and human rights treaties were drafted and began to figure in relations between states.

In what was to become the European Union, the European Court of Justice moved quickly to establish the supremacy and reach of EU law.[32] Nonetheless, its significant decisions on media issues, which were largely focused on the sensitive broadcast sector, occurred later once its foundational decisions on the penetrating character of European economic obligations took effect.[33] The European Court of Human Rights, its cousin court, charged with interpreting and applying the European Convention on Human Rights, proceeded more cautiously. Its foundational decisions on the character of European human rights law did not present as great a challenge to domestic controls on the media. Not surprisingly, the Court's first major cases concerning the Article 10 right to freedom of expression, including *Handyside, Sunday Times*, and *Lingens*, concerned print publications.[34] Its broadcasting cases came later and were less momentous than those of the ECJ.[35]

In the international sphere, matters moved even more slowly. The GATT had little application to the media. Limited to trade in goods, the GATT's ostensible reach was limited to those media traded in a tangible form, such as the limited cross border trade in newspapers and periodicals. This potential impact on the media was further restricted by the GATT's provisions that grant state parties the right to maintain tight controls on the screening of foreign films, which at the time was the most significant form of international trade in media goods.[36] In the international human rights field, the participating UN member states took until 1996 to agree on the terms of the core multilateral human rights treaties, the International Covenant on Civil and Political Rights, and the International Covenant on Economic, Social and Cultural Rights.[37]

The practical irrelevance of European and international law to the media began to change rapidly in the last decade of the Cold War. Lifted by economic growth and thawing east–west relations, multilateral institutions entered a period of expansion and greater sophistication. Cross border relationships of all kinds became thicker and more complex, feeding into a general growth in the numbers and scope of European and international legal agreements and decisions.[38] The focus for this

---

[32] Case 26/62, *NV Algemene Transport-en Expeditie Onderneming van Gend & Loos v. Netherlands Inland Revenue Administration* [1963] ECR 1 and Case 6/64, *Flaminio Costa v. E.N.E.L.* [1964] ECR 585.

[33] Case C-352/85, *Bond van Adverteerders v. The Netherlands State* [1988] ECR 2085.

[34] *Handyside v. UK* [1976] 1 EHRR 737; *Sunday Times v. UK* [1970] 2 EHRR 245; *Lingens v. Austria* [1986] 8 EHRR 407.

[35] *Groppera Radio v. Switzerland* [1990] 12 EHRR 321; *Autronic AG v. Switzerland* (1990), Application No. 12726/87, 12 EHRR 485.

[36] GATT (1947), Article IV.

[37] For an overview of the two Covenants in context, see Steiner, H., Alston, P., and Goodman, R., (eds), *International Human Rights in Context*, 3rd edn (Oxford University Press, 2007).

[38] Held, D. and McGrew, A., 'Political Globalization: Trends and Choices' in Kaul, I., Conceicao, P., Le Goulven, K., and Mendoza, R.U. (eds), *Providing Global Public Goods: Managing Globalization* (Oxford University Press, 2003), 185–199 at 187.

new era of multilateral cooperation and treaty making was however undoubtedly the stimulation of market based, economic relations.

In the European Union, the member states launched the Single Market, an ambitious initiative aimed at the reinvigoration and extension of the principles of free movement. Apart from major changes to the EC Treaty, introduced through the 1986 Single European Act, this initiative brought a raft of new legislation to foster a genuine common market.[39] These included specific measures intended to break down market barriers in targeted sectors, such as telecommunications and broadcasting. They also, unavoidably, brought the impact of free movement obligations deeper into specialized domestic regulatory regimes. In the broadcasting sector, the adoption of the Television Without Frontiers Directive in 1989 (now entitled the Audiovisual Media Services Directive), marked a decisive acceleration in the integration of European media markets.[40]

In the international sphere, the United States, the Europeans, and their major developed trade partners had thrown their weight behind the ambitious goals of the Uruguay Round. These difficult, lengthy negotiations culminated in the creation of the WTO and expansion of international trade law into major new areas, including trade in services and the protection of intellectual property rights.[41] For the media, the new General Agreement on Trade in Services (GATS) held the potential for greater access to hitherto protected domestic audiovisual sectors. However, the GATS, limited by its complex structure and the resistance of participating states, had little impact in the most contentious area: trade in broadcast media services.[42] On the other hand, the agreement not only established the principle that media services should be subject to trade obligations, but it also made significant headway in liberalizing trade in related services that were rapidly becoming essential to the delivery of information and entertainment content. These developments included several GATS based global agreements on trade in telecommunication services.[43]

The fall of the Soviet Union was an extraordinary catalyst for the expansion of public and private multilateral projects.[44] The end of the Cold War brought the United States, in particular, an apparent double global triumph of market economics

---

[39]　Single European Act [1987] OJ L169/4.

[40]　Council Directive 89/552/EEC of 3rd October 1989 on the coordination of certain provisions laid down by Law, Regulation or Administrative Action in Member States concerning the pursuit of television broadcasting activities.

[41]　Renewal and expansion of the GATT during the multilateral Uruguay Round negotiations that lasted from 1986 to 1994. The final package of agreements concluded in Marrakech created the World Trade Organization and not only broadened the trade liberalization regime to include services, but also fortified international intellectual property obligations and created a stronger trade dispute resolution system. GATS and TRIPS Agreement (Trade Related Aspects of Intellectual Property Rights). For an overview, see Barton, J., Goldstein, J., Josling, T., and Steinberg, R., *The Evolution of the Trade Regime: Politics, Law, and Economics of the GATT and the WTO* (Princeton University Press, 2006).

[42]　See Chapter 5 on International Trade Law and the Media.

[43]　Most notably, the WTO, Fourth Protocol to the General Agreement on Trade in Services (30 April 1996) (entry into force), which secured the liberalization of basic telecommunications services through much of the world.

[44]　See Barnett, M. and Finnemore, M., 'The Power of Liberal International Organizations' in Barnett, M. and Duvall, R. (eds), *Power in Global Governance* (Cambridge University Press, 2005), 161–184.

and liberal democracy.[45] It was, in hindsight, a decade of exceptional opportunity for efforts to universalize liberal economic and political principles.[46] The manifest failures of state socialism appeared to have convincingly demonstrated that liberal democracy is a necessary condition for long term economic prosperity.

During this relatively short period, market based public policies, often associated with a return to classical liberal principles, became powerfully influential in many governments and organizations. This policy environment was sceptical of state intervention in markets, except where demonstrably necessary to correct proven market failures. From this view, the liberalization of markets was not only an efficient way to deliver goods and services, but would also provide the foundations for an integrated world economy. As Thomas Freedman commented in 1999, '[g]lobalisation means the spread of free-market capitalism to virtually every country in the world. Globalisation also has its own set of economic rules—rules that revolve around opening, deregulating and privatising your economy.'[47]

These market based public policies became widely known, especially by their opponents, as 'neoliberalism'.[48] In the trade and development field, they were also collectively referred to as the policies of the 'Washington Consensus'.[49] This term described several prescriptive principles of economic governance that included fiscal austerity, privatization, market liberalization, and the encouragement of foreign investment.[50] The rising influence of the Washington Consensus policies also marked the end of 'embedded liberalism', the long standing system of trade relations in which social policy measures were, in general, exempt from market access obligations.[51] That system had, '...respected sovereignty, and left it to internal domestic policy to control the redistribution of wealth, with the essential caveat that trade restrictions should not be used for any protectionist purpose. However, fiscal policy, monetary policy, and welfare policies were means of domestic control over redistributive justice that, at least in theory, trade left untouched.'[52]

---

[45] See, for example, Fukuyama, F., *The End of History and the Last Man* (Penguin Books, 1992).

[46] Kagan, R., 'End of Dreams, Return to History', *Policy Review*, No. 144 (Hoover Institute, Stanford University, 2007): 'Clinton's grand strategy of building post-Cold War order around expanding markets, democracy, and institutions was the triumphant embodiment of the liberal vision of international order'. See, more generally, Drezner, D.W., *All Politics is Global* (Princeton University Press, 2007).

[47] Friedman, T., *The Lexus and the Olive Tree* (HarperCollins, 1999), 8.

[48] Bordieu, P., 'The Essence of Neoliberalism' *Le Monde Diplomatique* (English edn), December 1998.

[49] Held, D. and McGrew, A., n. 38 above, 185–199. See also Held, D., *Global Covenant: The Social Democratic Alternative to the Washington Consensus* (Polity Press, 2004).

[50] Stiglitz, J., *Globalization and its Discontents* (Penguin Books, 2002), 53 and 67. The term 'Washington Consensus' was coined in 1990 by the economist John Williamson to refer to 'the lowest common denominator of policy advice being addressed by the Washington-based institutions to Latin American countries as of 1989'. Williamson, J., 'What Should the World Bank Think About the Washington Consensus?' 15(2) *World Bank Research Observer* (2000) (The International Bank for Reconstruction and Development), 251–264.

[51] See Ruggie, J.G., n. 15 above, 379–415.

[52] Patterson, D. and Afilalo, A., *The New Global Trading Order: The Evolving State and the Future of Trade* (Cambridge University Press, 2008), 5.

Market based public policies were particularly influential in the closing years of the Uruguay Round. As one leading American trade official commented, the objective in creating the GATS was 'the creation of conditions for fair and predictable global market competition that stimulate productivity and innovation and drive out low quality, high cost, and outdated services'.[53] In short, the GATS was built on a strong belief in the benefits of market competition. Yet this global ascendancy was transient and always contested.[54] Opponents of neoclassical economic policies criticized their apparent 'market fundamentalism' or, as one critic alleged, their reduction of '[a]ll dimensions of human life, including the social, cultural and political, to market based economic principles'.[55] Alternatively, the neoclassical model of market based economics and minimal state intervention was simply a programme to further the interests of particular businesses and governments under the guise of the public good.[56]

In the past decade, the influence of neoclassical economic policies has waned in much of the world, while the legitimacy of state intervention for non-market policy purposes has recovered considerably.[57] In Europe, the concept of essential non-market public policies has become embodied in the increasingly important legal category of 'services of general interest', whose importance is now affirmed in a protocol to the Treaty of Lisbon.[58] Internationally, China's rise to become a leading economic power has also provided a powerful alternative model of growth that features heavy state involvement in the economy and managed commercial relations.[59] That is not to say that market based approaches to public policy are no longer heavily influential in Europe or elsewhere. With different degrees of qualification, supporters have continued to argue that the easing of government restrictions on cross border trade in goods, services, and investment remains essential to greater prosperity and personal autonomy.[60] That argument will always have a substantial place in regional and international policy debates.

---

[53] Feketekuty, G., 'Regulatory Reform and Trade Liberalization in Services' in Sauvé, P. and Stern, R. (eds), *GATS 2000: New Directions in Services Trade Liberalisation* (Brookings Institution, 2000), 225–240.

[54] Stiglitz, J., *Globalization and Its Discontents* (W. W. Norton & Company, 1999) and Stiglitz, J., *Making Globalization Work* (W. W. Norton & Company, 2006); Rodrik, D., 'Rethinking Growth Policies in the Developing World' (Harvard University, Luca d'Agliano Lecture in Development Economics, 2004). See political and legal theorists Gray, J., *False Dawn: The Delusions of Global Capitalism* (Granta Books, 1998); Braithwaite, J. and Drahos, P., *Global Business Regulation* (Cambridge University Press, 2000).

[55] See Bourdieu, P., n. 48 above.

[56] Duménil, G. and Lévy, D., *Capital Resurgent: Roots of the Neoliberal Revolution* (Harvard University Press, 2004).

[57] Wallerstein, I., '2008: The Demise of Neoliberal Globalization' *Monthly Review*, Commentary No. 226, (1 February 2008).

[58] Treaty of Lisbon amending the Treaty on European Union and the Treaty establishing the European Community, signed at Lisbon, 13 December 2007, Protocol on Services of General Interest.

[59] Ramo, J.C., *The Beijing Consensus* (The Foreign Policy Centre, 2004). For a recent restatement of that argument in relation to China, see Hutton, W., *The Writing on the Wall: China and the West in the 21st Century* (Little, Brown, 2007).

[60] See, for example, Wolf, M., *Why Globalization Works* (Yale University Press, 2004) and Bagwati, J., *In Defense of Globalization* (Oxford University Press, 2004). See also World Bank, *Economic Growth in the 1990s: Learning from a Decade of Reform* (2005).

A further, and much less noticed, change has also occurred since the end of the Cold War. This is simply that the once closely aligned twin goals of entrenching liberal economic and political values in global institutions and agreements has come apart. Two decades of prodigious efforts to foster a global market economy have overshadowed the political aspirations of the liberal democratic project. Unlike the European Union, the GATT never demanded democracy in its participating states, requiring only a commitment to market based trade. Since its founding in 1994, the WTO has embraced that position fully, accepting non-democratic countries, notably China, that are willing to open their domestic markets to greater foreign competition. For the WTO, market based trade has no necessary link with democracy, liberal or otherwise.[61] Indeed, there is arguably no longer any sustainable connection between policies aimed at fostering market based, global economic growth and those that seek to spread liberal democratic forms of government.[62]

The consequences of this change for international media law are enormous. Once the relationship between the liberty to publish and its restraint is detached from political liberalism, the boundaries of legitimate state conduct are much wider. As discussed above, the major trade treaties recognize the right of state parties to derogate from their primary obligations, which typically include a greater or lesser degree of liberalized trade in media content. In European Union law, those rights of derogation are conditioned by liberal democratic principles, which therefore have a major role in defining the legitimate objectives of national public policy. Without this close association with liberal democracy, or any other concept of political legitimacy, world trade law lacks a fundamental orientation that can similarly define the contours of its public policy exceptions. It may therefore block valid liberal democratic interventions in media markets just as it may also approve illiberal ones.

The loss of momentum in the international liberal democratic project since its brief post Cold War ascendancy has many important implications for international media law. These include the shift in political and economic influence away from the transatlantic axis towards rising powers in Asia and elsewhere.[63] While some of these are major democratic states, including India and Brazil, they are not historic partners in American liberal internationalism. Consequently, globalization is losing its once distinctive westernized character and the Atlantic powers no longer set the rules for international relations as they once did.

---

[61] Bardhan, P., 'Capitalism: One Size Does Not Suit All' *Yale Global* (7 December 2006): 'Shaped by many cultures, some forms of capitalism are more palatable to anti-globalization activists than others. . .'.

[62] Lieven, A. and Hulsman, J., *Ethical Realism: A Vision for America's Role in the World* (Pantheon Books, 2006). See also D'Aspremont, J., '1989–2010: The Rise and Fall of Democratic Governance in International Law', in Crawford, J., (ed.), *Select Proceedings of the European Society of International Law*, Vol. 3, (Hart Publishing, 2011).

[63] A widely discussed and celebrated phenomenon. See, for example, Gungwu, W., 'China Rises Again' *YaleGlobal* (25 March 2009); Northrup, D., 'Globalization and the Great Convergence: Rethinking World History in the Long Term', 16(3) *Journal of World History* (2005), 249–267; Schiller, D., 'Poles of Market Growth? Open Questions about China, Information and the World Economy', 1(1) *Global Media and Communication* (2005), 79–103.

This does not simply imply a change in global seating arrangements. Political and economic relations are more complex and unpredictable than only a few decades ago. The steady proliferation of states since World War II, swollen by the break up of the Soviet regional order, has destabilized methods of cooperation and control. While many governments are reasonably effective, others struggle to carry out their domestic and external responsibilities, undermined by endemic poverty, corruption, and instability. Tensions between values and beliefs have also spread along the networks of a globalized world, relaying the impact of local conflicts and violence instantaneously. In these turbulent conditions, the optimistic assumption that, in conditions of freedom, liberalism is universally welcome has faded, usurped by the more pessimistic view that liberalism is historically specific, only flourishing in the right conditions.

Multilateral obligations in the broadcast era

In the last decade of the Cold War, the pressure of European and international economic obligations on domestic media regimes began to rise sharply. In most countries, the domestic broadcasting sector was both heavily regulated and closely guarded from foreign competition, serving a range of state directed or fostered social and political purposes.[64] In a relatively short period, satellite broadcasting technologies leapt forward, enabling commercial operators to break into these potentially lucrative markets. Using new technologies that permitted direct home reception of satellite signals, foreign based operators could now draw advertising and subscription revenue from these markets, while avoiding their regulatory controls.

Many governments were alarmed by this intrusion.[65] These foreign broadcasts not only avoided their content restrictions and obligations, but also tapped into the revenue streams that sustained domestic audiovisual production. They consequently mounted a determined resistance, creating a variety of legal and administrative measures to obstruct foreign access and the outflow of revenue.[66] In this struggle, commercial satellite broadcasters turned to national trade obligations in their efforts to have these barriers to market access dismantled. While international trade law gave them little assistance, European Union commitments to the free movement of services were immensely valuable in breaking down barriers to cross border broadcasting in Europe.[67]

---

[64] For example, public service broadcasting in Europe attempted to safeguard national languages, cultural identity, and social cohesion.

[65] In 1993, Rupert Murdoch said that satellite television was 'an unambiguous threat to totalitarian regimes everywhere'. BBC News, 'Murdoch hits Chinese "brick wall"', (19 September 2009).

[66] For example, Case C-17/00, *De Coster v. Collège des Bourgmestre et Échevins de Watermael-Boitsfort* (2001) ECR I-9445.

[67] See Chapter 4 on the application of the rules of free movement to satellite television services. See also Chapter 5 on the failure of the Uruguay Round to liberalize trade in cross border television services.

The legal issues were however clouded with uncertainties. Underlying this contest between the primary obligation to ensure fair market access and the permitted exceptions for legitimate public policy purposes lay an irresolvable problem. Genuine social and cultural policy measures in the media sector also serve the purposes of genuine economic protectionism. Protective restrictions on advertising for children, for example, will create a regulatory barrier for satellite broadcasts that conform to the more lenient standards of a foreign country.[68] Consequently, while the specific legal issues in this struggle have often been technical, they have also tapped into fundamental questions about the limits of national autonomy and the relationship between economic policy and social and cultural policy. These were not questions that could be decided permanently through supranational legislation or adjudication and have continued to figure prominently in international as well as European media law. They have dogged the EU Audiovisual Media Services Directive since its first adoption in 1989 and subsequent long evolution through amendments and judicial interpretation.[69] They were also directly at issue in the protracted Uruguay Round negotiations over trade in audiovisual services.[70]

This also meant that disputes in European and international media law have often been highly strategic, extending their arguments to areas as diverse as the conceptual development of human rights law and the legal interfaces between key European and international bodies. It is certainly no surprise that human rights law has played a pivotal role in these disputes, given that political freedom and economic freedom are often linked in liberal democratic public policy. There are however important reasons why the interplay of economic obligations and human rights has been particularly complex and strategically driven in the media law field. The argument for greater liberty to publish and distribute media content has strong foundations in both economic and human rights law. Indeed, as discussed above, this tandem argument, which draws on both the right to freedom of expression and the right to fair market access, is a formidable weapon for battering down national measures that obstruct foreign media.[71]

In contrast, the argument for restricting media content in order to protect individual or collective well being rests almost entirely on human rights law foundations. This has forced supporters of media restrictive measures to develop the human rights arguments for well being as far as possible and to ensure that human rights considerations are integrated into economic law decisions. European and international human rights treaties certainly contain a substantial array of protected rights and recognized interests that support well being in various ways. However, these are a loose collection compared to the comparatively concise,

---

[68] For example, Joined Cases C-34/95, C-35/95, and C-36/95, *Konsumentombudsmannen (KO) v. De Agostini (Svenska) Förlag AB and TV–Shop i Sverige AB* [1997] ECR I-3843.

[69] On the Audiovisual Media Services Directive, see Chapter 4.

[70] GATS negotiations in the Uruguay Round.

[71] *Autronic AG v. Switzerland*, 22 May 1990, Application No. 12726/87, 12 EHRR 485, para. 47.

concentrated statement of the right to freedom of expression found in the same treaties.

Consequently, arguments favouring well being in relation to freedom of expression benefit considerably from wider efforts to develop better cohesion for this concept within human rights theory and law. Perhaps the most significant development in this direction is the rising importance of 'human dignity' in liberal democratic human rights jurisprudence.[72] While a notoriously elastic concept, human dignity does provide a common thread that can pull together many disparate elements in human rights and at least a semblance of greater coherence. In this guise, human dignity acts as protective buffer against the deep penetration of market based, economic globalization.[73] On the other hand, any liberal argument for the protection of human dignity or well being will always contain a significant emphasis on personal and collective freedom of expression. This also opens the way to the argument that well being in the form of greater liberty is best enhanced through economic as well as political liberty.

The fact that arguments for restricting the media in order to protect well being depend so heavily on human rights law has a further consequence for media related disputes in the European and international spheres. In most circumstances, these arguments are best made in forums where decisions are grounded in human rights law and where trade and market access obligations are not at issue. Conversely, policy and law making forums whose competence rests on economic rights and obligations are more likely to favour arguments for greater liberty to publish and distribute media content. As a result, forum shifting and other tactics for using the authority of regional and international bodies to best advantage have been exceptionally important to the development of European and international media law.[74] In Europe, the most important entities for forum shifting tactics are the various judicial and law making bodies of the Council of Europe and European Union. In the more fragmented international sphere, the interplay between different legal regimes may be less sophisticated, but can still be equally important.[75] In both spheres, moreover, states with greater financial and personnel resources are typically best positioned to work strategically across these organizational boundaries.

---

[72] McCrudden, C., 'Human Dignity and Judicial Interpretation of Human Rights', 19(4) *European Journal of International Law* (2008), 655–724.

[73] Smits, J., 'Human Dignity and Uniform Law: An Unhappy Relationship' in Moréteau, O., Romanach, J., and Zuppi, A. (eds), *Essays in Honor of Saul Litvinoff* (Baton Rouge, 2008), 749–760.

[74] Forum shifting is described as avoiding discussion or negotiation of a matter in one regional or international organization, while pursuing the same matter in another which is more likely to produce the desired outcome. See Braithwaite, J. and Drahos, P., *Global Business Regulation* (Cambridge University Press, 2000), 29–31 and Alvarez, J., 'International Organizations: Then and Now', 100 *American Journal of International Law* (2006), 324–347, at 329. On forum shifting in relation to the negotiation of intellectual property treaties, see Helfer, L.R., 'Regime Shifting: The TRIPs Agreement and the New Dynamics of International Intellectual Property Lawmaking', 29(1) *Yale Journal of International Law* (2004), 1–84.

[75] For example, the UNESCO Convention on Cultural Diversity and the GATS.

Deregulation in the internet era

It took several decades for the complex tensions between domestic media regimes and national market access and human rights obligations to develop, many of which only came into focus with the arrival of satellite broadcasting. Yet, despite the pivotal importance of satellite broadcasting, its central role was also extraordinarily brief. Even in the early 1990s, just as the Uruguay Round was deadlocked over trade in audiovisual services via satellite, the potential impact of the internet was beginning to become apparent to media entrepreneurs and governments. For the former, its decentralized and open character was ideally suited to the delivery of information and entertainment content through deregulated markets.[76] The latter, however, were cautiously enthusiastic. While immediately perceiving the threat to their control over the domestic media, many governments also saw the possible economic, social, and political benefits of the internet and introduced legal and financial measures to speed its growth within their borders.[77]

As both the first home of the internet and the world's dominant economic power, the United States was in a formidable position to set the international ground rules for this global growth.[78] American domestic communications and media policy had already taken a decisive turn towards deregulation a decade earlier. In the 1980s, the Federal Communications Commission deregulated several key aspects of broadcasting, largely abandoning the principle that broadcasters should operate as regulated trustees for the public good.[79] The FCC was therefore more than ready to apply a policy of market competition and limited intervention to the internet.[80] As one senior FCC official wrote at the time, 'Information technology has demolished time and distance, but instead of validating Orwell's vision of Big Brother watching the citizen, just the reverse as happened; the citizen is watching Big Brother and so the virus of freedom, for which there is no antidote, is spreading by myriad electronic networks to the four corners of the world.'[81]

---

[76] See for example, Barlow, J., 'The Economy of Ideas: Selling Wine Without Bottles on the Global Net', in Ludlow, P., *High Noon on the Electronic Frontier: Conceptual Issues in Cyberspace* (MIT Press, 1996).

[77] See, for example, in Britain, the 1998 Green Paper issued by the Department of Culture, Media and Sport and the Department of Trade and Industry, *Regulating Communications: Approaching Convergence in the Information Age* (1998) CM4022 (July).

[78] Müller, M., 'Who Owns the Internet? Ownership as a Legal Basis for American Control of the Internet', 15 *Fordham Intellectual Property, Media and Entertainment Law Journal* (2005), 709.

[79] Advisory Committee on Public Interest Obligations of Digital Television Broadcasters, Final Report: *Charting the Digital Broadcasting Future* (Washington DC, 1998), 24. Fowler, M. and Brenner, D., 'A Marketplace Approach to Broadcasting Regulation', 60 *Texas Law Review* (1982), 209–257.

[80] William Kennard, former FCC Chairman, 'The Unregulation of the Internet: Laying a Competitive Course for the Future' speech, 20 July 1999, <http://www.fcc.gov/commissioners/previous/kennard/speeches.html>.

[81] Nelson, M., 'Sovereignty in the Networked World' in *The Emerging Internet: The 1998 Report of the Internet* (Institute for Information Studies, Aspen Institute, 1998).

The Clinton administration moved swiftly to ensure that American internet policies would spread as rapidly and as far as possible. In its 1997 *Framework for Global Electronic Commerce*, the White House set out its principles for internet governance, emphasizing market forces and minimal state intervention.[82] The American government urged other states to adapt their laws and regulatory systems to accommodate the internet's decentralized nature and its culture of bottom-up governance. The Framework declared that '[w]here governmental involvement is needed, its aim should be to support and enforce a predictable, minimalist, consistent and simple legal environment for commerce'.[83] In essence, American internet policy emphasized the *sui generis* nature of internet based services and exhorted foreign governments not to attempt to confine them within their existing communications or media regulatory rules.

In many quarters, the United States found a receptive audience for its internet regulatory policies. European and other governments were persuaded that strong regulatory controls would stifle the growth of the domestic information economies they were so keen to foster. At their 1997 Ministerial Conference on 'Global Information Networks: Realising the Potential', EU governments jointly declared that the expansion of global information networks should be market-led and left to private initiative.[84] The Ministerial Declaration also stressed the importance of self regulation in protecting the interests of consumers and in promoting ethical standards.[85] Even in the international sphere, the European Commission recommended greater multilateral cooperation to manage the globalization of new communications and media services, but also suggested that formal treaties and institutions would be inappropriate.[86]

Major international bodies dedicated to the growth of market based economic relations adopted a similar argument for regulatory restraint. In 1988, the OECD declared that,

[a]s governments, industry and consumers venture into this new platform, they are looking to ensure that effective protection is provided in the digital marketplace, and that unnecessary barriers to electronic commerce are addressed. Legal frameworks should be established

---

[82] United States Government, *A Framework for Global Electronic Commerce* (The White House, 1997).

[83] Ibid, Principle 3. See also Kennard, W., *Connecting the Globe: A Regulator's Guide to Building a Global Information Community* (Federal Communications Commission, 1999).

[84] European Ministerial Conference at Bonn, 'Global Information Networks: Realising the Potential', Ministerial Declaration, 1997, para. 14. This Declaration followed the influential Bangemann Report to the European Commission from communication industry experts, which exhorted the European Union to 'put its faith in market mechanisms as the motive power to carry us into the Information Age'. High Level Group on the Information Society, *Europe and the Global Information Society: Recommendations to the European Council* (The Bangemann Report, 1994).

[85] 'Global Information Networks', ibid., para. 19.

[86] See Communication from the Commission of 4 February 1998 to the Council, the European Parliament, the Economic and Social Committee and the Committee of the Regions: 'The Globalisation of the Information Society: the need for strengthened international coordination' COM (98) 50 final.

only where necessary, should promote a competitive environment and should be clear, consistent and predictable.[87]

This wide consensus on regulatory restraint, even for a provisional period, was striking, given the vast range of goods and services that could potentially be sold online.[88] For a time, it seemed that communications technologies were finally achieving what constitutional principles had failed to do: emancipating expression, both politically and economically, from the state.

In contrast, concerns about the internet's potentially destructive impact on the liberal democratic state and its public policies were less audible. Yet these were also influencing the now rapid growth of communications and media law. The Europeans, for example, mixed enthusiasm with caution. In 1997, the European Commission released its *Green Paper on the regulatory implications of communications convergence*, which urged public authorities to avoid over-regulating the internet or subjecting it to their existing media content regulatory rules.[89] Nonetheless, the Commission also called for clear and effective rules relating to privacy and data protection, the promotion of cultural diversity, and the protection of minors and public order.[90] The following year, the Commission's *Oreja Report of Media Experts* forcefully defended the continuing relevance of European media models. The report's authors stated, 'we see that the starting point for Europeans was different: namely, that it has never been assumed in Europe that the broadcasting

---

[87] Organisation for Economic Cooperation and Development (OECD) Ministerial level Conference, 'A Borderless World: Realising the Potential of Global Electronic Commerce' (Ottawa, 1998), see 'Conference Conclusions' SG/EC(98)14/REV6. See also the OECD Committee for Information, Computers and Communications Policy, *Global Information Infrastructure—Global Information Society (GII-GIS) Policy Recommendations for Action* (OECD) (approved by OECD Council at Ministerial level, May 1997). This key policy document argued against stifling the internet with excessive or premature regulations and recommended that the Internet should be allowed the same free flow as paper based information and that any restrictions should reflect fundamental rights such as free speech and privacy (16).

[88] See, for example, Commission on E-Business, IT and Telecoms, 'The Impact of Internet Content Regulation' *International Chamber of Commerce, Policy Statement*, 2002 Doc. No. 373–37/1; Islam, R., 'Into the Looking Glass' in Islam, R. (ed.), *The Right to Tell: The Role of Mass Media in Economic Development* (World Bank Institute, 2002); Coordinating Committee of Press Freedom Organisations (2002), *Statement of Vienna: Press Freedom on the Internet* issued as a contribution to the pre-WSIS (United Nations World Summit on the Information Society, Geneva 2003); the WSIS (2003), *Declaration of Principles* Doc. WSIS-03/GENEVA/DOC/4-E, (ITU), Principle 39. OECD (2004), *Recommendation of the Council on Broadband Development* [C (2003)259]; Moeller, C. and Amouroux, A., 'Introduction' in Moeller, C. and Amouroux, A. (eds), *The Media Freedom Internet Cookbook* (OSCE Representative on Freedom of the Media, 2004), 12; Einzinger, K., 'Media Regulation on the Internet' in Moeller, C., and Amouroux, A. (eds), ibid., 142–143.

[89] European Commission, *Green Paper on the Convergence of the Telecommunications, Media and Information Technology Sectors and the Implications for Regulation* COM (97) 623, Chapter V, Principle 1. See also Council of Europe, Committee of Ministers, Declaration on Freedom of Communication on the Internet (Strasbourg, 28.05.2003), Principle 1: Content rules for the Internet, Principle 3: Absence of prior state control.

[90] European Commission ibid., Chapter IV(3). See also European Commission, *Green Paper on the Protection of Minors and Human Dignity in Audiovisual and Information Services* COM (96) 483 final.

and audiovisual sector should be treated as an economic subject only or that the market per se would guarantee a pluralistic service'.[91]

In non-democratic countries, the response to the internet was less equivocal.[92] In China, the government never wavered from the view that the internet should be integrated into its existing methods of controlling communications and media content.[93] This system, first established in the Communist Party's remote base areas in the 1930s and guided ever since by its Central Propaganda Department, ensures that the editors and journalists follow Party policies.[94] It also ensures that any organized opposition to the Party's rule cannot gain a foothold in the national media. In its efforts to protect its vital hold over the country's public information environment, the Chinese government has confounded early expectations that the internet would overwhelm its media controls. Instead, it has created the world's best resourced and most sophisticated internet control system.[95]

The structure of European and international media law

Throughout the world, the ongoing communications revolution has brought wrenching changes to the media state relationship. While the advent of direct-to-home satellite broadcasting brought the latent tensions between domestic autonomy and foreign obligations into the open, the internet and other new communications services have brought them into crisis. Long established controls over media content have failed to cope with the explosion of domestic content sources and the breakdown of the barrier between foreign and domestic content. In this torrent of digitized content, social and commercial relationships have changed dramatically. The ability to communicate instantaneously and to exchange large volumes of information and entertainment content has plainly enriched many peoples' personal lives and vastly extended the opportunities for commerce. It has also eroded the security and authority of the state and threatened the well being of individuals and communities.

The communications revolution has consequently thrown domestic media regimes into disorder. While governments have sought to adapt quickly to changing communications and media services, the pace of change has frequently outrun

---

[91] European Commission, Report from the High Level Group on Audiovisual Policy, *Digital Age: European Audiovisual Policy*, Directorate-General X (1998), 'Part I: The Media and the European Model of Society'.

[92] Compare Iran to China. See the OpenNet Initiative Internet Filtering in Iran (2009), <http://opennet.net/sites/opennet.net/files/ONI_Iran_2009.pdf>.

[93] Keller, P., 'Privilege and Punishment: Press Governance in China', 21(1) *Cardozo Arts and Entertainment Law Journal* (2003), 87–138.

[94] Ibid., Liebman, B., 'Watchdog or Demagogue? The Media in the Chinese Legal System', 105(1) *Columbia Law Review* (2005), 1–157. See also Privacy International and the GreenNet Educational Trust, *Silenced: An International Report on Censorship and Control of the Internet* (2003); OpenNet Initiative, *A Country Study Internet Filtering in China* (2009), <http://opennet.net/research/profiles/china>.

[95] See Brady, A., *Marketing Dictatorship: Propaganda and Thought Work in Contemporary China* (Rowman and Littlefield, 2008), ch 2: 'Guiding Hand: The Role of the Propaganda System'.

their efforts.[96] For liberal democracies, these new legal and regulatory measures must fit within constitutional principles that compel the state to safeguard an open public sphere and accept some consequent risks to security and well being. This has frequently involved a reassessment of the limits of freedom of expression and the degree of harm that needs to be borne to ensure its adequate protection. For European states, adjusting to the internet era has been especially complicated. Changes in domestic media regimes are often tightly constrained by their far reaching regional economic and human rights commitments. Yet in addition to those constraints, the European regional order has also provided avenues for effective cooperation with other neighbouring states to address the challenges of the communications revolution. The wider international sphere has echoed these effects. Its multilateral trade and other obligations have pinched domestic autonomy, but also enabled participating states to coordinate their efforts more broadly.

While governments have struggled over the past decade to respond effectively to fast moving changes in communications and media services, they have also frequently intervened to speed the pace of change to achieve their public policy goals. In many countries, governments have for example directly or indirectly funded expensive broadband infrastructure development to achieve economic growth and social policy goals.[97] Yet, much more than government funding and other policy measures, the commercial pursuit of revenue and profit has driven the communications revolution forward in much of the world.[98] For this reason, the primary legal and policy perspective on the cross border flow of information and entertainment content is an economic one. Whether in Europe or in the global sphere, forums that specialize in trade in goods and services are the most influential in breaking down or legitimizing barriers to content production and distribution.

All other fields of law important to European and international media law, most notably human rights, have thus developed in an environment dominated by market based economic principles. In Europe, this has largely meant the application of the rules of free movement and their exceptions to the media sector. The international rules for trade in media goods and services are, in comparison, less well defined. The core rules are located within the WTO regime, but during the Doha Round stalemate momentum on cross border communications and media issues shifted to bilateral and other preferential trade agreements.[99]

To be sure, human rights based arguments have continued to bear heavily on these developments, especially for liberal democratic states. Human rights law not only has a deep interface with market based economic issues, but also provides alternative forums in which disputes over restraints on the media can be resolved.

---

[96] For example, efforts in the European Union to maintain a conceptual and regulatory distinction between linear and non-linear audiovisual content. See Chapter 4.

[97] See Chapter 14 on moves towards broadband access as a universal service obligation.

[98] The commercialization of China's media has also given market forces a powerful role in the development of the media in China. See Hu, S., ch 2 'The Rise of the Business Media in China', and, Miao, D., ch 3 'Struggling Between Propaganda and Commercials', in Shirk, S. (ed.), *Changing Media, Changing China* (Oxford University Press, 2010).

[99] On bilateral trade agreements, see Chapter 5.

These forums are especially important when they are able to address issues that cannot be dealt with fully in economic forums because they fall within recognized exceptions to the market access and other economic obligations of participating states. Human rights law has its own related problems in penetrating domestic autonomy, particularly in sensitive problems of national security, but it can be used to compel the state to justify itself in ways not possible under economic law. Nonetheless, in many circumstances media companies, and the governments that support them, have turned to economic obligations first to force the removal of disputed restrictions on the publication and distribution of media content.[100] These economic obligations may be open to non-market public policy arguments, but contain them with necessity tests. The remedies for their breach, moreover, even when not compensatory, are based on principles of economic loss. Consequently, the economic obligations set out in core treaties and supplementary instruments are the primary framework for the development of European and international media law.

As a result, for both the economic and human rights law, their impact on the domestic media state relationship occurs chiefly through the interpretation of the obligations undertaken by states. This means that methods used to interpret the breadth and depth of these obligations play an immensely important role in defining the nature of national autonomy in media matters. This will initially involve some combination of literal and purposive methods of interpretation to determine whether the obligation at issue covers the challenged domestic measure.[101] In general, domestic measures that restrict the publication or distribution of media content will easily fall within the scope of the economic or human rights obligations that protect the free flow of information, either as prohibited barriers to trade in goods and services or as prohibited fetters on freedom of expression.

It is therefore the interpretation of the recognized exceptions, rather than the obligations themselves, that more often determines whether a domestic measure must comply with European or international obligations. There is moreover an abundance of public policy purposes that are used to justify national restrictions on the media. Consequently, almost every recognized exclusion, derogation, or limitation to free flow obligations has become vitally important to European and international media law. These diverse exceptions have the potential to legitimize a great range of restrictive domestic measures.[102] They are however also subject to necessity conditions intended to ensure that they are only used for legitimate purposes and in a legitimate manner.[103]

---

[100] See, for example, Case C-211/91, *Commission v. Belgium* [1992] ECR I-6757.

[101] Note, for example, the broad scope of the 'public morals' exception recognized in economic and human rights law. See Chapter 12.

[102] See Part III: Restricting the Liberty to Publish.

[103] Necessity is a key term in the major exception provisions affecting the media in the EU Treaty on the functioning of the European Union, the CE European Convention on Human Rights, the WTO General Agreement on Tariffs and Trade, and the General Agreement on Trade in Services, as well as the UN International Covenant on Civil and Political Rights.

The depth that an economic or human rights obligation penetrates into domestic law and administration is as important as its breadth. A domestic measure that obstructs the purposes of an obligation will thus not necessarily constitute non-compliance if it is beyond the intended reach of the obligation. The measure may be within the area of discretion left to each state to decide the manner of implementation that best suits local conditions. European human rights law famously permits state parties a variable 'margin of appreciation' when implementing their convention obligations.[104] Alternatively, the measure may violate the literal meaning of the obligation, but be beyond its purposes. In economic law terms, this is often referred to as a question of the standard or intensity of review. Accordingly, a market access obligation may not apply to a domestic measure that is applied equally and pursues a legitimate purpose, despite the fact that it disadvantages competing foreign goods or services.

It therefore becomes apparent that the question whether a state has breached a human rights or economic obligation involves a determination not only of the extent of the violation, but also of the extent the state has acted for any other legitimate purpose. This consideration of opposing obligations and legitimate purposes, which in human rights law typically arises in the form of rights or interests, naturally lends itself to balancing or proportionality methods of adjudication. Indeed, proportionality analysis has become the principal model for adjudicating questions of treaty compliance in European and international media law.[105] Aside from its obvious use in evaluating of incommensurable commitments, proportionality analysis has other advantages for supranational adjudication. By ostensibly not requiring specific forms of compliance, it allows greater flexibility for national differences within the same set of obligations. At the same time, it can still be used to force governments to set out a reasoned justification for non-compliance with a European or international obligation.

Proportionality analysis is also deeply implicated in grander conceptual debates over the future of European and international public order. Through balancing and cross comparison, proportionality offers a method of reconciling the diverse legal and policy objectives that sit on different sides of the external and internal fault lines of European and international law. In this way, judges or other decision makers are able to chart the proper limits of national autonomy and resolve the difficult interface between economic and human rights law. The comprehensive perspective of proportionality analysis offers a framework for the integration and principled coherence sought by constitutionalism.[106]

---

[104] Letsas, G., 'Two Concepts of the Margin of Appreciation', 4 *Oxford Journal of Legal Studies* (2006), 705.

[105] This model is not uniform and is seen to vary considerably, often falling short of proportionality *stricto sensu*. See generally, Andenas, M. and Zleptnig, S., 'Proportionality: WTO Law in Comparative Perspective', 42(3) *Texas International Law Journal* (2007), 370–427, and Stone Sweet, A. and Mathews, J., 'Proportionality Balancing and Global Constitutionalism', 47(1) *Columbia Journal of Transnational Law* (2008), 72–164.

[106] On the role of constitutionalism in contemporary international law and policy, see Dunoff, J. and Trachtman, J., 'A Functional Approach to International Constitutionalization', in Dunoff, J. and

Proportionality, as a tool of constitutionalism, is directed towards greater doctrinal coherence and order across the breadth of an integrated legal and political regime.[107] This project is therefore not directed towards the strengthening of constitutional institutions in the European or international spheres, although it assumes the development of independent judicial institutions. Instead, it concerns the constitutional principles that constrain and unify the exercise of public authority within those spheres. Like other constitutionalist objectives, the goal of fundamental doctrinal coherence is grounded in the principles of the contemporary liberal democratic state. These include the protection of democracy, human rights, and good governance. In short, the constitutionalist vision is, amongst other important things, a further twist in long running efforts to entrench liberal economic and political values into European and international public order.[108]

In Europe, these efforts are conceptually sophisticated and institutionally well supported. While the western European regional order was always self consciously liberal democratic, two events of the 1980s were critically important in propelling European constitutionalism forward: the renewal of European common market objectives and the absorption of former Soviet states. The 1986 Single European Act not only broadened the scope of EU law but also extended its reach further into the regulatory regimes of the member states.[109] For the media sector, this was the essential legal step to accompany the technological breakthrough of direct-to-home satellite broadcasting, which together brought about the first genuine foreign competition in the most heavily protected domestic markets. This kind of deep intrusion into sensitive national regulatory policy forced EU institutions and law to develop the fundamental principles and methods to address the difficult relationship between market and non-market public policy.

The failure of Soviet power in the same decade soon brought the progressive expansion of the European regional system eastwards. Accession to the Council of Europe and then the European Union was necessarily limited to those former socialist states that could demonstrate adequate progress in transforming themselves into stable, market based liberal democracies on the European model. Yet this process of tutelage also required greater clarity in the principles and rules that define the legitimate European state, including the legal and regulatory foundations of a pluralist, independent media.[110]

The achievement of constitutionalism in the international sphere is, in comparison to Europe, a far greater challenge. There is no comparable consensus on the

---

Trachtman, J., (eds), *Ruling the World? Constitutionalism, International Law, and Global Governance* (Cambridge University Press, 2009).

[107] See also Koch, C., 'Envisioning a Global Legal Culture', 25(1) *Michigan Journal of International Law* (2003), 1–76.

[108] Kumm, M., 'Democracy is Not Enough: Rights, Proportionality and the Point of Judicial Review' in Klatt, M. (ed.), *The Legal Philosophy of Robert Alexy* (Oxford University Press, 2009), 134.

[109] See Pescatore, S., 'Some Critical Remarks on the "Single European Act"', 24(1) *Common Market Law Review* (1987), 9; Ehlermann, C., 'The Internal Market Following the Single European Act', 24(3) *Common Market Law Review* (1987), 361.

[110] On the Council of Europe, see Chapter 6.

character of any nascent international public order. Nor is there an integrated set of core institutions capable of sustaining that order. Nonetheless, while international constitutionalism is more aspiration than project, it has obvious foundations in the major multilateral treaties and forums important to global political and economic relations. In the human rights field, the composite 'international bill of rights' carries long standing claims of universality and supremacy and its principles easily support an explicitly liberal democratic interpretation.[111] More importantly, the creation of the WTO in 1994 made international trade law the obvious focus for the advance of constitutionalism in the international sphere.[112] The concurrent expansion of trade law beyond goods into services and intellectual property rights created a much bigger interface with national law and regulation, which sharpened debate over the purposes of domestic regulation, the scope of recognized exceptions to trade obligations, and the limits of WTO review. In these circumstances, the strengthening of dispute resolution under the authority of the WTO Appellate Body has created the potential for the constitutional doctrinal development of these issues.

Objections to constitutionalism

Constitutionalism that focuses on multilateral legislative institutions and instruments and lays particular emphasis on constitutional adjudication is highly problematic. Constitutionalism in this form necessarily assumes that regional and international bodies have the potential to exercise competent authority over the diverse economic and social relations that arise locally within their far flung constituent states. Yet these supranational bodies are distant from the local conditions and preferences their decisions are intended to affect. Inevitably, they lack the local understanding or supervisory capacity needed for the effective exercise of democratically responsive, governmental authority.[113] 'It is much easier to design institutions that are locally democratic than globally democratic, particularly in terms of responsiveness to the "cultural" aspects of what counts as democratic decision making; moreover, preferences and social circumstances are likely to be more homogeneous within localities than across a set of boundaries.'[114] These objections apply with special intensity to the media state relationship, which is

[111] On the 'International bill of rights', see Chapter 6.
[112] Cass, D.Z., *The Constitutionalization of the World Trade Organization* (Oxford University Press, 2005); Krajewski, M., 'Democratic Legitimacy and Constitutional Perspectives of WTO Law', 35(1) *Journal of World Trade* (2001), 167–186.
[113] 'Sustained and focused control by an agency is not achieved by simply passing a law, but requires detailed knowledge of and intimate involvement with the regulated activity', Majone, G., 'The Rise of the Regulatory State in Europe' in Baldwin, R., Scott, C., and Hood, C., *A Reader on Regulation* (Oxford University Press1998), 204.
[114] Charny, D., 'Regulatory Competition and the Global Coordination of Labor Standards', 3(2) *Journal of International Economic Law* (2000), 281–302. See also Kaul, I. and Mendoza, R., 'Advancing the Concept of Public Goods' in Kaul, I., Conceicao, P., Le Goulven, K., and Mendoza, R., *Providing Global Public Goods* (Oxford University Press, 2003), 78–111.

thickly enmeshed the culture, politics, and even geography of societies and communities.

The problem of insensitivity to locality plainly afflicts major states as much as supranational entities. Yet it has also produced innumerable forms of flexibility in law making and public administration in countries that have sought to resolve the problem of distance between central authority and local conditions. In the European and international spheres, however, the number and diversity of participating states as well as their collective resistance to significant structural reform makes this problem much larger and difficult to resolve. As Dani Rodrik has argued, regarding the international sphere, deep integration, national sovereignty, and democracy are mutually incompatible.[115]

European and international regimes are undoubtedly constructed to accommodate multiple differences between participating states. But even in Europe, where member states are committed to a common liberal democratic identity, the boundaries of permitted national discretion inevitably exclude public policy choices that are justifiable within the broad principles of liberalism. On the one hand, a state may find that its fundamental commitments to the protection of liberty violate its European obligations because these require a different balance between personal liberty and well being. European human rights law, for example, does not permit the radical denial of legal remedies for injury to reputation for prominent public figures, although that position is defensible on liberal principles and entrenched in the constitutional law of other liberal democracies.[116] On the other hand, a state may find that its non-market policy goals are heavily restricted by its EU market based economic obligations. Here, it is often European Union law that restricts the freedom of member states to intervene in media markets for valid social and cultural purposes.[117]

The international obligations of states are less extensive and less well articulated, but they can present an even greater challenge for participating non-liberal democratic states. From their perspective, constitutionalism is merely a new guise for the liberal democratic strategy of changing their character through international legal obligations. There is consequently no area of international law more contested than civil and political human rights, whose implicit foundations in liberal democratic thought constantly presses on these states.[118] Even international economic obligations, which many non-democratic states have found conditionally acceptable, are difficult to reconcile with a government controlled media sector.[119]

---

[115] Rodrik, D., 'How to Save Globalization from its Cheerleaders' KSG Working Papers No. RWP07-038 (2007), 25 at 30.

[116] See *Lindon, Otchakovsky-Laurens and July v. France* (2007) ECHR 21279/02, 36448/02. See also *New York Times Company v. Sullivan* (1964) 376 U.S. 254.

[117] See Chapters 14 and 15.

[118] For example, China's reluctance to ratify the ICCPR despite ratification of the ICESCR. Lee, K., 'China and the International Covenant on Civil and Political Rights: Prospects and Challenges', 6(2) *Chinese Journal of International Law* (2007), 445–474.

[119] See, for example, *China—Measures Affecting Trading Rights and Distribution Services for Certain Publications and Audiovisual Entertainment Products*, (WT/DS363/AB/R), Appellate Body (December 2009).

Where supranational obligations are subject to binding adjudication, the traditional methods of avoiding or softening their unwelcome implications through
auto-interpretation are greatly reduced. On this front, the ubiquitous use of
balancing or proportionality analysis has only added to concerns about the excessive
reach of these obligations and their insensitivity to local needs. Its neutrality, which
is often seen as one of the chief strengths of proportionality analysis in a supranational setting, has ironically become one of its major faults. As discussed in Chapter
2, proportionality analysis has difficulty in maintaining a consistent moral position
grounded in a particular conception of the person. This is especially true in the
European or international spheres, where solutions need to apply across a range of
legal and political systems. In those contexts, the balancing exercise is inevitably
drawn towards the middle ground, looking for the apparent consensus position and
moderating out exceptional practices.[120]

As the European experience demonstrates, proportionality analysis can be firmly
situated within the liberal democratic tradition. Nonetheless, it is essentially a
mechanism to force states and other parties to account for their conduct rather
than to establish principles and doctrines that give clarity and predictability within
a particular moral and political tradition. In relation to freedom of expression, this
leads to two difficulties. First, proportionality is unlikely to yield a consistent
understanding of the relationship between liberty and well being. In each instance,
they are both core aspects of individual autonomy and dignity and must be weighed
afresh in any balancing exercise. As a result, European media law depends heavily
on the consequential arguments for freedom of expression that focus on the needs
of democracy and the benefits of openness. Where the moral claims of liberty and
well being are roughly balanced, these consequential arguments, at least in principle, provide the critical element needed to break these stalemates. In this manner,
protection for the well being of the individual must give way where there is a
compelling argument for publication that serves democratic processes or ensures
the exposure of falsity or wrongdoing for other public purposes.

Yet even here, proportionality analysis can leave uncertainty. Balancing may
routinely turn to consequential reasoning to justify decisions that favour the liberty
to publish, but it is not a form of adjudication that readily yields the kind of
certainty that can be found in a developed line of doctrinal argument. The
protection of individual or societal well being will therefore always retain a residual
capacity to upset well developed consequential arguments. As the European Court
of Human Rights concluded in decision in *Lindon*, ' . . . regardless of the forcefulness of political struggles, it is legitimate to try to ensure that they abide by a
minimum degree of moderation and propriety, especially as the reputation of
a politician, even a controversial one, must benefit from the protection afforded
by the Convention'.[121]

---

[120] See n. 25 above.
[121] *Lindon, Otchakovsky-Laurens and July v. France* (Application Nos 21279/02 and 36448/02)
(22 October 2007), para. 57.

From a liberal democratic perspective, proportionality analysis can be further
faulted for permitting the balancing of fundamental rights against the mere interests
of the state, the general public, or of individuals. An individual's right to freedom of
expression may thus be weighed directly against the state's interest in national
security. This, however, is contrary to the liberal jurisprudential argument that
freedom of expression and other fundamental rights lose their special quality as
rights when they become elements in a general balancing exercise.[122] According to
that argument, it is the special status and treatment of rights that protect a society's
basic values from encroachment by the state, which by its nature is prone to
unwarranted secrecy and narrow self interest.

Despite these difficulties, there is no obvious alternative to balancing and
proportionality analysis in supranational adjudication. Adjudication based on the
'moral vision' of a constitutional document requires a combination of close textual
analysis and keen attention to the social, political, and cultural circumstances of the
society bound by that constitution. This arguably can only be done effectively
within a specific political community that enjoys sufficient social cohesion and
shared values. The result however will be a moral vision distinctive to that
community and less suited to others, which is of little use to regional or international legal regimes that must find outcomes that encompass differences between
member states.

From treaties to networks

From a wider perspective, concerns about constitutional adjudication in supranational regimes appear parochial and even misdirected. While the Westphalian
notion of a community of states acting in accordance with common rules is the
archetypical model of regional and world order, it also seems increasingly anachronistic in a world that throngs with states that range widely in every possible
capacity. Non-compliance, deliberate or inadvertent, is commonplace. Even in
Europe, the capacity and willingness of states to fulfil the obligations of European
public order varies considerably. In these circumstances, the quest for supranational
constitutionalism appears narrowly law based and state centred.

That question of relevance becomes all the more pressing when the state is seen
in the full context of contemporary international relations, including in particular
the host of non-state actors that have become a prominent part of regional and
global affairs. States now jostle with international organizations, multinational
corporations, business associations, labour unions, charities as well as terrorist
and criminal groups in the struggle for resources, influence, and advantage. As
this transformation has occurred, there has also been a wholesale re-evaluation of
the character of the contemporary state and its future.[123] 'In this post-Westphalian

[122] Dworkin, R., *A Matter of Principle* (Harvard University Press, 1985).
[123] See, for example, Strange, S., *The Retreat Of The State: The Diffusion Of Power In The World
Economy* (Cambridge University Press, 1996) and Mathews, J., 'Power Shift', 76(1) *Foreign Affairs*

order there is a marked shift towards hierarchy—a divided authority system—with states seeking to share the tasks of governance with a complex array of institutions, public and private, transnational, regional, and global, representing the emergence of overlapping "communities of fate".'[124] Consequently, national territorial boundaries have become less important in containing and shaping the use of power.[125]

Just as states no longer wield their historic authority over global political and economic relations, the treaty, on which much supranational constitutionalism is founded, is no longer the omnipresent instrument of multilateral relations. In the post World War II decades, it was well suited to the ambitious construction of new European and international regimes.[126] Indeed, without the multilateral treaty, the legalization of regional and international relations over the past half century could not have taken place.[127] These treaty based regimes, however, could only operate effectively when the participating states acted in close cooperation, ensuring that their obligations were interpreted similarly and enforced domestically.[128] This 'club model' was moreover centred on the western democracies and was only successful so long as they collectively dominated the major multilateral forums and agencies.[129]

As the influence of assertive, newly independent states grew, the international law making process became more complex and unwieldy. In looking for other methods to manage their relations, states developed innovative forms of agreement, including a wide variety of soft law instruments.[130] By sacrificing the legally binding character of the treaty obligation, these instruments provided a method

(1997), 50–66: 'The end of the Cold War has brought . . . a novel redistribution of power among states, markets, and civil society. National governments are not simply losing autonomy in a globalizing economy. They are sharing powers . . . with businesses, with international organizations, and with a multitude of citizens groups known as non-governmental organizations'; See also Khanna, P., *How to Run the World: Charting a Course to the Next Renaissance* (Random House, 2011).

[124] Held, D. and McGrew, A., n. 38 above, at 186.

[125] Raustiala, K., 'The Architecture of International Cooperation: Transgovernmental Networks and the Future of International Law', 43(1) *Virginia Journal of International Law* (2002), 1–92 at 13–14.

[126] Although contractual in nature, the treaty, in its endless versatility, serves formidable constitutional and legislative purposes just as well as the mundane aims of innumerable bilateral exchanges of letters. See Jennings, R. and Watts, A., *Oppenheim's International Law* (Oxford University Press, 2008); Aust, A., *Modern Treaty Law and Practice*, 2nd edn (Cambridge University Press, 2007); Boyle, A. and Chinkin, C., *The Making of International Law* (Oxford University Press, 2007).

[127] Goldstein, J., Kahler, M., Keohane, R.O., and Slaughter, A-M., 'Introduction: Legalization and World Politics', 54(3) *International Organization* (2000), 385–399. On the legalization of economic relations, see Jackson, J.H, 'International Economic Law: Reflections on the "Boiler Room" of International Relations' 10 *The American Journal of International Law and Policy* (1995), 509–606.

[128] Keohane, R. and Nye, J., n. 13 above.

[129] Ibid.

[130] Chinkin, C., 'Normative Development in the International Legal System' in Shelton, D. (ed.), *Commitment and Compliance: The Role of Non-Binding Norms in the International Legal Systems* (Oxford University Press, 2001), 21–42; Shelton, D., 'Normative Hierarchy in International Law', 100(2) *American Journal of International Law* (2006), 291–323; Shelton, D., 'Soft Law' *Handbook of International Law* (Routledge Press, 2008); Schäfer, A., 'Resolving Deadlock: Why International Organisations Introduce Soft Law', 12(2) *European Law Journal* (2006), 194–208. For a critical discussion of the concept of international 'soft law', see Raustiala, K., 'Form and Substance in International Agreements', 99(3) *American Journal of International Law* (2005), 581–614;

of achieving reasonable precision in the responsibilities of states. When used in multilateral regimes where acts of non-cooperation have serious practical consequences for member states, soft law instruments can often rival treaties in effective compliance.[131] Both the European Union and the Council of Europe consequently have increasingly resorted to soft law instruments to set out common principles for member states.[132] They also have an important role in bridging the gap between state and non-state parties, the latter lacking the capacity in public international law to become parties to treaties. Consequently, soft law is now a major dimension of European and international media law.

These changes in the instruments of cooperation between states are also a symptom of the evolving nature of the state itself.[133] As global communications and transportation services improved, government departments and agencies found it increasingly convenient to cooperate closely with foreign counterparts over great distances.[134] They could, as a result, engage in coordinated cross border policy and rule making while simultaneously taking responsibility for domestic implementation.[135] By the 1990s, governmental relationships of this kind were seen as part of the new phenomenon of global network relationships. These, in simple terms, are loosely structured, horizontal relationships that link key individuals and organizations through shared goals or responsibilities.[136] Their development however has radically changed the scale and complexity of cross border relations.[137] In

Shaffer, G. and Pollack, M., 'Hard vs. Soft Law: Alternatives, Complements and Antagonists in International Governance' 94 *Minnesota Law Review* (2010), 706–799.

[131] Slaughter, A-M., *A New World Order* (Princeton University Press, 2004), 224.

[132] See, for example, the European Parliament and Council, *Recommendation on the protection of minors and human dignity and on the right of reply in relation to the competitiveness of the European audiovisual and on-line information services industry* (2006/952/EC). See also *Recommendation on the development of the competitiveness of the European audiovisual and information services industry by promoting national frameworks aimed at achieving a comparable and effective level of protection of minors and human dignity* (98/560/EC, 1998); Council of Europe, Committee of Ministers, *Declaration on freedom of communication on the Internet* (Strasbourg, 28 May 2003) (Adopted by the Committee of Ministers at the 840th meeting of the Ministers' Deputies). Dawson, M., 'Soft Law and the Rule of Law in the European Union: Revision or Redundancy?' EUI Working Papers (RSCAS) 2009/24.

[133] No longer the state envisioned in the post World War II Bretton Woods Agreements. See Patterson, D. and Afilalo, A., *The New Global Trading Order: The Evolving State and the Future of Trade* (Cambridge University Press, 2008), 2.

[134] Slaughter, A-M., 'The Real New World Order', 76(3) *Foreign Affairs* (1997), 183–197 at 189.

[135] Krisch, N. and Kingsbury, B., 'Introduction: Global Governance and Global Administrative Law in the International Legal Order', 17(1) *European Journal of International Law* (2006), 1–13 at 3.

[136] The European Commission has defined networks as 'interaction between individuals and/or organisations (communities, regional and local authorities, undertakings, administrations, research centres and so on) in a non-hierarchical way and where every participant is responsible for a part of the resources needed to achieve the common objective, electronic communication being the most preferred tool', European Commission, *Report from the Commission on European Governance* COM (2002) 705 final.

[137] Castells, M., *The Rise of Network Society,* Vol. 1 of *The Information Age: Economy, Society and Culture* (Blackwell, 1996); Raustiala, K., 'The Architecture of International Cooperation: Transgovernmental Networks and the Future of International Law', 43(1) *Virginia Journal of International Law* (2002), 1–92 at 15; Picciotto, S., 'Networks in International Economic Integration: Fragmented States and the Dilemmas of Neo-Liberalism', 17 *Northwestern Journal of International Law and Business* (1996), 1014–1056.

intergovernmental relations, they are most often associated with national regulatory bodies, but they also link ministries, courts, and legislatures, enabling the harmonization of national legal and regulatory standards, administrative practices, and policy objectives.[138] As Anne-Marie Slaughter has argued, '[d]isaggregating the state into its functional components makes it possible to create networks of institutions engaged in a common enterprise even as they represent distinct national interests'.[139] Somewhat counter-intuitively, formal treaty relations may even be enhanced by these parallel forms of obligation and cooperation, which can smooth treaty negotiation, fill in gaps, and otherwise improve implementation.[140]

Relationships between governments however are only a small part of the thick web of networks that now connect businesses, professions, research institutions, and civil society organizations across the world.[141] States therefore may often find themselves in competition with financial and commercial networks that are centred on powerful non-state entities, both domestic and foreign.[142] The boundaries between governmental and non-governmental networks have moreover been eroded by new communications services that allow instantaneous and continuous contact between state and non-state agents.[143]

---

[138] On regulatory networks, see Stephan, P.B., 'Regulatory Cooperation and Competition: The Search for Virtue' in Bermann, G. et al. (eds), *Transatlantic Regulatory Cooperation: Legal Problems and Political Prospects* (Oxford University Press, 2000), 167–282. See also Shaffer, G.C., 'The Blurring of the Intergovernmental: Public-Private Partnerships behind U.S. and EU Trade Disputes' in Pollack, M.A. and Shaffer, G.C. (eds), *Transatlantic Governance in the Global Economy* (Rowman & Littlefield, 2001), 97–123; Shaffer, G.C., 'What's New in EU Trade Dispute Settlement? Judicialisation, Public-Private Networks and the WTO Legal Order', 13(6) *Journal of European Public Policy* (2006), 832–850. On the controversy in the United States over the use of foreign law in interpreting the American Constitution, the availability of legal and judicial networks that familiarize judges with foreign law, see Slaughter, A-M., n. 131 above, 3 and Anderson, K., 'Foreign Law and the U.S. Constitution', 131 *Policy Review* (2005), 33–50.

[139] Slaughter, A-M., n. 131 above, 195.

[140] Raustiala, K., 'The Architecture of International Cooperation: Transgovernmental Networks and the Future of International Law', 43(1) *Virginia Journal of International Law* (2002), 1–92 at 72. On the operation of treaties as a continuing dialogue between the state parties, international officials, and non-governmental organizations, see Chayes, A. and Handler Chayes, A., *The New Sovereignty: Compliance with International Regulatory Agreements* (Harvard University Press, 1995).

[141] Higgott, R., Underhill, G.R.D., and Bieler, A. (eds), *Non-State Actors and Authority in the Global System* (Routledge, 2000); Hongju Koh, H., 'The Globalization of Freedom', 26 *Yale Journal of International Law* (2001), 305.

[142] See Held, D. and McGrew, A., n. 38 above, 185–199 at 189; Scott, C., 'Regulation in the Age of Governance: The Rise of the Post Regulatory State' in Jordana, J. and Levi-Faur, D. (eds), *The Politics of Regulation: Institutions and Regulatory Reforms for the Age of Governance* (Edward Elgar, 2004), 145–174.

[143] See, for an example of the role of private interests in the making of public international law, Sell, S., *Private Power, Public Law: The Globalization of Intellectual Property Rights* (Cambridge University Press, 2003). Europe: 'a more systematic and proactive approach to working with key networks to enable them to contribute to decision-shaping and policy execution, and examining how the framework for transnational cooperation of regional or local actors could be better supported at EU level for the purpose of presenting proposals.' 3.1.4. Fourth line of action: connecting with networks. See the European Commission, *Report from the Commission on European Governance* COM (2002) 705 final, 15. For a European example of the special position of businesses in network relationships with governments, see the European Union Publishers' Forum. It was established in 1996 as a contact forum between newspaper, magazine, and online publishers and European institutions. It is co-presided

The global media sector abounds with commercial and professional network relationships. Media companies and professionals tend to have a natural affinity for communications technologies and have put them to use to secure a favourable regulatory environment across borders. Many of the world's largest media companies provide, in themselves, substantial bases for international networks and support a large number of media related organizations and centres.[144] These are complemented, both domestically and internationally, by commercial media associations, such as the International Federation of the Periodical Press, the World Association of Newspapers, and the International Association of Broadcasting. In Europe, the commercial and public service media sectors are also well organized to protect their interests in Brussels and abroad. European media business associations include the European Newspaper Publishers' Association, the European Publishers Council, the Association of Commercial Television in Europe, the Association Européenne des Radios, and the European Broadcasting Union.

In the internet era, the strengthening of network relationships based in the United States and the European Union have helped to project their cultural and political policies internationally and strengthen their influence in global communications and media policy debates.[145] More generally, these western based networks have also helped to suffuse liberal democratic values more widely through the growth of common standards and practices. While this is not constitutionalism in the form of multilateral institutions, rights, and obligations, or formal adjudication, it is at least consistent with the underlying vision of a liberal democratic regional and global public order.[146] Accordingly, while the more formal, state centred liberal democratic project may have faltered, it has arguably continued through the synergy between governmental, commercial, and professional networks.[147]

The influence of the commercial media in Europe and internationally on liberal democratic public policy through network relationships can however also be distinctly undemocratic and selective in its liberalism. Networks tend to be closed to public scrutiny and lack the openness and accountability that are essential to

---

by the President of the Federation of European Publishers and the Director-General of the Office for Official Publications of the European Communities.

[144] On multinational media ownership, consult Columbia Journalism Review, 'Who Owns What' resource, <http://www.cjr.org>.

[145] Krisch, N., 'International Law in Times of Hegemony: Unequal Power and the Shaping of the International Legal Order', 16(3) *European Journal of International Law* (2005), 369–408; Raustiala, K., 'The Architecture of International Cooperation: Transgovernmental Networks and the Future of International Law', 43(1) *Virginia Journal of International Law* (2002), 1–91 at 16; Castells, M., *End of Millennium*, Vol. 3 of *The Information Age: Economy, Society and Culture* (Blackwell, 1998), 70–165; Tully, J., 'Communication and Imperialism' in Tully, J., *Public Philosophy in a New Key*, (Vol. 2, Imperialism and Civic Freedom), (Cambridge University Press, 2008), and De Sousa Santos, B., *Toward a New Legal Common Sense: Law, Globalization and Emancipation* (Butterworths, 2000).

[146] Constitutionalism does not necessarily mean a unitary hierarchy or a hierarchy among legal systems or interpretive institutions. Constitutionalism can be achieved through heterarchy. See Halberstam, D., 'Constitutional Heterarchy: The Centrality of Conflict in the European Union and the United States' in Dunoff, J. and Trachtman, J. (eds), *Ruling the World? Constitutional, International Law and Global Government* (Cambridge University Press, 2009).

[147] See Slaughter, A-M., 'The Real New World Order', 76(3) *Foreign Affairs* (1997), 183–197 at 184; Slaughter, A-M., n. 131 above.

democratic decision making. In addition, the commercial media have a very particular and often self interested relationship with liberal arguments for freedom of expression. For many journalists and editors, the most compelling argument is the dual freedom of speech and free market one that emphasizes liberty from state restrictions on the publication and distribution of media content.[148] It will rarely be in the media's interest to champion the cause of individual or collective well being or the security of the state where those are threatened by the media publications. The commercial media moreover is unlikely to welcome the creation or expansion of any public service media that offer subsidized information or entertainment services.[149]

The pluralist perspective

In the years since the collapse of the Soviet Union, European and international public order have undergone an enormous transformation. Despite setbacks, liberal democratic principles are deeply entrenched in an expanded European order and influential across the rest of the world, even in states that reject the liberal democratic project.[150] Despite its many internal inconsistencies, the liberal democratic media state relationship has consequently become the leading model for media law, regulation, and policy. From a structuralist perspective, this model has become part of the global institutional culture that determines the legitimate structure, purposes, and methods of liberal democratic states.[151]

In Europe, the domestic media state relationship is thoroughly enmeshed in European regional law and public administration. European supranational courts, holding exclusive authority over the meaning of the foundational treaties, have pushed European economic and human rights law deep into the domestic realm, leaving no aspect of media policy untouched. Eastward expansion has intensified this process, demanding much greater clarity in the principles and rules that define the legitimate European democratic state. Even the deep fault line between Europe's

---

[148] For many journalists and editors, the most compelling argument is the dual freedom of speech and free market one that emphasizes liberty from state restrictions on the publication and distribution of media content.

[149] Murdoch, J., 'Your Compass in a Changing World', *The Marketing Society Annual Lecture*, 24 April 2008.

[150] In China, the domestic debate is not liberal democratic but is acutely conscious of liberal democratic arguments. On the influence of the Enlightenment and liberalism on ideas of modernity in China, see Zhang Yongle, 'The Future of the Past: On Wang Hui's Rise of Modern Chinese Thought', 62 *New Left Review*, March–April 2010.

[151] Structuralist perspectives have emphasized the ways in which states are shaped by globalized concepts of state structure and domestic public order, leading to constitutional and institutional isomorphism. See Goodman, R. and Jinks, D.,'Toward an Institutional Theory of Sovereignty', 55(5) *Stanford Law Review* (2003), 1749–1788; Drezner, D.W., *All Politics is Global: Explaining International Regulation* (Princeton University Press, 2007), 17. But see also Dixon, R. and Posner, E., 'The Limits of Constitutional Convergence', (2010) University of Chicago, Public Law Working Paper No. 329.

human rights and economic regional regimes is being gradually resolved.[152] Consequently, as media issues are ineluctably drawn into the European sphere, a distinctive European media law is emerging.

The strengthening hold of European law on the domestic media state relationship has also placed that relationship under acute strain. Media law and policy is intensely local in nature and the tensions running between the liberty to publish and the protection of the state and public are rooted in local concerns, beliefs, and preferences. The authority and legitimacy of the state therefore rests, in part, on its ability to manage those tensions. The common European model, however, inevitably reduces the range of solutions available to member states, leaving scant room for exceptional solutions to the problems of reconciling liberty and the risk of harm.[153] There is consequently a troubling incompatibility between the constitutionalist vision of a coherent, integrated European order and the thickly domestic nature of the media state relationship.

International public order, which in comparison to Europe is a patchwork of ill coordinated regimes loosely connected by an arguably fragmented legal system, ostensibly offers far fewer challenges to the media state relationship.[154] Yet, for non-liberal democracies, the international sphere is fraught with difficulties. There is now a global consciousness of the importance of human rights and human dignity, which every state must acknowledge and address in some manner. While the liberal democratic human rights project may have been fought to a standstill, it still retains the potential to question the legitimacy of illiberal and non-democratic governments. International trade law also poses problems for states with extensive or arbitrary controls on domestic and foreign media content. Even with careful negotiation, national treatment and transparency obligations will inevitably affect the many goods and services involved in the domestic information and entertainment sectors.[155] The WTO obligation to negotiate further liberalization of trade in services is moreover likely to bring greater pressure on protected media sectors over the long term.

For liberal democracies, it is the unresolved direction of the liberal democratic project that causes difficulties for domestic media law and policy. The international human rights field is a subject for immense shared disappointment, especially in the area of civil and political rights. Nonetheless, the fundamental principles entrenched in the UDHR and the ICCPR sustain a unified argument for liberal democratic freedom of expression that can be made to run seamlessly from domestic or regional law to international law. Ironically, the undeveloped state of

---

[152] See Chapter 4.
[153] Schauer, F., 'The Exceptional First Amendment' in Ignatieff, M., (ed.) *American Exceptionalism and Human Rights* (Princeton University Press, 2005), 29–56.
[154] International Law Commission, *Conclusions of the Work of the Study Group on Fragmentation of International Law: Difficulties arising from the Diversification and Expansion of International Law*, Report to the UN General Assembly, 2006, A/61/10, para. 251.
[155] See, for example, *China—Measures Affecting Trading Rights and Distribution Services for Certain Publications and Audiovisual Entertainment Products*, (WT/DS363/AB/R), Appellate Body (December 2009).

international human rights law has meant that liberal democratic disagreements over the proper limits of the liberty to speak and publish have remained largely below the surface.

International trade law, in contrast, has been a focus for sharp debate over the proper role of the state in media markets and the legitimacy of restraints on trade in media goods and services. Its market based approach to this trade is however only half built and many of the essential questions have been put off. The exceptions necessary for member states to derogate from trade obligations for non-market public policy reasons are still incomplete and contentious. In this respect, although the interface between WTO law and human rights law is the subject of much constitutionalist academic debate, it remains open and unresolved.[156] The dominant interface in international trade law therefore lies between trade liberalization obligations and the domestic autonomy of state parties.

In the face of these many limitations, the obvious question is whether the constitutionalist vision of order and coherence in the international sphere is anything more than a stimulus for creative thinking about global governance.[157] Indeed, much the same question could be asked about the European enterprise, given the refusal of many politicians and voters to accept the goals of the failed European Constitution. Alternatively, it can also be argued that the costs to national autonomy of the significant constitutionalist goals already realized in Europe are an excessive and unnecessary burden on the member states. Certainly, European principles and rules outlining the legitimate media state relationship have gradually become more prescriptive and confining.

These concerns suggest that a pluralist perspective on European and international public order is not only more realistic, but better suited to the prospects for liberal democracy in a world that is fissured by differences in moral and political values. Legal and political pluralism accepts this pervasive diversity and the endurance of incompatible regimes.[158] Unlike full blooded constitutionalism, pluralism therefore has no difficulty in reconciling the co-existence of regions dominated by liberal and non-liberal concepts of public order.[159] '[P]luralist approaches...assume the existence of a plurality of distinct and separate entities without any overall community,

---

[156] Petersmann, E-U., 'Time for a United Nations "Compact" for Integrating Human Rights into the Law of Worldwide Organizations: Lessons from European Integration', 13(3) *European Journal of International Law* (2002), 621–650; Alston, P., 'Resisting the Merger and Acquisition of Human Rights by Trade Law: A Reply to Petersmann', 13(4) *European Journal of International Law* (2002), 815–844.

[157] For example, global administrative law.

[158] On legal pluralism as a conceptual framework for international order, see, for example, Berman, P., 'Global Legal Pluralism', 80(6) *Southern California Review* (2007), 1155–1238; Burke-White, W., 'International Legal Pluralism', 25(4) *Michigan Journal of International Law* (2004), 963–980; Krisch, N., 'The Pluralism of Global Administrative Law', 17(1) *European Journal of International Law* (2006), 247–278; Krisch, N., The Case for Pluralism in Postnational Law. LSE Legal Studies Working Paper No. 12/2009, Tamanaha, B., 'Understanding Legal Pluralism: Past to Present, Local to Global' St. John's Legal Studies Research Paper No. 07-0080, 2007; Michaels, R., 'Global Legal Pluralism', 5 *Annual Review of Law & Social Science* (2009), 243–262.

[159] Borgen, C., 'Whose Public, Whose Order? Imperium, Region, and Normative Friction', 32(2) *Yale Journal of International Law* (2007), 331–362.

they emphasize the autonomous, authoritative decision-making processes and autochthonous values of each, and they envisage communication and conflict resolution through agonistic political processes, ad-hoc negotiation and pragmatic adjustment.'[160]

As an intellectual perspective, pluralism is also helpful in recognizing the irrepressible diversity in governmental, economic, and social practices that flourishes under the skin of ostensible conformity with regional and international models.[161] Law and government are rooted in locality, however much constrained and shaped by supranational models of the legitimate state. This is especially true of the media state relationship, which is uniquely structured by the history and circumstances of its place and operates according to its overriding concerns, values, and beliefs. While constitutionalism addresses the need for more effective cooperation to resolve the host of public policy issues that are regional or global in scale. Pluralist arguments are a healthy reminder of the underlying importance of locality and the need to accommodate exceptional norms and practices in supranational models of the legitimate state.

---

[160] De Búrca, G., 'The European Court of Justice and the International Legal Order after *Kadi*' Jean Monnet Working Paper 01/09, 2009.

[161] Goodman, R. and Jinks, D., 'Toward an Institutional Theory of Sovereignty', 55(5) *Stanford Law Review* (2003), 1749–1788.

PART II

THE MEDIA IN EUROPEAN AND INTERNATIONAL LEGAL REGIMES

4

The Media in the European Single Market

European media law rests on the mixed foundations of economic and human rights law. While human rights law captures public attention more often, it is Europe's economic laws that set the basic contours and dynamics for media law. This follows simply from the fact that the production and distribution of information and entertainment content in Europe is primarily driven by the pursuit of profit and market share. Plainly, political, social, and cultural interests are hugely important in creating demand for the consumption of media content, but the satisfaction of that demand will generally depend on prevailing market economic conditions. Consequently, European Union law, which protects the market foundations of content production and distribution, creates the background framework in which European human rights law operates in the media sector. Nevertheless, it is also true that European media law has developed in the mid ground between persistent efforts to break down barriers to European market integration and powerful resistance claiming to protect vital political, social, and cultural values.

The media sector has presented a huge challenge for the project of creating a European single market. Member states have resisted each step in the further integration of national media into that regional market, anxious at the dismantling of established local media structures and practices and with it a loss of vital leverage over the domestic public information environment. For the EU's western member states, national media policies have been historically structured around the fact of heavy state involvement in the broadcast sector. This state presence, ostensibly to advance the political and social goals of a democratically oriented concept of freedom of expression, gave the European media model its distinctive character. The state provision of media services along with close control of media content standards has therefore often blunted the market opening potential of EU rules on free movement and market competition.

Yet the relationship between EU law and the media sector has also been dynamic and unpredictable. When the European Economic Community was founded in 1957, television had only recently become a mainstay of domestic entertainment and national culture. After a period of consolidation and dominance for national broadcasting systems, commercial satellite television arrived, breaking into the comparative isolation of national markets. That transformation was hardly under-way when the internet arrived, which promised and eventually delivered a complete media revolution.

Throughout these changes, European Union law has also been constantly evolving. The core textual provisions of the original Treaty of Rome (now transformed into the Treaty on the Functioning of the European Union, the 'TFEU'), guaranteeing free movement and fair competition, have remained largely unchanged. Yet their meaning has undergone a radical evolution through judicial interpretation as well as far reaching primary and secondary EU legislation.[1] Some of the most important of these developments occurred through the work of the European Court of Justice in establishing the supremacy of EU law and creating the principles needed to penetrate deep into domestic law and public administration. In that process, European economic law has evolved beyond the basic question of whether a national measure is discriminatory to the more intrusive question of whether it creates a barrier to market integration.[2] The development of competition law disciplines has also increased market competition, limiting favouritism and reliance on national champions.

In the media sector, this strengthening of EU law has progressively tipped the balance towards a more expansive liberty to publish and distribute media content across Europe. While Europe's linguistic and cultural barriers to media market integration remain formidable, the EU has forced open domestic media sectors that were effectively closed for centuries to foreign based competition. That however has also significantly raised the stakes for the future of the European media state relationship. In the face of this challenge to national control over content standards, member states have forcefully demanded protection of regulatory regimes and subsidies from the obligations of free movement and fairer competition. This confrontation over media policy is therefore closely bound to other developments in EU law, in particular the rising importance of non-market public policy.

The liberty to publish and free movement

European law has undoubtedly undergone a transformation from an almost exclusive focus on economic goals to the pursuit of a wider set of public policy concerns. Yet despite the encroachment of non-market public policy, European Union law remains centred on its market based principles of free movement and fair competition. It consequently retains a heavy bias towards the liberty to publish, generally treating the protection of the state and the public from the harmful effects of media content as secondary concerns, albeit important ones. For new media competitors pioneering the use of satellite television in the 1980s, the EU's rules of market integration were therefore essential to the commercial success of their cross border ventures. Many of these were designed to escape the reach of media regulation in their target markets by using more congenial regulatory regimes located elsewhere

[1] Barnard, C., *The Substantive Law of the EU: The Four Freedoms* (Oxford University Press, 2010), 8–24.
[2] Ibid., 165–170.

in the European Union as a base of operations.[3] Those cross border television services could not have been achieved without the rules of free movement, which were subsequently essential to the phenomenal growth of electronic commerce in information and entertainment content across Europe.

This process of liberalization was not inevitable. It required continuous pressure from commercial media companies, acting individually and through their associations, sometimes backed by sympathetic member state governments. For several decades, they have sought to enforce and expand the EU's market based rules and thereby dismantle protective national measures.[4] Along the way, they have pressured the Commission to limit member state intervention in media markets and have turned regularly to the European Court of Justice for assistance.[5]

Given the immense importance of the EU's rules of free movement to the development of European media law, it is ironic that media disputes and concerns have seldom featured in the developing law of free movement of goods. In the first decades of the European Economic Community, liberalizing trade in goods between member states was the organization's dominant purpose. In comparison, trade in services was then a much less important element in European national economies and thus ranked far behind trade in goods in the processes of market integration. Free movement of goods thus provided the basis for much of the European Court of Justice's work on the meaning and scope of EU treaty obligations.[6] These notably included the Court's *Dassonville* and *Cassis de Dijon* decisions, in which it radically extended the scope of the free movement principle, potentially capturing domestic measures only remotely capable of hindering cross border trade.[7]

---

[3] Syvertson, T., and Skogerbo, E., 'Scandinavia, Netherlands and Belgium', in Smith, A. (ed.), *Television: An International History*, 2nd edn (Oxford University Press, 1998), 223.

[4] Prominent European media business associations include the European Newspaper Publishers' Association, the European Publishers Council, the Association of Commercial Television in Europe, and the Association Européenne des Radios.

[5] See, for example, the Joint Letter to European Commissioner Kroes regarding the European Commission Review of the Broadcasting Communication from the Association of Commercial Television in Europe (ACT), the European Publishers Council (EPC), the German Association of Commercial Radio and Telecommunications Providers (VPRT), the European Newspaper Publishers' Association (ENPA), and the European Radio Association (AER), (10 February 2009) <http://www.epceurope.org>. Commercial resort to the European Court of Justice has been a driving force in the development of European media law. See, for example, one of the earliest broadcasting cases, Case C-352/85, *Bond van Adverteerders v. Netherlands* [1988] ECR 2085.

[6] The Treaty on the Functioning of the European Union, Articles 28, 34, and 35, which establish the customs union covering all trade in goods and the prohibition of quantitative restrictions (quotas) on trade in goods.

[7] In *Dassonville* the Court interpreted the provisions on quantitative restrictions on the free movement of goods (now TFEU, Articles 34–35) to mean that 'measures having equivalent effect to a quantitative restriction to imports' include 'all trading rules enacted by Member States which are capable of hindering, directly or indirectly, actually or potentially, intra-Community trade': Case C-8/74, *Procureur du Roi v. Benoît and Gustave Dassonville* [1974] ECR 837. In *Cassis de Dijon*, the Court declared that this included indistinctly applicable measures, (i.e. those that apply to domestically and imported goods: Case C-120/78, *Rewe-Zentral v. Bundesmonopolverwaltung für Branntwein* [1979] ECR 649. However, the Court later limited this scope when it excluded indistinctly applicable measures that concern the marketing of goods rather than matters relating to their composition or presentation: Cases C-267 and 268/91, *Criminal Proceedings against Keck and Mithouard* [1993] ECR I-6097.

These decisions on the liberalization of European trade in goods plainly apply to all media content that is traded in the form of goods. This includes all printed media, films, CDs, DVDs, and other media products where information or entertainment content is bound to a carrier medium and traded in that form.[8] Historically, however, language barriers and transport difficulties have generally limited European cross border trade in bulk for newspapers, magazines, and books.[9] The development of cinema films brought a new form of media good into European and international trade, yet most film titles only required the purchase or lease of a few copies, given that they could be screened multiple times. More recently, CDs and DVDs have become an important part of European and international trade in media goods, although even this relatively vibrant sector has already been eclipsed by online consumption of entertainment content, both legal and illegal.[10]

Over the past century, the use of new communications technologies has progressively shifted the media away from its formative connection with printed paper and later plastic into electronic forms of delivery. This shift has been especially significant for cross border delivery. It not only surmounts many of the traditional costs of distribution over distance, but also vaults customs barriers, making it more difficult for the receiving state to impose content controls.

As far as EU law is concerned, 'a television signal must, by reason of its nature, be regarded as provision of services'.[11] This conclusion made trade in services the primary conceptual framework for European media law, not only for broadcasting and other electronic distribution systems, but also for advertising and other economic services carried by broadcasters and other operators.[12] This transition towards trade in services also came in two phases. Initially, the basic questions about the free movement of media services were worked out in the sensitive broadcast sector, which was, and in many places still is, subject to intense state regulation. The focus for trade in media services has now moved to the new media, which have grown rapidly under a less intensive regulatory approach. The current era is consequently full of anomalies as consumers can easily purchase the same foreign sourced digital content on an imported CD or DVD or through downloading from the internet. In EU law, the former involves trade in goods, whereas the latter involves trade in services, and different European and domestic rules and standards may therefore apply.

---

[8] Case C-155/73, *Sacchi v. Italy* [1974] ECR 409, para. 7.

[9] Where two or more countries share a common language and transport distances are commercially viable, cross border regional markets in print media may be signficant. In *Vereinigte Familiapress*, the Court dealt with barriers to the import of German langauge periodicals in to the Austrain market: Case C-368/95, *Vereinigte Familiapress v. Heinrich Bauer Verlag* [1997] ECR I-3689.

[10] See Case C-244/06, *Dynamic Medien Vertriebs GmbH v. Avides Media AG* (2008) 2 CMLR 23, where the Court applied the rules of free movement of goods to restrictions on the import of video games into Germany.

[11] Case C-155/73, *Sacchi v. Italy* [1974] ECR 409, para. 6.

[12] Case C-352/85, *Bond van Adverteerders v. The Netherlands State* [1988] ECR 2085.

Free movement of services and the Television Without Frontiers Directive

The free movement principle underlies all trade in media services, offering a powerful lever to break down national restrictions on the cross border flow of information and entertainment content in Europe.[13] This potential was first realized in the 1980s. Until that time, most European trade in media content was largely carried on between media companies based in their own national territories with little cross border integration of content production and distribution.[14] Television in western Europe however had begun to change rapidly as the last public broadcasting monopolies came to an end and new opportunities for satellite based delivery appeared. For a few commercial broadcasters, this was an extraordinary chance to break into lucrative but hitherto closed national advertising and subscription markets.[15]

In a series of judgments, primarily arising out of the Netherlands and Belgium, the European Court of Justice confirmed that EU law does not, in principle, permit restrictions on cross border television services.[16] This did not however unleash a dramatic process of negative harmonization in the broadcast media markets of the member states. While the Court asserted the fundamental importance of free movement of broadcast services, it was unwilling to challenge the basic validity of national controls over broadcasters as well as programme content, conceding that member states may restrict the inward flow of television services for legitimate public policy reasons. Yet, as discussed below, the Court also insisted that these national regulatory regimes should be neither deliberately protectionist nor disproportionate in their effects on trade.[17]

In this first phase in the liberalization of broadcast services, the ECJ had thus made good progress in elucidating the basic principles of European media law, but its even handed approach left a host of questions unanswered. Commercial broadcasters were disappointed by the wide scope for restrictions on access that seemed to overwhelm the principle of free movement. Public broadcasters and their governments, on the other hand, were left uncertain about the legitimate scope and durability of their broadcasting regulatory regimes and activities.

---

[13] TFEU, Article 56.
[14] Graham, A., 'Technology, Talent and Production', in Carter, P. (ed.), *Television and Beyond: The Next Ten Years* (Independent Television Commission, 2002), 70.
[15] Levy, D., *Europe's Digital Revolution* (Routledge, 1999), 161–164.
[16] See, for example, Case C-52/79, *Procureur du Roi v. Marc JVC Debauve* [1980] ECR 833; Case C-352/85, *Bond van Adverteerders v. The Netherlands State* [1988] ECR 2085; Case C-288/89, *Stichting Collectieve Antennevoorziening Gouda v. Commissariaat voor de Media* [1991] ECR I-4007; Case C-353/89, *Commission v. Netherlands* [1991] ECR I-4069; Case C-260/89, *Elliniki Radiophonia Tiléorassi AE and Panellinia Omospondia Syllogon Prossopikou v. Dimotiki Etairia Pliroforissis* [1991] ECR I-2925; Case C-211/91, *Commission v. Belgium* [1992] ECR I-6757; Case C-148/91, *Vereiniging Veronica Omroep Organisatie v. Commissariaat voor de Media* [1993] ECR I-487; Case 23/93, *TV10 SA v. Commissariaat voor de Media* [1993] ECR I-4824.
[17] Ibid.

The European Commission and member states soon stepped in to take direct control of the confrontation between commercial satellite broadcasters and protective national media regimes. As part of the Single Market renewal of European market integration, they agreed to adopt secondary legislation in the form of a directive on television broadcasting services.[18] This was a deliberately narrow piece of legislation. Radio broadcasting was excluded and left to the general principles of EU law. As a media platform, radio was of declining importance and most member states had already adapted to substantial cross border, terrestrial radio broadcasting.[19] The proposed directive was also separate from parallel work commencing on the liberalization of telecommunications services.[20] In addition, the television and telecommunications related work of the 1980s came well in advance of EU general legislation on the liberalization of access to services markets. It was not until the end of 2006 that the EU finally adopted the long debated Services Directive, which coincidentally excludes audiovisual services due to their complexity as well as their comprehensive treatment in this earlier legislation.[21]

The negotiation of a legal instrument to govern cross border television services between EU member states was nevertheless a lengthy and acrimonious business. Their divergent national broadcasting regimes and policy objectives could not be reconciled without awkward, interlocking compromises. France and Britain were, in particular, divided over the degree to which market forces or state regulation should be used to achieve social policy objectives.[22] These arguments were made with equal force in the Council of Europe, where the same states were negotiating a parallel treaty on transfrontier television broadcasting.[23]

The new EU Directive, known until 2007 as the 'Television Without Frontiers Directive', quickly became the key reference point on audiovisual content for EU

[18] Collins, R., *Broadcasting and Audiovisual Policy in the European Single Market* (John Libbey, 1994), Nitsche, I., *Broadcasting in the European Union*, (T.M.C. Asser Press, 2001), ch 4, Harrison, J., and Woods, L., *European Broadcasting Law and Policy* (Cambridge University Press, 2007), chs 4 and 5.

[19] On Luxembourg's role as a base for cross border broadcasting, see 'Luxembourg: Changing Anatomy of an International Broadcasting Power', in Dyson, K., and Humphreys, P. (eds), *The Political Economy of Communications: International and European Dimensions* (Routledge, 1990).

[20] See, for example, Commission Directive 88/301/EEC of 16 May 1988 on competition in the markets in telecommunications terminal equipment.

[21] Directive 2006/123/EC of the European Parliament and of the Council of 12 December 2006 on Services in the Internal Market. Article 2(2): 'This Directive shall not apply to the following activities: (g) audiovisual services, including cinematographic services, whatever their mode of production, distribution and transmission, and radio broadcasting', see also Recital (24). For general background, see De Witte, B., 'Setting the Scene: How Did Services Get to Bolkestein and Why? (July 2007) EUI Working Paper No. LAW 2007/20.

[22] Collins, R., 'The European Union Audiovisual Policies of the U.K. and France', in Scriven, M. and Lecomte, M., *Television Broadcasting in Contemporary France and Britain* (Berghahn Books, 1999), 198–221.

[23] *European Convention on Transfrontier Television* 1989 (as amended), ETS 132. See also Mowes, B., *A Media Policy for Tomorrow*, prepared for the 6th European Ministerial Conference on Mass Media Policy, and, Humphreys, P., *Mass Media and Media Policy in Western Europe* (Manchester University Press, 1996).

law and policy.[24] The Directive is founded on the combined principles of free movement of services and the recognition of country of origin regulatory authority. The member states, and by agreement certain non-member European states, are accordingly obliged to permit the reception and retransmission of broadcasts by any television service provider under the jurisdiction of another member state.[25] The Television Without Frontiers Directive was therefore a strong legal stimulus for greater liberty to broadcast audiovisual content across the borders of member states. Yet, as discussed below, this legislation also balanced that element with a range of measures giving most member states enough leeway to retain their broadcasting regulatory regimes largely intact.

The Council of the European Union declared in 2002 that the goals of the Directive included the promotion of 'cultural and linguistic diversity and the strengthening of the European audiovisual industry' and reinforcement of 'the indispensable role of television broadcasting in the democratic, social, and cultural life of society'.[26] This declaration underscores the unique nature of the Television Without Frontiers Directive. While based on the core principles of European market integration, the Directive also incorporated a substantial range of social and cultural policy objectives, some of which required the harmonization of television content standards across the member states.

These notably included the obligation to ensure that broadcasters reserve a majority proportion of their transmission time for a wide genre of programmes for European works.[27] Although a necessary part of the compromise underpinning the Directive, this foray into cultural policy initially appeared to exceed the bounds of EU legislative competence.[28] This nagging question was only resolved when the

---

[24] This Directive, now known as the Audiovisual Media Services Directive, has been consolidated as 'Directive 2010/13/EU of the European Parliament and of the Council of 10 March 2010 on the coordination of certain provisions laid down by law, regulation or administrative action in Member States concerning the provision of audiovisual media services'. It was originally adopted as 'Council Directive 89/552/EEC on the coordination of certain provisions laid down by law, regulation or administrative action in Member States concerning the pursuit of television broadcasting activities' (as amended by Directive 97/36/EC and Directive 2007/65/EC). See also Drijber, B., 'The Revised Television without Frontiers Directive' 36 *Common Market Law Review* (1999), 87–122.

[25] Directive 2010/13/EU, ibid., Article 3(1). See also *Commission v. Belgium* [1996] ECR I-4115 and Case C-14/96, Criminal Proceedings against Paul Denuit [1997] ECR I-2785.

[26] Council Conclusions of 19 December 2002 on the 'Television without Frontiers' Directive, 2003/C 13/01. See also Commission Communication on the Principles and Guidelines for the Community's Audiovisual Policy in the digital age. 14 December 1999, COM (1999) 657 final, and Communication on the Future of European Regulatory Audiovisual Policy, European Commission, 15 December 2003 COM (2003) 784 final.

[27] Directive 2010/13/EU, n. 24 above, Article 16: '1. Member States shall ensure, where practicable and by appropriate means, that broadcasters reserve for European works a majority proportion of their transmission time, excluding the time allotted to news, sports events, games, advertising, teletext services and teleshopping. This proportion, having regard to the broadcaster's informational, educational, cultural and entertainment responsibilities to its viewing public, should be achieved progressively, on the basis of suitable criteria.' See Chapter 15.

[28] De Witte, B., 'The European Content Requirement in the EC Television Directive', 1 *The Yearbook of Media and Entertainment Law* (Oxford University Press, 1995), 101.

member states expressly incorporated a limited range of cultural objectives into the purposes of the EU through the amendment process of the 1992 Maastricht Treaty.[29]

The communications revolution and the new Directives

The Television Without Frontiers Directive was largely created to deal with the impact of direct-to-home satellite broadcasting on European media law. Yet, the Directive had hardly entered into force before a new revolution in communications technologies arrived, overturning many of the assumptions about boundaries and national control on which the Directive was based. At that time, digitization of information and entertainment content and internet delivery of media services were still a long way from the contemporary world of mass broadband access, but the promise of a convergent communications and media sector had already begun to transform commercial strategies and public policy. By the mid 1990s, the European Commission, anxious that Europe not be left behind the United States, began a wholesale reconsideration of EU law and policy in the communications sector.[30]

As part of these efforts, the Commission accepted that the media and telecommunications sectors should shift from vertical regulation, in which each communications platform is regulated according to the content service it carries, to horizontal regulation, in which regulation is broadly divided between infrastructure and content. On the infrastructure side, the Commission launched a review of EU law governing telecommunications and related fields, leading in 2002 to the adoption of a new set of Directives creating a comprehensive regulatory framework for electronic communications.[31] These Directives encourage regulatory neutrality between competing communications platforms, which is intended to ensure that market forces determine which technologies and services become the mainstay of European electronic communications. The Framework Directives are also firmly based on the principles of free movement of services and establishment as well as market competition.

---

[29] See Article 167 TFEU, (ex Article 128/Maastricht Treaty): 'The Union shall take cultural aspects into account in its action under other provisions of the Treaties, in particular in order to respect and to promote the diversity of its cultures.'

[30] See European Commission, *Green Paper on the protection of minors and human dignity in audiovisual and information services*, COM (96) 483 final.

[31] Directive 2002/21/EC of the European Parliament and of the Council of 7 March 2002 on a common regulatory framework for electronic communications networks and services (Framework Directive), Directive 2002/20/EC of the European Parliament and of the Council of 7 March 2002 on the authorisation of electronic communications networks and services (Authorisation Directive), Directive 2002/19/EC of the European Parliament and of the Council of 7 March 2002 on access to, and interconnection of, electronic communications networks and associated facilities (Access Directive), Directive 2002/22/EC of the European Parliament and of the Council of 7 March 2002 on universal service and users' rights relating to electronic communications networks and services (Universal Service Directive), Directive 2002/58/EC of the European Parliament and of the Council of 12 July 2002 concerning the processing of personal data and the protection of privacy in the electronic communications sector (Directive on privacy and electronic communications).

These Directives are aimed at European communications infrastructure issues and therefore do not apply to audiovisual and other media content services.[32] Nonetheless, one of the principal tools of the state in restricting or enabling the production and distribution of media content, as well as controlling public access to such content, is to control the right to own or use communication facilities. The Framework Directives consequently have significant effects on this aspect of media law and regulation. The ECJ has, for example, determined that the main Framework Directive, amongst others, obliges member states to grant spectrum usage rights on objective, transparent, non-discriminatory, and proportionate criteria.[33] The electronic communications regulatory framework thus supports the liberty to publish and distribute content by limiting the ability of member states to impose arbitrary or discriminatory access conditions.

The adoption of the Television Without Frontiers Directive seriously complicated the European Union's subsequent efforts to respond to the digitization of media content production and distribution. As the communications revolution gathered pace, television services, once a unique and extraordinarily powerful element in the European media, gradually began to merge with new forms of mass audiovisual services. Yet the Directive's principal rules setting out the conditions for the free movement of television services and the harmonization of their content standards have stayed in place through two major amendment processes.[34] While the technological distinctiveness of traditional linear television services may have broken down, many major television channels have remained important vehicles for the delivery of national political and social policy objectives through positive content obligations.[35] In addition, long established restrictions on programme and advertising content have also remained important to public expectations of protection from harmful and offensive content.

---

[32] Under Article 2(2) of Directive 2002/21/EC, an 'electronic communications service' means a service normally provided for remuneration which consists wholly or mainly in the conveyance of signals on electronic communications networks, including telecommunications services and transmission services in networks used for broadcasting, but exclude services providing, or exercising editorial control over, content transmitted using electronic communications networks and services; it does not include information society services, as defined in Article 1 of Directive 98/34/EC.

[33] Case C-380/05, *Centro Europa 7 Srl v. Ministero delle Comunicazioni e Autorità per le garanzie nelle comunicazioni*, (ECJ, 31 January 2008): '116 . . . Article 49 EC and, from the date on which they became applicable, Article 9(1) of the Framework Directive (2002/21/EC), Article 5(1), the second subparagraph of Article 5(2) and Article 7(3) of the Authorisation Directive (2002/20/EC), and Article 4 of the Competition Directive (2002/77/EC) must be interpreted as precluding, in television broadcasting matters, national legislation the application of which makes it impossible for an operator holding rights to broadcast in the absence of broadcasting radio frequencies granted on the basis of objective, transparent, non-discriminatory and proportionate criteria.'

[34] See Directive 97/36/EC of the European Parliament and of the Council of 30 June 1997 amending Council Directive 89/552/EEC on the coordination of certain provisions laid down by law, regulation or administrative action in Member States concerning the pursuit of television broadcasting activities, and, Directive 2007/65/EC of the European Parliament and of the Council of 11 December 2007 amending Council Directive 89/552/EEC on the coordination of certain provisions laid down by law, regulation or administrative action in Member States concerning the pursuit of television broadcasting activities.

[35] On the continuing importance of public service television, as well as new media, in European law and public policy, see Part IV: Intervention in Media Markets.

During the internet boom of the 1990s, there was certainly support from some member states and in the European Parliament for comprehensive EU legislation to deal with all forms of audiovisual electronic media. During the 1997 amendment process for the Directive, the Culture Committee of the Parliament urged that it be broadened to capture video-on-demand and other new audiovisual content services.[36] However, the European Parliament as a whole rejected this proposal, persuaded that any move towards direct regulation of internet based content was inappropriate for this emerging, dynamic communications platform. This reflected the anxious concern that Europe would fail to grasp the economic potential of online services if it imposed broadcasting style regulatory controls.[37]

Instead, the European Union created an alternative regulatory framework for these internet based services, introducing a formal distinction in law between television and online audiovisual content. This distinction hinged on the question of whether the consumer is able to request audiovisual content individually, or whether the content provider determines its time and manner of delivery. Services that deliver content at the individual request of the recipient, such as video-on-demand, were classed as 'information society services'.[38] This left traditional linear television channels, including channels with some interactive elements, subject to the rules of the Television Without Frontiers Directive. Information society services, such as non-linear, pay-per-view television services and internet based

[36] Keller, P., 'The New Television Without Frontiers Directive', *The Yearbook of Media and Entertainment Law 1997/1998* (Oxford University Press, 1998), 188.

[37] These tensions can be seen in the deregulatory recommendations of the 'Bangemann Report' on 'Europe and the Information Society' (Europe and the Global Information Society—Recommendations of the High-level Group on the Information Society to the Corfu European Council, 26 May 1994). See also Ministerial Conference at Bonn 'Global Information Networks: Realising the Potential', 6–8 July 1997, Ministerial Declaration: Section entitled 'Responsibility of the actors' (paras 41–43). The sense of uncertainty in European internet policy at that time is also evident in the 1998 Oreja Report: 'The Internet environment, however, functions in a different way, involving infrastructure suppliers, service providers, access providers and content providers (which may be located in different countries for the same service). The question of liability is therefore far more complex. Neither it nor the matter of which state has jurisdiction has yet been resolved.' Digital Age: European Audiovisual Policy, Report from the High Level Group on Audiovisual Policy, (the 'Oreja Report', 1998) Directorate General X, [ch III, 6].

[38] Information society services were defined in Directive 98/34/EC of the European Parliament and of the Council of 22 June 1998 laying down a procedure for the provision of information in the field of technical standards and regulations and of rules on information society services, which states that an information society service is 'any service normally provided for remuneration, at a distance, by electronic means and at the individual request of a recipient of services'. See also Recitals (17) and (18) of Directive 2000/31/EC of the European Parliament and of the Council of 8 June 2000 on certain legal aspects of information society services, in particular electronic commerce, in the Internal Market (Electronic Commerce Directive). The latter states that television and radio broadcasting are not information society services because they are not provided at individual request; by contrast, services which are transmitted point to point, such as video-on-demand or the provision of commercial communications by electronic mail are information society services. See also Case C-89/04, *Mediakabel BV v. Commissariaat voor de Media* ECR I-4891 (2 June 2005), in which the ECJ affirmed that a service comes within the concept of 'television broadcasting' referred to in Article 1(a) of the Television Without Frontiers Directive if it consists of the initial transmission of television programmes intended for reception by the public, that is, an indeterminate number of potential television viewers, to whom the same images are transmitted simultaneously.

audiovisual services, on the other hand, were dealt with under new legislation, most notably the 2000 Electronic Commerce Directive.[39]

This Directive is also based on the twin principles of free movement and regulation by country of origin, affirming the EU's basic support for the liberty to publish and distribute media content in the new electronic services sector.[40] In contrast to the Television Without Frontiers Directive, the Electronic Commerce Directive was very much a product of the early internet era. Reflecting the policy consensus that the internet should not be brought under existing media regulatory regimes, it assumes that the basic principles of free movement can be applied to 'information society services' without the need for harmonization of national content rules. It therefore has a broader but simpler sphere of application than the TWF Directive.[41]

The major exception to this avoidance of content issues in the Electronic Commerce Directive lies in special rules limiting criminal and civil liability for internet intermediaries, that is to say information society services that enable consumers to access third party content. These include services that permit third parties to use their facilities to make content available to the public, such as video hosting services.[42] Hosting services of this kind are protected from liability where the service provider does not exercise prior control over the content that third parties make available and has not received notice that its facilities are being used to make unlawful content available. The Directive does not however attempt to dictate what kind of liability should be imposed in any circumstance. That is left to the determination of the member states, subject to other European obligations, including those of the European Convention on Human Rights. In addition, the Directive does not limit liability where a service provider chooses to make content available to the public in the same way as a broadcaster or newspaper. Indeed, European Union law and policy stresses that content providers should bear legal responsibility for such content.[43] While considerably less extensive than its

---

[39] As early as 1997, the Commission began work on specific legislation to create a common European legal framework for electronic commerce. European Commission Communication 'A European Initiative on Electronic Commerce' (16 April 1997), IP/97/313. See also McGonagle, T., 'Does the Existing Regulatory Framework for Television Apply to the New Media?' *IRIS Plus*, 2001–6.

[40] Directive 2000/31/EC, n. 38 above. Article 3: '1. Each Member State shall ensure that the information society services provided by a service provider established on its territory comply with the national provisions applicable in the Member State in question which fall within the coordinated field. 2. Member States may not, for reasons falling within the coordinated field, restrict the freedom to provide information society services from another Member State.'

[41] The Electronic Commerce Directive consequently covers all content services, unless they are specifically excepted under Article 1(5) from the very broad 'coordinated field' set out in Article 2(h), which covers, 'requirements laid down in Member States' legal systems applicable to information society service providers or information society services, regardless of whether they are of a general nature or specifically designed for them'.

[42] The rules of liability for mere conduits, caching and hosting are set out in Articles 12–14 of the Electronic Commerce Directive.

[43] Despite uncertainties regarding intermediaries, this position was clear in EU internet policy from the outset, which required 'full and complete liability of content providers, with special emphasis on their editorial role'. European Commission, Protection of Minors and Human Dignity in Audiovisual and Information Services, Consultations on the Green Paper, Commission Working Document SEC

American counterpart provisions, it is nonetheless a significant contribution to the liberty to publish in the new media environment, both in limiting liability and in harmonizing liability principles across the member states.[44]

In effect, the Electronic Commerce Directive rules on liability created a halfway house between the two pre-existing models for content regulation: the telecommunications model, in which service providers generally escape liability for the third party content they carry; and the broadcasting model, in which providers carry full responsibility for all the content they broadcast. The first was deemed unsuitable for internet based services as it ignored the ability of internet providers to exert some control over the content they make available. The broadcast model was however equally unsuitable as it assumes complete provider control over content. The Directive rules are therefore an attempt to bridge that gap.

By the early 2000s, broadband or high speed internet access had begun to transform the nature of electronic content services. New non-linear, audiovisual programme services, such as video-on-demand, had developed to the point that they were beginning to compete directly with traditional linear television services in broadband homes. In many countries, media companies were offering the same programmes on parallel broadcast and on-demand services.[45] The broadcast services offered programmes on a daily schedule, while their sister on-demand services offered the same programmes on a menu. Not surprisingly, these developments also made the recently settled distinction in EU law between television and all other electronic audiovisual services appear unsustainable. In the dawn of broadband internet access, it was simply no longer self evident that the content standards for television services should be different from those applied to other audiovisual services now equally accessible in the home.

In 2003, the Commission launched a consultation exercise on the future of EU legislation on audiovisual media services.[46] This initiative culminated four years later in a major revision of the Television Without Frontiers Directive, which among other things gave it a new name: the Audiovisual Media Services Directive

(97) 1203. See also Commission Communication on 'Illegal and Harmful Content on the Internet' COM (96) 487, which declared that '[t]he responsibility of member states to ensure the application of existing laws. What is illegal off-line remains illegal online.'

[44] See s. 230, Communications Decency Act 1996, (47 U.S.C. s. 230), which US courts have interpreted expansively to provide extensive immunity for internet intermediaries. See, for example, *John Doe v. SexSearch.com*, 502 F.Supp. 2d 719. See also Tushnet, R., 'Power Without Responsibility: Intermediaries and the First Amendment', 76 *George Washington Law Review,* (2008), 986–1016, Harper, J., 'Against ISP Liability' 28(1) *Regulation* (2005), 30, and Levmore, S., 'The Internet's Anonymity Problem', in Nussbaum, M. and Levmore, S., (eds), *The Offensive Internet: Speech, Privacy and Reputation* (Harvard University Press, 2011), 50.

[45] In Britain, the major broadcasters developed parallel on-demand services, notably including the BBC iPlayer service.

[46] Commission Proposal for a Directive of the European Parliament and of the Council amending Council Directive 89/552/EEC on the coordination of certain provisions laid down by law, regulation or administrative action in Member States concerning the pursuit of television broadcasting activities, COM (2005) 0646 final. See also European Commission, *Communication on the Future of European Regulatory Audiovisual Policy* COM (2003) 784 final, (15 December 2003). European Commission, *TV without Frontiers: Commission proposes modernised rules for digital era TV and TV-like services,* IP/05/ 1573 (13 December 2005).

(the AVMS Directive).[47] The most important change introduced in the 2007 amendments to the Directive was the transfer of 'on-demand audiovisual services' out of the legal category of information society services, which are principally governed by the Electronic Commerce Directive, into the amended AVMS Directive.[48] The Commission and the member states had agreed that the two services should be brought under the same legislative framework to reduce regulatory disparities between them.

Initially, the Commission had proposed that the Directive's provisions concerning the protection of children should be extended to a much wider variety of internet based, audiovisual content made available by providers based in the European Union.[49] In the face of determined resistance by Britain and other member states, the EU institutions reached a compromise, which limits the extension of these obligations to online video-on-demand services and also gives member states the right to use coregulation to achieve appropriate levels of protection.[50] This compromise was intended to bring the services most closely resembling television under similar controls, while ensuring that member states were not compelled to take action against user generated content services and websites. There was moreover no fundamental reason why on-demand services could not be carved out of one Directive and grafted into the other, given that both Directives are based on principles of free movement and country of origin jurisdiction and thus generally support greater liberty to publish and distribute media content in the European Single Market.

On-demand services, which in many ways are unlike traditional broadcasting services, could not however be rationally forced into the AVMS Directive's broadcasting regulatory model. Consequently, new concepts and definitions needed to be created within the AVMS Directive. The resulting definitional complexity of the AVMS Directive illustrates some of the legislative problems arising out of convergence and the blurring of technological distinctions. Legislative drafters, who could once clearly identify a service using as little as a one word, such as 'television' or 'telecommunications', have struggled to select and articulate the key elements that distinguish one electronic service from another. Even in the 1990s, the Directive could still use simple concepts, such as 'television programmes' and 'reception by the public', to identify television services as the exclusive subject of the legislation.[51]

---

[47] Directive 2010/13/EU, n. 24 above.
[48] Directive 2010/13/EU, ibid., Article 4: '8. Directive 2000/31/EC shall apply unless otherwise provided for in this Directive. In the event of a conflict between a provision of Directive 2000/31/EC and a provision of this Directive, the provisions of this Directive shall prevail, unless otherwise provided for in this Directive.'
[49] European Commission: Proposal for a Directive amending Council Directive 89/552/EEC, COM (2005) 646 Final [December 2005].
[50] Tryhorn, C., 'Minister attacks EU media plans', *The Guardian* (29 June 2006). See also Broadband Stakeholders Group, *Audiovisual Media Services Draft Directive: Opinions and Recommendations of Stakeholders in the UK* (April 2006), <http://www.broadbanduk.org/>.
[51] Council Directive 89/552/EEC on the coordination of certain provisions laid down by law, regulation or administrative action in Member States concerning the pursuit of television broadcasting activities, Article 1: 'For the purpose of this Directive: (a) 'television broadcasting' means the initial transmission by wire or over the air, including that by satellite, in unencoded or encoded form, of

The AVMS Directive now contains the umbrella category of 'audiovisual media service', 'the principal purpose of which is the provision of programmes, in order to inform, entertain or educate, to the general public'.[52] That category is further divided into 'television broadcasting' and 'on-demand audiovisual media service'. In either form of audiovisual media service, the programme content offered must be 'under the editorial responsibility of the service provider', in contrast to an internet video hosting service, such as YouTube. However, a television broadcasting service offers 'simultaneous viewing of programmes on the basis of a programme schedule'.[53] Whereas on-demand audiovisual media services offer 'programmes at the moment chosen by the user and at his individual request on the basis of a catalogue of programmes selected by the media service provider'.[54] These definitional boundaries are plainly open to uncertainty and dispute.

Protecting the interests of state and society in EU law

At its core, the interface between the liberty to publish and European Union law is conceptually simple. It essentially involves the removal of state restrictions on the production and distribution of media content. Additionally, as discussed below, the liberty to publish is enhanced generally by intervention to maintain fair market competition. In contrast, the protection of the state as well as the public collectively and individually from the harmful consequences of that liberty has a much more complicated relationship with EU law. In the original architecture of the Treaty of Rome (now present in the TFEU), these concerns were addressed by including specific exceptions or rights of derogation in relation to the primary principles. These include several broadly stated, non market public policy objectives, such as the protection of public order and public morals.[55] Consequently, the primary obligations of European economic law, unlike human rights law, are all weighted in favour of the liberty to publish. There are, for example, no primary obligations similar to the rights to privacy or to a fair trial in the European Convention on

---

television programmes intended for reception by the public. It includes the communication of programmes between undertakings with a view to their being relayed to the public. It does not include communication services providing items of information or other messages on individual demand such as telecopying, electronic data banks and other similar services...'

[52] Directive 2010/13/EU, n. 24 above, Article 1. See also Recitals (21)–(31) of the Directive 2007/65/EC, which amended the AVMS Directive.

[53] Directive 2010/13/EU, Article 1, ibid.

[54] Ibid.

[55] TFEU, Article 36: 'The provisions of Articles 34 and 35 shall not preclude prohibitions or restrictions on imports, exports or goods in transit justified on grounds of public morality, public policy or public security; the protection of health and life of humans, animals or plants; the protection of national treasures possessing artistic, historic or archaeological value; or the protection of industrial and commercial property. Such prohibitions or restrictions shall not, however, constitute a means of arbitrary discrimination or a disguised restriction on trade between Member States.' Article 52(1) 'The provisions of this Chapter and measures taken in pursuance thereof shall not prejudice the applicability of provisions laid down by law, regulation or administrative action providing for special treatment for foreign nationals on grounds of public policy, public security or public health.'

Human Rights that squarely favour the interests of individuals in limiting the liberty to publish.[56]

As drafted, the Treaty of Rome did nonetheless present the appearance of balance between primary obligations and broad exceptions. That appearance was however short lived. The European Court of Justice soon established the principles of supremacy and direct effect, overwhelming a traditional public international law understanding of the limits of the Treaty.[57] In these bold moves, the Court cut away the legal basis on which member states could resist the principles of free movement and fair competition. The Court's success in strengthening these primary obligations however came at a price. It was forced to recognize that more effective market integration could not occur without also accepting that free movement may be lawfully obstructed for a wider range of public policy purposes than those expressly stated in the Treaty.[58] This was certainly the case in the sensitive media sector. Here, many member state governments resisted the principle of free movement where it threatened essential public policy goals, including pluralism and cultural diversity, despite the lack of an obvious anchor in the text of the Treaty.

The Court accordingly determined that the principle of free movement includes a secondary form of exception. Member states may obstruct free movement when using universally applicable (non-discriminatory) measures that pursue overriding requirements of general public importance, provided those measures meet the requirements of proportionality.[59] This concept of overriding or mandatory public policy exceptions is nevertheless not well adapted for distinguishing legitimate, incidental protectionist measures from illegitimate or excessive ones. Indeed, governments may even prefer a particular non-discriminatory measure precisely because it is not only well suited to the protection of an important public policy goal, but it also conveniently impedes foreign competitors. In the media state relationship, the state may also have a strong interest in protecting national media providers because they are vehicles for the delivery of many public policy objectives. This mixture of legitimate, even laudable, policy goals and determined protectionism has severely complicated the pursuit of European market integration in the media sector.

It has therefore long been evident that the right of member states to limit the impact of European market integration must become more sophisticated and better defined. That process is undoubtedly constrained by the need to respect the legitimate autonomy of the member states.[60] Yet EU law is nonetheless strengthening its grasp on questions of non-market public policy through the ongoing effort

---

[56] Articles 6, 8, and 10, European Convention on Human Rights. More generally, see Chapter 6.
[57] Case C-26/62, *N.V. Algemene Transport- en Expeditie Onderneming van Gend & Loos v. Nederlandse administratie der belastingen* [1963] ECR 1. See also Barnard, C., n. 1 above, 46.
[58] Case C-120/78, *Rewe-Zentral AG v. Bundesmonopolverwaltung für Branntwein ('Cassis de Dijon')* [1979] ECR 649; Case C-288/89 *Stichting Collectieve Antennevoorziening Gouda v. Commissariaat voor de Media* [1991] ECR I-4007.
[59] See Barnard, C., n. 1 above, 165 and 171.
[60] Article 5(3) of the Treaty on European Union (TEU).

to integrate fundamental human rights into European economic law. The recognition of these fundamental rights in EU law has come from two sources: the constitutional principles common to the member states and the human rights treaties to which they are parties.[61] The latter are centred on the European Convention of Human Rights and the growing body of case law decided by the European Court of Human Rights in Strasbourg.

The introduction of fundamental rights has brought about a broad transformation in EU law. In successive revisions to the principal treaties, the member states have drawn on human rights principles to ground the EU's expanding legislative competence in non-market public policy areas. Article 19 of the TFEU, originally introduced in 1998 by the Treaty of Amsterdam, has for example been fused with fundamental rights to become an important basis for EU legislation outside the traditional economic fields.[62] In addition, the EU Charter of Fundamental Rights, which was only declaratory when first introduced, is now legally binding for most member states as a consequence of the Lisbon Treaty.[63] By establishing a defined body of express rights in place of an implied body of rights dependant on ad hoc identification by the Court, the Charter has brought greater clarity into the somewhat hazy field of EU fundamental rights.[64] At the same time, it has bolstered the authority of the European Union to move deeper into the human rights dimensions of EU law and policy.[65] That however complicates not only the

[61] TEU, Article 6(3). Fundamental rights, as guaranteed by the European Convention for the Protection of Human Rights and Fundamental Freedoms and as they result from the constitutional traditions common to the Member States, shall constitute general principles of the Union's law. Case C-11/70, *Internationale Handelsgesellschaft v. Einfuhr-und Vorratstelle für Getreide und Futtermittel* [1970] ECR 1125: 'Respect for fundamental rights forms an integral part of the general principles of law protected by the Court of Justice. The protection of such rights, whilst inspired by the constitutional traditions common to the Member States, must be ensured within the framework of the structure and objectives of the Community'; see also Case C-4/73, *Nold v. Commission* [1974] ECR 49: '[I]nternational treaties for the protection of human rights on which the Member States have collaborated or of which they are signatories, can supply guidelines which should be followed within the framework of Community law.' Weiler, J. and Lockhart, N., 'Taking Rights Seriously: The European Court and its Fundamental Rights Jurisprudence', Part I, 32 *Common Market Law Review* (1995), 84, and Part II, 32 *Common Market Law Review* (1995), 579.
[62] TFEU, Article 19(1): 'Without prejudice to the other provisions of the Treaties and within the limits of the powers conferred by them upon the Union, the Council, acting unanimously in accordance with a special legislative procedure and after obtaining the consent of the European Parliament, may take appropriate action to combat discrimination based on sex, racial or ethnic origin, religion or belief, disability, age or sexual orientation.'
[63] Charter of Fundamental Rights of the European Union (2000/C 364/01). TEU, Article 6 (1): 'The Union recognises the rights, freedoms and principles set out in the Charter of Fundamental Rights of the European Union of 7 December 2000, as adapted at Strasbourg, on 12 December 2007, which shall have the same legal value as the Treaties.' See also Protocol on the Application of the Charter of Fundamental Rights of the European Union to Poland and to the United Kingdom.
[64] On the weaknesses of human rights protection within the EU, see De Búrca, G., 'The Road Not Taken: The EU as a Global Human Rights Actor', 105 *American Journal of International Law* (forthcoming 2011).
[65] This will occur largely through the processes of proportionality analysis. See Charter of Fundamental Rights, Article 52(1): 'Any limitation on the exercise of the rights and freedoms recognised by this Charter must be provided for by law and respect the essence of those rights and freedoms. Subject

interface between EU law and the member states, but also its interface with the European Convention on Human Rights and the other treaty and policy instruments of the Council of Europe.[66]

In its relations with the member states, the European Union has now long shed its reluctance to become involved in the political, social, or cultural implications of market integration.[67] It has instead joined the Council of Europe in setting and interpreting human rights standards for an expanding European regional sphere. The enlargement of the EU eastwards over the past decade also strengthened the argument for using the EU's formidable powers and authority to assist the transition to liberal democracy in new and applicant member states.[68] But this expanding role for the EU in non-economic policy fields has also heightened concerns about the erosion of member state autonomy in key public policy areas and securing the proper limits of EU intrusion into these sensitive domestic affairs.[69]

The Lisbon Treaty attempted to address these concerns by prominently reasserting the principle of member state autonomy in the Treaty on European Union (TEU).[70] The TEU also makes plain that the Charter, while legally binding, is not an autonomous instrument, but remains firmly grounded in the constitutional traditions common to the member states.[71] This creates a powerful argument

---

to the principle of proportionality, limitations may be made only if they are necessary and genuinely meet objectives of general interest recognised by the Union or the need to protect the rights and freedoms of others.'

[66] See Chapter 6.

[67] See, for example, TEU, Article 2: 'The Union is founded on the values of respect for human dignity, freedom, democracy, equality, the rule of law and respect for human rights, including the rights of persons belonging to minorities. These values are common to the Member States in a society in which pluralism, non-discrimination, tolerance, justice, solidarity and equality between women and men prevail.'

[68] Following the Cold War, the European Union expanded to include Austria, Cyprus, Malta, Sweden, Finland, Hungary, Poland, Romania, Slovakia, Latvia, Estonia, Lithuania, Bulgaria, Czech Republic, and Slovenia. The current applicant states are Turkey, Croatia, Macedonia (FYROM), Montenegro, Albania, Iceland and Serbia. See Sadurski W., 'The Role of the EU Charter of Rights in the Process of Enlargement', in Bermann, G.A, and Pistor, K. (eds), *Law and Governance in an Enlarged European Union,* (Hart Publishing, 2004), 61.

[69] This is an especially complex issue for new member states that are endeavouring to balance national autonomy with external supervision they accepted as the price of EU membership. See Sadurski, W., 'Solange, Chapter 3: Constitutional Courts in Central Europe', 14(1) *European Law Journal* (2008), 1–35.

[70] TEU, Article 4(2): 'The Union shall respect the equality of Member States before the Treaties as well as their national identities, inherent in their fundamental structures, political and constitutional, inclusive of regional and local self-government. It shall respect their essential State functions, including ensuring the territorial integrity of the State, maintaining law and order and safeguarding national security. In particular, national security remains the sole responsibility of each Member State.' This provision is in addition to TEU Article 5(1), which states that '[t]he use of Union competences is governed by the principles of subsidiarity and proportionality'. See also Protocol on the Application of the Principles of Subsidiarity and Proportionality (Treaty of Lisbon), Craig, P., 'Competence and Member State Autonomy: Causality, Consequence and Legitimacy', in Micklitz, H.W. and De Witte, B. (eds), *The European Court of Justice and the Autonomy of the Member States*, (Hart Publishing, forthcoming, 2011).

[71] TEU, Article 6(3): 'Fundamental rights, as guaranteed by the European Convention for the Protection of Human Rights and Fundamental Freedoms and as they result from the constitutional traditions common to the Member States, shall constitute general principles of the Union's law.'

that the ECJ should be slow to disregard national constitutional norms that conflict with the uniform and effective enforcement of EU law.[72] Conversely, it also underscores the continuing authority of EU institutions to determine which principles of national law are sufficiently shared to be recognized as fundamental rights.

The rising importance of fundamental freedoms in EU law has focused attention on the relationship between the treaties and other legal instruments of the European Union and the Council of Europe. It is of course a well established principle of EU law that fundamental rights should be interpreted and applied consistently with the European Convention on Human Rights, including its case law.[73] The Lisbon Treaty has moreover paved the way for the European Union to become a party to the Convention, which will further cement the supremacy of the Convention over the interpretation of EU fundamental rights.[74] The European Union and the Council of Europe have also increased their institutional cooperation to ensure better coordination of their diverse human rights related activities and measures.[75] These moves

---

[72] Kumm, M., 'The Jurisprudence of Constitutional Conflict: Constitutional Supremacy in Europe Before and After the Constitutional Treaty', 10 *European Law Journal* (2005), 262. On the argument that EU institutions must respect national constitutional traditions as well as their legislative and policy choices, see Gerards, J., 'Pluralism, Deference and the Margin of Appreciation Doctrine', 17(1) *European Law Journal* (2010), 80–120.

[73] Charter of Fundamental Rights, Article 52(3), In so far as this Charter contains rights which correspond to rights guaranteed by the Convention for the Protection of Human Rights and Fundamental Freedoms, the meaning and scope of those rights shall be the same as those laid down by the said Convention. This provision shall not prevent Union law providing more extensive protection. Memorandum of Understanding between the Council of Europe and the European Union (2007), 16. The Council of Europe and the European Union will base their co-operation on the principles of indivisibility and universality of human rights, respect for the standards set out in this field by the fundamental texts of the United Nations and the Council of Europe, in particular the Convention for the Protection of Human Rights and Fundamental Freedoms, and the preservation of the cohesion of the human rights protection system in Europe.

[74] TEU, Article 6. European Union accession to the Convention became possible after Protocol 14 of the European Convention on Human Rights came into force on 1 June 2010. Official talks on the European Union's accession to the European Convention on Human Rights (ECHR) began on 7 July 2010. In addition, robust European Court of Human Rights supervision of national measures taken to fulfil EU law will also depend on its reconsideration of its *Bosphorus* judgment, in which it refused to review measures taken by an EU member state action based on a binding EC legislative measure where the European Court of Justice undertook the general protection of human rights. See Costello, C., 'The Bosphorus Ruling of the European Court of Human Rights: Fundamental Rights and Blurred Boundaries in Europe', 6(1) *Human Rights Law Review* (2006), 87–130, and Lock, T., 'Beyond Bosphorus: The European Court of Human Rights' Case Law on the Responsibility of Member States of International Organisations under the European Convention on Human Rights', 10(3) *Human Rights Law Review* (2010), 529–545.

[75] The 1987 Arrangement between the Council of Europe and the European Community, the 2001 Joint Declaration on Cooperation and Partnership between the Council of Europe and the European Commission, the 2007 Memorandum of Understanding between the Council of Europe and the European Union and the 2008 Agreement between the European Community and the Council of Europe on Cooperation between the European Union Agency for Fundamental Rights and the Council of Europe. The European Union Fundamental Rights Agency was established by Council Regulation No. 168/2007 of 15 February, 2007 and it has been working since 1 March 2007. The Fundamental Rights Agency replaces and builds on the work of the European Monitoring Centre on Racism and Xenophobia. Joris, T. and Vandenberghe, J., 'The Council of Europe and the European Union: Natural Partners or Uneasy Bedfellows?', 15 *Columbia Journal of European Law*, (2008–2009), 1. De Schutter, O., The Two Europes of Human Rights: The Emerging Division of

towards closer integration of European economic and human rights law ironically come at a time when the EU Court of Justice has emphasized the autonomy of EU law in relation to public international law, emphasizing the primacy of European fundamental norms.[76]

In principle, the fault line in European public order between economic and human rights law has been remedied by placing the European Convention on Human Rights and its Court at the apex of both legal systems. There are nevertheless significant differences between the Charter and the Convention. Notably, the Charter is wider in scope than the ECHR, which opens avenues for innovation in EU law where the European Court of Human Rights cannot lead.[77] Yet even when the rights in both instruments are closely aligned, such as the right to freedom of expression, consistency is not assured. Where the European Court of Human Rights has yet to clarify a particular application of a right, the ECJ may well impose its own conception of that right, either on the basis of a common practice among the member states or perhaps on the authority of the Charter alone.

Market integration is moreover not a primary concern for the Council of Europe. Its purposes are to protect human rights, democracy, and the rule of law and, while those presuppose a market based economy, the Council's focus is necessarily on those non-market policy objectives.[78] The members of the CE also include several important non-EU states, including Russia and Turkey, whose governments are less likely to be concerned that decisions taken in the Council are closely coordinated with those of the EU. In some instances, these differences in priorities and membership may well lead to gaps opening between the fundamental rights of the EU and the human rights of the CE.

The liberal concept of human rights is enormously useful in illuminating what is at stake in the relationship between the media and the liberal democratic state. Certainly, given the great breadth of liberal thought, human rights offers few definitive conclusions, but it does provide an essential common language for evaluating the benefits and harms of the liberty to publish. When liberal human rights are injected into economic law, they can therefore place the economic arguments in a rich moral and political context. The transformation of the Charter into a legally binding instrument for most member states has therefore provided a firmer basis that enables EU law to draw on that rich understanding of the media state relationship.

On one level, the right to freedom of expression powerfully reinforces the economic argument for greater liberty to publish and distribute media content. Liberal human rights assume that personal freedom fundamentally includes a large measure of economic freedom, including the freedom to engage in commerce and

---

Tasks between the Council Of Europe and the European Union in Promoting Human Rights in Europe', 14 *Columbia Journal of European Law* (2008), 509.

[76] See De Búrca, G., 'The EU, the European Court of Justice and the International Legal Order after Kadi', 1(51) *Harvard International Law Journal* (2009), 1.

[77] The Charter, for example, expressly enshrines the principle of human dignity in Article 1, while this principle only receives an oblique mention in the preamble to Protocol 13 of the Convention.

[78] On the Council of Europe, see Chapter 6.

to exercise rights of property.[79] This association is explicit in the Charter, which protects the freedom to conduct business and the right to own and dispose of property.[80] The Convention is somewhat less fulsome on the question of commerce and property. Protocol 1 of the ECHR nonetheless sets out the right to peaceful enjoyment of possessions and the right to engage in commerce is arguably implicit in the Convention's approach to questions of liberty in Europe.[81]

The presence of these rights in the Charter and the Convention help to tie the economic arguments for market efficiency and consumer choice together with the political and moral arguments for personal freedom. On that basis, the liberty to publish free from restraint or interference by the state can be articulated as an economic, moral, and political necessity. This is the compelling double argument, based in both economic and human rights law, that features so often in liberal democratic disputes over the proper relationship of the media and the state. There is however an obvious mismatch between the two. The European Court of Human Rights has largely crafted the ECHR right to freedom of expression around democratic arguments for greater liberty to speak and publish. Doubling up European economic and human rights arguments to support the liberty of the media will therefore only gain full weight when the democratic argument is fully engaged. The liberty to publish pornography, for example, may be justified on economic grounds but is rarely contributes to the processes of democratic debate and participation.

On a different plane, European human rights law sustains a bundle of assorted arguments for restricting the liberty to publish and intervening in media markets. The Charter and the Convention both include significant rights to privacy and fair judicial proceedings that can be balanced directly against the right to freedom of expression. They also expressly state that the right to freedom of expression includes a right of access to information, which is often deployed in support of state intervention to achieve greater pluralism in the media.[82]

Aside from these competing rights, the Charter and Convention also contain equivalent exceptions to the right to freedom of expression.[83] These recognize the

[79] On Europe's fundamental commitment to market economics, see Szyszczak, E., *The Regulation of the State in Competitive Markets in the European Union* (Hart Publishing, 2007), 3–7.

[80] European Charter of Fundamental Rights, Article 16, 'The freedom to conduct a business in accordance with Community law and national laws and practices is recognised', and Article 171. 'Everyone has the right to own, use, dispose of and bequeath his or her lawfully acquired possessions. No one may be deprived of his or her possessions, except in the public interest and in the cases and under the conditions provided for by law, subject to fair compensation being paid in good time for their loss. The use of property may be regulated by law in so far as is necessary for the general interest', and 2: 'Intellectual property shall be protected.'

[81] European Convention on Human Rights, Protocol 1, Article 1(1): 'Every natural or legal person is entitled to the peaceful enjoyment of his possessions. No one shall be deprived of his possessions except in the public interest and subject to the conditions provided for by law and by the general principles of international law.' Note that the European Court of Human Rights has emphasized the importance of private sector participation in the media. See, for example, *Informationsverein Lentia and others v. Austria* (Application No. 13914/88 et al.) (24 November 1993).

[82] See Chapter 14.

[83] Compare Article 10(2) of the Convention and Article 52 of the Charter.

conditional legitimacy of state measures that restrict individual or collective free-dom where they conflict with the fundamental interests of the state or society. As discussed in Chapter 2, these interests may formally rank below the right to freedom of expression in priority, but they are also essential to the realization of those rights. The security of the territorial state, and by extension its capacity to maintain public order, is inseparable from the secure enjoyment of freedom of expression in a stable liberal democratic society. Restraints on extreme expression may also be justified by the need to maintain peaceful relations between individuals and groups in societies divided by incommensurable differences in values.

General exceptions to free movement

In European economic law, the interests of the state, communities, and individuals in restricting the liberty to publish must be established through the recognized exceptions to the principles of free movement and fair competition. These include the express exceptions set out in the TFEU as well as other EU legislative instru-ments and the implied exceptions developed by the European Court of Justice. Under Articles 36 and 52 of the TFEU, member states may exceptionally impose discriminatory restrictions on the free movement of goods or services for specified public purposes.[84]

For the media sector, the most important of the justifications for impeding the free movement of goods are the protection of public morality, public policy, and public security. The Court has however refused to give these categories an expan-sive definition and has also imposed rigorous conditions on their application.[85] These exceptions merit this restrictive approach and intense scrutiny because they involve overtly discriminatory domestic measures that directly oppose the funda-mental principles of European market integration. In the *Bond van Adverteerders* case, for example, the ECJ rejected the Dutch government's argument that its restrictions on the transmission of foreign sourced advertising could be justified on grounds of public policy under Article 52.[86] The Court found that even if public policy encompasses consumer protection, the measures used were disproportionate as the Dutch authorities could not show that they were necessary for the protection of the public interest concerned.

While the Court kept the Article 36 and 52 exceptions within strict boundaries, it has also recognized the special importance of these grounds when legitimately used. While secondary to the EU principles of free movement, the public policy grounds recognized in these articles are important expressions of national autonomy. They are also closely connected to the fundamental rights of the European Union. For the same reasons, the ECJ has shown considerable pragmatism in finding additional ways to ensure that the deepening of market integration remains sensitive

---

[84] Articles 36 and 52(1), n. 55 above.
[85] Kessedjian, C., 'Public Order in European Law', 1(1) *Erasmus Law Review* (2007), 25.
[86] See Case C-352/85, n. 16 above.

to political and social realities in the member states. Most importantly, as noted above, the Court developed the concept of overriding or mandatory public policy requirements to give European Union law needed additional flexibility. EU law therefore permits significant obstruction of free movement where universally applicable measures are necessary to achieve legitimate public policy goals.

In the view of the ECJ, each member state is entitled to determine the level of protection needed for a legitimate public policy objective, but the manner in which that level of protection is pursued must be proportionate.[87] In most cases, the Court has focused its proportionality inquiry on the question of whether the measures used are more restrictive of free movement than necessary to achieve the declared objectives.[88] It has rarely raised the additional proportionality *stricto sensu* question of whether the measures, even if no more restrictive than necessary, nonetheless impose a disproportionate burden on free movement. This would involve the Court in a critical balancing of the EU's main economic objectives with domestic public policy concerns often rooted in fundamental rights. This is certainly the case where member states have imposed restrictive measures on the publication or distribution of media content, arguing that these are necessary for the protection of core social and political values. So far, the ECJ has shied away from taking a direct role in these sensitive public policy decisions.

For the same reason, the Court has declared that there is no closed list of overriding or mandatory public policy objectives that potentially justify restrictions on free movement. Nor is there any requirement that a common fundamental value should be defined or applied in a similar way across the member states.[89] In addition, the ECJ has not kept a strict separation between the Articles 36 and 52 grounds for exceptional treatment and those identified under the doctrine of mandatory public policy interests. In the *Dynamic Medien Vertriebs* case, for example, it found that the objective in question, the protection of young people, was linked to the Article 36 public morality and public policy grounds.[90] The Court then went on to cite other sources that demonstrate that the protection of young people is a major public policy objective warranting recognition in EU law. These included international and European legal obligations of member states to protect children, including the UN Convention on the Rights of the Child and the Charter of Fundamental Rights of the European Union.[91]

The Court has however also pointed out that even where a domestic regulatory measure can be justified under the exceptions permitted by European economic

---

[87] See Barnard, C., n. 1 above, 171.

[88] '[A]s the Court has consistently held, the application of national provisions to providers of services established in other Member States must be such as to guarantee the achievement of the intended aim and must not go beyond that which is necessary in order to achieve that objective. In other words, it must not be possible to obtain the same result by less restrictive rules', Case C-288/89, *Stichting Collectieve Antennevoorziening Gouda v. Commissariaat voor de Media* [1991] ECR I-4007.

[89] Case C-36/02, *Omega Spielhallen- und Automatenaufstellungs GmbH v. Oberbürgermeisterin der Bundesstadt Bonn* (14 October 2004).

[90] Case C-244/06, *Dynamic Medien Vertriebs GmbH v. Avides Media AG*, para. 42.

[91] Ibid., at paras 39–40.

law, it may nonetheless infringe European human rights obligations.[92] Here the Court is in effect alluding to a potential problem within the double economic and human rights argument for an expansive liberty to publish. In principle, it is possible that a restrictive measure, which satisfies the conditional exceptions permitted under the rules of free movement, will nevertheless fall foul of the requirements of the right to freedom of expression.[93] On the other hand, the ECJ has acknowledged that the Convention and Charter protected right to freedom of expression has its own permitted grounds for exceptions.[94] These are also broadly similar to those permitted under the EU's rules of free movement. Before the Charter became legally enforceable as a consequence of the Lisbon Treaty, the Court had no basis on which to test for potential conflicts between economic and human rights principles. It could only leave that matter to the determination of the member states.[95] In the future, the Court may well take on both sides of the double argument in media cases, comparing the allied but different demands of free movement with those of free expression and weighing both against their permitted exceptions. On the other hand, the Court may adopt the view that, in most cases, the right to freedom of expression does not bring anything to the argument that cannot already be accomplished through the rules of free movement.[96]

In the media sector, media pluralism has undoubtedly been the most important public policy interest invoked to justify restrictions on the publication or distribution of media content.[97] As Advocate General Poiares Maduro stated in the *Centro Europa 7* case,

the part often played by the media as editors of the public sphere is vital to the promotion and protection of an open and inclusive society in which different ideas of the common good are presented and discussed. In this regard, the European Court of Human Rights has stressed that the fundamental role of freedom of expression in a democratic society, in particular where it serves to impart information and ideas to the public, 'cannot be successfully accomplished unless it is grounded in the principle of pluralism, of which the State is the ultimate guarantor'. Accordingly, the application of Community law in the area

---

[92] 'In particular, where a Member State relies on the combined provisions of Articles 56 and 66 in order to justify rules which are likely to obstruct the exercise of the freedom to provide services, such justification, provided for by Community law, must be interpreted in the light of the general principles of law and in particular of fundamental rights. Thus the national rules in question can fall under the exceptions provided for by the combined provisions of Articles 56 and 66 only if they are compatible with the fundamental rights the observance of which is ensured by the Court', Case C-260/89, *Elliniki Radiophonia Tiléorassi AE and Panellinia Omospondia Syllogon Prossopikou v.Dimotiki Etairia Pliroforissis ('ERT')* [1991] ECR I-2925, para. 43.

[93] Ibid., para. 44.

[94] Case C-368/95, *Vereinigte Familiapress v. Heinrich Bauer Verlag* [1997] ECR I-3689, para. 26.

[95] For example, ibid.

[96] See, for example, the pre-Treaty of Lisbon case Case C81/09, *Reference for a preliminary ruling from the Simvoulio tis Epikratias (Greece)—Idrima Tipou AE v. Ipourgos Tipou kai Meson Mazikis Enimerosis* (21 October 2010), in which the Court found that Greek measures aimed at the protection of honour or reputation constituted a disproportionate burden on the freedom of establishment and the free movement of capital. Reference to the right to freedom of expression, which in the future may well be necessary to reflect the post-Lisbon constitutional arrangements, would have had no practical effect on the outcome in this case.

[97] On media pluralism in European law, see Chapter 14.

of national broadcasting services is guided by the principle of pluralism and, moreover, assumes special significance where it strengthens the protection of that principle.[98]

In comparison, human dignity has not played a similarly prominent role in media cases, but this fundamental human rights value without doubt underpins many of the specific justifications for restricting the liberty to publish, such as the suppression of hate speech or the protection of pluralism.[99]

The biggest impact of mandatory public policy requirements on European media law has been in the broadcasting sector. Here, EU member states have struggled for decades to defend their broadcasting content regimes from the demand for free movement of services. Indeed, the Court developed the principles of mandatory requirements in part through cases dealing with these efforts. Despite their blatant obstruction of free movement and fair competition, the ECJ could hardly invalidate the concept of intensive state control over the broadcast media for political and social policy purposes. State intervention in radio and television for these sweeping and varied purposes was, after all, not only common throughout the member states, but was also woven into the fabric of political and social life in leading member states.

Nevertheless, the Court's strengthening of the rules of free movement had placed enormous pressure on these regimes, which were often elaborate legal and institutional constructions carrying a host of domestic interests and concerns. In several countries, such as the Netherlands and Belgium, linguistic, ethnic, religious, and other divisions were buffered through the provision of special access and programme obligations.[100] In others, such as France, national cultural and social solidarity was deliberately reinforced through the broadcast media.[101] In these systems, advertising was typically a critically important issue, rigorously controlled for quality purposes, but also often protected as a source of revenue for domestic broadcasters fulfilling government policy objectives.

In the Netherlands, the arrival of foreign based satellite television services presented an immense threat to its system of public funding through centrally retained advertising revenues. To defend this system, the Dutch government required that foreign broadcasts retransmitted by cable in the Netherlands should be produced in a non-commercial manner equivalent to those imposed on domestic providers. When these measures were challenged before the ECJ, the Court

---

[98] Case C-380/05, *Centro Europa 7 Srl v. Ministero delle Comunicazioni e Autorità per le garanzie nelle comunicazioni* (ECJ, 31 January 2008).

[99] On human dignity as a general principle in EU law, see Case C-36/02, n. 89 above. See also TEU, Article 2: 'The Union is founded on the values of respect for human dignity, freedom, democracy, equality, the rule of law and respect for human rights, including the rights of persons belonging to minorities. These values are common to the Member States in a society in which pluralism, non-discrimination, tolerance, justice, solidarity and equality between women and men prevail'; EU Charter of Fundamental Rights, Article 1; McGonagle, T., 'Safeguarding Human Dignity in the European Audiovisual Sector' *IRIS Plus*, 2007–6.

[100] Brants, K. and Jankowski, N., 'Cable television in the Low Countries', in Negrine, R. (ed.), *Cable Television and the Future of Broadcasting* (Croom Helm, 1985).

[101] Mazdon, L., 'Cinema and Television', in Scriven, M. and Lecomte, M. (eds), *Television Broadcasting in Contemporary France and Britain* (Berghahn Books, 1999), 71.

accepted the Dutch government's argument that the pluralist social, cultural, religious, and philosophical objectives behind these content control measures were within the bounds of legitimate public policy.[102] However, it also concluded that there was no necessary connection between the objective of media pluralism and the measures imposed on the retransmission of foreign broadcasts.

As noted above, decisions of this kind left most parties in a state of uncertainty. The new commercial satellite broadcasters had to accept that national broadcasting regimes could lawfully impose major obstructions on the free movement of their television services. Governments, anxious to protect the status quo, also had to accept that these regimes were now highly vulnerable to the requirement that the measures employed should be no more restrictive than necessary. Yet these complex public service broadcasting regimes had been developed to suit other public purposes and had never been designed to meet that test.

Audiovisual Media Services Directive and content standards

The core provisions governing cross border television services in the Audiovisual Media Services Directive, previously known as the Television Without Frontiers Directive, have remained unchanged through the 1997 and 2007 amendments. These provisions are constructed around the strained compromises achieved when the Directive was first negotiated in the 1980s. The combined principles of free movement and country of origin regulation are ordinarily powerful levellers of standards across member states. In principle, service providers will tend to base themselves in the most commercially convenient member state, putting pressure on states with more restrictive standards to eliminate unnecessary differences. However, agreement on free movement and country of origin regulation in the AVMS Directive was only secured through the inclusion of substantial harmonization of content standards. This in effect combined an underlying concept of generic television services open to competition across the EU with a heavy overlay of common obligations.

The Directive is thus a complex intrusion into the domestic media state relationship, supporting the liberty to publish, but also limiting and shaping that liberty to suit a range of non-market public policy objectives. The Directive is therefore much more than a detailed version of the principles of the TFEU applied to cross border television services. It obliges member states to impose restrictions on broadcast services in place of the TFEU's permissive approach to national restraints on the free movement of services. These prescriptive rules include negative restrictions aimed at the protection of children and the suppression of incitement to hatred as well as aspects of consumer protection in relation to advertising.[103]

---

[102] Case C-288/89 and Case C-148/91, n. 16 above.
[103] Directive 2010/13/EU, n. 24 above, Articles 6 (incitement to hatred), Article 9 (advertising restrictions relating to the protection of human dignity and health), and Articles 12 and 27 (protection of children from harmful programmes).

Beyond these restrictions on harmful or offensive programmes and advertising, the Directive also requires member states to impose positive content obligations on broadcasters under their jurisdiction. This further assortment of non-market public policy obligations includes minimum quotas for European and independent works in programme content, limits on the exercise of exclusive rights to sports and other major events, and public rights of reply to personally injurious or offensive reports.[104]

In a further contrast to the TFEU, the Directive only permits derogation from the obligation to permit reception and retransmission of television services from other member states on very limited grounds. This narrow right of derogation can be invoked where another member state has failed to fulfil its Directive obligations regarding the protection of children or the prohibition of incitement to hatred in broadcast programmes.[105] It also reflects the long standing principle that public morals are not uniform across Europe.[106] EU law therefore recognizes that member states have legitimate differences in how public morality is addressed in law and public administration and cannot be held to a common European standard.

Obligations on member states to intervene in the editorial decisions of television broadcasters are a heavy constraint on the media's liberty to choose programme content. The justification for this burden on free movement and freedom of expression is that they foster pluralism, cultural heritage, cultural diversity, social cohesion, and other legitimate social and political objectives. They are consequently a legislative articulation of common European values, which are moreover ostensibly grounded in the right to human dignity and other fundamental rights. Yet the AVMS Directive is also a deep intrusion into the dynamics of the domestic media state relationship that cannot be unpicked at the national level. Its many constraints on the liberty to publish were reached through negotiations between the EU member states, the Commission, and latterly the European Parliament. They are also broadly in line with the now settled fundamentals of European media law as developed by the Luxembourg and Strasbourg Courts, which permit substantial state restriction of the liberty to publish. This stands in sharp contrast to the strongly sceptical view of the state, which is entrenched in American constitutional jurisprudence and is now outside the European model of the legitimate media state relationship.

Despite its importance to the audiovisual sector, there are many content matters that fall outside the fields covered by the AVMS Directive.[107] The manner in which goods and services are advertised, taxed, or otherwise regulated will frequently intersect with questions of media content regulation, yet these

---

[104]   Ibid., Articles 12, 16–17 (European and independent works), Article 14 (listed events), Article 15 (short news reports), and Article 28 (rights of reply).

[105]   Ibid., Article 3(2).

[106]   *Handyside v. United Kingdom*, Application No. 5493/72 [1976] ECHR 5 (7 December 1976), para. 49.

[107]   Directive 2010/13/EU, n. 24 above, Article 3(1).

matters are principally governed by other EU laws.[108] The Directive only requires that any measures taken to regulate such matters should not amount to a form of secondary control that restricts the reception or retransmission of audiovisual media services from other member states.[109] National restrictions on partisan political advertising and programmes, for example, undoubtedly affect the free movement of these services between member states.[110] This field, however, is outside the scope of the Directive. Instead, it falls under the public policy exceptions of EU law and is thus a matter for member states to determine, subject to the limits of those exceptions and the requirements of European human rights law.

The Directive's commitment to the free movement of services is also somewhat deceptive. Article 4 gives member states the right to impose stricter obligations on media service providers under their jurisdiction than those required by the Directive.[111] This, in effect, allows member states to take advantage of the linguistic, cultural, and economic factors that create barriers between Europe's regional and national media markets. Major producers of original audiovisual content are typically based in their principal markets to maintain good access to local locations, creative staff, and other facilities as well as national cultural subsidies or tax relief. Re-establishing the business under the jurisdiction of another member state to avoid stricter local content requirements is therefore often financially and logistically impractical. Nonetheless, Article 4 creates an unpredictable regulatory space that is always vulnerable to technological and commercial change. Established national media companies may choose to accept local regulatory rules, however burdensome, but for many of their new media competitors EU law offers real alternatives.

Some member states are moreover particularly vulnerable to significant cross border media penetration. A country, such as Ireland or Austria, may share a language with a larger neighbouring state and therefore provide a convenient secondary market for adapted programmes and advertising content. For these states, the AVMS Directive has forced them to permit reception and retransmission of these channels, regardless of their impact on smaller domestic producers. Some member states have not however been willing to accept that the Directive's free movement rules should also apply to media providers who target one national market while established in another member state where they have no substantial

---

[108] See, for example, Joined Cases C-34/95, C-35/95, and C-36/95, *Konsumentombudsmannen (KO) v. De Agostini (Svenska) Förlag AB and TV-Shop i Sverige AB* (9 July 1997).

[109] Ibid., para. 33: 'Although the Directive provides that the Member States are to ensure freedom of reception and are not to impede retransmission on their territory of television broadcasts coming from other Member States . . . it does not have the effect of excluding completely and automatically the application of rules other than those specifically concerning the broadcasting and distribution of programmes. 34 Thus the Directive does not in principle preclude application of national rules with the general aim of consumer protection provided that they do not involve secondary control of television broadcasts in addition to the control which the broadcasting Member State must carry out.'

[110] See, for example, s. 92(1), Representation of the People Act 1983 (as amended), which concerns programme services broadcast from outside the United Kingdom intended to influence British elections.

[111] Directive 2010/13/EU, n. 24 above, Article 4(1).

connections. These governments have argued that 'delocalized' providers of this kind, who are in reality domestic media operating under a flag of convenience, ought instead to fall under the jurisdiction of the member state where their primary target audience resides. Although this argument is apparently at odds with the country of origin principle, it has found support in the European Court of Justice.[112] The delocalization principle was then partially recognized in the 1997 amendments to the AVMS Directive, before receiving more substantial treatment in the 2007 amendments. These created a new procedure that provides an avenue for states to pursue claims of delocalization, while also restraining potential protectionism.[113]

Content standards for on-demand and information society services

With the arrival of broadband internet access in many households across Europe, the intensive harmonization of content standards for broadcasting had begun to create unsustainable differences with new competing online audiovisual services. In 2005, the Commission argued that an outdated view of internet access in the home was leaving children exposed to significant harm.[114] While it failed to gain support for a comprehensive shift of audiovisual content services into the AVMS Directive, it did secure agreement that restrictions on harmful content should be applied to those new media services that closely resemble television. Consequently, as discussed above, on-demand audiovisual media services were carved out of the information society services category and moved to the Directive.

That move also entailed major adaptations in the Directive's content standards to bring the treatment of on-demand audiovisual services into line with television services. The Directive therefore requires that member states ensure that on-demand audiovisual media services under their jurisdiction abide by content restrictions protecting children and prohibiting incitement to hatred that parallel those imposed on television services.[115] The Directive's positive content obligations for on-demand services are however limited to the soft requirement that they promote the production and access to European works.[116]

The question of rights of derogation presented a particular problem. The AVMS Directive's narrow rights of derogation applicable to television broadcasting services were unsuitable for on-demand services. These are often unlicensed and governed by self regulatory regimes, making it difficult, as compared to licensed television services, for governments to ensure that the on-demand services under their jurisdiction abide by the Directive's content standards. Given that greater potential for public exposure to harmful or offensive content, other member states wishing to

---

[112] Case C-148/91, n. 16 above, para. 12. See also Case C-56/96, *VT4 Ltd v. Vlaamse Gemeenschap* [1997] ECR I-3143, and Case C-212/97, *Centros v. Erhvervs-og Selskabsstyrelsen* [1999] ECR I-1459.
[113] Directive 2010/13/EU, n. 24 above, Article 4. See also Recital (40).
[114] Commission Proposal, n. 46 above.
[115] Articles 6, 9 and 12.
[116] Directive 2010/13/EU, n. 24 above, Article 12.

block access to such content required more extensive rights of derogation from the Directive's free movement and country of origin obligations. The drafters of the amended Directive therefore imported the more extensive rights of derogation for on-demand audiovisual services from the Electronic Commerce Directive.[117] A member state may therefore conditionally derogate from the obligation to permit reception and retransmission of on-demand audiovisual services from other member states for reasons of public policy, public health, public security, and consumer protection. It is however notable that the 'public policy' ground for derogation in the AVMS Directive, as defined by an indicative list of objectives, appears narrower than that available under general EU law for 'public policy' exceptions.[118]

In contrast to the AVMS Directive, the Electronic Commerce Directive is in essence a more detailed version of the rules of the TFEU as they apply to 'information society services'. As noted, this Directive is based on the linked principles of free movement and country of origin regulation that underpin the TFEU. Accordingly, it does not contain a battery of prescriptive content rules similar to the negative restrictions on harmful or offensive content and the positive obligations to intervene in media markets included in the AVMS Directive. Instead, the Electronic Commerce Directive follows the permissive approach of the TFEU in allowing conditional derogations from the primary obligations.[119] These conditions include not only the ubiquitous requirement of proportionality, but also procedural steps for consultation with the member state having jurisdiction over the information society service provider concerned. As just noted, the AVMS Directive contains identical rules of derogation for on-demand audiovisual services.

This radically different model for information society services reflects the internet policy preferences of the 1990s, which discouraged state regulation of internet content. In that vein, the Electronic Commerce Directive only obliges member states to encourage trade, professional, and consumer associations to draw up codes of conduct regarding the protection of minors and human dignity.[120] This emphasis on self and co regulation followed the regulatory model previously established by the 1998 EU Recommendation on Minors and Human Dignity.[121] That non-binding instrument recommends that member states promote, 'as a supplement to the regulatory framework, the establishment on a voluntary basis of national frameworks for the protection of minors and human dignity in audiovisual and information services'.[122] Although the Recommendation covers all audiovisual

---

[117] Ibid., Article 3(4), Directive 2000/31/EC, n. 38 above, Article 3(4).

[118] Barnard, C., n. 1 above, 149.

[119] Directive 2000/31/EC, n. 38 above, Article 3(4). See also Recitals (24)–(26).

[120] Directive 2000/31/EC, n. 38 above, Article 16.

[121] Council Recommendation of 24 September 1998 on the development of the competitiveness of the European audiovisual and information services industry by promoting national frameworks aimed at achieving a comparable and effective level of protection of minors and human dignity (1998 Recommendation protection of minors and human dignity).

[122] Ibid., Article I.

and information content services, including broadcasting, it is primarily directed at the regulation of content provided by online and other new media services.[123]

Outside the AVMS Directive and the Electronic Commerce Directive, European Union law also contains a very different type of prescriptive measure that obliges member states to restrict the liberty to publish. Unlike the provisions of the Directives, these are not based on the nature of the content service, but are instead based on the class of expression that is deemed to be extremely harmful. The three main areas of concern are therefore incitement to terrorism, child pornography, and incitement to racial and other forms of hatred. In these areas, three Council Framework Decisions require the criminalization of various forms of publication of content that falls within these prohibited classes.[124] Following the Treaty of Lisbon, these Framework Decisions are now subject to adjudication by the European Court of Justice.[125]

Intervention in media markets and restrictions on the liberty to publish

In comparison to the rules of free movement, European Union competition law has a more ambiguous impact on the relationship between the media and EU member states. Competition law limits the activities of media and communication businesses in many ways, such as prohibitions on mergers in media markets and restrictions on the ways in which sports rights may be sold or licensed.[126] Certainly, any business subject to these restraints has had its liberty to publish or distribute content restricted. The well known justification for EU competition rules is however that they promote fair market competition, which potentially increases the efficiency of firms and the availability of a wider range of better products and services for consumers.[127] On that reasoning the removal of barriers to entry and unfair practices in the media sector will improve the quantity and quality of information and entertainment goods and services. From this wider perspective, while competition rules may restrict the liberty to publish for particular businesses, they enhance that liberty generally.

The European Union's rules restricting subsidies and other forms of state aid are similarly an important restraint on national public service media regimes. In

---

[123] Ibid., 'Indicative Guidelines for the Implementation, at National Level, of a Self-Regulation Framework for the Protection of Minors and Human Dignity in On-Line Audiovisual and Information Services'.

[124] Framework Decision 2002/475/JHA on combating terrorism, as amended by Council Framework Decision 2008/919/JHA of 28 November 2008, Council Framework Decision 2004/68/JHA of 22 December 2003 on combating the sexual exploitation of children and child pornography, and Council Framework Decision 2008/913/JHA of 28 November 2008 on combating certain forms and expressions of racism and xenophobia by means of criminal law.

[125] See TFEU, Title V, Area of freedom, security and justice, and Article 10, Protocol 36 to the Treaty of Lisbon (Transitional Provisions). See also on pre-Treaty of Lisbon arrangements, Borgers, M., 'Implementing Framework Decisions', 44(5) *Common Market Law Review* (2007), 1361–1386.

[126] See Chapter 14.

[127] Whish, R., *Competition Law*, 6th edn (Oxford University Press, 2008), ch 1.

relation to free movement, the ECJ has never prohibited the member states from intervening in media markets, even to the point of maintaining partial monopolies in the broadcast sector.[128] It has however determined that the rules of free movement require that state broadcasting regimes operate in a strictly proportionate manner according to their designated purposes.[129] The Commission, however, prodded to action by commercial competitors to publicly funded broadcasters, has engaged in a long running effort to contain public service media schemes through the use of state aid law. While this again restricts the liberty to publish for state owned or supported media, it potentially widens opportunities for their competitors.

While competition law measures can therefore be used to restrict the liberty of individual businesses, the resulting increase in market opportunities will, in principle, lead to the improved production and distribution of information and entertainment content generally. Ideally, this achieves both the economic goal of market efficiency and greater consumer choice and the political and social goal of media pluralism. The main difficulty here is that competition rules do not always constrain ownership and control sufficiently to maintain an adequate level of media pluralism for those political and social purposes.

Competition law, for example, prohibits the abuse of dominance, but can also tolerate the dominance of markets by companies that have grown large through innovation and opportunity.[130] The concept of media pluralism, on the other hand, precludes significant market dominance, regardless of the dominant company's conduct, because it enjoys an excessive influence on the flow of news and other current affairs information, which often also excludes other voices. EU law therefore permits member states to restrict media ownership and control beyond the needs of competition law to achieve the more rigorous standards of media pluralism. The Merger Regulation accordingly provides that '...Member States may take appropriate measures to protect legitimate interests other than those taken into consideration by this Regulation and compatible with the general principles and other provisions of Community law...plurality of the media...shall be regarded as legitimate interests...'.[131]

In addition to restrictions on company ownership and control, most EU member states have also attempted to bolster media pluralism through various state supported public service media enterprises or schemes.[132] These are intended to complement the external pluralism of the wider media market with an internally regulated pluralism in which providers offer diverse programmes that include a

---

[128] Case C-260/89, n. 92 above.
[129] See Chapter 14.
[130] Whish, R., n. 127 above, 173.
[131] Article 21(4) of Council Regulation 139/2004 of 20 January 2004 on the control of concentrations between undertakings.
[132] On contemporary public service media in Europe, Bron, C., 'Financing and Supervision of Public Service Broadcasting', in *Public Service Media: Money for Content*, *IRIS Plus*, 2010–4 (Strasbourg, June 2010).

broad range of information and opinion.[133] This kind of intervention is arguably necessary in Europe's linguistically and culturally fragmented media market, especially for those countries or areas that are too small and cannot sustain a pluralist media through market forces alone. European public service media are traditionally based in the broadcasting sector, reflecting their origins in Europe's state broadcast monopolies. In the past decade, they have developed on-demand programme services, interactive websites, and other new media services that offer traditional and new forms of content.

These public service media enterprises present a major challenge for the European Union's principles of free movement and fair competition. Their activities are plainly a substantial intervention in media markets that inevitably disadvantages some domestic and foreign media businesses operating in, or wishing to enter, these markets. The long running argument over the proper balance between national public service media and fair competition across the EU has consequently had a pervasive influence on the development of EU law. As a general rule, the sovereign right of member states to allocate their public funds should be consistent with their European Union obligations.[134] Yet, given the importance of these enterprises to national politics and public life over the past half century, EU law has not surprisingly embraced the principle that member states are entitled to provide major financial support to the media to sustain a sufficiently rich and diverse range of programming that educates, informs, and entertains.[135] Even the European Union itself funds multiannual subsidy programmes to help strengthen the capacity of the European media sector to produce and deliver European content.[136]

In EU law, the question of public service media funding and other support has primarily been resolved through the rules concerning state aid.[137] However, it took well over a decade of administrative decisions, dispute resolution, and supplementary legislation within the EU before the basic principles governing the financing of public service media were settled. Their application moreover continues to be contentious as communications technologies and media services evolve and markets change.[138] In this process, the Commission was forced to concede substantial

---

[133] On internal pluralism in the British broadcast media regime, see Humphreys, P., 'Media Freedom and Pluralism in the United Kingdom (UK)', in Czepek, A., Hellwig, M., and Nowak, E., *Press Freedom and Pluralism in Europe: Concepts and Conditions,* (Intellect, 2009), 197.

[134] See Szyszczak, E., n. 79 above, 178.

[135] See, for example, Protocol on the System of Public Broadcasting in the Member States, Treaty of Amsterdam amending the Treaty on European Union, the Treaties establishing the European Communities and certain related Acts (2 October 1997).

[136] See Decision No. 1718/2006/EC of the European Parliament and of the Council of 15 November 2006 concerning the implementation of a programme of support for the European audiovisual sector (MEDIA 2007). See also Chapter 15.

[137] This principally occurs under the umbrella of the concept of Services of a General Interest set out in Article 106(2) of the TFEU. See Chapter 15.

[138] Compare for example, European Broadcasting Union (EBU), *Comments on the second draft revised Broadcasting Communication of 8 April 2009* (May 2009), <http://www.ebu.ch>, and Association of Commercial Television in Europe (ACT), *Comments on the second draft Communication on State Aid and Public Broadcasting* (May 2009), <http://www.acte.be>.

authority to the member states over the scope of public service media activities, yet it was also able to strengthen the rules of financial accountability of these services.[139]

In terms of the TFEU, the proper limits to public service media funding involve a compromise between Article 107, which prohibits state aid, and Article 106, which creates an exception to EU competition law for 'services of a general economic interest' (SGEI).[140] This concept goes well beyond the typical core purposes of the liberal democratic state, such as public order and basic social security measures. It also encompasses significant state supported services whose delivery affects economic conditions for commercial providers in a broad range of market sectors.[141] Under Article 106(2), member states may exercise a conditional right of derogation from Community competition law to grant exclusive powers or rights as well as funding to particular undertakings carrying out these services of general economic interest.[142] This makes SGEI the logical vehicle for the protection of public service media from the prohibition on state aid. As the Commission has acknowledged,

The broadcast media play a central role in the functioning of modern democratic societies, in particular in the development and transmission of social values. Therefore, the broadcasting sector has, since its inception, been subject to specific regulation in the general interest. This regulation has been based on common values, such as freedom of expression and the right of reply, pluralism, protection of copyright, promotion of cultural and linguistic diversity, protection of minors and of human dignity, consumer protection.[143]

Exporting European media law

In the decades following World War II, the United States was the most influential media law model in the liberal democratic world. Its market based media system and innovative constitutional law developments in media matters were not always copied, but certainly helped to change media law in many countries.[144] In this era,

---

[139] Protocol on the System of Broadcasting in the Member States, n. 135 above.

[140] SGEI fall within the wider EU category of Services of a General Interest: 'These services, for instance traditional state prerogatives such as police, justice and statutory social security schemes are not subject to specific EU legislation, nor are they covered by the internal market and the competition rules of the Treaty.' Communication from the Commission to the European Parliament, the Council, the European Economic and Social Committee and the Committee of the Regions accompanying the Communication on 'A single market for 21st century Europe' Services of general interest, including social services of general interest: a new European commitment COM (2007) 725 final, Brussels, 20 November 2007.

[141] In recent years, the concept of SGEI has become critically important in efforts to rebalance European Union law to give greater recognition to non-market public policy goals. See Article 36, Charter of Fundamental Rights of the European Union; TFEU, Article 14, and, Protocol on Services of General Interest (Treaty of Lisbon).

[142] See Szyszczak, E., n. 79 above, ch 4: The Regulation of State Monopolies.

[143] Communication from the Commission—*Services of general interest in Europe* (2001/C 17/04).

[144] See, for example, Chapter 10 regarding the influence of United States constitutional law concerning defamation on European human rights law.

the dual economic and political argument for freedom of speech, often referred to as 'the free flow of ideas' became synonymous with American media law and its advocacy of an open media marketplace. In western Europe, the United States exerted a powerful influence on national as well as regional developments, but its insistence on a minimal state presence in media markets and relatively unrestrained expression in the public sphere just as often made it a counter example.[145] As European market integration progressed, a different model of the legitimate liberal democratic media state relationship began to emerge from the often fractious compromises of European law making. Here, the state was not only restrained to allow liberty to speak and publish, but also obliged to intervene to protect the public from multiple harms and to foster public goods.

In the past half century, American participation in international media law and policy has carried a heavy strategic interest in the export of domestic political and economic values.[146] In contrast, the European Union has more often been protective and internally focused. It is only in recent decades that the EU has become an exporter of legal principles and regulatory models for the media sector. The wealth of European experience in market integration has given the EU a clear advantage in anticipating developments in international cooperation. Europe's successes in exporting its laws and regulatory regimes, notably including data protection principles, are certainly due in part to their multilateral design.[147] European law must be flexible enough to accommodate different domestic policies and circumstances, but still be broadly effective. On the other hand, many aspects of European integration are specific to Europe and are not easily transferred out of that context.[148] For similar reasons, European Union states have found that their international trade and other obligations place great strains on the intricate compromises achieved within European institutions.[149] There are also major questions about the relevance of a model for supranational order that is so heavily dependent on compromise between states and positive cooperation in maintaining protective domestic standards. Few countries would, moreover, look to the EU for clear principles to govern the media in the internet era. The preservation of the European public service media ethos and the broad protection of the public from harm and offence have sat awkwardly with a strong commitment to the freedom to provide media services across frontiers.

[145] Schauer, F., 'The Exceptional First Amendment.' in Ignatieff, M. (ed.), *American Exceptionalism and Human Rights* (Princeton University Press, 2005), 29–56. See also Patterson, O., 'The Speech Misheard Round the World', *New York Times* (22 January 2005).
[146] See, for example, Bollinger, L., *Uninhibited, Robust and Wide Open* (Oxford University Press, 2010), ch 4.
[147] *The External Dimension Of The Single Market Review* (Commission Staff Working Document accompanying the Commission Communication: A Single Market for 21st Century Europe (SEC (2007) 1519).
[148] On the global spread and limitations of constitutional and institutional models, see Goodman, R. and Jinks, D., 'Toward an Institutional Theory of Sovereignty', 55(5) *Stanford Law Review* (2003), 1749–1788.
[149] Young, A., 'The Incidental Fortress: The Single European Market and World Trade', 42(2) *Journal of Common Market Studies* (2004), 393–414.

5

International Trade in Media Goods and Services

At the end of the Cold War, the centre of gravity in international media law and policy shifted decisively from human rights to trade relations. Forty years earlier, the UN General Assembly had adopted the 1948 Universal Declaration of Human Rights, proclaiming the beginning of a new era in international public order. The Declaration made plain that human rights standards had now become an external measure of the legitimacy of state conduct. The right to freedom of expression, moreover, occupied a central place in that assembly of civil, political, and other rights, which made the domestic relationship between the media and the state a matter of international concern.

Defining the proper balance between the liberty to publish and other opposing state and public interests under the mantle of this new international principle soon became a key ideological and tactical issue in Cold War politics.[1] Certainly, in that same period, barriers to trade in media products, in particular films and television programmes, proved a major irritant in transatlantic trade relations. Yet, for the western democracies, the geopolitical importance of the 'free flow of information' overshadowed the question of how to liberalize trade in media goods and services.

With the end of the Cold War, coinciding with the arrival of commercial satellite broadcasting, those economic issues came to the fore. In a period of unchallenged liberal democratic ascendency, the United States led the construction of a new legal and institutional framework for a market based, integrated, global economy. Despite disagreements between the major negotiating states, that project took an enormous step forward in 1994 with the conclusion of the Uruguay Round trade negotiations. The resulting agreements created the World Trade Organization, which was intended to become the principal vehicle for the ongoing process of multilateral trade liberalization.[2]

Aside from establishing the WTO, the Uruguay Round updated the General Agreement on Trade and Tariffs (GATT) and put in place a new General Agreement

---

[1] See Chapter 6.
[2] The Uruguay Round was initiated in 1986 by the GATT member states and finally concluded in 1994 with the Marrakech Declaration, which among other things announced the creation of the World Trade Organization. 'The Organisation's main tasks are to manage the results of the multilateral trade negotiations, organise further negotiations on trade liberalisation and, with the help of the common dispute settlement mechanism, resolve any disputes arising between Members.'

on Trade in Services (GATS) as well as an agreement on Trade-Related Aspects of Intellectual Property Rights (TRIPS).[3] It also created a compulsory, dispute resolution process that provides for independent adjudication on a relatively short timescale. This move was instrumental in transforming the pre-existing GATT trade regime into a much more formal, law based institution in which adjudication and legal doctrine play a leading role.[4]

Since this bright beginning, the reputation of the WTO multilateral process has suffered in the doldrums of the Doha Development Round negotiations.[5] Initiated in 2001, after the 1999 debacle at the WTO ministerial conference at Seattle, the Doha Round negotiations repeatedly failed to achieve mandated deadlines and goals. During the Uruguay Round, negotiations were dominated by the United States and the western Europeans, who achieved substantial gains in global market access, but in the process created an institution with weak global credibility.[6] WTO negotiations are now far more complex, involving a wider range of states operating in vastly different economic and political circumstances. These stalled multilateral negotiations have thus pushed the development of global trade relations in two directions: resort to the dispute resolution processes of the WTO, with a consequent demand for the judicial development of its vaguely stated treaty provisions, and resort to bilateral and regional preferential trade agreements, which have proliferated across the world.

Despite this multilateral disarray, the WTO remains the central hub of the world trade system. It provides the master template for economic relations, establishing the essential concepts and principles for global trade and, consequently, the foundations for the rough patchwork that is international media law. In these foundations, moreover, international media law has clear structural parallels with its European counterpart, in which media goods and services are subject to broadly similar principles. In the domestic media state relationship, the liberty to publish therefore aligns with international as well as European obligations on the state to remove barriers to trade. The interests of the state in restricting the publication and distribution of media content are similarly aligned with permissive exceptions requiring varying proofs of 'necessity'. Finally, this primary, market based orientation towards a greater cross border flow of information and entertainment content is inherently unsympathetic to domestic measures that restrict or foster particular kinds of content. This, in turn, brings the tensions of the media state relationship back into the evolving rules of international and European economic law.

---

[3] Marrakesh Agreement establishing the World Trade Organization, (15 April 1994), 33 ILM 1144 (1994), General Agreement on Tariffs and Trade 1994 (incorporating GATT 1947), 33 ILM 1153 (1994), General Agreement on Trade in Services, 33 ILM 1167 (1994). See, generally, van den Bossche, P., *The Law and Policy of the World Trade Organization*, 2nd edn (Cambridge University Press, 2008), ch 2.

[4] WTO, Understanding on Rules and Procedures Governing the Settlement of Disputes (DSU) (15 April 1994), 33 ILM 1226 (1994).

[5] Fourth WTO Ministerial Conference (Doha, November 2001): Ministerial Declaration (20 November 2001), Wt/Min(01)/Dec/1. See also Adlung, R., 'Services Negotiations in the Doha Round: lost in flexibility?' 9(4) *Journal of International Economic Law* (2006), 865–893.

[6] Cottier, T., 'The Legitimacy of WTO Law', NCCR Trade Working Paper No. 2008/19.

Nonetheless, there are also striking differences between the European Union and the WTO, which lacks the EU's capacity to integrate itself into the legal and institutional fabric of the member state. In principle, European Union law seeks to achieve a single European market, in which national measures that unreasonably impede trade between member states are eliminated, regardless of whether those measures are discriminatory.[7] In other words, it seeks improved conditions for trade per se and not merely non-discriminatory trade. In contrast, the primary WTO rules only require the opening of domestic markets to foreign competition on a non-discriminatory basis. The member states may therefore maintain extensive restrictions on media content, provided that these are applied to imported and domestic media goods and services in an equivalent, non-discriminatory manner.

On that basis, measures that are deliberately discriminatory, such as restrictions intended to protect the cultural or social character of the domestic media, are likely to violate the member state's WTO obligations.[8] Non-discrimination is moreover an expansive concept in international trade law, capturing not only formally discriminatory domestic measures, but also ostensibly neutral measures that have direct discriminatory consequences. In the view of the WTO Appellate Body, this approach to non-discrimination under the national treatment provisions of the GATT and GATS reflects their basic purpose, which is to avoid protectionism.[9] Universally applicable measures prohibiting or restricting public access to harmful or offensive media content will, for example, breach WTO non-discrimination rules if they are shown to have adverse material effects on the sale of imported media content that is in substance comparable to domestic media content.[10] As discussed below, discriminatory national measures may nonetheless be protected by the exception provisions of the GATT and GATS.

The scope of WTO non-discrimination obligations is certainly not limited to domestic measures that are overtly discriminatory as a matter of law.[11] They also prohibit measures that are universally applicable but which cause direct discrimination in practice for foreign competitors, which hugely extends the range of the domestic measures that are potentially in breach of WTO rules. In addition, WTO law imposes a number of secondary obligations that go beyond the primary goal of non-discrimination. These require, for example, that the trade related laws and regulations of member states must be transparent, which not only forces the disclosure of WTO inconsistent measures but also creates a more predictable regime for foreign competitors.[12]

---

[7] Barnard, C., *The Substantive Law of the EU: The Four Freedoms* (Oxford University Press, 2010), 19–24.

[8] See, for example, *Canadian Periodicals: Canada—Certain Measures Concerning Periodicals*, AB-1997-2, WT/DS31/AB/R (WTO Appellate Body) (30 July 1997).

[9] *Japan—Alcoholic Beverages II*, AB-1996-2, *WT/DS8/AB/R*, WT/DS10/AB/R, WT/DS11/AB/R, (WTO Appellate Body) (4 October 1996), 16. *Korea—Taxes on Alcoholic Beverages*, AB-1998-7, WT/DS75/AB/R, WT/DS84/AB/R (WTO Appellate Body) (18 January 1999), para. 120.

[10] On the application of WTO non-discrimination disciplines to harmful or offensive media content, see Chapter 12.

[11] Diebold, N., 'Non-Discrimination and the Pillars of International Economic Law', *Institute for International Law and Justice*, IILJ Emerging Scholars Paper 18 (8 June 2010).

[12] GATT, n. 3 above, Article X. GATS, n. 3 above, Article III.

Yet, the goals of the WTO trade regime remain fairly modest. It is aimed at the shallow, negative integration of a global market for goods and services, which is far from the European Union's ambitious programme of positive integration and selective harmonization of domestic standards.[13] Within the rules of the WTO, the liberty to publish is thus primarily served by the principle of non-discriminatory trade in media goods and services. Even negative integration on that limited basis, moreover, remains a stiff challenge, particularly in relation to trade in services, which are often intensively regulated in ways that exclude or severely disadvantage foreign competitors. To obtain the benefits of trade liberalization, member states must accept disciplines that grind away differences in domestic regulatory standards and requirements. This frequently means accepting foreign goods or services subject to different national standards.

The non-market public policy objectives of WTO member states are mainly protected by the general exceptions built into the treaties.[14] These cover a broadly defined concept of public policy, which encompasses a substantial, but not unlimited, range of media related policy objectives. WTO general exceptions do not, however, have a close relationship with international human rights, unlike comparable general exceptions in EU law, which have gradually become tightly bonded with European human rights law.[15] In European Union law, human rights principles, such as the right to a private life or the right to a pluralist media, help to define the substance and limits of the exceptions to free movement and market competition.[16] Conversely, a well developed liberal interpretation of freedom of expression law combines easily with these economic obligations to strengthen arguments for greater liberty to publish. There is no comparable development in international economic law.

The weak interface between WTO law and the United Nations based field of international human rights law reflects both the wider fragmentation of international law and the conceptual as well as practical difficulties of its various regimes.[17] Within the WTO, the Appellate Body has had great difficulty in settling the limits of trade law and the degree to which it recognizes the competing international obligations of member states. The organization emerged out of Uruguay Round as the world's most developed multilateral regime and quickly made its influence felt in almost every aspect of cross border relations. It possessed not only a wide mandate over the economic activities of its members, but also a law based, binding

---

[13] On the limited objectives of the Uruguay Round agreements, see Lawrence, R.Z., *Regionalism, Multilateralism, and Deeper Integration* (The Brookings Institution, 1996).

[14] GATT, n. 3 above, Article XX. GATS, n. 3 above, Article XIV.

[15] See Chapters 4 and 6.

[16] See, for example, Case C-368/95, *Vereinigte Familiapress v. Heinrich Bauer Verlag* [1997] ECR I-3689.

[17] Pauwelyn, J., *Conflict of Norms in Public International Law: How WTO Law relates to other Rules of International Law* (Cambridge University Press, 2003). See also Report of the International Law Commission, *Conclusions of the Work of the Study Group on the Fragmentation of International Law: Difficulties arising from the Diversification and Expansion of International Law* 2006, A/CN.4/L.682, and A/CN.4/L.682/Add.1, and Voon, T., *Cultural Products and the World Trade Organization* (Cambridge University Press, 2007), 130–142.

dispute resolution system. This combination of sweeping substantive scope and an authoritative, independent tribunal is virtually unique in the international sphere. From a liberal democratic perspective, these qualities gave the WTO an alluring potential to serve as the core institution for the construction of a constitutionalized world order.[18]

The question of how the WTO regime should operate in relation to other areas of international law and public administration has run in two directions. One concern is that the immense scope of WTO trade law, backed up by binding adjudication, has unbalanced the development of international public order. Trade law has thus become the central field of international cooperation and dispute resolution, its disciplines exerting a constant, disproportionate pressure on non-market public policies.[19] In the media sector, which is enmeshed in political, social, and cultural policy objectives, this apparent over-extension is an acute problem for many states.[20]

The other concern is that attempts to resolve the relationship between legal regimes from inside WTO law will seriously undermine its capacity to sustain the liberalization of global trade in goods and services.[21] It was apparent from the outset that this expanded trade regime could not blindly ignore the other international legal obligations of its member states. In an early decision, the Appellate Body made plain that the WTO legal regime would draw on the basic principles and methods of international law and could not be read in 'clinical isolation from public international law'.[22] The difficulty for the Appellate Body and panels since then has been to develop that relationship, while also remaining within the strictures placed on their competence by the founding states.[23] By relying on the accepted rules of treaty interpretation, they have cautiously opened the way to greater interaction between WTO law and other fields of international law.[24] In this manner, the Appellate Body closed the gap between international trade and

---

[18] Cass, D., *The Constitutionalization of the World Trade Organization: Legitimacy, Democracy, and Community in the International Trading System* (Oxford University Press, 2005); Trachtman, J.P., 'The Constitutions of the WTO', 17(3) *European Journal of International Law* (2006), 623–646.

[19] Dunoff, J., 'The Death of the Trade Regime', 10 *European Journal of International Law* (1998), 733; Guzman, A., 'Global Governance and the WTO', 45 *Harvard International Law Journal* (2004), 303; McGinnis, J. and Movsesian, M., 'Against Global Governance in the WTO', 45 *Harvard International Law Journal* (2004), 353.

[20] See Chapter 15 on trade and cultural policy.

[21] The problem of 'linkage' between WTO disciplines and external legal regimes is widely discussed. For an overview, see Patterson, D. and Afilalo, A., *The New Global Trading Order: The Evolving State and the Future of Trade* (Cambridge University Press, 2008), 86–93.

[22] *United States—Standards for Reformulated and Conventional Gasoline*, 1996, WT/DS2/AB/R, 17.

[23] Under the Dispute Settlement Understanding, the Appellate Body or the Panels are not permitted, in their recommendations or rulings, to add to or diminish the rights and obligations provided in the WTO covered agreements: *WTO Understanding on Rules and Procedures Governing the Settlement of Disputes*, Article 3.2. Yet the same article also directs those tribunals to clarify WTO agreements in accordance with customary rules of interpretation of public international law.

[24] While their approach reflects the deliberate constraints of the DSU, n. 4 above, the Appellate Body and Panels have also been urged to take account of a broader range of international legal principles and rules when adjudicating complaints. See, for example, Report of the International Law Commission, n. 17 above, paras 169 and 170.

environmental law by using international agreements relating to the environment to interpret the meaning of Article XX exceptions to the GATT in the 2001 *US— Shrimp* case.[25]

This has resulted in an increasingly 'cosmopolitan' WTO regime. Ideally, this cosmopolitanism will be based on 'a coherent and open relationship to other trade related public international norms and private standards' as well as embracing 'a multi-levelled regulatory jurisdiction linking multilateral disciplines with regional and domestic regulatory autonomy'.[26] The WTO however has a long way to travel before it reaches that ideal. The textual and doctrinal basis for a more open relationship with external norms and standards is still uncertain.[27] While the Appellate Body has found sufficient basis in the WTO treaties to accommodate some member state obligations under environmental treaties, linkage by textual interpretation has obvious limits.

In addition, there is a compelling argument that a coherent relationship between WTO law and other international regimes will not work unless it is grounded in common normative values, including respect for human rights.[28] This would require a reasonably clear, shared understanding of the content and application of international human rights obligations. Yet the content of specific human rights, not least civil and political rights, is instead contentiously ill defined. There is certainly no global consensus on the meaning and limits of the right to freedom of expression, which is too intimately connected to the character of the state to allow even rough uniformity.[29] In the current state of global relations, in which the influence of the western democracies has declined markedly since their post Cold War ascendency, these divisions are likely to continue if not widen. The many tensions between different strands of liberal democratic thought on the limits of free speech are also sure to continue, as they reflect, in part, the deep differences in this broad tradition of political and moral thought.[30] Plainly, in some areas where the fields of international trade and human rights law substantially overlap, such as labour standards, a wider common understanding is not as elusive. Bridges between the two fields are therefore likely to be constructed selectively and cautiously.

---

[25] *United States—Import Prohibition of Certain Shrimp and Shrimp Products*, AB-2001-4, WT/DS58/AB/RW. See also Perez, O., 'Multiple Regimes, Issue Linkage and International Cooperation: Exploring the Role of the WTO'. 26(4) *University of Pennsylvania Journal of International Economic Law* (Spring 2006), 735.

[26] Panizzon, M. and Pohl. N., 'Beyond regulatory control and multilateral flexibility: Gains from a cosmopolitan GATS', in Panizzon, M., Pohl, N., and Sauvé, P. (eds), *GATS and the Regulation of International Trade in Services*, (Cambridge University Press, 2008), 6.

[27] On, for example, the gap between the provisions of the UNESCO Convention on Cultural Diversity and WTO law, see Chapter 15.

[28] See, for example, Aaronson, S.A., 'Seeping in Slowly: How Human Rights Concerns are Penetrating the WTO', 6(3) *World Trade Review* (2007), 413–449; Thomas Cottier, 'The Legitimacy of WTO Law', in Yue, L. (ed.), *The Law and Economics of Globalisation*, (Edward Elgar Publishing Ltd, 2009), 11; and Eeckhout, P., 'The Scales of Trade—Reflections on the Growth and Functions of the WTO Adjudicative Branch', 13(1) *Journal of International Economic Law* (2010), 3–26.

[29] See Chapter 6.

[30] On freedom of expression and liberalism, see Chapter 2.

This will occur largely through the ongoing interpretation of the general exceptions to the primary trade obligations of the GATT and GATS. While hardly systematic or certain, the ad hoc approach pursued by the Appellate Body at least acknowledges the need for flexibility where significant non-market public policy objectives are at issue. In developing these exceptions, however, the chief concern of the WTO panels and Appellate Body has been to balance the right of member states to pursue their unique domestic policy goals with the essential integrity of their WTO obligations. The Appellate Body is therefore unlikely to follow the Court of Justice of the European Union in deciding that the balancing exercise is conditioned by general principles of human rights.[31] In the absence of an international tribunal similar to the European Court of Human Rights able to impose coherence on human rights law, it would have to undertake that task itself, which is plainly beyond its competence.

Trade in goods and the liberty to publish

Despite the relative shallowness of WTO obligations, they do have sufficient depth and scope to engage two distinctly different policy divides in the media field. The first of these arises within the diverse sphere of liberal democratic public policy. As noted above, liberal democracies are famously divided in their treatment of the media and their justifications for their restraints and interventions in the media sector. The mandatory criminalization of incitement to ethnic and religious hatred under European Union law, for example, stands in obvious contrast to American First Amendment doctrine.[32] Beyond these iconic free speech issues, the EU has grounded its efforts to integrate European media markets through compromises that accept a high level of state intervention and subsidization to protect national cultural and social objectives. In principle, the protectionist character of this fusion of market and non-market public policy is incompatible with the WTO's basic principles of non-discriminatory, progressive trade liberalization.[33]

The second policy divide occurs between the WTO's liberal democratic member states and those that are neither liberal nor democratic. Here as well, the differences lie in the justifications for restraints on the liberty to publish and state intervention in media markets. Yet, without a shared commitment to liberal principles of personal autonomy in relation to state and society, these differences are much deeper and harder to bridge. They are also a huge barrier to efforts to move trade liberalization beyond the principle of non-discriminatory trade to deeper market access commitments. This would require a more rigorous standard of review regarding the necessity of domestic media measures, which would no doubt bring

---

[31] On the role of European human rights law in European Union law, see Chapter 4.
[32] Council Framework Decision 2008/913/JHA of 28 November 2008 on combating certain forms and expressions of racism and xenophobia by means of criminal law.
[33] Young, A., 'The Incidental Fortress: The Single European Market and World Trade', 42(2) *Journal of Common Market Studies* (2004), 393–414.

to the surface political differences presently beyond the reach of the non-discrimination principle.

The WTO's commitment to non-discriminatory trade, which is its chief contribution to the liberty to publish and distribute media content across borders, originated in the 1947 GATT treaty. This treaty served as an improvised framework for the liberalization of trade in goods between market economies throughout the Cold War decades.[34] While severely limited in many respects, the GATT was a useful legal and institutional basis for tariff reduction and other work on non-tariff barriers. Through the GATT, contracting states accumulated a wealth of experience in trade liberalization through the principles of equal treatment with domestic competitors ('national treatment') and equal treatment between foreign competitors ('most favoured nation' or MFN).[35] These, in addition to the prohibition of import quotas, provide the principal tools of the GATT to achieve non-discrimination in trade in goods between state parties.[36]

In simple terms, the GATT national treatment obligation requires state parties to provide equality of competitive opportunity between domestic and foreign goods. This helps to ensure tariff reductions and other market access commitments undertaken by the member states are not replaced by discriminatory legal or regulatory measures.[37] The GATT's national treatment discipline captures non-compliant measures regardless of whether they are formally discriminatory or simply discriminatory in their effects. This discipline is not however intended to reach domestic measures that merely have incidental adverse effects on foreign competitors. It therefore functions as a boundary keeper between simple liberalization of trade and deeper market integration.[38]

The GATT MFN discipline requires state parties to offer the most favourable treatment they accord to any of their trading partners unconditionally to all other GATT parties. Like national treatment, the MFN discipline applies equally to legal measures and administrative practices.[39] Yet, despite the apparent breadth of this trade discipline, the MFN obligation has had a variable impact. It is subject to the right of member states to enter, on conditions, preferential trade agreements that discriminate between trading parties.[40] These regional and bilateral trade agreements, including the European Union, NAFTA, and Mercosur, have multiplied to

---

[34] On the origins of the 1947 GATT, see George Bronz, 'The International Trade Organization Charter', 62(7) *Harvard Law Review* (1949), 1089–1125.

[35] GATT, n. 3 above, Article 1 (most favoured nation—MFN) and Article III, (national treatment). See also Vranes, E., 'The WTO and Regulatory Freedom: WTO Disciplines on Market Access, Non-Discrimination and Domestic Regulation relating to Trade in Goods and Services', 12(4) *Journal of International Economic Law* (2009), 953–987.

[36] GATT, ibid., Article XI 'General Elimination of Quantitative Restrictions'.

[37] Verhoosel, G., *National Treatment and WTO Dispute Settlement: Adjudicating the Boundaries of Regulatory Autonomy* (Hart Publishing, 2002), 12.

[38] Ibid, 2.

[39] Working Group On The Interaction Between Trade And Competition Policy, *The Fundamental WTO Principles of National Treatment, Most-Favoured-Nation Treatment and Transparency*, Wt/Wgtcp/W/114 (14 April 1999).

[40] GATT, n. 3 above, Article XXIV, and GATS, n. 3 above, Article V.

create what is often described as a 'spaghetti bowl' of discriminatory preferences.[41] There are consequently hundreds of MFN exempt preferential agreements registered with the WTO and more come into existence every year.[42] The full application of the WTO most favoured nation principle is therefore more an exception than a general rule.

The determination of whether a challenged measure is discriminatory under the GATT turns on the question of whether it has negatively affected 'like' imported goods. The requirement that discrimination must be shown in relation to specific comparable goods, which has no counterpart in EU law, reflects the GATT's focus on questions of discrimination rather than barriers to trade per se. If the WTO were to move towards the prohibition of unnecessary barriers to trade, regardless of discriminatory effects, this close attention to 'likeness' would no longer play such a key role.[43]

The tests for likeness under the GATT raise difficult questions about the factors that should be used to identify the similarity of goods.[44] National laws or other measures that limit the import of foreign media goods, such as magazines or films, are frequently based on claims of distinctiveness or specificity in the relationship between media content and domestic social and cultural values.[45] The liberalization of trade however requires that goods should, as much as possible, be treated as generic things. Social or cultural differences associated with the content can therefore only be recognized if they significantly limit the substitutability of ostensibly competing goods.[46] Yet these factors, while often important for public policy purposes, are frequently less important to consumers than price and editorial quality. While this economic based approach to likeness tends to be insensitive to the non-economic distinctiveness of media content, it would be impossible to define major markets for substitutable goods and services or to identify the conditions for equality and fairness in trading without this generic perspective.

The foregoing discussion implies that the GATT had a decisive impact on the development of international trade in media content in the decades between the end of World War II and the disintegration of the Soviet Union. Yet, the GATT, although richly supplemented by additional agreements and case decisions, had a

---

[41] *The Future of the WTO: Addressing institutional challenges in the new millennium*, Report by the Consultative Board to the former Director-General Supachai Panitchpakdi, ch 2: The erosion of non-discrimination; See also Hufbauer, G.C. and Schott, J.J., The Doha Round After Hong Kong, *Policy Briefs in International Economics*, Institute for International Economics, No. Pb06-2, February 2006; and Roy, M., Marchetti, J., and Lim, H., *Services Liberalization in the New Generation of Preferential Trade Agreements (PTAs): How Much Further than the GATS?*, Staff Working Paper ERSD-2006-07 September 2006, World Trade Organization, Economic Research and Statistics Division.

[42] Heydon, K., *After the WTO Hong Kong Ministerial Meeting: What is at Stake?* OECD Trade Policy Working Paper No. 270 (2006).

[43] Pauwelyn, J., 'The Unbearable Lightness of Likeness', in Panizzon, M., Pohl, N., and Sauvé, P., n. 26 above, 358.

[44] GATT, n. 3 above, Article III.

[45] Carmody, C., 'When Cultural Identity was not at Issue; Thinking about Canada: Certain Measures concerning Periodicals', 30 *Law and Policy in International Business* (1999), 231.

[46] Voon, n. 17 above, ch 1: Trade and Culture.

relatively small impact on the world's media in that period. Newspapers, magazines, and other media products that passed national borders in a tangible form were certainly classed as goods for the application of customs tariffs and other domestic measures.[47] These barriers to trade however were often less important than linguistic and cultural differences and the distribution costs of paper in bulk.

Logically, the non-discrimination disciplines of the GATT should have helped to ease the international trade in cinema films and television programmes, as these were clearly also traded in the form of tangible goods. Claims of cultural distinctiveness, however, overwhelmed that potential during the drafting of the 1947 GATT Treaty. To satisfy European concerns, the agreement expressly permits the protection of national cinema industries through the use of screen quotas, which some GATT parties later extended unilaterally to include domestic quotas restricting the broadcast of foreign television programmes.[48]

Digitization has radically changed the nature of international trade in media goods. Although suffering from fierce competition from other convergent media platforms, the print media have increased their reach, not only through online delivery, but also through the digital supply of content to remote printing facilities. There are, as a result, many new circumstances in which the GATT applies to what are effectively cross border deliveries of printed media goods, although these invariably include cross border services as well.[49] For the most part, however, the digitization of audiovisual entertainment has moved the focus for media trade firmly into the sphere of trade in services.

Trade in services and the liberty to publish

More than any other achievement of the Uruguay Round, the GATS carries the greatest potential to force changes in national media laws and policies.[50] The GATS sets out the foundations for the liberalization of global trade in services, including insurance, finance, tourism, communications, and media content. The aim of this treaty is to improve market opening for services through

---

[47] When media content is bound to a tangible carrier medium, such as newsprint, videotape, or plastic discs, and is sold across national frontiers in that form, it is usually treated as a good for the purposes of trade law. More often, information and entertainment content passes through those frontiers by wireless or wired electronic transmission. In these intangible forms, the delivery of content is typically classed as a service.

[48] See Chapter 7.

[49] In *Canada—Certain Measures Concerning Periodicals*, n. 8 above, the Appellate Body stated that 'a periodical is a good comprised of two components: editorial content and advertising content. Both components can be viewed as having services attributes, but they combine to form a physical product—the periodical itself.' See also Hoekman, B., 'Towards a More Balanced and Comprehensive Services Agreement', in Schott, J. (ed.), *The WTO After Seattle* (Institute for International Economics, 2000), 127.

[50] Footer, M. and Graber, C., 'Audiovisual Policy: the Stumbling Block of Trade Liberalisation', *Journal of International Economic Law* (2000) 115–144.

non-discriminatory trade rules, supported by common regulatory principles and binding dispute resolution.[51]

Liberalization of trade in services is however frequently more technically complex and politically sensitive than the use of equivalent disciplines to liberalize trade in goods. Negotiations under the GATT were initially directed at the reduction of tariffs imposed on imported goods. Once tariff levels had fallen, the GATT process began to focus on non-tariff and taxation barriers, such as sanitary standards for food products and other protective measures, which were growing in complexity and limiting the entry of foreign goods.[52] The liberalization of trade in services has opened a much wider range of domestic regulatory measures to possible review.

Unlike goods, which are subject to regulatory controls at the customs port of entry, foreign based services typically enter a country at the place of consumption, which may be anywhere within its borders. Foreign competitors therefore often become directly enmeshed in domestic regulatory regimes, such as radio and television content standards, that were never designed to incorporate foreign service providers. Under the principles of the GATS, these domestic measures may constitute illicit barriers to trade when they have discriminatory effects.[53] The GATS therefore has the capacity to overturn long established regulatory measures and, as a result, constrain public policy choices that governments and citizens have historically regarded as being purely domestic in nature.[54]

The drafters of the GATS, as much as possible, attempted to follow the structure and principles of the GATT. Consequently, the treaty uses the same basic commitment to non-discrimination through national treatment and most favoured nation obligations as well as the prohibition of quotas and other quantitative restrictions.[55] The GATS national treatment obligations however go further in applying the principle not only to services but also to the suppliers of services.[56] In contrast, the GATT does not extend national treatment obligations to the suppliers of goods. The effect of the GATS national treatment principle is also complicated by the ambiguous relationship between this discipline and the market access obligations set out in Article XVI.[57] These provisions prohibit a large range of quantitative

[51] Sauvé P., and Stern, R., 'New Directions in Services Trade Liberalization: An Overview', in Sauvé and Stern, *GATS 2000: New Directions in Services Trade Liberalisation* (Brookings Institution, 2000), 1.
[52] WTO Sanitary and Phytosanitary Measures Agreement, contained in the Final Act embodying the results of the Uruguay Round of Multilateral Trade Negotiations. See also Noll, R., 'Regulatory Reform and International Trade Policy', in Ito, T. and Krueger, A.O. (eds), *Deregulation and Interdependence in the Asia-Pacific Region* (University of Chicago/NBER, 2000), 13–54.
[53] Feketekuty, G., 'Assessing and Improving the Architecture of GATS', Sauvé, P. and Stern, R. (eds), *GATS 2000: New Directions in Services Trade Liberalisation* (Brookings Institution, 2000), 85–111 at 90.
[54] Sauvé, P., 'Completing the GATS Framework: Addressing the Uruguay Round Leftovers', *Aussenwirtschaft*, 57, Jahrgang (2002), vol. III, Zurich, Rueger, S., 301–341, at 328.
[55] Article XVI (Market Access) and Article XVII (National Treatment) and Article II MFN.
[56] According to Article XVII, WTO Members are obligated 'to accord to services and service suppliers of any other WTO Member, in respect of all measures affecting the supply of services, treatment no less favourable than that it accords to its own like services and service suppliers'.
[57] Mattoo, A., 'National Treatment in the GATS: Corner-Stone or Pandora's Box?' 31(1) *Journal of World Trade* (February 1997), 107–135.

restrictions on services or service suppliers, regardless of whether they are discriminatory. Under the GATS, quantitative restrictions, such as quotas, are in principle unjustifiable restrictions on trade and are therefore broadly defined. Qualitative restrictions, including restrictions on offensive or harmful publications, are however beyond the scope of Article XVI.

In the *US—Gambling* case, the Appellate Body concluded that a measure is prohibited under Article XVI if it is numerical or quantitative in nature, regardless of whether it is explicitly quantitative in form.[58] In this case, the absolute prohibition of online gambling on moral grounds under various American laws was deemed to be a quantitative restriction. This expansive view arguably imperils important non-discriminatory restrictions used by governments in regulating services, possibly including significant media content related measures.[59] At the very least, the decision makes it hazardous for governments to prohibit particular ways of delivering a service. Nonetheless, the *US—Gambling* decision apparently leaves purely qualitative restrictions outside the scope of Article XVI, even where they have quantitative effects.[60]

The GATS drafters sought to create as much consistency as possible with the GATT. But the demand from member states for flexibility, both in cushioning domestic regulation from the effects of market opening obligations and in allowing selective liberalization, produced a markedly different instrument with many novel features. The most striking of these is that the GATS does not require across the board liberalization. Its trade disciplines only apply to those service sectors in which member states have made specific commitments in schedules to the agreement to open their markets to foreign services and their providers.[61] This sectoral approach gave governments much needed flexibility, enabling them to commit selectively to market opening where possible, while also continuing to protect domestically sensitive services.[62]

The GATS not only divides services into exclusive sectoral categories, but also creates further flexibility based on the manner in which a particular service is delivered. When making positive commitments in relation to a services sector, member states therefore have the additional right to specify which of four named modes of supply are subject to those commitments.[63] This further deviation from the GATT framework, which makes no equivalent distinctions in the supply of

[58] Appellate Body Report, *United States—Measures Affecting the Cross-Border Supply of Gambling and Betting Service*, WT/DS285/AB/R (7 April 2005).

[59] Pauwelyn, J., 'WTO Softens Earlier Condemnation of U.S. Ban on Internet Gambling, but Confirms Broad Reach into Sensitive Domestic Regulation', *ASIL Insight*, (12 April 2005).

[60] 'Nondiscriminatory domestic regulations that address the quality of the service supplied or the quality of the service supplier can be maintained as long as they do not constitute "unnecessary barriers" to trade in services', Wunsch-Vincent, S., *The WTO, The Internet and Trade in Digital Products* (Hart Publishing, 2006), 39.

[61] Article XX: Schedules of Specific Commitments.

[62] Hoekman, B., n. 49 above, 119.

[63] The four modes of supply under the GATS are (1) 'cross border supply' which means the delivery of services from one member state to another by electronic or other means; (2) 'consumption abroad' which refers to travel to another member state to consume services; (3) 'commercial presence' which involves the establishment of a subsidiary, branch or other commercial presence in another member

goods, created a flexible geometry of sectors and modes in which specific commitments could be substantially qualified by member states. Accordingly, member states may modify their commitments in their schedules by adding additional 'terms', 'limitations', and 'conditions' regarding any prohibited quantitative measures and 'conditions' and 'qualifications' regarding any prohibited discriminatory measures.[64]

Securing agreement on the basic architecture of the GATS required years of negotiation, which left an array of basic issues unresolved and therefore open to interpretation and doctrinal development by dispute resolution panels and the Appellate Body. It was not, for example, even clear whether the national treatment discipline applied across all modes of supply or whether a member state could freely discriminate between identical services on the basis of their different modes.[65] In short, the agreement was far from complete when adopted. As Panagiotis Delimatsis has described it,

The breadth of the GATS coverage, the novelty of the issues at stake, the sectoral diversity, the specificities associated with services where the state used to be the monopoly supplier or was actively involved in their supply, the regulatory intensity of several services sectors, and the inherent complexity of the GATS due to the multiple modes of supply are only a few of the justifications for the deficiencies of the GATS.[66]

The GATS, in parallel with the GATT, uses the concept of 'like services and service suppliers' to test for discriminatory treatment. However, determining the likeness of services can be extraordinarily difficult, especially where those services are evolving through the rapid exploitation of new communication technologies. In negotiating their initial commitments during the Uruguay Round, the participating states adopted a framework for the classification of services called the Services Sectoral Classification List (SSCL).[67] The categories of services set out in the SSCL were adapted from a United Nations product classifications code and the Uruguay Round negotiating states were encouraged to follow this classification scheme.[68] However, there was no binding obligation to use it or any other common nomenclature.[69] Moreover, even the majority of member states, who chose to schedule

---

state; and (4) 'presence of natural persons' which refers to entry to another member state to supply services.

[64] GATS, n. 3 above, Articles XVI and XVII.

[65] See Sauvé, P., n. 54 above, 326.

[66] Delimatsis, P., *International Trade in Services and Domestic Regulations* (Oxford University Press, 2007), 33.

[67] WTO, Services Sectoral Classification List, MTN.GNS/W/12 (10 July 1991).

[68] The United Nations Provisional Central Product Classification (CPC) is intended to be an exhaustive guide to non-tradable as well as tradable goods, services and assets, which is used for international statistical purposes. Provisional Central Product Classification, Statistical Papers, Series M No. 77, United Nations (1991). The United Nations Central Product Classification has been revised on several occasions. The latest version is the Central Product Classification, Version 1.1, Statistical Papers, Series M No. 77, United Nations (2004). See Scheduling of Initial Commitments in Trade in Services: Explanatory Note, MTN.GNS/W/164, (1993). Guidelines for the Scheduling of Specific Commitments under the General Agreement on Trade in Services (GATS) Adopted by the Council for Trade in Services on 23 March 2001.

[69] *United States—Gambling and Betting Service*, n. 58 above, para. 176.

their commitments by reference to the SSCL and the related UN code, also used their own national interpretations to resolve ambiguities. Other countries, including the United States, referred to the SSCL, but chose to modify them, using their own domestic classifications for some services.

This inevitably led to textual ambiguities and disputes between member states over their respective rights and obligations under the GATS. In March 2003, Antigua and Barbuda initiated WTO dispute resolution procedures over its dispute with the United States regarding the cross border supply of online gambling and betting services.[70] According to the United States, it had not included gambling and betting services in its GATS commitments. The American commitment to open 'recreational services' to foreign access expressly excluded 'sporting' services, which the United States claimed included gambling and betting under its own definitional rules. In 2005 the WTO Appellate Body found against the United States, deciding that unless states make their own definitions explicit, they are assumed to have followed the SSCL and the corresponding United Nations classifications.[71] The *US—Gambling* case, the first purely GATS case to reach the Appellate Body, resolved several issues regarding its proper interpretation, but also confirmed that confusion over likeness could yield extraordinary commercial opportunities for internet based services.

The great flexibility of the GATS Treaty was fully expected to yield a diversity of commitments across the various services sectors identified in the SSCL. In the field of basic telecommunications, for example, liberalization has re-shaped much of the world's voice and data communications sector. The Uruguay Round negotiations produced the GATS Annex on Telecommunications which obliges state parties to grant access to public telecommunications services on reasonable and non-discriminatory terms. In 1997, WTO member states representing two thirds of the world telecommunications market concluded a further agreement containing substantial commitments to market access for basic telecommunications services.[72] In contrast, European demands for recognition of the distinct cultural importance of audiovisual services in the face of American demands for greater access to European media markets led to an impasse. This was only partially resolved through a pragmatic compromise that left the GATS audiovisual sector without significant liberalization commitments.[73]

Under the structure of the GATS, by refusing to make commitments for audiovisual services, member states forestalled the application of the treaty's domestic regulation, national treatment, and market access obligations. To prevent the application of the MFN obligation, which applies regardless of sectoral commitments, countries determined to protect their audiovisual media resorted to an ad hoc dispensation. During the Uruguay Round, the negotiating states agreed to

---

[70] Ibid.   [71] Ibid., para. 204.

[72] Fourth Protocol to the General Agreement on Trade in Services, S/L/20.

[73] See Chapter 15. See also Graber, C., 'Audiovisual Policy: The Stumbling Block of Trade Liberalisation' in Geradin, D. and Luff, D. (eds), *The WTO and Global Convergence in Telecommunications and Audiovisual Services* (Cambridge University Press, 2003).

permit a one off opportunity for member states to create exemptions from the GATS MFN obligation before the treaty entered into force.[74] In this way, the European Union and its member states put in place a block of protective exemptions relating to various pan-European and country specific measures.[75]

Despite the rift over audiovisual services, the creation of a legal framework for the liberalization of trade in services was a major feat, regardless of its structural deficiencies and the modest commitments of the member states.[76] The negotiators had focused their attention on the conceptual and architectural work needed to bring the basic elements of the agreement into being. These included the definitions of trade in services, the rules and principles to govern liberalization and the mechanisms for determining the scope of the treaty.[77] As far as actual liberalization was concerned, their goal for the Uruguay Round of services negotiations was simply to lock member states into existing levels of market access.[78] This strategy was, in the event, not entirely successful. 'Not only is the coverage of specific commitments limited for many countries, but in many cases the commitments are less liberal than the policies that are actually applied—that is, many governments refrained from binding the status quo.'[79]

The major achievement of the GATS was therefore to set in motion the process of reducing barriers to trade in services, rather than to achieve substantial reductions. Despite these cautious beginnings, the Uruguay Round launched the GATS as a legal and institutional project for the progressive liberalization of trade in services.[80] Its provisions compelled member states to participate in future negotiations not only to open services markets to more foreign competition but also to widen and deepen the scope of the GATS disciplines.[81] This ambitious second phase of services liberalization was however soon to become mired in the setbacks of the Doha Round.

---

[74] GATS Annex on Article II MFN Exemptions. See also Adlung, R. and Carzaniga, A., 'MFN Exemptions Under the General Agreement on Trade in Services: Grandfathers Striving for Immortality?' 12(2) *Journal of International Economic Law* (2009), 357–392.

[75] See WTO, *Communication from the European Communities and Its Member States*, TN/S/O/EEC (10 June 2003).

[76] See Sauve, P., n. 54 above, 302–304.

[77] See Hoekman, B., n. 49 above, 120.

[78] See Feketekuty, G., n. 53 above, 85–111, at 91.

[79] See Hoekman, B., n. 49 above, 121.

[80] See GATS, n. 3 above, Articles XIX to XXI.

[81] Article XIX of the GATS required that new negotiations begin not later than five years after the WTO Agreement entered into force with the goal of achieving a progressively higher level of liberalization. The resulting GATS 2000 negotiations were later merged into the comprehensive trade negotiations finally launched in November 2001 at Doha following the debacle at Seattle. See Doha Ministerial Declaration WT/MIN(01)DEC/W/1 ('Doha Declaration endorses the work already done, reaffirms the negotiating guidelines and procedures, and establishes some key elements of the timetable...').

The media in the Doha Round

The Doha Development Round agenda includes major objectives that are immensely important to the further liberalization of multilateral trade in media goods and services. In the services negotiations, however, little has been accomplished. This is moreover the form in which most cross border trade in information and entertainment content now occurs as a consequence of the digitization of content and the rise of the internet and other electronic delivery platforms. Given that services negotiations began well before the Doha Round, this lack of progress underscores the general complexity of market access in services sectors.[82] It also reflects the intense social and political sensitivity of the media sector and the resistance of member states to external obligations that would require significant changes in their media laws or regulatory controls.

The stagnation of the Doha Round led to two important shifts in the halting liberalization of global trade in services. Within the WTO, negotiation, once the principal method of multilateral liberalization, gave way to a judicially led evolution in trade law.[83] As discussed below, the work of the WTO panels and Appellate Body has, for example, substantially developed the rules governing general exceptions to the primary obligations.[84] These exceptions for recognized public policy purposes, such as the protection of public morals and public order, are of great relevance to the domestic media state relationship. They provide essential justifications for restrictions on the media that have a discriminatory effect on foreign sourced media goods and services.

The second shift in trade law occurred outside the WTO. In the absence of a collective Doha Round set of agreements, many countries turned to bilateral or regional preferential trade agreements to achieve gains currently unobtainable on a multilateral basis.[85] While the rules of the WTO constitute the basic framework for most of these agreements, many contain a range of additional or 'WTO plus'

---

[82] On the limited progress of negotiations on trade in services during the Doha Round, see Sauvé, P., 'Been There, Not [Quite] [Yet] Done That: Lessons and Challenges in Services Trade', in Panizzon, M., Pohl, N., and Sauvé, P. (eds), n. 26 above, 599, and Adlung, R., *Services Liberalization from a WTO/GATS Perspective: In Search of Volunteers*, World Trade Organization, Staff Working Paper ERSD-2009-5, February 2009.

[83] Goldstein, J. and Steinberg, R.H., *Regulatory Shift: The Rise of Judicial Liberalization at the WTO*. UCLA School of Law, Law-Econ Research Paper No. 07-15.

[84] GATT, Article XX and GATS, Article XIV.

[85] 'Uncertainty over the outcome has highlighted the growing importance of bilateral free trade agreements (FTAs) concluded by the United States and the European Union in breaking new ground in trade liberalisation', Hufbauer G.C. and Schott, J.J., n. 41 above; 'The PTAs (*Preferential Trade Agreements*) reviewed highlight that the United States, the main *demandeur* and home to leading international suppliers, has made significant headway in terms of obtaining certain guarantees of access in this sector (audiovisual)', Roy, M., Marchetti, J., and Lim, H., n. 41 above, 38; Bhagwati, J. and Panagariya, A., 'Bilateral trade treaties are a sham', *Financial Times* (London, 13 July 2003); Abbott, F.M., 'A New Dominant Trade Species Emerges: Is Bilateralism a Threat?' 10(3) *Journal of International Economic Law* (2007), 571–583; Herrmann, C., 'Bilateral and Regional Trade Agreements as a Challenge to the Multilateral Trading System' (February 2008). EUI LAW Working Paper No. 2008/9.

elements.[86] In several bilateral agreements between the United States and specific trade partners, for example, there are major obligations to remove restrictions on trade in audiovisual services, sidestepping the standstill compromise of the Uruguay Round in this sector.[87] Secondary rule making of this kind will undoubtedly have an impact on the future development of trade rules in the WTO. Indeed, these agreements are partly driven by a quest 'to shape an emerging legal order and to do so in novel ways that move policy and open markets beyond WTO approaches, rules and architectures'.[88]

One of the central issues that has developed both judicially within the WTO and by negotiated agreement outside the WTO is the treatment of electronic commerce.[89] While the purchase of digitized content through the internet now occurs globally on a vast scale, its status under the rules of the WTO remains unresolved.[90] The technical issue of classification sits at the heart of these arguments. Classification is critically important in WTO law because it not only governs the legal boundary between goods and services, but is also essential in determining whether particular goods or services are 'like', which is a prerequisite to the ultimate decision whether a domestic measure discriminates against foreign sourced goods or services and their suppliers.[91] The arguments over the proper classification of electronic commerce are moreover being played out against the background of the increasingly anachronistic classifications of the SSCL.[92] These classifications, decided in the early 1990s, have made it difficult to ground the debate over electronic commerce in the framework of the GATS, as its own classifications for services have become part of the disagreement.

When the potential for global internet based commerce became apparent, the United States was concerned that this promising new form of globalized commerce would be stifled by foreign domestic regulation.[93] Consequently, it argued that

---

[86] Roy, M., Marchetti, J., and Lim, H., 'The Race Towards Preferential Trade Agreements in Services: How Much Market Access is Really Achieved?' in Panizzon, M., Pohl, N., and Sauvé, P. (eds), n. 26 above, 77.

[87] See, for example, *Australia—United States Free Trade Agreement: Non-Conforming Measures*, Annexes One and Two. See also Chapter 15.

[88] Delimatsis, P., Diebold, N., Molinuevo, M., Panizzon, M., and Sauvé, P., 'Developing Trade Rules for Services: A Case of Fragmented Coherence?' Working Paper No. 2009/38.

[89] World Trade Organization, Council for Trade in Services, *Audiovisual Services: Background Note by the Secretariat* (S/C/W/40) (15 June 1998). See also Peng, S., 'Trade in Telecommunications Services: Doha and Beyond', 41(2) *Journal of World Trade* (2007), 293–317.

[90] 'Electronic commerce' has been defined in the following terms, '[e]xclusively for the purposes of the work programme, and without prejudice to its outcome, the term "electronic commerce" is understood to mean the production, distribution, marketing, sale or delivery of goods and services by electronic means', Work Programme on Electronic Commerce, adopted by the General Council on 25 September 1998, WT/L/274 (30 September 1998). See also Wunsch-Vincent, S., 'Trade Rules for the Digital Age, in Panizzon, M., Pohl, N., and Sauvé, P. (eds), n. 26 above, 497.

[91] Cossy, M., 'Some Thoughts on The Concept of 'Likeness' in the GATS', in Panizzon, M., Pohl N. and Sauvé P., n. 26 above, 327.

[92] The United Nations Central Product Classification has been updated several times since it was used to create the SSCL in 1991. The most recent version, CPC Ver. 2, was completed in December 2008.

[93] The United States has worked to protect the interests of its computer programme and games producers as well as its films and television programmes industries in the development of the rules for trade in digitized products. Wunsch-Vincent, S., n. 60 above, 109.

electronically delivered products fell outside established trading rules. Or, at the very least, they should be subject to the disciplines of the GATT rather than the opt-in flexibility of the GATS.[94] The American government also urged the global adoption of principles for regulating electronic commerce based on transparency, light regulation, and no customs duties.[95] While other governments conceded that the internet was something radically new, many were opposed to the creation of a *sui generis*, liberalized field of trade law, which seemed likely to destabilize domestic regulatory regimes. From that perspective, electronic commerce was neither *sui generis* nor subject to the GATT, but fell properly within the GATS 'cross border' mode of supply.[96] This would allow states to absorb the impact of cross border electronic commerce on a piecemeal, sector by sector basis.

In 1998, the Second WTO Ministerial Conference created a work programme to resolve differences over the application of WTO law and practice to electronic commerce. The working group responsible for this programme reached an informal consensus that the vast majority of transactions on the internet are services that are covered by GATS.[97] Several member states, including the United States, have however not conceded that downloaded products are governed by the GATS.[98] Yet, so far, there is no formal declaration that the WTO's rules and obligations apply to digital trade. The Appellate Body has nonetheless determined in the *US— Gambling* case that online gambling, a form of electronic commerce, is a cross border mode of service under the GATS, but did not address the question of downloaded products.[99] Thus judicial conclusion has yet to be collectively affirmed by the member states in a negotiated WTO instrument.

The application of GATS rules to cross border electronic commerce is of great importance to the future treatment of trade in media content. It is also hugely contentious as it concerns both the distinction between goods and services and the classification of specific services.[100] The cross border supply of broadcast, linear television to the public is plainly within the scope of the GATS 'audiovisual services' sector, which was left ring fenced under the Uruguay Round settlement between the United States and the European Union.[101] Yet, in reaching that pragmatic compromise, they left open the question of whether new methods of

---

[94] Baker, S.A., Lichtenbaum, P., Shenk, M., and Yeo, M., 'E-Products and the WTO', 35 *International Lawyer* (Spring 2001), 5.

[95] United States Government, *A Framework for Global Electronic Commerce* (The White House, 1997).

[96] See Wunsch-Vincent, S., n. 60 above, 52–60.

[97] WTO, Economic Commerce Briefing Note: *Work Programme Reflects Growing Importance,* 2001. See also Wunsch-Vincent, S., n. 60 above, 171.

[98] Wu, T., 'The World Trade Law of Censorship and Internet Filtering', 7 *Chicago Journal of International Law* (2006), 263 at 270.

[99] *United States—Gambling and Betting Service*, n. 58 above. See also Wunsch-Vincent, n. 60 above, 175.

[100] Voon, n. 17 above, 70–75.

[101] Under the WTO Services Sectoral Classification List, n. 67 above, 'Audiovisual Services' (a subset of Communications Services) divided into motion picture and video tape production, motion picture projection, radio and television, radio and television transmission, sound recording, and other (audiovisual) services.

delivering audiovisual content would also fall within that classification.[102] Further-more, even if a service that supplies audiovisual programmes over the internet at the individual request of a consumer in another country is indeed an 'audiovisual service' under the GATS, it is not clear what mode of supply is involved.[103] Should electronically delivered service transactions be classified as cross-border transactions (mode 1) or as consumption abroad (mode 2), which is typically subject to less restrictions in scheduled commitments?[104] In the *US—Gambling* case, the Appellate Body seems to assume, but does not make explicit, that online gambling services are classified as mode 1.

While these questions have lingered for a decade without clear resolution in the WTO, electronic commerce has become a common element in recent preferential trade agreements,[105] although these are generally limited to what is necessary to secure the benefits of greater electronic commerce between the states concerned without prejudging the final outcome of WTO decisions on classification. It is moreover apparent that despite uncertainty in the trade rules, global electronic commerce has continued to grow and change. In place of the once highly managed international trade in films and programmes, content digitization and internet based distribution has created a globalized marketplace for media content.

This occurred in part because, in most countries, internet based transactions began to develop in an apparent regulatory void. Consequently, the growth of cross border trade in electronic commerce has not required the pruning of dense, long standing regulatory regimes, as is necessary in the broadcast media sector. Instead, it has merely required governmental restraint in bringing those legal and regulatory restrictions to bear on emerging electronic services. Initially, this also involved the question whether states even had the capacity to impose such restrictions on internet based services.[106] As that question has been largely resolved in their favour, the focus is now on the terms on which those restrictions are imposed.

In short, the sale of information and entertainment content over the internet has been absorbed into the centuries old relationship between the media and the state. Certainly, the demand for digitized content over evolving electronic networks creates new opportunities to escape existing controls on the publication and distribution of media content. Settling the trade rules for electronic commerce is thus directly connected to the question of how a state should legitimately conduct itself and, more particularly, the extent to which it is liberal democratic

---

[102] '[M]ost of the digital content delivery services, like video-on-demand over the internet, are inseparable combinations of telecommunications, software and audiovisual services that rely on commitments on these content services themselves and their digital transmission', Wunsch-Vincent, S., n. 60 above, 71.

[103] Ibid., 67–70.

[104] Wunsch-Vincent has argued that the 'audiovisual services' classification is not suited to new media services, given the different elements involved. Ibid., 74.

[105] See the 2003 United States–Singapore Free Trade Agreement. See also n. 26 above.

[106] For example, Murray, A., *The Regulation of Cyberspace* (Routledge-Cavendish, 2006).

in character.[107] Classification decisions that circumvent existing barriers to foreign content are grounded in market based economic justifications for greater liberty, which readily combine with political and moral ones. This is, in effect, the dual argument for the liberty to publish. The preference to integrate electronic commerce into existing media laws and regulatory regimes is, on the other hand, grounded in the security, authority, and legitimacy needs of the state and through it collective and individual interests in restricting expression.

Few states attempt a complete prohibition on the inflow of foreign information and entertainment content, which is difficult to enforce, causes domestic resentment and blocks information that the regime also finds useful. The interest of the state is to ensure that international rules do not interfere with the measures it deems necessary to filter foreign content of harmful or objectionable information and ideas. This of course applies to liberal democracies as much as theocracies. The GATS therefore offers several assurances to the state in this regard, providing a flexible architecture that allows cautious liberalization in sensitive sectors and a principle of non-discrimination that preserves domestic autonomy in content rules. Within this context, the treatment of electronic commerce under WTO law is a key issue for national media law and regulation.

Nonetheless, the impact of the GATS on the domestic media state relationship is not simply a question of old versus new media regulatory regimes. It is also enmeshed in Doha Round debates over whether to deepen the disciplines that govern trade in services, including the curbs on domestic regulations that unnecessarily obstruct cross border trade. In the Doha Round, work on the domestic regulation of services has focused on the incomplete provisions of GATS Article VI.[108] This article sketches out several obligations intended to discipline the manner in which domestic measures are applied and thereby minimize their trade distorting effects. Article VI:1 provides that 'measures of general application affecting trade in services' must be 'administered in a reasonable, objective and impartial manner'. This vague language was as close as the Uruguay negotiators could come to an agreement on how to treat non-discriminatory, non-quantitative measures affecting trade in services.[109] Aside from the obligations of Article VI:2, which concern the right of access to objective and impartial review of administrative measures, the provisions of Article VI only apply to the sectors and modes in which a member state has made scheduled commitments.[110]

---

[107] Anupam Chander, 'Trade 2.0', 34 *Yale Journal of International Law* (2009), 281.

[108] Delimatsis, P., 'Due Process and "Good" Regulation Embedded in the GATS—Disciplining Regulatory Behaviour in Services through Article VI of the GATS', 10(1) *Journal of International Economic Law* (2006), 13–50, Wouters, J., and Coppens, D., 'GATS and domestic regulations: balancing the right to regulate and trade liberalization', in Andenas, M., and Alexander, K. (eds), *The World Trade Organization and Trade in Services* (Brill/Nijhof, 2007), 57, Woll, C. and Artigas, A., 'When Trade Liberalization Turns into Regulatory Reform: The Impact on Business-Government Relations in International Trade Politics', 1(2) *Regulation and Governance* (2007), 121–138.

[109] Delimatsis, P., n. 66 above, 167.

[110] Adlung, R., 'Public Services and the GATS', 9(2) *Journal of International Economic Law* (2006), 455–485.

To remedy their failure to reach concrete conclusions in the Uruguay Round, the drafters included a commitment in Article VI:4 to further negotiations. These are supposed to develop disciplines ensuring that, *inter alia*, domestic measures relating to standards and licensing do not form unnecessary barriers to trade in services.[111] This work, which is ongoing, began in 2000 under the specially constituted GATS Working Party on Domestic Regulation and was formally reinvigorated in 2005 at the Hong Kong WTO Ministerial Conference.[112] One of the key issues for the Working Group is the meaning of 'necessity' in Article VI:4, which states that any disciplines negotiated shall aim to ensure that 'qualification requirements and procedures, technical standards and licensing requirements' are 'not more burdensome than necessary to ensure the quality of the service'.[113]

Efforts to establish a 'necessity' test for domestic regulations under Article VI have encountered strong resistance from member states acutely concerned about the potential intrusion of trade law into sensitive public policy choices. The Article VI:4 standard of 'not more burdensome than necessary' suggests the development of a 'least restrictive measure' test.[114] Yet necessity tests of this kind vary considerably and may even include an assessment of whether a measure's restrictive effects on trade outweigh its claimed contribution to the public good in the state concerned.[115] The Appellate Body has, for example, created a least restrictive measure test along these lines in developing the general exceptions to trade disciplines of the GATT and the GATS.[116] While an expansive test of this sort may be justifiable when used to limit avoidance of the WTO's primary non-discrimination obligations, it seems less so when applied to universally applicable domestic measures, which are presumed to be legitimate under WTO principles.

Over the past decade, trade specialists have also argued that the GATS will not become a fully effective trade instrument until it acquires a general necessity test

---

[111] GATS, n. 3 above, Article VI 4: 'With a view to ensuring that measures relating to qualification requirements and procedures, technical standards and licensing requirements do not constitute unnecessary barriers to trade in services, the Council for Trade in Services shall, through appropriate bodies it may establish, develop any necessary disciplines.'

[112] Hong Kong Ministerial Declaration (WT/MIN(05)/DEC) on the Doha Work Programme.

[113] GATS, Article VI:4(b).

[114] The mandate creation of a 'not more burdensome than necessary' standard suggests that Article VI should be patterned after the GATT Agreement on the Application of Sanitary and Phytosanitary Measures and the Agreement on Technical Barriers to Trade (TBT), which create similar necessity standards for certain categories of regulations on goods. Article 2.2 of the TBT states that 'Members shall ensure that technical regulations are not prepared, adopted or applied with a view to or with the effect of creating unnecessary obstacles to international trade. For this purpose, technical regulations shall not be more trade-restrictive than necessary to fulfil a legitimate objective, taking account of the risks non-fulfilment would create.'

[115] Mattoo, A. and Sauvé, P., 'Domestic Regulation And Trade In Services: Looking Ahead', in Mattoo, A., and Sauve, P., (eds), *Domestic Regulation and Service Trade Liberalization* (World Bank and Oxford University Press, 2003), 221. See also Communication from the European Communities and their Member States, *Domestic Regulation: Necessity and Transparency*, S/WPDR/W/14 (1 May 2001), For a discussion of the concept of 'necessity' as used in Article VI:4 and other GATS articles, see Trachtman, J.P., 'Lessons for the GATS from Existing WTO Rules on Domestic Regulation', in Mattoo and Sauvé (eds), *Domestic Regulation & Services Trade Liberalization* (World Bank and Oxford University Press, 2003), 57–81.

[116] GATT, n. 3 above, XX and GATS, n. 3 above, XIV.

rather than one limited to the scope of Article VI.[117] This proposed horizontal test would therefore apply to the GATS national treatment and most favoured nation obligations. According to this argument, a general necessity test would improve the effectiveness of these non-discrimination obligations, shifting the focus of the legal inquiry away from the issue of likeness towards its proper concern, which is the evaluation of de facto discrimination.[118] In 2009, however, the Working Party retreated from the difficult question of how to refine the 'not more burdensome than necessary' requirement. Instead, it accepted draft Disciplines on Domestic Regulations that only required that 'measures relating to licensing requirements and procedures, qualification requirements and procedures, and technical standards shall be pre-established, based on objective and transparent criteria and relevant to the supply of the services to which they apply'.[119] If the Disciplines are finally adopted by the member states in this form, the Article VI necessity test would simply apply in a limited, provisional form.[120]

While the Working Party's retreat from a robust Article VI necessity test is undoubtedly a lost opportunity to make the GATS a more effective restraint on domestic measures that inhibit trade, it is also a realistic response to the concerns of the member states.[121] The GATS is still a relatively young and institutionally weak trade law regime. It has yet to achieve the basic goal of bringing most global trade in services under WTO disciplines prohibiting discrimination against foreign services or their suppliers.[122] A necessity discipline aimed at non-discriminatory measures, which would potentially cut much deeper into member state regulatory autonomy, may well have to wait until the nature of GATS obligations have become clearer through trade practice and case decisions.[123]

As Dani Rodrik has argued, deepening economic integration through a reduction in domestic 'policy space' is likely to push the WTO into crisis by placing too

---

[117] See Delimatsis, P., n. 66 above. See also Mattoo, A., and Sauvé, P., n. 115 above, 221. Delimatsis, P., 'Concluding the WTO Services Negotiations on Domestic Regulation—Walk Unafraid' (24 August 2009). TILEC Discussion Paper No. 2009-032.

[118] Delimatsis, P., n. 66 above, Part IV. See also Pauwelyn, J., n. 43 above.

[119] Working Party on Domestic Regulation, Informal Note by the Chairman, *Draft Disciplines on Domestic Regulation pursuant to GATS Article VI:4* (Second Revision), 20 March 2009, para. 11. See also the draft 'Disciplines on Domestic Regulation Pursuant to Gats Article VI:4'—Annotated Text, 14 March 2010, and, Delimatsis, P., n. 117 above.

[120] According to Article VI:5, in the absence of disciplines created to fulfill the requirements of VI:4, member states shall not apply licensing and qualification requirements and technical standards that nullify or impair scheduled commitments in a manner which do not comply with the criteria outlined in subparagraphs VI:4(a), (b) or (c); and could not reasonably have been expected of that Member at the time the specific commitments in those sectors were made.

[121] For an example of those concerns, see Gould, E., 'Developments in the GATS Domestic Regulation Negotiations', *Canadian Centre for Policy Alternatives* (4 September 2009).

[122] Mattoo, A., 'Services in a Development Round: Three Goals and Three Proposals', World Bank Policy Research Working Paper No. 3718 (September 2005).

[123] Hoekman, B., n. 49 above, questions whether adopting the 'necessity' principle (familiar to the EU) to determine whether domestic regulation is legitimate can work in the WTO context. See also Mattoo, A. and Sauvé, P., (2003) 'Domestic Regulation and the GATS: Looking Ahead', in Mattoo, A. and Sauvé, P. (eds), *Domestic Regulation and Service Trade Liberalization* (World Bank and University Press, 2003), 221–230.

much pressure on the fault lines between 'deep integration, national sovereignty, and democracy'.[124] From this political economy perspective, a pure economic analysis of the costs and benefits of trade liberalization fails to capture the inherently political nature of the balance between market and non-market public policy choices.[125]

Individual member states' perceptions of what policies fall on one side of the line and what falls on the other are going to vary depending on ideology, regulatory traditions, and so forth, all of which generate intuitions about whether someone's regulatory behaviour looks like 'normal' public policy or, rather, like something that might only be done in the circumstances for protectionist reasons.[126]

Consequently, substantial economic integration in the European Union has required the development of common political, social, and cultural standards balanced against the autonomy interests of the member states.[127] In the WTO, where there is no equivalent capacity to develop common standards for non-market public policy, even negative integration carries high risks for regulatory autonomy.[128]

Many governments participating in the Uruguay Round were thus determined to limit the capacity of the GATS to interfere in their choice of non-discriminatory regulatory policies or methods.[129] The preamble to the treaty therefore expressly recognizes, 'the right of Members to regulate—and to introduce new regulations, on the supply of services within their territories in order to meet national policy objectives'. More recently, the Appellate Body has determined that while the 'right to regulate' is an inherent right of member states, it must be exercised in a manner consistent with WTO Agreements.[130] However, in the same case, it also decided that this right must be exercised in a manner consistent with the WTO obligations assumed by the member state. The GATS 'right to regulate' is therefore likely to operate as a factor in interpreting the extent of member state obligations,

---

[124] Rodrik, D., 'How to Save Globalization from its Cheerleaders', KSG Working Papers, No. RWP07-038, 25. Similarly Keohan and Nye have argued that '[m]ultilateral institutions do not compete so much with domestic institutions as rely on them. They will only thrive when substantial space is preserved for domestic political processes.' Keohane, R. and Nye, J.S. Jr, 'The Club Model of Multilateral Cooperation and Problems of Democratic Legitimacy', in Keohane, R. (ed.), *Power and Governance in a Partially Globalized World* (Routledge, 2002), 225.

[125] Howse, R. 'From Politics to Technocracy—and Back Again: The Fate of the Multilateral Trading Regime', 96 *American Journal of International Law* (2002), 94 at 95. See also Ruggie, J., 'Embedded Liberalism and the Postwar Economic Regimes' in 62 *Constructing The World Polity: Essays On International Institutionalization* (1998).

[126] Howse, n. 125 above, 96.

[127] '[N]ational differences and customs and the need for the regulator to take account of local realities, as far as frequency management is concerned, require full respect for the subsidiarity principle in this field to the benefit of the national bodies set up by each member state.' *Digital Age: European Audiovisual Policy*, Report from the High Level Group on Audiovisual Policy.

[128] Rodrik, D., 'How Far Will International Economic Integration Go?' *Journal of Economic Perspectives*, Winter 2000. See also Rodrik, D., n. 124 above.

[129] Pauwelyn, J.H.B., 'Rien ne Va Plus? Distinguishing Domestic Regulation From Market Access in GATT and GATS', 4(2) *World Trade Review* (2005), 131–170.

[130] *China—Measures Affecting Trading Rights and Distribution Services for Certain Publications and Audiovisual Entertainment Products* (WT/DS363/AB/R), (Appellate Body Report, December 2009), paras 221–222.

but not as the basis for any substantive balancing of member state regulatory autonomy and those obligations. Consequently, if the member states do not resolve the question of how WTO obligations should affect non-discriminatory measures that impair scheduled services commitments, this may well occur through the WTO panel and Appellate Body adjudication.[131]

The development of GATS disciplines governing domestic regulation could potentially reach deep into the domestic media state relationship. In most countries, many aspects of media content are subject to legal or other restrictions. The range and diversity of these measures therefore constitutes a significant obstacle to trade in information and entertainment content, not only because of the high cost of compliance in different national markets, but also because qualitative content standards are easily abused and exercised in bad faith. The removal of non-discriminatory measures that excessively hamper trade in media services would therefore substantially enhance the liberty to publish and distribute media content across borders. Yet, to achieve that result, those disciplines will demand that states justify their non-market public policy measures according to external standards, which many states are plainly unwilling to accept.

Investment and subsidies in the media sector

Restrictions on foreign investment can also have profoundly limiting effects on the liberty to publish and distribute media content. Indeed, these restrictions are often put in place precisely because the owners or controllers of a media company are presumed to wield huge influence over its editorial decisions. Restrictions on foreign ownership or control of media enterprises are therefore common through-out the world, including the United States and other liberal democracies.[132] They also tend to be especially restrictive in the broadcast media sector, which is still widely regarded as having the greatest influence over public attitudes and beliefs.

In this area, WTO law has no counterpart to the European Union's well developed rules on the freedom of establishment.[133] There is also no multilateral agreement comparable to the GATT and GATS establishing comprehensive rules for global foreign direct investment based on principles of transparency and non-discrimination. Instead, the WTO offers a number of piecemeal solutions. In the Uruguay Round, the member states negotiated the Agreement on Trade Related Investment Measures (TRIMS), which only applies to measures affecting trade in goods.[134] This agreement is chiefly aimed at ensuring that member states do not

---

[131] See Delimatsis, P. et al., n. 88 above.

[132] See, for example, United States, Communications Act of 1934, s. 310, which, *inter alia*, creates restrictions on foreign investment in United States companies that hold a broadcast or common carrier radio.

[133] See Barnard, C., n. 7 above, ch 10.

[134] Agreement on Trade-Related Investment Measures, (15 April 1994), Marrakesh Agreement Establishing the World Trade Organization, Annex 1A. See also Dimascio, N. and Pauwelyn, J., 'Nondiscrimination in Trade and Investment Treaties: worlds apart or two sides of the same coin', 102 *American Journal of International Law* (2008), 48–89.

discriminate against foreign goods by imposing conditions on foreign investors that favour domestic products. The TRIMS does not therefore directly address the question of restrictions on foreign ownership or control of producers of media products, such as newspapers and magazines.

The GATS prohibits discriminatory restrictions under its rules concerning the establishment of a service through a 'commercial presence' in the territory of another member state.[135] These rules come into effect where a member state has made scheduled commitments in a services sector and permits cross border supply of services through a commercial presence under mode 3. This means that the GATS only addresses investment issues in relation to this mode of supply of services and not more broadly as a distinct subject for non-discriminatory treatment. Given the impasse over audiovisual services, it also has no immediate application to media services for most member states.

The Doha Development Round agenda provided for negotiations to work towards a broader WTO investment agreement. These negotiations, however, began under the shadow of the OECD sponsored project to create a Multilateral Agreement on Investment (MAI), which collapsed acrimoniously in 1998.[136] Despite the exclusion of developing countries from the MAI negotiations, the leading market economies could not overcome their differences to reach a consensus on politically sensitive aspects of foreign investment.[137] These included demands for the right to restrict foreign investment for cultural and social policy purposes.[138]

These negotiations were also hampered by the difficulties of factoring investment related issues into complex multilateral negotiations relating to trade in goods and services. In the Doha Round, the WTO entrusted this objective to the Working Group on Trade and Investment, which was charged with preparations for the launch of full negotiations on a multilateral investment agreement at the fifth

---

[135] Sauvé, P., 'Multilateral Rules on Investment: Is Forward Movement Possible?' 9(2) *Journal of International Economic Law* (2006), 325–355. See also Sauvé, P. and Wilkie, C., 'Investment Liberalization in GATS' in Sauvé, P. and Stern, R. (eds), n. 51 above, 331–363.

[136] The MAI negotiations were launched by governments at the Annual Meeting of the OECD Council at Ministerial level in May 1995. See Multilateral Agreement on Investment Documentation from the Negotiations, Introduction, <http://www.oecd.org>.

[137] Kobrin, S., 'The MAI and the Clash of Globalizations', *Foreign Policy* (Fall 1998), 112. See also Kennedy, K.C., 'A WTO Agreement on Investment: A Solution in Search of a Problem?' 24 *University of Pennsylvania Journal of International Economic Law* (2003), 77, and Kurtz, J., 'NGOs, the Internet and International Economic Policy Making: The Failure of the OECD Multilateral Agreement on Investment', 3(2) *Melbourne Journal of International Law* (2002), 213.

[138] These concerns quickly shifted to the Doha Round negotiations. See, for example, Neil, G., 'WTO's New Round of Trade Negotiations: Doha Development Agenda Threatens Cultural Diversity', *Report to International Network on Cultural Diversity*, 20 November 2001: 'An investment agreement could force a re-evaluation of a significant number of cultural policies, including: prohibitions, limits or restrictions on foreign ownership in the cultural industries; public service broadcasters and other public institutions, since these might be perceived as unfair competitors for private foreign investors; regulations that discriminate against foreign broadcasting or publishing interests; co-production treaties; even financial subsidy programs if these discriminate against foreign firms or individuals. Should the agreement include an investor-state dispute settlement system that permits individual firms to sue foreign governments, the potential for challenges by multinational firms in the entertainment business would be great.'

WTO Ministerial Conference in 2003.[139] By that year, however, it had become obvious that the member states were too divided to include an investment agreement in the already delayed and tortuous negotiations on trade in goods and services. The following year, the WTO General Council therefore ruled out substantive negotiations on investment rules during the Doha Round.

In the absence of progress towards a multilateral agreement, many governments have shifted their attention to securing bilateral and regional investment agreements. These frequently include non-discrimination and other market access obligations that apply to media related investments.[140] Some of these are sufficiently long standing to have yielded arbitral decisions on the treatment of foreign investors in the media sector, including radio and television.[141] Consequently, while a multilateral agreement of investment is not presently on the horizon, the development of common principles is ongoing. Arbitral decisions on bilateral or regional agreements coupled with WTO adjudication on TRIMS obligations or GATS mode 3 services commitments could therefore gradually yield a 'a more coherent international framework for investment in services through the interpretation of similar principles in a uniform manner'.[142]

WTO work on subsidies has also moved forward in a similar piecemeal fashion. However, unlike rules on investment, subsidies involve positive rather than negative state intervention in markets for goods and services. In other words, international trade law chiefly concerns the removal of discriminatory and some non-discriminatory restraints on trade. In that context, establishing disciplines to control positive state intervention is a secondary, and still largely undeveloped, goal for multilateral trade law.

In principle, the WTO trade regime should also bring about reductions in subsidies and other forms of positive intervention in media markets that disadvantage foreign competitors. The use of state resources to support the delivery of services is however an exceptionally well developed, universal public policy tool. 'Subsidies are the most efficient instrument for pursuing non-economic objectives—to ensure universal service, to promote regional development, to offset income inequalities, and so forth.'[143] Many governments have therefore resisted external controls on their freedom to subsidize domestic goods and services, especially when those controls are proposed in the wider international sphere where their evolution is unpredictable.

Since the distant beginnings of the mass media, governments have used state ownership, monopolies, subsidies, and other forms of state intervention to achieve

---

[139] Doha Ministerial Declaration, n. 5 above, 'Relationship Between Trade and Investment', paras 20–22. Fifth WTO Ministerial Conference (Singapore, November 2001): Ministerial Declaration (13 December 2001), Wt/Min(01)/Dec/1, 'Investment and Competition', para. 20.

[140] For example, Australia–United States Free Trade Agreement.

[141] Peterson, L., 'International investment law and media disputes: a complement to WTO law', *Columbia FDI Perspectives*, No. 17, 27 January 2010. See also Treaty between the United States of America and Ukraine Concerning the Encouragement and Reciprocal Protection of Investment, and ICSID Case No. ARB/06/18. *Joseph C. Lemire v. Ukraine.*

[142] See Delimatsis, P. et al., n. 88 above.

[143] See Hoekman, B., n. 49 above.

their media policy goals. While these methods of direct control are a well known hallmark of military dictatorships and one party states, they are just as often found in liberal democracies.[144] In Europe, where media public policy in the member states is essentially market based, market failure arguments sustain a wide range of public ownership and subsidy interventions. From a trade law perspective, these tend to skew the functioning of media markets by privileging selected content providers or distributors and disadvantaging others, including foreign competitors. The European Union attempts to control the use of subsidies in the media sector for precisely this reason.[145]

The creation of subsidies disciplines for services is, as one would expect, one of the more contentious elements in the evolving rules of the GATS. Subsidies fall within the treaty's definition of measures affecting trade and are therefore caught by its non-discrimination obligations. However these only apply in sectors where a member state has made a scheduled commitment, but has not excluded subsidies from that commitment.[146] Consequently, the Uruguay Round pragmatic compromise on audiovisual services has left domestic media services outside the reach of non-discrimination obligations. Moreover, even where a scheduled commitment does include subsidies, the GATS non-discrimination obligations will only apply to the providers of 'like' services located within its territory.[147]

At the conclusion of the Uruguay Round, the negotiating states could not agree on any specific rules for subsidies, but did include a general statement in Article XV of the GATS on the potential negative effects of subsidies on trade in services.[148] This article mandated negotiations to establish horizontal disciplines to limit the trade distorting effects of subsidies.[149] These negotiations, which were absorbed into the Doha Round agenda, have centred on the adaptation of the WTO Agreement of Subsidies and Countervailing Measures (SCM), which applies to export subsidies for goods, to the more complicated problems of domestic services subsidies.[150] Some member states have resisted the inclusion of strict definitions or conditions for services subsidies and have even proposed adopting an SCM type 'green box' exemption for subsidies granted for recognized social or non-economic objectives.[151] Recent bilateral trade agreements have encountered

---

[144] On the role of public service media in Europe, see Part IV: Intervention in Media Markets.
[145] Ibid.
[146] Poretti, P., 'Waiting for Godot: subsidy disciplines in services trade', in Panizzon, M., Pohl, N., and Sauvé, P., n. 26 above, 466–488. See also Poretti, P., *The Regulation of Subsidies within the General Agreement on Trade in Services—Problems and Perspectives* (Kluwer Law International, 2009), ch 8.
[147] Poretti, P., n. 146 above.
[148] GATS, n. 3 above, Article XV, which states that '[m]embers recognize that, in certain circumstances, subsidies may have distortive effects on trade in services'. See Herold, A., 'European Public Film Support Within The WTO Framework' *IRIS Plus*, 2003–6, 2.
[149] Sauvé, P., n. 54 above.
[150] WTO Rules Negotiations: Chairperson's Texts 2007, Draft Consolidated Chair Texts of the AD and SCM Agreements, TN/RL/W/213, (30 November 2007). See also Voon, n. 17 above, 96–100.
[151] See Sauvé, P., n. 54 above, 332.

similar difficulties in introducing controls on the abuse of services subsidies for protectionist purposes.[152]

The media and general exceptions

The GATT and GATS treaties impose a range of obligations that effectively oblige member states to maintain or increase the liberty to publish and distribute media content across borders. These are supported or exceeded by a host of other agreements, bilateral, regional, and multilateral, that contain trade and investment liberalization obligations. While these international obligations are often substantially weaker than comparable European Union ones, they collectively express the principle that media goods and services should be allowed to cross borders on a non-discriminatory basis. To limit the scope of this principle, these agreements also contain provisions that shelter broadly defined state and public interests in restricting the publication and distribution of media content. In the GATS, this balancing of market and non-market public policies is most obvious in the flexible architecture of the treaty, which was largely constructed on an opt-in basis. Beyond this structural flexibility, the negotiators also introduced other elements designed to protect critically important public policies from the reach of trade disciplines. These include the permanent exclusion of core government activities from the scope of the treaty and a broad, conditional exception permitting discrimination against foreign services or their suppliers.

In excluding the core functions of the state from the reach of trade disciplines, Article I:3 of the GATS excludes services supplied in the exercise of governmental authority from the definition of 'services' that are subject to the treaty. Without this provision, the treaty could be applied to executive or administrative measures in areas traditionally excluded from market principles, such as the protection of public order and national security.[153] On its face, the GATS exclusion of 'services supplied in the exercise of governmental authority' potentially applies to state funding or other support for media organizations, in particular public service media. As noted above, many forms of state assistance given to public service media are potentially vulnerable to GATS disciplines. Article 1:3 is however unlikely to give them much protection as public services do not necessarily equate with government services. Article I:3 defines 'a service supplied in the exercise of governmental authority' as any service that is supplied neither on a commercial basis nor in competition with other service suppliers. Narrowly interpreted, this does not include most public

---

[152] Grosso, G., 'Analysis of Subsidies for Services: The Case of Export Subsidies', OECD Trade Policy Working Papers (2008) No. 66.

[153] In principle, GATS Article I captures 'any service in any sector' unless expressly excluded. Article XXVIII moreover sets out several expansive definitions that bring a wide range of government measures within the scope of the treaty's disciplines, In *European Communities—Regime for the Importation, Sale and Distribution of Bananas*'(WTDS27/AB/R), the Appellate Body rejected the argument notion that the GATS is limited to measures 'regulating' or 'governing' trade.' See Adlung, R. n. 110 above.

media services, as these are normally provided independently from the government and usually compete with commercial services.[154] Alternatively, this article could be read more broadly to refer only to profit-seeking activities, which would bring publicly funded media services within its protective scope.[155]

It is more likely that the position of state supported media services will be resolved through the development of general GATS law and not through the government services exclusion. Certainly, if the exclusion of audiovisual services not only remains in place, but the WTO member states agree to extend the definition of audiovisual to new media services, the GATS will continue to have limited application to media services. The liberalization of trade in media services would also remain a special issue for bilateral and regional preferential trade agreements. It is however more likely that developments in those agreements foreshadow eventual multilateral acceptance that trade in audiovisual services should be managed within the GATS.

Where media services are subject to GATS disciplines, the main protection for discriminatory measures based on non-market public policies lies in the Article XIV general exceptions. This article is closely modelled on Article XX of the GATT, ensuring that both treaties take the same approach to the question of whether a specific discriminatory measure can be excluded from WTO disciplines. Consequently some of the most important issues in WTO law affecting the media are located in this interface between its non-discrimination disciplines and domestic public policy. At this critical boundary, trade law expressly legitimizes a set of state purposes, while implicitly rejecting or minimizing others.

Under GATS Article XIV, the permitted grounds for exceptional treatment most relevant to the media are significantly wider than those permitted under GATT Article XX. Article XIV permits measures necessary to protect public morals and to maintain public order, while Article XX only permits measures necessary to protect public morals, which is a subset of the much broader concept of public order. WTO panels and the Appellate Body have taken a flexible approach to the meaning of these grounds, recognizing the diversity of public policy across the member states that must be reasonably accommodated.[156] In the *US—Gambling* case, for example, the Appellate Body found that the challenged American measures prohibiting online gambling were justified under the public morals exception of Article XIV.[157]

---

[154] European Broadcasting Union, *Audiovisual services and GATS negotiations: EBU contribution to the public consultation on requests for access to the EU market* (17 January 2003). See also Krajewski, M., 'Public Services and Trade Liberalization: Mapping the Legal Framework', 6(2) *Journal of International Economic Law* (2003), 341–367, who argues that this provision is likely to be interpreted narrowly and that most public services will fall within the sectoral scope of GATS, and see Voon, n. 17 above, 90–92.

[155] See Adlung, R., n. 110 above, 9.

[156] Wunsch-Vincent, S., 'Cross-Border Trade in Services and the GATS: Lessons from the WTO US–Internet Gambling Case', 5 *World Trade Review* (2006), 319. Note that GATS Article XIV contains GATS Footnote 5, which states that '[t]he public order exception may be invoked only where a genuine and sufficiently serious threat is posed to one of the fundamental interests of society'.

[157] Diebold, N.F., 'The Morals and Order Exceptions in WTO Law: Balancing the Toothless Tiger and the Undermining Mole', 11(1) *Journal of International Economic Law* (2008), 43–74. See also Delimatsis, P., 'Protecting Public Morals in a Digital Era: Revisiting the WTO Rulings in

Furthermore, the Appellate Body has also determined that member states have the right to determine for themselves the level of protection they consider necessary for any permitted public policy purpose, deferring to the autonomy of the member states and their better knowledge of their own societies and interests.

This flexible approach to the grounds for exceptional treatment has however firm limits. In the *Canada—Periodicals* case, the narrower grounds of Article XX proved to be an insurmountable obstacle to Canadian efforts to protect discriminatory measures affecting foreign magazines, which it argued were necessary 'to provide Canadians with a distinctive vehicle for the expression of their own ideas and interests'.[158] The Canadian position was however fatally weakened by the lack of any appropriate ground under Article XX that plausibly covered these cultural objectives. It is moreover not clear that the broader GATS Article XIV concept of 'public order' would encompass other cultural measures, such as local content and language quotas.[159]

The WTO panels and Appellate Body have shown flexibility over the permitted grounds for exceptional treatment, in part, because the texts of GATT Article XX and GATS Article XIV also provide the basis for stringent conditions.[160] These conditions are applied in two steps, the first of which addresses the requirement that the challenged domestic measure must be 'necessary' for the claimed public policy purpose.[161] Under WTO case law, necessary, in this context, means that no alternative measure exists that the member state could reasonably be expected to employ and which is not inconsistent with other GATT or GATS provisions or which at least entails the least degree of inconsistency with other GATT or GATS provisions.[162] In short, a 'necessary' measure, under this interpretation, is one that has no reasonable alternative.

US—Gambling and China—Publications and Audiovisual Products', Tilburg University: TILEC Discussion Paper No. 2010-041.

[158] Panel Report, *Canadian Periodicals: Canada—Certain Measures Concerning Periodicals*, WT/DS31/R, (14 March 1997), para 3.5. See also Appellate Body Report: *Canadian Periodicals: Canada Certain Measures Concerning Periodicals*, n. 8 above.

[159] EBU, *Audiovisual Services and GATS: EBU Comments on US Negotiating Proposals of December 2000* (12 March 2001).

[160] Verhoosel, n. 37 above, 34–37.

[161] Not all of the public policy purposes recognized in GATT Article XX or GATS Article XIV include an express necessity requirement. Those most relevant to the media under Article XX are '(*a*) necessary to protect public morals; (*b*) necessary to protect human, animal or plant life or health; and (*d*) necessary to secure compliance with laws or regulations which are not inconsistent with the provisions of this Agreement, including those relating to . . . the protection of patents, trade marks and copyrights, and the prevention of deceptive practices'. Under Article XIV '(a) necessary to protect public morals or to maintain public order; (b) necessary to protect human, animal or plant life or health; (c) necessary to secure compliance with laws or regulations which are not inconsistent with the provisions of this Agreement including those relating to: (i) the prevention of deceptive and fraudulent practices or to deal with the effects of a default on services contracts; (ii) the protection of the privacy of individuals in relation to the processing and dissemination of personal data and the protection of confidentiality of individual records and accounts; (iii) safety'

[162] See *Thailand—Restrictions on Importation of and Internal Taxes on Cigarettes*, (DS 10/R-37S/200), (Panel Report, 7 November 1990), para. 75. Note also the comment of Wu Xiaohui, 'The unfortunate upshot of this approach is that a complaining party can almost always propose some less trade-restrictive alternatives which would likely be endorsed by the panels with little regard to national

The necessity test is one of the critical devices used in WTO law to determine the appropriate relationship between its basic trade disciplines and member state autonomy. It is also a particularly difficult test to apply with clarity as it uses an abstract qualitative standard to determine the validity of domestic measures.[163] The Appellate Body has extended the necessity test to include the 'weighing and balancing' of a series of factors to determine whether the discriminatory measures is the least restrictive available. These include 'the contribution made by the compliance measure to the enforcement of the law or regulation at issue, the importance of the common interests or values protected by that law or regulation, and the accompanying impact of the law or regulation on imports or exports'.[164] The introduction of 'weighing and balancing' has pushed the necessity test towards a full fledged balancing ('proportionality *stricto sensu*') of competing public policy purposes.[165] So far, however, the Appellate Body has arguably kept within the lesser 'least restrictive measure' concept of necessity, albeit exploring its full potential.[166] The factors included in this weighing and balancing exercise are directed at the question of whether an alternative measure exists that protects the public policy objective of the member state equally well, but is also less restrictive of the member state's WTO trade obligations.[167]

The second step, following the necessity test, is to address the matching conditions set out in the first paragraphs or 'chapeaux' of GATT Article XX and GATS Article XIV. These prohibit domestic measures applied in a manner which constitutes a means of arbitrary or unjustifiable discrimination between countries where like conditions prevail or a disguised restriction on trade.[168] The purpose

---

conditions and policy constraints. Put simply, it is too easy for a complaining party to establish less trade-restrictive alternatives and too difficult for a responding party to prove that the alternatives are not reasonably available.' Wu, X., 'Case Note: China—Measures Affecting Trading Rights and Distribution Services for Certain Publications and Audiovisual Entertainment Products (WT/ DS363/AB/R)', 9(2) *Chinese Journal of International Law* (2010), 415–432. See also Qin, J., 'Pushing the Limit of Global Governance: Trading Rights, Censorship, and WTO Jurisprudence—A Commentary on China-Audiovisual Services' (23 November 2010), Wayne State University Law School Research Paper, <http://ssrn.com/abstract=1713886>.

[163] Mattoo, A. and Subramanian, A., 'Regulatory Autonomy and Multilateral Disciplines: the Dilemma and a Possible Resolution', 9(2) *Journal of International Economic Law* (1995), 303–322.

[164] *Korea—Measures Affecting Imports of Fresh, Chilled and Frozen Beef*, Appellate Body Report WT/ DS161/AB/R (11 December 2000), para. 164. See also *European Communities—Measures Affecting Asbestos and Asbestos-Containing Products*, WT/DS135/AB/R (Appellate Body Report, 5 April 2001), para. 172, and *Brazil—Measures Affecting Imports of Retreaded Tyres*, WT/DS332/AB/R (Appellate Body Report, 17 December 2007), para. 221.

[165] On proportionality analysis, see Chapter 2.

[166] Ortino, F., 'United States—Measures Affecting the Cross-Border Supply of Gambling and Betting Services', 7 *World Trade Review* (2008), 115–119. See also Eeckhout. P., n. 28 above.

[167] *United States—Gambling and Betting Services*, n. 58 above, para. 291. See also *Brazil— Retreaded Tyres*, n. 164 above, para. 178, McGrady, B., 'Necessity Exceptions in WTO Law: Retreaded Tyres, Regulatory Purpose and Cumulative Regulatory Measures', 12(1) *Journal of International Economic Law* (2009), 153–157, and see *China—Publications and Audiovisual Entertainment Products*, n. 130 above, para. 240.

[168] Given the similar language of the GATT Article XX and GATS Article XIV chapeau texts, the Appellate Body has stated that decisions made under Article XX are relevant to its analysis under Article XIV (*United States—Gambling and Betting Services*, n. 58 above, para. 291) and, vice versa, (*China—Publications and Audiovisual Entertainment Products*, n. 130 above, para. 239).

of these additional chapeaux provisions is to prevent the abuse or misuse of the right to claim exceptional treatment for measures that pursue important non-market public policy goals. This further scrutiny can be justified on the grounds that these domestic measures are discriminatory and therefore violate one of the WTO's fundamental principles of trade liberalization.[169]

The Appellate Body famously addressed this issue in the *US—Shrimp* case, stating

The task of interpreting and applying the chapeau is, hence, essentially the delicate one of locating and marking out a line of equilibrium between the right of a Member to invoke an exception under Article XX and the rights of the other Members under varying substantive provisions ... so that neither of the competing rights will cancel out the other and thereby distort and nullify or impair the balance of rights and obligations constructed by the Members themselves in that Agreement. The location of the line of equilibrium, as expressed in the chapeau, is not fixed and unchanging; the line moves as the kind and the shape of the measures at stake vary and as the facts making up specific cases differ.[170]

Beyond Article XX and XIV, the GATT and GATS also permit exceptional treatment of discriminatory national measures intended to protect national security, under GATT Article XXI and GATS Article XIV*bis*.[171] The grounds for exceptional treatment set out in these articles potentially affect the media in two ways. They permit discriminatory measures taken in time of war or other international emergency, which could include many restrictions on the publication or distribution of foreign media. They also recognize the right of a member state not to supply any information it controls if that state considers that disclosure would be contrary to its essential security interests.[172] This exception places an important limit on the use of WTO transparency or other obligations to force the disclosure of government held information.[173]

The international media law patchwork

Trade in media content is just one of several deeply controversial issues affecting the further development of the GATT and GATS. Determining the rules for trade in media content is therefore only part of the trade law puzzle and will only be resolved within that general process. Nonetheless, the media state relationship, with its many claims to distinctiveness, will continue to be a source of contention within the WTO. The importance of these claims to distinctiveness for many member states cannot be easily overridden, but the demand for politically and socially grounded exceptions is also broad enough to overwhelm the principle of non-discriminatory access to media markets.

[169] *US—Shrimp*, n. 25 above, para. 156.
[170] Ibid., para. 159.
[171] Lindsay, P., 'The Ambiguity of GATT Article XXI: Subtle Success or Rampant Failure', 52 *Duke Law Journal* (2003), 1277.
[172] GATT XXI(a) and GATS XIV:1(a).
[173] On rules of access to state held information, see Chapter 9.

Other states are hardly likely to accept willingly the foreclosure of valuable markets in information and entertainment content. For many, as well, the question of trade in media goods and services is powerfully linked to equally important liberal democratic principles supporting open media markets. The governments of the western democracies responsible for laying the foundations of the WTO regime have tended to assume that its obligations of openness and transparency not only demand a market based economy, but are also inconsistent with autocracy. Nonetheless, admission of China, Vietnam, Russia, and other non-liberal democratic states into the WTO implies an acceptance that the media will continue to be only lightly bound by trade law disciplines.[174]

While trade law cannot ignore the potential for overt and disguised economic protection, it must also respect the right of states to pursue important media related public policies. In many situations, however, it will take extraordinary ingenuity to satisfy these two goals. If demands for market access cut too far into essential domestic media policies, governments can be expected to fight hard to protect these state and public interests.[175] Nor will these compromises between market and non-market public policy goals be worked out exclusively within the forums and rules of the WTO. While trade law tends to exclude or confine the non-economic attributes of media goods and services, other international legal regimes are receptive to their protection or promotion. Insulated from market access disciplines, these regimes provide a space in which alternative forms of consensus and cooperation on media content issues can develop.[176] The United Nations Educational Scientific and Cultural Organization (UNESCO), has a well known history as a forum for dissent against market based media policies. UNESCO has wide responsibilities for cultural as well as social matters and it is therefore an ideal institution for the promotion of these aspects of media policy. It has also placed this work squarely on

---

[174] China is in a different position compared to many other WTO member states, having agreed to open parts of its media sector to GATT and GATS disciplines under its Accession Protocol (Protocol of Accession of the People's Republic of China to the World Trade Organization (11 December 2001), WT/L/432), which has opened the way to dispute applications concerning China's laws and regulations affecting media goods and services. (See, for example, *China—Publications and Audiovisual Entertainment Products*, n. 130 above. For comment on this decision, see Bollinger, L., *Uninhibited, Robust, and Wide-Open* (Oxford University Press, 2009), ch 3.) On China's Accession Protocol, see Qin, J., '"WTO-Plus" Obligations and Their Implications for the World Trade Organization Legal System: An Appraisal of the China Accession Protocol', 37(3) *Journal of World Trade* (2003), 483–522.

[175] As Daniel Drezner has argued, 'In the case of the Internet, when the United States and the European Union saw significant benefits and low adjustment costs from coordination, the effective global governance of Internet-related issues was achieved—even if the great powers voluntarily delegated the management of these regulatory regimes to private actors. When Internet issues intersected with larger public policy questions—such as privacy or speech rights—the adjustment costs for governments dramatically increased. In the absence of a great power concert, governments used all of the tools of statecraft at their disposal to protect their preferred set of regulatory standards—even if such a decision heavily restricted Internet use.' Drezner, D., 'The Persistent Power of the State in the Global Economy', *Cato Unbound*, 6 June 2007. See also Drezner, D., *All Politics is Global: Explaining International Regulatory Regimes* (Princeton University Press, 2007), ch 4.

[176] On forum shifting, See Braithwaite, J. and Drahos, P., *Global Business Regulation* (Cambridge University Press, 2000), 29–31.

an international human rights foundation, which provides a robust alternative to international trade law.[177]

The International Telecommunications Union (ITU), another UN agency, has played a different role in the development of international communications law and policy.[178] In the past century, when electronic communication services were publicly owned and operated in much of the world, the ITU was the key forum for multilateral cooperation on communications matters. It consequently had considerable influence over cross border media matters, especially in relation to satellite broadcasting. In the current era of privatized communication infrastructures and internet based delivery, the ITU has lost influence and practical importance. The determination of the United States to keep the organization on the margins of global internet policy and rule development was highly effective in sidelining the organization. In the 1990s, the American government took the view that the ITU was structurally bound to a state centred perspective on communications policy.[179] It was thus poorly equipped to allow participation by commercial communications companies and other non-governmental stakeholders or to respond to the market driven character of deregulated communications facilities and services.[180] Consequently, the United States rejected the ITU and any other traditional international organization, when it established the Internet Corporation for Assigned Names and Numbers (ICANN), the principal international organization for the coordination of internet domain names and Internet Protocol addresses in the form of a non-profit corporation registered under the laws of California.[181] Successive US governments have since then fended off recurring calls for ICANN to be reconstituted as a treaty based, international organization.[182]

The ITU has nonetheless gained a foothold in the internet policy sphere. Its sponsorship of the World Summit on the Information Society (WSIS) attracted considerable press attention, but the organizations more mundane responsibilities for the coordination of global telecommunications account for its presence in the internet policy field. The WSIS did however provide an opening for greater UN sponsored involvement in internet policy making. At the 2005 second phase

---

[177] On the UNESCO Convention on Cultural Diversity, see Chapter 15.

[178] The International Telecommunications Union (ITU) is the direct institutional descendant of the International Telegraph Union, formed in 1865 to support the administration of the first International Telegraph Convention. In 1947 the ITU became a specialized agency of the United Nations and it remains one of the key forums for international agreement and cooperation on communication matters. The ITU is responsible for coordination of national activities in telecommunication and radio communication, including the primary allocation of radiospectrum for various communications uses and the registration of satellite orbital positions.

[179] Huston, G., 'Opinion: ICANN, the ITU, WSIS, and Internet Governance' 8(1) *Internet Protocol Journal* (March 2005). See also Cukier, K., 'Who will Control the Internet', *Foreign Affairs,* (November/December 2005), 7.

[180] Huston, n. 179 above.

[181] The United States has agreed to greater international accountability for the ICANN under the 2009 Affirmation of Commitments between the United States Department of Commerce and ICANN. See 'ICANN be Independent: Regulating the Internet', *The Economist* (25 September 2009).

[182] See Cukier, K., n. 179 above.

meeting of the WSIS at Tunis, the participating governments agreed instead to establish a permanent multi-stakeholder forum under the authority of the UN Secretary General.[183] This body, the Internet Governance Forum, has provided a novel public international space for non-governmental discussion of internet related issues. Although its influence over internet policy and rule making is limited, the IGF carries many of the aspirations of liberal democratic public order.[184]

The WTO is, nonetheless, vastly more consequential in international affairs than the ITU, UNESCO, or other any other international organization of importance to the media. Yet it is not the only significant international body that seeks the development of a global market economy. The Organisation for Economic Cooperation and Development (OECD) has, in particular, had a major role in coordinating policies amongst developed, market economies in areas that bear directly on the media.[185] The OECD provides a forum for the negotiation of joint policies amongst developed countries formally committed to market based economics and liberal democracy.[186] Aside from its research projects, the OECD sponsors both legally binding treaties as well as other multilateral agreements and guidelines. The organization has also played an important role in promoting policy consensus across international organizations on trade matters, including the major regional groups such as the European Union and the North American Free Trade Agreement. Its limited influential membership has made the OECD a useful forum for the negotiation of agreements that can serve as building blocks for wider agreements. In the media sphere, its work on data protection and electronic commerce has, for example, been an important influence on the development of international principles.[187]

The position of WTO law in this array of specialized and regional regimes is both central and precarious. Institutional and network relationships between the

---

[183] The Working Group on Internet Governance (WGIG) was established by the United Nations following first phase of the World Summit on the Information Society in 2003: ITU Council Working Group on the World Summit on the Information Society, *Beyond Internet Governance,* Document WG-WSIS 7/13-E (2004). The Internet Governance Forum was created following the WGIG (2005) report to the WSIS Tunis Summit in 2005. See also Mayer-Schoenberger, V. and Ziewitz, M., 'Jefferson Rebuffed—The United States and the Future of Internet Governance' (May 2006), Kennedy School of Government, Working Paper No. RWP06-018.

[184] See Mathiason, J., *Internet Governance: The New Frontier of Global Institutions* (Routledge, 2008), chs 7 and 8.

[185] Mahon, R. and McBride, S., 'Standardizing and disseminating knowledge: the role of the OECD in global governance', 1(1) *European Political Science Review* (2009), 83–101. See also, for example, the work of the OECD paving the way for the global spread of common internet public policies, OECD, Committee for Information, Computers and Communications Policy, Global Information Infrastructure—Global Information Society (GII-GIS) *Policy Recommendations for Action* (1997).

[186] Convention on the Organisation for Economic Co-operation and Development, (Paris, 14 December 1960): First Recital, 'CONSIDERING that economic strength and prosperity are essential for the attainment of the purposes of the United Nations, the preservation of individual liberty and the increase of general well-being.'

[187] C(80)58 Recommendation of the Council concerning Guidelines Governing the Protection of Privacy and Transborder Flows of Personal Data; C(85)139 Declaration on Transborder Data Flows; and C(98)177 Declaration on the Protection of Privacy on Global Networks, <http://www.oecd.org>.

WTO and other trade related organizations has certainly aided policy coordination. Equally, specialist organizations, such the ITU and UNESCO, have provided havens for the development of non-market centred commitments on media related matters, while regional trade organizations have forged their own pre-emptive compromises on trade in media content. In media matters, the WTO is therefore severely challenged. It must control the interfaces between trade law and other fields of international law while respecting the autonomy of member states and developing common rules for trade in media goods and services. It must also do this in a global environment in which the goal of integrating national economies no longer enjoys the support it once had in major national governments.

6

The Media in European and International Human Rights Law

Part I—The media in European human rights law

European human rights law is widely celebrated as one of the continent's foremost achievements in its long journey back from the cataclysm of World War II. It has given the European conception of liberal democratic human rights and public order a global reach that often exceeds the political and social influence of its individual member states.[1] Yet the celebrity status of European human rights law tends to obscure the fact that European media law rests primarily on economic rather than human rights foundations. Like much of the world's media, the publication and distribution of media content in Europe is driven by market forces and the primary legal framework in which it operates is consequently commercial. European media law has accordingly developed along the avenues and openings created by the European Union's rules on free movement and fair competition.[2]

Nonetheless, European human rights law retains an extraordinary power to shape the relationship between the media and the European state, supporting as well as blunting the effects of the EU's market based economic principles. The right to freedom of expression, declared in the European Convention on Human Rights (ECHR), provides one half of the powerful liberal, double argument for the liberty to publish, giving moral and political force to the economic justifications. The Convention moreover has an essential role in defining the scope and limits of non-market public policy. It is therefore present within the EU's exceptions and derogations to the free movement of media goods and services as well as the permitted scope for positive state intervention in media markets.

The idea of freedom of expression in European human rights law has always been closely connected with the problems of Europe's Cold War division and subsequent unification. The Council of Europe (CE), the institutional home of the European Human Rights Convention, was founded in London in 1949 at a

---

[1] Bertoni, E.A., 'The Inter-American Court of Human Rights and the European Court of Human Rights: A Dialogue on Freedom of Expression Standards', 3 *European Human Rights Law Review* (2009), 332.
[2] See Chapter 4.

moment when memories of fascism were fresh and Soviet power was close at hand.[3] Consequently, its views on freedom of expression in the media have always been coloured by its primary mission to protect and foster democratic government in Europe. From this perspective, the liberty to publish in European human rights law is, first and foremost, an essential element in a healthy democratic state.

The end of the Cold War did not change this dynamic. In fact, the dissolution of Yugoslavia and the Soviet Union and the hasty creation of fragile new democracies in east and southeast Europe, only strengthened the importance of that focus for the Council of Europe. In the 1990s, the organization embarked on a major programme of standard setting to guide the transition to democracy in these countries.[4] Using principles developed in western Europe, the Council has aggressively promoted the independence of the media from government and political parties, while also encouraging the establishment of publicly funded media.[5] It also works closely with a variety of other regional organizations devoted to similar aims, such as the Organization for Security and Co-operation in Europe (OSCE) and the Venice Commission.[6] At the same time, the Council has used its full array of instruments to address both the need to keep internet based service free from unnecessary constraints and the need to counter the harmful effects of internet use.[7]

The Council of Europe's many treaties, declarations, resolutions, recommendations, and other instruments bearing on media issues all rest on the European Convention on Human Rights and, more particularly, the body of Convention case law developed by the European Court of Human Rights in Strasbourg.[8] It is of course the Strasbourg Court that has turned the Convention into a living

---

[3] Statute of the Council of Europe (Treaty of London, 1949), ETS 001. The core objectives of the Council of Europe are the protection and promotion of human rights, democracy, and the rule of law (Council of Europe Summit of Heads of State and Government, Final Declaration, Warsaw, 2005).

[4] Varju, M., 'Transition as a Concept of European Human Rights Law', 2 *European Human Rights Law Review* (2009), 170. See also Greer, G., *The European Convention on Human Rights* (Cambridge, 2006), 108.

[5] See, for example, Council of Europe, Committee of Ministers Recommendation on the Independence and Functions of Regulatory Authorities for the Broadcasting Sector, REC (2000), 23.

[6] The OSCE has made freedom of expression a key concern in its work in the transition to liberal democracy. In 1997, the OSCE appointed a Representative on Freedom of the Media (Council Decision No. 193, Mandate of the OSCE Representative on Freedom of the Media, 137th Plenary Meeting). The Representative's tasks include calling attention to violations of freedom of expression and advocating and promoting full compliance with OSCE principles and commitments regarding freedom of expression and free media. The European Commission for Democracy through Law (the Venice Commission) is the Council of Europe's advisory body on constitutional matters. Founded in 1990, the Commission has, *inter alia*, assisted the post 1989 new democracies to adopt constitutions consistent with Council of Europe standards.

[7] See, for example, Council of Europe, Committee of Ministers Recommendation states on self-regulation concerning cyber content, Rec (2001) 8, Council of Europe, Committee of Ministers Declaration on freedom of communication on the Internet (May 2003), and Council of Europe, Committee of Ministers, Declaration on freedom of communication on the Internet (Strasbourg, 28 May 2003).

[8] The European Convention for the Protection of Human Rights and Fundamental Freedoms, (ETS No. 005), was adopted in Rome in November 1950 and came into force three years later. It was the first international treaty to guarantee a wide range of civil and political rights.

instrument at the centre of an expanding body of case law.[9] It not only holds the exclusive power to interpret the Convention but also exercises compulsory jurisdiction over all CE member states, which are bound to find legal or other remedies for violations of Convention protected rights.[10] The member states have moreover repeatedly increased the number of those rights and also enhanced the powers of the Court.[11] The Court consequently has enjoyed sufficient authority to develop the meaning of European human rights law through its case decisions, overcoming national resistance and bringing a degree of harmonization to European domestic law.

In principle, the Court holds extraordinary powers to shape European media law and create a common template for the legitimate media state relationship in Europe. Yet the Court is structurally incapable of achieving that degree of supremacy over the evolving principles of European human rights or the affairs of the state parties to the Convention. It is an unwieldy body that must often resort to generality rather than clarity to maintain consistency or direction in its judgments. While reforms are under way, the Court remains overburdened with individual applications and has limited ability to focus its scarce resources on the continent's most pressing human rights issues.[12]

The Court of Human Rights is also compelled to use a method of adjudication that is unsuited to the breadth of its responsibilities. It must ensure that the state parties implement the Convention's principles in an effective manner, while also allowing them sufficient flexibility to do so in a way best suited to their domestic conditions.[13] The meaning of those principles must also evolve with changing European social and cultural norms, yet pay sufficient respect to enduring traditions and customs in the state parties.[14] All of which must be accomplished within a highly fact specific system of supervisory adjudication, which is closely focused on the circumstances of each individual applicant. As a consequence, the Court must

[9] Letsas, G., 'Strasbourg's Interpretive Ethic: Lessons for the International Lawyer', 21(3) *European Journal of International Law* (2010), 509–541.

[10] Article 1: 'The High Contracting Parties shall secure to everyone within their jurisdiction the rights and freedoms defined in Section I of this Convention.'

[11] Aside from substantive rights, the protocol procedure has been used to reform the Court's structure and procedures. Notably, Protocol 1, which came into force in 1998, abolished the European Commission on Human Rights and created a right of direct application to the Court. More recently, Protocol 14 introduces various reforms to increase the efficiency and effectiveness of the Court, including a new admissibility criterion that permits the Court to declare an application inadmissible if the applicant did not suffer a significant disadvantage. It also paves the way for EU accession to the Convention. See also Caflisch, L., 'The Reform of the European Court of Human Rights: Protocol No. 14 and Beyond', 6(2) *Human Rights Law Review* (2006), 403–415.

[12] High Level Conference on the Future of the European Court of Human Rights (Interlaken Conference), *Interlaken Declaration: The Future of the European Court of Human Rights*, (19 February 2010).

[13] Mahoney, P., 'Marvellous Richness of Diversity or Invidious Cultural Relativism', 19(1)*Human Rights Law Journal* (1998), 1.

[14] Gerards, J., 'Judicial Deliberations in the European Court of Human Rights', in Huls, N., Adams, M., and Bomhoff, J. (eds), *The Legitimacy Of Highest Courts' Rulings* (T.M.C. Asser Institute, 2008), 407–436.

stretch to situate an application in the full context of relevant domestic law and policy, yet also bring to bear the relevant human rights principles.[15]

Outside the EU's principles of free movement, no European legal provision has shaped European media law more than Article 10 of the European Convention on Human Rights, which requires state parties to protect the right to freedom of expression.[16] Yet, the primacy of the Convention easily obscures the wealth of other Council of Europe instruments intended to guide member states in the media sector. While the Court works in an intensely case specific manner, the CE's Committee of Ministers and the Parliamentary Assembly routinely use their authority to issue wide ranging guidance that addresses overlapping legal, political, and social issues.[17] These include declarations and recommendations underscoring the importance of the media in a democratic society and the dangers posed by violence against journalists, repressive laws on defamation and sedition, as well as censorship by government authorities and excessive intervention by media regulators.[18]

Plainly, the disadvantage of CE declarations and recommendations it that, while sometimes influential, they are not legally binding on the member states, unlike the judgments of the Court or the Council of Europe's other treaties. Even participation in these treaties is optional, unlike the CE's requirement that every member state must become a party to the Convention. Moreover, apart from the Convention, Council of Europe treaties are not subject to binding, third party adjudication, although some make provision for an administrative body charged with conciliating agreement on implementation.[19]

Thus, while European media law is centred on Article 10 of the Human Rights Convention, it is also enlarged considerably by this constellation of soft and hard instruments.[20] Collectively, they give a comprehensive portrait of the media state relationship in a legitimate European liberal democracy, supporting the liberty to

[15] Greer, S., 'What's Wrong with the European Convention on Human Rights?' 30(3) *Human Rights Quarterly* (2008). See also Chapter 14 regarding the Court's decisions in the field of political advertising.

[16] For a general overview, see Voorhoof, D., 'Freedom of Expression under the European Human Rights System. From Sunday Times (n° 1) v. U.K. (1979) to Hachette Filipacchi Associés ("Ici Paris") v. France (2009)', 1(2) *Inter-American and European Human Rights Journal* (2009), 3–49.

[17] Under Article 15.*b* of the Statute of the Council of Europe, the Committee of Ministers may make 'recommendations to the governments of members, and the Committee may request the governments of members to inform it of the action taken by them with regard to such recommendations'. In the media sector, the Committee of Ministers is assisted by the Steering Committee on the Media and New Communications Services as well as various short term, expert bodies, such as the Committee of Experts on New Media and the Ad-hoc Advisory Group on Cross-border Internet.

[18] See, for example, the Committee of Ministers Declaration on the freedom of expression and information (April 1982), Recommendation (1996) 10 on the guarantee of the independence of public service broadcasting, Recommendation (2000) 23 on the independence and functions of regulatory authorities for the broadcasting sector, Declaration on freedom of political debate in the media (February 2004), and Declaration on measures to promote the respect of Article 10 of the European Convention on Human Rights (January 2010).

[19] See, for example, the Standing Committee of the 1989 European Convention on Transfrontier Television (ETS No. 132), established under Articles 20–21.

[20] Krisch, N., 'The Open Architecture of European Human Rights Law', 71 *Modern Law Review* (2008), 183–216.

publish across a wide range of areas subject to restrictive measures. The principles concerning the protection of journalist's sources, for example, oblige CE member states to force the disclosure of these sources only so far as necessary and only where all other means of investigation have been exhausted.[21] On the other hand, Council of Europe treaties are also used to coordinate state restrictions on harmful or offensive expression, obliging participating states to criminalize or restrict media content. These notably include efforts to restrict the production and distribution of child pornography and incitement to hatred or violence.[22] All of these varied Council of Europe initiatives are however grounded in the principles of the ECHR and are intended to reflect the Court's case law, however much they consolidate, enhance, or fill gaps.

The substantial coherence of European media law across the economic and human rights divide owes much to the close and often well coordinated relationship between the European Union and Council of Europe.[23] This is based on a deep conceptual affinity within the liberal democratic tradition, in which economic and human rights law presuppose each other's existence. European human rights law therefore protects a sphere of personal autonomy that includes a general right to hold property and engage in commerce.[24] The importance of this economic dimension of freedom of expression in human rights law has moreover risen with the rapid growth of commercial, cross border media services, which has brought about a pronounced alignment of EU and CE concerns regarding new media services.[25]

In the same vein, European Union law assumes the fundamental legitimacy of both domestic and European measures that pursue recognized human rights goals. Indeed, one of the chief strengths of non-market public policies in relation to EU principles of free movement and fair market competition law is that they are typically as well grounded in European human rights law as they are in the constitutional principles of the member state. There is conversely a very strong coherence between European economic freedoms and human rights freedoms. In the media sector, this is most obvious in the double argument for greater liberty to publish and distribute content. Free movement of media goods and services is thus an argument based on economic efficiency but is also imbued with the political and

---

[21] On the protection of journalists' sources, see Chapter 9.

[22] See, for example, Council of Europe, Convention on Cybercrime, (ETS No. 185) including its Additional Protocol to the Convention on cybercrime, concerning the criminalisation of acts of a racist and xenophobic nature committed through computer systems, (ETS No. 185), See also Council of Europe, Convention on the Protection of Children Against Sexual Exploitation and Sexual Abuse 2007 (ETS No. 201), Convention on the Prevention of Terrorism (2005) (ETS No. 196).

[23] Memorandum of Understanding between the Council of Europe and the European Union (2007).

[24] ECHR, Protocol 1, Article 1 provides for the rights to the peaceful enjoyment of one's possessions.

[25] In the media sector, the parallel, if not always smooth, development since the mid 1980s of the EU Audiovisual Media Services Directive and the CE European Transfrontier Television Convention (ETS No. 132) reflects this close relationship. The European Commission also regularly participates in the meetings of various Council of Europe standard setting bodies, including the Steering Committee on Media and New Communication Services.

moral weight of the right to freedom of expression, as developed by the European Court of Human Rights.

The conceptual and practical affinity between European economic and human rights law has fed long running efforts to integrate human rights principles into EU law. The granting of treaty status to the EU Charter of Fundamental Rights under the Treaty of Lisbon, which has made it legally binding in most member states, has taken this integration project a major step forward.[26] On the Council of Europe side, beyond the recognition of rights to hold property and engage in commerce, it has a well developed institutional relationship with the European Commission and other EU bodies, such as the Fundamental Rights Agency. Formal cooperation agreements, including the 2007 Memorandum of Understanding between the European Commission and the Council of Europe, have enabled observer status in CE negotiations and participation in joint programmes.[27] The Memorandum declares the indivisibility and universality of human rights and that the Council of Europe is the 'Europe-wide reference source for human rights'.[28] It also provides for cooperation in areas especially important to the media, including efforts to combat discrimination, racism, xenophobia and intolerance, the protection of the rights of the child, and the promotion of freedom of expression and information.[29] The most important step in the integration of the EU into European human rights law will however occur when the EU becomes a party to the Convention, which is now legally possible.[30]

Despite the pre-eminent position of the Council of Europe and European Convention on Human Rights in Europe's emerging constitutional order, the European Union is, without doubt, a vastly more powerful organization. Its broader and more effective legislative and judicial processes give EU law a more pervasive presence in domestic law and regulation. This has made it an attractive alternative forum for European social and political policy initiatives, many of which were historically outside or on the margins of its legislative competences.[31]

---

[26] See Chapter 4 discussion of the Charter of Fundamental Freedoms. See also Johan Callewaert, 'The European Convention on Human Rights and European Union Law: a Long Way to Harmony', 6 *European Human Rights Law Review* (2009), 768–783.

[27] The 2007 Memorandum of Understanding between the Council of Europe and the European Union (CM (2007) 74 10 May 2007). See also the 1987 Arrangement between the Council of Europe and the European Community, the 2001 Joint Declaration on Cooperation and Partnership between the Council of Europe and the European Commission, and the 2008 Agreement between the European Community and the Council of Europe on cooperation between the European Union Agency for Fundamental Rights and the Council of Europe. And see Joris, T. and Vandenberghe, J., 'The Council of Europe and the European Union: Natural Partners or Uneasy Bedfellows?' 15 *Columbia Journal of European Law* (2008–2009), 1. De Schutter, O., 'The Two Europes Of Human Rights: The Emerging Division of Tasks between the Council of Europe and the European Union in Promoting Human Rights in Europe', 14 *Columbia Journal of European Law* (2008), 509.

[28] Memorandum of Understanding, Clauses 16–17.

[29] Ibid., clause 21.

[30] European Union accession to the Convention became possible after Protocol 14 of the European Convention on Human Rights came into force on 1 June 2010. Official talks on the European Union's accession to the European Convention on Human Rights (ECHR) began on 7 July 2010.

[31] See, for example, Framework Decision 2002/475/JHA on combating terrorism, as amended by Council Framework Decision 2008/919/JHA of 28 November 2008; Council Framework Decision

On the other hand, the Council of Europe's status as an independent organization and the participation of major non-EU states has given it a special role as an alternative regional forum. Its strong competence in social, cultural, and political affairs gives the CE the authority to tackle these issues directly, rather than in the often oblique manner of the EU. It therefore provides a forum where governments can seek to blunt the effects of EU initiatives or advance issues that challenge the market based assumptions of EU law. This can be readily seen in the parallel drafting and amendment of the main EU and CE instruments that specifically address cross border television broadcasting: the EU Audiovisual Media Service Directive and the CE Convention on Transfrontier Television. While aligned with the Directive on major points, the Convention contains several provisions not found in the Directive, including the requirement that broadcasters ensure that news fairly present facts and encourage the free formation of opinions.[32] In 2010, however, the EU through the European Commission effectively blocked planned amendments to the Convention on Transfrontier Television because of unacceptable divergences from the AVMS Directive, throwing the Convention's future in doubt.[33]

ECHR Article 10 and the media state relationship

Despite the obvious mismatch in the political and legislative authority of the European Union and the Council of Europe, the EU is not in a position of absolute dominance. While the European Union may wield greater legislative and judicial powers, its member states are all parties to the European Convention on Human Rights, which has given the Strasbourg Court powerful leverage over the development of European media law. This leverage is grounded in the Convention, which directly bears on all important aspects of the relationship between the media and the state, either through the obligations of the state parties or through conditional exceptions.

The liberty to publish is principally stated in the comprehensive Article 10(1) right to freedom of expression.[34] The state's interest in restricting that liberty for

2004/68/JHA of 22 December 2003 on combating the sexual exploitation of children and child pornography; Council Framework Decision 2008/913/JHA of 28 November 2008 on combating certain forms and expressions of racism and xenophobia by means of criminal law.

[32] European Convention on Transfrontier Television (ETS No. 132), Article 6(2).

[33] Council of Europe, Standing Committee On Transfrontier Television (T-TT), 45th Meeting Report (Executive Summary), (21 July 2010) T-TT(2010)2.

[34] ECHR, Article 10: '1. Everyone has the right to freedom of expression. This right shall include freedom to hold opinions and to receive and impart information and ideas without interference by public authority and regardless of frontiers. This article shall not prevent States from requiring the licensing of broadcasting, television or cinema enterprises. 2. The exercise of these freedoms, since it carries with it duties and responsibilities, may be subject to such formalities, conditions, restrictions or penalties as are prescribed by law and are necessary in a democratic society, in the interests of national security, territorial integrity or public safety, for the prevention of disorder or crime, for the protection of health or morals, for the protection of the reputation or the rights of others, for preventing the disclosure of information received in confidence, or for maintaining the authority and impartiality of the judiciary.'

reasons of security, authority, and legitimacy is secured through the Article 10(2) grounds for restricting expression.[35] Those grounds include the 'rights of others', which extends the scope of legitimate exceptions to other articles in the Convention that legitimize restrictions on expression. These notably include the Article 8 right to a private life and the Article 6 right to a fair trial. The 'rights of others' also encompasses other individual and collective interests in the restriction of expression, including prohibitions on the publication or distribution of grossly offensive content.[36]

The Court has worked within this framework of rights and exceptions to create an evolving set of principles that govern critical aspects of the media state relationship. Its early decisions in media cases under Article 10 continue to provide important landmarks, containing statements of principle repeated verbatim in scores of subsequent decisions.[37] Since that formative period, the Court has explored the implications of these simple, and often bold, statements, in a process that has produced a more complex, nuanced body of case decisions.[38] At the same time, the Court's case law concerning the media has needed to reflect rapid changes in communications technologies, media services, and social attitudes. A once well established European culture of deference to public figures has, for example, shifted towards one of greater scrutiny, criticism, and even ridicule in the major media as well as in Europe's vast range of new media services.[39] Yet within that shift, the Court has tempered its robust support for scrutiny and criticism with a concern that public figures should retain a meaningful right to private life and reputation, regardless of their fame or notoriety.[40] That picture however suggests judgments of great clarity and direction. However, the Court, burdened with thousands of applications and served by a diverse cadre of judges, is more often accused of a drift towards inconsistent and ambiguous case law.[41]

Article 10(1) covers a wide array of interests furthering the liberty to publish information and entertainment content. These include the interests of content publishers, distributors, and potential recipients as well as the wider public interest in maintaining the public flow of diverse information and ideas. In contrast to a more rights centred interpretation of a constitutional right to free speech, the Court has taken an expansive view of what forms of expression are within the scope of

---

[35] Ibid.

[36] *Otto-Preminger-Institut v. Austria* (Application No. 13470/87) [1994] ECHR 26 (20 September 1994).

[37] See, for example, *Handyside v. the United Kingdom* (Application No. 5493/72) (7 December 1976), *Lingens v. Austria* (Application No. 9815/82) (8 July 1986), and *Sunday Times v. the United Kingdom* (Application No. 6538/74) (26 April 1979).

[38] On the relationship between the protection of reputation and the ECHR Article 8 right to respect for private life, see Chapter 10.

[39] See, for example, *Vereinigung Bildender Künstler v. Austria* (Application No. 68354/01), (25 January 2007).

[40] See, for example, *Lindon, Otchakovsky-Laurens and July v. France* (Application Nos 21279/02 and 36448/02) (22 October 2007), para. 57. See also Millar, G., 'Whither the spirit of Lingens?' 3 *European Human Rights Law Review* (2009), 277–288.

[41] Gerards, J., n. 14 above, 498.

Article 10(1).[42] Indeed, the Court has had comparatively little to say about the boundaries of expression protected under the Convention.[43]

The court's expansive view of Article 10(1) sits awkwardly with the two part structure of Article 10, which implies that the liberty to publish will normally take precedence over competing interests. This indicates that a broadly defined concept of expression under Article 10(1) will lead to a powerfully entrenched liberty to publish. That possibility is however belied by the structure of the Convention as a whole, which creates a fundamental equality between the Article 10 right to freedom of expression and other competing rights. The Court has moreover applied a method of analysis that largely ignores the structural anomalies of the Convention. It has used the conditions set out in Article 10(2) to create a set of tests or hurdles to determine the legitimacy of any state measure that interferes with the Article 10(1) composite right to freedom of expression.[44] While these tests use the specific language of Article 10(2) as a point of departure, the underlying approach is inspired by proportionality analysis.[45] The Court has, in this way, taken the textual requirement that any legitimate interference must be 'necessary in a democratic society' to include the key condition that it must be proportionate. On this basis, the Court has been able to use Article 10(2) to force state parties to justify a challenged domestic measure that restricts the liberty to publish in a rigorous, principled manner.

Certainly, the Court has found in many cases that a domestic measure violates the Convention right to freedom of expression without proceeding to a full blown balancing of competing rights and interests. Like the Court of Justice of the European Union, it frequently decides cases on the grounds that the measure is not the least restrictive means of achieving a legitimate objective.[46] It is however also willing to use the full range of proportionality *stricto sensu* balancing to determine whether a domestic measure, for which there is no less restrictive alternative, pursues an objective that in the circumstances must outweigh the right to freedom of expression.[47] This method stands in obvious contrast to a

---

[42] Schauer, F., 'Freedom of Expression Adjudication in Europe and the United States: A Case Study in Comparative Constitutional Architecture', in Nolte, G., *European and US Constitutionalism*, (Cambridge University Press, 2005), 47–64 at 52. Gerards, J. and Senden, H., 'The Structure of Fundamental Rights and the European Court of Human Rights', 7(4) *International Journal of Constitutional Law* (2009), 619–653.

[43] Gardbaum, S., 'A Democratic Defense of Constitutional Balancing', 4(1) *Law & Ethics of Human Rights* (2009).

[44] Under Article 10(2), the Court has determined that a state party may only legitimately restrict the liberty to speak or publish or deny access to information where it demonstrates that the measures used are prescribed by law for a legitimate aim, which is based on the express grounds set out in Article 10(2), and are necessary in a democratic society. To satisfy the latter condition, the state party must also demonstrate that the measures address a pressing social need and are proportionate to that objective. See Nicol, A., Millar, G., and Sharland, A., *Media Law and Human Rights*, 2nd edn (Oxford University Press, 2009), 13–35.

[45] On proportionality analysis, see Chapter 2.

[46] See, for example, *Informationsverein Lentia and Others v. Austria* (Application No. 37093/97) (24 November 1993).

[47] See, for example, *Stoll v. Switzerland* (Grand Chamber) (Application No. 69698/01) (10 December 2007).

more rights centred approach to constitutional adjudication, in which a narrowly defined right is given a more assertive and categorical application in the face of competing interests.[48]

To give this interpretative method sufficient stability, the Court has needed to identify the core purposes of Article 10(1) or, in other words, the most important interests served by the liberty to speak and publish. Where those core purposes are restricted or otherwise frustrated by domestic measures, the right to freedom of expression will weigh more heavily and the measure concerned, however legitimate in itself, will be held to a higher standard of review. In these circumstances, the risk or burden of harm will consequently tip towards the state, the general public, or the specific individuals affected by the expression at issue. The core purposes of Article 10 identified by the Court are consequential in nature. In its view, the essence of this Convention right to freedom of expression is the protection of democratic processes and the scrutiny of public institutions and public affairs more generally.[49] This does not mean that expression outside those, such as artistic or commercial expression, does not merit protection under Article 10.[50] Where state parties impose restrictions on these forms of expression for legitimate purposes, however, the Court tends to use a lesser standard of review.[51]

To determine whether a challenged measure interferes with freedom of expression in a manner that engages the core purposes, the Court uses several indicative factors. The most important of these, although somewhat vaguely defined, is whether the substance of the matter in dispute is of general interest. This is a wide category taking in matters of purely local concern, such as an alleged act of surgical malpractice, as well as matters of international controversy, such as the operation of the Norwegian seal hunting industry.[52] While this principle of general interest can only begin to clarify the issues, its breadth and flexibility has one obvious advantage. It weakens the liberal democratic objection that the state in the form of judges, or even worse a supranational court, should not decide what is a legitimate matter for public debate or comment.

Within this extensive field of matters of general interest, the Court has developed more specific factors to help determine when Article 10(1) is most deeply engaged. Given the Court's intense concern to protect and foster democracy in the member states, it is plain that expression directly connected to democratic elections, especially

---

[48] Schauer, F., n. 42 above. See also Wagner DeCew, J., 'Free Speech and Offensive Expression,' 21 *Social Philosophy and Policy* (2004), 81–103.

[49] The Court has thus frequently stated, '[t]here is little scope under Article 10 para. 2 of the Convention for restrictions on political speech or on debate of questions of public interest', *Lingens v. Austria*, n. 37 above, para. 42. See also *Thorgeir Thorgeirson v. Iceland* (Application No. 13778/88) (25 June 1992), para. 63.

[50] On commercial expression, see *Markt Intern Verlag Gmbh and Klaus Beermann v. Germany* (Application No. 10572/83) (20 November 1989), para. 26, and Randall, M., 'Commercial Speech under the European Convention on Human Rights: Subordinate or Equal?' 6(1) *Human Rights Law Review* (2006). On artistic expression, see *Müller and Others v. Switzerland* (Application No. 10737/84) (24 May 1988), para. 33.

[51] See Nicol, A., Millar, G., and Sharland, A., n. 44 above, 214–218. See below, discussion of the margin of appreciation.

[52] *Bladet Tromsø and Stensaas v. Norway* (Application No. 21980/93) (20 May 1999).

speech or publications that seek to persuade voters to support a candidate or policy position, will draw greater protection. Article 10 will also give similarly robust protection to expression that not only concerns a matter of general interest, but also concerns a person who has a significant role in public affairs, such as a politician or other public figure.[53] On that basis, the Court found the decision of the Austrian Court of Appeal to grant damages and an injunction to a politician, pictured naked and engaged in vivid sexual activities in a satirical painting, to be a violation of Article 10.[54]

The Court also takes into account whether the expression at issue is contained in a media publication or at least a publication that is directed at the general public.[55] Article 10 does not expressly refer to the media, but it does protect the right 'to receive information and ideas', which among other things is a prerequisite for informed democratic participation. In the Court's view, that right cannot be properly satisfied without an independent media capable of performing an essential watchdog role in a democratic society.[56] As a result, in Article 10 applications, a state party that has restricted a media publication will bear a heavier burden of justification. The Court has also extended this principle in several directions. Editors and journalists are entitled to a wide discretion not only in the substance of what they publish, but also in their methods of expression, which may be deliberately exaggerated or provocative.[57] They are also entitled to keep the identity of their sources secret, unless the state can show compelling reasons to force disclosure.[58]

The Court's conclusion that the core purposes of Article 10 are to protect democratic participation and the scrutiny of public institutions and public affairs makes good sense from several perspectives. As an institutional matter, it reflects the original goal of the Council of Europe to renew democracy in western Europe in the aftermath of World War II.[59] It also accords with public international law rules of treaty interpretation, which the Court frequently uses to develop the meaning of

---

[53] On public figure status, see Chapter 10.

[54] *Vereinigung Bildender Künstler*, n. 39 above.

[55] 'The most careful scrutiny on the part of the Court is called for when, as in the present case, the measures taken or sanctions imposed by the national authority are capable of discouraging the participation of the press in debates over matters of legitimate public concern': *Bladet Tromsø and Stensaas v. Norway*, n. 52 above, para. 64.

[56] 'Not only does the press have the task of imparting such information and ideas: the public also has a right to receive them. Were it otherwise, the press would be unable to play its vital role of "public watchdog"': *Observer and Guardian v. the United Kingdom*, (Application No. 13585/88) (26 November 1991), para. 59. 'In this respect, the pre-eminent role of the press in a State governed by the rule of law must not be forgotten. Although it must not overstep various bounds set, inter alia, for the prevention of disorder and the protection of the reputation of others, it is nevertheless incumbent on it to impart information and ideas on political questions and on other matters of public interest': *Castells v. Spain* (Application No. 11798/85) (23 April 1992), para. 43. See also Kelley, D., and Donway, R., 'Liberalism and Free Speech', in Lichtenberg, J., (ed.), *Democracy and the Mass Media* (Cambridge, 1990), 66–101.

[57] *Prager and Oberschlick v. Austria* (Application No. 15974/90) (26 April 1995), para. 38.

[58] On the protection of journalists' sources, see Chapter 9.

[59] See recitals of the 1949 Treaty of London (Statute of the Council of Europe), n. 3 above.

the Convention.[60] These rules require the Court to interpret each provision according to the 'object and purpose' of the ECHR, which includes 'effective political democracy'.[61] This orientation towards liberal democracy, plainly of great importance during the Cold War, found a new focus with the sudden change of governments and national boundaries in eastern Europe and the Balkans. The accession of a large number of young democracies to the Convention has made the Court a key institution in safeguarding the growth of democratic institutions in these countries.[62]

In addition, the Court's consequential view of freedom of expression has enabled it to sidestep, at least partially, the irresolvable tensions in liberal thought between the liberty to publish and the protection of collective and personal well being. In the Convention, that latent tension is most acute in the relationship between the Article 10 right to freedom of expression and the voluminous Article 8 right to respect for private life. As these Convention rights, in principle, have equal weight, a balancing exercise directed at the deontological values of the liberty to publish as compared to the protection of mental and physical well being from the consequences of that liberty would be a comparison of incommensurables. The Court's consequential approach to freedom of expression therefore gives it a reasonably objective method for overcoming that impasse.

Ironically, the Court's identification of the core purposes of Article 8 is more deontological in nature. As the Court stated in *Von Hannover v. Germany,* 'private life, in the Court's view, includes a person's physical and psychological integrity; the guarantee afforded by Article 8 of the Convention is primarily intended to ensure the development, without outside interference, of the personality of each individual in his relations with other human beings'.[63] The values of personal and psychological integrity, evoking fundamental concepts of autonomy and human dignity, are also important to the liberty of the individual to speak and publish. However, by emphasizing the importance of democracy and openness in public affairs under Article 10, the Court has created a set of principles that can be used to determine when that Article ought to take precedence over Article 8. Clearly, where there is a direct clash between the core interests protected by Articles 10 and 8, a proportionality analysis will be finely balanced, demanding an exceptional public interest to overcome the need to respect the most intimate personal and psychological concerns of the individual.[64] As discussed below, that sphere of confrontation becomes wider if the core purposes of these Articles are described in generalities.

---

[60] Vienna Convention on the Law of Treaties, UN Doc. A/Conf.39/27, Article 31.

[61] See European Convention on Human Rights, n. 8 above, Preamble. See also Article 3 of Protocol No. 1 to the Convention, which states that '[t]he High Contracting Parties undertake to hold free elections at reasonable intervals by secret ballot, under conditions which will ensure the free expression of the opinion of the people in the choice of the legislature'.

[62] See, for example, *Manole a.o. v. Moldova* (Application No. 13936/02) (17 September 2009), *Meltex Ltd and Mesrop Movsesyan v. Armenia,* (Application No. 32283/04) (17 June 2008), and *Glas Nadezhda Eood and Elenkov v. Bulgaria* (Application No. 14134/02) (11 October 2007). See also Chapter 14.

[63] *Von Hannover v. Germany* (Application No. 59320/00) (24 June 2004), para. 50.

[64] See, for example, *Plon* (Société) *v. France* (Application No. 56148/00) (18 May 2004).

The consequentialist orientation of Article 10 can also be used to determine the proper limits of the liberty to publish when state security and public order interests are threatened. These are listed as mere legitimate interests in Article 10(2) and are therefore in principle secondary to the Article 10(1) right to freedom of expression. These interests however are rooted in the territorial state's claim to be the exclusive entity capable of sustaining an effective, large scale liberal democracy. Article 10 thus harbours one of the oldest conundrums of political liberalism, that liberty requires the state. If the core purposes of Article 10 are to protect democracy and openness in public affairs, the tension between liberty and security is certainly not dissolved, but it does give the Court a clearer focus in weighing the competing arguments.[65]

Nonetheless, the Court has not been able to capitalize on its consequential interpretation of Article 10 as much as the foregoing discussion would suggest. Determining when the argument for democracy and openness will override the well being interests of others, or the security needs of the state, depends on the conception of democracy used. In its judgments, the Court has however only sketched out a loose picture of democracy, referring expansively to its qualities of pluralism, tolerance, and broadmindedness and insisting on the importance of democratic elections.[66] As membership in the Council of Europe has expanded, the already dim prospects for a more specific idea of European democracy have receded further. While a thick concept of democracy would certainly give the consequential perspective on freedom of expression greater depth and clarity, the Convention must retain a definition that is flexible enough to apply from one edge of Europe to the other. 'And because the Court has only a "thin" conception of a democratic society to work with, engaging in a debate on what a pluralistic, democratic society should look like will be fraught with difficulties.'[67]

The sphere of direct confrontation between Articles 10 and 8 is therefore exceptionally broad and not well defined. The Court is simply unable to give a consistent explanation of the circumstances in which a public figure's right to a private life should yield to the needs of democracy and transparency in public affairs. Nor can it give a consistent explanation of the legitimate purposes of the state outside the core area of democratic government As Jacco Bomhoff has argued, constitutional adjudication ideally places 'the relationship between individual rights and governmental powers on a thick, substantive, historically and culturally con-tingent conception of democracy'.[68] Instead, 'the Court has centred its conceptual apparatus around what may count as the safe, central element of its mandate; the

---

[65]   See, for example, *Ceylan v. Turkey* (Application No. 23556/94) (8 July 1999), *Özgür Gündem v. Turkey* (Application No. 23144/93) (16 March 2000), and *Yalçin Küçük (No. 3) v. Turkey* (Application No. 71353/01) (22 April 2008).

[66]   'Such are the demands of that pluralism, tolerance and broadmindedness without which there is no "democratic society"': *Oberschlick v. Austria (No. 1)* (Application No. 11662/85) (23 May 1991), para. 57. See also *Bowman v. United Kingdom* (Application No. 24839/94) (19 February 1998).

[67]   Bomhoff, J., 'The Rights and Freedoms of Others: The ECHR and its Peculiar Category of Conflicts between Individual Fundamental Rights' in Brems, E. (ed), *Conflicts Between Fundamental Rights* (Intersentia, 2008), 619–654, at 635.

[68]   Ibid.

definition of individual rights'.[69] From this perspective, the protection of democracy and the scrutiny of public affairs under Article 10 is thin because it is essentially no more than the clustered rights of individuals.

Uncertainty over the concept of democracy in European human rights law inevitably spills over into the special role the Court has given to the media under Article 10. If the media deserves exceptional protection because it serves the core purposes of Article 10, the boundaries of that zone of protection will be defined by the Court's notion of democracy and transparency. A broad, flexible view of democracy will thus yield a similarly broad and flexible definition of the media, which becomes not only a watchdog to inform the public, but also a vehicle for political pluralism, cultural diversity, and social solidarity.[70] At some point however this breadth becomes excessive and it is not clear when or why the involvement of the media should decisively shift the balancing exercise towards the liberty to publish.

This problem has grown as the communications revolution has eroded distinctions between mass and personal communications as well as professional journalism and private correspondence. As the Court has repeatedly made clear, the news media's privileged position under Article 10 will often depend on whether the journalists or editors concerned have acted in good faith and in accordance with the ethical standards of the profession.[71] Keying the application of Article 10 into the professional standards of journalists usefully helps to clarify the media's proper zone of protection, excluding sloppy journalism as well as the realm of private expression. Yet the erosion of boundaries that once defined journalism has challenged the very idea of a distinct, professional news media. In the internet era, the news media now includes many individuals who are not trained journalists and do not operate under the control of dedicated media organizations, but nonetheless provide current affairs information to the general public. The most obvious solution is to develop a more functional and less status based approach to the information watchdog role in a democratic society. That solution however requires a clearer definition of the democratic purposes of Article 10, which the Court will be hard pressed to do without cutting into the autonomy of the state parties.

Questions about the role of the new media in European democracy are not confined to the problem of determining when the state may properly restrict content publication or distribution. They have risen even more sharply in relation to positive state interventions in the media to achieve social and cultural policy

---

[69] Ibid.

[70] *Demuth v. Switzerland* (Application No. 38743/97) (5 November 2002), para. 33.

[71] 'By reason of the "duties and responsibilities" inherent in the exercise of the freedom of expression, the safeguard afforded by Article 10 to journalists in relation to reporting on issues of general interest is subject to the proviso that they are acting in good faith in order to provide accurate and reliable information in accordance with the ethics of journalism': *Bladet Tromsø and Stensaas v. Norway*, n. 52 above, para. 65. See also *Fressoz and Roire v. France* (Application No. 29183/95) (Grand Chamber, 21 January 1999), para. 54, which states that Article 10 'protects journalists' rights to divulge information on issues of general interest provided that they are acting in good faith and on an accurate factual basis and provide "reliable and precise" information in accordance with the ethics of journalism'.

goals. Here, the communications revolution has intensified the strained relationship between the economic liberty aspects of freedom of expression and the European public service media model.[72] The destruction of the barriers that once separated traditional media markets has brought the public service broadcasting model into a radically new, convergent media context. This has reopened basic questions about the rationale and methods of state participation in the media and their effects on the general liberty to publish.

In 1950, when the CE Committee of Experts on Human Rights was drafting the Convention, the Council of Europe member states were all directly involved in the provision of national broadcasting services. The contemplated right to freedom of expression, which embraces the liberal democratic principle of liberty from the state, posed an obvious threat to these broadcasting regimes, which were dominated by the state through monopolies and restrictions on broadcast licensing as well as content restrictions and obligations. It is presumably for this reason that the Committee of Ministers decided to include a third sentence in the final draft of Article 10(1), which states that, '[t]his article shall not prevent States from requiring the licensing of broadcasting, television or cinema enterprises'.[73] In time, the Court would use this short statement to justify not only the licensing of broadcast services, but also for the entire edifice of public service media in Europe.

In its early decisions, the Court found that this sentence permits the selective licensing of broadcasting services on technical grounds, such as the prevention of radio signal interference.[74] Later, it extended its scope to include content requirements. In its important *Informationsverein Lentia* decision, the Court stated that the third sentence of Article 10(1) justifies licensing restrictions based on 'the nature and objectives of the proposed station, its potential audience at national regional or local levels, the rights and needs of a specific audience, and obligations deriving from international legal instruments'.[75] In doing so, the Court has treated this sentence as if it were included in the Article 10(2) legitimate grounds for exception, subjecting any licensing measures aimed at these social policy goals to the full range of 10(2) conditions. It has also yoked these grounds to the core democratic purposes of Article 10. National licensing systems must therefore support media pluralism, which now means that extensive state monopolies are prohibited and private media must be reasonably accommodated.[76] In this vein, the Court has also found violations of Article 10 in where broadcast licensing is tainted with arbitrariness and favouritism.[77]

---

[72] See Chapter 14.

[73] European Commission of Human Rights, *Preparatory Work on Article 10 of the European Convention on Human Rights*, DH (56)15, 17 August 1956.

[74] *Groppera Radio AG v. Switzerland* (Application No. 10890/84) (28 March 1990).

[75] *Informationsverein Lentia and Others v. Austria* (Application No. 37093/97) (24 November 1993), para. 32.

[76] See *Verein Alternatives Lokalradio Bern and Verein Radio Dreyeckland Basel v. Switzerland* (Application No. 10746/84), Commission decision of 16 October 1986, cited *inter alia* in *Informationsverein Lentia and Others v. Austria*, n. 75 above. See also Article 1 of Protocol No.1 to the European Convention on Human Rights, which safeguards a right to property.

[77] See, for example, *Meltex Ltd and Mesrop Movsesyan v. Armenia*, n. 62 above. See also Chapter 14.

Digitization has of course exponentially increased the carrying capacity of radio-spectrum, cable, and other transmission platforms, which has made licensing a minor administrative requirement for many audio and audiovisual services. Consequently, the third sentence of Article 10(1) is no longer a key provision protecting the national power to allocate broadcasting frequencies. It is nonetheless still hugely relevant to the legitimacy of licensing conditions or restrictions, especially those affecting public service media. State parties may therefore use this sentence to justify restrictions on particular sources or kinds of information or entertainment content, effectively favouring domestic content for social and cultural reasons. In addition, they are entitled to mandate positive content obligations to achieve other public service objectives, such as children's or news and current affairs programmes. Indeed, the CE Committee of Ministers has strenuously emphasized the benefits of public service media to its member states in advancing pluralism and social cohesion.[78]

This support for state mandated media content does not always sit comfortably with the underlying Article 10 commitment to the liberty to speak and publish. As mentioned, the Court has rejected the extensive state broadcast monopolies that were once the essence of the European media model in times of transmission scarcity. As well, the Court has opposed sweeping restrictions on broadcast political advertising, even for allegedly pluralist purposes, insisting that these schemes cannot exclude marginal parties and groups from major media platforms.[79] In contrast, there have been no major Article 10 decisions overturning the discriminatory use of European content quotas or challenging the selective use of subsidies for public service media. While these measures may disadvantage competitors, they do not directly interfere with the rights of specific individuals to freedom of expression, which is the primary concern of Article 10. All of which reflects the unresolved character of European human rights law, which attempts to accommodate the great diversity of liberal democratic thought and must therefore reconcile, or at least sidestep, contradictory notions of the state as both foe and friend of liberty.[80]

For the Council of Europe member states, Article 10 has always been a wayward cannon when directed at their national broadcast media regimes. These developed over many years through complex interplays between social and cultural policy and revenue and production requirements. They also depended on the comparative isolation of national broadcasting systems. As satellite television broadcasting began

---

[78] See, for example, Committee of Ministers Recommendation on media pluralism and diversity of media content CM/Rec (2007) 2, Committee of Ministers Recommendation to member states on the remit of public service media in the information society Rec (2007) 3, and Committee of Ministers, Declaration on Cultural Diversity (7 December 2000). See also Chapter 15.

[79] See *Verein Gegen Tierfabriken Schweiz (Vgt) v. Switzerland (No. 2)*, (Grand Chamber), (Application No. 32772/02) (30 June 2009) and *TV Vest As & Rogaland Pensjonistparti v. Norway* (Application No. 21132/05) (11 December 2008). See also Chapter 14.

[80] Contrast with contemporary American constitutional doctrine, which assumes that the motive of the state is invariably to burden disfavored speech or speakers. See Kagan, E., 'Private Speech, Public Purpose: The Role of Governmental Motive in First Amendment Doctrine', 63 *University of Chicago Law Review* (1996), 413, 443–505.

to break into these markets in the 1980s, new foreign based television channels frequently transmitted prohibited commercial content in determined efforts to tap into domestic advertising revenue. The welcoming attitude of the Court to this development underscored the power of twinned political and economic arguments for the freedom to transmit content across national borders.[81] In the face of these developments, the member states sought to develop a stable legal and policy framework through other Council of Europe instruments, in particular the Trans-frontier Television Convention.[82] This treaty, created in parallel with the EU Television Without Frontiers Directive, necessarily accepted the principle of cross border television broadcasting, but attempted to counter its disruptive potential by including common European content standards.[83]

The margin of appreciation

The Court's interpretation of Article 10 has not only put concerns about democracy and governance at the heart of European media law, but has also made those concerns a rationale for deeper penetration into domestic law. According to the Court's doctrine of the margin of appreciation, state parties to the Convention are entitled to greater leeway or discretion to impose restrictions on expression when the central purposes of Article 10 are not directly engaged.[84] This judicial self restraint is intended to respect the autonomy of the state parties.[85] It leaves the implementation of the Convention to them as much as possible, especially in matters where the influence of local culture and beliefs are particularly important.[86]

Accordingly, the Court has declared that, 'a wider margin of appreciation is generally available to the Contracting States when regulating freedom of expression

---

[81] In *Autronic AG v. Switzerland* (Application No. 12726/87) (22 May 1990), the Court found that national laws, which prohibit the reception of foreign satellite broadcasts lawfully transmitted from other states regardless of content, violate Article 10.

[82] Draft Explanatory Report to the revised European Convention on Transfrontier Audiovisual Media Services, 25: 'Given the risk that increased international competition between the new services which were developing in Europe could induce a purely market approach to broadcasting and a general lowering of standards to the detriment of the effective choice of the public, the public service concept of broadcasting (whether publicly or privately organised) and Europe's cultural heritage were at the heart of concerns in those days about the development of transfrontier broadcasting in Europe.' See also Bernd Möwes, *Fifty years of media policy in the Council of Europe—a Review*, 6th European Ministerial Conference on Mass Media Policy (June 2000).

[83] European Convention on Transfrontier Television, n. 32 above, Article 10.

[84] As the Court has stated, 'Article 10(2) leaves to the Contracting States a margin of appreciation. This margin is given both to the domestic legislator ... and to the bodies, judicial amongst others that are called upon to interpret and apply the laws in force ...' 'Nevertheless, Article 10(2) does not give the Contracting States an unlimited power of appreciation': *Sunday Times v. the United Kingdom* (Application No. 6538/74) (26 April 1979), para. 59.

[85] Mahoney, P., n. 13 above.

[86] 'The Convention leaves to each Contracting State, in the first place, the task of securing the rights and liberties it enshrines. The institutions created by it make their own contribution to this task but they become involved only through contentious proceedings and once all domestic remedies have been exhausted (Article 26)': *Handyside v. the United Kingdom* (Application No. 5493/72) (7 December 1976), para. 48.

in relation to matters liable to offend intimate personal convictions within the sphere of morals or, especially, religion'.[87] Where artistic or commercial expression offends widely held moral or religious beliefs, but does not engage the core purposes of Article 10, review of restrictive domestic measures will thus be less intensive. When considering restrictions on purely commercial expression, the Court should therefore 'confine its review to the question whether the measures taken on the national level are justifiable in principle and proportionate'.[88] In contrast, the intensity of review deepens considerably whenever a state restriction on expression engages those core purposes. As discussed above, this is typically indicated by the presence of key factors, such as the fact that the expression at issue concerns a matter of general interest.[89] Here, the narrow margin of appreciation is intended to protect the integrity of the Convention, compelling state parties into compliance with its principal purposes.

Where the margin of appreciation is limited, the Court will pay close attention to the legal and factual circumstances of the application and its decision may depart from the findings of the domestic courts or authorities on essential points.[90] This fine grained review leads to an expectation of more finely meshed compliance, which tightly curtails the autonomy of the state parties.[91] It also results in a negative harmonization of domestic laws at a greater level of specificity in areas where politically and socially important expression are at issue. This is certainly a reasonably effective way to identify and curb illiberal state practices that violate the purposes of Article 10. In these areas, however, this harmonization necessarily imposes a common view of liberal freedom of expression that, while broad, inevitably eliminates important opposing or divergent strands of liberal thought. This is most noticeable where the Convention right to freedom of expression is

---

[87] *Wingrove v. the United Kingdom* (Application No. 17419/90) (25 November 1996), para. 58. The Court also declared in *Handyside v. the United Kingdom*, n. 86 above, para 48, '[I]t is not possible to find in the domestic law of the various Contracting States a uniform European conception of morals. The view taken by their respective laws of the requirements of morals varies from time to time and from place to place, especially in our era which is characterised by a rapid and far-reaching evolution of opinions on the subject. By reason of their direct and continuous contact with the vital forces of their countries, State authorities are in principle in a better position than the international judge to give an opinion on the exact content of these requirements as well as on the "necessity" of a "restriction" or "penalty" intended to meet them.'

[88] *Markt Intern Verlag GmbH and Klaus Beermann v. Germany*, n. 50 above, para. 33. See also Randall, M.H.,'Commercial Speech under the European Convention on Human Rights: Subordinate or Equal?' 6(1) *Human Rights Law Review* (2006). The Court's view of commercial expression is notably less even handed than that of the United States Supreme Court, although even there commercial expression is also less well protected. See *Central Hudson Gas & Electric Corp. v. Public Service Commission of New York* 447 U.S. 557 (1980).

[89] See, for example, *Bladet Tromsø and Stensaas v. Norway*, n. 52 above, para. 59, in which the Court stated, '. . . in cases such as the present one the national margin of appreciation is circumscribed by the interest of democratic society in enabling the press to exercise its vital role of "public watchdog" in imparting information of serious public concern.'

[90] In *Bladet Tromsø and Stensaas v. Norway*, ibid., for example, the Court disregarded the conclusions of the Norwegian courts regarding the status and significance of a confidential report to a Norwegian government ministry.

[91] Lord Hoffmann, 'The Universality of Human Rights', *Judicial Studies Board Annual Lecture*, 19 March 2009.

opposed by another fundamental treaty right, such as the Article 8 right to a private life. When this occurs, the Court is forced to balance these opposing rights on highly specific terms.[92]

Balancing rights and interests

The structure of the Convention, coupled with the dense case law of the Court, has created major differences in how specific restrictions on the liberty to publish are evaluated. Other Convention rights are, for example, given greater weight than the legitimate interests set out in Article 10(2), which must, in principle, be narrowly interpreted and rigorously justified.[93] It is consequently sensible to anchor, if at all possible, a domestic measure that restricts expression in a suitable Convention right, rather than rely on a mere legitimate interest. In recent years, Article 8 has provided a major target for these efforts and the Court has had difficulty in determining the boundary between its right to respect for private life and related interests set out in Article 10(2). According to the Court, in exceptional circumstances the protection of reputation will engage the protection of Article 8, but ordinarily it is only a legitimate Article 10(2) interest.[94]

Aside from the pressure to expand the scope of Convention rights, the Court has also had difficulty in giving appropriate weight to the diverse legitimate interests that are not enclosed within a Convention right. These include individual or collective interests in not being exposed to expression that is seriously offensive to moral or religious beliefs. Plainly, Article 10(2) recognizes a legitimate state interest in the protection of 'public morals' and the Court has used the 10(2) reference to the 'rights of others' expansively to include the protection of religious beliefs.[95] The difficulty here lies in the fact that moral and religious beliefs are vitally important to democratic politics and are therefore thickly woven into domestic law and public policy.[96] This turns the core democratic purpose of Article 10 in a circle as majority preferences, including moral beliefs, are the very stuff of democratic life, which presents the Court with the classic problem of illiberal democratic majorities. In

---

[92] See, for example, *Lindon, Otchakovsky-Laurens and July v. France*, n. 40 above, para. 57, in which the Court stated, that, '... regardless of the forcefulness of political struggles, it is legitimate to try to ensure that they abide by a minimum degree of moderation and propriety, especially as the reputation of a politician, even a controversial one, must benefit from the protection afforded by the Convention'.

[93] See, for example, *Observer and The Guardian v. the United Kingdom* n. 56 above, para. 59. See also Gerards, J.H., 'Fundamental rights and other interests—should it really make a difference?' in: E. Brems (ed.), *Conflicts between Fundamental Rights* (Intersentia, 2008), 655–690.

[94] See, for example, *Karako v. Hungary* (Application No. 39311/05) (28 April 2009).

[95] Note that the European Convention on Human Rights, Article 9 right to freedom of thought, conscience, and religion requires that the state protect individuals from interference with their religious beliefs, but does not oblige the state to protect them from expression that is offensive to religious beliefs. See *Choudhury v. The United Kingdom* (Application No. 17439/90) (5 March 1991).

[96] On the historic role of religion in many Council of Europe member states, including the importance of Christian Democratic parties in establishing the post World War II western European regional order, see Kalyvas, S., *The Rise of Christian Democracy in Europe* (Cornell University Press, 1996).

response, the Court has decided that a restrictive measure will not violate the Convention right to freedom of expression, provided that the expression at issue has no obvious political or social importance and also causes gross offence to significant moral or religious sensibilities.[97] Convention case law thus arguably reveals an implicit right not to be gratuitously offended, which is rooted in majoritarian democracy as well as influential concepts of human dignity.[98]

The Court's problems in maintaining clear positions of principle when confronted with opposing rights or interests that claim equally to engage the core purposes of Article 10 is to some extent a problem of proportionality analysis. This method of adjudication has important benefits in forcing state parties to justify their restrictions on the media in a thorough, principled manner. However, it is a method that can turn into an open ended, ad hoc balancing exercise that depletes the notion of rights of their jurisprudential significance.[99] It is moreover particularly difficult for a supranational court to ground proportionality analysis in a specific political or moral perspective, as this normally requires allegiance to a particular society's constitutional values. The mandate of the European Court of Human Rights is however to develop principles that are flexible enough to apply in all Council of Europe member states, regardless of their local conditions or particular liberal democratic values. Consequently, even if the Court wished to develop a clearer conception of the priorities of Article 10, it is poorly placed to graft the text of Article 10 onto specific political or moral commitments. Quite reasonably, the Court prefers to invoke consequentialist principles, which it applies as narrowly as possible to the individual applicant's circumstances, thus treading lightly between complex domestic contexts and wider conceptual issues.[100] This narrow focus however leaves it in danger of blundering into domestic regulatory regimes or public policy fields without the capacity to evaluate the full range of relevant issues.[101]

---

[97] See *Otto Preminger Institut v. Austria* (Application No. 13470/87) (20 September 1994) and *I.A. v. Turkey* (Application No. 42571/98) (13 September 2005).

[98] McCrudden, C., 'Human dignity and judicial interpretation of human rights', 19 *European Journal of International Law* (2008), 655–724 at 702: 'Dignity sometimes functions as a justification for limiting the protection of rights or obligations, similar to a public order or public morals exception, allowing the state to place limits on what particular rights would otherwise require.' See also McGonagle, T., 'Safeguarding Human Dignity in the European Audiovisual Sector' *IRIS Plus*, 2007–6.

[99] Gerards, J., n. 14 above. See also Tsakyrakis, S., 'Proportionality: An Assault on Human Rights?' 7(3) *International Journal of Constitutional Law* (July 2009), 468–493.

[100] See Bomhoff, J., 'The Rights and Freedoms of Others: The ECHR and its Peculiar Category of Conflicts between Individual Fundamental Rights', in Eva Brems (ed.), *Conflicts Between Fundamental Rights* (Intersentia, 2008), 619–654.

[101] Criticism of this kind has been levelled at the Court in its treatment of the complex field of political advertising. See, for example, *R. (on the Application of Animal Defenders International) v. Secretary of State for Culture, Media and Sport* (House of Lords) [2008] UKHL 15. But see Sackman, S., 'Debating "Democracy" and the Ban on Political Advertising, 72(3) *The Modern Law Review* (2009), 475–487.

Part II—International human rights law and the media

International human rights law has many obvious parallels with European human rights law in its interface with the domestic media state relationship. The liberty to publish is secured, as a general principle, in the 1948 Universal Declaration of Human Rights (UDHR).[102] Article 19 of the UDHR proclaims that, '[e]veryone has the right to freedom of opinion and expression; this right includes the right to hold opinions without interference and to seek, receive, and impart information and ideas through any media and regardless of frontiers'. These provisions were soon restated at greater length in Article 19 of the draft International Covenant on Civil and Political Rights (ICCPR).[103] The UN General Assembly, however, did not adopt that treaty or its companion, the International Covenant on Economic, Social and Cultural Rights (ICESCR),[104] until 1966.[105] The UDHR and the ICCPR not only declare the fundamental obligation of states to guarantee freedom of expression, but also set that principle in a nest of related rights and interests. Article 19 is therefore the chief point of reference for international debates over the proper limits to the liberty to publish and distribute media content.

In its structure, Article 19 is a close cousin of Article 10 of the 1950 European Convention on Human Rights.[106] Indeed, it was already available in draft form for

---

[102] The Universal Declaration of Human Rights, GA Resolution 217A (III), UN Doc A/810 at 71 (1948). On the UDHR generally, see Klug, F., 'The Universal Declaration of Human Rights: 60 years on', *Public Law* (Spring 2009) and Risse, M., 'Securing Human Rights Intellectually: Philosophical Inquiries about the Universal Declaration', in Kosslyn, S. and Hammonds, E. (eds), in the series *The New Harvard Bookshelf: Towards a Liberal Education for the 21st Century*.

[103] International Covenant on Civil and Political Rights, GA Resolution 2200A (XXI), UN Doc. A/6316 (1966). On the history of the ICCPR drafting negotiations, see Bossuyt, M., *Guide to the 'Travaux Préparatoires' of the International Covenant on Civil and Political Rights*, (M. Nijhoff, 1987). See also Joseph, S., Schultz, J., and Castan, M., *International Covenant on Civil and Political Rights, Cases, Materials, and Commentary*, 2nd edn (Oxford University Press, 2004).

[104] International Covenant on Economic, Social, and Cultural Rights, GA Resolution 2200A (XXI), 21 UN GAOR Supp. (No. 16) at 49, UN Doc. A/6316 (1966); Craven, M., *The International Covenant on Economic, Social, and Cultural Rights: A Perspective on its Development* (Clarendon Press, 1995), 56–57; Choukroune, L., 'Justiciability of economic, social, and cultural rights: the UN Committee on Economic, Social and Cultural Rights' review of China's first periodic report on the implementation of the International Covenant on Economic, Social and Cultural Rights' 19 *Columbia Journal of Asian Law* (2005), 30–49.

[105] It took a further ten years after the adoption of the texts by the General assembly for the two Covenants to gain a sufficient number of ratifications to come into force. Several major states, dissatisfied with the outcome, declined to become parties. The American government had declared as early as 1953 that it would assist in drafting the Covenants and would not become a party. It was not until 1977 that the United States government under the Carter administration changed its position, signing both Covenants that year and later ratifying its signature to the ICCPR in 1992. It has chosen not to ratify the ICESCR. While Russia, through its predecessor state the Soviet Union, became a party to both treaties in 1973, China has proceeded more cautiously, ratifying its accession to the ICESCR in 2001. It has yet to ratify its 1998 signature to the ICCPR.

[106] ICCPR, Article 19: '1. Everyone shall have the right to hold opinions without interference. 2. Everyone shall have the right to freedom of expression; this right shall include freedom to seek, receive and impart information and ideas of all kinds, regardless of frontiers, either orally, in writing or in print, in the form of art, or through any other media of his choice. 3. The exercise of the rights provided for in paragraph 2 of this article carries with it special duties and responsibilities. It may therefore be

the Council of Europe's Committee of Experts to consider when they began their work on Article 10, which partly accounts for the drafting similarities.[107] Both set out the right to freedom of expression in broad terms followed by the grounds and conditions necessary for any legitimate state restrictions on the liberty to speak or publish. Much like ECHR Article 10, Article 19 of the ICCPR is also related to other rights in the Covenant, including Article 18, which requires state parties to protect the right to freedom of thought, conscience, and religion.

The United Nations, like the Council of Europe, has its own constellation of human rights treaties. Article 19 is therefore connected to derivative provisions in these treaties that buttress the Covenant right to freedom of expression. Article 13 of the Convention on the Rights of the Child declares, for example, that '[t]he child shall have the right to freedom of expression; this right shall include freedom to seek, receive and impart information and ideas of all kinds, regardless of frontiers, either orally, in writing or in print, in the form of art, or through any other media of the child's choice'.[108] These links with other rights, in the Covenant and in other UN human rights treaties, also imply that state party obligations regarding the Article 19 right to freedom of expression are not only negative restraints on the state, but also carry positive responsibilities to ensure freedom of expression is universally available within the state.[109]

On the opposite side of the media state relationship, the ICCPR and ECHR take a similar approach to the protection of state, collective, and individual interests from the harmful effects of expression. In the Covenant, these interests are primarily covered by the public policy grounds set out in Article 19(3), which set out the conditions for legitimate restrictions on freedom of expression. As compared to Article 10(2) ECHR, the public policy grounds set out in Article 19(3) of the Covenant are expressed in fewer but broader terms.[110] Most notably, Article 19(3) includes the protection of public order (*ordre public*) as a legitimate ground for restricting speech or publications, which encompasses a broad range of measures necessary for effective government and social stability. The ECHR and the ICCPR are also similar in providing that a state party may only restrict expression on these recognized grounds if it has demonstrated that its measures are 'provided by law' and 'necessary'.[111]

The public policy grounds identified in Article 19(3) have direct links with protected rights set out in other articles of the Covenant. In common with the

---

subject to certain restrictions, but these shall only be such as are provided by law and are necessary: (a) For respect of the rights or reputations of others; (b) For the protection of national security or of public order (ordre public), or of public health or morals.'

[107] European Commission of Human Rights, Preparatory Work on Article 10 of the European Convention on Human Rights (17 August 1956).

[108] United Nations, Convention on the Rights of the Child, GA Resolution 44/25, annex, 44 UN GAOR Supp. (No. 49) at 167, UN Doc. A/44/49 (1989).

[109] See, for example, Article 27 of the ICCPR, which protects minority rights to language and culture. These provisions, which potentially limit majority rights of expression, are supported by the right to take part in cultural life protected by Article 15 of the ICESCR.

[110] ICCPR, Article 19, n. 106 above.

[111] ECHR Article 10(2), n. 44 above.

ECHR, the Article 19(3) reference to the 'rights of others' includes the right to a fair trial protected by Article 14 and the right to privacy protected by Article 17.[112] Beyond the Covenant, the 'rights of others' links the 19(3) recognized grounds for restricting freedom of expression with rights contained in other United Nations human rights treaties. For example, Article 16 of the Convention on the Rights of the Child requires that state parties protect the privacy rights of children.[113]

These links to other Covenant rights and associations with other UN treaty obligations make clear that the grounds set out in Article 19(3) are not merely permissive, but in some circumstances are connected to obligations to restrict speech or publication to protect competing rights. In this manner, the Article 19(3) national security and public order grounds are linked to Article 20 of the Covenant, which requires that states prohibit 'any advocacy of national, racial or religious hatred that constitutes incitement to discrimination, hostility or violence'. That provision leads on to the Convention on the Elimination of All Forms of Racial Discrimination (CERD), which notably requires that state parties criminalize the 'dissemination of ideas based on racial superiority or hatred, incitement to racial discrimination, as well as all acts of violence or incitement to such acts against any race or group of persons of another colour or ethnic origin', while also criminalizing participation in 'propaganda activities, which promote and incite racial discrimination'.[114] Plainly, it is necessary to be a state party to each of these treaties to be bound by their terms.[115] However, aside from the fact of near universal participation in the major UN human rights treaties, international human rights law is in theory indivisible and the core treaties are regarded as expressing common principles.

Yet, in spite of the many structural similarities between the European and international human rights regimes, they are more often characterized by their differences in principles as well as practice. As compared to the Council of Europe, the United Nations has a much larger body of human rights treaties that range more widely in subject matter. The relationship between these treaties is moreover strained by differences between state parties not just over the meaning of specific treaty obligations, but even regarding the fundamental nature of international human rights. For many states, the principles of universality and indivisibility are

---

[112] ICCPR, Article 14: '. . . . everyone shall be entitled to a fair and public hearing by a competent, independent and impartial tribunal established by law'. Article 17: '1. No one shall be subjected to arbitrary or unlawful interference with his privacy, family, or correspondence, nor to unlawful attacks on his honour and reputation. 2. Everyone has the right to the protection of the law against such interference or attacks.'

[113] UN Convention on the Rights of the Child, Article 16: '1. No child shall be subjected to arbitrary or unlawful interference with his or her privacy, family, or correspondence, nor to unlawful attacks on his or her honour and reputation. 2. The child has the right to the protection of the law against such interference or attacks.'

[114] United Nations, Convention on the Elimination of All Forms of Racial Discrimination, GA Resolution 2106 (XX), Annex, 20 UN GAOR Supp. (No. 14) at 47, UN Doc. A/6014 (1966).

[115] On treaty obligations, see Jennings, R. and Watts, A., *Oppenheim's International Law* (Oxford University Press, 2008); Aust, A., *Modern Treaty Law and Practice*, 2nd edn (Cambridge University Press, 2007).

acceptable because this great assemblage of treaty rights and obligations can be made, with some effort, to align with their own constitutional values and principles.

In communications and media matters, liberal democracies have tended to view the right to freedom of expression as the essential core right, which other rights and interests variably support or limit. This also reflects the traditional liberal democratic emphasis on the first generation rights of the ICCPR and more cautious acceptance, or even rejection, of the positive obligations contained in the ICESCR. That resistance is often much stronger for third generation rights, such as the collective rights of peoples to self determination and to development, which can have significant effects on the meaning and implications of the right to freedom of expression.[116] The right to development has, for example, provided a basis on which to claim better access to international communications infrastructures as well as liberalized use of information and products protected by intellectual property rights.[117]

There is therefore no hierarchy of treaties or conceptual framework of rights and obligations akin to the Council of Europe's consciously liberal democratic regime. The ICCPR does not dominate the United Nations human rights regime in the way that the ECHR sits at the heart of European public order. At the very least, it must share its premier rank status in the informal international bill of rights with the ICESCR.[118] There is moreover no United Nations adjudicatory body in the human rights field possessing powers remotely comparable to the European Court of Human Rights. The ICCPR, for example, is only supported by its well leashed Human Rights Committee.[119] This Committee is charged with reviewing the periodic reports of the state parties to the Covenant and is also empowered to examine individual complaints regarding alleged violations of the ICCPR by those state parties that have accepted its jurisdiction under the treaty's Optional Protocol.[120]

---

[116] Declaration on the Right to Development, United Nations General Assembly (4 December 1986), A/RES/41/128.

[117] See, for example, World Summit on the Information Society, Plan of Action, WSIS-03/GENEVA/DOC/5-E (12 December 2003), Part B: Objectives, Goals and Targets, and see also Stiglitz, J., 'Knowledge as a Global Public Good', in Kaul, I., Grunberg, I., and Stern, M. (eds), *Global Public Goods: International Cooperation in the 21st Century* (Oxford University Press, 1999), 308–326.

[118] Despite the shared history of the two Covenants, there is no obligation to become a party to both. While the United States is a party to the ICCPR, it has signed but not ratified the ICESCR; the People's Republic of China in contrast is a party to the ICESCR but has only signed and not ratified the ICCPR.

[119] On the strengths and weaknesses of the United Nations Human Rights system, see Alston, P., 'Reconceiving the UN Human Rights Regime: Challenges Confronting the New UN Human Rights Council', Center For Human Rights And Global Justice Working Paper, Number 4, June 2006. On the ICCPR Human Rights Committee, see Joseph, Schultz, and Castan, *The International Covenant on Civil and Political Rights*, 2nd edn (Oxford University Press, 2005), 46–52; Nowak, M., 'The Need for a World Court of Human Rights', 7(1) *Human Rights Law Review* (2007); and Buergenthal, T., 'The U.N. Human Rights Committee', 5 *Max Planck Yearbook of United Nations* Law (2001), 341–398.

[120] Optional Protocol to the International Covenant on Civil and Political Rights, GA Resolution 2200A (XXI), 21 UN GAOR Supp. (No. 16) at 59, UN Doc. A/6316 (1966).

The ICCPR Human Rights Committee also enjoys limited powers to clarify the meaning of the ICCPR by adopting 'General Comments' concerning specific articles of the treaty or special issues relating to the responsibilities of the state parties.[121] Although their precise legal status is open to question, the Committee's General Comments are often regarded as authoritative or at least persuasive interpretations of the Covenant.[122] Yet these are unmistakably modest powers. The Committee has focused on the urgent task of maintaining the treaty's basic integrity without embarking on significant doctrinal development. Its powers are essentially too weak to impose an authoritative interpretation and thereby deny the state parties their normal rights of interpretation.

In addition, as discussed in Chapter 5, there is little supranational coordination of international economic law and human rights law. In contrast to the deepening integration of European economic and human rights law, in the international sphere this interface is largely governed by the internal rules of these very separate fields of law. It therefore falls to the state parties to trade and human rights treaties to determine for themselves the proper relationship between these obligations where they overlap or conflict.

The reasons for the striking differences between European and international human rights are certainly obvious enough. In the immediate post World War II period, the idea of using international law to place legal limits on the conduct of states in their treatment of individuals and communities was driven forward by the United States, in the face of British and Soviet reluctance.[123] Soviet apprehensions were well justified as this made the conduct of the state towards its citizen a matter of legitimate external scrutiny and criticism under international law. Where the western Europeans subsequently made human rights the basis for a shared public order, the newly created United Nations created a forum for the clash of Cold War values and strategic interests.

In that clash, the proper relationship between the media and the state was, from the outset, one of the main issues of contention. The American government had shown its determination to advance the cause of liberal democratic freedom of expression beyond its borders long before the end of World War II. In his 1941 Address to the US Congress, President Roosevelt spoke of four essential freedoms: freedom of speech, freedom of religion, freedom from want, and freedom from fear. Of these, he stated, '[t]he first is freedom of speech and expression—everywhere in the world'. In the immediate post war years, the United States championed an international right to freedom of expression with the expectation that it should be defined in a broadly liberal democratic manner.

Given the dominant position of the United States in the fledgling United Nations organization, it was inevitable that the newly established UN Human

---

[121] Under Article 40(4) of the ICCPR, the Human Rights Committee may adopt 'general comments' on specific articles in order to provide guidance to states when submitting national reports to the Committee.

[122] Buergenthal, T., n. 119 above.

[123] Hunt, L., *Inventing Human Rights* (Norton & Company, 2007), 202–203.

Rights Commission, once entrusted with the task of creating a statement of fundamental human rights, would include a prominent right to freedom of expression in the UDHR. Yet in creating that international legal right, the UDHR dramatically raised the stakes for non-liberal democratic states. This effectively made the relationship between the media and the state a subject of international law, which necessarily brought with it the larger question of the legitimate political and social character of the state itself. For the Soviet Union and its newly constituted dependencies in eastern Europe and other non-liberal democracies, the strategic and tactical issues were unmistakable.[124]

Opposition to the liberal democratic project, which began in the immediate post war years, rejected negative harmonization through human rights law, but nonetheless used similar legal tools and methods. The proliferation of human rights treaty regimes has continued a process that began with the drafting of the UDHR, in which the influence of distinctively liberal democratic elements has been diluted with social democratic and socialist elements. International civil and political rights can thus only be properly understood in the context of economic, social, and cultural rights and the collective needs of peoples for development and autonomy. In this process, concepts, such as human dignity, rather than personal liberty have come to symbolize the universal character of human rights.[125]

The principles of state sovereignty and consent to be bound have always been vitally important to international human rights strategies. As noted above, the fact that treaties do not bind non-parties has allowed states to tailor their human rights obligations according to their domestic policies.[126] States may also accede to a treaty but selectively limit their obligations through reservations and interpretive declarations.[127] Nonetheless, for a number of reasons, states have tended to become parties to human rights treaties containing problematic obligations and have not resorted to reservations or declarations on a wholesale basis. In fact, reservations to Article 19 of the ICCPR are relatively uncommon. It is also ironic that the best known reservations to the ICCPR concerning freedom of expression were made by

---

[124] On the role of the Soviet Union in the development of United Nations human rights instruments, see Normand, R., and Zaidi. S., *Human Rights at the UN: The Political History of Universal Justice* (Indiana University Press, 2008), ch 6.

[125] McCrudden, C., n. 98 above. See, for example, the Preamble to the United Nations Charter, which states that 'faith in fundamental human rights, in the dignity and worth of the human person, in the equal rights of men and women . . . ', as well as the Preamble to the Universal Declaration of Human Rights, which states that, 'recognition of the inherent dignity and of the equal and inalienable rights of all members of the human family is the foundation of freedom, justice and peace in the world'. See also Universal Declaration of Human Rights, Article 1, which states, *inter alia*, that '[a]ll human beings are born free and equal in dignity and rights'. The Preambles to the International Covenant on Civil and Political Rights and the International Covenant on Economic, Social and Cultural Rights both also state, 'these rights derive from the inherent dignity of the human person'.

[126] The Peoples Republic of China has signed but not ratified the ICCPR, but is nonetheless a state party to several other United Nations human rights treaties, including the International Convention on the Elimination of All Forms of Racial Discrimination, International Covenant on Economic, Social and Cultural Rights, Convention on the Elimination of All Forms of Discrimination against Women, Convention against Torture and Other Cruel, Inhuman or Degrading Treatment or Punishment, Convention on the Rights of the Child, and Convention on the Rights of Persons with Disabilities.

[127] Aust, A., n. 115 above, ch 8.

the United States, which was concerned that the weak protection of freedom of speech under the Covenant might conflict with American constitutional law.[128] Reservations to the ICCPR must in any event be consistent with the Covenant's objects and purposes, a point of treaty law that the ICCPR Human Rights Committee has underscored in its General Comment No. 24.[129] Yet, that rule notwithstanding, a broadly worded and wide ranging treaty of this nature offers considerable scope for state parties to modify the effect of particular obligations through reservations and declarations without manifestly violating its diverse objects and purposes. The United States made its accession to the Covenant subject to an array of reservations, declarations, and understandings, which set a benchmark for selective participation.[130]

One of the reasons that state parties seldom use reservations to limit the potential impact of Article 19 is that its permitted grounds for restricting expression are broad and the limiting conditions are vague. The state parties may restrict expression for the purpose of protecting the rights or reputations of others, national security, public order, public health, and public morals, so long as the measures used are provided by law and are necessary.[131] The potential impact of Article 19 on the domestic media state relationship therefore turns on the meaning of the word 'necessary'.[132] Under European economic and human rights law, as well as WTO law, the word necessary, when used in this manner, opens the door to a series of tests associated with proportionality analysis.[133] To what extent this is also true of the word 'necessary' as used in Article 19(3) is a matter of debate. Although it is found in many forms around the world, proportionality analysis is most often linked to European styles of liberal democratic constitutional review.[134] It is therefore resisted by non-liberal democracies, while also viewed with scepticism in the United States.[135]

Even where state parties are in irrefutable contravention of their ICCPR obligations, the UN human rights system has also proven to be largely incapable of bringing sustained, meaningful sanctions to bear on these states. The Covenant suffers from a major weakness that limits the practical effectiveness of all multilat-

---

[128] United States of America, Reservations to the International Covenant on Civil and Political Rights: '(1) That article 20 does not authorize or require legislation or other action by the United States that would restrict the right of free speech and association protected by the Constitution and laws of the United States.' Article 20 of the ICCPR requires the prohibition by law of advocacy of national, racial or religious hatred that constitutes incitement to discrimination, hostility, or violence.

[129] ICCPR Human Rights Committee, General Comment 24 (52), General comment on issues relating to reservations made upon ratification or accession to the Covenant or the Optional Protocols thereto, or in relation to declarations under article 41 of the Covenant, UN Doc. CCPR/C/21/Rev.1/Add.6 (1994). See also Vienna Convention on the Law of Treaties, Article 31.

[130] Henkin, L., 'U.S. Ratification of. Human Rights Treaties: The Ghost of Senator Bricker', 89 *American Journal of International Law* (1995), 341 and Bradley , C. and Goldsmith, J., 'Treaties, Human Rights, and Conditional Consent', 149 *Pennsylvania Law Review* (2000), 399.

[131] Article 19(3), n. 106 above.

[132] Negotiators rejected the proposal that 'necessary' should be modified by the phrase 'in a democratic society', Bossuyt, M.J., n. 103 above, 391.

[133] On proportionality analysis, see Chapter 2.

[134] Ibid.

[135] Ibid.

eral human rights treaties. As a treaty, the ICCPR is undoubtedly legally binding on the state parties and, in principle, engages their state responsibility when breached.[136] However, while the state parties owe their legal obligations under the Covenant directly to the other parties, the purpose of the treaty is to impose duties on states regarding the treatment of individuals under their jurisdiction, including their own citizens. This triangular relationship, while innovative in harnessing the idea of international obligation to domestic conduct, lacks the practical quid pro quo that supports the enforceability of more traditional treaties.[137] Quite simply, there are often few effective sanctions or counter measures available to deploy against a state for a violation of human rights obligations that do not also harm or stigmatize the individuals and communities those obligations are supposed to assist.

Resisting liberal democracy

The adoption of the UDHR by the UN General Assembly in 1948 occurred during a remarkable moment of relative accord in international relations.[138] The member states were able to negotiate an instrument that contained both civil and political rights as well as economic and social rights. The United States, uncharacteristically receptive to government intervention after the experience of the Great Depression and the World War II, agreed to the inclusion of the latter while gaining universal recognition of civil and political rights. The last minute decision of the Soviet Union and its socialist allies to abstain from the adoption of the UDHR, along with Saudi Arabia and South Africa, however, signalled the closing of this period of wary consensus. The UDHR itself revealed the shallowness of their agreement, barely addressing the relationship between its declared rights and any legitimate restrictions on their exercise.

At this point, the struggle over the meaning of freedom of expression in the newly created UN human rights regime began in earnest. During its 1946 inaugural session, the UN General Assembly passed Resolution 59(I), which called for an 'International Conference on Freedom of Information'. This Resolution also declared that '[f]reedom of information is a fundamental human right and the touchstone of all the freedoms to which the United Nations is consecrated'. The General Assembly notably adopted two other resolutions in 1947: one condemning all forms of propaganda likely to encourage threats to international peace and another concerning false or distorted news reports likely to injure friendly relations

---

[136] On state responsibility and the breach of international obligations, see Crawford, J., *The International Law Commission's Articles on State Responsibility. Introduction, Text and Commentaries* (Cambridge University Press, 2002), ch 3.

[137] Hathaway, O., 'Do Human Rights Treaties Make a Difference?' 111(8) *Yale Law Journal* (June 2002), 1935–2042.

[138] When the United Nations General Assembly adopted the Declaration, 48 member states voted in favour, none voted against, eight abstained (these were the six Communist member states led by the Soviet Union, which had participated in the drafting of the Declaration, as well as Saudi Arabia, and South Africa) and two states were absent. UN General Assembly Resolution 217A(III), 10 December 1948.

between states.[139] The UN Conference on Freedom of Information convened in 1948 and met over the next four years, producing two draft conventions (the Convention on Freedom of Information and the Convention on the International Transmission of News) and several recommendations. After strong opposition from western press organizations, who were concerned about draft clauses restricting criticism of foreign governments, neither treaty was opened for signature or ratification.[140]

As the Cold War deepened, the meaning of the right to freedom of expression became a recurring point of contention between the NATO democracies and the Soviet bloc states. It soon also became a sore spot in relations between the United States and western Europeans on one side and many newly independent Asian and African states on the other. These western governments became concerned as former colonies began to voice their opposition to the dominance of American and European news agencies in the supply of international and local news. This simmering argument eventually came to a head within the United Nations Educational, Scientific and Cultural Organization (UNESCO) during the late 1970s. UNESCO's wide and ill defined areas of responsibility, including its obligation to advance knowledge and to promote the free flow of ideas, made it a natural forum for media related projects and disputes.[141] Although the issue of news supply had been under discussion for several years, the confrontation centred on the recommendations of the UNESCO appointed McBride Commission.[142] This Commission was created to examine the state of world communications, including ways to achieve a free and balanced flow of information as part of a New World Information and Communication Order (NWICO).

The NWICO idea was an outgrowth of the New International Economic Order proposals of the 1970s.[143] Its proponents sought a restructuring of the world's news media to change an apparent imbalance in the international flow of information.[144]

---

[139] United Nations General Assembly Resolution A/RES/110(II), and United Nations General Assembly Resolution A/RES/127(II).

[140] Whitton, J.B., 'The United Nations Conference on Freedom of Information and the Movement Against International Propaganda', 43(1) *The American Journal of International Law* (January 1949), 73–87, Binder, C., 'Freedom of Information and the United Nations', 6(2) *International Organization* (May 1952), 210–226.

[141] UNESCO Constitution, Article I, 1. The purpose of the Organization is to contribute to peace and security by promoting collaboration among the nations through education, science and culture in order to further universal respect for justice, for the rule of law and for the human rights and fundamental freedoms which are affirmed for the peoples of the world, without distinction of race, sex, language or religion, by the Charter of the United Nations. 2. To realize this purpose the Organization will: (a) Collaborate in the work of advancing the mutual knowledge and understanding of peoples, through all means of mass communication and to that end recommend such international agreements as may be necessary to promote the free flow of ideas by word and image.

[142] The Commission, established in 1979, was formally titled the International Commission for the Study of Communication Problems, but is commonly known after its chairman Sean McBride. See Thussu, D., *International Communication: Continuity and Change*, (Arnold, 2000), 43–52.

[143] Ibid., 39.

[144] UNESCO Mass Media Declaration 1978 (Declaration on Fundamental Principles concerning the Contribution of the Mass Media to Strengthening Peace and International Understanding, to the Promotion of Human Rights and to Countering Racialism, Apartheid and Incitement to War,

In 1980 the McBride Commission released its final report *Many Voices One World*, which included several major recommendations later accepted by a vote of UNESCO member states.[145] These included the need for an NWICO and a range of measures aimed at putting greater control over the production and distribution of news about developing countries into their hands. UNESCO's launch of its NWICO initiative however coincided with the coming to power of the Reagan administration in the United States and the Thatcher government in Britain. Although they had previously participated in UNESCO media development programmes, under new leaders the United States and Britain led a concerted attack on the NWICO project and on UNESCO for supporting it.[146] Many large media western based companies and media organizations joined in condemning a plan that appeared to endorse the transfer of control over the news into the hands of governments.[147] As a sign of their disapproval of UNESCO's policies and its mismanagement, the United States, Britain, and Singapore withdrew from UNESCO in 1984, 1985, and 1986 respectively.[148] This confrontation severely damaged UNESCO as a forum for the development of international policy or law relating to communications and the media.

The collapse of the Soviet Union appeared to herald the dawn of a new liberal democratic global public order. In this atmosphere of liberal democratic triumph, the United Nations General Assembly agreed to launch a major review of international human rights law and policy that culminated in the 1993 World Conference on Human Rights held in Vienna.[149] This review was, in part, intended to put the divisions of the Cold War into the past and to give the UN's human rights system a more explicitly liberal democratic character. The World Conference was, however, preceded by a series of preparatory conferences, including the Asian regional conference at Bangkok, which famously placed conditions on the universality of UN recognized human rights.[150] The meeting at Bangkok is best known for raising the issue of 'Asian values' and how they should be reflected in human rights principles.[151] Although criticized for offering governments a cultural cover for

UNESCO document 20C/20 Rev., November 1978). See Masmoudi, M., 'The New World Communication Order', 29(2) *Journal of Communication* (1979), 172–185.

[145] UNESCO, *Many Voices, One World*, Paris: UNESCO, 1980. See also Resolution 4/19, International Commission for the Study of Communication Problems, UNESCO, Records of the General Conference Twenty-first Session, Belgrade, 1980.

[146] Cate, F., 'The First Amendment and the International "Free Flow" of Information', 30 *Virginia Journal of International Law* (1990), 372–420.

[147] Thussu, D., n. 142 above.

[148] Britain returned to UNESCO in 1997 and the United States returned in 2003.

[149] United Nations General Assembly Resolution A/RES/45/155.

[150] 1993 Bangkok Declaration on Human Rights, Clause 8. 'Recognize that while human rights are universal in nature, they must be considered in the context of a dynamic and evolving process of international norm-setting, bearing in mind the significance of national and regional particularities and various historical, cultural and religious backgrounds...' Report of the Regional Meeting for Asia of the World Conference on Human Rights, A/CONF.157/ASRM/8, A/CONF.157/PC/59.

[151] 14 *Indiana International and Comparative Law Review* (2003), 1–85; Peerenboom, R., 'Human Rights, China and Cross-Cultural Inquiry: Philosophy, History and Power Politics', 55 *Philosophy East & West* (2005), 283–320.

the denial of civil and political rights, the resulting Bangkok Declaration underscored the limits of liberalism as the foundation for a universal system of human rights.[152] This warning shot against universality delivered in the Bangkok Declaration was nonetheless muffled at the global Vienna World Conference. The 1993 Vienna Declaration and Programme of Action, adopted at the Conference, found sufficient common ground to reiterate the basic principles of universal human rights.[153] Article 1 of the Declaration included the simple statement that, '[t]he universal nature of these rights and freedoms is beyond question'.

The Declaration also addressed liberal concerns, including the importance of democracy itself. It defined democracy as being based on 'the freely expressed will of the people to determine their own political, economic, social and cultural systems and their full participation in all aspects of their lives'. The difficulty here, as in other international human rights instruments, was a lack of essential detail. The language of the Vienna Declaration does not, for example, directly rebut the position of the Chinese Communist Party that its rise to power in the 1940s was a free expression of the will of the Chinese people.[154]

The 'Asian values' debate arose in relation to debates over the policies of some Asian governments and leaders in the early 1990s.[155] But serious arguments regarding the cultural roots and limits of liberalism and alternative perspectives on human dignity continue.[156] China, whose economic successes have made it a powerful alternative model of political and social order, has based its opposition to liberal freedom of expression on a mix of arguments that emphasis the public's need for economic development and social stability.[157] More recently, the Chinese government has begun to emphasize its distinctive cultural heritage, making explicit links to Confucianism.[158] Elsewhere, opposition to liberal freedom of expression on religious grounds has also grown dramatically over the past decade, highlighting the limits of the post Cold War liberal democratic ascendancy.[159]

---

[152] On the relationship between universal human rights principles and the development of public policy in east Asia, see Bell, D., *Beyond Liberal Democracy* (Princeton University Press, 2006) and Peerenboom, R., 'Beyond Universalism and Relativism: The Evolving Debates about "Values in Asia"', 14 *Indiana International and Comparative Law Review* (2003), 1–85.

[153] The Vienna Declaration and Programme of Action (A/CONF.157/23).

[154] Saich, T., *Governance and Politics of China* (Palgrave, 2001), ch 2.

[155] Peerenboom, R., 'Beyond Universalism and Relativism: The Evolving Debates about "Values in Asia"', n. 152 above.

[156] On alternative concepts of human dignity and human rights, see Bell, D., n. 152 above, ch 3; Dembour, M.-B., *Who Believes in Human Rights? Reflections on the European Convention* (Cambridge University Press, 2006), ch 6; Krotoszynski, Jr, R., *The First Amendment in Cross-Cultural Perspective: A Comparative Legal Analysis of the Freedom of Speech* (New York University Press, 2006), ch 5; Donnelly, J., 'The Relative Universality of Human Rights', 29 *Human Rights Quarterly* (2007), 281–306; and Donnelly, J., *Universal Human Rights in Theory and Practice*, 2nd edn (Cornell University Press, 2003).

[157] See, for example, State Council of the Peoples Republic of China, *Human Rights Developments in China in 2009.* (State Council Information Office, 26 September 2009).

[158] Bell, D., *China's New Confucianism: Politics and Everyday Life in a Changing Society* (Princeton University Press, 2010), Part 1.

[159] Cerone, J., 'The Danish Cartoon Row and the International Regulation of Expression', *ASIL Insights*, Vol. 10, Issue 2, (2006).

A decade later, the United Nations sponsored the World Summit on the Information Society (WSIS).[160] This event, held in two phases—first in Geneva in 2003 and then in Tunis in 2005—principally concerned cooperation on development and governance issues in relation to new information and communications services.[161] Human rights organizations, with some government support, also put the WSIS under pressure to incorporate a substantial human rights dimension into its Declaration and Plan of Action.[162] While these organizations did gain some rights of participation in the WSIS process, their influence on the agenda was modest. The Summit was largely devoted to the technical and administrative challenges of developing a global information society, including the complex problems of internet governance. While the right to freedom of expression inevitably arises in all these contexts, it did not become a focal issue for the WSIS. The 2003 WSIS Declaration nevertheless included a provision on freedom of expression and the role of the media in the global information society.[163] The participating states reaffirmed their commitment to freedom of the press and freedom of information, as well as independence, pluralism, and diversity in the media.[164] Although falling far short of activist goals, this was in fact a moderate success, given the determination of the Chinese and other representatives to delete the provision entirely.[165]

The WSIS proceedings also carried echoes of the NWICO dispute. An umbrella activist organization, Communication Rights in the Information Society (CRIS), proposed the inclusion of a general 'right to communicate' in the final Declaration.[166] Advocates of this proposed right have argued that it encompasses the communication aspects of all three generations of international human rights. It draws together the idea of freedom of expression as a negative restriction on the state with rights of empowerment, including equitable access to media and communications services, the right to cultural identity, and rights of access to

---

[160] In 2002 the UN General Assembly endorsed the ITU's proposal to host a World Summit on the Information Society (WSIS) General Assembly Resolution 56/183, 31 January 2002.

[161] Plans for the WSIS formally initiated by UN General Assembly Resolution 56/183 (December 2001).

[162] Drake, W. and Jørgensen, R.F., 'Introduction', *Human Rights in the Global Information Society* (MIT Press, 2006), 1–51.

[163] WSIS, Geneva Declaration of Principles, WSIS-03/GENEVA/DOC/0004, Part B9: Media, Clause 55.

[164] See, for example, European Commission Communication *Towards a Global Partnership in the Information Society* (April 2006), IP/06/542: 'The Commission welcomes the clear and unequivocal statement of the World Summit on the primary importance of the information society for democracy and the respect for human rights and fundamental freedoms; in particular the freedom of expression and opinion, as well as the freedom to receive and access information. Therefore, the Commission notes with concerns the cases of cyber-repression, which means the misuse of ICT to help repressive regimes to restrict the free flow of information on the Internet. The Commission encourages the companies concerned to work on a code of conduct on this crucial issue, in close cooperation with NGOs.'

[165] Wagner, M.A., 'Free, independent and pluralistic media recognized as an essential element of the Information Society Report on the first phase of the World Summit on the Information Society', published in the *Final Report of the World Electronic Media Forum* (March 2004), European Broadcasting Union.

[166] Drake, W. and Jørgensen, R., n. 162 above.

information.[167] The 'right to communicate' also carries a strong association with the NWICO proposals of the UNESCO MacBride Commission. Given these associations and the broad mixture of ideas underlying this proposed right, its supporters faced sharp criticism at the WSIS from more traditionally liberal media organizations.[168] The right to communicate initiative consequently failed to gain wide support, amidst concerns that formal recognition of a new omnibus communications right would dilute the potency of the right to freedom of expression.[169]

The inconclusive sparring in the WSIS over the meaning of freedom of expression in the internet era reflected the continuing dissension occurring in the United Nations human rights institutions more generally. In the past decade, a sufficient number of member states agreed to a substantial reform of the UN human rights system in an effort to reduce the opportunities for manipulation and obstruction by some member states. In 2006, the UN General Assembly replaced the Commission on Human Rights, the UN's principal intergovernmental body responsible for human rights policy and implementation, with a new Human Rights Council.[170] This institutional change however failed to produce a dramatic transformation in the politics of human rights within the United Nations.[171] As one would expect, the UN member states' positions on questions of freedom of expression continue to reflect their particular concerns and the diversity of their own media state relationships. This can be readily seen in the recent debate between member states

[167] On the origins of the 'right to communicate' see Hamelink, C.J., *The Politics of World Communication* (Sage, 1994); see also d'Arcy, J., 'Direct Broadcast Satellites and the Right to Communicate,' 118 *EBU (European Broadcasting Union) Review* (1969); D'Arcy, J., 'Direct Broadcast Satellites and the Right to Communicate', in Harms, S., Richstad, J. and Kie, K.A. (eds), *Right to Communicate: Collected Papers* (University of Hawaii Press, 1977), 1–9. McIver Jr, W.J., Birdsall, W. F., Rasmussen, M., 'The Internet and the right to communicate' 8(12) *First Monday* (2003); Galtung, J. and Vincent, R., *Global Glasnost: Toward a New Information and Communication Order?* (Hampton Press, 1992), ch 3.

[168] See, for example, Article 19, *Statement on the Right to Communicate*, Document WSIS/PC-2/CONTR/95-E (London, February 2003). See also Bullen, D., 'What's Wrong with a "Right to Communicate"', in *New Code Words for Censorship* (World Press Freedom Committee, 2002).

[169] Padovani, C. and Nordenstreng, K., 'From NWICO to WSIS: Another World Information and Communication Order?' 1 *Global Media and Communication* (2005), 264–272; Mueller, M., Kuerbis, B., and Pagé, C., 'Democratizing Global Communication? Global Civil Society and the Campaign for Communication Rights in the Information Society', 1 *International Journal of Communication* (2007), 267–296.

[170] Resolution adopted by the General Assembly, 60/251. *Human Rights Council*, 3 April 2006. The Human Rights Commission was established in 1946 by the UN Economic and Social Council. In March 2006, the UN General Assembly voted to replace the Commission with a new body, the UN Human Rights Council. According to a BBC report 'UN creates new human rights body' (15 March 2006) 'the United States, the Marshall Islands, Palau, and Israel voted against the Council's creation, claiming that it would have too little power and that there were insufficient safeguards to prevent human rights-abusing nations from taking control'. See also Alston, P., n. 119 above, and Rodley, N., 'United Nations Human Rights Treaty Bodies and Special Procedures of the Commission on Human Rights—Complementarity or Competition?' 25(4) *Human Rights Quarterly* (November 2003).

[171] Callejon, C., 'Developments at the Human Rights Council in 2007: A Reflection of its Ambivalence', 8 *Human Rights Law Review* (2008), 323–342 and Hampson, F.J., 'An Overview of the Reform of the UN Human Rights Machinery', 7(1) *Human Rights Law Review* (2007).

over the adoption of a Human Rights Council Resolution on the defamation of religions.[172]

The liberal democratic project—purposes and achievements

In spite of decades of dogged resistance from a changing cast of opponents, the liberal democratic project of securing a distinctively liberal democratic vision of human rights, universalized through international legal standards and supervisory procedures, has secured many notable successes. These significantly include the international consensus that states are under a moral and legal duty to respect the human rights of individuals. The debate is centred on the nature of those rights and rarely on their existence.

Freedom of expression remains however far from the core areas of global consensus, which include, for example, the right to life and the right to an education. The reasons for this lack of success in a field where successes are always modest are plain enough. A liberal democratic conception of freedom of expression necessarily challenges the foundations of the non-liberal and non-democratic state and their governments are not slow to recognize that sobering implication. The liberal democratic cause of global press freedom has accordingly been advanced not only out of a genuine concern for liberty, but also out of a strategic calculation that its acceptance would inexorably bring about the spread of liberal democratic government. Indeed, it has been an article of faith that once implanted, liberal freedom of expression will grow in a virtuous circle, as exposure to a more open media will kindle a desire for yet more freedom.

The failure to achieve a liberal democratic global public order should not overshadow the immense importance of what has been achieved. The recognition of the right to freedom of expression in the UDHR and the ICCPR is first of all a robust statement capable of sustaining a liberal democratic interpretation without any textual difficulties. It is therefore a vitally important point of reference in international law that strengthens solidarity amongst liberal democracies. While there are points of difficulty, such as the obligation to criminalize hate speech, the open character of Article 19 of the ICCPR and its flexible relationship with other rights important to liberal autonomy and democratic concerns ensures that it is not deeply incompatible with the constitutional order of any liberal democracy.

It is therefore a solid foundation for efforts to strengthen the liberal democratic position within the UN human rights system. While major western democracies were strongly critical of the UN Human Rights Commission, they also worked to use this body as a forum to advance freedom of expression and media pluralism. During its existence, the Commission was responsible for many activities and measures concerning freedom of expression, including its annual resolutions on the right to freedom of opinion and expression. These Resolutions contained a set

---

[172] United Nations, Human Rights Council, Resolution 7/19, *Combating defamation of religions*. On opposition, see Article 19, Statement on Human Rights Council: ARTICLE 19 Calls on HRC Members to Vote Against Proposed Resolution on 'Defamation of Religions', 25 March 2009.

of carefully negotiated phrases, accumulated over many years, that demonstrate the persistence of liberal democratic efforts as well as the determined resistance they have faced. The UN Human Rights Commission's 2005 Resolution, for example, called on member states not to restrict freedom of expression in the media and broadcasting, in particular the editorial independence of the media.[173] That Resolution also called on states to refrain from imposing restrictions which are inconsistent with paragraph 3 of Article 19 of the ICCPR and set out a further list of politically important forms of expression.[174] Yet this statement is ultimately limited by the exceptions set out in Article 19(3), including the meaning of the crucial term 'necessity' in that paragraph. The 2005 Resolution does not address those issues.

UNESCO has provided an equally useful forum for similar efforts. With the loss of American funding and the easing of Cold War tensions, the appetite within UNESCO for confrontation over freedom of expression faded. By the 1990s, UNESCO chose to sponsor a series of regional declarations on media issues that reflected the new politics of the brief post Cold War liberal democratic ascendency. While lacking detail, these declarations endorsed the principles of media autonomy from the state and pluralism in national news media.[175] UNESCO has continued to play a role in the international promotion of freedom of expression through its various programmes.[176] Even the UN World Summit on the Information Society, which advanced no new ground on the question of freedom of expression in the new media, at least reiterated the basic principles. This was sufficient for the European Commission to conclude that,

---

[173] United Nations Human Rights Commission Resolution 2005/38 on the Right to Freedom of Opinion and Expression, Clause 4(g).

[174] Ibid., Clause 4, '[c]alls *upon* all States: . . . (p) While noting that article 19, paragraph 3, of the International Covenant on Civil and Political Rights provides that the exercise of the right to freedom of opinion and expression carries with it special duties and responsibilities, to refrain from imposing restrictions which are not consistent with paragraph 3 of that article, including on: i) Discussion of government policies and political debate; reporting on human rights, government activities and corruption in government; engaging in election campaigns, peaceful demonstrations or political activities, including for peace or democracy; and expression of opinion and dissent, religion or belief, including by persons belonging to minorities or vulnerable groups; ii) The free flow of information and ideas, including practices such as the banning or closing of publications or other media and the abuse of administrative measures and censorship; iii) Access to or use of information and communication technologies, including radio, television and the Internet . . .'

[175] UNESCO: The 1991 Windhoek Declaration on the Promotion of Free and Pluralistic African Press, The 1992 Declaration of Alma Ata on Promoting Independent and Pluralistic Asian Media, The 1994 Declaration of Santiago de Chile on Promoting the Independent and Pluralistic Media, The 1996 Declaration of Sana'a on Promoting Independent and Pluralistic Arab Media, The 1997 Sofia Declaration on Promoting European Pluralistic and Independent Media.

[176] UNESCO at its 34th session UNESCO's General Conference adopted the Medium-Term Strategy for 2008–2013 (34 C/4): Strategic Programme Objective 13: Fostering pluralistic, free and independent media and infostructures: para. 122: 'UNESCO will undertake advocacy for press freedom and the free flow of information, openness, inclusiveness, ethical and professional standards of all media, including Internet media and communication in cyberspace. Special attention will be paid to the protection of press freedom and the rights and safety of media and information professionals, especially within the framework of alert monitoring networks for the protection of freedom of expression.'

[t]he Summit has reaffirmed the primary importance of democracy, of policy objectives such as sustainable development and cultural diversity, and of the respect for human rights and fundamental freedoms, including the freedom of expression and opinion, as well as the freedom to receive and access information. These are indispensable if information and communication technologies (ICTs) are to contribute to economic and social progress in emerging and developing countries.[177]

The relative successes of the liberal democratic project in the media field owes as much to commercial and professional as well as activist media organizations as it does to the efforts of governments. These include professional associations, such as the International Federation of Journalists, International Press Institute, and the International News Safety Institute, that work to promote the interests of journalists. These in turn rely on a great range of regional and national organizations, including the European Federation of Journalists and the Inter American Press Association. These commercial and professional associations also have important connections with media related research and campaign organizations. The Canadian based International Freedom of Expression Exchange, for example, provides information and support to media related bodies in many countries that share a liberal democratic view of press freedom. While these networks are genuinely international, reaching every continent, the better funded and more influential organizations have historically been based in the United States and Europe. These include the American based Electronic Frontier Foundation, Freedom Forum, Media Law Resource Center, World Press Freedom Committee and the European based Reporters sans Frontières, ARTICLE 19, and Privacy International.

These organizations have worked energetically to advance the idea that the right to freedom of expression recognized in the ICCPR is essentially liberal democratic in nature. Although kept to the margins of the UN system, they have been instrumental in the creation of non-governmental declaratory instruments that have subsequently acquired a semi-official status. In relation to the ICCPR, the most important of these are the 1984 Siracusa Principles on the Limitation and Derogation Provisions in the International Covenant on Civil and Political Rights.[178] The Siracusa Principles were adopted at a conference of human rights experts in Italy organized by human rights NGOs.[179] Their purpose was to clarify

---

[177] Communication from the Commission to the Council, the European Parliament, the European Economic and Social Committee and the Committee of the Regions, *Towards a Global Partnership in the Information Society: Follow-up to the Tunis Phase of the World Summit on the Information Society* (WSIS) COM (2006) 181 final.

[178] See United Nations, Economic and Social Council, UN Sub-Commission on Prevention of Discrimination and Protection of Minorities, Siracusa Principles on the Limitation and Derogation of Provisions in the International Covenant on Civil and Political Rights, Annex, UN Doc E/CN.4/1984/4 (1984). The Siracusa Principles by regional courts, such as the European Court of Human Rights (see *A. and others v. the United Kingdom*, (Application No. 3455/05)) and also by domestic courts, such as the House of Lords in Britain (see, for example, *A and others v. The Secretary of State for the Home Department*, [2004] UKHL 56).

[179] The Siracusa conference was attended by representatives from the International Commission of Jurists, the International Association of Penal Law, the American Association for the International Commission of Jurists, the Urban Morgan Institute for Human Rights, and the International Institute of Higher Studies in Criminal Sciences.

the circumstances and manner in which a state may rely on permitted exceptions to the rights set out in the ICCPR. More specifically, the Siracusa Principles elaborated the meaning of 'necessity' as used in Article 19 and other ICCPR articles. Principle 11, for example, introduces the least restrictive means element of proportionality analysis, stating that, 'in applying a limitation, a state shall use no more restrictive means than are required for the achievement of the purpose of the limitation'.

Other declarations of this kind concerning freedom of expression have similarly gained a quasi-official status in the international human rights field. The Johannesburg Principles on National Security, Freedom of Expression and Access to Information, for example, focus on questions of freedom of expression in the context of threats to national security.[180] They aim to limit the ability of governments to suppress politically sensitive expression by spuriously alleging that it threatens public order or national security.[181] The Johannesburg Principles have been cited several times in the UN Human Rights Commission's annual resolutions on the right to freedom of opinion and expression and are often cited in advocacy to UN bodies as well as national authorities.[182]

The Siracusa, Johannesburg, and other statements of principle relating to freedom of expression are influential precisely because they supply the clarity and specificity that the human rights processes of the United Nations cannot provide. They are also the product of the networks that connect governments, media corporations, human rights organizations, and academic bodies across the liberal democratic world. The growth of these network relationships has advanced the effectiveness of efforts to entrench a liberal understanding of freedom of expression into international law and practice. The weakness of these statements of principle is also plain enough. They cannot substitute for clear, justiciable international legal obligations.[183]

---

[180] The Johannesburg Principles were adopted in 1995 by a conference of experts in international law, national security, and human rights organized by ARTICLE 19, the International Centre Against Censorship in collaboration with the Centre for Applied Legal Studies of the University of Witwatersrand in Johannesburg. UN Doc. E/CN.4/1996/39 (annex).

[181] Johannesburg Principle 7: 'Protected Expression: (a) Subject to Principles 15 and 16, the peaceful exercise of the right to freedom of expression shall not be considered a threat to national security or subjected to any restrictions or penalties. Expression which shall not constitute a threat to national security includes, but is not limited to, expression that: (i) advocates non-violent change of government policy or the government itself; (ii) constitutes criticism of, or insult to, the nation, the state or its symbols, the government, its agencies, or public officials, or a foreign nation, state or its symbols, government, agencies or public officials; (iii) constitutes objection, or advocacy of objection, on grounds of religion, conscience or belief, to military conscription or service, a particular conflict, or the threat or use of force to settle international disputes; (iv) is directed at communicating information about alleged violations of international human rights standards or international humanitarian law. (b) No one may be punished for criticizing or insulting the nation, the state or its symbols, the government, its agencies, or public officials, or a foreign nation, state or its symbols, government, agency or public official unless the criticism or insult was intended and likely to incite imminent violence.'

[182] See, for example, Human Rights Commission Resolution 2003/42.

[183] See Raustiala, K., 'Form and Substance in International Agreements', 99(3) *American Journal of International Law* (2005), 581–614.

In the same period that non-governmental organizations were attempting to push the necessity issue forward, the ICCPR Human Rights Committee had begun to develop its own interpretation of Article 19. Using its adjudications of individual applications under the ICCPR Optional Protocol, the Committee took the word 'necessary' in Article 19(3) to mean that state parties must use the least restrictive means to achieve their legitimate public policy goals.[184] In 1983, however, the Committee failed to say anything significant about this issue when it issued its General Comment on Article 19, merely stating opaquely that, '...[h]owever, when a State party imposes certain restrictions on the exercise of freedom of expression, these may not put in jeopardy the right itself...and they must be justified as being 'necessary' for that State party for one of those purposes'.[185] Despite that silence, the Committee has since then referred to the principle of least restrictive measure in relation to Article 19 on several occasions.[186] It has also made plain in other General Comments that it forms part of other ICCPR Articles that include a similar necessity condition for resort to recognized objectives.[187]

These trends are undoubtedly significant. Certainly, the rules of treaty interpretation do not lead decisively to the conclusion that 'necessary' in Article 19(3) requires some form of proportionality analysis. Despite the influence of the participating western democracies, differences between the parties during the drafting negotiations show that Article 19 does not have an unequivocally liberal democratic object and purpose.[188] In addition, neither the Siracusa Principles nor even the HRC General Comments and application decisions legally bind any state and are perhaps only persuasive or indeed relevant to states already committed to those principles. Yet, this kind of work has at least helped to solidify a consensus amongst liberal democracies on the meaning of the ICCPR.

It is difficult to draw general conclusions about the influence of international human rights on the media state relationship. The majority of UN member states are parties to the Covenant and are therefore formally committed to its obligations. Yet there is a widespread view that the UN human rights system is nearly broken as it seems incapable of compelling any state to do more than what its government is

---

[184] *Alba Pietraroia v. Uruguay*, Communication No. 44/1979, UN Doc. CCPR/C/OP/1 at 76 (1984) (para. 16).
[185] Human Rights Committee, General Comment No. 10: Freedom of expression (Article 19).
[186] See also, for example, *Kim Jong-Cheol v. Republic of Korea*, Communication No. 968/2001, UN Doc. CCPR/C/84/D/968/2001 (2005), in which the Committee stated in paragraph 8.3, '...It is not, therefore, in a position to conclude that the law, as applied to the author, is disproportionate to its aim. Accordingly, the Committee does not find a violation of article 19 of the Covenant in this regard.' See also Nowak, M., *UN Covenant on Civil and Political Rights: CCPR Commentary* (N.P. Engel, 1993), 355–357.
[187] Human Rights Committee, General Comment No. 27: Freedom of movement (Article 12), CCPR/C/21/Rev.1/Add.9, 14. Article 12, para. 3, clearly indicates that it is not sufficient that the restrictions serve the permissible purposes; they must also be necessary to protect them. Restrictive measures must conform to the principle of proportionality; they must be appropriate to achieve their protective function; they must be the least intrusive instrument amongst those which might achieve the desired result; and they must be proportionate to the interest to be protected.
[188] Bossuyt, M., n. 103 above.

already willing to do.[189] Yet, on another view, these criticisms fail to grasp the complexity or depth of contemporary global public order. While states may use the rules of treaty law to avoid hard obligations, as participants in the international community they are drawn into its common practices, assumptions, and obligations.[190] To avoid becoming bound by apparent acquiescence, a state must consciously and continuously make its opposition obvious to other states or parties. Without express opposition, the least restrictive measure principle could therefore become universally accepted without formal consent. States and societies are nonetheless not lulled into liberal democracy. Accepting the principle of least restrictive measure is only a small step towards restraint and accountability. Article 19(3) also sets out broadly stated public policy grounds that a state may pursue when legitimately restricting freedom of expression. The struggle is to determine what level of protection a state may adopt when relying on these grounds to limit the harmful effects of expression. The liberal democratic project will gain little if the least restrictive measure principle only operates in relation to the level of protection chosen by the state party.

The development of the right to freedom of expression in international human rights law is part of the gradual, halting move towards the greater accountability of states. It is strong evidence that the liberal democratic project still has vitality and the potential to shape the emerging global public order. There is, however, much evidence that this project has become thin, its efforts diluted into general principles of transparency and accountability, which are no longer explicitly liberal and only vaguely democratic. Yet perhaps this is the nature of supranational order. Liberal democracy is flexible enough to be adapted to any culture or place, but it grows out of local conditions and demands. Global public order cannot create that process. Instead, its essential importance is to develop general principles that are readily adapted to liberal democratic purposes.

---

[189] Posner, E., 'Human Welfare, Not Human Rights', 108 *Columbia Law Review* (2008), 1758.

[190] See Goodman and Jinks, 'Incomplete Internalization and Compliance with Human Rights Law', 19(4) *European Journal of International Law* (September 2008), 725–748. But see Mushkat, R., 'Incomplete Internalization and Compliance with Human Rights Law: A Reply to Ryan Goodman and Derek Jinks', 20(2) *European Journal of International Law* (2009), 437–442.

7

Jurisdiction and the Media

State control over the media is rarely, if ever, solely a matter of coercion, whether exercised through legal or other means. The shared loyalties and values of owners, political leaders, editors, and government officials are equally important in setting the boundaries for permissible content. Nonetheless, the threat of coercion has always underpinned the close connection between the rise of the territorially defined nation state and its national media. In the last resort, a state's capacity to manage its public information environment rests on its ability to exert physical control over the production and distribution of content within its territory. This relationship has evolved and endured through centuries of change in communication technologies and methods. As these have become more efficient and accessible, and often less vulnerable to state controls, governments have looked for new ways to maintain their grip on the media state relationship.

In the printing press era, governments directed their coercive efforts in two directions: firstly towards the individuals who published, printed, and distributed illegal publications and, second, towards the printed works and the presses needed to produce them. The cumbersome process of printing and distributing publications was vulnerable at multiple points to state control, especially when compared to the instantaneous and elusive nature of the internet. Governments could require licences at every step, from the commissioning of the work to the final sale.[1] As the production and distribution of printed works expanded regionally and nationally, authorities discovered new vulnerabilities, including the taxation of paper and the imposition of exorbitant postal rates on journals.[2] Criminal offences and civil rights of action applicable to the media also burgeoned, ranging from sedition, contempt of court, obscenity, and defamation to infringement of copyright. Other methods could be equally effective. Police surveillance and harassment of editors and journalists has, for example, provided an effective way to curb an investigative or critical press.

Yet complete state control over public information, even in the print era, was plainly impossible. Even in more recent times, only a few governments, such as the

---

[1] See Brady, A., *Marketing Dictatorship: Propaganda and Thought Work in Contemporary China* (Rowman and Littlefield, 2008), ch 2, 'Guiding Hand: The Role of the Propaganda System', and Keller, P., 'Privilege and Punishment: Press Governance in China', 21(2) *Cardozo Arts and Entertainment Law Journal* (2003), 87–138.

[2] On the evolution of state control over the communication technologies and media goods and services, see Chapter 1.

Chinese Communist Party under Mao Zedong, have attempted that degree of public discipline and ideological conformity.[3] Governments have historically concentrated their efforts on the mass media, recognizing that comprehensive control of personal communications was beyond their grasp. Effective state control over printed works was usually sufficient to blunt the influence of unwanted information and ideas.

In confronting the printing press, states developed methods to control domestic public information and frequently enforced heavy political and religious censorship. Yet this was also the age of the Enlightenment and the revolutionary politics that followed. Even when banned, books and journals circulated quietly and liberal minded rulers frequently provided safe havens for their production. Political and religious dissenters, as well as pornographers, could take advantage of these more relaxed regimes to publish locally and to send their works into more restrictive places.[4] The diversity of regimes in Europe was therefore important not only to its fertile intellectual life, but also to the developing character of state control over media content. Control over territorial boundaries became an essential part of the media state relationship.

Territory, sovereignty, and jurisdiction

Through these centuries, international law had very little to say about state controls on public information within the national territory. This fell within the ample sphere of state sovereignty. The autonomous, territorially sovereign state consequently possessed an unfettered right to suppress publication and distribution within its borders as it saw fit.[5] It was moreover fully entitled to use coercive force where necessary to achieve that end. International law was nonetheless directly concerned with the boundaries of that sovereign authority, which were determined in large part by the principles of jurisdiction.[6] These principles were, and still are, largely located in customary international law, which arises out of the settled practice of states, where it can be discerned. In the case of jurisdiction, that practice has developed through two related avenues: first, the application of public laws and regulatory regimes to domestic and foreign based businesses and individuals; and, second, through the domestic resolution of private or civil disputes that involve a significant foreign element, which is commonly known as private

---

[3] See Kenneth Lieberthal, K., *Governing China: From Revolution to Reform* (New York: W.W. Norton & Company, 2003), chs 3 and 4, and see also Dikötter, F., *The Age of Openness: China before Mao*, (University of California Press, 2008).

[4] These have included Karl Marx, who took refuge in London after the suppression of his journalistic publications, notably the *Neue Rheinische Zeitung*, by various German authorities.

[5] On Westphalian territorial sovereignty, Raustiala, K., *Does the Constitution Follow the Flag? Territoriality and Extraterritoriality in American Law* (Oxford University Press, 2009), 222.

[6] Jennings, R. and Watts, A., *Oppenheim's International Law*, 9th edn (Longman, 1996), 456–457.

international law or conflict of laws.[7] While domestic public law jurisdiction includes prosecutions related to the foreign publications, private international law concerns civil actions, such as claims of defamation against foreign based publishers.

The international law of jurisdiction was initially formed through the efforts of European states to create rules for durable peaceful relations. Its principles reflect the critical importance of defined territories and identifiable citizens that arose with the Westphalian concept of the sovereign state.[8] Rights of jurisdiction based on any simple model of territory and nationality could not however hope to capture the fluidity of human activities and, in particular, the harmful consequences of events occurring beyond national borders. The principles of jurisdiction therefore evolved under a powerful tension. They preserve the essential role of territory and nationality in defining the boundaries of the state, while also recognizing the right of states to protect critical interests from foreign based acts.[9] The international law of jurisdiction is therefore both intricate and uncertain. States have frequently re-interpreted and extended the principles of territory and nationality to acquire greater extraterritorial reach.[10] Nationality is, for example, used to assert jurisdiction over foreigners who have caused harm to a state's own citizen beyond its borders.[11] More often, governments have inflated and adapted the idea of territory to create a sufficient basis on which to exercise jurisdiction over acts occurring abroad. Assertions of jurisdiction of this sort, based on the local consequences of foreign based activities, have become increasingly common as states have attempted to make their complex domestic regulatory systems more effective.[12]

The effects of overlapping sovereignty are softened, to some extent, by the additional distinctions that have developed between kinds of jurisdiction. A state may thus claim prescriptive jurisdiction over a foreign based activity because of its local effects, but not assert adjudicative jurisdiction over the foreign nationals involved because they are located abroad.[13] These distinctions between kinds of state authority create a useful check on the crude exercise of extraterritorial jurisdiction, but the contemporary problem of jurisdiction creep continues. These changes in the rules of jurisdiction are especially important to the media state relationship, in which the cross border flow of information and ideas has always challenged the notion of exclusive territorial sovereignty.

---

[7] Private international law is often divided into three areas: choice of governing law, jurisdiction, and recognition and enforcement of foreign judgments.

[8] Raustiala, K., n. 5 above, 10–12.

[9] See, for example, the *Lotus Case* (France v. Turkey) PCIJ, Ser. A., No. 10, 1927, in which the Permanent Court of International Justice sought to balance these interests in its discussion of the relative nature of territoriality.

[10] See, for example, Reydams, L., *Universal Jurisdiction: International and Municipal Legal Perspectives* (Oxford University Press, 2004), ch 2.

[11] On 'passive personality' jurisdiction, Jennings, R. and Watts, A., n. 6 above, 472.

[12] See Raustiala, K., 'The Evolution of Territoriality: International Relations and American Law', in Kahler, M. and Walter, B. (eds), *Territoriality and Conflict in an Era of Globalization* (Cambridge University Press, 2006), 236 and Berman, P., 'The Globalization of Jurisdiction', 151(2) *University of Pennsylvania Law Review* (December 2002), 311–426.

[13] Jennings, R. and Watts, A., n. 6 above, 457.

In the age of the printing press, the limitations of jurisdiction based on territory and nationality were less often apparent. Through those centuries, the practicalities of effective control over public information sat more comfortably within the framework of sovereignty, territory, and jurisdiction. Even as print publishing grew from a local trade into a major industry, it remained largely contained by national borders and controlled by domestic law. Prescriptive jurisdiction over writers and publishers located in foreign countries was certainly limited by territoriality, although the principles of jurisdiction permitted selective extraterritorial reach. Domestic laws on illicit publications could, for example, apply to nationals regardless of their place of residence. States claimed exceptional rights to extend their laws to foreigners located abroad who seriously endangered their national security.[14] In any event, the difficulties of legislating against publishers and printers in foreign places were not likely to be a first concern for most states. The practical barriers to the import and local distribution of any printed work in quantity gave an effective state ample opportunity to limit the influence of foreign publications on the public information environment. The state's capacity to control published works within its territories was therefore not unduly restricted by the boundaries of territorial sovereignty.

For European states and societies, the more pressing question was to determine the legitimate purposes and limits of that capacity to restrict the flow of public information. In the evolution of liberal thought, the primary focus had shifted from God and ruler to the rational individual, whose freedom to speak openly and to put thoughts into print had assumed a new, overwhelming importance.[15] Without those freedoms, a liberal state could neither be achieved nor sustained. Consequently, the drafters of the formative declarations of liberal public order, including the Bill of Rights of the United States Constitution and the French revolutionary Declaration of the Rights of Man and Citizens, both adopted in 1789, gave this principle a prominent position.[16] These instruments became the vital forerunners to Articles 19 of the Universal Declaration on Human Rights and the International Covenant on Civil and Political Rights, as well as Article 10 of the European Convention on Human Rights.

The individual was not the only beneficiary of the Enlightenment's celebration of reason. The rational state also emerged as a new focus for ideas and methods of moulding the character of society and the individual. Even where it was honoured, liberal freedom of the press was invariably limited by the expanding demands of the state. In revolutionary France, Napoleon brought public order and a return to strong press controls, which the subsequently restored Bourbon monarchy reinforced.[17] The diversity of print media regimes in Europe and elsewhere reinforced the close fit between the territorially sovereign state, the principles of jurisdiction,

[14] Jennings, R. and Watts, A., n. 6 above, 466–478.
[15] Dupre, L., *The Enlightenment and the Intellectual Foundations of Modern Culture* (Yale, 2004), 154–162.
[16] Hunt, L., *Inventing Human Rights* (Norton, 2007), 131.
[17] Ibid., 179–180.

and the domestic media. Unless bound by a treaty agreement, a state was entitled to reject the local application of foreign laws. Even where treaty obligations were undertaken, reserved rights to derogate where necessary to protect essential public policies provided a safety barrier against the extraterritorial application of unacceptable foreign laws. In this manner, international law helped to sustain the capacity of liberal and non-liberal states to maintain their distinctive media regimes. This defensive use of territorial sovereignty remains a potent element in contemporary international arguments over cross border flows of media content.[18]

Radio broadcasting and the territorial state

Radio broadcasting brought a new world of legal and practical difficulties for the media state relationship. As a mass media platform, radio not only challenged the state's ability to control public information, but also eroded the importance of territorial boundaries. Governments responded with innovative methods of control, both unilateral and cooperative. In several ways, the state's hold on the new broadcast media was similar to its relationship with the press. Broadcast programmes, carried invisibly across the country by radio waves, were certainly unlike the static, printed word. Yet broadcasting transmission facilities were just as tangible as printing presses and gave the state obvious points of physical control within the national territory. Programme editors were also as vulnerable as their print media colleagues to the coercive power of the state. To this extent, governments could set effective rules for domestic broadcast content through general law and sector regulation, backed by an obvious power to seize facilities and prosecute individuals.

In other critical respects, broadcasting was entirely unlike the print media. Signal interference was an immediate problem for the operation of radio broadcast services. Interference was not only a threat to any competing broadcast, but more importantly for many states, it could disrupt military communications, which had hitherto driven the development of radio communications.[19] There were also severe limits on the amount of usable spectrum available for analogue radio. But, in contrast to the supply of printing presses and newsprint, rationing through the operation of market forces alone appeared unworkable even in wealthier economies. These fundamental problems of signal interference and spectrum scarcity pushed all governments towards compulsory or monopoly licensing and spectrum allocation. As matter of territorial sovereignty, states enjoyed rights of exclusive authority over the allocation management of spectrum use. Yet effective national control over domestic radio communication depended on cooperation with foreign

---

[18] See, for example, the World Summit on the Information Society (WSIS), Declaration of Principles, WSIS-03/GENEVA/DOC/0004, (12 December 2003): '49 a) Policy authority for Internet-related public policy issues is the sovereign right of States. They have rights and responsibilities for international Internet-related public policy issues . . .'

[19] Starr, P., *The Creation of the Media: Political Origins of Modern Communications* (Basic Books, 2004), 330–340.

states. Instantaneous communication over distance, one of the principal benefits of radio signals, was also one of the chief obstacles to the maintenance of domestic spectrum order. Foreign radio broadcasts spilled over national frontiers and merged into the domestic radio communications sphere. Reducing cross border frequency interference therefore became a pressing foreign policy objective, especially for smaller countries surrounded by neighbouring states.

In 1927, the representatives of 74 countries and territories met at the Washington International Radiotelegraph Conference to adopt a multilateral treaty creating the first comprehensive international obligations on radio communications. This major step in multilateral cooperation led, in 1932, to the creation of the International Telecommunications Union.[20] The 1927 International Radiotelegraph Convention confirmed the principal obligations of states in the joint use of the radio spectrum, including the duty to prevent unauthorized transmission and to ensure that authorized domestic users do not interfere with the communication services of other states.[21] Those obligations have remained in place through successive generations of ITU conventions.[22]

The ITU treaties, combined with regional and bilateral agreements, collectively formed the basis for a comparatively durable and effective global regime that grew to encompass satellite orbits and operations as well as technical cooperation in radio and telecommunications.[23] Under this layer of global public order, however, national control has remained the cornerstone of multilateral cooperation on the use of radio spectrum. Despite the non-territorial nature of radiospectrum, international principles of cooperation reinforced the central role of territoriality and nationality in maintaining spectrum order. States were consequently able to fashion relatively coherent regimes regulating broadcasting and maintaining control over the domestic public information environment.

Using this international framework, a state could distinguish between authorized domestic and foreign broadcasters as well as identify pirate operators. These unauthorized operators, who broadcast between and over the frequencies allocated to authorized broadcasters and radio users, were an inevitable and persistent hazard of international system based on spectrum licensing. In European states, where private or commercial broadcasting was widely prohibited, considerable efforts, both unilateral and in collaboration with foreign governments, were needed to suppress or at least curb unauthorized broadcasting. Britain, for example, faced an

---

[20] Following the 1927 Washington International Radiotelegraph Conference, the delegates to the 1932 Madrid Conference agreed to combine the International Telegraph Convention of 1865 and the International Radiotelegraph Convention of 1906 to form the International Telecommunication Convention and to change the name of the Union to International Telecommunication Union.

[21] 1927 International Radiotelegraph Convention, Articles 5 and 10.

[22] ITU, International Telecommunications Constitution, Article 45. See also Luther, S.F., *The United States and the Direct Broadcast Satellite: The Politics of International Broadcasting in Space* (Oxford University Press, 1988); Lyall, F., *Law and Space Telecommunications* (Gower, 1989) and Taishoff, M.N., *State Responsibility and the Direct Broadcast Satellite* (Pinter, 1987).

[23] The four main treaties establishing the contemporary International Telecommunications Union ITU are the Constitution, Convention, Radio Regulations, and International Telecommunications Regulations.

upsurge in pirate radio broadcasts during the 1960s. A growing number of unauthorized operators had begun broadcasting popular music and other commercial content to Britain and other northern European countries. Several were based on ships or disused offshore military installations that were then outside national territorial waters, including the famous ship based stations *Radio Caroline* and *Radio Veronica*.[24] These North Sea broadcasters gained large audiences in Britain, the Netherlands, and adjacent broadcast markets.

In 1967, the British government enacted legislation that prohibited British nationals or residents from operating or supplying unlicensed marine broadcast facilities.[25] Britain also collaborated with other states in the Council of Europe to adopt a treaty that required parties to take similar measures in their own territories and against their nationals.[26] These measures, together with the opening of the domestic broadcasting sphere to licensed non-state commercial broadcasters and the transmission of more popular programming by public broadcasters, effectively suppressed the sea based operators.[27] Nonetheless, pirate broadcasters, usually operating secretly inside national territory, remain a constant element in British and other national broadcast systems.[28] The suppression of the North Sea broadcasters demonstrated the potential effectiveness of the state based, international division of jurisdiction over the radiospectrum. Yet, just as often, states have failed to cooperate to achieve closer control over radio communications. Not long after the North Sea broadcasters were put out of business, Switzerland looked unsuccessfully to Italy to help suppress a pirate operator broadcasting into Switzerland from the top of the Groppera peak in the Italian Alps.[29] This broadcaster eventually ceased operations permanently only after Swiss authorities banned the retransmission of its programmes through domestic cable networks and other factors made the service uneconomic to operate.[30]

[24] Crissell, A., *An Introductory History of British Broadcasting* (Routledge, 1997), 136–142.

[25] Marine, etc., Broadcasting (Offences) Act 1967; see also Woodliffe, J., 'The Marine, etc., Broadcasting (Offences) Act 1967', 30(6) *The Modern Law Review* (November 1967), 676–680.

[26] Council of Europe, 1965 European Agreement for the Prevention of Broadcasts Transmitted from Stations Outside National Territories, (ETS No. 53), Article 2. Each Contracting Party undertakes to take appropriate steps to make punishable as offences, in accordance with its domestic law, the establishment or operation of broadcasting stations referred to in Article 1, as well as acts of collaboration knowingly performed.

[27] In the United Kingdom, licensed private commercial radio began to operate following the Sound Broadcasting Act 1972, while the BBC extended its range of programming into genres served by the pirate broadcasters, in particular pop: Crissell, A., n. 24 above, 140–147; Seymour-Ure, C., *The British Press and Broadcasting*, 2nd edn (Blackwell, 1996), 78–79.

[28] See United Kingdom, Office of Communications, (OFCOM), Report, *Illegal broadcasting: Understanding the issues* (April 2007).

[29] This situation was described in detail in the *Groppera Radio v. Switzerland* judgment of the European Court of Human Rights, which cites Swiss claims that Italy was in violation of its ITU obligations in permitting a large number of private radio and television broadcasting stations in the Po valley to broadcast into Switzerland on frequencies not coordinated by the Swiss government ... *Groppera Radio AG v. Switzerland* (Application No. 10890/84) (28 March 1990), para. 41.

[30] Ibid.

Liberal democracy perspectives on broadcasting jurisdiction

The advent of radio broadcasting had little impact on the substance of domestic media law. A radio broadcast, as much as a newspaper, could incite crime, transmit blasphemy, breach standards of obscenity and indecency, harm reputations, breach confidences, and infringe copyright. Yet broadcasting had radically changed the nature of the mass media. Radio entered the home with an immediacy and influence that no newspaper or journal could hope to match. An illiterate listener living in the remote countryside could enjoy the same access to programmes as an educated, urban resident. This increased public access was however widely seen as an unprecedented threat to state information and entertainment policies. Broadcasters, more than newspaper publishers, could deliver programmes and advertising of their own choosing directly into the home without prior notice. Consequent state anxieties about the potential influence of radio on the public fed into the wider question of how radio communications should be properly managed. Most governments determined that the state should use its control over access to the airwaves to impose standards on broadcast content. Even in the United States, where publishers were increasingly successful in using the First Amendment to challenge state controls on the print media, Congress gave newly created federal regulators broad powers over radio content, which the courts subsequently upheld.[31]

Democratic governments may have shared a conviction that broadcast content should be subject to closer control than their print media, but they were divided on methods and standards. Famously, the United States chose to license private providers, fostering the growth of flourishing commercial markets for broadcasting services long before they appeared in western Europe.[32] European governments generally preferred a larger role for the state in the broadcast media, building powerful public service broadcasters that had no American equivalent.[33] European and American colonial authorities, moreover, frequently adapted their national regulatory models to create familiar, but also distinctively colonial, broadcasting regimes through much of Asia and Africa.[34] While liberalism and democracy ebbed and flowed in Europe, European states adapted controls over the media to the character and needs of colonial rule in their overseas possessions.

During the Cold War decades, broadcasting policies in the western democracies remained markedly different in substance and structure. Even as west European states relinquished their state monopolies over broadcasting, their continuing

---

[31] Starr, P., n. 19 above 363–367.

[32] Ibid., 330–339.

[33] European broadcast regimes have never been uniform and have varied considerably in their development, often incorporating elements of non-state participation. See, for example, Humphrey, P., *Media and Media Policy in Germany: The Press and Broadcasting since 1945* (Berg, 1994); Kuhn, R., *The Media in France* (Routledge, 1995).

[34] In British India, for example, the colonial government's Indian State Broadcasting Service began broadcasting in 1930, while in the American Philippines, a nascent system of private broadcasting was legitimized under the colonial government's 1931 Radio Control Law.

attachment to publicly funded broadcasters was in stark contrast to the resolutely market based, American broadcast media system. European restrictions on film and programme imports from the United States were also a growing irritant in transatlantic trade relations. Yet despite their notable differences, they shared a rough consensus on the principles governing state regulation of the media. The western Europeans, as much as the United States, were politically, and often constitutionally, committed to liberal principles of tolerance, plurality of opinion, and diversity in information and entertainment content. Without these, a state could not be a legitimate liberal democracy in either American or western European terms.

The projection of a liberal model of the legitimate state through multilateral conventions had obvious implications for the exercise of sovereignty, particularly for non-democratic states.[35] The scope of internal sovereignty was now subject to external legal constraints that were intended to strengthen or foster domestic democratic institutions. At least as a matter of principle, these international obligations hardly counted as constraints for viable liberal democracies. From a liberal perspective, the state's claims to sovereignty are only valid when constituted by citizens who are free to exercise individual and collective choices within the protected sphere of political and social tolerance. In this broadly construed model, states nonetheless retained exclusive authority over their domestic public information spheres. The legitimate liberal democratic state was still firmly rooted in the tradition of the territorially sovereign, Westphalian state. The architecture of multilateral economic and human rights treaties, for example, carefully preserved the autonomy of the sovereign state in critical areas of public policy through express and implied exceptions.[36]

In comparison to these initiatives, the western democracies put less effort into multilateral collaboration to assert more effective control over harmful media content. In the circumstances, this was hardly surprising. Their goal was to advance a liberal democratic model of the state that would, among other things, ease government restrictions on the international flow of information, ideas, and opinions. Collaboration on minimum standards for offensive or harmful content was an unwelcome distraction from this goal. The abortive work on the 1948 United Nations Freedom of Information Conference conventions had already made the risks of such obligations clear.[37] Even when carefully drafted, any treaty obliging states to impose restrictions on information or entertainment content offered a potential pretext for states to justify more extensive curbs on freedom of expression. Western democracies were also relatively untroubled by the cross border intrusion of foreign supplied, harmful content. Common restrictions on print and

---

[35] On the ICCPR and other UN based human rights initiatives, see Chapter 6.

[36] See Article 19 of the International Covenant on Civil and Political Rights, GA Resolution 2200A (XXI), 21 UN GAOR Supp. (No. 16) at 52, UN Doc. A/6316 (1966). See also Article XX and XXI of the General Agreement on Tariffs and Trade 1994 (incorporating GATT 1947), (15 April 1994), 33 ILM 1153 (1994), and Article XIV and XIV*bis* of the General Agreement on Trade in Services (15 April 1994), 33 ILM 1167 (1994). See also Chapters 5 and 6.

[37] The Conference yielded the draft Convention on Freedom of Information and the draft Convention on the International Transmission of News. See Chapter 6.

broadcast content as well as the practical difficulties of mounting cross border media businesses kept violent and pornographic material out of mainstream circulation in most states. It was only later with changing moral standards in many western countries and new communications technologies, such as direct-to-home satellite television, that the intrusion of foreign sourced, restricted, or illicit content became a more prominent issue. Consequently, international legal obligations to control the export of harmful content developed slowly and cautiously through a thin patchwork of general and special obligations.

Customary international law, at most, prohibits states from broadcasting, or permitting others to use their territory to broadcast, some forms of extreme content. Failure to do so will give rise to state responsibility, but what content falls within this category is disputed. A broadcast transmitted to another state could potentially put the state where it originated in violation of its obligation not to intervene in the domestic affairs of other countries through force or other means.[38] This obligation includes indirect forms of support for violent subversive activities and therefore logically extends to direct incitement to violence through broadcasts aimed at the residents of other states.[39] This is plainly a relatively small area of international consensus. Democratic governments have been reluctant to recognize a positive legal duty in international law to prevent harmful broadcasts that goes beyond content inciting violence or other serious criminal activities. Any wider obligation would increase pressure on the right to freedom of expression, as protected by the UDHR and the ICCPR, which protect the transmission of peaceful political dissent across national frontiers. Western democracies, for example, opposed efforts to incorporate a requirement into the ITU treaties that a state must seek the express permission of another state before allowing a domestic broadcaster to transmit broadcasts to that state.[40]

For liberal democracies, the distinction is usually made between permissible support for peaceful dissent and prohibited incitement of violence. However, making that highly qualitative distinction is often difficult and controversial in practice. For several years in the 1990s, Britain permitted the locally licensed Kurdish language television channel MED TV to broadcast by satellite to Turkey its support for the Kurdish independence movement, despite strong Turkish government objections.[41] The British television regulatory authority imposed

---

[38] *Case Concerning the Military and Paramilitary Activities in and against Nicaragua* (Nicaragua v. United States of America) [1986] ICJ Reports 14, paras 202–209). See also Declaration of Principles of International Law Concerning Friendly Relations and Co-operation Among States in Accordance with the Charter of the United Nations, GA Resolution 2625, UN GAOR, 25th Sess., Supp. No. 28.

[39] Declaration on the Inadmissibility of Intervention into the Domestic Affairs of States, GA Resolution 2131, 20th Sess., Supp. No. 14, at 108, UN Doc. A/6014 (1965). No state has the right to intervene, directly or indirectly, for any reason whatsoever, in the internal or external affairs of any other state. Consequently, armed intervention and all other forms of interference or attempted threats against the personality of the state or against its political, economic, and cultural elements, are condemned.

[40] Fisher, D., *Prior Consent to International Direct Satellite Broadcasting*, Utrecht Studies in Air and Space Law, Vol. 8 (M. Nijhoff, 1990).

[41] See also Monroe Price, Satellite Broadcasting as Trade Routes in the Sky', 11(2) *Public Culture* (1999), 387–403.

penalties on the channel for violations of its licence, but was not persuaded that these merited the removal of its licence to broadcast. The regulator did however finally revoke the operator's licence after MED TV began advocating violent opposition to the Turkish government.[42]

Conversely, a commitment to liberal democracy and market economics leaves scant ground on which to object to foreign broadcasts that do not incite violence, but nonetheless frustrate national media policies. Where a foreign based broadcaster lacks any valid government authorization, a state that receives its broadcasts can legitimately treat it as a pirate broadcaster. It is free to obstruct signal reception or use other anti-piracy measures.[43] But where that broadcaster is authorized by the relevant state, a liberal democratic state is likely to violate rights to freedom of expression if it frustrates domestic reception.[44] On this basis, Radio Luxembourg was famously able to broadcast popular radio programmes unobstructed to the southeast of Britain for many years, effectively breaching the BBC's domestic monopoly.[45] Similarly, in Canada, the national history of radio and television broadcasting has been one of fierce competition between the domestic media and American cross border broadcasters.[46] Even in this unequal struggle, the Canadian government has been reluctant to interfere with the reception of American broadcasts, not least because of the liberal democratic foundations of the Canadian state. It has resorted instead to subsidies, quota restrictions on the local rebroadcast of foreign content, and prohibitions on foreign ownership to sustain national media policies.[47]

General international law thus imposes few uncontested positive duties regarding harmful or injurious communications content. There are, nonetheless, important special regimes containing positive obligations, including for example the responsibilities of ITU member states.[48] The most potent special regime affecting media content, however, was created during the Uruguay Round negotiations that established the WTO. The inclusion of the TRIPS agreement in the WTO trade system introduced obligations on member states to ensure that their domestic

---

[42] United Kingdom, Independent Television Commission, Bulletin No. 8 (1998), 'Med TV's licence was suspended on 22 March by the ITC under section 45A of the Broadcasting Act 1990, following four broadcasts which included inflammatory statements encouraging acts of violence in Turkey and elsewhere. These were judged by the ITC as "likely to encourage or incite crime or lead to disorder". This is against UK law, as set out in the 1990 and 1996 Broadcasting Acts.'

[43] See *Groppera*, n. 29 above.

[44] *Autronic AG v. Switzerland* (Application No. 12726/87) (22 May 1990).

[45] Radio Luxembourg broadcast in English to the United Kingdom from 1951 to 1992 from the Grand Duchy of Luxembourg. See Dyson, K., 'Luxembourg: Changing Anatomy of an International Broadcasting Power', in Dyson, K., and Humphreys, P. (eds), *The Political Economy of Communications: International and European Dimensions* (Routledge, 1990).

[46] Raboy, M., 'Canada' in Smith, A. (ed), *Television: An International History* (Oxford University Press, 1998), 162–168.

[47] Raboy, M. and Taras, D., 'Canada', in d'Haenens, L. and Saeys, F. (eds), *Western Broadcast Models: Structure, Conduct and Performance* (Mouton De Gruyter, 2007), 361–378.

[48] See, for example, Constitution of the International Telecommunications Union, Article 6: Execution of the instruments of the Union.

intellectual property laws meet specified international minimum standards.[49] TRIPS was a dramatic break from the traditional resistance of democratic states to positive duties regarding media content, although its protection of property rights is plainly within the liberal tradition. There is at yet no other comparable international regime imposing duties on states to restrict information and entertainment content. The Council of Europe Cybercrime Convention, for example, is limited to selected states and contains piecemeal rather than comprehensive obligations.[50]

Broadcasting jurisdiction and the Audiovisual Media Services Directive

In Europe, the evolving balance between multilateral obligations and national autonomy in the broadcasting field has been altogether different. The original architecture for western European regional cooperation was one of sovereign, liberal democratic states bound by limited domestic and international restraints on their powers to interfere with social and economic liberties. They retained substantial autonomy in media matters through express and implied exceptions to these basic obligations.[51] The European Union, moreover, did little initially to address the welter of discordant national rules concerning advertising, obscenity, violence, and other content matters that hindered cross border trade in broadcast content. Nor were the European Court of Justice and the European Court of Human Rights inclined to make a frontal assault on the privileges and powers of state supported broadcasters.[52] While they had begun to delineate the boundaries of the legitimate European liberal democracy, they were careful to acknowledge the importance of state owned or supported broadcasters to the member states.

European economic obligations were certainly more complex and demanding than any comparable international ones. The Treaty of Rome's requirements concerning free movement of goods and services and the right of establishment obliged member states to open their national media sectors to competing firms based anywhere in the European Union.[53] Discriminatory quotas supporting domestic programmes or bans on local retransmission of broadcast services from other member states were therefore, in principle, unlawful. In practical terms,

---

[49] TRIPS: Agreement on Trade-Related Aspects of Intellectual Property Rights, (1994), Marrakesh Agreement Establishing the World Trade Organization, Annex 1C, 1869 U.N.T.S. 299.

[50] The 2001 Council of Europe Convention on Cybercrime, (ETS No. 185), requires state parties to create legal offences concerning unauthorized access, interception, or interference with data or systems as well as misuse of devices, computer-related forgery, computer-related fraud, offences related to child pornography and offences related to copyright and neighbouring rights.

[51] In relation to media goods and services, see the Treaty on the Functioning of the European Union (TFEU), Article 36 and Article 52(1). On express and implied exceptions to the rules of free movement in European Union law, see Chapter 4.

[52] See Chapters 4 and 6.

[53] See TFEU, Articles 28, 34, and 35, which concern the free movement of goods, and Article 56, which concerns the free movement of services. On the rules of free movement in European Union law as they apply to the media, see Chapter 4.

however, these EU obligations provided few advantages for European terrestrial broadcasters attempting to gain audiences in neighbouring states. Cross border services were hampered as much by restrictive radiospectrum agreements between states as they were by local laws affecting reception or retransmission. Europe's major media markets were also comparatively isolated. Linguistic and cultural differences between states and localities meant that only a few entertainment genres could attract a significant audience in more than one country. National markets were also dominated by well established public and private broadcasters whose privileges created dense barriers to market entry.[54] In that era of spectrum starved analogue broadcasting, the reservation of radiospectrum and cable capacity for preferred national providers left few opportunities for new entrants.

The advent of satellite broadcasting opened enormous breaches in these barriers, radically changing the dynamics of the media state relationship. Through satellites, broadcasters acquired the frequencies and range to transmit their programmes and advertising to entire populations in other states. This became a catalyst not only for a commercial revolution in European media, but also for major developments in regional economic and human rights law.[55] Media entrepreneurs pushed the Commission and member states to overcome differences in national content and technical standards that limited the free movement of broadcasting services. At the same time, defensive governments looked for ways to protect national broadcasting systems from revenue loss and an influx of foreign content.

The Commission and member states sought to resolve this tangle of interests and new services in a comprehensive directive spanning economic, social, and cultural policy objectives. This legislation, previously known as the Television Without Frontiers Directive and now renamed the Audiovisual Media Services Directive, opened the way to significant market integration for European television services.[56] To do so, it relies on specially defined rules of jurisdiction to set the rights and obligations of the member states. The state holding jurisdiction over a broadcaster has a pivotal role, not only for enforcing the Directive's minimum European standards for programmes and advertising, but also in imposing its own more restrictive national standards. This exclusive relationship, however, requires a clarity and certainty that the Directive has not always delivered.

The Directive did not follow international practice in basing jurisdiction on the place of transmission or the nationality of the responsible individual or corporate

---

[54] On the transition in Britain from a monopoly broadcast regime under the BBC to a regime of limited public–private competition dominated by the BBC and ITV, see Curran, J. and Seaton, J., *Power Without Responsibility: Press, Broadcasting and the Internet in Britain*, (Routledge, 2010), chs 11 and 12.

[55] On changes in European economic law, see Levy, D., Europe's Digital Revolution: Broadcasting Regulation, the EU and the Nation State (Routledge, 1999). On the influence of human rights based principle of pluralism on European broadcast media rules, see Craufurd Smith, R., *Broadcasting Law and Fundamental Rights* (Oxford University Press, 1997), 174–196.

[56] On the Audiovisual Media Services Directive (Directive 2010/13/EU of the European Parliament and of the Council of 10 March 2010 on the coordination of certain provisions laid down by law, regulation or administrative action in Member States concerning the provision of audiovisual media services) (AVMS Directive), see Chapter 4.

body. After a period of uncertainty, the European Court of Justice conclusively determined that the Directive requires member states to take jurisdiction according to the place in which a broadcaster is established.[57] This principle is consistent with EU law more generally and can usually be applied without difficulty to major national broadcasters. Yet the place of establishment of many smaller European broadcasters is not readily apparent. If a broadcaster has its head office in one member state, but engages in substantial editorial and production work in one or more other member states, the Directive's jurisdictional sub-rules are far from conclusive.[58] This situation can easily arise when a satellite broadcaster has targeted the market in a particular member state and produces programmes and advertising in that state, but also maintains a head office and significant presence in another member state.[59]

The rapid proliferation of digital channels across Europe has also made it much harder for national authorities to determine the place of establishment, as many of these channels are small commercial operations that may open and close within months, possibly backed by unknown investors and operators. Yet even this situation appears manageable when compared to Europe's internet based media, which are also subject to the principle of country of origin jurisdiction. As discussed in Chapter 4, in 2007 on-demand audiovisual services were carved out of the Electronic Commerce Directive, which governs 'information society services', and transferred into the AVMS Directive. While this legislative surgery required major changes to the AVMS Directive, the fact that both Directives are based on the principles of free movement and country of origin meant there was a basic consistency of approach.[60] Nonetheless, given that there are innumerable internet based services in Europe delivering information and entertainment content, it is clearly very difficult, if not impossible, to know where many are established. The

[57] AVMS Directive, Article 2. Initially, the British government determined that jurisdiction under the Directive arose in the country where the broadcast was first transmitted or, in the case of satellite broadcasting, the country of uplink. Britain was the only member state to reject the principle of establishment and, in so doing, created a significant loophole that allowed broadcasters to base their operations in Britain and avoid the Directive's mandatory European content quotas. This situation finally concluded in 1996 when the ECJ found against Britain (C-383/92, *Commission v. United Kingdom*), which was expressly reinforced in the 1997 amendments to the Directive.

[58] Ibid.

[59] For example, CLT-UFA SA, a satellite broadcaster, licensed in Luxembourg, which directed its services RTL 4 and 5 to the Dutch market. The Dutch broadcast authorities claimed that despite its presence in Luxembourg, it had sufficient ties to the Netherlands to be subject to Dutch jurisdiction. The dispute almost led to a Commission infringement action against the Netherlands, but was settled through Dutch law and an agreement between the government and the broadcaster. See the Fourth Report from the Commission to the Council, the European Parliament, the European Economic and Social Committee, and the Committee of the Regions on the application of Directive 89/552/EEC 'Television without Frontiers',/* COM/2002/0778 final */; see also Fifth Report from the Commission to the Council, the European Parliament, the European Economic and Social Committee and the Committee of the Regions on the application of Directive 89/552/EEC 'Television without Frontiers' (SEC (2006) 160).

[60] On the free movement and country of origin rules of the AVMS Directive and the Electronic Commerce Directive (Directive 2000/31/EC of the European Parliament and of the Council of 8 June 2000 on certain legal aspects of information society services, in particular electronic commerce, in the Internal Market), see Chapter 4.

practical answer to this problem, which is built into both Directives, is to permit wide, if conditional, powers of derogation that allow member states to resort to national measures that restrict domestic access or possibly sanction the service provider.[61]

On its face, the Directive substantially curtails the freedom of European member states to manage their domestic media sectors. The substantive fields covered by the Directive are subject to the country of origin principle, which forces member states to accept broadcasts governed by the standards of other member states.[62] Consequently, television programmes transmitted by broadcasters established in another EU state can effectively become part of the national media while remaining largely outside national control. This loss of autonomy was, however, only intended to occur within a protected regional broadcasting sphere. Member states are bound by the Directive and other European laws to maintain minimum common standards that protect not only public morality, but also essential liberal values of tolerance and human dignity.[63] The goal is a European broadcast media space in which content standards are maintained through a mix of unilateral and collaborative controls. And in some situations, the system is reasonably effective.

International jurisdiction in the internet era

The digitization of media content and the convergence of services have broken down once reliable assumptions about state control over the individuals and facilities essential to modern communications. For many states, the most troubling aspect of this transformation has been the public's ability to access a cornucopia of foreign content through the internet. Content safe havens have become a global phenomenon as providers have found congenial places to locate their online distribution services cheaply and efficiently. Pornographers and neo-nazis prohibited from transmitting content under European laws can thus operate from the United States under the protection of the First Amendment.[64]

This revolution in accessibility thrust the question of jurisdiction to the forefront of media law and policy making. As the boundaries separating domestic and foreign media eroded, the existing rules of jurisdiction could not answer pressing questions about the limits of the state. Foreign content was now freely accessible in the home, but if the computers hosting that content were located abroad and the individuals responsible had no other local connections, when should the state exercise its prescriptive or adjudicative powers? The most difficult issue was whether the simple

---

[61] See AVMS Directive Article 3 and Electronic Commerce Directive, Article 3(4).

[62] See Case C-11/95, *Commission v. Belgium* and Case C-34/95, *Konsumentombudsmannen (KO) v. De Agostini (Svenska) Förlag AB*. See Chapter 4.

[63] See AVMS Directive Articles 6 (incitement to hatred), Article 9 (advertising restrictions relating to the protection of human dignity and health), and Articles 12 and 27 (protection of children from harmful programmes). See Chapter 4.

[64] On the critically important United States *Brandenburg v. Ohio* distinction in constitutional law between incitement to hatred and incitement to violence, see Chapter 13.

act of making content available on the internet was sufficient in itself for any state to assert jurisdiction if that content resulted in local harm or injury. While most states have since reached some conclusions on these questions, there is as yet no international consensus.

As discussed above, entertainment and information content has always flowed, and sometimes trickled, across borders. The regular adjustment of content controls to cope with new communications technologies has been an equally constant concern for national governments. The borderless nature of radio communications presented an enormous challenge to state authority, but governments found ways to blunt its potential effects through unilateral and cooperative measures. The arrival of the internet was therefore not unprecedented, although its challenges are undoubtedly of a greater magnitude. Unlike the print and broadcast sectors, the internet operates as a single, unified entity. It is technically a network of networks, but those constituent networks are bound together by common communication protocols, including a universal address system. No other communications infrastructure has this degree of unity and interdependence. This technological unity, which appeared to render national boundaries irrelevant, also inspired new ideas about the limits of state authority and the special character of internet based activities. One particularly important and broadly shared idea was that online content and transactions existed in a unique conceptual space called 'cyberspace'.[65] In its radical version, cyberspace was entirely outside the legitimate or practical scope of territorially defined, national media and communications regimes.

This libertarian understanding of cyberspace arose in the early years of general public access to the internet in the United States, when the flow of online content was still astonishingly open and unstructured. Since then, the power of governments and commerce to shape the architecture of the internet and to target the online activities of specific individuals has demonstrated the weaknesses of the cyberspace argument. Its proponents underestimated the inventiveness of the states and markets in finding ways to manage the public information environment.[66] And yet the idea of cyberspace remains an important contribution to the evolving debate over the relationship between the state and the internet. Online communication is an extraordinary challenge for the state and the grasp of individual states on internet based activities is still weak when compared to the control they can wield over broadcasting and the print media.

In these efforts, governments have returned to familiar methods and concepts, looking for discrete functions that are vulnerable to the coercive powers of the state. Domestic content producers, host computer services, and internet access providers are all susceptible to state legal and regulatory measures through the local presence of companies, individuals, facilities, and revenues. In addition, national citizens or

---

[65] See, for example, Johnson, D. and Post, D., 'Law and Borders—The Rise of Law in Cybespace', 48 *Stanford Law Review* (1996), 1367.

[66] On the power of the state over internet content providers, see Reidenberg, J., 'Technology and Internet Jurisdiction', 153 *University of Pennsylvania Law Review* (2005), 1951; Goldsmith, J., 'Against Cyberanarchy', 65 *University of Chicago Law Review* (1998), 1199; and Goldsmith, J. and Wu, T., *Who Controls the Internet* (Oxford University Press, 2006).

companies can be held responsible for their participation in foreign based services. Consequently, from the state's perspective, the contemporary, commercialized internet offers a host of vulnerable points that are potentially within jurisdictional reach.

Beyond the challenge of sheer numbers, the state must also disentangle domestic and foreign sources of content to determine the legal and practical limits of its authority. But the lack of clear distinctions between domestic and foreign based, online services has meant that the reach of national laws and enforcement processes is not easily calculated or controlled. Prosecutions or civil actions may, for example, require foreign resident companies to appear before local courts for inadvertent content related offences. National regulatory authorities may, moreover, demand that service providers monitor and report user activities, regardless of the user's local connections. Consequently, the contemporary state cannot assert effective control over communications and media services without deliberately or accidentally extending its authority into foreign states.

This clash of sovereign authority is not simply a consequence of the cross border nature of the internet. States have been managing the risks occasioned by the cross border delivery of media content for centuries, just as they have dealt with interactive communications across their borders through generations of telecommunications services. It is the sheer breadth and complexity of interactive services available instantaneously across multiple borders that have propelled the state into the current morass of jurisdictional uncertainty. In these circumstances, the key determinants, such as the geographical location of an act or its responsible party, often confuse as much as resolve the issue of proper jurisdiction. Parties in different locations may, for example, all contribute to the relevant online activity and yet also be entirely and reasonably unaware of the alleged harm in the state that wishes to assert jurisdiction. For governments, the problem has been to create regulatory controls over public access to harmful online content and activities that are effective, but do not provoke unnecessary jurisdictional disputes with foreign states. Businesses, on the other hand, wish to ward off the spectre of universal liability and to reduce the potential for exorbitant or multiple claims for their internet based services.[67]

Jurisdiction and transatlantic differences

As governments worked their way through the practical problems of internet jurisdiction, they gained scant assistance from the relevant principles of public international law. Those principles of jurisdiction are anchored in the idea of a community of territorially constituted states, each holding primary authority over

---

[67] International Chamber of Commerce, *Policy Statement: The Impact of Internet Content Regulation*, Doc no. 373-37/1 (18 November 2002), '5. Jurisdiction and applicable law mechanisms should not plague business with the risks of unexpectedly being subjected to laws and judgments in other countries.'

its citizens.[68] Consequently, any solutions to the conundrums of jurisdiction over internet based content must recognize the overriding importance of territoriality and nationality to questions of jurisdiction under international law. Yet, as noted above, those principles have already been stretched considerably by states seeking to square the circle of territorial sovereignty and the cross border reach of human activities. In the absence of consistent state practice in the difficult area of jurisdiction, customary international law offers little more than broad consensus on basic principles.

The resolution of these uncertainties through a multilateral treaty on jurisdiction is also unlikely in the next decade. During the 1990s, the United States and the major European states attempted to bridge the differences between their models for harmonizing civil and commercial jurisdictional rules. That project, which they initiated within the Hague Conference on Private International Law, collapsed in 2002, although it did proceed as far as a draft 'Convention on Jurisdiction and Enforcement of Judgements in Civil and Commercial Matters'.[69] Despite many points of agreement, the American and European representatives could not overcome their different approaches to the basic problems of jurisdiction. The obstacles to a successful conclusion of the Hague jurisdiction treaty were formidable. Although the American and European models both arose in liberal economic and political environments, they developed through remarkably different processes. They diverged on matters of principle as well as specific rules, including the nature and extent of the connection with national territory needed to assert a valid claim to jurisdiction.

In the United States, the states of the union shared a common language and legal system, which substantially reduced the legal and practical objections to litigation in other states. The United States Supreme Court was also well placed to use federal constitutional guarantees of 'due process' to curb the excessive assertion of 'long arm' jurisdiction by the states, or under federal law.[70] As a matter of fundamental principle, the Supreme Court determined that a defendant cannot be required to appear before an American domestic court without having sufficient 'minimum contacts' with the forum.[71] The forum court must moreover show that

[68] On the problems of adapting that idea to cross border media, see Decroos, M., 'Criminal Jurisdiction Over Transnational Speech Offenses', 13(3) *European Journal of Crime, Criminal Law and Criminal Justice* (2005), 365–400.

[69] *Some Reflections on the Present State of Negotiations on the Judgments Project in the Context of the Future Work Programme of the Conference*, Permanent Bureau, Hague Conference on Private International Law, General Affairs, Prel. Doc. No 16, (February 2002). The extent of these transatlantic differences became clear in 1999 when the Preliminary Draft Convention was unveiled. See Hague Conference on Private International Law, Report of the Special Commission on Jurisdiction, Recognition and Enforcement of Foreign Judgments in Civil and Commercial Matters, Preliminary Document, No. 11. One part of the negotiations was successfully rescued and led to the 2005 Hague Convention on Exclusive Choice of Courts Agreements. See Brand, R., 'The New Hague Convention on Choice of Court Agreements', *ASIL Insights*, 16 July 2005. See also Clermont., K.M., 'A Global Law of Jurisdiction and Judgments: Views from the United States and Japan'), *Cornell Law School Legal Studies Research Paper Series.* Paper 10 (8 September 2004).

[70] United States Constitution, Fifth and Fourteenth Amendments.

[71] *International Shoe Co. v. Washington,* 326 U.S. 310.

its exercise of jurisdiction does not violate 'traditional notions of fair play and substantial justice'.[72]

Constitutionalization has benefited American rules of jurisdiction in important ways, not least by linking the legitimacy of personal jurisdiction directly to the right of the individual to judicial 'due process'. Through decades of judicial precedent, US courts have drawn on these principles to find innovative solutions to the rigidity and arbitrariness of territorially defined jurisdiction.[73] The result is a broadly comprehensive set of jurisdictional principles, embracing public and private as well as state and federal law.[74] Yet constitutionalization has also made compromise with foreign partners more difficult, if not impossible, as witnessed in the failure of the Hague jurisdiction convention.

In that project, one of the major difficulties stemmed directly from the constitutionally based categories of general and specific jurisdiction in US law. General jurisdiction permits the exercise of personal jurisdiction where a defendant has engaged in substantial, systematic, and continuous activities in or directed at the forum state.[75] Having thus 'purposefully availed' itself of the benefits of the forum economy and legal system, a non-resident party is subject to local jurisdiction on any civil matter, whether related to its local activities or not. This is commonly known as 'doing business' jurisdiction and plays a prominent part in American commercial litigation. It also poses a serious risk for foreign companies entering transactions with parties resident in an American state, who may find themselves subject to suit in that state for unrelated activities occurring elsewhere. In contrast, specific jurisdiction permits the exercise of personal jurisdiction only for matters directly related to the forum state under the 'minimum contacts' principle. According to the US Supreme Court, '[I]t is essential in each case that there be some act by which the defendant purposefully avails itself of the privilege of conducting activities within the forum State, thus invoking the benefits and protections of its laws.'[76]

In some situations, an American court may thus exercise specific jurisdiction over a defendant whose activities ostensibly occurred outside the territory of the forum state, provided those acts were intentionally directed towards the forum state and caused harmful effects or consequences to occur there.[77] This use of 'effects' jurisdiction is, in public international law terms, related to both the objective territorial and protective principles of jurisdiction. Objective territoriality concerns the exercise of jurisdiction for actions that began abroad but culminated in the national territory, whereas the protective principle concerns actions occurring

---

[72] Ibid.

[73] Borchers, P., 'Jones v. Flowers: An Essay on a Unified Theory of Procedural Due Process'. 40 *Creighton Law Review* (2007), 343.

[74] On personal jurisdiction under United States constitutional law, see Hay, P., Borchers, P., and Symeonides, S., *Conflict of Laws* (West, 2010).

[75] *Helicopteros Nacionales de Colombia, S.A. v. Hall*, 466 U.S. (408).

[76] *Hanson v. Denckla*, 357 U.S. 235 (1958).

[77] *Calder v. Jones*, 465 U.S. 783 (1984).

entirely abroad that harm essential national interests.[78] Under the American domestic effects doctrine, the defendant's final positive act need not take place in the forum state so long as its foreseeable harmful consequences occur there.[79] Additionally, that harm may concern significant private as well as public interests. A broadcast may, for example, cause injury to an individual's reputation in foreign states where it is received, or also violate the laws of the receiving state prohibiting publications that prejudice judicial proceedings. The effects doctrine is therefore a genuinely extraterritorial claim to rights of jurisdiction.[80]

The chief advantage of effects jurisdiction lies in its flexible and pragmatic awareness of the complex relationship between human activities and geographical places. Yet the disadvantages are equally plain. Effects jurisdiction is based on the quality of the relationship between the activity and the place, including questions of intention and the degree of involvement with the forum. Aside from the inherent unpredictability of that qualitative analysis, the deeper concern is that effects jurisdiction is a convenient vehicle for the extraterritorial projection of domestic policies.[81] The effects doctrine is clearly a potential threat to information and entertainment businesses seeking consumers across different geographical markets. Their profitability often rests on many thousands of individual transactions, each of which has, by itself, little value. These businesses are, therefore, typically geared towards high volume, cross border transactions and often differentiate their content services for different geographical markets. They therefore will often be at risk of liability for consequential harm or injury under local laws.[82]

In the United States, however, the effects doctrine does not pose an exceptional risk to the domestic media. The rights of US states to make extensive claims to jurisdiction and to demand the enforcement of resulting judgments by other states of the Union are subject to constitutional principles of substantive and procedural justice.[83] There is, in particular, an underlying assurance that the needs of the media are taken into account in every state through the application of the First Amendment. The common law of defamation in the United States, for

---

[78] Jennings, R., and Watts, A., n. 6 above.

[79] *Calder v. Jones*, n. 77 above.

[80] The effects principle was first developed in United States anti-trust law cases, such as *United States v. Aluminum Company of America*, 148 F.2d 416 (2d Cir. 1945). See also Huffman, M., 'A Retrospective on Twenty-Five Years of the Foreign Trade Antitrust Improvements Act', 44 *Houston Law Review* (2007), 285.

[81] As Raustiala has argued, '[w]eaker states tend to rely more heavily on traditional concepts of territorial sovereignty to bolster their claims to autonomy and security, whereas powerful states are more likely to find territoriality a fetter on their policy objectives. These states are in a better position to use the contemporary unbundling of territory, sovereignty and state power to find innovative ways of protecting their national interests.' Raustiala, K., n. 12 above, 221. See also Raustiala, K., *Does the Constitution Follow the Flag? Territoriality and Extraterritoriality in American Law* (Oxford University Press, 2009), ch 4.

[82] See, for example, the Australian case of *Dow Jones & Company, Inc v. Gutnick* [2002] HCA 56.

[83] United States Constitution, Article IV, states that, 'Full Faith and Credit shall be given in each State to the public Acts, Records, and judicial Proceedings of every other State'. Consequently, state public policy exceptions are narrowly construed in relation to judgments issued by the courts of other American states.

example, has been substantially curtailed through judicial efforts to protect freedom of speech.[84]

Free speech concerns have also had a direct impact on the rules of jurisdiction affecting defamation and privacy actions through the 'single publication rule', widely adopted in US state law. This rule dictates that the publication of multiple copies of the same publication should be treated as a single publication occurring in one place, subject to the laws of one state.[85] This rule protects publishers from the possibility of multiple lawsuits in different forums for the same publication and the resulting chilling effect on publication. Although, as a consequence of the effects principle, that single jurisdiction is almost certain to be a state where the publication has a substantial circulation.[86]

The First Amendment also plays an important role in filtering the recognition and enforcement of foreign civil judgments. Unlike the domestic judgments of states of the union, American courts may use a broadly construed public policy defence when considering whether to recognize a foreign judgment. Any found to be inconsistent with the requirements of the First Amendment, among other essential principles of American public policy, are rejected.[87] On the other hand, United States constitutional law cannot, plainly, protect American publishers from enforcement actions in foreign countries where they have revenues or assets.

Across the Atlantic, the harmonization of the law of jurisdiction in Europe has taken a radically different course in both substance and process. This reflects not only the greater rights of sovereignty enjoyed by EU member states, but also the important differences in their domestic laws and public policies. Harmonization of jurisdiction, moreover, has occurred through direct negotiations between the member states and through the legislative proposals of the European Commission. While the European Court of Justice has an important role in implementing these agreements and legislation, it has not used basic principles of EU law to lead the evolution of European law concerning jurisdiction. Human rights principles have certainly influenced the development of the rules of jurisdiction, especially Article 6 of the European Convention on Human Rights, which concerns the fairness of judicial processes. Yet this influence is modest in comparison to developments in American jurisdictional law.

---

[84] See Chapter 10.

[85] See Torts Restatement (Second), § 577A. Single and Multiple Publications. See also *Keeton v. Hustler Magazine, Inc*, 465 U.S. 770 (1984).

[86] *Calder v. Jones*, n. 77 above.

[87] On the refusal to enforce British libel judgments, see Youm, K.H., 'The Interaction between American and Foreign Libel Law: US Courts Refuse to Enforce English Libel Judgments', 49(1) *The International and Comparative Law Quarterly* (January 2000), 131–165. See also United States, Securing the Protection of our Enduring and Established Constitutional Heritage Act of 2010, which amends United States Code, Part VI of Title 28 by adding Chapter 181: Foreign Judgments. This Chapter states, *inter alia*, that 'a domestic court shall not recognize or enforce a foreign judgment for defamation unless the domestic court determines that . . . the defamation law applied in the foreign court's adjudication provided at least as much protection for freedom of speech and press in that case as would be provided by the first amendment to the Constitution of the United States and by the constitution and law of the State in which the domestic court is located'.

By choosing not to ground the harmonization of laws on jurisdiction directly in European constitutional principles, EU law in this field lacks the comprehensive character of equivalent American law. So far, the EU has restricted harmonization to civil and commercial law. In that sphere, the Brussels I Regulation is the principal instrument setting out binding rules regarding jurisdiction as well as the enforcement of judgments.[88] The Regulation, which is the product of years of legal development, including a large body of ECJ decisions, is directed principally at civil litigation concerning parties or matters directly related to the European Union and associated states. Under its default principle, the right to exercise exclusive jurisdiction arises in the member state where the defendant is domiciled.[89] In addition, the Regulation's rules regarding the recognition of judgments only concern those given in a member state.[90] Supplementary rules, however, significantly extend the scope of jurisdiction where the matter in dispute arose out a contract, tort, or other specified matters.[91] This means that the Regulation can easily apply where neither party is domiciled in a member state. Nevertheless, the European Union law jurisdiction regime is inward focused and member states are free to apply other domestic rules of jurisdiction to disputes that are unconnected to the EU, or associated states, according to the rules of the Regulation.[92] These may include grounds to assert jurisdiction prohibited under the Regulation.[93]

In public law matters the member states have retained the right to determine their rules of jurisdiction independently, unless jurisdiction is determined by EU legislation or by other special instrument.[94] In some fields, notably competition law, the European Union also asserts jurisdiction in public law matters in its own right. In this field, the EU has developed a variation of the effects doctrine, following the lead of the United States in the exercise of extraterritorial jurisdiction

---

[88] The Brussels I Regulation (Council Regulation (EC) No. 44/2001 on Jurisdiction and the Recognition and Enforcement of Judgements in Civil and Commercial Matters [2000] OJ L12/1) is an adaptation of the Brussels Convention on Jurisdiction and the Enforcement of Judgements in Civil and Commercial Matters (supplemented by the Lugano Convention on Jurisdiction and Enforcement of Judgments on Civil and Commercial Matters which brought EFTA countries, such as Norway, under the same set of rules). In 2000, the European Union replaced the Brussels and Lugano Conventions with the Brussels I Regulation, which is now the primary European instrument on matters of jurisdiction and recognition of judgments. The Regulation covers all the member states except Denmark, which remains subject to the Brussels Convention. Switzerland, Iceland, and Norway are subject to the Lugano Convention.

[89] Brussels I Regulation, Article 2.

[90] Brussels I Regulation, Article 33.

[91] Brussels I Regulation, Article 5 is the main article in the Brussels I Regulation concerning special jurisdiction. In relation to tort claims, it states, 'A person domiciled in a Member State may, in another Member State, be sued . . . 3. in matters relating to tort, delict or quasi-delict, in the courts for the place where the harmful event occurred or may occur.'

[92] See, for example, the application of the doctrine of *forum non conveniens* by English courts, Brand, R. and Jablonski, S., *Forum Non Conveniens* (Oxford University Press, 2007), ch 2.

[93] For example, Annex I of the Brussels I Regulation, which lists specific national rules that are deemed to be exercises of exorbitant jurisdiction, prohibits the use of the British rule permitting jurisdiction when 'the document instituting the proceedings having been served on the defendant during his temporary presence in the United Kingdom'.

[94] See for example, Article 2 of the Audiovisual Media Services Directive.

in anti-trust cases.[95] The great variety of public and private law grounds on which EU states, collectively or individually, assert jurisdiction has given the outward face of European law on jurisdiction a fragmented and confusing appearance. In comparison, the United States has benefited from a more unified jurisdictional law, which has allowed it greater strategic flexibility in choosing areas in which to exercise extraterritorial jurisdiction.[96] European private international law does, however, have some important advantages as a model for the wider harmonization of jurisdictional law. It rests on common principles that apply collectively to states with distinctively different legal systems, unlike the American model, which developed entirely within a relatively uniform, albeit federal, system.

European private international law, however, lacks the flexibility of related law in the United States, which is more coherently meshed with public policy objectives outside the direct concerns of jurisdiction. Liberal freedom of the press, which is such a prominent strand in American jurisdictional law, is considerably less evident in the Brussels I Regulation and its associated treaties. There is certainly no equivalent to the single publications rule. European rules concerning tort allow a claimant to bring an action in the place where the harmful event occurred, which can be either the place where the act causing the injury occurred or where the injury arose.[97] Accordingly, parties claiming tortious injury to reputation or breach of privacy are entitled to bring an action in the place where the injury occurred rather than the place of initial publication. Where significant injury has resulted in more than one member state, a publisher may face multiple legal actions.

This does not mean that liberal concerns about media freedoms have little influence on European private international law. Given the avowed liberal democratic foundations of Europe's regional institutions, the impact of legal developments on freedom of the press will always be an influential factor. When the European Court of Justice determined that a defamation action may be brought in any member state where injury to reputation occurred, it also decided that compensation may only be awarded for the local injury.[98] A claim for all injury to reputation can therefore only be made in the defendant's place of domicile or establishment.

Media issues have also had a significant influence on recent developments regarding the harmonization of European principles concerning choice of governing law. During the lengthy negotiation of the Rome II Regulation on the law applicable to non-contractual obligations, European legislative institutions could

---

[95] In the view of the General Court the application of the Merger Regulation to a merger between companies located outside EU territory, involving an extraterritorial exercise of EU jurisdiction, 'is justified under public international law when it is foreseeable that a proposed concentration will have an immediate and substantial effect in the Community': T-102/96, *Gencor Ltd v. Commission* [1999] ECR II-0753, at paras 89–92.

[96] Raustiala, K., 'The Evolution of Territoriality: International Relations and American Law', n. 12 above.

[97] Brussels I, Article 5, n. 91 above. See also Case 21/76, *Handelskwekerij Bier v. Mines de Potasse d'Alsace* [1976] ECR 1735.

[98] Case C-68/93, *Shevill v. Presse Alliance SA* [1995] ECR I-415.

not agree on what law should govern obligations relating to privacy and defamation.[99] Media companies were particularly concerned that they would become subject to a uniform rule that the law of the place of alleged injury would apply.[100] They would be at greater risk of defamation and privacy claims being brought under multiple foreign laws. Yet these concerns, couched in terms of economic burden and freedom of the press, could not be reconciled with the protection of claimants from unfamiliar laws unrelated to the place of injury.[101] In the text finally adopted, privacy, defamation, and related rights of personality were therefore excluded from the scope of the Regulation.[102]

While freedom of the press may have a stronger direct influence on American law, the necessary foundations for the harmonization of European private international law are strikingly similar to those of the United States. The common European rules are underpinned by guarantees of fundamental liberal justice secured by judicial and other institutions.[103] Without those assurances, the EU member states could not have accepted limits on their rights of jurisdiction or obligations to enforce judgments issued by other member states. It was only within a bounded, liberal democratic regime that European states could create a shared system of private international law.

Thus, in both Europe and the United States, public policy barriers to the enforcement of judgments issued within each common system can be tightly restricted. Under the European law, courts may still refuse to recognize a judgment from a state subject to the Brussels I Regulation or associated treaties where recognition would be manifestly contrary to domestic public policy.[104] Nonetheless, the ECJ has determined that a state may only invoke this right when recognition of the foreign judgment would manifestly breach a law essential to the legal order of the state concerned.[105] Resort to a public policy is therefore an ultimate defence in a regional system that, in principle, operates according to shared values.

---

[99] Regulation (EC) No. 864/2007 of the European Parliament and of the Council of 11 July 2007 on the law applicable to non-contractual obligations. The Regulation applied from 11 January 2009, to events giving rise to damage occurring after its entry into force.

[100] van Eechoud, M.M.M., 'The Position of Broadcasters and Other Media under the Proposed EC 'Rome II' Regulation on the Law Applicable to Non-Contractual Obligations'. *IRIS Plus*, 2006–10. See European Publishers Council press release, *Europe's publishers and journalists in joint plea to protect press freedom in Rome II Key vote in Legal Affairs Committee*, 15 December 2006.

[101] Similarly, see, for example, media representations to the United Kingdom's Law Commission, regarding its report *Defamation and the Internet, A Preliminary Investigation,* Scoping Study No. 2, December 2002, para. 4.33. As the Commission summary states 'Rather, they wish to remove the likelihood of *any* defamation action, by ensuring that they could only be held liable according to the law they are most familiar with, namely that of their home jurisdiction. This, they argue, would allow them to predict and avoid legal actions.'

[102] Rome II Regulation, Article 2. 'The following shall be excluded from the scope of this Regulation: (g) non-contractual obligations arising out of violations of privacy and rights relating to personality, including defamation.' See also Chapter 10.

[103] Mills, Alex, 'The Dimensions of Public Policy in Private International Law', 4(2) *Journal of Private International Law* (August 2008).

[104] Brussels I Regulation, n. 88 above, Article 34(1) .

[105] Case C-7/98, *Krombach v. Bamberski* [2000] ECR I-1935.

For that reason, the ECJ has also found that a state may refuse recognition if a foreign judgment has been reached in a manner inconsistent with Article 6 of the ECHR, which protects the right to a fair and public hearing within a reasonable time by an independent and impartial tribunal.[106]

In the United States, the safety barrier is more restrictive. It is virtually impossible for the courts of any state to refuse to recognize or enforce civil judgments issued by other states of the Union on public policy grounds.[107] However, no such constitutional restriction applies when an American court considers the recognition of a civil judgment rendered by a court outside the United States legal system.[108] In this respect, courts in the United States and Europe are alike in retaining broad powers to reject judgments issued outside their respective spheres of protected substantive and procedural justice. This position is, arguably, within the principles of customary international law, in which there is no clear obligation to recognize or enforce civil judgments issued by other states. Where a state does recognize foreign judgments, it is consequently free to use an armoury of domestic legal objections to filter out those that are manifestly flawed or incompatible with domestic public policy.

The Hague judgments project

Given the differences between American and European laws concerning jurisdiction and judgments, the obstacles to both US and EU participation in a multilateral agreement in this field are plainly formidable. With hindsight, it seems inevitable that the attempt in the 1990s to negotiate such an agreement would fail. Yet, at that time, there was considerable goodwill and sound logic behind the ultimately unsuccessful Hague Convention on Jurisdiction and Enforcement of Judgements in Civil and Commercial Matters.

The Hague judgments treaty was initiated in the years of optimistic multilateralism that followed the end of the Cold War. At that time, the Uruguay Round was moving towards completion and the United States and other western democracies were keen to solidify the emerging market based, global economy. Aside from the Hague judgments project, negotiations had also begun within the OECD on the Multilateral Agreement on Investment, which failed in 1998.[109] These agreements were intended to strengthen the security of international commercial relations by harmonizing basic principles of domestic law while introducing elements of mutual recognition.

---

[106] See Fawcett, J., 'The Impact of Article 6(1) of the ECHR on Private International Law', 56 *International Comparative Law Quarterly* (2007), 1–48.

[107] *Baker v. General Motors Corp.*, 522 U.S. 222.

[108] See, for example, *Matusevitch v. Telnikoff*, 877 F Supp 1 (DDC, 1995) and *Bachchan v. India Abroad Publications Inc*, 585 NYS 2d 661 (NY County SC, 1992). See also United States, Securing the Protection of our Enduring and Established Constitutional Heritage Act of 2010, n. 87 above.

[109] See Kobrin, S. 'The MAI and the Clash of Globalizations', *Foreign Policy* (Fall 1998), 112.

The Hague Conference on Private International Law was the obvious international organization to host the judgments treaty project. For the past half century, the Hague Conference has been the chief multilateral institution concerned with the progressive unification of the rules of private international law.[110] During that period, the Conference also sponsored many successful multilateral private international law treaties.[111] The judgments project was, nonetheless, surprisingly ambitious for a Hague Conference private international law treaty. Historically, Hague treaties have tended to be limited in scope, addressing specific areas of law where a consensus among the participating states appeared achievable. In 1993, the United States proposed a treaty on the recognition and enforcement of civil and commercial judgments.[112] In 1996, following European proposals, the proposed treaty was further expanded to include jurisdiction.[113] While this expansion logically connected recognition of judgments to the key underlying question of whether the court responsible properly exercised jurisdiction over the parties, it also turned a major project into a vast one.

By the mid 1990s, European influence on the negotiations had also become decisive. The participating European governments, a numerically powerful block within the Hague Conference, used their voting strength to shape the judgments project to conform with EU precedents. Following their proposals, the 1998 draft Hague judgments treaty was closely modelled on the formative European agreements on jurisdiction and recognition of foreign judgments.[114] In the circumstances, this was a reasonable way to proceed. While the United States had initiated the project, it had no experience in multilateral treaties in this field and no alternative model to offer, aside from domestic law. It was nonetheless also a fortuitous opportunity for the EU and its member states to entrench European rules into the fabric of international law.

Yet the 1998 draft treaty was only a temporary success for the European negotiators. The transatlantic divide over basic concepts as well as details remained unbridged.[115] In the area of tort, the draft followed the Brussels model, stating that

---

[110] See Article 1 of the Statute of the Hague Conference on Private International Law. The Hague Conference is a permanent intergovernmental organization and currently has 70 Members, including the European Union.

[111] The texts of the Hague Conference sponsored treaties can be accessed through the organization's website: <http://www.hcch.net>.

[112] Letter of 5 May 1992 from Edwin D. Williamson, Legal Advisor, US Department of State, to Georges Droz, Secretary General, The Hague Conference on Private International Law, distributed with Hague Conference document L.c. ON No. 15 (1992). The Hague Conference approved this work in 1993 at its Seventeenth Session and ordered the creation of a special commission to take the work forward. See also Clermont, K.M., n. 69 above.

[113] Final Act of the Eighteenth Session of the Hague Conference on Private International Law, 19 October 1996, at 21.

[114] See Brussels and Lugano Conventions, n. 88 above.

[115] *Some Reflections on the Present State of Negotiations on the Judgments Project in the Context of the Future Work Programme of the Conference*, n. 69 above. The extent of these transatlantic differences became clear in 1999 when the Preliminary Draft Convention was unveiled. See Hague Conference on Private International Law, Report of the Special Commission on Jurisdiction, Recognition and Enforcement of Foreign Judgments in Civil and Commercial Matters, Preliminary Document,

a claimant may bring a tort action in the place where the act causing the injury occurred or where the injury arose.[116] American negotiators objected that this tort rule was mechanistic and inferior to their own principles of jurisdiction.[117] They argued that US general and specific grounds for exercising jurisdiction could better take into account the array of territorial and non-territorial factors relevant to jurisdiction.[118] In the European view, the Brussels model offered the clarity and certainty needed for a global treaty covering diverse systems of civil justice. The Europeans objected that doing business in a particular place was an ambiguous and insufficient ground for the exercise of personal jurisdiction for any matter, regardless of whether the claim was connected to the forum.[119] American general 'doing business' jurisdiction, referred to in the negotiations as 'activity based jurisdiction', consequently had no place in the Convention. For the United States, however, the right to exercise general jurisdiction was rooted in constitutional law and could not be abandoned or modified to suit the needs of a multilateral treaty.

In 2002, the negotiating states formally accepted that the obstacles to completion of the treaty could not be resolved. The parties did however salvage something from this stalemate, successfully concluding a much smaller treaty on choice of court agreements.[120] The judgments treaty negotiations also gave the states involved an opportunity to work through the problems of multilateral agreement on jurisdiction and the recognition of judgments, identifying points of consensus and disagreement. Any further multilateral work in this area will no doubt draw on these negotiations, although resumption of this work is unlikely in the near future.[121]

No. 11, and Borchers, P.J., 'A Few Little Issues for the Hague Judgments Negotiations' 24 *Brooklyn Journal of International Law* (1998), 157.

[116] A plaintiff may bring an action in tort or delict in the courts of the State—in which the act or omission that caused injury occurred, or in which the injury arose, unless the defendant establishes that the person claimed to be responsible could not reasonably have foreseen that the act or omission could result in an injury of the same nature in that State. Hague Conference on Private International Law, *Towards a worldwide Convention on jurisdiction and foreign judgments in civil and commercial matters*, Edinburgh Informal Meeting of Delegates, April 2001, Proposed Revisions to Article 10, <http://www.cptech.org/ecom/jurisdiction/hague.html#cptdocs>.

[117] Brand, R., 'The 1999 Hague Preliminary Draft Convention Text on Jurisdiction and Judgments: A View from the United States' in Pocar, F., and Honorati, C. (eds), *The Hague Preliminary Draft Convention on Jurisdiction and Judgements 3*, (Cedam, 2005).

[118] Proposed Revisions to Article 10, n. 116 above: 'A plaintiff may bring an action in tort or delict in the courts of the State in which the defendant has engaged in frequent or significant activity, or has [intentionally] directed such activity into that State, provided that the claim arises out of that activity.'

[119] Brand, R., n. 117 above.

[120] Hague Convention on Choice of Court Agreements of 2005. See Brand, R.,'The New Hague Convention on Choice of Court Agreements', *ASIL Insights*, 16 July 2005. See also Clermont, K.M., n. 69 above.

[121] *Some Reflections on the Present State of Negotiations on the Judgements Project in the Context of the Future Work Programme of the Conference*, n. 69 above, See also Brand, R., n. 117 above, 7, and Brand, R.,'Current Problems, Common Ground, and First Principles: Restructuring the Preliminary Draft Convention Text', in Barcelo III, J. and Clermont K. (eds), *A Global Law of Jurisdiction and Judgments: Lessons from the Hague Convention* (Kluwer Law International, 2002), 75–116.

Territory, jurisdiction, and the internet

The commercial promise of the internet underscored the importance of finding global solutions to the conflicts and uncertainties of jurisdiction affecting international trade. Yet, ironically, the rise of the internet deepened divisions between the parties to the Hague judgments negotiations. American negotiators considered the Brussels model ill equipped for a more fluid and unpredictable global communications system.[122] If anything, the online delivery of goods and services demanded closer attention to the connections between the parties and less to the strong territoriality embedded in European rules. If the internet appeared to embody liberal principles of economic, social, and political liberty, European rules appeared designed to obstruct this expanding sphere of commercial and personal freedom.[123]

No country has had more influence on the international development of internet jurisdiction and liability issues than the United States.[124] As both the original home of the internet and a complex federal state, the United States was the first to confront problems of harm arising out of internet based communications crossing jurisdictional boundaries. American courts and legislators developed solutions that were both innovative but also squarely within the contours of American constitutional law and public policy. Inevitably, the First Amendment provided an essential guide for jurisdictional issues closely tied to the information and entertainment media. Within the sphere of First Amendment doctrine, American courts have thus developed two lines of useful precedent to determine the question of personal jurisdiction in cases where the essential activities occurred online. The first of these concerns the degree and quality of interactivity in the internet based connection between the parties.[125] A website hosted on a computer in one state that is passive and lacks any significant interactive relationship with users in other states will rarely provide a connection between provider and user sufficient to sustain a claim of jurisdiction in the user's place of residence. In contrast, a website that is used for the interactive supply of goods or services will usually sustain a claim of specific, if not general, jurisdiction. This approach makes the important assumption that making content available to internet users is not, in itself, a local act in the place where the user is located.[126]

---

[122] Haines, A., *The Impact of the Internet on the Judgements Project: Thoughts for the Future*, Permanent Bureau of the Hague Conference, Preliminary Document 17 (February 2002).

[123] Schultz, T., 'Carving Up the Internet: Jurisdiction, Legal Orders, and the Private/Public International Law Interface', 19(4) *European Journal of International Law* (2008), 799–839.

[124] See Wilske, S., and Schiller, T., 'International Jurisdiction in Cyberspace: Which States May Regulate the Internet?' 50 *Federal Communications Law Journal* (1998), 117–178, Goldsmith, J., 'Against Cyberanarchy', 65 *University of Chicago Law Review* (1998), 1199, Geist, M., 'Is There a There There? Toward Greater Certainty for Internet Jurisdiction', 16 *Berkeley Technology Law Journal* (2001), 1345, and Koh, H.K., 'The Globalisation of Freedom', 26 *Yale Journal of International Law* (2001), 305.

[125] See *Zippo Mfg. Co. v. Zippo Dot Com Inc.*, 952 F. Supp. 1119 (1997). See also Geist, M., n. 124 above.

[126] See, for example, *Cybersell, Inc. v. Cybersell, Inc.*, 130 F.3d 414 (9th Cir. 1997).

The second line of American case law relies on the effects doctrine. In some circumstances, content available on a passive basis through the internet may cause serious, intentional harm to a person located in another state. That content may, for example, be defamatory or may breach personal privacy rights. In these cases, American courts are sometimes willing to exercise extraterritorial jurisdiction on the basis that the defendant intentionally caused harm in the forum state through acts carried out in a different state.[127] The effects doctrine does not, however, open the way to universal liability through the simple act of making content available on the internet. US Courts have looked for intentional targeting of the claimant in the forum and will only exercise jurisdiction where it was foreseeable to the defendant and reasonable in all the circumstances.[128]

This approach to internet jurisdiction is also imbued with a sensitivity to freedom of speech concerns, as developed under the First Amendment. The act of making content available on the internet is therefore protected, unless that content threatens serious harm to private or state interests and has no redeeming public importance.[129] American law on internet jurisdiction and liability thus takes a cautious position on interference with content simply made available on the internet, but can nonetheless be very assertive where online activities breach US law. While American developments in the field of internet jurisdiction are widely known, their close association with US constitutional law has blunted their influence in other legal systems with different legal traditions and public policies.[130] In Europe, clarity and certainty have had a greater role in the development of jurisdictional rules, enabling the integration of national markets operating under different domestic legal orders. The problems of jurisdiction in civil and commercial cases over online activities have, as a result, been resolved through the application of the Brussels I Regulation combined with other internet specific legislation.[131]

In many areas, differences between domestic principles of jurisdiction do not result in significant differences in practical outcomes. When purely commercial transactions are conducted through the internet, American and European rules will frequently yield a similar conclusion on the question of personal jurisdiction over a party to the contract.[132] There is, however, no such rough consensus on jurisdiction or liability where a party has simply made content available on the internet,

---

[127] See *Calder v. Jones*, n. 77 above, and *Keeton v. Hustler Magazine, Inc*, n. 85 above.

[128] The defendant's conduct and connection with the forum must be such that he or she should reasonably anticipate being made subject to the jurisdiction of the courts there: *WorldWide Volkswagen Corp. v. Woodson*, 444 U.S. 286, 297 (1980).

[129] *ACLU v. Reno* 521 U.S. 844 (1997).

[130] Timofeeva, Y., 'Worldwide Prescriptive Jurisdiction in Internet Content Controversies: Comparative Analysis', 20 *Connecticut Journal of International Law* (Fall 2004).

[131] Note that while 'on-demand audiovisual media services' and 'information society services' are normally subject to the regulatory jurisdiction of the member state in which they are established, in accordance with the relevant provisions of the AVMS Directive n. 56 above, and the Electronic Commerce Directive, n. 60 above, these Directives do not supplant the jurisdiction of the courts. See Electronic Commerce Directive, Recital (23) and Article 1(4).

[132] Under United States jurisdiction rules, the commercial provider is likely to satisfy the minimum contacts test (*International Shoe Co. v. Washington*, n. 71 above), whereas under the Brussels I

which then causes harm to users in other locations. For media content providers, lack of agreement on this issue is a serious problem in extending the distribution of their information and entertainment services. They face not only the risk of civil claims in foreign courts, but also the threat of foreign criminal and regulatory sanctions as well.

Two controversial cases, one French and the other Australian, marked the growing resistance to American principles of internet jurisdiction, even amongst fellow liberal democratic states. The first of these concerned the internet company Yahoo!, which a French court found had unlawfully given French residents online access to auction websites under its control that offered nazi artefacts for sale.[133] This case is often described in strikingly different terms because of a subsequent decision of a US federal court that this French judgment could not be enforced in the United States.[134] In that decision, the court invoked American public policy regarding freedom of speech to reject the French decision in strong terms, which remains consistent with United States constitutional law, despite the successful appeal of the decision on technical grounds.[135] Consequently, the *Yahoo!* case demonstrated the willingness of states to exercise jurisdiction where a foreign based provider has made content available to local users and also the continuing importance of safe havens in the patchwork of national media regimes. While Yahoo! obtained a declaration of support in the American courts, it also decided to refuse to host the sale of offending goods in the future, ostensibly as a matter of internal policy and not in compliance with the French judgment.

The second case arose in Australia, where Joseph Gutnick, a businessman resident in the state of Victoria, brought an action for defamation against the American publishing company Dow Jones. In this case, the High Court decided that Australian law permitted the exercise of jurisdiction over the defendant American company because it had made its online content available to local users.[136] In both the *Yahoo!* and *Gutnick* cases, the issues of jurisdiction were mixed with questions of liability, as the defendant companies would not have been

Regulation, n. 88 above, the commercial provider will be similarly subject to the jurisdiction of the place of performance of the obligation.

[133] *Yahoo! v. La Ligue Contre Le Racisme et L'Antisemitisme,* See also Reimann, M., 'Introduction: The Yahoo! Case and Conflict Of Laws in the Cyberage', 24 *Michigan Journal of International Law* (2003), 663; Watt, H.M.,'Yahoo! Cyber-collision of cultures: who regulates?', 24 *Michigan Journal of International Law* (2003), 673. While symbolically important, the French *Yahoo!* decision stated a principle already widely accepted in Europe. In 1997, the European Commission had, for example, stated that 'according to the principle of territorial jurisdiction, the law applies on the national territory of the state and hence also applies to on-line services'. European Commission, *Protection of Minors and Human Dignity in Audiovisual and Information Services, Consultations on the Green Paper,* Commission Working Document SEC (97) 1203.

[134] *Yahoo!, Inc v. La Ligue Contre Le Racisme et l'Antisemitisme, et al.,* 169 F Supp 2d 1181.

[135] *Yahoo!, Inc v. La Ligue Contre Le Racisme et l'Antisemitisme, et al.,* 433 F.3d 1199.

[136] *Dow Jones & Company, Inc v. Gutnick,* n. 82 above, The Barron's Magazine website, owned by Dow Jones, was available to users in Australia and a number had subscribed to the service containing the defamatory statement. See also Kohl, U., 'Defamation on the Internet—Nice Decision, Shame about the Reasoning, Dow Jones & Co v Gutnick', 52 *International and Comparative Law Quarterly* (2003), 1049–1058, and Garnett, R., 'Dow Jones & Company Inc v Gutnick: An Adequate Response to Transnational Internet Defamation?' 4 *Melbourne Journal of International Law* (2003), 196.

liable under relevant US law. Accordingly, the defendants sought to avoid the exercise of local jurisdiction or, alternatively, to have American legal principles regarding internet content recognized, directly or indirectly, by the local courts.[137] However, these hopes of universalizing American jurisdictional principles, at least amongst liberal democracies, faced an insurmountable objection. The adoption of American principles would effectively disable a sovereign foreign state from protecting state and public interests concerning internet content that diverged from American public policy.[138] This problem would be particularly acute in areas such as defamation and privacy law, where First Amendment free speech protections are stronger than in many other liberal democracies.

Consequently, many states looked to the basic principles of territoriality and nationality to re-assert their authority over the national public information environment in the face of the internet revolution. Foreign based content providers will, as a result, find themselves subject to local prescriptive jurisdiction on the grounds that their content is locally prohibited and accessible. The extraordinary commercial opportunities of universal availability are thus also clouded by the spectre of universal liability.[139] Yet the pleas of online content providers for privileges against local jurisdiction and liability have met a sceptical response in many states. As the English Court of Appeal has stated, 'A global publisher should not be too fastidious as to the part of the globe where he is made a libel defendant . . . in an Internet case the court's discretion will tend to be more open-textured than otherwise; for that is the means by which the court may give effect to the publisher's choice of a global medium.'[140] Certainly, for the major commercial services coming to dominate the internet, sensitivity to local content rules was rapidly becoming a standard cost of business.[141]

Even in the United States, state and federal governments were not slow to use this vulnerability to wage a concerted campaign against foreign internet based gambling companies that attempt to attract American online users.[142] The laws of Louisiana, for example, prohibit any online commercial gambling operator,

---

[137] *Dow Jones & Company, Inc v. Gutnick*, n. 82 above.
[138] Reidenberg, J., 'Technology and Internet Jurisdiction', 153 *University of Pennsylvania Law Review* (2005), 1951. See also United Kingdom, Law Commission, *Defamation and the Internet A Preliminary Investigation,* Scoping Study No. 2, December 2002, 'A place where the content is hosted rule would put claimants in an unreasonable position, forcing them in every instance to bring an action at a place chosen by the content provider.'
[139] 'Jurisdiction and applicable law mechanisms should not plague business with the risks of unexpectedly being subjected to laws and judgments in other countries': International Chamber of Commerce, 'Business Recommendations to Governments, No. 5', *Policy Statement: The Impact of Internet Content Regulation,* Doc no. 373–37/1 (18 November 2002).
[140] *Lewis v. King* [2004] EWCA Civ 1329. In this case, the Court of Appeal, adopting the approach taken by the Australian High Court in *Dow Jones & Company, Inc v. Gutnick,* n. 82 above, stated that 'it makes little sense to distinguish between one jurisdiction and another in order to decide which the defendant has "targeted", when in truth he has "targeted" every jurisdiction where his text may be downloaded'. See also Borchers, P.J., 'Internet Libel: The Consequences of a Non-rule Approach to Personal Jurisdiction', 98(2) *Northwestern Law Review* (2004), 473–492.
[141] Swire, P., 'Elephants and Mice Revisited: Law and Choice of Law on the Internet', 153 *University of Pennsylvania Law Review* (2005), 1978–1979.
[142] Morse, E., 'The Internet Gambling Conundrum: Extraterritorial Impacts of Domestic Regulation', in Kierkegaard, S. (ed.), *Cyberlaw, Security and Privacy* (IAITL, 2007), 443–460.

regardless of physical location, from accepting a wager from a person located in Louisiana.[143] The claim to jurisdiction is grounded in the gambling transactions between the foreign gambling service providers and the users resident in Louisiana, including the flow of payments from those users. The difficulty for Louisiana and other state authorities was in enforcing their prescriptive jurisdiction against individuals located outside the state.[144] In view of that limitation, the United States government buttressed its own federal laws concerning online gambling by enacting the Unlawful Internet Gambling Enforcement Act of 2006.[145] This Act made it unlawful for gambling providers or financial intermediaries to process payments for illicit gambling transactions. Financial institutions that do business in the United States can thus be compelled to shut down revenue streams to offshore gambling operators.

As states have fastened on local intermediaries and revenue flows, they have improved the effectiveness of their claims of jurisdiction over foreign based content providers. Yet the consequences of liability in multiple jurisdictions have also become somewhat more predictable through the gradual harmonization of content related laws in fields such as intellectual property, data protection, computer crime, and child pornography.[146] This convergence of domestic laws concerning information and entertainment content has occurred, especially amongst liberal democracies, through a variety of formal and informal means. The American inspired 'public figure' doctrine, for example, has had a profound influence on laws concerning reputation and privacy in other liberal democracies.[147] Yet the international harmonization of laws concerning internet based content should not however be overplayed. The sensitivity of media issues and the difficulties of coordinating criminal and other public laws with foreign states are huge barriers to multilateral agreement. The European model of broad harmonization between states of domestic laws concerning media content is unique.

The risk of civil claims or prosecution in multiple jurisdictions under diverse foreign laws remains a serious problem for major content providers. Their choice is increasingly to withhold content that is unlawful in any significant foreign market or to use technical means to block access by users located in those places.[148] Yet

---

[143] Louisiana Revised Statutes, Annotated, s.14:90.3.

[144] Ward, A. and Pimlott, D., 'Ex-Sportingbet boss free to return to UK in New York', *Financial Times*, 29 September 2006.

[145] Title VIII of the Safe Port Act the Unlawful Internet Gambling Enforcement Act of 2006 (UIGE Act).

[146] See for example, Goldstein, P., *International Copyright: Principles, Law and Practice*, (Oxford University Press, 2001), 63–64, and Dinwoodie, G.B., 'The International Intellectual Property Law System: New Actors, New Institutions, New Sources'. *Marquette Intellectual Property Law Review* (2006), 210. See also Council of Europe, Convention on Cybercrime (ETS No. 185), which is open to several major non-European states and contains provisions obliging state parties to establish the legal and administrative basis for data preservation orders, production orders, search and seizure orders, as well as important obligations concerning jurisdiction, extradition, and mutual assistance in investigations and prosecutions by state parties.

[147] See Chapter 10.

[148] See, for example, Day, J., 'UK readers blocked from NY Times terror article', *The Guardian* (29 August 2006); Mathieson, S., 'Why the NYT web block doesn't work', *The Guardian* (30 August 2006).

while the technologies and problems of the global internet may be radically new, the underlying relationship between the state and major content producers and distributors is not. The state has always aimed its primary efforts to control its national information and entertainment environment at the largest or most influential organs of the mass media.[149] For editors, the choice of what to publish and where to distribute has therefore always depended in part on the legal consequences; especially when the media organization concerned is an elephant that cannot hide from the eye of the state.

In contrast, personal communications, from dinner table conversations to telephone calls and letters, have historically constituted a communications sphere that the state has had great difficulty in monitoring or controlling.[150] This is the sphere from which Peter Swire's elusive internet mice have evolved. In the broadband internet era, personal communications have become public as new services have given individuals ways of making their personal views and videos available to the world. Although even in this new era, they depend on major service providers, such as Myspace, Facebook, and YouTube, who are increasingly expected to take responsibility for the third party content they carry.

The rise of individual participation in the media through interactive, online services has deepened the tension between the territorial state and the global internet. There is, firstly, greater access to foreign information and entertainment content that is subject to foreign content standards or none at all. This has plainly weakened the capacity of the state to maintain the boundaries of the national public information environment, although governments continue to evolve methods to restrict access to illicit, foreign based content. Conversely, the application of national rules to internet based content has drawn the state well beyond its territorial boundaries. The uncertainty of where internet based activities are essentially located has encouraged the outward creep of jurisdictional claims.[151] Territoriality, which historically constrained the exercise of jurisdiction and maintained boundaries between states, has become instead a device that permits the state to claim internal sovereignty over any internet based activity.[152]

American principles of jurisdiction, which have left strict territoriality behind, may be better suited to the global reach of the internet. By focusing on the relationship between the parties rather than the simple fact that content can be accessed in the territory, in principle, reduces the risks of universal liability for media companies that make their content available online. This approach, not surprisingly, has found favour with the International Chamber of Commerce, which has stated that, the '[l]aws and regulations of a particular country should

---

[149] Brady, A.M., *Marketing Dictatorship: Propaganda and Thought Work in Contemporary China* (Rowman & Littlefield, 2008), ch 2: Guiding Hand: The Role of the Propaganda System.

[150] Plainly, the twentieth century produced highly effective systems of pervasive loyalty, surveillance, and terror in which ordinary personal communication is self censored even when unmonitored. Yet conformity on this scale is evidently difficult to sustain.

[151] Timofeeva, Y., n. 130 above.

[152] Kobrin, S., 'The Trans-Atlantic Data Privacy Dispute, Territorial Jurisdiction and Global Governance', 30 *Review of International Studies* (2004), 111–131.

apply where content is specifically directed to the country in question. For example, does the site solicit, either directly or by its degree of interactive content, an exchange of information with the users in a particular jurisdiction.'[153] The risks are, moreover, not only commercial, as publishers in liberal democracies may well choose to censor their online content to avoid liability under the more restrictive, foreign laws.

Consequently, while US rules of jurisdiction have sometimes met with a cool response, the argument that strict territoriality is incompatible with the global internet has an obvious logic.[154] In this respect, the internet has become a focus for wider arguments over the future of territorial sovereignty.[155] The problems of jurisdiction over internet based content demonstrate, with acute clarity, the limitations of the Westphalian model of the territorially defined state in an era of globalization and multilayered interdependence. Within the WTO, for example, there has been considerable uncertainty how trade rules based on assumptions of territoriality should be applied to global electronic commerce.[156] Yet, it is the same state that remains the pre-eminent institution in matters of public order and security, whether in the domestic or international sphere. Moreover, where its laws and coercive powers are reasonably effective, commerce has readily segmented global communications to replicate territorial boundaries.

---

[153] International Chamber of Commerce, *Policy Statement: The Impact of Internet Content Regulation*, Doc no. 373–37/1 (18 November 2002).

[154] For example, Berman, P.S., 'The Globalization of Jurisdiction', 151(2) *University of Pennsylvania Law Review* (December 2002), 311–426.

[155] On the problem of sovereignty in relation to internet based activities, see Bartelson, J., 'The Concept of Sovereignty Revisited', 17(2) *The European Journal of International Law* (2006), 463–474. See also Engel, C., 'The role of law in the governance of the internet', 20(1–2) *International Review of Law, Computers & Technology* (July 2006), 201–216.

[156] Wunsch-Vincent, S., The WTO, The Internet and Trade in Digital Products: EC-US Perspectives (Hart Publishing, 2006), 67–70.

PART III

RESTRICTING THE LIBERTY TO PUBLISH

8

Criticism of the State and Incitement to Violence

Public knowledge and discussion of the state and political elites has always posed a threat to ruling authority. Public criticism, whether accurate or not, can quickly undermine the state's claims to authority and legitimacy, spreading public disaffection and increasing resistance to its laws and other demands on citizens. Public knowledge of the inner workings of the state can also undercut its effectiveness and even destroy the secrecy needed to safeguard state security and public safety.[1] Yet scrutiny and criticism of the state also have their obvious uses in limiting the risks of excessive secrecy and isolation in state administration and exposing maladministration and miscarriages of justice.

The dilemma for the state has always been to determine how much scrutiny and comment is necessary for these purposes and who should be entrusted with that task. The preference for internal rather than external scrutiny and criticism is near universal. This is obviously the case in China, for example, where the Communist Party government relies on internal reporting and inspection methods and limits public debate, but it also occurs often enough in democratic governments, which make their own arguments for state secrecy and internal review.[2] These questions about the proper limits of public comment about the state and knowledge of its internal workings have been a defining issue in the emergence of the modern state and its relationship with subjects and citizens. Throughout much of Europe, monarchical states sought to suppress early newsletters, pamphlets, and other publications through internal surveillance and criminal sanctions.[3] That drive to control and limit the liberty to publish became, and remains, the central dynamic of

---

[1] See Holmes, S., 'Liberal Constraints on Private Power: Reflections on the Origins and Rationale of Access Regulation', in Lichtenberg, J. (ed.), *Democracy and the Mass Media* (Cambridge University Press, 1990), 21 and 33.

[2] On internal Communist Party methods of accountability, see Heilmann, S., 'Regulatory Innovation by Leninist Means: Communist Party Supervision in China's Financial Industry', 181 *The China Quarterly* (2005), 1–21, and Sapio, F. 'Shuanggui and Extralegal Detention in China', 22(1) *China Information* (2008), 7–37. On the problem of ensuring accountability for intelligence services in liberal democracies, see Born, H., and Leigh, I., 'Democratic Accountability of Intelligence Services', *SIPRI Yearbook 2007: Armaments, Disarmament and International Security*, ch 5.

[3] See, for example, Darnton, R., *The Devil in the Holy Water, or, The Art of Slander from Louis XIV to Napoleon* (Pennsylvania, 2009).

the media state relationship, which has broadened and deepened through centuries of technological and commercial change.

In the current communications revolution, powerful changes are occurring in the public scrutiny and criticism of the state. Digitization and new communications platforms, most notably the internet, have given individuals the ability to make ideas and information directly and widely available.[4] For the state, new technologies have exponentially increased its capacity to process and store information, which often goes unchallenged in an era also marked by public anxiety about safety and security.[5] These changes have left the state's power over the media weaker and stronger in different respects. It has become less effective in suppressing unwanted criticism or unauthorized disclosures of information. Yet state institutions have also been able to use the turmoil of a rapidly changing media sector to their advantage, not only managing the release of information into the media more effectively, but also becoming public information providers themselves.

From a liberal democratic perspective, these changes in the media state relationship do not require any change in fundamental principles. The right of the press to subject the state to constant scrutiny and comment is a cornerstone of liberal democracy. Media criticism of the state serves not only the functional goal of exposing maladministration and injustice, but also the broader one of maintaining the democratic character of the state and public life. Quite apart from this democratic argument, the freedom to speak openly about the state is essential to liberalism's emancipation of the individual. At its worst, the state is liberalism's nightmare, a wielder of immense power used arbitrarily and oppressively for illegitimate purposes that suppress and confine individual liberty. Yet, even the benign, enabling state is a frequent target for liberal suspicions that its powers will be carelessly used to restrict liberty, despite well meant public policy goals.[6] It is only through constant watch and criticism that this is kept at bay.

It is consequently a universal principle of liberal democracy that freedom of expression must encompass a broad right to subject the state to robust public scrutiny and criticism. This must moreover include disloyal as much as loyal criticism, which even when rejected may force governments to explain their policies and actions. For these reasons, the existence of a diverse, pluralist media sector capable of sustaining investigative reporting and informed commentary on public affairs has become a key measure of successful liberal democracy. In the sphere of public debate on matters of common concern, the liberal democratic state comes closest to the liberal ideal of the unrestricted market place of ideas. It is therefore a sphere of expression in which the arrival of the internet has caused few conceptual problems, though many practical ones. Simply put, it makes little difference in principle if the speaker is a national news broadcaster or a pensioner sitting at home

---

[4] See, for example, Lynch, L., '"We're Going to Crack the World Open": Wikileaks and the future of investigative reporting' *Journalism Practice* (August 2010).

[5] Birnhack, M., and Elkin-Koren, N., 'The Invisible Handshake; the Re-emergence of the State in the Digital Environment', 8 *Virginia Journal of Law & Technology* (2003).

[6] See Wilson, B., *What Price Liberty?* (Faber and Faber, 2009), ch 8.

writing her blog or tweeting if most public comment about the state is protected by the right to free speech.

This is not however an unbounded market place of ideas. While the liberty of the individual is traditionally understood as freedom from the state, liberty no less than democracy needs the protection of an effective state.[7] Scrutiny and criticism must therefore be restrained when they put the security and effectiveness of the state at serious risk of harm. The need to determine the proper limits for public scrutiny and criticism has not only shaped the development of the media since the beginnings of the liberal state, but also its constitutional principles. Ultimately, the state sets limits for public criticism and comment, determining the boundary between reasonable and unreasonable risks of harm. Yet here, in the interplay of constitutional principles, the concept of 'public interest' does not play the decisive boundary setting role that it does in other areas, such as the protection of privacy and reputation. The security and effectiveness of the state is itself a matter of public interest, which needs to be set against the democratic interest in scrutiny and criticism of public affairs. At a certain point, liberal constitutional presumptions against the state's exercise of coercive power inevitably run into the dependence of both liberalism and democracy on the protection of the territorial state.

Vigorous scrutiny and comment on the state cannot be achieved by simply expanding the liberty to speak and publish. It also requires good access to information about the state. Yet, despite the close connection between comment and knowledge, they have tended to yield two distinct areas of media law and policy. The right to criticize institutions and agents of the state is a classic negative freedom that the liberal democratic state may not restrict without convincing justifications.[8] In contrast, more recently developed legal rights of access to government held information are positive obligations on the state to provide reasonable access for public applicants. This second field, often called 'freedom of information' is the subject of Chapter 9.

The liberty to comment on the institutions of the state is also structured according to its particular vulnerabilities. The state's security functions are routinely shielded from external view and held to more limited accountability through closed internal methods. Even important public functions of the state, in particular trials and other judicial proceedings, are also protected from public comment in many liberal democracies where fairness to the parties is deemed to be at risk.[9] These areas of greater sensitivity, moreover, lie behind a more general line that the state draws between robust, legitimate criticism and incitement to violence. Determining when that threshold has been crossed is a famously difficult question for the liberal democratic state. The risk to the state and the public must be considered against

---

[7] Heyman, S., *Free Speech and Human Dignity* (New Haven: Yale University Press, 2008), 114.

[8] This field is itself divided between laws that concern exposure and criticism of state institutions, including threats to state security and public safety, and laws that concern exposure and criticism of politicians, public officials and other individuals who wield influence over public affairs. The latter field is the subject of Chapter 10.

[9] Cram, I., *A Virtue Less Cloistered: Courts, Speech and Constitutions* (Hart Publishing, 2002).

the chilling effects of any restraints or sanctions on public debate of issues that are often of great democratic importance.

In the United States, the Supreme Court has created a test that demands that the state demonstrate that the expression at issue creates a serious and imminent risk of unlawful conduct.[10] These principles, summarized in the Court's judgment in *Brandenberg v. Ohio*, reflect not only a jurisprudential commitment to the market place of ideas, but also a deep confidence in the resilience of American political institutions.[11] Yet even this test is flexible enough for the Court to allow restrictions on expression that present only an indirect threat of terrorism to the United States or friendly foreign states.[12] Indeed, in the past decade, liberal democracies have generally shifted the balance against comment that appears to celebrate or support organized violent acts.[13] Outside the United States, the *Brandenberg v. Ohio* doctrine has had a strong influence on policy debates, but much less so on constitutional principles.[14] While this rejection may well reflect the illiberal tendencies of the state, it no doubt also stems from genuine concerns about the threats to national stability where the institutions of the state are weak or tensions between ethnic or religious groups are volatile and easily exploited. Where the territorial unity of the state is threatened by a major secessionist campaign, the contradiction between democracy and security becomes especially problematic. Liberal principles suggest that a democracy must bear secessionist agitation to the point of non-violent dissolution. Yet, secession is typically the political aim of a minority whose separatist cause often features some organized violence against the resisting majority. In these circumstances, there is often no sensible distinction between expression that is merely hostile to the state and expression that can be interpreted as an incitement to violence.

In these circumstances, journalists may well refuse to take up the responsibility and risk being a public watchdog on the state. The publication of a critical evaluation of an apparent incitement to violence may well involve security sensitive information that the state does not wish divulged.[15] Governments may also

---

[10] *Brandenburg v. Ohio*, 395 U.S. 444 (1969).

[11] Waldron, J., 'Free Speech & the Menace of Hysteria', 55(9) *The New York Review of Books* (29 May 2008).

[12] See, for example, *Holder, Attorney General v. Humanitarian Law Project*, USSC, where the Court found that a federal law that prohibited non-violent assistance, including training in international law and dispute resolution, to designated terrorist organizations did not violate the First Amendment. The Court distinguished this assistance from independent advocacy of a cause.

[13] Donohue, L., 'Terrorist Speech and the Future Of Free Expression', 27(1) *Cardozo Law Review* (2005), 233. See also United Kingdom, Terrorism Act 2006, s. 1(2): 'A person commits an offence if—(a) he publishes a statement to which this section applies or causes another to publish such a statement; and (b) at the time he publishes it or causes it to be published, he—(i) intends members of the public to be directly or indirectly encouraged or otherwise induced by the statement to commit, prepare or instigate acts of terrorism or Convention offences; or (ii) is reckless as to whether members of the public will be directly or indirectly encouraged or otherwise induced by the statement to commit, prepare or instigate such acts or offences.'

[14] See below on the principles of European human rights law regarding permissible restraints on expression that potentially incites violence.

[15] Mendel, T., 'National Security vs. Openness: An Overview and Status Report on the Johannesburg Principles', in *National Security and Open Government: Striking the Right Balance*. Campbell Public Affairs Institute, The Maxwell School of Syracuse University (2003), 7.

prohibit the media from reporting ideas or other expression associated with groups or individuals who seek to overthrow or break up the state.[16] This however puts the media in great difficulty where it attempts to report on what is plainly a matter of acute public importance. An attempt at fully impartial reporting could well constitute unlawful support for terrorism. At the same time, groups opposed to the state often view the mainstream media as an arm of the police or intelligence services and therefore make journalists the targets of violent attacks or hostage taking.

Criticism and incitement in the European Union

Determining the principles for legitimate criticism of the state in Europe exposes some of the deepest fault lines in European public order. Legal obligations on member states to advance economic and political liberty have expanded the flow of information across borders and increased the transparency of state administration. While these obligations can be found in a diverse array of secondary legislative and other measures, they are firmly rooted in the primary European obligations concerning the free movement of goods and services and freedom of expression. Yet, as much as Europe's regional regime is avowedly liberal democratic, it is also founded on a legal and political structure established by sovereign, territorial states. The effectiveness of European media law therefore depends on the effective exercise of state power to enforce economic, social, and political rights and duties, which requires commitment and cooperation by the participating states. Conversely, European rules must allow member states sufficient leeway to safeguard national security and domestic public order, which is well recognized in the basic principles of the European Union.[17] In short, the rules concerning criticism of the state, including incitement to violence, have developed in a regional regime that accords considerable weight to the needs of the state. The result is a very state oriented perception of the media state relationship, in which thresholds for measures protecting core interests of the state from speech and publications can be quite low.

This is most apparent in the reluctance of European institutions to challenge state restrictions on the liberty to publish or demand public access to information when national security or public safety is potentially at issue. The origins of this sensitivity are not difficult to fathom. Despite their rejection of historic conflicts and commitment to a common future, the European Union and Council of Europe were both creations of the early Cold War era. The western European founding states were military allies in the confrontation with the Soviet Union, sharing intelligence links and secrecy obligations. Subsequent national crises have also played an important part in defining the sphere of state autonomy in European

---

[16] See Donohue, L., n. 13 above.

[17] Treaty on the Functioning of the European Union, Article 67(1). The Union shall constitute an area of freedom, security, and justice with respect for fundamental rights and the different legal systems and traditions of the Member States.

law. During the 'Troubles' in Northern Ireland, the British and Irish governments resorted to extensive restrictions on the media that the European Court of Human Rights accepted as legitimate and necessary.[18] In Turkey, wide ranging efforts to suppress secessionist expression have contributed an extraordinary number of decisions in the same Court on the proper limits to criticism of the state and its representatives.[19]

Since the end of the Cold War, fresh crises have kept the problems of state security and public order high on the agendas of the European Union and Council of Europe. The breakup of the former socialist bloc, not least the violent dissolution of Yugoslavia, brought a flood of politically and institutionally weak states into the European regional system. Even as those concerns of indigenous violence and instability quieted, the influence of islamist terrorism filtered across Europe. This new challenge to state authority is notable not only for its wholesale rejection of European liberal democracy, but also for the innovative use of internet based communication to proselytize and organize. In response, European media law has acquired new prohibitions on expression that glorifies or apologizes for terrorist acts. This turn to prescriptive European rules limiting expression puts heavy demands on European public order, which must also restrain abuses of state power, especially in member states where domestic controls on the state are inadequate.

In practice, national measures restricting criticism of the state or incitement to violence are not significant barriers to the free movement of media goods and services in the European Union. The obvious reason for this is that liberal democracy is a prerequisite for EU membership. For many applicant states, both in the west and the east, accession has involved a process of democracy strengthening in domestic politics, law, and public administration. In this process, few elements have greater importance than the principle that all aspects of the state are open to intrusive and robust public scrutiny and criticism, provided this does not cause a serious threat to the public interest in security and order. The EU has however taken decades to acquire the competences and doctrinal resources to articulate a fully liberal democratic balancing of freedom and security. Certainly, the original principles of free movement provided a clear, market based demand for openness and restraint by the state in its treatment of the media. This economic perspective, however, gave EU institutions a limited basis on which to assess

---

[18] See *Brind v. United Kingdom* (Application No. 18714/91), (9 May 1994), (ECmHR), and *Purcell v. Ireland* (Application No. 15404/89), (16 April 1991) (ECmHR). These application concerned legal restrictions on media interviews with members of a lawful political party, Sinn Fein, which was deemed to be the political wing of IRA, a proscribed organization. The Commission concluded that the restrictions, which were designed to deny representatives of identified terrorist organizations and their supporters the ability to use the broadcast media as a platform to gain popular support and legitimacy, were proportionate and the applications were manifestly inadmissible.

[19] Application to the European Court of Human Rights against Turkey form for example, the majority of the cases cited in Council of Europe, Committee of Experts on Terrorism, Freedom of Expression and 'Apologie du Terrorisme', CODEXTER (2008) 30. See also Davis, H., 'Lessons from Turkey: Anti-Terrorism Legislation and the Protection of Free Speech', 1 *European Human Rights Law Review* (2005), 80.

legitimate non-market policy reasons to restrict media publications. In contrast, Article 10 of the European Convention on Human Rights offered a much broader framework in which to elaborate tests for restrictions on freedom of expression. It was therefore only with the gradual infusion of human rights law that the European Union developed its capacity to address the substance of national assertions of state security and public safety.

Nonetheless, in terms of the EU Single Market, the basic legal structure has not changed since it was created in the Treaty of Rome and then fundamentally shaped by the European Court of Justice. A domestic measure restricting public criticism of the state or incitement to violence will, in principle, constitute a breach of free movement obligations to the extent it affects trade in media goods and services, unless saved by an express or implied exception. In most cases, restrictions of this kind on the liberty to publish are non-discriminatory, applying equally to domestic and foreign based media. Member states can therefore safely assume that, where these measures substantially hinder market access, they will fall under the mandatory public policy exceptions of EU economic law, which are less rigorously reviewed than discriminatory measures, although also subject to the requirements of proportionality.[20]

It is here, where non-market public policy exceptions meet the rules of free movement, that the EU's economic principles must be integrated with European human rights obligations as well as the member states' assertions of autonomy in essential domestic affairs. Undoubtedly, the link with European human rights law strengthens the case for placing as few restrictions as possible on any discussion of the state. Liberal economic freedom and political freedom are close companions in opposition to the power of the state. The transparency of public administration is essential to the goal of free movement in the single market, just as informed comment on the activities of the state is essential to European democracy. Consequently, the potential effects of the right to freedom of expression, as a European fundamental right, must be taken into account when considering the free movement obligations of the member states.[21] The European Union is however also founded on the security and effectiveness of its member states and those needs are well represented in the legitimate grounds for exceptions to the rules of free movement. Any confrontation between the economic and political arguments for greater liberty to publish and the security and public order responsibilities of the state must therefore be worked out through the methods of proportionality analysis. As a general principle, however, properly tailored restrictions on criticism of the state, such as restraints on prejudicial commentary on judicial proceedings or public incitements to violence, are plainly legitimate national measures under EU law.

Despite the adoption of two major directives governing various aspects of trade in media services, the use of proportionality analysis at the nexus between the

---

[20] On public policy exceptions in European Union law, see Chapter 4.
[21] Case C-260/89, *Elliniki Radiophonia Tiléorassi AE v. Dimotiki Etairia Pliroforissis and others* [1991] ECR I-2925, para. 43. See also Chapter 4.

primary rules of free movement and mandatory public policy exceptions remains the chief device for resolving the validity of restrictions on public criticism of the state or incitement to violence under EU law.[22] The Audiovisual Media Services Directive only applies directly to domestic content measures that fall within the fields it coordinates.[23] These include the protection of children from harmful or offensive content and the protection of the public more generally from incitement to hatred, but do not include the protection of the state from criticism or even the public from incitement to violence unconnected with incitement to hatred. As a result, the general rules of free movement and their exceptions continue to govern national restrictions on these forms of public comment or incitement in audiovisual media services, although any national measures that take the form of secondary controls on the free movement of audiovisual services would violate the Directive.[24] It is only where these are mixed with content that comes within one of the Directive's coordinated fields that its rules apply. This is most likely to occur where an incitement to violence is also an incitement to hatred based on 'race, sex, religion or nationality', which are specifically prohibited from inclusion in audiovisual programmes under the AVMS Directive.[25] If a member state concludes that a television or on-demand audiovisual service under the jurisdiction of another member state is in serious breach of this obligation, it may conditionally derogate from the Directive's free movement obligation under the very narrow grounds permitted for television services and the much wider grounds permitted for on-demand audiovisual services.[26]

The much simpler Electronic Commerce Directive combines the basic free movement of services obligation with the country of origin principle for information society services. A member state may however impose proportionate restrictions on these services for reasons of public policy that include the prevention, investigation, detection, and prosecution of criminal offences, and public security, including the safeguarding of national security and defence.[27] This is, in effect, a legislative restatement of the exceptions already permitted under EU law described above. In addition, the Directive's rules on the conditional liability of service providers and operators are important in protecting these parties from liability for unlawful criticism or incitement of third parties.[28] Under these rules, a provider or operator that hosts third party content will not be shielded from liability where it is

---

[22] Directive 2010/13/EU of the European Parliament and of the Council of 10 March 2010 on the coordination of certain provisions laid down by law, regulation or administrative action in Member States concerning the provision of audiovisual media services (AVMS Directive), and Directive 2000/31/EC of the European Parliament and of the Council of 8 June 2000 on certain legal aspects of information society services, in particular electronic commerce, in the Internal Market (Electronic Commerce Directive). On these Directives generally, see Chapter 4.
[23] Directive 2010/13/EU, n. 22 above, Article 3.
[24] Case C-34/95, *Konsumentombudsmannen (KO) v. De Agostini (Svenska) Förlag AB* (9 July 1997), para. 33.
[25] Directive 2010/13/EU, n. 22 above, Article 6.
[26] Ibid., Article 3, and Directive 2000/31/EC, n. 22 above, Article 3.
[27] Directive 2000/31/EC, n. 22 above.
[28] Ibid., Articles 12–15. See also Chapter 4.

both reasonable for it to know that offensive or harmful material has been posted on its service and technically feasible for it to control access to that material. On this basis, a newspaper website that permits online readers to post comments may be held liable for comments posted by a reader that prejudice current criminal proceedings in breach of local law if it fails to act expeditiously to remove the post once it has reasonable notice of its content. The Directive does not however attempt to dictate what kind of liability should be imposed in any circumstance. That is left to the determination of the member states, subject to other European obligations, including those of the European Convention on Human Rights.

Given the liberal democratic foundations of the European Union, there is only a marginal legitimacy in EU law for national measures that restrict criticism or comment on state institutions. There are certainly no prescriptive obligations in EU secondary legislation that oblige member states to institute measures restricting public criticism of the state, including its judicial processes. This is not the case however for incitement to violence. The development of the EU's Third Pillar powers, now absorbed into its general powers following the Lisbon Treaty, created the legal basis for a coordinated extension of state power, which, for the media, has been most evident in the field of counter-terrorism. Here, the legislative centrepiece is the 2002 Framework Decision on Combating Terrorism, which built on earlier Third Pillar counter-terrorism measures.[29] This Framework Decision requires that member states recognize and punish specified terrorist acts, including numerous secondary activities that might otherwise escape prosecution.[30] These included incitement to commit a terrorist offence.[31]

In 2008, the scope of the Framework Decision was extended, after a long, contentious debate in the European Parliament and elsewhere over its implications for personal liberty.[32] These new obligations addressed, in part, the use of internet based communication to motivate groups or individuals to participate in terrorist acts and to provide them with information on how to carry out attacks.[33] Under

---

[29] Framework Decision on Combating Terrorism 2002/475/JHA. Earlier measures include, Council Joint Action 96/610/JHA of 15 October 1996 concerning the creation and maintenance of a Directory of specialised counter-terrorist competences, skills and expertise to facilitate counter-terrorism cooperation between the Member States of the European Union, Council Joint Action 98/428/JHA of 29 June 1998 on the creation of a European Judicial Network, with responsibilities in terrorist offences, in particular Article 2, Council Joint Action 98/733/JHA of 21 December 1998 on making it a criminal offence to participate in a criminal organisation in the Member States of the European Union, and, Council Recommendation of 9 December 1999 on cooperation in combating the financing of terrorist groups.

[30] Framework Decision on Combating Terrorism 2002/475/JHA, n. 29 above, which sets out and defines the main terrorist offences in Articles 1–3.

[31] Ibid., Article 4(1): 'Each Member State shall take the necessary measures to ensure that inciting or aiding or abetting an offence referred to in Article 1(1), Articles 2 or 3 is made punishable.'

[32] Council Framework Decision 2008/919/JHA of 28 November 2008 amending Framework Decision 2002/475/JHA on combating terrorism. See also O'Neill, M., 'A Critical Analysis of the EU Legal Provisions on Terrorism', 20(1) *Terrorism and Political Violence* (January 2008), 26–48, and Boyne, S.M., 'Free Speech, Terrorism, and European Security: Defining and Defending the Political Community', 30(2) *Pace Law Review* (2010), 417.

[33] Council Framework Decision 2008/919/JHA, n. 32 above, Recital (4).

the amendments, member states must criminalize provocations to commit terrorist offences as well as recruitment and training for terrorism.[34] According to Article 3(1)(a):

public provocation to commit a terrorist offence' means the distribution, or otherwise making available, of a message to the public, with the intent to incite the commission of a terrorist offence listed in the Framework directive, where such conduct, whether or not directly advocating terrorist offences, causes a danger that one or more such offences may be committed.

Opposition to the inclusion of this new offence focused on the broad phrase 'causes a danger', which goes well beyond the more limited offence of incitement.[35] It blurs the already difficult distinction between robust, even angry, commentary on a matter of public concern and express incitements to violence. To meet these criticisms, the drafters included Article 2, which constrains the interpretation of the new offences in stating that the Framework Decision does not require member states to take any measure that violates European or domestic standards regarding the protection of freedom of expression, in particular freedom of the press and other media.[36] Nonetheless, it is also obvious from the text of the Framework Decision that public provocation to commit a terrorist offence must mean less than actual incitement and that such an offence is within the legitimate exceptions to freedom of expression in Europe.

Plainly, prescriptive measures of this kind, which bolster the powers of the state and reduce the sphere of public liberty, challenge liberal ideas about the proper relationship between the media and the state. This is moreover a point at which the European prescriptive model of the legitimate liberal democratic state has excluded alternatives that are well within the traditions of liberalism. It is true that drafters of the Framework Decision attempted to balance its coercive elements with a strong assertion that fundamental European human rights were unaffected.[37] One of the difficulties here however is that requiring member states to take coercive measures is easier than creating effective European constraints on the exercise of state power. European human rights are very much a case in point. The supervisory power of the European Court of Human Rights ultimately depends on the persistence of

---

[34] Ibid. These obligations are contained in new Articles 3 and 4.

[35] European Parliament legislative resolution of 23 September 2008 on the proposal for a Council Framework Decision amending Framework Decision 2002/475/JHA on combating terrorism (COM (2007)0650 – C6–0466/2007–2007/0236(CNS)). See also International Commission of Jurists, *Briefing Paper: Amendment to the Framework Decision on Combating Terrorism—Provocation to Commit a Terrorist Offence.*

[36] Council Framework Decision 2008/919/JHA, n. 32 above, Article 2. See also Recital (14): '[N]othing in this Framework Decision may be interpreted as being intended to reduce or restrict the dissemination of information for scientific, academic or reporting purposes. The expression of radical, polemic or controversial views in the public debate on sensitive political questions, including terrorism, falls outside the scope of this Framework Decision and, in particular, of the definition of public provocation to commit terrorist offences.'

[37] Ibid., Article 1(2): 'This Framework Decision shall not have the effect of altering the obligation to respect fundamental rights and fundamental legal principles as enshrined in Article 6 of the Treaty on European Union.' See also Recital (10).

individual applicants who are willing to fight through domestic and Strasbourg processes to reach a decision. Victory in Strasbourg is moreover no guarantee of an effective domestic remedy, much less reform of the offending domestic law.[38]

Criticism and incitement in the Council of Europe

The basic elements of European public policy regarding media criticism of the state and incitement to violence have developed within the Council of Europe. Unlike the European Union, the Council of Europe has always enjoyed ample competence to consider directly the political and social aspects of the conflict between liberty and public order. Founded to protect and foster the liberal democratic character of western Europe, it is moreover ostensibly dedicated to limiting both the coercive powers of the state and the illiberal demands of democratic majorities. Yet, just as much as the European Union, it must also advance these aims without undermining essential state security and public safety in the member states, which are the guarantors of liberalism and democracy in Europe.

These contrasting objectives were drafted into the language and structure of the European Convention on Human Rights, which the European Court of Human Rights has developed expansively in its Article 10 case law. In unequivocal language, the Court has repeatedly stated that the liberal democratic state must endure robust criticism in all aspects of public policy and the conduct of its institutions and officials. As the Court declared in *Castells v. Spain*,

> There is little scope under Article 10 § 2 of the Convention for restrictions on political speech or on debate on questions of public interest. Furthermore, the limits of permissible criticism are wider with regard to the government than in relation to a private citizen or even a politician. In a democratic system the actions or omissions of the government must be subject to the close scrutiny not only of the legislative and judicial authorities but also of public opinion. Moreover, the dominant position which the government occupies makes it necessary for it to display restraint in resorting to criminal proceedings, particularly where other means are available for replying to the unjustified attacks and criticisms of its adversaries.[39]

---

[38] On the need to increase the efficiency and effectiveness of the European Court of Human Rights, see High Level Conference on the Future of the European Court of Human Rights (Interlaken Conference), *Interlaken Declaration: The Future of the European Court of Human Rights* (19 February 2010).

[39] *Castells v. Spain* (Application No. 11798/85) (23 April 1992), para. 46. See more generally *Handyside v. the United Kingdom* (Application No. 5493/72) (7 December 1976), para. 49 on the breadth of offensive expression protected by Article 10. The Council of Europe Committee of Ministers has drawn on the case law of the ECHR in its *Of Europe, Declaration on Freedom of Political Debate in the Media* (12 February 2004), in which it declares 'The state, the government or any other institution of the executive, legislative or judicial branch may be subject to criticism in the media. Because of their dominant position, these institutions as such should not be protected by criminal law against defamatory or insulting statements' (Principle II. Freedom to criticise the state or public institutions).

The Court has also set out the consequences of this principle for the European media state relationship. In *Başkaya and Okçuoğlu v. Turkey*, the Court noted that 'the most careful scrutiny on the part of the Court is called for when the measures taken by the national authority are capable of discouraging the participation of the press, one of society's "watchdogs", in the public debate on matters of legitimate public concern, even measures which merely make access to information more cumbersome'.[40]

Enunciating the principle of robust criticism of the state is fundamental to a liberal definition of freedom of expression, but is also an incomplete description of this facet of the media state relationship. There are few more definitive images of liberal democracy than the freedom of the newspaper editor to abuse the state in printed word and, in these statements, the European Court of Human Rights has simply demanded that state parties, at a minimum, fulfil that basic qualification. Yet, for reasons of historical and contemporary politics, treaty language, and its supranational status, the Court has shown considerable deference to the state where expression presents a significant threat to its core interests. All of those factors bear on the Court's cautious treatment of national laws restricting criticism of the courts or the administration of justice. As a first principle, critical public comment regarding the courts and the judiciary, like any other institution of the state, is protected under Article 10, especially where that comment concerns a matter of general concern.[41] As the Court stated in the seminal *Sunday Times* case, '[w]hilst the mass media must not overstep the bounds imposed in the interests of the proper administration of justice, it is incumbent upon them to impart information and ideas concerning matters that come before the courts just as in other areas of public interest'.[42] Nonetheless, state parties may legitimately restrict that principle, in a proportionate manner, not only where public expression threatens the fairness of a specific hearing or other judicial process, but also where it endangers the authority or impartiality of the judiciary more generally. Article 10 consequently offers scant protection for media speculation on guilt and innocence or even on civil liability.[43]

There is undoubtedly clear support for this approach in the text of the Convention. The legitimate public policy reasons for restricting freedom of expression set out in Article 10(2) include, first, the generic 'rights of others', which provides a link to the Article 6 right to a fair hearing, and, second, the more specific public interest in 'maintaining the authority and impartiality of the judiciary'.[44] The text

[40] *Başkaya and Okçuoğlu v. Turkey*, (Application Nos 23536/94 and 24408/94) (8 July 1999), para. 62. See also *Tarsasag a Szabadsagjogokert v. Hungary* (Application No. 37374/05) (14 April 2009).
[41] On the distinction under ECHR Article 10 between scrutiny and comment about judicial proceedings generally and scrutiny and comment about individual judges, see Chapter 9.
[42] *Sunday Times v. United Kingdom* (Application No. 22083/93), (22 October 1996), para. 29. See also *De Haes and Gijsels v. Belgium* (Application No. 19983/92) (24 Feburary 1997), para. 37. 'The Court reiterates that the press plays an essential role in a democratic society. Although it must not overstep certain bounds in particular in respect of the reputation and rights of others, its duty is nevertheless to impart—in a manner consistent with its obligations and responsibilities—information and ideas on all matters of public interest, including those relating to the functioning of the judiciary'.
[43] *Sunday Times v. United Kingdom*, ibid., para. 63.
[44] European Convention on Human Rights, Article 6, states, *inter alia*, that, 'everyone is entitled to a fair and public hearing within a reasonable time by an independent and impartial tribunal established by law'. On the right to a public hearing, see *Håkansson and Sturesson v. Sweden*, (Application No. 11855/85) (21 February 1990).

of Article 10 is of course no great barrier to a more assertive application of the principle of robust comment on state institutions to courts and judicial processes. The Court has often enough treated the Convention as a living document, whose terms need to be interpreted according to developments in European human rights principles as well as public expectations.[45] Courts and judges are however often viewed as unique institutions of the state that are especially vulnerable to public criticism, particularly in countries where public confidence in the rule of law is weak. The Council of Europe has moreover always included member states where the judiciary struggle to maintain their independence from external pressures. Working within the limits of its supervisory authority, the Court must accommodate the needs of these states, where the administration of justice would arguably suffer if exposed to the kind of harsh and often abusive criticism permitted for other branches of government. The doctrinal force of the democratic argument for greater liberty to publish is moreover rather weak when weighted against these concerns. As discussed above, the public interest in the open discussion of all matters relating to the state must be weighted against the public interest in an effective state capable of delivering justice, which is a matter of appearance as well as fact. On that basis, the Court has interpreted the 'authority of the judiciary' under Article 10(2) as including the confidence which the courts in a democratic society must inspire not only in those before the courts but also the public at large.[46] This has had the ironic consequence of creating a parallel in European human rights law between the treatment of public figures and the treatment of the courts, both of which are entitled to restrain publications that injure their different forms of dignity.[47]

The Court's case law in this area has also created what is effectively a significant margin of appreciation for state parties when seeking to restrain public comment concerning matters before the domestic courts or similar tribunals. It remains to be seen how much discretion the state parties to the ECHR enjoy when pursuing different approaches to the problem of achieving effective and fair justice in an open society. In the midst of a communications revolution that has opened the public sphere to comment by a vast number of individuals, groups, and organizations, the imposition of stiff sanctions for major instances of prejudicial reporting is ripe for review. The American alternative, in which the risk of prejudice borne by the courts and not the media, is expensive for the public purse and arguably less effective in protecting the fairness of the proceedings from trial by media. It does however offer

---

[45] See Mowbray, A., 'The Creativity of the European Court of Human Rights', 5(1) *Human Rights Law Review* (2005), 57–79.

[46] 'The courts—the guarantors of justice, whose role is fundamental in a State based on the rule of law—must enjoy public confidence. They must accordingly be protected from destructive attacks that are unfounded, especially in view of the fact that judges are subject to a duty of discretion that precludes them from replying to criticism', *De Haes and Gijsels v. Belgium*, n. 42 above, para. 37. See also *Worm v. Austria* (83/1996/702/894) (29 August 1997).

[47] 'A clear distinction must, however, be made between criticism and insult. If the sole intent of any form of expression is to insult a court, or members of that court, an appropriate punishment would not, in principle, constitute a violation of Article 10 § 2 of the Convention', *Skalka v. Poland* (Application No. 43425/98) (27 May 2003), para. 38.

the clear advantage of imposing fewer burdens on the liberty to publish and opening the courts up to more intense public scrutiny. Yet the Court's interpretation of Article 10, in connection with Article 6, may have blocked that avenue.

Incitement to disorder and violence

Restrictions on expression that incites violence open up fundamental questions about the boundary between public debate in democratic societies and the core interests of the state. European human rights law is founded on the legitimacy of the state's security interests and its obligation to protect public safety as much as it is on liberal ideals of liberty of thought, speech, and action. It must therefore take on the task of determining when expression causes a real risk of violence and, more controversially, what degree of risk the state and the public must bear before restrictions on freedom of expression are permissible. This immediately raises the question whether these issues, which are closely tied to the particular vulnerabilities of member states and the relative stability of their societies, can be definitively addressed at the supranational level. Viewed optimistically, inclusion in a strong European regional order has provided member states with greater security, for which they must pay in part with greater tolerance of domestic dissent and criticism of the state. Yet, given Europe's recurring regional and national security crises, running from ideologically motivated terrorism through violent separatist movements across the breadth of Europe to more recent islamist terrorism, a common standard based on expansive protection for the liberty to speak and publish would arguably impose undue risks of incited violence for some member states. In these circumstances, the European Court of Human Rights has created a loosely stated standard, which may better accommodate differences between Europe's many democracies, but also creates the potential for unjustifiably restrictive national measures. The controlling device lies in the Court's careful application of proportionality analysis. This however raises other objections, which include the excessive breadth of judicial discretion where proportionality balancing includes the weighing of conflicting public policies.

In developing principles to govern incitement to violence, the Court has found no great obstacles in the Convention's assorted rights, obligations, and interests. Article 10 gives strong protection to expression that is critical of the state up to the point that particular expression directly or indirectly advocates violence against the state or members of the public.[48] The Article 10(1) right to freedom of expression is offset by several relevant legitimate grounds for restricting expression, including the interests of national security, territorial integrity, or public safety and the prevention of disorder or crime. The Court has drawn on these when stating that, 'it remains open to the competent State authorities to adopt, in their capacity as guarantors of public order, measures, even of a criminal-law nature, intended to

---

[48] See *Handyside v. United Kingdom*, n. 39 above, para. 49, on the basic protection Article 10 affords to expression that offends, shocks, or disturbs the state.

react appropriately and without excess...'.[49] States are therefore entitled to adopt special measures to combat terrorism, which may extend to media restrictions.[50] In addition, under Article 15, state parties may provisionally derogate from certain Convention rights, including Article 10, in time of 'war or other public emergency threatening the life of the nation'.[51] On this basis, the Court has declared the basic rule that the words at issue must be capable of being an incitement to violence, the key factor being whether, taken as a whole, they advocate violence, armed resistance, or insurrection.[52] Caustic criticism of the institutions, agents, or policies of the state is not, in itself, incitement, even where that criticism is provocative, insulting, or involves serious allegations of wrong doing by public authorities.[53]

This is notably an approach that imposes less risk on the state or the public than the one developed by the United States Supreme Court.[54] In 1999, in the case of *Sürek v. Turkey (No. 3)* 24735/94, Judge Bonello wrote in his concurring opinion that,

[t]hroughout these, and previous Turkish freedom-of-expression cases in which incitement to violence was an issue, the common test employed by the Court seems to have been this: if the writings published by the applicant supported or instigated the use of violence, then his conviction by the national courts was justifiable in a democratic society. I discard this yardstick as insufficient. I believe that punishment by the national authorities of those encouraging violence would be justifiable in a democratic society only if the incitement were such as to create 'a clear and present danger'. When the invitation to the use of force is intellectualised, abstract, and removed in time and space from the foci of actual or impending violence, then the fundamental right to freedom of expression should generally prevail.[55]

That argument may well be gaining ground in the European Court of Human Rights. In its 2010 Chamber decision in *Gül v. Turkey*, the Court combined its established test of advocacy of violence with a further requirement that the Turkish government show that there was 'a clear and imminent danger which required an interference such as the lengthy criminal prosecution faced by the applicants'.[56]

In determining whether an incitement to violence has occurred and whether the response of the state party concerned was proportionate, the Court has placed great weight on how the words at issue were reasonably understood in their context, highlighting several factors relevant to whether there is a pressing need for the restriction and whether the form of restriction or sanction is proportionate to

---

[49] See *Castells v. Spain*, n. 39 above. See also *Incal v. Turkey* (Application No. 22678/93) (9 June 1998), para. 54.

[50] *Brogan and others v. United Kingdom* (Application No. 11209/84 et al.) (29 November 1988), para. 61.

[51] Article 15, however imposes strict limitations on the permissible circumstances and duration for any derogation from Convention obligations.

[52] *Ceylan v. Turkey*, (Application No. 23556/94) (8 July 1999), paras 33–36.

[53] Ibid., paras 33–34. See also *Özgür Gündem v. Turkey* (Application No. 23144/93), (16 March 2000), para. 60, and *Yalçin Küçük (No. 3) v. Turkey* (Application No. 71353/01) (22 April 2008).

[54] *Brandenburg v. Ohio*, n. 10 above.

[55] Concurring Opinion of Bonello J., *Sürek v. Turkey (No. 2)* (Application No. 24122/94).

[56] *Gül v. Turkey* (Application No. 4870/02) (8 June 2010), para. 42.

that need.[57] These include the status of the individual who expressed the statement at issue. If, for example, the words were spoken by a public figure active in politics, they may have greater influence on the general public and if spoken by the leader of a banned violent organization, they may have a special significance to its supporters.[58] The nature of the expression and its form of publication can also be as important to the question of incitement of violence as the actual words.[59] Clearly, where sanctions are imposed directly on the media, the necessity of those measures will need to be convincingly established, given the importance of the media's watchdog role in a democratic society.[60] In addition, words expressed in a literary or artistic form that also only reach a limited audience are less likely to merit serious sanction than an inflammatory political declaration in a popular newspaper or radio station.[61]

Expression is not however guaranteed protection under Article 10 simply because of its artistic form or satirical intent. In its decision in *Leroy v. France*, the Court considered a conviction and fine imposed for the publication two days after the destruction of the World Trade Towers in 2001 of a cartoon that satirized the attack with a caption parodying the advertising slogan of a famous brand: 'We have all dreamt of it... Hamas did it'.[62] In the view of the Court, the cartoon was not only a criticism of the American government and its policies, but also glorified the violent destruction of the Trade Towers, which therefore justified the interference with freedom of expression. Moreover, 'the impact of such a message in a politically sensitive region, namely the Basque Country, was not to be overlooked; the weekly newspaper's limited circulation notwithstanding, the Court noted that the drawing's publication had provoked a certain public reaction, capable of stirring up violence and demonstrating a plausible impact on public order in the region'.[63]

---

[57] The Court, 'must, with due regard to the circumstances of each case and a State's margin of appreciation, ascertain whether a fair balance has been struck between the individual's fundamental right to freedom of expression and a democratic society's legitimate right to protect itself against the activities of terrorist organisations', *Zana v. Turkey* (Application No. 18954/91) (25 November 1997), para. 55, and *Gul v. Turkey*, n. 56 above, para. 38. See also *Gündüz v. Turkey* (Application No. 3507/97) (14 June 2004), para. 48. 'In the Court's view, such comments demonstrate an intransigent attitude towards and profound dissatisfaction with contemporary institutions in Turkey, such as the principle of secularism and democracy. Seen in their context, however, they cannot be construed as a call to violence or as hate speech based on religious intolerance.'

[58] *Zana v. Turkey*, n. 57 above, para. 60, '... the support given to the PKK—described as a "national liberation movement"—by the former mayor of Diyarbakır, the most important city in south-east Turkey, in an interview published in a major national daily newspaper, had to be regarded as likely to exacerbate an already explosive situation in that region'. See also *Ceylan v. Turkey*, n. 52 above, (which concerned a trade-union leader), and *Hogefeld v. Germany* (Application No. 35402/97) (20 January 2000), (which concerned an imprisoned leader of a terrorist group whose statements could amount to an implicit incitement to violence, given her status and previous activities).

[59] In *Özgür Radyo-Ses Radyo Televizyon Yayın Yapım Ve Tanıtım A.Ş. v. Turkey* (Application No. 11369/03) (4 December 2007), (which concerned the broadcast of a well known political song).

[60] *Ürper a.o. v. Turkey* (Application No. 14526/07 et al.) (20 October 2009).

[61] *Karatas v. Turkey* (Application No. 63315/00) (5 January 2010), (which involved a private individual who expressed his views in a book of poetry rather than mass media, a fact that substantially limited any impact on national security). See also *Baskaya and Okçuoglu v. Turkey* (Application Nos 23536/94 and 24408/94) (8 July 1999).

[62] *Leroy v. France* (Application No. 36109/03) (2 October 2008).

[63] Ibid., para. 64.

Despite the reference in *Gül* to the need to show a 'clear and imminent danger' to warrant a proportionate degree of restriction, a large body of ECHR case law suggests that Article 10 requires that the state party do no more than demonstrate that the expression at issue causes a genuine risk of violence. Moreover, an incitement to violence may only be apparent when the words are viewed in their full context. European human rights law therefore leaves a significant burden on the media to judge whether its reporting on a controversial issue or individual raises a substantial risk of violence. Plainly, that burden increases where the media seeks to report on an organized group that uses violence for its political or other ends. As the Court has stressed,

... the 'duties and responsibilities' which accompany the exercise of the right to freedom of expression by media professionals assume special significance in situations of conflict and tension. Particular caution is called for when consideration is being given to the publication of the views of representatives of organizations which resort to violence against the State lest the media become a vehicle for the dissemination of hate speech and the promotion of violence.[64]

In these special circumstances, state parties may also take precautionary measures to prohibit direct access to the media by groups or individuals dedicated to violence.[65] The Court has however sought to balance this affirmation of the importance of state security and public safety by underlining the public's right of access to information about contentious political and social matters, including the objectives and motivations of terrorist groups.[66] Article 10 therefore protects the media when it is attempting in good faith to inform the public about these matters and its reporting cannot reasonably be categorized as an incitement to violence. In a similar vein, the Committee of Ministers of the Council of Europe has called on public authorities in member states to refrain from adopting measures equating media reporting on terrorism with support for terrorism.[67]

In principle, the case law of the European Court of Human Rights on incitement to violence only creates a minimum standard for the protection of freedom of expression. Member states therefore enjoy a substantial margin of discretion to adopt domestic standards that shift the risk of expression leading to violence towards the state and the public, provided any domestic standard fulfilled the ECHR positive obligations to protect life and personal security.[68] Judge Bonello, in advocating adoption of the American *Brandenburg v. Ohio* standard, obviously did not see a potential clash with these positive obligations that required discussion.[69]

---

[64] *Sürek and Özdemir v. Turkey* (Application Nos 23927/94 and 24277/94) (8 July 1999), para. 63.
[65] *Purcell v. Ireland, Brind v. United Kingdom*, n. 18 above.
[66] *Sürek and Özdemir v. Turkey*, n. 64 above, para. 61. See also *Gündüz v. Turkey*, n. 57 above.
[67] Council of Europe, Committee of Ministers, Declaration on freedom of expression and information in the media in the context of the fight against terrorism, (2 March 2005).
[68] *L.C.B. v. United Kingdom* (Application No. 23413/94) (9 June 1998), and *A. v. United Kingdom*, (Application No. 25599/94) (23 September 1998).
[69] Concurring Opinion of Bonello J., *Sürek v. Turkey (No 2)*, n. 55 above. 'The guarantee of freedom of expression does not permit a state to forbid or proscribe advocacy of the use of force except when such advocacy is directed to inciting or producing imminent lawlessness and is likely to incite or

Other developments in the European Union and Council of Europe however have
cast doubt on the freedom of member states to adopt an exceptional position on
legal standards for incitement.

In the past decade, Europe's regional bodies have joined or supported various
measures that identify terrorism as a matter of international concern and create
obligations to criminalize acts related to terrorism and to prosecute those responsible when they are perpetrated. The Council of Europe's treaty making powers were
first turned to this purpose in 1977, when it adopted the European Convention on
the Suppression of Terrorism.[70] In 2003, this Convention was strengthened and
broadened as part of the new coordination of anti-terrorism measures amongst
democratic and non-democratic states that followed the September 2001 attacks.[71]
The Council of Europe's Committee of Ministers, underscoring this shift in
European public policy, stated the previous year that, '[s]tates are under the
obligation to take the measures needed to protect the fundamental rights of
everyone within their jurisdiction against terrorist acts, especially the right to
life'.[72] For the media, the most important development in this outpouring of
legal and policy instruments was the Council of Europe's 2005 Convention on
the Prevention of Terrorism, which followed on the heels of UN Security Council
Resolution 1624.[73] Article 5 of the Convention obliges state parties to criminalize
public provocation to commit terrorist acts.[74]

The criminalization of provocation to commit terrorist offences, which includes
not only direct incitement but also the glorification of terrorism, is an obvious

produce such action (*Brandenburg v. Ohio*, n. 10 above at 447). It is a question of proximity and degree
(*Schenck v. United States* 294 U.S. 47 (1919) at 52).'

[70] Council of Europe, 1977 European Convention on the Suppression of Terrorism, (ETS
No. 090), which includes an obligation on state parties to extradite or prosecute several defined actions
endangering life, such as the seizure of an airplane.
[71] Council of Europe, 2003 Protocol amending the European Convention on the Suppression of
Terrorism, (ETS No. 190).
[72] Council of Europe, Committee of Ministers, *Guidelines on human rights and the fight against
terrorism*, (adopted on 11 July 2002). See also Council of Europe, Committee of Ministers, Declaration on the Fight against International Terrorism (12 September 2001), and Decision on the Fight
against International Terrorism (21 September 2001).
[73] United Nations Security Council Resolution 1624 (14 September 2005), discussed below. The
Council of Europe, 2005 Convention on the Prevention of Terrorism (ETS No. 196) builds on
previous international agreements that define terrorist acts. These are listed in Annex 1 to the 2005
Convention and run from the 1970 Hague Convention for the Suppression of Unlawful Seizure of
Aircraft to the 1999 International Convention for the Suppression of the Financing of Terrorism
(United Nations General Assembly Resolution 54/109). The 2005 Convention laid the ground for the
2008 amendments to the European Union Framework Decision on Combating Terrorism, n. 29
above, which imposes a similar obligation on EU member states. See also Hunt, A., 'The Council of
Europe Convention on the Prevention of Terrorism', 12(4) *European Public Law* (2006), 603.
[74] Article 5—Public provocation to commit a terrorist offence: '1.... "public provocation to
commit a terrorist offence" means the distribution, or otherwise making available, of a message to
the public, with the intent to incite the commission of a terrorist offence, where such conduct, whether
or not directly advocating terrorist offences, causes a danger that one or more such offences may be
committed. 2. Each Party shall adopt such measures as may be necessary to establish public provocation to commit a terrorist offence... when committed unlawfully and intentionally, as a criminal
offence under its domestic law.' See also Council of Europe, Committee of Experts on Terrorism,
Freedom of Expression and 'Apologie du Terrorisme', CODEXTER (2008) 30.

threat to liberal democratic freedom of expression. The Council of Europe has consequently sought to underscore the importance of freedom of expression while broadening the concept of incitement to include provocation.[75] The 2005 Convention contains substantial provisions in this vein, which require that state parties ensure that the measures taken to fulfil the main Convention obligations, including Article 5, 'are carried out while respecting human rights obligations, in particular the right to freedom of expression, freedom of association and freedom of religion'.[76] The same article also subjects those measures to 'the principle of proportionality, with respect to the legitimate aims pursued and to their necessity in a democratic society, and should exclude any form of arbitrariness or discriminatory or racist treatment'.[77] Nonetheless, unlike the Convention's provisions on the criminalization of terrorist related acts, these obligations do not specific how they should be implemented in domestic law or practice. As a matter of European law, it therefore falls to the Convention on Human Rights and its Court to provide the background standards to limit the scope of these prescriptive obligations. That however is a major task for a regional human rights system that is not equipped to provide relief for individual applicants from across the furthest breadth of Europe. Consequently, the effect of Article 5, in combination with the EU Framework Decision discussed above, is to narrow the scope of the liberty to publish across Europe, tightening the model of the legitimate European state.

Criticism and incitement in international trade law

The relationship between international trade law and national measures restricting public criticism of the state or inciting disorder or violence is distinctly different from the one that has developed between European economic law and these domestic measures. In contrast to the European debate over the proper limits of state power, which rests on conclusively liberal democratic foundations, the liberal democratic project in the international sphere is still engaged in a long running, inconclusive effort to set the global terms for the legitimate exercise of state power. That effort has been obstructed not only by the determined resistance of non-democratic states, but also by the common pursuit of stability and security by all states. In this wider sphere, the liberal economic argument for greater liberty to publish operates in trade law without close support from its twin, the liberal political argument for greater liberty, which has only achieved a modest place in international human rights law, despite bursts of rhetorical dominance in international politics. In the absence of clear human rights instruments or effective enforcement machinery, the institutional and legal strengths of international

---

[75] Council of Europe, Committee of Ministers, *Guidelines on human rights and the fight against terrorism* (adopted on 11 July 2002) II. 'All measures taken by States to fight terrorism must respect human rights and the principle of the rule of law, while excluding any form of arbitrariness, as well as any discriminatory or racist treatment, and must be subject to appropriate supervision.'
[76] 2005 Convention on the Prevention of Terrorism, n. 73 above, Article 12(1).
[77] Ibid., Article 12(2).

trade law, centred on the WTO, have instead become an attractive alternative conceptual vehicle to advance ideas about the deep liberalization of domestic media sectors.[78]

That aspiration however faces formidable obstacles. International trade obligations to liberalize trade in media goods and services are much weaker than their European counterparts. Trade law is primarily directed at the removal of discriminatory barriers to trade and has only moved tentatively towards deeper market integration, which would provide much greater leverage to force the removal of domestic restraints on the publication and distribution of media content. Consequently, most national restrictions on the media for criticism of the state or incitement to violence are currently beyond the reach of trade rules as they typically apply to domestic and foreign media equally. Yet, even ostensibly non-discriminatory restrictions can be applied in discriminatory ways that breach national treatment obligations, owing to differences in domestic versus foreign ownership, control, and methods of content publication and distribution and thus fall within the scope of national treatment obligations.[79] In China, for example, the domestic media are governed through institutional networks of state ownership or sponsorship that are closely coordinated by Communist Party networks directing the work of key management and editorial staff.[80] China's abundant media licensing requirements and regulatory rules, which are thus only one element in the control of the domestic media, are however the primary means of excluding or controlling the operations of foreign media.[81] These are effectively two different, albeit overlapping, systems of media regulation and control whose application depends on whether the media organization is domestic or foreign. There is therefore substantial room for different treatment that is also discriminatory in trade law terms, especially given the difficulty of separating commercial and political policy goals where restraints on foreign media goods and services serve both.

Under the rules of the WTO, if a national measure restricting criticism of the state or incitement to violence were to violate a state's GATT or GATS non-discrimination obligations, the immediate question is whether such a highly political measure also fell within the relevant general exceptions in those treaties.[82] These general exceptions have near identical introductory or 'chapeau' conditions, as Article XIV of the GATS was modelled on Article XX of the GATT. However their lists of permitted grounds for exceptional treatment vary considerably. Measures

---

[78] Bollinger, L., *Uninhibited, Robust and Wide-Open* (Oxford University Press, 2010).

[79] On the scope of WTO non-discrimination obligations, see Chapter 5.

[80] McGregor, R., *The Party: The Secret World of China's Communist Rulers* (Harper, 2010), 235–255. See also Wu, T 'The World Trade Law of Censorship and Internet Filtering', 7 *Chinese Journal of International Law* (2006), 263.

[81] See, for example, *China—Measures Affecting Trading Rights and Distribution Services for Certain Publications and Audiovisual Entertainment Products*, (WT/DS363/AB/R), Appellate Body (December 2009).

[82] Article XX, General Agreement on Tariffs and Trade 1994 (incorporating GATT 1947), (15 April 1994), 33 ILM 1153 (1994), and Article XIV, General Agreement on Trade in Services, (15 April 1994), 33 ILM 1167 (1994). On the general exception provisions of the GATT and the GATS, see Chapter 5.

taken against foreign media goods, such as printed newspapers, for criticism of state institutions have no obvious protection under the legitimate grounds set out in GATT Article XX. This apparent lacuna in such a politically sensitive area arguably reflects the assumption of the American and western European drafters that the GATT exceptions should generally follow the core needs and expectations of a liberal democratic state and there was therefore no need to protect measures falling short of a threat to public safety.[83] Measures that prohibit or restrict the publication of incitement to violence against the state or the public will thus arguably fall within the exception for measures that are 'necessary to protect human, animal or plant life or health'. Any measure falling within the scope of a legitimate ground for exceptional treatment would also have to satisfy not only the necessity condition, which may involve 'weighing and balancing' different factors to determine if it was the least restrictive measure, but also the Article XX chapeau provisions concerning arbitrary or disguised trade discrimination.[84]

Article XIV of the GATS is notably more expansive, permitting measures that are 'necessary to . . . maintain public order', which is described in a footnote to Article XIV as meaning the protection of 'fundamental interests of society'.[85] It was surely not the intention of the United States or the other principal drafting states when including 'public order' as a ground for exceptional treatment to open the door to illiberal and non-democratic restrictions on the media. Nevertheless, China's accession to the WTO in December 2001 brought that lurking possibility into the open, given that it acceded as a well established one party state with a history of tight control over its media. It can therefore be expected to make full use of Article XIV in the future, challenging liberal democratic concepts of legitimate fundamental interest.[86] How those challenges will be dealt with under the various conditions that must be satisfied under GATS Article XIV, which follow those of GATT Article XX, will be key development in international media law. While most member states refrained from making positive commitment in the audiovisual sector during the Uruguay Round, which significantly reduced the impact of the GATS non-discrimination obligations on trade in media services, under its Accession Protocol, China agreed to major liberalization commitments in the audiovisual sector. For China, Article XIV is therefore an important element in its defence of wide ranging restrictions on published criticisms of the state and the Communist Party that have discriminatory consequences for foreign media services.

---

[83] Article XX, ibid., includes measures 'necessary to protect public morals', which, as discussed in Chapter 10, can encompass the privacy and reputation interests of politicians and public officials.

[84] Article XX, 'Subject to the requirement that such measures are not applied in a manner which would constitute a means of arbitrary or unjustifiable discrimination between countries where the same conditions prevail, or a disguised restriction on international trade, nothing in this Agreement shall be construed to prevent the adoption or enforcement by any contracting party of measures . . .'

[85] GATS XIV, n. 82 above, and GATS Footnote 5. See also Appellate Body Report, *United States—Measures Affecting the Cross-Border Supply of Gambling and Betting Service*, WT/DS285/AB/R, (7 April 2005), para. 296.

[86] Eeckhout, P., 'The Scales of Trade—Reflections on the Growth and Functions of the WTO Adjudicative Branch', 13(1) *Journal of International Economic Law* (2010), 3–26.

In addition to the GATT and GATS general exceptions, both treaties also contain security exceptions that are also potentially relevant to restraints on criticism of the state or incitement of violence. Article XXI of the GATT and Article XIV*bis* of the GATS permit member states to take 'any action which it considers necessary for the protection of its essential security interests...taken in time of war or other emergency in international relations'.[87] While these provisions are limited to circumstances of war or international emergency, they may be applied when a state considers such action necessary.[88] Indeed, this sweeping discretion appears to reserve the power to self judge the necessity and scope of any measures taken under the security exceptions, limited only by principles of good faith and the necessity principle of least restrictive measure.[89] In addition, the GATT and GATS security exceptions permit any national measures taken to fulfil 'obligations under the United Nations Charter for the maintenance of international peace and security'. In principle, this 'peace and security' exception is relevant to the 2005 UN Security Council Resolution concerning the criminalization of incitements to commit terrorist acts, which is discussed below. That Resolution covers all forms of media but is particularly important for incitement to terrorism through internet based forms of public communication. For most WTO member states, however, that connection is currently theoretical. Given the Uruguay Round agreement to disagree on audiovisual services and uncertainties over the status of electronic commerce under WTO law, there are few direct WTO obligations affecting trade in media services.[90] Moreover, criminalization of incitement to terrorist activities should, in any event, apply equally to domestic and foreign media goods and services.

Criticism and incitement in international human rights law

Public criticism of the state has been one of the defining issues for international media law since the adoption of the Universal Declaration of Human Rights in 1948. Since then, it has played a crucial part in efforts to entrench liberal democratic principles into international human rights law and use them to define the character of the legitimate state. Article 19(1) of the International

---

[87] GATT, Article XXI(b)(iii) and GATS, Article XIV(b)(iii), See also TRIPS, Article 73 Security Exceptions.

[88] GATT, Article XXI: Security Exceptions, Nothing in this Agreement shall be construed,... (*b*) to prevent any contracting party from taking any action which it considers necessary for the protection of its essential security interests.

[89] See Decision Concerning Article XXI of the General Agreement, GATT Doc. L/5426 (1982), GATT B.I.S.D. (29th Supp.), at 23 (1983). See also Lindsy, P., 'The Ambiguity of GATT Article XXI: Subtle Success or Rampant Failure?' 52 *Duke Law Journal* (2003), Hahn, M., 'Vital Interests in the Law of GATT: An Analysis of GATT's Security Exception', 12 *Michigan Journal of International Law* (1991), 558, and, *Resource Book on TRIPS and Development,* UNCTAD-ICTSD, (Cambridge University Press, 2005), 805–806.

[90] On the Uruguay Round pragmatic compromise concerning 'audiovisual services', see Chapters 5 and 15.

Covenant on Civil and Political Rights lays the foundations for this work by stating that, '[e]veryone shall have the right to hold opinions without interference', which the treaty leaves free from exceptions or restrictions.[91] The broad language of the right to freedom of expression stated in paragraph 19(2) lays the path open for a strong right to criticize the institutions, agencies, and representatives of the state without fear of sanction or hindrance. The scope of that right depends however on how far that expansive interpretation is safeguarded by the Article 19(3) conditional exceptions.

The ICCPR Human Rights Committee has declared that 'the right to freedom of expression is of paramount importance in any democratic society, and that any restrictions on its exercise must meet strict tests of justification'.[92] Yet the Committee's diverse membership and limited competence has hampered its efforts to work out the substance of those tests of justification and their application.[93] Under the Optional Protocol, there have also been comparatively few individual communications concerning freedom of expression. Its decisions in these cases have moreover often turned on the failure of the state to provide evidence for its assertions or to address key questions, rather than on decisive doctrinal issues.[94] The Committee's most important statement regarding political expression is contained in its General Comment on Article 25, which concerns the right to participate in public affairs, voting rights, and the right of equal access to public service. Unlike its bland 1983 General Comment on Article 19, in this General Comment the Committee captured the spirit of the post Cold War moment, declaring that,

[i]n order to ensure the full enjoyment of rights protected by article 25, the free communication of information and ideas about public and political issues between citizens, candidates and elected representatives is essential. This implies a free press and other media able to comment on public issues without censorship or restraint and to inform public opinion. It requires the full enjoyment and respect for the rights guaranteed in articles 19, 21 and 22 of the Covenant, including freedom to engage in political activity individually or through political parties and other organizations, freedom to debate public affairs, to hold peaceful demonstrations and meetings, to criticize and oppose, to publish political material, to campaign for election and to advertise political ideas.[95]

The right to freedom of expression in international human rights law remains nonetheless open to limitations that hinge on the Article 19(3) grounds for exceptional treatment, including the protection of national security and public order (*ordre public*). In common with the European Convention on Human Rights

---

[91] International Covenant on Civil and Political Rights (ICCPR), GA Resolution 2200A (XXI), UN Doc. A/6316 (1966). See ICCPR, Human Rights Committee, *General Comment No. 10: Freedom of expression (Art. 19)*, (29 June 1983).

[92] *Korneenko and Milinkevich v. Belarus*, Communication No. 1553/2007.

[93] On the ICCPR Human Rights Committee, see Chapter 6.

[94] See, for example, *Kim v. Republic of Korea*, Communication No. 574/94, *Svetik v. Belarus*, Communication No. 927/2000, *Velichkin v. Belarus*, Communication No. 1022/2001, *Korneenko and Milinkevich v. Belarus*, n. 92 above.

[95] ICCPR, Human Rights Committee, *General Comment No. 25: The right to participate in public affairs, voting rights and the right of equal access to public service (Art. 25)* (12 July 1996).

law, the ICCPR faces the problem that it is founded on the existence of states and presumes that state parties are free to take necessary measures to preserve their own security as well as the safety of the public. Democratic states as much as non-democratic ones therefore retain the power to impose restrictions and sanctions on criticism that crosses over into incitement to violence against the state. Not only acknowledged in Article 19(3), but also in Article 4 of the ICCPR, which permits exceptions to freedom of expression, among other rights, in times of emergency.[96] The further question of when public criticism harms the state by putting the stability of the state and public order at risk without direct risk of violence is a relatively uncharted area in international human rights law, although the subject of sustained advocacy by media and human rights organizations as well as governments.[97]

Aside from this recognition of the importance of national security and public safety in the ICCPR and other UN human rights treaties, the United Nations Security Council has created major international obligations for states to act against terrorist activities.[98] For international media law, the most important of these are contained in United Nations Security Council Resolution 1624.[99] Adopted in September 2005, Resolution 1624 calls on states to adopt necessary and appropriate measures to prohibit by law and to prevent incitement to commit a terrorist act or acts, which has provided a basis in international law for the criminalization of incitement to terrorist acts and recruitment through any communication medium, including the internet.[100] The need to implement this obligation with due regard

---

[96] ICCPR, Article 4(1), 'In time of public emergency which threatens the life of the nation and the existence of which is officially proclaimed, the States Parties to the present Covenant may take measures derogating from their obligations under the present Covenant to the extent strictly required by the exigencies of the situation, provided that such measures are not inconsistent with their other obligations under international law and do not involve discrimination solely on the ground of race, colour, sex, language, religion or social origin.' See also ICCPR *General Comment No. 29: States of Emergency (Art. 4)* (31 August 2001).

[97] See, for example, Johannesburg Principles on National Security, Freedom of Expression and Access to Information, UN Doc. E/CN.4/1996/39 (1996). See also ARTICLE 19, *Statement on the Encouragement of Terrorism,* 2005.

[98] See, for example, United Nations Security Council Resolution 1624 (2005), doc. S/RES/ 1624 (2005). See also Keller, H., and Fischer, A., 'The UN Anti-terror Sanctions Regime under Pressure', 9(2) *Human Rights Law Review* (2009), 257–266, Bianchi, A., 'Security Council's Anti-terror Resolutions and their Implementation by Member States: An Overview', 4 *Journal of International Criminal Justice* (2006), 1044–1073, Bianchi, A., 'Assessing the Effectiveness of the UN Security Council's Anti-terrorism Measures: The Quest for Legitimacy and Cohesion', 17(5) *European Journal of International Law* (2006), 881–919, Ronen, Y., 'Incitement to Terrorist Acts Under International Law', 23(3) *Leiden Journal of International Law* (2010), and Amnesty International Report, *Security and Human Rights Counter-Terrorism and the United Nations* (3 September 2008).

[99] United Nations Security Council Resolution 1624, n. 98 above.

[100] Ibid. 'Condemning also in the strongest terms the incitement of terrorist acts and repudiating attempts at the justification or glorification (apologie) of terrorist acts that may incite further terrorist acts . . .' Under Article 25 and Chapter VII of the UN Charter, the United Nations Security Council has the authority to pass resolutions that have binding legal force on UN member states. See, Talmon, S., 'The Security Council as World Legislature', 99 *The American Journal of International Law,* (2005) 175. See also ICCPR, Article 46 of the ICCPR, which gives the provisions of the UN Charter priority over the Covenant.

for the right to freedom of expression and other international human rights is also widely noted in United Nations guidance.[101] Resolution 1624 itself states that implementing measures must be in accordance with the obligations of states under international law. But what these assurances precisely mean for domestic measures prohibiting incitement to terrorist activities is open to argument as every state enjoys a margin of discretion to implement the Resolution in a manner appropriate to local circumstances. For campaigning organizations, the principle declared by the United States Supreme Court in *Brandenburg v. Ohio* is the gold standard.[102] It is moreover a recurring inspiration in international human rights debates. In their annual joint declaration of 2008, the UN Special Rapporteur on Freedom of Opinion and Expression and regional rapporteurs were clearly influenced by this standard when they declared that,

[t]he criminalisation of speech relating to terrorism should be restricted to instances of intentional incitement to terrorism, understood as a direct call to engage in terrorism which is directly responsible for increasing the likelihood of a terrorist act occurring, or to actual participation in terrorist acts (for example by directing them). Vague notions such as providing communications support to terrorism or extremism, the 'glorification' or 'promotion' of terrorism or extremism, and the mere repetition of statements by terrorists, which does not itself constitute incitement, should not be criminalised.[103]

This position is plainly at odds with the position adopted in European Union law, whose formal response to Resolution 1624 in the 2008 revisions to the Framework Decision on Combating Terrorism contains precisely these types of broadly stated provisions.[104]

---

[101] See United Nations Global Counter-Terrorism Strategy, (United Nations General Assembly Resolution A/RES/60/288) (8 September 2006), which states that 'States must ensure that any measures taken to combat terrorism comply with their obligations under international law, in particular human rights law, refugee law and international humanitarian law'. See also General Assembly Resolution A/RES/60/158 (16 December 2005) on the protection of human rights and fundamental freedoms while countering terrorism, and Secretary-General of the United Nations Report, *Uniting against terrorism: recommendations for a global counter-terrorism strategy* (27 April 2006).

[102] *Brandenburg v. Ohio*, n. 10 above. See also Johannesburg Principles on National Security, Freedom of Expression and Access to Information, n. 97 above, Principle 6, which asserts that the *Brandenburg v. Ohio* standard is also the applicable standard in international law.

[103] See *Joint Declaration on Defamation of Religions, and Anti-Terrorism and Anti-Extremism Legislation* 2008 of the UN Special Rapporteur on Freedom of Opinion and Expression, the OSCE Representative on Freedom of the Media, the OAS Special Rapporteur on Freedom of Expression and the ACHPR (African Commission on Human and Peoples' Rights) Special Rapporteur on Freedom of Expression and Access to Information, (9 December 2008). See also *Joint Declaration on International Mechanisms for Promoting Freedom of Expression* 2005 by the UN Special Rapporteur on Freedom of Opinion and Expression, the OSCE Representative on Freedom of the Media and the OAS Special Rapporteur on Freedom of Expression (21 December 2005).

[104] Framework Decision on Combating Terrorism 2002/475/JHA, n. 29 above.

9

Access to State Information

The freedom to express public criticism of the institutions and agents of the state is perhaps the most defining element in the relationship between the media and the state. Effective scrutiny and criticism of the state depends, however, not only on the nature of any state restrictions on the liberty to publish, but also on the limits on access to information held or controlled by the state. The celebrated liberal democratic right to subject the state to robust scrutiny and comment can therefore easily be ineffectual or misdirected if those seeking to exercise the right have no access to critically important facts held by the state. Yet, while constitutional rights to criticize the state arose at the birth of liberal democracy, rights of access to state information were absent in many liberal democratic states until recent decades.[1]

Resistance to the development of a right of access to state information, often known as the right to freedom of information, has stemmed from various concerns about the need to protect information necessary to the security of the state, the maintenance of public order, and the effectiveness of state administration more generally as well as the inevitable desire to retain the power that comes from the control of knowledge. Indeed, for centuries, governments have been developing ever more complex information classification and control systems and creating legal duties of secrecy and confidentiality for servants of the state and the public to prevent the disclosure of information. In the face of these arguments and defences, the liberal democratic right to freedom of expression has historically been a conceptually weak device when used to force the disclosure of state information. Its origins as a negative right made it often very effective when used to counter state restrictions on the liberty to speak or publish, but courts have been reluctant to use this fundamental right to create positive rights of access to state held information.[2] This would have involved them in a host of consequent decisions about the necessity of disclosing or protecting allegedly sensitive information.

Courts have consequently tended to follow in the wake of legislative and administrative changes in this field brought about by economic and political

---

[1] Mendel, T., *Freedom of Information: A Comparative Legal Survey*, (UNESCO, 2008). See also Vleugels, R., *Overview of all 86 FOIA Countries*, Statewatch, (22 September 2008), and Banisar, D., *Freedom of Information: International Trends and National Security*, paper presented at the Democratic and Parliamentary Oversight of Intelligence Services Workshop (Geneva Centre for the Democratic Control of Armed Forces, October 2002).

[2] In the United States, there is for example no constitutional First Amendment right of access to government information: Bollinger, L. and Stone, G., *Eternally Vigilant: Free Speech in the Modern Era* (University of Chicago Press, 2002), 17–18.

pressures for greater transparency in the operation of the state. With the rise of the regulatory state and resulting increases in the range and quantity of government held information, the commercial value of access to that information rose as well. At the same time, access to the burgeoning information resources of the state became increasingly important to informed participation in democratic self government.[3] The media, whose need for access to information is relentless, seized on these and other arguments to join in campaigns for freedom of information rights.

As the balance has shifted in much of the liberal democratic world towards legal rights of freedom of information, the arguments for greater transparency and openness have also shifted to the details of access, turning on technical questions about definitions, presumptions, and discretions. The rules for each freedom of information regime must determine who is entitled to apply for access; what information is subject to any rights of access and in what form; what exceptions may be used to deny access; and, whether denials of access are subject to third party review. If the entitlement to apply is narrowly limited to those directly affected, the media may well be virtually barred from access. Where rights of access are limited to formal, named documents, then a substantial body of state held information will be kept outside the freedom of information regime. The digitization of information has moreover not only vastly increased the capacity of the state to gather and store information, but has also created new ways of holding and processing data that are unrelated to the older concept of the administrative document, which has been the cornerstone of many freedom of information regimes. Rules of access to government information must therefore continually evolve with changes in technologies and administrative practices to maintain standards of access. In that process, however, the changing confidentiality needs and responsibilities of the state also have their impact. The growth in state information processing has brought, for example, greater demands for the protection of personal privacy and commercial confidentiality. Cross border terrorism and other criminal activities have also vastly increased the exchange of security sensitive information between governments and consequent mutual data protection arrangements. In these sensitive areas, governments have insisted on limited external scrutiny and wide margins of discretion in the release of information.

In recent decades, commercial and political demands for access to state information have often been voiced in the language of good governance, which includes the ideals of transparency and accountability in public institutions. The public policy language of good governance has not only enhanced the legitimacy of demands for freedom of information rights, but has also put unauthorized disclosures of state information in a new light. States have traditionally used an array of legal duties to maintain the secrecy of state information, often imposing these on state employees and third parties alike, effectively gagging media publication through sudden injunctions and fear of sanctions. There is plainly no clash in principle between such measures and liberal democratic values, which recognize the state's legitimate

---

[3] On government responses to demands for access to government held data, see Rogers, S., 'Official government data sites around the world', *The Guardian* (26 May 2010).

Restricting the Liberty to Publish

need to enforce secrecy and confidentiality, albeit through proportionate obligations and sanctions. The problem has always been how to devise legal rules to govern the unauthorized disclosure of corruption and other wrongdoing within state institutions. This is acutely important in the security and public order aspects of government policy making and administration that are usually shielded from freedom of information access rules. While liberal political theory, which views the state with varying degrees of suspicion or hostility, provides powerful arguments for the public disclosure of wrongdoing, a workable public interest defence for disclosures that breach secrecy and confidentiality law must balance those objectives with the legitimate needs of the liberal democratic state. Whistleblower laws and similar public interest defences for unauthorized disclosure are therefore only applicable where gravity of the wrongdoing and the surrounding circumstances warrant revelation to the public.[4]

For the media, the unauthorized publication of state information creates the twofold problem of potential complicity in an unlawful act and probable demands for the revelation of the identity of the source of the information. Both issues are open to persuasive democratic arguments in favour of the liberty to publish. First, where disclosure of information is in the public interest, it is arguably a disproportionate fetter on freedom of expression for the state to impose liability on anyone who publishes leaked state information in those circumstances. Criminal culpability or civil liability for third parties should, on that basis, be limited in general terms and also open to public interest defences.[5] Secondly, it is arguably an even greater fetter on free speech if the media are subject to the normal rules of law regarding the disclosure of evidence relevant to to criminal or civil wrongdoing. The concern here is that forced disclosure of journalists' sources will chill the flow of information to the media and thereby diminish the quality of public discourse, undermining participation in democratic self government. On this argument, there is an important public interest in the protection of sources, which should be embodied in an overarching principle of law that journalists cannot be compelled to reveal sources, except in narrowly defined circumstances.[6] The well recognized difficulty here is that it is also in the public interest for all individuals, who possess information of wrongdoing, to disclose that information when required to do so.[7] Where the law does provide a shield against lawful demands for the disclosure of sources, the breadth of that defence will depend on the strength of the overarching presumption, which will determine whether the shield covers the disclosure of documents, electronic data, and other source material, whether it applies regardless of an express promise of confidentiality and other key questions. Yet here, as well, the communications revolution is forcing a redefinition in terms as the concept of the journalist

---

[4] See, for example, United Kingdom, Public Interest Disclosure Act 1998.

[5] See, for example, the reasoning of the United States Supreme Court in the Pentagon Papers case, *New York Times Co. v. United States* (403 U.S. 713). See also *Bartnicki v. Vopper*, 532 U.S. 514 (2001), and see Stone, G., 'Free Speech and National Security', 84 *Indiana Law Journal* (2009), 939.

[6] See, for example, United Kingdom, Contempt of Court Act, s. 10. See also New York State, Civil Rights Law, Article 7, Section 79-h.

[7] *Branzburg v. Hayes*, 408 U.S. 665 (1972).

has dissolved into a wider range of individuals who comment on public affairs or make information available to the public.

Access to state information in the European Union

The European Union principles of free movement, when first set out in the 1957 Treaty of Rome, were primarily concerned with the removal of legal and other restraints on basic economic relations within the EEC and raised few positive obligations for member states. Even as those positive obligations have grown, the major EU treaties have never been amended to incorporate a general right of access to information held by public bodies in the member states. Nonetheless, several primary EU obligations compel greater disclosure of state information. EU transparency requirements concerning national laws, regulations, and administrative measures are, for example, a major element in the achievement of a more effective European Single Market. These include the obligation to notify the Commission of new technical standards or regulations.[8] Furthermore, when a member state does make information available that affects the European Single Market, the manner of that disclosure to companies or consumers is conditioned by European Union law, in particular by the principle of non-discrimination.

In theory, the rules of free movement have a direct role to play where the production or distribution of media content is prohibited on the grounds that it involves the unauthorized disclosure of state information. If a prohibition of this kind seriously impedes trade in media goods or services in the European single market, it will in principle breach free movement obligations, unless saved by an express or implied exception. That proviso is however not a difficult hurdle to cross for restrictions on the publication of classified government information, which are typically non-discriminatory and therefore fall under the less stringent terms of the mandatory public policy exceptions to the free movement obligations.[9] Prohibiting the disclosure of confidential state information is clearly a rational means of safeguarding national security and public order, which are essential functions of the state well recognized in EU law. Indeed, European Union law recognizes the necessary autonomy of member states in carrying out these public policy objectives.[10] Where prohibitions on the disclosure of state information are intended to protect personal data of third parties, the member state concerned may also invoke the European fundamental right to respect for private life.[11] EU secondary

---

[8] Directive 98/34/EC of the European Parliament and of the Council of 22 June 1998 laying down a procedure for the provision of information in the field of technical standards and regulations.

[9] On overriding or mandatory public policy exceptions, see Chapter 4.

[10] Barnard, C., *The Substantive Law of the EU: The Four Freedoms* (Oxford University Press, 2010), 165.

[11] See Charter of Fundamental Rights of the European Union, Article 7. Everyone has the right to respect for his or her private and family life, home and communications. See also Regulation 1049/2001 of the European Parliament and of the Council of 30 May 2001 regarding public access to European Parliament, Council and Commission documents (Transparency Regulation), Article 4(1).

legislation on media services has also had little impact in this area. Restrictions on the unauthorized publication of state information do not fall within a field coordinated by the Audiovisual Media Services Directive, which is therefore inapplicable. The Electronic Commerce Directive has a much broader application to national measures affecting content supplied by an information society service, which will include restrictions of this kind. Its primary obligation to permit free movement on a country of origin basis is nonetheless subject to detailed exceptions modelled on those available in EU law generally and therefore lead to the same conclusions. On this basis, measures taken to prevent or sanction the leaking of classified government information on internet websites are permissible under the Directive provided they satisfy the requirements of proportionality. The Electronic Commerce Directive's provisions on the liability of internet intermediaries will however conditionally protect information society services that host third party content, including unlawfully disclosed information.[12]

Plainly, the fundamental right to freedom of expression must also be taken into account when assessing the proportionality of the restrictive classification of state information and legal rules that prevent its disclosure.[13] At present, the ECHR Article 10(1) argument for greater liberty to publish largely duplicates the economic one contained in the free movement obligations of the member states. Article 10(2) moreover permits restrictions on expression for the same public policy aims that are permitted under the rules of free movement and imposes broadly equivalent conditions. Nonetheless, recent decisions of the European Court of Human Rights have cautiously recognized a positive right to state information under Article 10.[14] This has created an opening for changes in European Union law, as the European Court of Justice begins to apply the European Charter of Fundamental Rights, incorporating and directly applying the case law of the ECHR.[15]

In European Union law there are however at present only secondary rights of access created under subordinate European Union legislation. These include the Directive on Public Access to Environmental Information, which was adopted in 2003 as a consequence of the EU's accession to the Aarhus Convention.[16] Article 3 of this Directive requires that public authorities in the member states are under an

---

[12] Directive 2000/31/EC of the European Parliament and of the Council of 8 June 2000 on certain legal aspects of information society services, in particular electronic commerce, in the Internal Market (Electronic Commerce Directive), Articles 12–15. See also Chapter 4.

[13] Case C-260/89, *Elliniki Radiophonia Tiléorassi AE v. Dimotiki Etairia Pliroforissis and others* [1991] ECR I-2925, para. 43.

[14] See discussion of *Sdružení Jihočeské Matky v. Czech Republic* (Application No. 19101/03), (10 July 2006) and subsequent cases, below.

[15] See Chapter 4.

[16] Directive 2003/4/EC of the European Parliament and of the Council of 28 January 2003 on public access to environmental information; Convention on Access to Information, Public Participation in Decision-making and Access to Justice in Environmental Matters, done at Aarhus, Denmark, on 25 June 1998, sponsored by the United Nations Economic Commission for Europe (UNECE or ECE). See also Directive 2003/35/EC of the European Parliament and of the Council of 26 May 2003 providing for public participation in respect of the drawing up of certain plans and programmes relating to the environment and amending with regard to public participation and access to justice, Council Directives 85/337/EEC and 96/61/EC.

obligation to make environmental information held by or for them available to any applicant on request and without statement of an interest. Other provisions require that environmental information is made widely available to the public regardless of whether a specific request for access is made.[17] In the same year, the European Union adopted the Public Sector Information Directive, which is intended to increase the re-use of public sector information for commercial and non-commercial purposes.[18] Unsurprisingly, a Commission consultation on the Directive in 2008 found that, '[d]iverging views exist between public sector bodies (the supply side) and re-users (the demand side) on the current PSI re-use environment. While the former group considers it to be satisfactory and working well, re-users are more critical and feel that implementation of the Directive has been much too slow.'[19] The Commission Review of the Directive, published in 2009 emphasizes the need for member states to terminate exclusive information re-uses arrangements and ensure fair competition between public sector bodies and re-users.[20]

The European Union has also responded, sometimes very reluctantly, to demands for greater openness and accountability in EU institutions as part of efforts to address the democratic deficit in European regional policy making and public administration.[21] The basic right of European Union citizens and residents of access to documents held by European Union institutions, bodies, offices, and agencies, whatever their medium, is now entrenched in Article 15 of the TFEU.[22] The language of this treaty right is also more expansive than Article 255 of the EC Treaty, which it replaces.[23] That narrower language was however also included in Article 42 of the EU Charter of Fundamental Rights, which states that '[a]ny citizen of the Union, and any natural or legal person residing or having its registered office in a Member State, has a right of access to European Parliament, Council and Commission's documents'. The wider scope of TFEU Article 15 therefore supersedes the earlier language of the Charter where they both apply. This right of access is mainly implemented through the EU Transparency Regulation and associated

---

[17] Directive 2003/4/EC, n. 16 above, Article 7: Dissemination of environmental information.

[18] Directive 2003/98/EC of the European Parliament and of the Council of 17 November 2003 on the Re-Use of Public Sector Information.

[19] Commission Staff Working Document accompanying the Communication from the Commission to the European Parliament, the Council, the European Economic and Social Committee and the Committee of the Regions on the re-use of Public Sector Information—Review of Directive 2003/98/EC—[COM (2009) 212 final], 16.

[20] Communication from the Commission to the European Parliament, the Council, the European Economic and Social Committee and the Committee of the Regions—Re-use of Public Sector Information: review of Directive 2003/98/EC—[SEC (2009) 597], Conclusions.

[21] On the recognition of the importance of openness for relations between the Union and its citizens, see in 1993 Declaration 17, attached to the Maastricht Treaty (Treaty on European Union, 1992). See also Code of Conduct concerning public access to Council and Commission documents 93/730/EC, OJ [1993] L340/41.

[22] Treaty on the Functioning of the European Union, Article 15(3): 'Any citizen of the Union, and any natural or legal person residing or having its registered office in a Member State, shall have a right of access to documents of the Union institutions, bodies, offices and agencies, whatever their medium, subject to the principles and the conditions to be defined in accordance with this paragraph.'

[23] Article 255 of the Treaty establishing the European Community introduced under the 1996 Treaty of Amsterdam.

Council, Commission, and Parliament Decisions.[24] The European Union's own Aarhus Convention obligations overlap with these, but in the field of environmental information also require the active collection and dissemination of information and public consultation on plans and programmes relating to the environment.[25] Inevitably, the Transparency Regulation has failed to please advocates of government openness while also worrying EU and member state officials that effective government will be compromised.[26]

Under the Transparency Regulation, citizens of the Union, as well as natural or legal persons residing or having a registered office in a member state, have a right of access to documents held by EU institutions.[27] In principle, information not held in an identifiable document is therefore not subject to that basic right of access. The 'document' provision has consequently always carried the risk that critical information will be recorded in ways that fall outside this category. In its *WWF-EPO v. Council of the European Union* decision, for example, the EU General Court held that there is no obligation under the Regulation to produce minutes for a meeting if formal minutes were not produced at the time, regardless of whether notes of some kind were recorded.[28] The risk that important information is not retained in a formal document has increased as digitization has not only changed information storage and retrieval methods, but has also failed to provide a generic concept to replace the document.[29] This focus on formal documents is moreover much more than a question of which information is shielded from disclosure. It also helps to determine who controls the process of disclosure. If the right of access were to extend to 'relevant information', for example, this would open government held information to extensive information trawling by the media, commercial companies, social organizations, and individuals. Whatever the benefits of that expansion in transparency of public institutions, it would also become more difficult to manage the disclosure process and guard essential confidentiality. On the other hand, retaining the concept of the document means that access decisions are narrowly focused on the security, privacy, and other implications of disclosing a

---

[24] Regulation 1049/2001 (Transparency Regulation), n. 11 above. See also Council Decision 93/731 on public access to Council documents, OJ [1993] L340/43, Commission Decision No. 94/90 on public access to Commission documents OJ [1994] L46/58 and Parliament Decision No. 97/632 on public access to parliament documents OJ [1997] L263/27 (as amended). For a history of the Transparency Regulation, see Bunyan, T., *Secrecy and openness in the European Union—the ongoing struggle for freedom of information*, Statewatch (2002).

[25] These were implemented through a European Union regulation in 2006: Regulation 1367/2006 of the European Parliament and of the Council of 6 September 2006 on the application of the provisions of the Aarhus Convention on Access to Information, Public Participation in Decision-making and Access to Justice in Environmental Matters to Community institutions and bodies.

[26] Dunin-Wasowicz, J., 'The Transparency Regulation in Context: A Proxy for Legitimacy or an Instrument of Regulatory Practice?' 16(3) *Columbia Journal of European Law* (2010), 497–520.

[27] Regulation 1049/2001, n. 11 above, Article 2(1).

[28] Case T-264/04, *WWF-EPO v. Council of the European Union*, Court of First Instance (25 April 2007). See also de Abreu Ferreira, S., 'The Fundamental Right of Access to Environmental Information in the EC: A Critical Analysis of WWF-EPO v. Council', 19(3) *Journal of Environmental Law* (2007), 1–10.

[29] Bunyan, T., *FOI in the EU: When is a 'Document' not a 'Document'?* Statewatch, <http://www.statewatch.org>.

discrete piece of information, which leaves a very wide margin of discretion in the hands of public authorities. In the current amendment process for the Transparency Regulation, the Council and Commission have resisted the European Parliament's efforts to discard the 'document' concept.[30]

Standards of transparency also tend to follow major changes in public policy. In the European Union, the rise of anti-terrorism and personal privacy concerns have put pressure on the right of access to state held information. In principle, the Transparency Regulation right of access applies to documents relating to security matters.[31] However, under Article 4(1)(a), European Union institutions must refuse access to a document where disclosure would undermine the protection of the public interest as regards 'public security', 'defence and military matters', 'international relations', and 'financial, monetary or economic policy'. This provision cannot be blocked on the grounds that there is 'an overriding public interest in disclosure' of the information at issue, which is the case with all other Article 4 permitted reasons for an exceptional denial of access.[32] Without this proviso, it is extremely difficult to challenge the decision of an EU institution to refuse disclosure under Article 4(1)(a).[33] In fact, the European Court of Justice has held that EU institutions enjoy a broad discretion under this sub-paragraph to determine whether disclosure of documents could undermine the public interest.[34]

The security provisions of the Transparency Regulation are also grounded in western European defence and intelligence arrangements that have governed inter-governmental information sharing since the early Cold War.[35] Although buttressed by networks of bilateral agreements between the western democracies, these arrangements

---

[30] European Parliament, P6_TA-PROV(2009)0114, *Public access to European Parliament, Council and Commission documents*. See also *Public access to European Parliament, Council and Commission documents* COM (2008)229 final, Proposal for a Regulation of the European Parliament and of the Council regarding public access to European Parliament, Council and Commission documents, and, Kierkegaard, S., 'Open access to public documents—More secrecy, less transparency!', 25(1) *Computer Law & Security Report* (2009), 3.

[31] Regulation 1049/2001, n. 11 above, Recital (7) '. . . the right of access also applies to documents relating to the common foreign and security policy and to police and judicial cooperation in criminal matters. Each institution should respect its security rules.'

[32] Ibid., Article 4(2).

[33] See, for example, the decision of the ECJ in Case C-39/05 and C-52/05, *Sweden and Turco v. Council and others* [2008] ECR I-4723, 392–3 in which the proviso was applicable under Article 4(2). In this case, which concerned the denial of access to opinions of the Council's legal service, the Court held that this Article does not permit a blanket refusal to disclose as 'an overriding public interest is constituted by the fact that disclosure of documents containing the advice of an institution's legal service on legal questions arising when legislative initiatives are being debated increases the transparency and openness of the legislative process and strengthens the democratic right of European citizens to scrutinize the information which has formed the basis of a legislative act'.

[34] Case C-266/05, *Sison v. Council* [2007] ECR I-1233, 390.

[35] See Lodge, J., 'Transparency and EU Governance: Balancing Openness with Security', 11(1) *Journal of European Area Studies* (2003), 95–117 (23). See also Roberts, A., 'NATO, Secrecy, and the Right to Information', *East European Constitutional Review* (Fall 2002/Winter 2003). On greater international cooperation and intelligence data exchanges following September 2001, Roberts, A., *Blacked Out: Government Secrecy in the Information Age* (Cambridge University Press, 2006), 132–146, and Banisar, D., n. 1 above.

are underpinned by the NATO Security of Information Agreement.[36] Under its terms, NATO member states must maintain a common classification system and institute a system of 'originator control', which ensures that the classification of information may not be reduced or removed without the consent of the originating government.[37] Distribution of information outside NATO is subject to a similar prohibition. In 1998, the European Union became a formal party to this security of information system.[38] Aside from the robust security and defence exceptions of Article 4 of the Transparency Regulation, the EU's security of information obligations in relation to NATO are also reflected in Article 9, which concerns the treatment of sensitive documents.[39] This article prohibits the registration or release of sensitive documents without the consent of the originating authority.[40] This obligation of secrecy includes the existence of the document and the identity of the originating authority.[41]

The Lisbon Treaty has however opened a small chink in this tightly woven net of agreements. Now that the EU Charter of Fundamental Rights is legally binding on most members states, it will provide a basis to challenge exceptions to the Transparency Regulation that potentially breach the Charter's freedom of expression obligations. The safeguarding of national security and public order are critically important issues for democratic self government and ought therefore to be open to the greatest possible public scrutiny that does not harm essential public interests. These arguments, when made in light of the nascent right of access to state information under Article 10 of the ECHR, could force changes in the Transparency Regulation. Yet, national security and public order will always remain areas where courts are cautious in demanding openness or external accountability that hobbles the state, whose effectiveness is a prerequisite for a secure democratic society. Supranational courts, aware of their distance from the local context, will be doubly mindful of this difficult balance.

---

[36] Reichard, M., *The EU-NATO Relationship: a legal and political perspective* (Ashgate, 2006), 312.

[37] *Security within the North Atlantic Treaty Organization*, C-M (55) 15 (final).

[38] *Agreement between the Parties to the North Atlantic Treaty for the Security of Information*, (Brussels, 6 March 1997) (in force 16 August 1998), OJ L80, 27 March 2003.

[39] Regulation 1049/2001, n. 11 above, Article 9(1). Sensitive documents are documents originating from the institutions or the agencies established by them, from Member States, third countries or International Organisations, classified as 'Très Secret/Top Secret', 'Secret' Or 'Confidentiel' in accordance with the rules of the institution concerned, which protect essential interests of the European Union or of one or more of its Member States in the areas covered by Article 4(1)(a), notably public security, defence, and military matters.

[40] See also Regulation 1049/2001, n. 11 above, Article 4(5). A Member State may request the institution not to disclose a document originating from that Member State without its prior agreement. See also European Commission, Proposal for a Regulation of the European Parliament and of the Council regarding public access to European Parliament, Council and Commission documents COM (2008) 229 final (30 April 2008), which includes modifications to Article 4(5) introduce a modest check on the member state veto, providing for an obligation to give reasons for a refusal to disclose and a power to review the adequacy of those reasons.

[41] Case C-266/05, n. 34 above, para. 101.

Access to state information in the Council of Europe

The importance of public access to information held or controlled by the state for European liberal democracy is a well recognized theme in the work of the Council of Europe. As the Committee of Ministers stated in 2002, the 'transparency of public administration and of the ready availability of information on issues of public interest' is essential to 'pluralistic, democratic society'.[42] Yet despite this consensus on transparency and openness, the European Court of Human Rights has found it immensely difficult to give force to that idea in the form of a clear principle of law under the Convention on Human Rights. While the text of Article 10 only includes an express right to receive information 'without interference by public authority', the Court's case law on freedom of expression as a tool of democratic self government readily supports a positive right of access to state information where that information is directly relevant to a matter of general concern. It is however only recently that it has moved cautiously in that direction. In 1979, the Court declared in *Leander v. Sweden* that, 'Article 10 does not . . . confer on an individual a right of access to a register containing information on his personal position, nor does it embody and obligation on the Government to impart such information to the individual', and that, 'the right to freedom to receive information basically prohibits a Government from restricting a person from receiving information that others wish or may be willing to impart to him'.[43]

There are abundant good reasons for a supranational human rights court to be cautious in developing a positive right of access. The court's legal analysis is necessarily bound to the concept of fundamental rights, which has proved exceptionally useful in curbing excessive or arbitrary uses of state power, but is less suited to the creation of regulatory regimes. The obvious danger for the Court, in creating a positive right of access to state information under Article 10, is that it will be drawn into the task of setting minimum standards for complex freedom of information regulatory regimes. That task is beyond the capabilities of many domestic courts and is certainly an immense one for the European Court of Human Rights, given its limited supervisory jurisdiction over dozens of countries with very different systems of public administration. The evidentiary problems alone are daunting. Where member states have refused access to information on grounds of national security or public safety, the Court is unlikely to have sufficient access to the information to determine the balance between the democratic interest in disclosure and the legitimate state interest in secrecy, except as a matter of general principle. This is inevitably a sphere in which the Court is under great pressure to give due regard to the core interests of the state parties.

---

[42] Council of Europe, Committee of Ministers, Recommendation on access to official documents, Rec (2002) 2.

[43] *Leander v. Sweden* (Application No. 9248/81) (26 March 1987), para. 74. In 2003 the Court reiterated that, 'it is difficult to derive from the Convention a general right of access to administrative data and documents'.

Since its decision in *Leander*, the Court has nonetheless picked its way carefully towards a right of access. Its development of positive rights under Article 8 have led it inexorably into the problems of access to information. In its 1979 decision in *Gaskin v. United Kingdom*, the Court held that the applicant had an Article 8 based right to government held information about his adoption, while also deciding that there had been no interference with his Article 10 right to receive information.[44] Since the fall of the Soviet Communist state, the Council of Europe's championing of freedom of expression in the new eastern European democracies and the growing importance of transparency and public accountability in European principles of good governance have put pressure on the Court to recognize a right of access to state information under Article 10.[45] The change of direction came in the 2006 *Sdruženi Jihočeské Matky v. Czech Republic* case in which it recognized that, in principle, a denial of access to information by the state could result in a breach of Article 10.[46] Three years later, the Court found a breach of Article 10 where government authorities had refused to disclose the information, despite a domestic court order to do so in its decision in *Kenedi v. Hungary*, declaring that 'access to original documentary sources for legitimate historical research was an essential element of the exercise of the applicant's right to freedom of expression'.[47] Nonetheless, the Court is sure to continue to tread carefully, using case decisions to build the general principle of access to state information while leaving state parties a wide margin of discretion in setting access criteria and procedures.

The Council of Europe Convention on Access to Official Documents

In contrast to the cautious journey of the European Court of Human Rights, the Council of Europe Committee of Ministers has repeatedly encouraged member states over the past three decades to establish domestic freedom of information regimes.[48] As the Committee declared in 1982, member states should pursue 'an

---

[44] *Gaskin v. United Kingdom* (Application No. 10454/83) (7 July 1989). See also *Guerra v. Italy* (Application No. 14967/89) (19 February 1998), in which the Court found Italy in breach of Article 8 for failure to provide a legal means for residents of a town to force the disclosure of information held by a local manufacturer regarding potentially harmful emissions.

[45] See Curtin, D. and Dekker, I., 'Openness and Participation' in Curtin, D. and Wessel, R. (eds), *Good Governance and the European Union* (Intersentia, 2005). See also European Commission, *European Governance: A White Paper*, COM (2001) 428 final (25 July 2001).

[46] *Sdruženi Jihočeské Matky v. Czech Republic* (Application No. 19101/03) (10 July 2006). In this case, the Court indicated that a positive right of access to government information may exist in some circumstances, although not in this case. In its 2009 decision in *Tarsasag a Szabadsagjogokert v. Hungary* (Application No. 37374/05) (14 April 2009) the Court declared that it had 'recently advanced towards a broader interpretation of the notion of "freedom to receive information" and thereby towards the recognition of a right of access to information', para. 35. See also Hins, W. and Voorhoof, D., 'Access to State-Held Information as a Fundamental Right under the European Convention on Human Rights', 3 *European Constitutional Law Review* (2007), 114–126.

[47] *Kenedi v. Hungary* (Application No. 31475/05) (26 May 2009), para. 43.

[48] Council of Europe, Committee of Ministers, Recommendation on the access to information held by public authorities Rec (81) 19, Committee of Ministers, Declaration on the freedom of expression and information (29 April 1982), Committee of Ministers, Recommendation on the communication to third parties of personal data held by public bodies, Rec (91) 10, Committee of Minsters,

open information policy in the public sector, including access to information, in order to enhance the individual's understanding of, and his ability to discuss freely political, social, economic and cultural matters'.[49] In 2008, these efforts culminated in the Council of Europe Convention on Access to Official Documents.[50] The Convention was the first legally binding international instrument to create a general right of access to official documents held by public authorities. It nonetheless also follows the Council of Europe's *à la carte* model of treaty drafting, offering state parties a set of flexible provisions and optional extensions.[51] It is also a work of considerable compromise. The Convention sets out a fundamental obligation for state parties to grant access to official documents that is in turn offset by a series of exceptions and limitations.[52] It also sets out a wide definition for 'official documents', which means that the right of access applies to 'all information recorded in any form, drawn up or received and held by public authorities'.[53] The treaty attempts to balance these elements, which represent the democratic public interest in disclosure of state information, with the core needs of the state through an extensive power to limit the general right of access. The legitimate grounds for limiting access include 'national security, defence and international relations; public safety; and, the prevention, investigation and prosecution of criminal

Recommendation concerning the protection of personal data collected and processed for statistical purposes, Rec (97) 18, Committee of Ministers, Recommendation on a European policy on access to archives, Rec (2000) 13, and Committee of Ministers, Recommendation on access to official documents, Rec (2002) 2.

[49] See, for example, Council of Europe, Committee of Ministers, Declaration on the freedom of expression and information (29 April 1982), Part II c. See also Council of Europe, Committee of Ministers, Recommendation on access to official documents, Rec (2002) 2, which states that '[c]onsidering that wide access to official documents, on a basis of equality and in accordance with clear rules:—allows the public to have an adequate view of, and to form a critical opinion on, the state of the society in which they live and on the authorities that govern them, whilst encouraging informed participation by the public in matters of common interest; fosters the efficiency and effectiveness of administrations and helps maintain their integrity by avoiding the risk of corruption;—contributes to affirming the legitimacy of administrations as public services and to strengthening the public's confidence in public authorities'.

[50] Council of Europe, Convention on Access to Official Documents (ETS No. 205) (27 November 2008). See also the critical opinion of the Parliamentary Assembly, which sought a partial re-draft of the treaty, Council of Europe, Parliamentary Assembly, *Draft Council of Europe convention on access to official documents*, Opinion No. 270 (2008).

[51] See, for example, Council of Europe, Convention on Access to Official Documents, n. 50 above, Article 1(2)(a)(ii), which states that the right of access applies to all bodies performing administrative functions, but also permits states to optionally extend the right to legislative and judicial bodies as well as private bodies performing public functions.

[52] Ibid., Article 2(1): 'Each Party shall guarantee the right of everyone, without discrimination on any ground, to have access, on request, to official documents held by public authorities.'

[53] Ibid., Article 1.2(b). See also the Explanatory Report to the Council of Europe Convention on Access to Official Documents, para. 11: 'any information drafted or received and held by public authorities that is recorded on any sort of physical medium whatever be its form or format (written texts, information recorded on a sound or audiovisual tape, photographs, e-mails, information stored in electronic format such as electronic databases, etc.)'. The Convention nonetheless leaves the state parties to decide what information constitutes an official document when information is contained in a database (Explanatory Report, para 12).

activities' as well as 'privacy and other legitimate private interests'.[54] State parties also enjoy a broad, but also conditional, discretion in deciding how these limitations should be exercised, whether through individual case decisions or through the governing rules.[55] As the Explanatory Report to the Convention states, 'The notion of national security should be used with restraint. It should not be misused in order to protect information that might reveal the breach of human rights, corruption within public authorities, administrative errors, or information which is simply embarrassing for public officials or public authorities.'[56] In this way, having cut large exceptions out of the right of access, the Convention attempts to contain resort by state parties to national security and other grounds through proportionality principles and interpretative restrictions.

The Convention's conditions and hortatory strictures are very much in line with other Council of Europe's guidance addressing the acute tension between the need for openness in a democratic society and the necessary preservation of state security and public order. The Committee of Ministers has, for example, emphasized the positive duty of member states to protect and assist journalists when they are reporting conflicts or other events connected to national security and public safety.[57] It has also urged CE member states to 'guarantee freedom of movement and access to information to media professionals in times of crisis'.[58] In relation to anti-terrorism measures, it has declared that they should, 'ensure access by journalists to information regularly updated, in particular by appointing spokespersons and organising press conferences, in accordance with national legislation'.[59] These specific points of guidance are solidly grounded in the core democratic purposes of Article 10 of the European Convention on Human Rights, but they are also non-legally binding guidance. They are certainly well rooted in the principles of Article 10 developed by the Court, but positive obligations of this kind are far beyond the reach of the ECHR.

---

[54] Convention on Access to Official Documents, Article 3(1). See also Council of Europe, Committee of Ministers, Recommendation on the communication to third parties of personal data held by public bodies, R (91) 10, and, Parliamentary Assembly, Recommendation on data protection and freedom of information, 1037 (1986).

[55] Convention on Access to Official Documents, Article 3(2). See also Article 3.1: 'Each Party may limit the right of access to official documents. Limitations shall be set down precisely in law, be necessary in a democratic society and be proportionate to the aim of protecting.'

[56] Explanatory Report, n. 53 above, para. 23. In addition, the Explanatory Report states at paragraph 38 that '[a]bsolute statutory exceptions should be kept to a minimum'.

[57] Council of Europe, Committee of Ministers, Recommendation on the protection of journalists in situations of conflict and tension, Rec (96) 4. See also Council of Europe, Committee of Ministers, Declaration on the protection and promotion of investigative journalism (26 September 2007), and Council of Europe, Committee of Ministers, Recommendation on the provision of information through the media in relation to criminal proceedings, Rec (2003) 13E.

[58] Council of Europe, Committee of Ministers, Guidelines on protecting freedom of expression and information in times of crisis (26 September 2007), Guideline 8. See also Guideline 11: 'Military and civilian authorities in charge of managing crisis situations should provide regular information to all media professionals covering the events through briefings, press conferences, press tours or other appropriate means', and, Guideline 12: 'The competent authorities in member states should provide information to all media professionals on an equal basis and without discrimination.'

[59] Council of Europe, Committee of Ministers, Declaration on freedom of expression and information in the media in the context of the fight against terrorism (2 March 2005).

Unauthorized disclosure of state information and the protection of journalists' sources

The European Court of Human Rights has underscored the importance of permitting the unauthorized publication of state information in the public interest.

Press freedom assumes even greater importance in circumstances in which State activities and decisions escape democratic or judicial scrutiny on account of their confidential or secret nature. The conviction of a journalist for disclosing information considered to be confidential or secret may discourage those working in the media from informing the public on matters of public interest. As a result the press may no longer be able to play its vital role as 'public watchdog' and the ability of the press to provide accurate and reliable information may be adversely affected.[60]

Yet the Court has sought to balance this application of Article 10(1) with the public interest in maintaining an effective state, which is disaggregated into various legitimate aims set out in Article 10(2). The public interest in disclosure of information concerning matters of general importance may consequently be nullified by this second form of public interest. The resulting opposition of incommensurable public interests can only be resolved by looking to other factors to determine whether a restriction on the unauthorized publication of state information amounts to a breach of Article 10. In this regard, the Court has stated that, 'Article 10 protects the right of journalists to divulge information on issues of public interest provided that they are acting in good faith and on an accurate factual basis and provide "reliable and precise" information in accordance with the ethics of journalism'.[61] Provided the journalists and editors concerned can clear this hurdle, they will in principle be entitled to rely on government documents as a source without further verification of the information contained in them or liability for its disclosure.[62]

The Court's Grand Chamber decision in *Stoll v. Switzerland,* however, demonstrated how very high that hurdle can be where the media publishes sensitive state information that potentially harms an important national interest.[63] In this case, Swiss courts convicted and imposed a fine on the journalist Martin Stoll for publishing a confidential report produced by the Swiss ambassador to the United States regarding the compensation due to Holocaust victims for unclaimed assets deposited in Swiss banks. In its initial decision in Stoll's favour, finding a breach of Switzerland's Article 10 obligations, a Chamber of the European Court of Human Rights declared that, '[i]n the context of a political debate such a sentence would be likely to deter journalists from contributing to public discussion of issues affecting

---

[60] *Stoll v. Switzerland* (Grand Chamber), (Application No. 69698/01) (10 December 2007).
[61] *Goodwin v. United Kingdom* (Application No. 28957/95) (11 July 2002), para. 39.
[62] *Bladet Tromsø and Stensaas v. Norway* (Application No. 21980/93) (20 May 1999), paras 68–71.
[63] *Stoll v. Switzerland*, n. 60 above.

the life of the community and was thus liable to hamper the press in performing its task as purveyor of information and watchdog'.[64] In December 2007, the Grand Chamber overturned that conclusion. In its view, the report undoubtedly concerned matters of public interest and the articles disclosing that information were published in the context of an important public, impassioned debate in Switzerland with an international dimension. Nevertheless, the Court also found that Switzerland had legitimate grounds to convict Stoll as disclosure of the report not only could have harmed its interests in the negotiations with the United States, but also undermined the climate of discretion necessary for the conduct of Switzerland's diplomatic relations.[65] The Grand Chamber, moreover, held that the articles were written in a sensationalist style with inappropriate allegations of anti-Semitism and contained misleading inaccuracies and therefore fell short of the requirements of good faith and the ethics of journalism.[66]

From the Court's perspective, the clash between one public interest in openness in matters of national importance and the other in secrecy in the conduct of negotiations with foreign states needed to be resolved by weighing other relevant factors, in particular the conduct of the journalist. That approach however faces two objections. First, the ethics of journalism are no more than general principles of conduct that the courts are ill equipped to assess in their proper context of news deadlines and other media pressures. Judgments about the professional conduct of journalists and editors are therefore likely to turn on the Court's evaluation of the specific facts of each case, creating decisions that obscure as much as they illuminate the applicable principles of law. In the *Stoll* decision, the Grand Chamber concluded that whether Stoll breached any law in obtaining the diplomatic report was not a determining factor, it was sufficient that he knew that disclosure of the report would be a breach of the Swiss Criminal Code. Yet in other decisions, the European Court of Human Rights has doubted whether the mere fact that the information at issue was unlawfully obtained by a third person can deprive the applicant of the protection of Article 10 of the Convention.[67] In *Guja v. Moldova*, for example, the Grand Chamber held that sanctions imposed on a civil servant, who had disclosed information about official wrongdoing to the media in breach of his duty of confidence, amounted to a violation of Article 10.[68] The court declared that, '[i]n a democratic system the acts or omissions of government must be subject to the close scrutiny not only of the legislative and judicial authorities but also of the media and public opinion. The interest which the public may have in particular information can sometimes be so

---

[64] *Stoll v. Switzerland* (Application No. 69698/01) (25 April 2006) (Chamber decision), para. 58.

[65] *Stoll v. Switzerland*, n. 60 above, para. 136.

[66] Ibid., para. 149.

[67] *Radio Twist S.A. v. Slovakia* (Application No. 62202/00) (19 December 2006). The Court has also determined that, where a journalist receives information from a third party, the lawfulness of that person's conduct does not determine whether the journalist should be compelled to disclose his or her identity: *Tillack v. Belgium* (Application No. 20477/05), (27 November 2007), para. 65. See also *Financial Times and others v. United Kingdom,* (Application No. 821/03) (15 December 2009), para. 63.

[68] *Guja v. Moldova* (Application No. 14277/04) (12 February 2008) (Grand Chamber).

strong as to override even a legally imposed duty of confidence.'[69] This leads to the second and more fundamental objection to the approach of the Court in *Stoll*, which is simply that it is the responsibility of the state, in a liberal democracy, to guard its own secrets. That task should therefore only be extended to the media in exceptional circumstances as their duty is to inform the public about matters of political and social importance.

This instinctively protective view of the state is also apparent in the case law of the European Court of Human Rights concerning the protection of journalists' sources. As a general matter, the Court has determined that state parties to the ECHR are under an obligation, stemming from Article 10, to ensure that journalists are not forced to divulge their sources of information, unless there are compelling reasons to override the public interest in protecting journalists' sources.[70] Yet the Court's decisions on the protection of sources have also created an apparent hierarchy of legitimate interests that weigh differently when balanced against that fundamental public interest in the protection of sources. In several cases involving the breach of commercial rights, the Court has decided that the interest of the party seeking disclosure of the identity of the source was insufficient to outweigh the general interest in non-disclosure.[71] It has however taken a less expansive view of this general interest in cases involving information sought in the course of criminal investigations. As the Court has declared in other circumstances, 'journalists cannot, in principle, be released from their duty to obey the ordinary criminal law on the basis that Article 10 affords them protection'.[72] In criminal cases, it has therefore tended to focus on the proportionality of the methods used by the state to force the disclosure of the journalist's source. If those methods are sufficiently proportionate, the Court is likely to favour disclosure, especially where the criminal matter is serious.[73] Accordingly, the disclosure demanded by

---

[69] Ibid., para. 74.

[70] *Goodwin v. United Kingdom*, n. 61 above, para. 39: '... Protection of journalistic sources is one of the basic conditions for press freedom, as is reflected in the laws and the professional codes of conduct in a number of Contracting States and is affirmed in several international instruments on journalistic freedoms. Without such protection, sources may be deterred from assisting the press in informing the public on matters of public interest. As a result the vital public watchdog role of the press may be undermined and the ability of the press to provide accurate and reliable information may be adversely affected. Having regard to the importance of the protection of journalistic sources for press freedom in a democratic society and the potentially chilling effect an order of source disclosure has on the exercise of that freedom, such a measure cannot be compatible with Article 10 of the Convention unless it is justified by an overriding requirement in the public interest.' Note that the Court and other Council of Europe institutions have restricted the right not to disclose the identity of sources to 'journalists'. This is defined as meaning 'any natural or legal person who is regularly or professionally engaged in the collection and dissemination of information to the public via any means of mass communication' (Council of Europe, Committee of Ministers, Recommendation on the right of journalists not to disclose their sources of information, Rec (2000) 7, Appendix to Recommendation No. R (2000) 7). This somewhat narrow definition is likely to exclude many individuals who carry out journalistic significant functions through internet based new media.

[71] *Goodwin v. United Kingdom*, n. 61 above, *Financial Times and others v. United Kingdom*, n. 67 above.

[72] *Fressoz and Roire v. France* (Application No. 29183/95) (21 January 1999), para. 52.

[73] Nonetheless, even when there is a serious threat to national security or public safety, such as terrorism, the state is not excused from its obligation to respect, so far as possible, the right of

the state should be no more than necessary to achieve the legitimate object and should be sought only when all reasonable alternatives have been exhausted.[74] Consequently, where the objective of disclosure is to uncover the source of allegations regarding malfeasance by the state, the interest in protecting the anonymity of people who wish to share accurate information about wrongdoing with the media is likely to outweigh the state's interest in disclosure.[75]

Access to state information in international law

In international trade law, obligations on states to disclose information, often referred to as transparency disciplines, serve several purposes. They deepen the effectiveness of obligations to remove discriminatory measures affecting trade by forcing governments to disclose information that may reveal discriminatory domestic measures. They also increase the predictability of international commerce more generally by reducing uncertainty about the content of domestic regulatory regimes and the risks of doing business under their rules. In this second aspect, transparency obligations are in effect an important first step towards the removal of non-discriminatory, yet also unnecessary, barriers to trade by bringing them under external scrutiny.

Within the World Trade Organization, the major transparency trade disciplines are contained in the GATT and the GATS,[76] although related transparency provisions occur in its other treaties and secondary instruments.[77] Article X of the GATT requires publication of trade relevant laws, regulations, judicial decisions, and administrative rulings of general application. Article III of the GATS more broadly requires that each member state publish promptly and, except in emergency situations, at the

journalists to protect their sources. See Council of Europe, Committee of Ministers, Declaration on freedom of expression and information in the media n. 59 above, and Council of Europe, Committee of Ministers, Guidelines on protecting freedom of expression and information in times of crisis (26 September 2007), Part III. Protection of journalists' sources of information and journalistic material.

[74] *Sanoma Uitgevers B.V. v. the Netherlands* (Application No. 38224/03) (14 September 2010) (Grand Chamber). See also *Ernst and others v. Belgium* (Application No. 33400/96) (July 2003), *Roemen and Schmit v. Luxembourg* (Application No. 51772/99) (February 2003), and Recommendation on the right of journalists not to disclose their sources of information, Appendix, n. 70 above, Principle 3b.

[75] *Voskuil v. the Netherlands* (Application No. 64752/01) (22 November 2007), para. 71.

[76] Article XX, General Agreement on Tariffs and Trade 1994 (incorporating GATT 1947), (15 April 1994), 33 ILM 1153 (1994), and Article XIV, General Agreement on Trade in Services, (15 April 1994), 33 ILM 1167 (1994). On the general exception provisions of the GATT and the GATS, see Chapter 5.

[77] In addition, to the GATT and GATS rules referred to in the text, the Trade-Related Aspects of Intellectual Property Rights (TRIPS), Agreement on Technical Barriers to Trade (TBT), Agreement on the Application of Sanitary and Phytosanitary Measure (SPS), Agreement on Subsidies and Countervailing Measures (SCM), Agreement on Safeguards, Agreement on Trade-Related Investment Measures (TRIMS), and the Agreement on Implementation of Article VI of the General Agreement on Tariffs and Trade 1994 (Anti-Dumping Agreement) all contain notice or publication provisions requiring disclosure by of laws or administrative rules and measures by member states.

latest by the time of their entry into force, all relevant measures of general application which pertain to or affect the operation of the GATS. The GATS Article VI:4 mandated negotiations on domestic regulation disciplines are also expected to yield a transparency obligation for domestic qualification requirements and procedures, technical standards, and licensing requirements.[78] These GATT and GATS transparency obligations are nonetheless subject to the general and security exceptions contained in both treaties. The latter permit a member state to refuse to disclose any information it controls where it considers disclosure to be contrary to their essential security interests.[79] These security exceptions are also potentially very broad, given their unusually subjective language.[80] They are consequently a potential obstacle for any effort to use WTO transparency or other obligations to gain access to government held information. On the other hand, since the 1999 debacle of the Seattle Ministerial Conference, the WTO has itself adopted several measures to increase its own transparency in ways that assist member states outside the core group of well funded, influential states as well as companies and civil society organizations outside the organization.[81] These measures also reflect changing expectations regarding the nature of global public order and the role of transparency in better global public administration.[82]

Outside the WTO, other international organizations have also sponsored transparency or disclosure initiatives for wide ranging economic purposes. The United Nations Convention Against Corruption, for example, requires that each state party take, 'such measures as may be necessary to enhance transparency in its public administration, including with regard to its organization, functioning and decision making processes, where appropriate'.[83] In contrast, the OECD has, among other things, urged its member states to make state held databases and

---

[78] On the work of the GATS Working Party on Domestic Regulation, see Chapter 5.

[79] GATT Article XXI and GATS Article XIV*bis*.

[80] On WTO security exceptions, see Chapters 5 and 8.

[81] The Doha Ministerial Declaration declared that '[r]ecognizing the challenges posed by an expanding WTO membership, we confirm our collective responsibility to ensure internal transparency and the effective participation of all members. While emphasizing the intergovernmental character of the organization, we are committed to making the WTO's operations more transparent, including through more effective and prompt dissemination of information, and to improve dialogue with the public. We shall therefore at the national and multilateral levels continue to promote a better public understanding of the WTO and to communicate the benefits of a liberal, rules-based multilateral trading system', WTO, Ministerial Conference, Ministerial Declaration adopted on 14 November 2001, WT/MIN(01)/DEC/1, para. 10. See also WTO, General Council, Procedures for the Circulation and De-restriction of WTO Documents, WT/L/452 (16 May 2002); and WTO, General Council, Decision on Transparency Mechanism for Regional Trade Agreements adopted on 14 December 2006, WT/L/671 (18 December 2006).

[82] See, for example, the Global Transparency Initiative (GTI) which is a network of civil society organizations promoting openness in the International Financial Institutions (IFIs), such as the World Bank, the IMF, the European Investment Bank and Regional Development Banks. See also Jenkins, B., 'The World Bank's new access to information policy: Conceptual leap with limits', Bank Information Center, *INFO BRIEF*, March 2010.

[83] *United Nations Convention Against Corruption*, General Assembly Resolution 58/4 (31 October 2003), Article 10 'Public Reporting'.

other information available for commercial and other public use.[84] These varied obligations and recommendations have an important place in international media law, potentially opening the state to greater external scrutiny and criticism. They are however also necessarily weighted towards the disclosure of state information related to international finance and commerce and therefore lack the comprehensive character of a freedom of information right grounded in the broader liberal democratic interest in an open state. Furthermore, even where they take the form of legally binding disclosure obligations, they do not create enforceable or even conceptual rights to information. Instead, they are obligations on states to make certain categories of information public, but typically leave considerable discretion for governments to decide what state information falls within those categories.

In these circumstances, the international human right to freedom of expression provides an obvious foundation for a broad, explicit right of access to information. The equally obvious difficulty here is that the United Nations has done comparatively little to develop this strand of Article 19 of the UDHR and the ICCPR. There are at best a scattering of non-binding recommendations to states on the development of freedom of expression as a positive right and the importance of establishing domestic freedom of information laws.[85] In the comparative absence of significant intergovernmental activity, media and civil society organizations have promoted an expansive international right to freedom of information grounded in Article 19, often in anti-statist terms. The 1995 Johannesburg Principles on National Security, Freedom of Expression and Access to Information, for example, declare that, '[e]veryone has the right to obtain information from public authorities, including information relating to national security' and that '[i]n all laws and decisions concerning the right to obtain information, the public interest in knowing the information shall be a primary consideration'.[86] The Principles also set out a comparatively strict view of permissible exceptions to this right of access under

---

[84] See, for example, the OECD Recommendation of the Council for Enhanced Access and More Effective Use of Public Sector Information, [C(2008)36], which recommends that OECD states adopt the principle of 'Openness': 'Maximising the availability of public sector information for use and re-use based upon presumption of openness as the default rule to facilitate access and re-use'.

[85] See, for example, UN Commission on Human Rights, *The Right to Freedom of Opinion and Expression*, Resolution 2005/38, which calls upon all states, '[t]o adopt and implement laws and policies that provide for a general right of public access to information held by public authorities, which may be restricted only in accordance with article 19 of the International Covenant on Civil and Political Rights'. See also the Joint Declaration by the UN Special Rapporteur on Freedom of Opinion and Expression, the OSCE Representative on Freedom of the Media, and the OAS Special Rapporteur on Freedom of Expression, *International Mechanisms for Promoting Freedom of Expression 2004* (6 December 2004), and, *Report of the Special Rapporteur on the promotion and protection of the right to freedom of opinion and expression, Abid Hussain*, E/CN.4/1998/40, 'The Special Rapporteur has consistently stated that the right to seek and receive information is not simply a converse of the right to freedom of opinion and expression but a freedom on its own.'

[86] Johannesburg Principles on National Security, Freedom of Expression and Access to Information, UN Doc. E/CN.4/1996/39 (1996), Principles 11 and 13. See also Mendel, T., 'National Security vs. Openness: An Overview and Status Report on the Johannesburg Principles', in *National Security and Open Government: Striking the Right Balance*, Campbell Public Affairs Institute, The Maxwell School of Syracuse University, 2003.

ICCPR Article 19(3), including 'national security'.[87] Yet advocates of the open state have had to accept the ultimate validity of the state's claims of confidentiality for purposes of security and public order, questioning the extent of that sphere rather than its existence.[88]

International law regarding the powers of the state to punish unauthorized disclosures of confidential state information is just as uncertain as it is about rights of access to state information. While trade law contains significant disclosure obligations, it is for the reasons mentioned above of only background relevance to this question. A WTO member state may violate its various transparency obligations by failing to disclose required information, provided that no relevant exceptions apply. Yet, as these obligations do not create rights of access to state information, non-discriminatory domestic measures taken to enforce restrictions on the unauthorized disclosure of government information are not directly at issue under WTO law.

In principle, the right to freedom of expression, as established by Articles 19 of the UDHR and the ICCPR, provide a strong legal basis for limiting the power of the state to sanction unauthorized disclosures of state information. Under Article 19(3) of the ICCPR, the state's need to exercise effective control over its internal information must be weighed against the importance of public access to politically and socially important information. From a liberal democratic perspective, that balance should tip heavily in favour of the liberty to publish where wrongdoing is exposed. The joint declarations of the UN Special Rapporteur on Freedom of Opinion and Expression and various regional rapporteurs, facilitated each year by the campaigning Article 19 organization, have accordingly insisted that the powers of the state to police unauthorized disclosures have clear limits. On this view, it is for the state and its staff to guard its secrets.[89] 'Other individuals, including journalists and civil society representatives, should never be subject to liability for publishing or further disseminating this information, regardless of whether or not it has been leaked to them, unless they committed fraud or another crime to obtain the information.'[90]

---

[87] Johannesburg Principles, n. 86 above, Principle 12: A state may not categorically deny access to all information related to national security, but must designate in law only those specific and narrow categories of information that it is necessary to withhold in order to protect a legitimate national security interest.

[88] See for example, the Article 19 assisted Joint Declaration by the UN Special Rapporteur on Freedom of Opinion and Expression, the OSCE Representative on Freedom of the Media and the OAS Special Rapporteur on Freedom of Expression, *International Mechanisms for Promoting Freedom of Expression 2004* (6 December 2004), which declares that '[e]xceptions to the right of access should be set out clearly in these policies and access should be granted unless (a) disclosure would cause serious harm to a protected interest and (b) this harm outweighs the public interest in accessing the information'.

[89] Ibid.

[90] Ibid. See also Joint Declaration by the UN Special Rapporteur on Freedom of Opinion and Expression, the OSCE Representative on Freedom of the Media, the OAS Special Rapporteur on Freedom of Expression, and the ACHPR (African Commission on Human and Peoples' Rights) Special Rapporteur on Freedom of Expression, *International Mechanisms for Promoting Freedom of Expression 2006*, 19 December 2006.

That position is however at odds with the case law of the European Court of Human rights, as demonstrated in the Grand Chamber's decision in *Stoll v. Switzerland*.[91] It also does not fit easily with the decisions of international criminal tribunals, such as the International Criminal Tribunal for the Former Yugoslavia, which has used its contempt powers to sanction journalists who have violated its orders not to publicize the names of witnesses.[92] In developing its own principles, the Court has attempted to balance its duty to protect of the fairness of its trials and the safety of witnesses with its obligation to protect the freedom of journalists to cover its work effectively.[93] These differences between ostensibly liberal democratic views on access to state information demonstrate the difficulties of setting a model for the legitimate relationship between the media and the state in international law. International legal principles are open to widely different interpretations. Without universally authoritative institutions and a clear consensus amongst leading states, there will continue to be a patchwork of projects and forays that attempt to deliver legal certainty in the face of economic and political power.

---

[91] See, for example, the frequently anti-statist Johannesburg Principles, n. 86 above, which take a more conditional stance on this issue. Principle 15: 'no person may be punished on national security grounds for disclosure of information if (1) the disclosure does not actually harm and is not likely to harm a legitimate national security interest, or (2) the public interest in knowing the information outweighs the harm from disclosure.'

[92] The Tribunal, for example, found Domagoj Margetić guilty of contempt in February 2007 for disclosing protected witness lists on his website and sentenced him to a prison term of three months and a fine of 10,000 euros (ICTY, Domagoj Margetić, Case No. IT 95-14 R77.6). See also the decision of the ICTY Appeals Chamber in May, 2010 to affirm the contempt conviction of Vojislav Šešelj, the leader of the Serb Radical Party, on trial for war crimes, for disclosing information on 11 protected witnesses in violation of Tribunal orders (ICTY, Vojislav Šešelj, Case No. IT-03-67-T).

[93] Brockman-Hawe, BE.,'ICTY Special Chamber Decision In the Case Against Florence Hartmann' *ASIL Insight Volume 13, Issue 17* (2009). See also International Criminal Tribunal for the former Yugoslavia (ICTY) decision in *Prosecutor v. Radoslav Brdjanin and Momir Talic*, Case IT-99-36-AR73.9, Decision on Interlocutory Appeal, 11 December 2002, in which the Tribunal ruled that war correspondents have a qualified privilege to not testify even where the material has already been published and the sources are identified. They are not therefore obliged to give evidence to it unless their testimony had a 'direct and important value in determining a core issue in the case' or there was no reasonable alternative for obtaining the evidence.

10

Information Privacy and Reputation

From a liberal democratic view, the proper limits to scrutiny and criticism of politicians, public officials, and other public figures are rooted in the same ground as the scrutiny and criticism of the institutions and agencies of the state. In principle, effective democratic self government requires an expansive sphere in which individuals may comment as freely as possible on any matter of general concern. That argument moreover applies as much to individuals in positions of power or influence over public affairs as it does to the state itself. Indeed, for those who wield power through the state, liberal suspicions about the state, regardless of whether governmental intentions are malicious or benign, apply with equal force. It is consequently in the sphere of democratic politics that the relationship between the media and the liberal democratic state comes closest to the ideal of open, uninhibited market place of ideas.

Public figures and government institutions also suffer similar harms from media scrutiny and criticism. Disclosure of confidential information may cause serious financial losses and false allegations may damage public perception and confidence for individuals as much as public entities. There are however also distinctive differences. For individuals, injuries may go well beyond material harm or loss of confidence in professional abilities and extend to severe emotional distress and embarrassment felt because of intrusions into personal life and exposure to public curiosity and ridicule. It is injuries of this kind that give breach of privacy and loss of reputation their universal recognition, albeit in many different forms, as harms to vital aspects of human identity and social standing.

In an era of constitutional rights, recognition of a right to respect for privacy has introduced a volatile element into the relationship between the media and the state. This volatility is largely a result of the breadth of the privacy concept, which covers personal physical integrity, intrusion into the home or other personal space, and the collection, use, and disclosure of personal information.[1] The right to respect for privacy, moreover, is unlike the right to freedom of expression, which is ultimately rooted in the liberty to carry out the simple acts of speaking and writing. At best, the privacy right grows out of the idea that each individual should have control over his or her personal sphere of space and identity, determining both access and disclosure. While that idea has considerable intuitive appeal, it also has a fluidity or formlessness that seems incompatible with the formality of rights. The boundaries of that sphere

---

[1] Solove, D., 'A Taxonomy of Privacy', 154(3) *University of Pennsylvania Law Review* (2006), 477.

are often obscure, especially when they must be determined in public spaces or in social relationships. The idea, for example, that the right to respect for privacy encompasses the protection of honour and reputation from allegations made against a individual's moral integrity has become a point of fierce division in European media law.[2]

Liberalism brings its own problems to the task of deciding how privacy fits within constitutionalized rights. Classical liberalism, as liberty from the state, values privacy because it is an aspect of individual freedom and therefore on this view, privacy complements rather than obstructs the liberty to publish, which is similarly hostile to the state and offers an easy, if shallow, version of liberal universality. As liberalism has matured, however, privacy has found associations with other liberal perspectives on human identity, notably including autonomy and dignity, which have broadened the focus from liberty to include recognition and empowerment.[3] This is also an embrace of the diversity of ethical beliefs and cultural practices that liberalism has traditionally attempted to avoid, importing culture and locality into fundamental rights.

This shift in thinking about privacy has had an enormous influence on the media state relationship, even in liberal democracies where liberty from the state is especially cherished.[4] For individuals, a positive right to respect for privacy has become a lever for blocking the disclosure of personal information in the media, which have the capacity to amplify the injury to privacy far beyond the damage caused by an initial disclosure. Making personal privacy a barrier to the liberty to publish has however created an apparently irresolvable frontier between the rights to respect for privacy and freedom of expression. Certainly, no form of law or regulation has been left untried in attempting to secure adequate respect for both. In Anglo-American law, the wrongful disclosure of personal information developed first as the basis for a civil action in tort or equity.[5] If the right to respect for privacy is extended to take in the protection of personal honour and reputation, it also acquires common and civil law traditions of prosecuting libel as a criminal offence as well as regulatory solutions, such as statutory rights of reply.[6] In the internet era,

---

[2] See *Karako v. Hungary* (Application No. 39311/05) (28 April 2009) and *Polanco Torres and Movilla Polanco v. Spain* (Application No. 34147/06) (21 September 2010).

[3] Rössler, B., *The Value of Privacy*, (Polity Press, 2004); Solove, D., *Understanding Privacy*, Harvard University, 2008); Rosen, J., *The Unwanted Gaze* (Vintage Books, 2001); Whitman, J., 'The Two Western Cultures of Privacy: Dignity Versus Liberty', *Yale Law Journal* (April 2004).

[4] On the importance of liberty from the state in the interpretation of the First Amendment of the United States Constitution, see Chapter 2.

[5] Warren, S. and Brandeis, L., 'The Right to Privacy', *Harvard Law Review* (1890); Prosser, W., 'Privacy', 48(3) *California Law Review* (1960), 383–423.

[6] While criminal prosecution for libel is often associated with civil law countries, it also has strong roots in the common law. It was only in 2009 that Britain repealed the criminal offences of sedition and seditious libel, defamatory libel, and obscene libel (Coroners and Justice Act 2009) and criminal prosecution for libel, while severely constrained, is not in principle contrary to the right to free speech as protected by the First Amendment of the United States Constitution (*Garrison v. Louisiana*, 379 U.S. 64 (1964). See also Dohel, I., 'Freedom from Fear', 38(2) *Index on Censorship* (2009). On rights of reply, see Youm, K.H., 'The Right of Reply and Freedom of the Press: An International and Comparative Perspective', 76 *The George Washington Law Review* (2008), 1017.

civil actions seeking compensation for disclosure of personal information in the new media as well as the old are a regular feature of the public lives of celebrities. The wider public's experience of information privacy is however more often centred on internet based services that process their personal data for a range of commercial purposes. Here, civil actions are often irrelevant to the problems of how to prevent misuses of personal data and provide effective remedies for breaches of privacy that may cause limited harm to each individual concerned, but those individuals may count in the millions. Instead, the solutions to data protection tend to be regulatory and the debates are over the proper roles of the state and the market in providing those solutions.[7]

The chief argument against the growing influence of the right to respect for privacy is still that fundamental human rights originate in the concept of liberty from the state. A privacy right that is grounded in concepts that potentially compete with liberty, such as human dignity, and is also transformed into a positive obligation for the state to provide remedies against third parties, is an obvious threat to that liberty. In this potent form, privacy can present a substantial barrier to the publication of information that ought to be made public in a liberal democratic state. The nature of the right to respect for privacy has therefore become a key problem in the contemporary media state relationship.

The liberal democratic argument against an expansive privacy right is well grounded in the need for openness in democratic societies and the effectiveness of a general right of liberty to publish free from external constraints in achieving that end. The liberty argument also rightly warns that the protection of privacy and reputation can be a potent shield for politicians and other powerful individuals who seek shelter from legitimate public scrutiny. Certainly, the wealthy and powerful have typically been the driving force in the push to expand privacy rights and curtail the media's freedom to report on their lives.[8] This view fails however to acknowledge that advances in communications and other technologies have also dramatically reduced the sphere of privacy enjoyed by everyone and that many individuals also want effective remedies for intrusions into their personal lives and disclosure of their personal information. At a deeper level, this argument also reflects liberalism's own conflicts of principle. It is, in simple terms, a contest between a spare, self reliant version of autonomy and an empowered one that is willing to set limits on the liberty of others.

The legal relationship between the liberty to publish and the protection of privacy and reputation will continue to evolve as technologies and cultures change. Liberal democracies are also in broad agreement that both are legitimate public policy goals, even when they are divided as to how these goals should be accommodated in constitutional and ordinary law. Their approaches to this issue are nonetheless similar in form. The liberty to publish and the protection of privacy and reputation must co-exist in an overlapping legal field and the value given to one

---

[7] On data protection, see Chapter 11.

[8] See, for example, *Von Hannover v. Germany* (Application No. 59320/00) (24 June 2004) and (United Kingdom) *Campbell v. Mirror Group Newspapers Ltd* [2004] UKHL 22.

will always be relative to the value attributed to the other. There is consequently a logical structure to this field of law amongst liberal democracies. There is first an underlying question about the level of protection that should be given when publication and privacy interests are not in conflict. The law will, for example, set by default or conscious design the extent of any right to limit the disclosure of personal medical treatment.[9] Secondly, where the media wishes to publish such information, the law must use some device to determine when the right to publish will override the ordinary rules limiting disclosure. Here, the democratic argument for freedom of expression has tended to dominate the development of the principles used to resolve conflicts between liberty and privacy.[10] These typically focus on the status of the person concerned ('public figure'), the importance of the surrounding circumstances ('public interest'), and the extent the matter is already known to the public ('public domain'). Where information privacy has allegedly been violated, the right to limit the disclosure of private information will thus diminish as these factors become relevant. Conversely, the liberty to publish will be less well supported where the democratic argument has little application.

The development of these key factors, often entrenched in principles of constitutional law, has focused the conflict between freedom of expression and respect for privacy on the nature each factor and its proper application. There is, for example, a certain logic in making the status of the individual who is claiming personal privacy or reputation rights a key factor in determining the limits to freedom of expression as the injury concerns the personal integrity of that individual. This, however, inevitably leads to weighted hierarchies of status, which are graded according to the importance of the individual concerned in public affairs. If the person concerned represents the state in some significant way, he or she will be deemed to merit the robust scrutiny and criticism normally permitted for state institutions.[11] The importance of status becomes more difficult to judge where the individual has little or no connection with the state, yet wields considerable power or influence in political, economic, or social affairs. There are consequently pressures to expand the concept of the public figure as far as possible. While that may be justifiable for powerful individuals who have no direct connection to the state, it is less so for individuals who are at best marginal 'public figures', but who are awarded that status simply to ensure that the underlying goal of openness in a matter of public importance is achieved.[12]

In contrast, public interest or 'newsworthiness' tests tend to be more flexible, allowing courts to assess various elements in the surrounding circumstances when determining the relative importance of privacy or reputation in comparison to the liberty to publish.[13] This however gives rise to different problems of uncertainty

---

[9] *Plon (Société) v. France* (Application No. 56148/00) (18 May 2004).

[10] On the democratic argument for freedom of expression, see Chapter 2.

[11] On scrutiny and criticism of state institutions, see Chapter 8.

[12] See, for example, *Dameron v. Washington Magazine*, 779 F.2d 736, *Lohrenz v. Donnelly*, 350 F. 3d 1272.

[13] See, for example, *Diaz v. Oakland Tribune*, 139 Cal. App. 3d 118, in which the court stated, '... the individual's right to keep private facts from the public's gaze versus the public's right to know.

and potential arbitrariness. Most disputes regarding the disclosure of personal information or the publication of damaging allegations are arguably linked in some way to a matter of public interest.[14] Public interest tests therefore give courts wide discretion to decide whether that public interest aspect is significant enough to limit the privacy or reputation interest of the claimant. The chief objection here is that courts, as institutions of the state, should not be the final arbiters of what constitutes the legitimate public interest. It should instead be left to members of the public to decide what information is relevant for their own informed participation in the democratic process.[15] Yet courts, in attempting to avoid criticism for determining the public interest too narrowly, may conclude that the public interest is present in almost every privacy or reputation dispute. That, however, creates a presumption in favour of publication that weighs against almost every privacy or reputation claim.[16]

The third factor that can often arise in privacy disputes is the question whether the personal information disclosed was already in the public domain. At its simplest, the issue is merely whether the claimant has previously consented to the disclosure of the information, or whether the unauthorized prior disclosure was so great that any sanction imposed on further disclosure would be pointless. Public domain however also points towards a more complicated question about privacy in public spaces. On the one hand, there is greater certainty and clarity when privacy rights are aligned with private spaces and there is a clear-cut presumption that those rights do not arise in public spaces.[17] Yet this approach can also ride roughshod over privacy interests that genuinely do arise in public spaces, such as medical emergencies, which are observable to passers-by but not to any wider audience, unless reported through the media.[18] To recognize that the right to respect for privacy has some application to these disclosures of personal information in public does however sacrifice much of that certainty and clarity. It also enhances privacy interests at the expense of a liberty to speak and publish in public spaces that is not

---

In an effort to reconcile these competing interests, our courts have settled on a three-part test for determining whether matter published is newsworthy: [1] the social value of the facts published, [2] the depth of the article's intrusion into ostensibly private affairs, and [3] the extent to which the party voluntarily acceded to a position of public notoriety' (para. 13).

[14] See, for example, *Mosley v. News Group Newspapers* Ltd [2008] EWHC 1777 (QB), in which the court found that the sexual activities of the claimant were not sufficiently connected to any legitimate public interest, despite his prominent occupation and well known family history.

[15] Volokh, E., 'Freedom of Speech and Information Privacy: The Troubling Implications of a Right to Stop People from Speaking About You', 52 *Stanford Law Review* (2000), 1049. See also Schwartz, P., 'Free Speech vs. Information Privacy: Eugene Volokh's First Amendment Jurisprudence', 52 *Stanford Law Review* (2000), 1559.

[16] See US Supreme Court discussion of this issue in *Gertz V. Robert Welch, Inc.*, 418 U.S. 323 (1974), 345–346, See also *Rosenbloom* v. *Metromedia, Inc.*, 403 U.S. 29, at 79.

[17] See, for example, *Shulman v. Group W Productions*, 59 Cal. Rptr. 2D 434. See also *Time, Inc. v. Hill* (1967) 385 U.S. 374 in which the court stated that '[e]xposure of the self to others in varying degrees is a concomitant of life in a civilized community. The risk of this exposure is an essential incident of life in a society which places a primary value on freedom of speech and of the press' (388).

[18] The European Court of Human Rights made this distinction in *Peck v. United Kingdom* (Application No. 44647/98) (28 January 2003).

focused exclusively on the needs of democracy, but is grounded in the wider concept of an open market place of ideas.

The concepts of public figure, public interest, and public domain play a critical part in structuring compromises between the protection of privacy and reputation and the liberty to publish in liberal democratic media law. They are also vehicles for determining underlying conclusions, or at least preferences, about the proper relationship between autonomy the control of personal information and autonomy expressed through freedom of speech. Where the liberty to publish is deemed to be fundamentally more important, the law uses public figure, public interest, and public domain defences to privacy and reputation rights to guard a wider sphere of speech and publication. This is generally still true of the United States.

The U.S. Constitution, then, offers little support for information privacy—the claim of individuals, groups, or institutions to determine for themselves when, how, and to what extent information about them is communicated to others... The Supreme Court has crafted a limited framework for protecting individuals' right to privacy in the context of government activities concerning personal information and no support at all for privacy rights outside the public sector.[19]

The argument that the right to free speech must take precedence over privacy and reputation rights serves not only the democratic interest in exposing state institutions and individuals in positions of authority to scrutiny and criticism, but also the economic one of opening markets to innovative uses of information. That latter argument has become especially important in the internet era, in which new combinations of social relationships and commercial services have had a transforming effect on many societies. For social networking services, the combined political and economic arguments for expanding the liberty to publish are essential to the vision they offer of a borderless world of open communication in which the division between personal and public disappears.[20] The position in Europe has however evolved in a different direction. In European media law, harm to privacy and reputation is understood as having its own deep significance for personal autonomy and human dignity.[21] The foundations of the media state relationship are seen from a perspective of moral order as well as liberty, which is expressed in an equality of right in the clash between the liberty to publish and privacy and reputation. The rise of the fundamental right to respect for private life has, in particular, made the liberty to publish information and comment on matters of public interest a much more contested field for European law and policy.

---

[19] Cate, F., *Privacy In The Information Age*, (Brookings Institution Press, 1997), 66. See also Cate, F., and Litan, R., 'Constitutional Issues in Information Privacy', 9 *Michigan Telecommunications and Technology Law Review* (2002), 35.

[20] Johnson, B., Privacy no longer a social norm, says Facebook founder, *The Guardian*, (11 January 2010). See also Bonneau, J. and Preibusch, S., 'The Privacy Jungle: On the Market for Data Protection in Social Networks', *The Eighth Workshop on the Economics of Information Security WEIS 2009* (2009).

[21] The argument that individuals should not be compelled to endure public scrutiny and comment is not only well known in Europe, but has attracted intellectual support across the Atlantic. See, for example, Rosen, J., *Unwanted Gaze*, n. 3 above.

Information privacy and reputation in the European Union

National criminal and civil laws safeguarding information privacy and reputation constitute a relatively small issue for European Union law, despite their inhibiting effects on the free movement of media goods and services.[22] This low profile is especially striking when viewed in the context of the EU's major legislation governing data processing and the protection of personal data.[23] Yet that comparison is also the most telling. Data processing occurs in every European economic sector and involves the personal data, from the minimal to the deeply intrusive, of most residents and visitors to Europe. Resort to criminal and civil laws protecting information privacy and reputation however occurs where a specific individual has suffered significant emotional or material harm, which typically arises out of some form of news or current affairs publication. While almost any commercial media publication has a European cross border connection through production and advertising, news, and current affairs markets in Europe remain highly fragmented by linguistic as well as political and social differences among the member states. Those differences are likely to remain strong, even though migration and new forms of media are softening the historic importance of national boundaries for these media markets. It is consequently reasonable to assume that privacy and libel claims are more likely to occur within particular politically or linguistically defined areas, even when arising out of internet based media.[24]

The other major reason these national laws have so little apparent connection with European economic law is the overwhelming importance of European human rights law in establishing the balance between the liberty to publish and the protection of privacy and reputation in European media law. In formal terms, national measures restricting the liberty to publish for reasons of privacy and reputation will often constitute barriers to free movement. Much like laws restricting public criticism of the state, however, these apparent violations of free movement obligations are likely to be covered by express or implied exceptions. In the same vein, restrictions of this kind on the publication and distribution of media content are usually non-discriminatory in form and will therefore probably fall under the mandatory public policy exceptions of EU law where they create a substantial barrier to market access.[25] It is within the proportionality tests of these exceptions, as they combine with the general principles of EU law, that the

---

[22] The notable exception to this low profile occurs in the area of jurisdiction and choice of law, where civil actions for privacy and libel have had a major impact on the development of EU case law and legislation. See Chapter 7.

[23] On data protection, see Chapter 11.

[24] Certainly, cross border libel actions originating in other English speaking countries have played an important role in the development of defamation law in England. See, for example, *Reynolds v. Times Newspapers Limited* [1999] UKHL 45, and *Jameel and others v. Wall Street Journal Europe* [2006] UKHL 44.

[25] On public policy exceptions in European Union law, see Chapter 4.

issues are subsumed into the complex relationship between Articles 8 and 10 of the European Convention on Human Rights.

European Union law recognizes that national measures aimed at the protection of information privacy and reputation have a legitimate aim. Privacy and reputation are key elements within personal autonomy and dignity, which are foundational concepts within European fundamental rights and are reflected in the provisions of the European Convention on Human Rights and the European Union Charter of Fundamental Rights.[26] On this basis, member states may derogate from the EU rules of free movement provided that the measures concerned are proportionate to their legitimate aims and restrictive effects. Yet, that axis between the EU's economic freedoms and the right to respect for private life largely operates according to principles established in the more important axis between privacy and the right to freedom of expression, which is also a general principle of European Union law.[27] The extent to which respect for privacy limits the liberty to publish in EU law thus closely reflects the developing relationship between Articles 8 and 10 of the ECHR. As discussed below, where the core democratic purposes of Article 10 are engaged, the liberty to publish expression that breaches privacy and reputation rights enjoys substantial protection, permitting extensive scrutiny and criticism of politicians, public officials, and other public figures. As a result, in EU law the economic liberty to publish and distribute media content is most extensive where it coincides with democratic liberty. As the European Court of Justice begins to exercise its new Lisbon Treaty powers to apply the Charter, it will need to consider, within the overarching framework of the ECHR, more fully whether a combined economic and political argument for greater liberty carries more weight than one of these arguments on its own.[28]

The two major directives most relevant to trade in media services, the Audiovisual Media Services Directive and the Electronic Commerce Directive, have not significantly shifted the legal framework or arguments in this area.[29] Privacy and reputation are outside the fields coordinated by the AVMS Directive.[30] Consequently, where domestic criminal and civil laws protecting privacy and reputation are applied to television and on-demand audiovisual services, the Directive only

---

[26] The right to respect for private life is stated in similar terms in Article 8 of the European Convention on Human Rights and Article 7 of the Charter of Fundamental Rights of the European Union.

[27] Case C-260/89, *Elliniki Radiophonia Tiléorassi AE v. Dimotiki Etairia Pliroforissis and others* [1991] ECR I-2925, para. 43. See also Chapter 4.

[28] On the application of the rules of free movement to restrictive national measures intended to protect honour or reputation, see Case C-81/09, *Reference for a preliminary ruling from the Simvoulio tis Epikratias (Greece)—Idrima Tipou AE v. Ipourgos Tipou kai Meson Mazikis Enimerosis* (21 October 2010). See also discussion at Chapter 4, n. 96.

[29] Directive 2010/13/EU of the European Parliament and of the Council of 10 March 2010 on the coordination of certain provisions laid down by law, regulation or administrative action in Member States concerning the provision of audiovisual media services (AVMS Directive), and Directive 2000/31/EC of the European Parliament and of the Council of 8 June 2000 on certain legal aspects of information society services, in particular electronic commerce, in the Internal Market (Electronic Commerce Directive). On these Directives generally, see Chapter 4.

[30] On the fields coordinated by the AVMS Directive, see Chapter 4.

requires that they should not be used as a form of secondary control over services under the jurisdiction of another member state.[31] While the scope of the Electronic Commerce Directive is much broader, and therefore applies to national laws concerning privacy and reputation where they significantly affect the free movement of information society services, the exceptions permitted under this Directive are much the same as those available under general EU law.[32] Its only notable impact is therefore the conditional protection from liability the Directive offers for providers, and operators are important in conditionally protecting these parties from liability when hosting third party content.

In one area directly related to the protection of reputation, as well as media pluralism, European Union secondary legislation has however acquired a significant foothold.[33] In the Council of Europe, there has been a long running effort to create common European standards for mandatory domestic rights of reply that provide a simple remedy for individuals who have suffered an injury to reputation or serious inconvenience from the publication of a factual error.[34] Like many social policy issues developed within the Council of Europe, supporters of this initiative have also attempted to use the more effective legislative powers of the European Union to achieve an obligation binding on member states. There is certainly a plausible argument for EU legislation in this area on the basis that different rights of reply obstruct the free flow of media services. The growing importance of non-market public policy in the European Union, including the rights to human dignity and respect for private life, also provides an additional basis on which to address the harmful effects of media expression. On the other hand, rights of reply are also a burden on the liberty to publish, potentially chilling investigative journalism. There is moreover a subsidiarity argument that EU legislation in this area is an unwarranted intrusion into matters that are best dealt with through domestic law, regulation, or self regulation, in particular where the imposition of formal rights overrides other more flexible methods of redress. In any event, there has been no consensus amongst European governments favouring a common obligation to create an unambiguous legal right of reply for the print or any other media sector.

There is therefore no comprehensive right of reply obligation in European Union law, which has left the issue dispersed in several legislative and other EU instruments. The first opportunity to address this issue occurred with the arrival of direct-to-home satellite television in Europe, which prompted the negotiation of the Audiovisual Media Services Directive in the 1980s (then known as the

---

[31] *Konsumentombudsmannen (KO) v. De Agostini (Svenska) Förlag AB* (Case C-34/95) and *TV-Shop i Sverige AB* (Joined Cases C-35/95 and C-36/95), para. 34.

[32] Directive 2000/31/EC, Article 3(4)(i) 'necessary' for one of the following reasons; (ii) taken against a given information society service which prejudices the objectives referred to in point (i) or which presents a serious and grave risk of prejudice to those objectives; (iii) proportionate to those objectives. (Note however that the Directive excludes questions concerning the protection of personal data held or processed by information society services (Article 1(5)). These matters are covered by Directives 95/46/EC and 97/66/EC. See Chapter 11.)

[33] On media pluralism, see Chapter 14.

[34] See 'Information privacy and reputation in the Council of Europe' section below.

'Television without Frontiers' Directive).[35] Under the Directive, member states are required to introduce a right of reply, or equivalent measures, for any natural or legal person whose legitimate interests have been damaged by an assertion of incorrect facts in a television programme.[36] The Directive however not only permits different methods of implementation, but also states that a person seeking a right of reply governed by the Directive must accept the remedies offered under the laws of the country in which the relevant television broadcaster is established.[37]

Since adoption of the Directive in 1989, the major policy question has been whether and how this obligation should be extended to new media services, which has involved two conflicting European communications issues. The first is the principle that content measures should be platform neutral, meaning that any content rule should be applied to similar content or services, regardless of the communications platform or means through which they are delivered.[38] The other came out of the public policy atmosphere of the 1990s, in which the European Union accepted the proposition that broadcast media regulatory regimes should not be imposed on internet services.[39] If the former principle appears to have prevailed, it has done so without achieving clear obligations. In 2006 the European Union adopted a supplementary Recommendation on the Protection of Minors and Human Dignity, which urges member states to introduce measures regarding the right of reply or equivalent remedies in relation to on-line media.[40] The Recommendation's guidelines on the implementation of this right of reply or similar remedy are modelled on the right of reply provisions of the Audiovisual Media Services Directive, leaving open the manner of implementation.[41] In the following year, however, the Directive was amended to incorporate on-demand

---

[35] Porter, V. and Gabriel, M., (1993) 'The Right Of Reply To Transfrontier Television Broadcasts: A Two-Speed Europe', 1(4) *Journal of Financial Regulation and Compliance* (1993), 335–346.

[36] These provisions have been retained in the consolidated Directive/2010/13/EU, Recital (102) and Article 28, which states that, '... any natural or legal person, regardless of nationality, whose legitimate interests, in particular reputation and good name, have been damaged by an assertion of incorrect facts in a television programme must have a right of reply or equivalent remedies'.

[37] In Britain, the requirements of the Directive are implemented through OFCOM Broadcasting Code, 7.11. If a programme alleges wrongdoing or incompetence or makes other significant allegations, those concerned should normally be given an appropriate and timely opportunity to respond.

[38] On platform neutrality, see Chapter 3.

[39] See European Commission, *Green Paper on the Convergence of the Telecommunications, Media and Information Technology Sectors and the Implications for Regulation COM (97) 623*, Chapter V, Principle 1. See also Council of Europe, Committee of Ministers, Declaration on freedom of communication on the Internet (Strasbourg, 28 May 2003), Principle 1: Content rules for the Internet, Principle 3: Absence of prior state control.

[40] Recommendation of the European Parliament and of the Council on the protection of minors and human dignity and on the right of reply in relation to the competitiveness of the European audiovisual and on-line information services industry—20 December 2006, Annex 1: Indicative Guidelines for the Implementation, at National Level, of Measures in Domestic Law or Practice so as to Ensure the Right of Reply or Equivalent Remedies in relation to On-line Media. See also Council Recommendation of 24 September 1998 on the development of the competitiveness of the European audiovisual and information services industry by promoting national frameworks aimed at achieving a comparable and effective level of protection of minors and human dignity (98/560/EC).

[41] They are also closely related to the Council of Europe, Committee of Ministers Recommendation to member states on the right of reply in the new media environment, Rec (2004) 16.

audiovisual media services, but did not extend the right of reply obligation beyond broadcasting to those new media services.[42]

Information privacy and reputation in the Council of Europe

Under European human rights law, the limits to public scrutiny and criticism of politicians, public officials, and other public figures are defined within the closely meshed relationship of Articles 8 and 10 of the European Convention on Human Rights. That relationship has in the process become one of European media law's most distinctive features. It is also an area where the Council of Europe has largely avoided taking the lead in developing general principles, leaving the European Court of Human Rights to develop the law through case decisions that are, in principle, grounded in local circumstances.[43] Yet, on occasion, other Council of Europe institutions have seized the moment to take the law in this area forward. Following the death of Princess Diana in 1997, widely seen as the result of paparazzi harassment, the Parliamentary Assembly of the Council of Europe adopted its Resolution on the Right to Privacy, 1165 (1998), which has been widely cited for its principles balancing freedom of speech and the privacy rights of public figures.[44] More typically, the Committee of Ministers has followed in the wake of the Court, summarizing its case law principles to provide comprehensive guidance on contemporary issues of importance.[45]

There is however one area concerning remedies for injury to reputation where the Council of Europe has not left matters to the Court. For nearly forty years, the Council of Europe has promoted the use of rights of reply in domestic media law and regulation, urging member states to adopt a form of positive intervention in media markets that the Court until very recently seemed unlikely to advocate.[46]

---

[42] Directive 2010/13/EU, Recital (103). The right of reply is an appropriate legal remedy for television broadcasting and could also be applied in the online environment. The Recommendation on the protection of minors and human dignity and on the right of reply already includes appropriate guidelines for the implementation of measures in national law or practice so as to ensure sufficiently the right of reply or equivalent remedies in relation to online media.

[43] Committee of Ministers, Reply to 'Towards decriminalisation of defamation Parliamentary Assembly Recommendation 1814 (2007)' (11 June 2008), 'Bearing in mind the role of the European Court of Human Rights in developing general principles on defamation through its case law and its power to adjudicate claims of violations of Article 10 in specific cases, the Committee of Ministers does not consider advisable at this point in time to develop separate detailed rules on defamation for member states.' See also CE Parliamentary Assembly, *Towards decriminalisation of defamation*, Resolution 1577 (2007).

[44] See, for example, *Von Hannover v. Germany*, n. 8 above, and *A v. B plc (Flitcroft v. MGN Ltd)* [2002] EWCA Civ 337.

[45] See, for example, Council of Europe, Committee of Ministers, Declaration on Freedom of Political Debate in the Media, (12 February 2004), or Council of Europe, Committee of Ministers, Guidelines on Protecting Freedom of Expression and Information in Times of Crisis (26 September 2007), Part IV. Guarantees against misuse of defamation legislation.

[46] Council of Europe, Committee of Ministers, Resolution on the right of reply—Position of the individual in relation to the press, Resolution (74) 26. On European Court of Rights changing position on a positive right of access to government information, see *Kenedi v. Hungary* (Application No. 31475/05), para. 43. See also Chapter 9.

Here, the organization acted, once again, as a European forum of first resort for non-market public policy matters in the media field and latterly as a forum for extending EU obligations to non-EU states, once the European Union had belatedly taken up the issue of rights of reply.[47] In the lead up to the major revisions to the Audiovisual Media Services Directive in 2007, the Committee of Ministers issued its Recommendation on the Right of Reply in the New Media Environment.[48] This Recommendation called for a much more extensive right of reply than later adopted in EU legislation, covering 'any means of communication for the periodic dissemination to the public of edited information, whether on-line or off-line, such as newspapers, periodicals, radio, television and web-based news services'.[49] Despite the inclusion of a recital declaring that 'the right of reply can be assured not only through legislation, but also through co-regulatory or self-regulatory measures', the British and Slovak governments reserved their rights not to comply in so far as the Recommendation referred to online services.[50] Against this background, the European Court of Human Rights has concluded that, in exceptional circumstances, a positive obligation may arise for a state party under Article 10 to ensure an individual's freedom of expression by requiring the media to provide a reasonable and effective opportunity to exercise a right of reply.[51]

This regulatory guidance and judicial work on rights of reply, however complicated, is only a small piece that fits within the much larger edifice of Convention case law on the relationship between freedom of expression and information privacy and reputation. Initially, the Article 8 right to respect for family life and the Article 10 right to freedom of expression were not bound closely together in the Court's jurisprudence. They were each treated as rights that are concerned with the limits of state power, imposing negative obligations on member states not to interfere with the expression and privacy rights of individuals or private bodies, unless necessary for legitimate purposes. Yet two developments have brought these articles into tight opposition. The first of these was the Court's reliance on democratic arguments for free speech to identify the core purposes of Article 10, which created a broad, protected sphere of expression that cut deep into the sphere of private life. The second was the development of positive obligations under Article 8 to provide effective remedies for violations of privacy at the hands of other private parties, which in effect demanded the creation of effective remedies against the media for breaches of privacy.

---

[47] See, for example, European Convention on Transfrontier Television (ETS No. 132), which contains, in Article 8, a parallel obligation to the right of reply obligations of the Audiovisual Media Services Directive.

[48] Council of Europe, Committee of Ministers Recommendation on the right of reply in the new media environment, Rec (2004) 16E.

[49] Ibid., 'Definition'.

[50] Ibid. 'When adopting this Recommendation, the Permanent Representatives of the United Kingdom and the Slovak Republic indicated that, in accordance with Article 10.2 *c* of the Rules of Procedure for the meetings of the Ministers' Deputies, they reserved the right of their Governments to comply or not with the Recommendation, in so far as it referred to online services.'

[51] See *Melnychuk v. Ukraine* (Application No. 28743/03) (Admissibility Decision, 5 July 2005), *Vitrenko v. Ukraine* (Application No. 23510/02) (Admissibility Decision, 15 December 2008).

The Court first addressed the question of legitimate public scrutiny and criticism of people in positions of power in a number of important cases dealing with defamation, which the Court dealt with entirely within the framework of Article 10. This was also a period in which the European Court of Human Rights looked closely at the work of the United States Supreme Court, which had been expanding the influence of the First Amendment in American constitutional law. Most importantly, the Supreme Court had decided in *New York Times v. Sullivan* and subsequent cases that the ordinary rules of defamation law imposed an unacceptable burden on freedom of speech, especially where they provided a tool for politicians and public officials to silence their critics.[52] The resulting American model used the status of the libel claimant as the key threshold device, denying 'public figures' access to the normal rules protecting reputation in US state common law.

The American model, if unacceptably extreme in effectively eviscerating libel protection for public figures, offered an attractive precedent for European human rights law. The structure of Article 10 indicated that the right to freedom of expression, set out in Article 10(1) should take precedence over the mere legitimate aim of protecting of reputation listed in Article 10(2). Domestic laws or other measures protecting reputation should therefore not impair the core purposes of Article 10, in particular public debate regarding matters of common concern. In the 1986 case of *Lingens v. Austria,* the European Court of Human Rights therefore adopted some of the Supreme Court's core reasoning, stating that, 'the limits of acceptable criticism are accordingly wider as regards a politician as such than as regards a private individual. Unlike the latter, the former inevitably and knowingly lays himself open to close scrutiny of his every word and deed by both journalists and the public at large, and he must consequently display a greater degree of tolerance.'[53] Having introduced a modified public figure principle, the Court proceeded to explore its logical implications. This led to the elaboration of a hierarchy of status based on the importance and voluntariness of an individual's position in public affairs, especially in relation to the conduct of government and participation in electoral politics.[54] The weight given to the reputation interest of the claimant will therefore decline as his or her voluntary participation in important public affairs grows. In contrast to the politicians and other public figures at the top of the status hierarchy, private individuals are entitled to the normal protections and remedies of defamation law, provided those are not themselves disproportionate,

---

[52] *New York Times Co. v. Sullivan,* 376 U.S. 254 (1964), and, *Gertz v. Welch,* 418 U.S. 323 (1974).

[53] *Lingens v. Austria* (Application No. 9815/82) (8 July 1986), para. 42. See also Committee of Ministers, Council of Europe, *Declaration on Freedom of Political Debate in the Media* (12 February 2004), III. Public debate and scrutiny over political figures: 'Political figures have decided to appeal to the confidence of the public and accepted to subject themselves to public political debate and are therefore subject to close public scrutiny and potentially robust and strong public criticism through the media over the way in which they have carried out or carry out their functions.'

[54] These principles are summarized in Committee of Ministers, Council of Europe, *Declaration on Freedom of Political Debate in the Media* (12 February 2004).

especially where they may have a chilling effect on publications concerning the general or public interest.[55]

As a general rule, senior civil servants must also accept greater exposure to criticism, but not as much as politicians as they are presumed to have less authority and did not thrust themselves into the limelight to the same extent as politicians.[56] However, in the view of the Court, these principles must be modified where the public official is a judge or has judicial responsibilities.

> Regard must ... be had to the special role of the judiciary in society. As the guarantor of justice, a fundamental value in a law-governed State, it must enjoy public confidence if it is to be successful in carrying out its duties. It may therefore prove necessary to protect such confidence against destructive attacks that are essentially unfounded, especially in view of the fact that judges who have been criticized are subject to a duty of discretion that precludes them from replying ...[57]

Criticism of the conduct of a judge when carrying out his or her official functions may therefore be grounds for legitimate restrictions on expression that would be unacceptable for other public officials. In a European liberal democracy, judges cannot be screened from legitimate public scrutiny or criticism, but that does not include expression whose sole purpose is to insult a judge.[58]

In two important respects, the European Court of Human Rights diluted the *New York Times v. Sullivan* model with its unwavering focus on public figures. First, the Court has adopted the concept of 'public interest' as an additional or alternative threshold to determine when defamation standards should be eased to widen the liberty to publish, effectively watering down the importance of the status of the claimant.[59] 'According to its constant case-law, there is little scope under Article 10(2) of the Convention for restrictions on political speech or on debate on questions of public interest and very strong reasons are required for justifying such

---

[55] See *Tammer v. Estonia* (Application No. 41205/98) (6 February 2001), which illustrates the difficulties of assessing public figure status where the individual is closely connected to a major politician through family or relationship ties.

[56] 'Civil servants acting in an official capacity are, like politicians, subject to wider limits of acceptable criticism than private individuals. However, it cannot be said that civil servants knowingly lay themselves open to close scrutiny of their every word and deed to the extent politicians do and should therefore be treated on an equal footing with the latter when it comes to criticism of their conduct', *Oberschlick v. Austria (No. 2)* (Application No. 20834/92) (1 July 1997), para. 47. See also *Janowski v. Poland* (Application No. 25716/94) (21 January 1999), (Grand Chamber), and *Saaristo v. Finland* (Application No. 184/06) (12 October 2010).

[57] *Prager and Oberschlick v. Austria* (Application No. 15974/90) (26 April 1995), para. 34.

[58] *Skalka v. Poland* (Application No. 43425/98) (27 May 2003), para. 38. See also *Barford v. Denmark* (Application No. 11508/85) (22 February 1989), *Prager and Oberschlick v. Austria* (Application No. 15974/90) (26 April 1995), and *De Haes and Gijsels v. Belgium* (Application No. 19983/92), (24 February 1997).

[59] The court uses different terms, including 'a debate of general interest', 'matters of public concern', and 'issues of general interest' to identify a matter of public interest. There is moreover no clear distinction in the Court's case law between discussion of political affairs and discussion of other matters of public concern. See *Thorgeir Thorgeirson v. Iceland* (Application No.13778/88) (25 June 1992), para. 64. Legitimate public interest may therefore include the safety of logical surgery techniques or skills, *Bergen Tidende and Selisto v. Finland* (Application No. 56767/00) (16 November 2004).

restrictions.'[60] As a result, where the domestic measure at issue restricts the work of the media, the Court has used the public interest concept as an additional or alternative factor indicating that the democratic public interest is at risk.[61] Consequently, as compared to the US First Amendment public figure doctrine, the Article 10 combined public figure and public interest tests potentially cover a much wider set of issues and circumstances. In its favour, the Court's expansive application of the notion of public interest defuses the liberal criticism that institutions of the state, including courts, should not be in a position to decide the limits of legitimate public debate. For the same reason, however, the Court's public interest test is open to the criticism that it limits the protection that an ordinary person can expect under defamation law if he or she becomes involved in a matter of public interest, as this test can be satisfied in the complete absence of any public figure.[62]

In its second divergence from the American model, the court has combined its expansive threshold tests with an alternative standard of liability that is much less protective of the media than the US constitutional privilege. Under the *New York Times v. Sullivan* standard, a media defendant will be liable only if proven to have been motivated by actual malice when publishing a defamatory statement about a public figure.[63] The European Court of Human Rights has required instead that the media defendant should have acted in good faith and in accordance with the ethics of journalism when publishing a defamatory statement regarding a public figure or other person involved in a matter of general concern.[64] Aside from the question whether this standard is too restrictive of freedom of expression, it gives rise to an immediate problem of interpretation. 'Ethics of journalism' indicates a standard of due professional care. Yet, at its best, journalism operates under general principles of good professional conduct that are far less precise or rigorous than the

---

[60] *Filatenko v. Russia*, (Application No. 73219/01) (6 December 2007), para. 40. 'Pluralist democracy and freedom of political debate require that the public is informed about matters of public concern, which includes the right of the media to disseminate negative information and critical opinions concerning political figures and public officials, as well as the right of the public to receive them.' See also Council of Europe, Committee of Ministers, *Declaration on Freedom of Political Debate in the Media* (12 February 2004), I. Freedom of expression and information through the media.

[61] 'Whilst the press must not overstep the bounds set, *inter alia*, in the interest of "the protection of the reputation and right of others", it is nevertheless incumbent on it to impart information and ideas of public interest. Not only does the press have the task of imparting such information and ideas: the public also has a right to receive them. Were it otherwise, the press would be unable to play its vital role of "public watchdog". Although formulated primarily with regard to the print media, these principles doubtless apply also to the audio-visual media.' *Jersild v. Denmark* (Application No. 15890/89), (Grand Chamber, 23 September 1994), para. 31.

[62] *Bladet Tromsø and Stensaas v. Norway* (Application No. 21980/93) (20 May 1999).

[63] *New York Times Co. v. Sullivan*, n. 52 above.

[64] 'By reason of the "duties and responsibilities" inherent in the exercise of the freedom of expression, the safeguard afforded by Article 10 to journalists in relation to reporting on issues of general interest is subject to the proviso that they are acting in good faith in order to provide accurate and reliable information in accordance with the ethics of journalism.' *Bladet Tromsø and Stenaas v. Norway*, n. 62 above, para. 65. This standard is not necessarily expected of a private person, even when making his or her views available to the public (for example, on personal website) on a matter of public importance, especially when direct at standards of government administration, *Renaud v. France* (Application No. 13290/07) (25 February 2010).

professional codes of conduct used, for example, in medicine or engineering. In the face of this uncertainty, courts must either defer to the editorial judgement of professional journalists or use a judge determined standard to evaluate whether the conduct at issue satisfies the requirements of 'good faith and ethics of journalism'.[65]

The Court's public figure and public interest threshold not only serves to mark a shift from strict liability for defamation to the more lenient standard of good faith and ethics of journalism, but also marks the stronger protection of value judgements on matters of public concern. As the Court stated in *Lingens v. Austria,* 'a careful distinction needs to be made between facts and value-judgments. The existence of facts can be demonstrated, whereas the truth of value-judgments is not susceptible of proof... unless they can prove the truth of their statements. As regards value-judgments this requirement is impossible of fulfilment and it infringes freedom of opinion itself.'[66] The Court has however struggled to clarify satisfactorily the crucial and much used distinction between facts and value judgements, which often turns on the context of the defamatory statement and whether that context is adequately known to the public.[67] More recent decisions show a new approach, which places more weight on whether the essence of the relevant statement was opinion rather than allegation of fact instead of attempting to categorize it definitively as fact or value judgement.[68] Finally, the public figure and public interest threshold also raises the importance of damages, fines, and other remedies for injury to reputation. Consequently, the use of penal sanctions against the media for defamatory publications, except in the most serious cases, will be a disproportionate interference with freedom of expression.[69] The member states of the Council of Europe remain divided on the whether criminal sanctions for the protection of reputation should be abolished entirely and the Court has so far declined to lead this change in European media law.[70]

The work of the European Court of Human Rights on defamation was immensely useful in identifying the core purposes of Article 10 and their consequences for public scrutiny and criticism of politicians and other individuals in positions of power. As noted above, these developments were also relatively unaffected by the Court's work on Article 8. There was undoubtedly a structural connection between

---

[65] In Britain, the problem of judge made rules of conduct as opposed to editorial discretion arose in the leading cases of *Reynolds v. Times Newspaper Limited* and *Jameel and others v. Wall Street Journal Europe,* n. 24 above.

[66] *Lingens v. Austria,* n. 53 above, para. 46.

[67] 'The assessment whether a certain statement constitutes a value judgment or a statement of fact might in many cases be difficult' and 'their difference finally lies in the degree of factual proof, which has to be established.' *Scharsach and News Verlagsgesellschaft v. Austria* (Application No. 39394/98) (13 November 2003), para. 39. The Court has also limited this principle by insisting on proof of a sufficient factual basis for any value judgement: *Jerusalem v. Austria* (Application No. 26958/95) (27 February 2001), para. 43.

[68] See, for example, *Karsai v. Hungary* (Application No. 5380/07) (1 March 2010), para. 33, in which the Court described the relevant statement of fact as being 'value-laden'.

[69] Council of Europe, Committee of Ministers, *Declaration on Freedom of Political Debate in the Media* (12 February 2004), VIII. Remedies against violations by the media.

[70] Committee of Ministers, Reply to 'Towards decriminalisation of defamation Parliamentary Assembly Recommendation 1814 (2007)', (11 June 2008).

the two articles through Article 10(2), which includes 'preventing the disclosure of information received in confidence' and more generally the protection of the 'rights of others' as legitimate aims for an interference with freedom of expression. That connection is mirrored in part through Article 8(2), which includes the legitimate aim of the 'protection of the rights and freedoms of others' for interferences with respect for private life. However, these connections were reasonably dormant until the Court developed the right to respect for private life as a positive obligation to protect personal privacy from other private parties.[71] As a result, a claim in domestic law against the media for a breach of privacy is now ultimately secured by the claimant's Article 8 Convention right.[72]

The importance of Article 8 for European media law has also grown as the Court has broadened and deepened its concepts of 'private life', reflecting different aspects of the underlying principles of personal autonomy and respect for human dignity.[73] In the view of the Court, 'private life is a broad term not susceptible to exhaustive definition'.[74] In its case law, private life therefore covers a diverse range of issues connected to moral and physical identity and integrity, including gender identification, name, sexual orientation, and sexual life.[75] These are moreover changing with shifting European public sensitivities about personal privacy, including those occurring through the adoption of new communications technologies and services. These changing views on privacy find their impact on Article 8 through the threshold Article 8(1) test of whether the individual concerned had a reasonable or legitimate expectation of privacy.[76] The evolving definition of privacy in European human rights law however also underscores the unpredictability of Article 8's impact on media law, including its potent capacity to limit scrutiny of individuals in positions of power or influence.

This preference for flexibility and sensitivity to factual context in the interpretation of Article 8 has consequently knocked away apparent certainties in the relationship between the concepts of public and private. This includes the intuition that respect for privacy is closely associated with private places. For the media, that intuition supports a general freedom to report and comment on what occurs in

---

[71] '[A]lthough the object of Article 8 is essentially that of protecting the individual against arbitrary interference by the public authorities, it does not merely compel the State to abstain from such interference: in addition to this primarily negative undertaking, there may be positive obligations inherent in an effective respect for private or family life. These obligations may involve the adoption of measures designed to secure respect for private life even in the sphere of the relations of individuals between themselves', *X and Y v. Netherlands* (Application No. 8978/80) (26 March 1985), para. 23. See also *Marckx v. Belgium* (Application No. 6833/74) (13 June 1979), para. 31.

[72] See, for example, (United Kingdom) *Campbell v. Mirror Group Newspapers Ltd*, n. 8 above.

[73] Marshall, J., *Personal Freedom through Human Rights Law? Autonomy, Identity and Integrity under the European Convention on Human Rights* (Martinus Nijhoff Publishers, 2009, Part II, entitled 'Privacy and Personal Autonomy at the European Court of Human Rights'), 52.

[74] *Sidabras and Dziautas v. Lithuania* (Application Nos 55480/00 and 59330/00) (July 27 2004), para. 43.

[75] In *Botta v. Italy* (Application No. 21439/93) (24 February 1998), the Court stated that private life, 'includes a person's physical and psychological integrity; the guarantee afforded by Article 8 of the Convention is primarily intended to ensure the development, without outside interference, of the personality of each individual in his relations with other human beings' (para. 32).

[76] *Von Hannover v. Germany*, n. 8 above, para. 51.

public, which arguably provides the general public as well as the media clarity and certainty about the boundaries of privacy. The Court has however developed a more nuanced understanding of privacy in public places that is not only intuitively realistic, but also highly contextual and unpredictable. In its view, Article 8

> also protects a right to identity and personal development, and the right to establish and develop relationships with other human beings and the outside world and it may include activities of a professional or business nature. There is, therefore, a zone of interaction of a person with others, even in a public context, which may fall within the scope of 'private life'.[77]

An individual's reasonable expectation of privacy under Article 8 may therefore operate on different levels within that zone of interaction between private and public. A person in a public place may reasonably expect to be viewed there by anyone who has physical access to that place and perhaps even by those who have access to any camera and other surveillance device that may be reasonably expected there. In this respect, the concepts of public place and public domain continue to play an important role in limiting the right to respect for private life.[78] Yet that person will not normally have a reasonable expectation that any images or information gathered from that place will be published more widely.[79] Indeed, the Court has determined that the use of photos or videos is often particularly intrusive and revealing of an individual's private life and, consequently, there is a greater legitimate expectation of privacy regarding the publication of such images.[80]

In its exploration of the meaning of the Article 8 right to respect for private life, the Court has been propelled forward, sometimes with apparent reluctance, by the logic of its precedents. Given the breadth of the privacy concept elaborated in Article 8 case law, there is an obvious logical connection between ideas of honour and reputation and the protection of personal identity under that article. As the Court stated in *Pfeiffer v. Austria*, 'a person's reputation, even if that person is criticised in the context of a public debate, forms part of his or her personal identity and psychological integrity and also falls within the scope of his or her "private life". Article 8 therefore applies.'[81] In later chamber decisions, however, its judges have wavered over the strength of that link, which seems to demand a new equality in the treatment of the liberty to publish and the protection of reputation.[82] Nonetheless, while not all attacks on honour and reputation will bring Article 8 into play, recent

---

[77] *Peck v. United Kingdom* (Application No. 44647/98) (28 January 2003), para. 57.

[78] In a similar vein, it is also important whether the personal information at issue was accessible by the public prior to its unauthorized disclosure: *Fressoz and Roire v. France* (Application No. 29183/95), (Grand Chamber, 21 January 1999), para. 53. See also *Flinkkilä a.o. v. Finland* (Application No. 25576/04) (6 April 2010), para. 83.

[79] *Peck v. United Kingdom*, n. 77 above, para. 57.

[80] See *Egeland and Hanseid v. Norway* (Application No. 34438/04) (16 April 2009) and *Reklos and Davourlis v. Greece* (Application No. 1234/05) (15 January 2009).

[81] *Pfeifer v. Austria* (Application No. 12556/03) (15 November 2007), para. 35. See also *White v. Sweden* (Application No. 42435/02) (19 September 2006), para. 26.

[82] *Karako v. Hungary*, n. 2 above, paras 22–23 See also *Polanco Torres and Movilla Polanco v. Spain* (Application No. 34147/06) (21 September 2010).

decisions make clear that any serious false allegation about a person's character and integrity is likely to do so.[83]

The expanding scope of Article 8 has created a merged legal field in which respect for privacy and freedom of expression are not only closely enmeshed but also jointly applied.[84] In this merged field, Article 8 and Article 10 possess equal importance or weight under the Convention and must be fairly balanced when both are engaged in a particular ECHR application.[85] European human rights law is therefore increasingly at odds with American constitutional law, in which respect for privacy is neither a consolidated right or positive obligation on the state. Yet, at least in one respect, European and American law has moved in a roughly parallel direction. The principles developed to define the purposes and scope of the right to freedom of expression are used to structure and limit the sphere of personal privacy. The European Court of Human Rights has, for example, used its 'public figure' and 'public interest' threshold tests to cut back the protection of Article 8 rights where the democratic interest in the liberty to speak and publish outweighs the need to protect personal identity and integrity.[86] In the view of the Court, 'it would be fatal for freedom of expression in the sphere of politics if public figures could censor the press and public debate in the name of their personality rights, alleging that their opinions on public matters are related to their person and therefore constitute private data which cannot be disclosed without consent'.[87] This plainly does not give the media carte blanche to expose the private lives of senior politicians, but operates to permit exposure of aspects of private life that are matters of a public concern, such as the health problems of a politician that may affect his or her ability to carry out public duties.[88] Where the Article 10 threshold of public figure or public interest is crossed, the media's liability standard for breach of privacy rights has followed the Court's approach to liability standards in defamation cases. Once

[83] *A. v. Norway* (Application No. 28070/06) (9 April 2009), paras 63–65. See also *Petrenco v. Moldova* (Application No. 20928/05) (30 March 2010).

[84] This merged legal field created by the interaction of Articles 10 and 8 is not exclusive and may incorporate other ECHR rights, including Article 6, for example, which has its own close relationship with Article 10 because of its potentially restrictive effects on the liberty to publish. Indeed, in some applications all three Articles may be engaged, *Egeland and Hanseid v. Norway*, n. 80 above. See also *Eerikäinen and others v. Finland* (Application No. 3514/02) (10 February 2009).

[85] See, for example, Council of Europe, Parliamentary Assembly, Resolution on the Right to Privacy: '10. It is therefore necessary to find a way of balancing the exercise of two fundamental rights, both of which are guaranteed by the European Convention on Human Rights: the right to respect for one's private life and the right to freedom of expression. 11. The Assembly reaffirms the importance of every person's right to privacy, and of the right to freedom of expression, as fundamental to a democratic society. These rights are neither absolute nor in any hierarchical order, since they are of equal value.'

[86] The principles developed in the Court's Article 8 and Article 10 case law are summarized in Committee of Ministers, Council of Europe, *Declaration on freedom of political debate in the media*, 12 February 2004, VII. Privacy of political figures and public officials.

[87] *Tarsasag a Szabadsagjogokert v. Hungary* (Application No. 37374/05) (14 April 2009), para. 37. See also *Von Hannover*, n. 8 above, para. 64: 'the public has a right to be informed, which is an essential right in a democratic society that, in certain special circumstances, can even extend to aspects of the private life of public figures, particularly where politicians are concerned'. As regards private persons, see *Sciacca v. Italy* (Application No. 50774/99) (11 January 2005).

[88] See, for example, *Plon (Société) v. France*, n. 9 above, para. 36.

again, '[Article 10] protects journalists' rights to divulge information on issues of general interest provided that they are acting in good faith and on an accurate factual basis and provide "reliable and precise" information in accordance with the ethics of journalism.'[89]

While the Court has used Article 10, sometimes aggressively, to limit the impact of Article 8 on the liberty to publish, it has also used the right to respect for private life to reverse effect, pushing back the scope of the public figure and public interest threshold tests for greater freedom of expression. The groundwork for this effect was laid as long ago as *Lingens v. Austria*. 'No doubt Article 10(2) enables the reputation of others—that is to say, of all individuals—to be protected, and this protection extends to politicians too, even when they are not acting in their private capacity; but in such cases the requirements of such protection have to be weighed in relation to the interests of open discussion of political issues.'[90] Even prominent politicians are thus entitled to respect for their private lives even when acting in their official or public capacities, which will vary according to the nature of any relevant general interest.[91]

The concept of the public figure is therefore the focus for a conflict of values in which he or she is a legitimate target for public scrutiny and criticism, but also a human being bearing fundamental rights to autonomy and dignity. For the Court, that conflict can be resolved by evaluating the factual context and weighing the relevant factors, which yields decisions that can be intuitively appealing but also hard to reconcile with similar cases. In *Lindon, Otchakovsky-Laurens and July v. France*, for example, the Court found that the reputation interest of the French politician Jean-Marie Le Pen outweighed the genuine public interest in his involvement in racist political struggles in France because of the tone and severity of the allegations made against him in a novel authored and published by the claimants. In the course of its decision, the Chamber stated that '[t]he Court moreover considers that, regardless of the forcefulness of political struggles, it is legitimate to try to ensure that they abide by a minimum degree of moderation and propriety, especially as the reputation of a politician, even a controversial one, must benefit from the protection afforded by the Convention'.[92]

The often murky relationship between Articles 8 and 10 of the ECHR leads to several conclusions about information privacy and reputation in European human rights law. Article 8 values must be taken into account in any instance of public scrutiny or criticism of politicians, public officials, and other public figures. Moreover, given the evolving nature of respect for private life, the impact of Article 8 on the liberty to publish will continue to produce new tensions in European

---

[89] *Fressoz and Roire v. France*, n. 78 above, para. 54.

[90] *Lingens v. Austria*, n. 53 above, para. 42.

[91] 'Anyone, even if they are known to the general public, must be able to enjoy a "legitimate expectation" of protection of and respect for their private life': *Von Hannover v. Germany*, n. 8 above, para. 69.

[92] *Lindon, Otchakovsky-Laurens and July v. France* (Application Nos 21279/02 and 36448/02) (22 October 2007), para. 57. See also Millar, G., 'Whither the spirit of Lingens?', 3 *European Human Rights Law Review* (2009), 277–288.

media law. As communications technologies and services develop, expectations of privacy once associated with personal communication are mixing with those derived from the sphere of public spaces and media. Yet the effort to create European standards in this changing environment is further complicated by principles emphasizing the autonomy of Council of Europe member states in privacy matters, which are often deeply rooted in moral expectations and cultural preferences for which there is no common European standard.[93] There is furthermore a strong European policy emphasis on leaving internet based services free from direct state regulation. As the Committee of Ministers has declared, 'Member states should promote frameworks for self- and co-regulation by private sector actors with a view to protecting the right to respect for private life and private correspondence.'[94] In the face of these uncertainties, it is ironically the Article 10 democratic argument for greater liberty to publish that has become one of the chief means of defining the proper limits of privacy in the relationship between the media and European state.

Information privacy and reputation in international law

Domestic measures concerning information privacy and reputation are largely beyond the reach of the current objectives of trade liberalization. In most cases, these measures will apply to both domestic and foreign media goods or services that are within the jurisdiction of the state and therefore comply with the national treatment and MFN obligations of the WTO treaties and preferential trade agreements modelled on those agreements.[95] Resort to criminal prosecutions or civil actions for publications that harm the privacy or reputation interests of specific individuals may often attract media attention, but these measures also have a very small impact on international trade in media goods and services, which is dominated by the entertainment media. Plainly, they can have a substantial chilling effect on news reports regarding particular national leaders or prominent individuals if unauthorized exposure or unfavourable comment about them usually leads to substantial fines or damages. Conversely, national data protection regulations, which also tend to be non-discriminatory in their terms of application, are the

---

[93] '[A] wider margin of appreciation is generally available to the Contracting States when regulating freedom of expression in relation to matters liable to offend intimate personal convictions within the sphere of morals or, especially, religion': *Wingrove v. the United Kingdom* (Application No. 17419/90) (25 November 1996), para. 58.

[94] Council of Europe, Committee of Ministers, Declaration on human rights and the rule of law in the Information Society, CM (2005) 56 final (13 May 2005), 2. The right to respect for private life and correspondence. See also Council of Europe, Committee of Ministers, Recommendation on Measures to Promote the Democratic and Social Contribution of Digital Broadcasting, Rec (2003) 9, Appendix, para. 11.

[95] General Agreement on Tariffs and Trade 1994 (incorporating GATT 1947) (15 April 1994), 33 ILM 1153 (1994), and General Agreement on Trade in Services (15 April 1994), 33 ILM 1167 (1994). On the GATT and GATS national treatment and most favoured nation obligations, see Chapter 5.

subject of substantial international cooperation aimed at achieving common standards. This work, which is discussed in Chapter 11, is being undertaken precisely
because these national measures have an enormous impact on global trade in goods
and services.

In spite of their small impact on world trade, national laws restricting public
scrutiny and criticism of politicians, public officials, and other public figures have a
huge symbolic importance for the goal of entrenching liberal democratic values in
international law. The liberty to publish extensive information and comment
regarding public figures and matters of public interest has become an article of
faith in contemporary liberal democratic law and public policy. In the internet era,
this principle has moreover been taken in new directions through the outpouring of
comment about the lives of others that occurs daily in social networking and other
new communications and media services. Public comment about newsworthy
individuals, whether local or national, which was once the preserve of professional
journalists, has become an activity that is potentially open to anyone with access to
the internet. In this global sphere of public communication, the political arguments
for greater liberty to publish have become bound up with economic arguments
about the nature of new media services and the detrimental effect that privacy and
defamation laws can have on their development. This fusion of economic and
political liberalism in relation to new media services has led to recurring expectations that the liberalization of economic relations will also achieve liberal democracy's political ends.[96] Given the failure of international human rights obligations
to secure liberal democratic media freedoms, the potential for greater liberty
through trade obligations will continue to draw keen interest.

As a general matter, international trade rules cannot serve the purposes of liberal
internationalism in the media sector, including the specific aim of exposing people
in positions of power to greater public scrutiny and comment, unless the domestic
measures that protect their privacy and reputations are discriminatory. Here the
question is likely to be whether ostensibly non-discriminatory measures have been
applied in a discriminatory manner to foreign media goods or services and their
suppliers.[97] This may, for example, occur where domestic media are not subject to
equivalent damages or sanctions for the publication of similar information or
comment. Where discriminatory treatment can be shown, the question will immediately be whether that treatment can be justified under the general exceptions
permitted by Article XX of the GATT and Article XIV of the GATS, both of which
permit derogation from core obligations necessary for the protection of 'public
morals'.[98] The concept of public morals covers a range of major public policy

---

[96] See, for example, Bollinger, L., *Uninhibited, Robust, and Wide-Open* (Oxford University Press,
2009), ch 3.
[97] Note that while few states made commitments for audiovisual media services at the conclusion of
the Uruguay Round, further liberalization is likely to occur. China made significant commitments in
this sector in its subsequent Protocol of Accession and media services commitments are contained in
many bilateral trade agreements. See Chapter 5.
[98] On the GATT Article XX and GATS Article XIV general exceptions, see Chapter 5. On other
applications of 'public morals', see Chapter 12.

concerns rooted in prevailing social expectations and member states enjoy considerable discretion in determining the matters that deserve special protection and the
means used to achieve the chosen level of protection.[99] On this basis, there is
substantial room for a state to assert that it has a consistent history of offering a high
level of protection for personal privacy and reputation and its refusal to introduce a
public figure or public interest defence in these areas is well within its discretion in
the area of public morals. A public figure or public interest defence may well be
essential to the goals of contemporary liberal democracy, but the WTO does not
require that its member states adopt liberal democratic values in their treatment of
the media. The difficulty for the state concerned would instead be to justify
discriminatory treatment under the necessity and other conditions imposed by
the GATT and GATS general exception provisions.[100] Even where differences in
treatment can be explained as a side effect of national regulatory regimes, the
necessity test will demand a convincing demonstration that no other set of domestic
measures could achieve the intended result in a less discriminatory way.[101]

International human rights law sits in the background of these trade law issues.
What is starkly different, when compared to European human rights law, is the
relative independence of freedom of expression and information privacy rights.
There is certainly no barrier in the text of the International Covenant on Civil and
Political Rights to a similar merger of these rights through a set of interdependent
principles.[102] Article 19 of the ICCPR permits restrictions on freedom of expression that are provided by law and are necessary for respect of the rights or
reputations of others, while Article 17 states that '[n]o one shall be subjected to
arbitrary interference with his privacy, family, home or correspondence, nor to
attacks upon his honour and reputation'. Indeed, the express reference to honour
and reputation in Article 17 means that, unlike the European Convention, these are
incorporated into a fundamental Covenant right without need of contentious
doctrinal development. The ICCPR Human Rights Committee has also emulated
basic developments in European human rights law in its work on freedom of
expression and respect for privacy.[103]

---

[99] The WTO Appellate Body affirmed in the *US—Gambling,* that under GATS Article XIV(a),
the term 'public morals' denotes standards of right and wrong conduct maintained by or on behalf of a
community or nation. Appellate Body Report, *United States—Measures Affecting the Cross-Border
Supply of Gambling and Betting Service,* WT/DS285/AB/R (7 April 2005), para. 296. See also
Charnovitz, S., 'The Moral Exception in Trade Policy,' *Virginia Journal of International Law* (Spring
1998), 689, Marwell, J.C., 'Trade and Morality: The WTO Public Morals Exception after Gambling',
81 *New York University Law Review* (2006), 802.

[100] See Chapter 5.

[101] See, for example, *China—Measures Affecting Trading Rights and Distribution Services for Certain
Publications and Audiovisual Entertainment Products* (WT/DS363/AB/R) (Appellate Body Report,
December 2009), para. 240.

[102] On the International Covenant on Civil and Political Rights, see Chapter 6.

[103] In relation to Article 19, the ICCPR Human Rights Committee has endorsed the concept of
'public figure' defence to libel actions. See UN Human Rights Committee, *Sixth Periodic Report,
United Kingdom of Great Britain and Northern Ireland,* 18 May 2007, CCPR/C/GBR/6. In relation
to Article 17, it stated that the right to respect for private life and reputation must be guaranteed
against all interferences and attacks whether they emanate from state authorities or from natural or
legal persons, adding that, 'Article 17 affords protection to personal honour and reputation and

The great obstacle to reaching an understanding of freedom of speech and privacy akin to the European model remains the failure to entrench an unequivocal liberal democratic purpose into Article 19, which would then firmly ground the development of public figure or public interest principles. This remains the case despite vigorous efforts to create soft law precedents that will lead to a common global understanding of freedom of expression.[104] The continuing refusal of non-democratic states to accept an international obligation to use liberal democratic standards when imposing restrictions on the media must however be seen in the context of the ongoing transatlantic dispute over the relative importance of information privacy. The United States has, for example, frequently opposed the development of fundamental privacy rights in international law on economic as well as constitutional grounds.[105] Consequently, there is no clear consensus even amongst liberal democracies that Articles 17 and 19 of the ICCPR should be meshed together through a right to freedom of expression rooted in democracy, a positive obligation on states to protect the right to respect for privacy from third parties, and a heavy reliance on proportionality analysis to ensure that information privacy and free speech are given equal weight when they are in conflict.

States are under an obligation to provide adequate legislation to that end. Provision must also be made for everyone effectively to be able to protect himself against any unlawful attacks that do occur and to have an effective remedy against those responsible.' Human Rights Committee, General Comment 16, (Twenty-third session, 1988), Compilation of General Comments and General Recommendations Adopted by Human Rights Treaty Bodies, UN Doc. HRI\GEN\1\Rev.1 at 21 (1994). In 2004, the Human Rights Committee also adopted a General Comment endorsing the argument that ICCPR rights in general 'will only be fully discharged if individuals are protected by the State, not just against violations of Covenant rights by its agents, but also against acts committed by private persons or entities that would impair the enjoyment of Covenant rights in so far as they are amenable to application between private persons or entities': General Comment No. 31 [80] Nature of the General Legal Obligation Imposed on States Parties to the Covenant: 26/05/2004. CCPR/C/21/Rev.1/Add.13.

[104] See for example the 1985 Siracusa Principles, which state that '[a] limitation to a human right based upon the reputation of others shall not be used to protect the state and its officials from public opinion or criticism'. Siracusa Principles on the Limitation and Derogation of Provisions in the International Covenant on Civil and Political Rights, Annex, UN Doc E/CN.4/1985/4 (1985). B. Interpretative Principles Relating to Specific Limitation Clauses, viii.'rights and freedoms of others' or the 'rights or reputations of others'. See also the Special Rapporteurs' Joint Statement of 2000, which states that, '[h]arsh civil defamation laws are often used in place of more overt forms of censorship and can effectively prevent open criticism of government, politicians and the powerful. Civil defamation laws should respect the following principles: *(public figure)* politicians and public officials should have to tolerate a greater degree of criticism; *(public interest)* publications regarding matters of public interest which are reasonable in all the circumstances should not be considered defamatory.' *Statement regarding Key Issues and Challenges in Freedom of Expression*, by the OAS Special Rapporteur on Freedom of Expression, the OSCE Representative on Freedom of the Media and the UN Special Rapporteur on Freedom of Opinion and Expression, February 2000.

[105] On United States government opposition to the European Union data protection principles, see Chapter 11.

11

Protection of Personal Data

Despite the frequent spectacle of major privacy actions before the courts, the anonymous world of data processing has become the central field for the development of privacy law and policy.[1] Over a few decades, data processing has grown from an activity once confined to record keeping within major firms or government departments on mainframe computers to a networked, globalized activity that has become essential to almost every form of commerce and activity of the state. Data processing has also evolved into a diverse set of computer based technologies that can be used to analyse the behaviour of large groups or populations as well as the consumer and social activities of a specific individual. From iris scans and geolocation to the data mining of social networking services, personal information is being collected, stored, processed, and dispersed around the world in ways that are not only growing exponentially but also changing rapidly.

Data processing has also become an indispensable part of the information and entertainment media. As media companies have developed their commercial relationships with individual consumers through subscription television channels, download services, and websites, they have also engaged in extensive data analysis to understand consumer preferences and develop marketing techniques. In this respect, media data processing is much like that carried out in other commercial sectors. Yet journalism also involves the collection and storage of huge amounts of personal information in the form of interviews, government and company records, as well as photographs and films. While much of this is never published, it is acquired in the process of investigating, compiling, and checking published reports and remains stored for reference or future publication. In one sense, this electronic activity is merely a continuation of the traditional practices of journalists. But when combined with contemporary computing and communications technologies, journalism has become much more effective in gathering and analysing personal information, whether uncovering major social trends or exposing the personal life of a politician. In short, data processing is now inseparable from news production.

Viewed optimistically, the rise of data processing is critically important to advances in the security, efficiency, and convenience of contemporary life in an information rich world. These technologies have improved the detection and prevention of crime, coordination of medical services, effectiveness of public

---

[1] Kuner, C., 'Regulation of Transborder Data Flows under Data Protection and Privacy Law: Past, Present, and Future', TILT Law & Technology Working Paper No. 016/2010.

administration, and the marketing of useful goods and services. The greater transparency of contemporary life is moreover not only the price for these advances, but also part of a historic process of cultural change. By voluntarily disclosing information through social and professional networking and other communication services, such as Facebook and Twitter, individuals are voluntarily abandoning the anonymity of twentieth century urban life and returning to the once ubiquitous openness of pre-industrial, small town life.

Despite these arguments, data processing has also had a dramatic impact on personal privacy in ways that are often involuntary or at least lacking in genuine informed consent.[2] At its worst, this is a world of constant and pervasive surveillance that has grown increasingly powerful and embedded in the routines of daily life.[3] While the tools needed to protect privacy are sometimes present within communication and information services, their changing features require a degree of knowledge and alertness beyond the day-to-day awareness of many individuals and families. Even when precautions are taken, personal data can be processed without seeking permission through the combination of commercial design, information, and communication technologies and legal or regulatory gaps.[4] The growth of cloud computing and other ways of seamlessly combining cross border communication and information services have made this more common. Millions of individuals, for example, upload personal information to social networking sites hosted on remote servers, which may well be located in places that permit forms of data processing they do not reasonably expect.[5] Demands by government agencies, commercial companies, as well as criminal and terrorist organizations for new means of accessing protected information are also pushing the pace of technological innovation.[6]

The protection of personal information when processed as data has become one of the most pressing public policy issues of the internet era.[7] There are however

---

[2] Gelman, L., 'Privacy, Free Speech, And "Blurry edged" Social Networks' 50(5) *Boston College Law Review* (2009).

[3] 'Lives of Others: Privacy and the Internet', *Economist* (20 May 2010). See also Solove, D., *The Future of Reputation: Gossip, Rumor, and Privacy on the Internet* (Yale University Press, 2007), ch. 2. Rosen, J., *The Unwanted Gaze: The Destruction of Privacy in America*, (Random House, 2000), chs 1 and 2.

[4] Lipton, J.D., 'Mapping Online Privacy', 104(2) *Northwestern University Law Review* (2010).

[5] On privacy and cloud computing, see *Comments of the Center for Democracy & Technology to the European Commission in the matter of the Consultation on the Legal Framework for the Fundamental Right to Protection of Personal Data* (31 December 2009) <http://www.cdt.org>. See also Gelman, L., n. 2 above.

[6] Recent developments include deep packet inspection, which involves the examination of the actual content of the digital packets used to transmit information across the internet, whose content was once thought to be completely secure. See Daly, A, *The Legality of Deep Packet Inspection* (17 June 2010). Available at SSRN: <http://ssrn.com/abstract=1628024>. Other developments include the identification of the source of anonymized data. See Ohm, P., 'Broken Promises of Privacy: Responding to the Surprising Failure of Anonymization' University of Colorado Law Legal Studies Research Paper No. 09–12 (13 August 2009). The Article 29 Working Party considered the problem of reverse identification of anonymized data in its *Opinion 4/2007 on the concept of personal data* (Opinion 4/2007), 01248/07/EN WP 136, 24. See also Article 29 Data Protection Working Party, *Opinion 1/2008 on Data Protection Issues related to Search Engines*, WP148.

[7] Kenyon, A., and Richardson, M., *New Dimensions in Privacy Law* (Cambridge University Press, 2006).

entrenched differences on whether that protection should be obligatory and how any standards of protection should be achieved.[8] It is at least plain enough that civil actions in the courts for the unauthorized disclosure of private information are inadequate to remedy many privacy concerns about data processing. Globalized commercial practices now affect hundreds of millions of individuals, causing misuses of personal information that are often unnoticed by data subjects, who may individually only suffer small losses or inconveniences. Efforts to achieve better privacy protection in the processing of personal information have therefore tended to concentrate on regulatory rules and codes of conduct, which typically involve some mix of state designed and enforced or market based and consumer driven methods. Yet under those choices between state and market lies the divisive issue of how to achieve the right balance between economic and social liberty and constraint in a world of borderless data processing.[9]

For liberal democratic states, the dual argument for economic and political liberty is especially compelling. Maintaining the free flow of data has become a key factor in economic growth and is well supported by liberal arguments in favour of property rights and the freedom to engage in commerce. On this basis, state interference in data processing ought to be as permissive as possible to accommodate fast changing technologies and commercial needs. At the same time, liberal democratic claims about the importance of the freedom to publish matters of political and social importance gives additional weight to the argument that gathering and publishing personal data should not be unduly encumbered by regulatory restraints. If these are unduly burdensome, how is the democratic scrutiny and criticism of politicians, public officials, and other public figures to be accomplished in an era of electronic work and communication?

Liberalism however also values privacy. Although here, as discussed in Chapter 10, liberal democratic divisions also run deep. Indeed, even the idea that respect for privacy is a fundamental right of equal importance to the right to freedom of expression is disputed. These differences in basic principle have helped to sustain a wide divergence in methods of protecting personal data amongst liberal democracies. In the European view, the human right to respect for privacy, and its special relationship with the right to freedom of expression, provides the foundation for data protection regulation. In the United States, information privacy protection has not been given a similar constitutional status. Instead, a preference for market based solutions has prevailed, largely based on contractual agreements to permit data processing that are subject to the normal rules of consumer protection and selective statutory intervention.[10] In this transatlantic divergence, however, Europe has the

---

[8] Solove, D. and Richards, N., 'Rethinking Free Speech and Civil Liability', 109 *Columbia Law Review* (2009).

[9] Wong, R. and Savirimuthu, J., 'Identity Principles in the Digital Age: A Closer View', *International Journal of Intellectual Property Management* (2009), 396–410.

[10] 'In America privacy is seen as an alienable commodity subject to the market. Disputes about personal information as well as mechanisms for its protection are cast in economic terms: questions about property rights; who "owns" the data collected in a commercial transaction; and who has the right to the rents flowing from its exploitation': Kobrin, S.J., 'Safe Harbours Are Hard to Find: The

weaker hand. In common with other media law policy arguments, the advocates of greater freedom to process data have a natural advantage over those seeking to use legal or regulatory rules to limit the flow of data to protect privacy interests. Commercial and other interests are sufficient to drive the gathering and processing of personal data, while the protection of data privacy requires constant innovation in the creation of regulatory rules and their effective enforcement.

Data protection in the European Union

In the wider sphere of privacy rights, European Union law has so far followed in the wake of the European Convention on Human Rights, accepting its judicially determined balance between the liberty to publish and the protection of the autonomy and dignity of the individual. Even in the field of data protection, efforts to harmonize national rules began in the Council of Europe, which performed its characteristic role as the path breaking European forum for the development of common principles on matters of shared social and political concern. The European Union has however long since taken over as the primary forum for data protection law and policy. The EU Data Protection Directive, adopted in 1995, immediately became Europe's core legislative measure on the protection of personal data.[11] While the Directive followed the privacy principles laid down in the Council of Europe's earlier Convention for the Protection of Individuals with regard to Automatic Processing of Personal Data, it also marked a decisive shift in European work on data protection towards an accommodation with the commercial value of data processing for the single market.[12]

The justification for this shift in forums was therefore largely economic. As banks and other key European service providers were digitizing their record keeping, data protection measures introduced in different member states were beginning to obstruct market integration. The Directive was thus a harmonization of national measures intended to resolve uncertainties regarding the relationship of free movement and non-market public policy exceptions and thereby enable the liberalization of data flows in the single market. It consequently meshes the EU's principles of free movement with information privacy principles derived from Article 8 of the European Convention on Human Rights, which are also general principles of EU law. That status is recognized in the Charter of Fundamental Rights of the European Union, which incorporated not only a parallel to Article 8, but also a

---

Trans-Atlantic Data Privacy Dispute, Territorial Jurisdiction and Global Governance', 30(1) *Review of International Studies* (January 2004), 111–131.

[11] Directive 95/46/EC of the European Parliament and of the Council on the protection of individuals with regard to the processing of personal data and on the free movement of such data (Data Protection Directive).

[12] Ibid., Recital (11): Whereas the principles of the protection of the rights and freedoms of individuals, notably the right to privacy, which are contained in this Directive, give substance to and amplify those contained in the Council of Europe Convention of 28 January 1981 for the Protection of Individuals with regard to Automatic Processing of Personal Data.

specific article on the right to protection of personal data.[13] That data protection right, following the Treaty of Lisbon, is also now set out in Article 16 of the TFEU.[14]

Inevitably, Article 8 of the ECHR also brings its antagonistic relationship with Article 10 into the Directive, as information privacy in European human rights law cannot be understood separately from the Convention right to freedom of expression.[15] In principle, the right to freedom of expression therefore joins the economic principle of free movement to act as a double counterweight to the right to protection of data privacy. That double effect should however not be overstated. The Article 10 right to freedom of expression is largely defined by the democratic interest in open debate regarding matters of general concern. Outside that admittedly large area, Article 10 offers little support for the argument for free flow of data. From a data privacy advocate's point of view, the shift to the European Union is also plainly double edged, placing the right to respect for privacy rights in a context dominated by the rules of free movement assisted by the right to freedom of expression. European Union law, however, also makes the protection of personal data enforcement more effective compared to the consensual legislative instruments of the Council of Europe. Indeed, the Commission's initial draft of the Directive was attacked by commercial companies and some member states, notably Britain, for excessive privacy based restrictions on the free movement of data.[16]

The Directive and the journalistic purposes exception

Despite the adoption of various secondary measures, the 1995 Data Protection Directive remains the chief EU legislative instrument governing the free movement of data and the protection of personal data. Other relevant EU measures implement its principles and supplement them where they are silent.[17] The most important of these is the 2002 Directive on Privacy and Electronic Communications (also

---

[13] Charter of Fundamental Rights of the European Union, Article 7 Respect for private and family life and Article 8 Protection of personal data, which provides that '1. Everyone has the right to the protection of personal data concerning him or her. 2. Such data must be processed fairly for specified purposes and on the basis of the consent of the person concerned or some other legitimate basis laid down by law. Everyone has the right of access to data which has been collected concerning him or her, and the right to have it rectified. 3. Compliance with these rules shall be subject to control by an independent authority.'

[14] TFEU, Article 16, (ex Article 286 TEC), 1. Everyone has the right to the protection of personal data concerning them. On the importance of Article 16, see the speech 'Next steps for Justice, Fundamental Rights and Citizenship' given by Viviane Reding, Vice-President of the European Commission responsible for Justice, Fundamental Rights and Citizenship, 18 March 2010, Brussels.

[15] On the relationship between Articles 8 and 10 in European Human Rights, see Chapter 10.

[16] Raab, C. and Bennett, C., 'Protecting Privacy Across Borders: European Policies and Prospects', 72 *Public Administration* (1994), 95–112 at 107–109; Bennett, C. and Raab, C.,'The Adequacy of Privacy: The European Union Data Protection Directive and the North American Response', 12 *The Information Society* (1997), 245–263 at 248.

[17] See, for example, Directive 2005/60/EC of the European Parliament and of the Council of 26 October 2005 on the prevention of the use of the financial system for the purpose of money laundering and terrorist financing, and, Framework Decision 2008/977/JHA on the protection of personal data in the framework of police and judicial cooperation in criminal matters.

known as the ePrivacy Directive), which is part of the EU regulatory framework for electronic communications and governs data protection and other privacy issues for communications operators.[18] These include network operators that provide access to the internet or other communications platforms through electronic networks, mobile, and telephone connections.[19] Other directives, such as the Electronic Commerce Directive, expressly state that their provisions do not apply to questions relating to data protection.[20] That exclusion does not, however, affect the scope of the Electronic Commerce Directive's rules on liability for internet access and hosting services offered by information society services. Finally, the European Union has adopted secondary legislation that applies the Data Protection Directive's provisions to EU institutions.[21] In this internal EU field, there is also an important interface between these rules and the EU's Transparency Regulation.[22] Under that legislation, EU institutions must refuse access to a requested document where disclosure would undermine the protection of the privacy and the integrity of the individual.[23]

To achieve the complex objective of protecting both the EU's economic interest in the free flow of data and its commitment to the protection of privacy rights, the Data Protection Directive imposes a substantial harmonization of data protection law and regulation on the member states. Under this common regime, when the 'processing of personal data' occurs, a deemed 'data controller' is responsible for the processing of all 'personal data', which includes the more protected category of 'sensitive personal data'.[24] In the EU data protection regime, the data controller,

---

[18] Directive 2002/58/EC of the European Parliament and of the Council concerning the processing of personal data and the protection of privacy in the electronic communications sector (ePrivacy Directive), (as amended by Directive 2009/136/EC).

[19] Directive 2002/58/EC, Article 1.

[20] Directive 2000/31/EC of the European Parliament and of the Council of 8 June 2000 on certain legal aspects of information society services, in particular electronic commerce, in the Internal Market (Electronic Commerce Directive). Article 1(5)(b). On the Electronic Commerce Directive generally, see Chapter 4.

[21] Regulation (EC) No. 45/2001 of the European Parliament and of the Council on the protection of individuals with regard to the processing of personal data by the Community institutions and bodies and on the free movement of such data, OJ L8/1, 12.01.2001.

[22] Transparency Regulation—Regulation (EC) No. 1049/2001 of the European Parliament and of the Council of 30 May 2001 regarding public access to European Parliament, Council and Commission documents. See Chapter 9.

[23] Ibid., Article 4(1). See also Case T-194/04, *The Bavarian Lager Co. Ltd v. Commission of the European Communities*, paras 75–79, in which the ECJ determined that, regardless of the economic interests at issue, transparency obligations do not automatically take priority over the right to protection of personal data. Note also that the privacy protection exception does not contain the overriding condition 'unless there is an overriding public interest in disclosure' that applies to some of the other listed exceptions. In current negotiations over amendments to the Transparency Regulation, the Commission has proposed moving privacy out of this highly protected category, although the European Parliament is opposed to that downgrading of the privacy exception: European Commission, *Proposal for a Regulation of the European Parliament and of the Council regarding public access to European Parliament, Council and Commission documents*, COM (2008) 229 final, European Parliament, *Public access to European Parliament, Council and Commission documents*, P6_TA-PROV(2009)0114.

[24] Directive 95/46/EC, n. 11 above, Article 2(a): 'personal data' shall mean any information relating to an identified or identifiable natural person; (b) 'processing of personal data' shall mean any operation or set of operations which is performed upon personal data, whether or not by automatic

who may be a specific individual or a corporate body, is the key responsible actor, whose residence or establishment in a member state founds its national jurisdiction under the Directive.[25] A data controller must ensure that any processing of personal data carried out under its authority conforms with the basic principles of the Directive, including the primary one that processing must be fair and lawful.[26] In addition, where that processing involves sensitive personal data, the controller must meet further conditions, which include obtaining the data subject's express consent unless narrow exceptions apply.[27]

Media companies become data controllers for many different processing purposes. Some of these are transactional, including the management of subscriber information and marketing efforts, and the Data Protection Directive's restrictions therefore do not give rise to significant freedom of expression concerns. The Directive's restrictions on processing personal data are however a major obstacle to the production and publication of news and current affairs content. Beyond their restrictive effects on investigative journalism when a news media organization is deemed to be a data controller or processor, these rules also create a general barrier blocking access to personal data held by non-media controllers. In terms of the media state relationship, they limit the media's ability to access, use, and publish information about politicians, public officials, and other public figures. In this area, consent, which is the key exception that most commercial data controllers will ordinarily attempt to use to satisfy the Directive's prohibitions, will frequently be difficult or impossible to obtain. Media organizations have therefore sought wherever possible to widen the Directive's exceptions. The European Publishers Council, a media lobbying organization in Brussels, has for example argued for a broader interpretation of consent to include personal information and images voluntarily disclosed online through social networking and other new communications services.[28]

means, such as collection, recording, organization, storage, adaptation or alteration, retrieval, consultation, use, disclosure by transmission, dissemination or otherwise making available, alignment or combination, blocking, erasure or destruction; (d) 'controller' shall mean the natural or legal person, public authority, agency or any other body which alone or jointly with others determines the purposes and means of the processing of personal data, In addition, Article 8 defines sensitive personal data as 'personal data revealing racial or ethnic origin, political opinions, religious or philosophical beliefs, trade-union membership, and the processing of data concerning health or sex life.'

[25] Changes in technologies and the development of new services have also extended the reach of the Data Protection Directive. An individual who does no more than post names and addresses on a community website is probably a data controller under the Directive (Case C-101/01, *Criminal proceedings against Bodil Lindqvist* [2003] ECR I-12971). There are nonetheless many social networking and other Web 2.0 activities that fall outside the scope of the Directive, which does not apply to individuals who process personal data as part of a purely personal or household activity (Article 3(2)). The Directive also arguably does not apply to the provider of a web service hosting third part content, unless it also processes the data posted or made available by users (Article 29 Data Protection Working Party, *Opinion 5/2009 on Online Social Networking*, 01189/09/EN, WP 163 (12 June 2009)).

[26] Directive 95/46/EC, n. 11 above, Article 6.

[27] Ibid., Article 8(2)(e).

[28] European Publishers Council, *Contribution to the Review of the EU Data Protection Directive* (18 December 2009), para. 1.2.2.

The drafters of the Directive certainly attempted to take the special concerns of the media into account. In essence, they accepted that the democratic argument for free speech adds an additional factor that needs to be recognized beyond the balance struck between free movement in the single market and the protection of personal privacy.[29] Article 9 of the Directive therefore obliges member states to provide exemptions or derogations from key obligations where personal data is processed solely for journalistic purposes or the purpose of artistic or literary expression.[30] This is not a blanket exception for the media. It is limited to journalistic or editorial purposes, which in the context of Article 10 of the ECHR must mean expression directed at a matter of general concern. In short, the journalist exception in the Directive is firmly tied to the democratic argument for freedom of expression, whose ambit is carefully contained by the Directive.[31] As the ECJ Grand Chamber has stated, 'Article 9 of Directive 95/46 is to be interpreted as meaning that the activities . . . must be considered as activities involving the processing of personal data carried out "solely for journalistic purposes", within the meaning of that provision, if the sole object of those activities is the disclosure to the public of information, opinions or ideas.'[32] This cautious interpretation reflects the Court's efforts to reconcile a broad view of 'journalism', as required by the right to freedom of expression, with the principle that derogations or limitations concerning the protection of personal data must only apply so far as strictly necessary, as required by the right to respect for privacy.[33] Article 9 also contains a final proviso that the journalism exception shall only apply where it is 'necessary to reconcile the right to privacy with the rules governing freedom of expression'. This proviso, added in the final negotiations over the draft Directive, highlights the Directive's finely wrought balance between privacy and freedom of expression.[34]

---

[29] Directive 95/46/EC, n. 11 above, Recital (37): 'Whereas the processing of personal data for purposes of journalism or for purposes of literary of artistic expression, in particular in the audiovisual field, should qualify for exemption from the requirements of certain provisions of this Directive in so far as this is necessary to reconcile the fundamental rights of individuals with freedom of information and notably the right to receive and impart information, as guaranteed in particular in Article 10 of the European Convention for the Protection of Human Rights and Fundamental Freedoms; whereas Member States should therefore lay down exemptions and derogations necessary for the purpose of balance between fundamental rights as regards general measures on the legitimacy of data processing, measures on the transfer of data to third countries and the power of the supervisory authority; whereas this should not, however, lead Member States to lay down exemptions from the measures to ensure security of processing.'

[30] Ibid., Article 9. See also Recital (17). These key obligations only concern the general rules on the lawfulness of the processing of personal data, the rules on transfer of data to third countries and the rules on the supervisory authority.

[31] As the ECJ stated in Case C-101/01, *Bodil Lindqvist*, n. 25 above, 'the provisions of Directive 95/46/EC do not, in themselves, bring about a restriction which conflicts with the general principles of freedom of expression or other freedoms and rights, which are applicable within the European Union and are enshrined inter alia in Article 10 of the ECHR'.

[32] Case C-73/07, *Reference for a preliminary ruling from the Korkein hallinto-oikeus—Finland— Tietosuojavaltuutettu v. Satakunnan Markkinapörssi Oy, Satamedia Oy* (Grand Chamber, 16 December 2008), para. 65. See also Article 29 Data Protection Working Party, Recommendation 1/97, *Data Protection Law and the Media*. XV/5012/97-EN, WP1 (25 February 1997).

[33] Case C-73/07, n. 32 above, para. 56.

[34] Case C-101/01, n. 25 above, para. 87.

The inclusion of the Article 9 journalism exception was however only an achievement in principle for the media. The Directive created a conceptual framework to permit freedom to use data for legitimate journalistic purposes while also maintaining a minimum level of protection for personal data. It left considerable leeway however for member states to interpret and implement these principles according to domestic conditions.[35] This includes responsibility for determining the proportionate balance between the fundamental rights to freedom of expression and personal privacy.[36] For the media, as well as other commercial data users, this has meant that domestic data protection laws are rife with inconsistencies, which often have different effects on cross border use of data within the EU.[37] In the view of the European Commission, however, media demands for greater consistency must be weighed against the autonomy of member states in determining privacy law and policy, which is often rooted in domestic cultural and ethical beliefs.[38]

Beyond the limitations of the journalistic purposes exception, the Directive as a whole has needed constant re-interpretation to maintain its relevance to new communications and information technologies.[39] Its basic principles were of course established well before the internet became a public communications platform. The common European data protection system introduced under the Directive has therefore struggled to adjust to the changes of the internet era, including mass disclosure of personal information online and the torrent of personal data that crosses borders for processing each day. Nonetheless, EU institutions have argued that the Directive is as a highly dynamic piece of legislation whose principles have been successfully adapted to meet these challenges.[40] In 2007, the European

---

[35] Directive 95/46/EC, n. 11 above, Article 5: 'Member States shall, within the limits of the provisions of this Chapter, determine more precisely the conditions under which the processing of personal data is lawful.'

[36] Case C-101/01, n. 25 above, para. 85, '[I]t is for the national authorities and courts responsible for applying the national legislation implementing the directive to ensure a fair balance between the rights and interests in question, including fundamental rights (for example the right to freedom of expression).' See also Case 275/06, *Productores de Musica de Espana (Promusicae) v. Telefonica de Espana* and Kuner, C., 'Data Protection and Rights Protection on the Internet: The Promusicae Judgment of the European Court of Justice', 5 *European Intellectual Property Review* (2008).

[37] See, for example, International Chamber of Commerce (ICC), *Response to the European Commission Consultation on the Legal Framework for the Fundamental Right to Protection of Personal Data* (December 2009). See also Article 29 Data Protection Working Party, Recommendation 1/97, *Data Protection Law and the Media*. XV/5012/97-EN, WP1 (25 February 1997) and European Publishers Council, *Contribution on the Review of the Data Protection Directive 1995/46/EC.*

[38] Communication from the Commission to the European Parliament and the Council on the follow-up of the Work Programme for better implementation of the Data Protection Directive, COM (2007) 87 final.

[39] Much of the re-interpretation has been carried out by the Article 29 Data Protection Working Party, which was set up under Article 29 of Directive 95/46/EC. It is an independent European advisory body on data protection and privacy. Its tasks are described in Article 30 of Directive 95/46/EC and Article 15 of Directive 2002/58/EC.

[40] 'Directive 95/46/EC has stood well the influx of these technological developments because it holds principles and uses concepts that are not only sound but also technologically neutral. Such principles and concepts remain equally relevant, valid and applicable in today's networked world': European Union, The Article 29 Data Protection Working Party and the Working Party on Police and Justice, *The Future of Privacy: Joint contribution to the Consultation of the European Commission on the*

Commission concluded that the Directive did not require revision and EU efforts should focus on better implementation by member states.[41] Three years later, however, the Commission announced plans for the amendment of the Directive to address major changes in the nature of data processing, such as social networking and behavioural advertising.[42] This policy change also follows the new Article 16 of the TFEU, adopted under the Treaty of Lisbon, which will provide a stronger legislative basis for a new comprehensive directive dealing with free movement of data and respect for personal privacy. An amended Directive could introduce many media significant provisions, including a clarification of the meaning of 'consent' for the processing of sensitive personal data, a requirement for more effective redress mechanisms for data subjects, and a greater emphasis on enforcement through self regulation and other alternative means.[43] The Commission has indicated that these will probably include the use of 'privacy by design', which means integration of privacy and data protection into the design and operation of information and communication technologies.[44]

While an amended Directive may achieve greater consistency in data protection laws and regulation across Europe, for the media, it also threatens to make data collection and processing more difficult. As the European Publishers Council has argued, rules that make notice and consent procedures more obvious to consumers could destroy some of the convenience and appeal of new media services for consumers without improving the protection of personal data.[45] In addition, privacy by design implies that privacy and personal data protection elements will potentially be built into communication and information systems at a level beyond human review. Media access to information could therefore be automatically and invisibly blocked, regardless of the pressing freedom of expression grounds for that information to be evaluated or made public.

legal framework for the fundamental right to protection of personal data (1 December 2009), 02356/09/EN, WP 168, para. 42.

[41] Communication from the Commission to the European Parliament and the Council on the follow-up of the Work Programme for better implementation of the Data Protection Directive, COM (2007) 87 final.

[42] Reding, V., speech, n. 14 above.

[43] The Article 29 Data Protection Working Party and the Working Party on Police and Justice, *The Future of Privacy* n. 40 above.

[44] See Reding, V., speech, n. 14 above. See also The Article 29 Data Protection Working Party and the Working Party on Police and Justice, *The Future of Privacy* n. 40 above, para. 47. See also Opinion of the European Data Protection Supervisor on Promoting Trust in the Information Society by Fostering Data Protection and Privacy, 18 March 2010.

[45] European Publishers Council, *Contribution to the Review of the EU Data Protection Directive* (18 December 2009).

The Directive outside Europe

Like other comprehensive European regimes designed to address a combination of economic and social issues, the Data Protection Directive must deal with the territorial limits of European public order. Its solutions are both defensive and offensive. On the first front, it attempts to ensure as much as possible that the processing of personal data sourced in Europe remains subject to the Directive's rules, regardless of the location of the processing or the responsible data controller.[46] Secondly, the Directive is part of a general policy of encouraging non-EU governments and businesses to adopt European data protection principles. The media, once again, has divided interests in these efforts to maintain European standards and also to export them globally. There are obvious commercial advantages in having a unified regime that operates on common principles, reducing barriers to cross border media services and making the business environment more predictable. The export of those principles also benefits companies already familiar with their requirements. Yet, less restrictive data processing laws in the United States and elsewhere clearly serve the media's commercial interests better and the export of European standards erodes those advantages.[47]

The provisions of Article 4 of the Directive extend its jurisdictional reach outward as far as possible. Under Article 4(1), the Directive's rules must be applied even where a non-EU service provider makes use of equipment on the territory of a member state, which can include accessing a personal computer located on the territory of a member state.[48] This may occur where a person located in Europe uses the internet to contact a non-European based website, which then automatically downloads a cookie onto the user's computer and processes his or her personal data via the cookie.[49] The 'use of equipment' rule was however created well before the development of cookies and similar information retrieval software. Its application can therefore turn on arbitrary differences in how this kind of software

---

[46] 'The EU and its Member States should guarantee this fundamental right for everybody, in so far as they have jurisdiction. In a globalised world, this means that individuals can claim protection also if their data are processed outside the European Union': The Article 29 Data Protection Working Party and the Working Party on Police and Justice, *The Future of Privacy* n. 40 above, para. 23.

[47] On the advantages of the American approach, see, for example, Swire, P. and Litan, R., *None of your Business: World Data Flows, Electronic Commerce and the European Privacy Directive* (Brookings Institution, 1998), 123.

[48] Article 29 Data Protection Working Party, Working document on determining the international application of EU data protection law to personal data processing on the Internet by non-EU based web sites, 5035/01/EN/Final, WP 56 (30 May 2002).

[49] A cookie is a small piece of text file placed on a user's computer hard drive by an internet web page server to assist in basic authentication and identification tasks, such as storing website preferences. The Article 29 Data Protection Working Party has stated that persistent cookies containing a unique user ID are personal data and therefore subject to applicable EU data protection legislation (*Opinion 1/2008 on Data Protection Issues related to Search Engines*, WP 148). See also Article 29 Data Protection Working Party, Working document on determining the international application of EU data protection law to personal data processing on the Internet by non-EU based web sites, 5035/01/EN/Final, WP 56 (30 May 2002).

collects personal data. As the International Chamber of Commerce has argued, '[d]eeming non-EU data controllers to be "using" equipment in the EU when an EU individual goes to their web sites using various automated tools (such as cookies) is a legal fiction that implies that the vast majority of foreign websites are subject to EU data protection rules, since most websites make use of such tools'.[50] European Union institutions have also come to accept that the Directive's rules need to be adjusted to take better account of changes in technologies and communication practices.[51]

Where the processing of personal data occurs beyond the jurisdictional reach of its rules, the Directive attempts to impose other solutions. In principle, member states must prohibit transfers of personal data to third countries unless any subsequent processing is governed by adequate data protection standards.[52] This sweeping prohibition can however be avoided if the data transfer is arranged in a manner that ensures that the data subjects concerned have given their informed consent.[53] In addition, the adequacy requirement can be satisfied through a variety of mechanisms aside from the full adoption of European equivalent standards by the country in question, including 'binding corporate rules' and 'standard contractual clauses'.[54] These permit non-EU companies to bind themselves to data protection standards that the Commission has deemed to be adequate.[55]

The development of these alternative mechanisms has been driven forward by the scale and importance of data flows between Europe and America. Yet that transatlantic trade has also grown in the face of deep policy divisions over the proper relationship of privacy to economic and political liberty.[56] In the 1990s, while

---

[50] International Chamber of Commerce, *Response to the European Commission Consultation on the Legal Framework for the Fundamental Right to Protection of Personal Data* (December 2009).

[51] The Article 29 Data Protection Working Party and the Working Party on Police and Justice, *The Future of Privacy* n. 40 above.

[52] Directive 95/46/EC, n. 11 above, Article 25(1): 'Member States shall provide that the transfer to a third country of personal data which are undergoing processing or are intended for processing after transfer may take place only if, without prejudice to compliance with the national provisions adopted pursuant to the other provisions of this Directive, the third country in question ensures an adequate level of protection'. Note that the Directive demands equivalent protection within Europe and only adequate protection outside Europe. See Article 29 Working Party, *Transfers of personal data to third countries: Applying Articles 25 and 26 of the EU data protection directive*, DG XV D/5025/98, WP 12 (24 July 1998). Note that the mere act of making personal data available to individuals in third countries through the internet does not constitute a transfer of that personal data to third countries, Case C-101/01, n. 25 above.

[53] Directive 95/46/EC, n. 11 above, Article 26.

[54] The Council and the European Parliament have given the Commission the power to determine, on the basis of Article 25(6) of Directive 95/46/EC, whether a third country ensures an adequate level of protection. See also the Article 29 Data Protection Working Party and the Working Party on Police and Justice, *The Future of Privacy* n. 40 above.

[55] See, for example, Commission Decision on standard contractual clauses for the transfer of personal data to processors established in third countries, under Directive 95/46/EC (2002/16/EC) (27 December 2001). Binding Corporate Rules were introduced by the WP 29 in 2003.

[56] Bennett, C., and Raab, C., n. 16 above.

Europe saw the right to respect for private life as the foundation for its new regional data protection regime, data processing policy in the United States put market mechanisms first and state intervention as a last resort.[57]

Liberty of thought presupposes that information be freely available, and thus is usually believed to conflict with government imposed restrictions. Second, sectoral restrictions, if any, are preferred over comprehensive rules on the treatment of personal information. Following the principle of free flow of information, legislatures respond only to specific issues. Legal standards are justified only where targeted for a particular problem: therefore standards often develop on an ad hoc basis, by reaction to public scandals.[58]

This public policy consensus was also firmly grounded in the US Constitution and its exceptionally strong protection afforded to freedom of expression.[59] While the abuse of personal privacy in online services has since become a major public concern in the United States, this has not led to comprehensive data protection legislation.[60] American personal data protection law therefore remains a patchwork of federal and state legislation directed at different privacy issues with various data protection elements. From the European Commission's perspective, this American mix of self regulatory regimes and limited state oversight falls far short of the Directive's adequacy requirements.

Given the economic importance of data flows to the transatlantic trade relationship, both sides have made serious efforts to negotiate a workable compromise. The centrepiece of these negotiations is the EU-US Safe Harbour Arrangement; a flawed, but moderately successful, mechanism that marries American volunteerism with European state supervision.[61] Under the Safe Harbour Arrangement, US based companies can formally agree, or 'self-certify', to operate under principles modelled on the main requirements of the Directive and its important exceptions, including the journalistic purposes exception. In principle, observance of these principles is ultimately subject to enforcement action by the US Federal Trade

---

[57] *Privacy and Self Regulation in the Information Age,* National Telecommunications and Information Administration, US Department of Commerce, 1997.

[58] Reidenberg, J., and Gamet-Pol, F., 'The Fundamental Role of Privacy and Confidence in the Network', 30 *Wake Forest Law Review* (1995), 105–125, 114. 'The law should serve as a gap filler, facilitating individual action in those situations in which the lack of competition has interfered with private privacy protection ... The purpose of these rights is to facilitate—not to interfere with—the development of private mechanisms and individual choice as a means of valuing and protecting privacy': Cate, F., *Privacy in the Information Age* (Brookings Institution, 1997), 131.

[59] See Swire, P. and Litan, R., n. 47 above, 152. See also DeCew, J.W., *In Pursuit of Privacy: Law, Ethics and the Rise of Technology* (Cornell University Press, 1997).

[60] See, for example, Rosen, J., 'The Web Means the End of Forgetting', *New York Times* (19 July 2010).

[61] On the Safe Harbour Arrangement, see Heisenberg, D., *Negotiating Privacy: The European Union, The United States and Personal Data Protection* (Lynne Rienner Publishers, 2005); Farrell, H., 'Constructing the International Foundations of E-Commerce—the EU-US Safe Harbor Arrangement', 57(1) *International Organization* (Spring 2003), 277–306; and Shaffer, G., 'Managing U.S.-EU Trade Relations Through Mutual Recognition and Safe Harbor Agreements: "New" and "Global" Approaches to Transatlantic Economic Governance?' 9(29) *Columbia Journal of European Law* (2002).

Commission.[62] In 2000, the European Commission formally recognized the Safe Harbour Arrangement as satisfying the adequacy requirement of the Data Protection Directive.[63] From the outset, however, there have been differences of interpretation over the meaning and implementation of the Safe Harbour principles.[64] The United States government's interpretation of the journalistic purposes exception is stated in distinctively American constitutional terms, contrasting the 'rights' of a free press under the First Amendment with privacy protection 'interests' rather than rights.[65] In spite of these differences, the importance of cooperation on data protection for economic and other shared goals has outweighed dissatisfaction with current arrangements. Indeed, following the destruction of the World Trade Towers, US requirements for access to foreign sourced personal data shifted the focus of the transatlantic debate from commerce to security.[66] Yet, while the security field remains a key element in US-EU cooperation on privacy and data protection, the rise of mass participation in social networking and other services has also brought renewed attention to the commercial uses of personal data.[67]

In contrast to its complex dealings with the United States, the European Union has had some success in exporting the Directive as a model for data protection to

---

[62] The introduction of FTC oversight, made possible by linking company self certification to Section 5 of the Federal Trade Commission Act which prohibits unfair or deceptive acts or practices in or affecting commerce, was necessary to satisfy the European demand for an impartial, independent regulatory body equipped with necessary enforcement powers. Article 29 Working Party, *Judging Industry Self Regulation*, 1998. Swire, P. and Litan, R., n. 47 above 162.

[63] Commission Decision 2000/520/EC pursuant to Directive 95/46/EC of the European Parliament and of the Council on the adequacy of the protection provided by the safe harbour privacy principles and related frequently asked questions issued by the US Department of Commerce. See also Kobrin, S.J., n. 10 above.

[64] European Commission Staff Working Document: The implementation of Commission Decision 520/2000/EC on the adequate protection of personal data provided by the Safe Harbour Privacy Principles and related Frequently Asked Questions issued by the US Department of Commerce, SEC (2004) 1323.

[65] 'A. Where the rights of a free press embodied in the First Amendment of the U.S. Constitution intersect with privacy protection interests, the First Amendment must govern the balancing of these interests with regard to the activities of U.S. persons or organizations. Personal information that is gathered for publication, broadcast, or other forms of public communication of journalistic material, whether used or not, as well as information found in previously published material disseminated from media archives, is not subject to the requirements of the Safe Harbor Principles': Safe Harbor Privacy Principles FAQ, issued by the US Department of Commerce on 21 July 2000.

[66] See, for example, Agreement between the European Union and the United States of America on the processing and transfer of Financial Messaging Data from the European Union to the United States for the purposes of the Terrorist Finance Tracking Program. EN. L 195/42. Official Journal Union, 27 July 2010. Note also that in 2006, the EU-US Justice and Home Affairs Ministerial Troika established the EU-US High Level Contact Group on information sharing and privacy and personal data protection to exchange of information for law enforcement purposes regarding the prevention and prosecution of terrorism and serious transnational crime. The HLCG presented a final report on 28 May 2008 and an addendum to this report on 28 October 2009, identifying common data protection principles and policy objectives.

[67] See, for example, Trans Atlantic Consumer Dialogue, *Resolution on Social Networking*, DOC NO: INFOSOC 39-09, May 2009, which urges the US and EU governments to enact and enforce laws, among other things, forbidding making access and use of consumers' data a condition for using social network sites and requiring social networks to protect users' data from unauthorized use and third party access.

some of its other major trade partners.[68] Aside from domestic demands for improved data protection, these governments have also seen the attraction of gaining EU adequacy approval for trade purposes. However, only a handful of countries have done so thus far and, realistically, the prospects for a European directed global regime are poor.[69] The Directive nonetheless provides a model for domestic groups demanding greater privacy protection in government and commercial handling of personal data. Even in the United States, the Directive's principles have influenced public debate and perception of the issues, giving privacy advocates practical examples of alternative standards.[70] The spread of the European data protection model outside Europe has also increased pressure on major US firms to adopt European compliant privacy practices over the past decade.[71]

Data protection in the Council of Europe

The European Union's 1995 Data Protection Directive is now well established as the region's primary source of rules for the protection of personal data. European data protection law, however, originated much earlier in the Council of Europe, which adopted its first resolutions on the protection of the privacy of individuals vis-à-vis electronic data banks in the private and public sectors in the mid 1970s.[72] The Council of Europe was moreover the logical European forum for this work, which involved social and cultural issues that at the time were on the far margins of EU competence. The protection of personal data was also an area the European Court of Human Rights seemed unlikely to address in any significant way, despite the obvious connection with the fundamental right to respect for private life under Article 8 of the Convention. This stemmed, first, from the fact that abuses of privacy in data processing typically have a slight impact on specific individuals, despite affecting millions of consumers or citizens. In these circumstances, there would be few suitable applications before the Court on which it could build a coherent body of case law. Secondly, it was also unclear within the Council of Europe whether Article 8 even possessed the necessary scope to create positive

[68] Birnhack, M., 'The EU Data Protection Directive: An Engine of a Global Regime', 24(6) *Computer Law & Security Report* (2008).
[69] Kong, L., 'Data Protection and Transborder Data Flow in the European and Global Context', 21(2) *European Journal of International Law* (2010), 441–456. See also Bali, V., 'Data Privacy, Data Piracy: Can India Provide Adequate Protection for Electronically Transferred Data?' 21 *Temple International & Comparative Law Journal* (2007), 103, 115.
[70] Shaffer, G., n. 61 above.
[71] See Birnhack, M., n. 68 above, and Shaffer, G., 'Globalization and Social Protection: The Impact of Foreign and International Rules in the Ratcheting Up of U.S. Privacy Standards', 25 *Yale Journal of International Law* (Winter 2000), 1–88.
[72] Committee of Ministers, Resolution (73) 22 on the Protection of the Privacy of Individuals vis-à-vis Electronic Data Banks in the Private Sector (1973) and Committee of Ministers, Resolution (74) 29 on the Protection of the Privacy of Individuals vis-à-vis Electronic Data Banks in the Public Sector (1974). See also Raab, C. and Bennett, C., n. 16 above, 100.

obligations to protect personal data.[73] It therefore fell to the Council of Europe's Committee of Ministers to set out common principles for data protection regulation in the member states.

That ground breaking work on positive obligations in the field of information privacy was however later overtaken by the Court's development of the Article 8 right to respect for private life as a positive obligation, which has both enriched and complicated the field of data protection.[74] In relation to information privacy, the obligation of state parties to provide effective remedies for breaches by private parties brought Article 8 into a close, mutually defining relationship with the Article 10 right to freedom of expression.[75] More specifically, the democratic purposes of freedom of expression, which the Court has identified as the core purpose of Article 10, has come to define key limits to information privacy rights. For the media, Article 10 is therefore a powerful instrument to penetrate data protection rules when furthering public scrutiny or comment on matters of general concern.[76]

In 1981, the Council of Europe adopted its Convention for the Protection of Individuals with regard to Automatic Processing of Personal Data, which built on the earlier Committee of Ministers data protection resolutions and created Europe's first binding data protection obligations.[77] This treaty was also part of a larger western European initiative that sought to achieve a parallel international agreement on data protection within the OECD. Opposition from the United States, however, ensured that that instrument, the 1980 OECD Guidelines on the Protection of Privacy and Transborder Flows of Personal Data, contains notable differences with the Council of Europe Convention. These included an obligation for state parties to incorporate the CE Convention's basic principles for data protection into domestic law as well as the creation of stronger safeguards for especially sensitive personal data.[78] More generally, unlike the OECD Guidelines,

---

[73] 'It is also doubtful whether the European Convention on Human Rights, of which Article 8 (1) guarantees to everyone "the right to respect for his private and family life, his home and his correspondence", offers satisfactory safeguards against technological intrusions into privacy. The Committee of Experts on Human Rights has noted, for example, that the Convention takes into account only interferences with private life by public authorities, not by private parties': Explanatory Report to Committee of Ministers, Resolution (73) 22 on the Protection of the Privacy of Individuals vis-à-vis Electronic Data Banks in the Private Sector.

[74] It is now well accepted that European data protection rules are grounded in Article 8 of the convention. See, for example, Council of Europe, Committee of Ministers, Declaration on human rights and the rule of law in the Information Society, CM (2005) 56 final (13 May 2005), 2. The right to respect for private life and correspondence. See also Purtova, N., 'Private Law Solutions in European Data Protection: Relationship to Privacy, and Waiver of Data Protection Rights', 28(2) *Netherlands Quarterly of Human Rights* (2010), 179–198.

[75] See Chapter 10.

[76] See, for example, *Fressoz and Roire v. France* (Application No. 29183/95), (Grand Chamber, 21 January 1999).

[77] Council of Europe, 1981 Convention for the Protection of Individuals with regard to Automatic Processing of Personal Data, (ETS No. 108), and Additional Protocol to the Convention for the Protection of Individuals with regard to Automatic Processing of Personal Data, regarding supervisory authorities and transborder data flows (ETS No. 181).

[78] Ibid., Articles 4 and 6. See also *Explanatory report on the convention for the Protection of Individuals with regard to the Automatic Processing of Personal Data*, Council of Europe, Strasbourg, 1991.

the Convention does not underscore the importance of protecting the free flow of data, focusing instead on the need to protect personal data from unauthorized or improper use. Nor does it take up the problem of the restrictive effects of data protection rules on journalists, referring only obliquely to the right to freedom of expression. Article 9 of the Convention permits conditional derogation from key provisions for measures that are necessary to protect, among other things, 'the rights and freedoms of others', which according to the Explanatory Report to the Convention includes freedom of the press.[79]

For over a decade, the Convention was Europe's main statement of common principles and obligations regarding the protection of personal data. Yet the very process the treaty encouraged, the creation of law based, domestic data protection regimes, created barriers to the flow of data in the single market. The broad language of the Convention left state parties free to design domestic regulations reflecting their particular social and economic circumstances, but emerging differences between national regimes raised the costs of compliance for cross border data flows. Their harmonization therefore became a pressing objective for the European Commission, which led to the EU Data Protection Directive.[80] While the creation of the Directive, which adopted and expanded the Convention's principles, made the CE treaty largely irrelevant for states within the European Economic Area, it continues to fulfil the secondary role of coordinating public policy and law across the divide between the EU and the rest of Europe.[81] The Council of Europe has also promoted the treaty internationally, inviting non-European states to become parties without success.[82] In the past decade, the Committee of Ministers has also been active in developing European policy regarding data processing through the

[79] Ibid., Article 9(2)(b). See also *Explanatory report on the convention for the Protection of Individuals with regard to the Automatic Processing of Personal Data*, Council of Europe, Strasbourg, 1991, para. 58.

[80] Directive 95/46/EC, n. 11 above, Recital (11): 'Whereas the principles of the protection of the rights and freedoms of individuals, notably the right to privacy, which are contained in this Directive, give substance to and amplify those contained in the Council of Europe Convention of 28 January 1981 for the Protection of Individuals with regard to Automatic Processing of Personal Data.' See also *Explanatory Memorandum on the Amendments to Convention 108 Allowing the Accession of the European Communities*.

[81] See, for example, Council of Europe, Committee of Ministers, Recommendation on measures to promote the public service value of the Internet, CM/Rec (2007) 16E, which urges CE member states to 'harmonise legal frameworks in this area without unjustifiably disrupting the free flow of information, in particular by: a. improving their domestic frameworks for privacy law in accordance with Article 8 of the European Convention on Human Rights and by signing and ratifying the Convention for the Protection of Individuals with regard to Automatic Processing of Personal Data (ETS No. 108); b. providing appropriate safeguards for the transfer of international personal data to states which do not have an adequate level of data protection.' This connection with the EU Data Protection Directive is maintained in various ways, the most obvious being the coordination of amendments: Additional Protocol to the Convention for the Protection of Individuals with regard to Automatic Processing of Personal Data, regarding supervisory authorities and transborder data flows (ETS No. 181).

[82] 'The Council has restated the potentially universal value of the Convention ETS No. 108, in particular during the World Summit on the Information Society in Tunis (November 2005) and within the framework of the Internet Governance Forum in Athens (2006) and Rio (2007)': Standards on Privacy and Personal Data: Resolution on the urgent need for protecting privacy in a borderless world, and for reaching a Joint Proposal for setting International Standards on Privacy and Personal Data Protection. 2009 31st International Conference of Data Protection and Privacy.

internet and other digitized communications networks. It has emphasized not only the general obligation of member states to protect privacy and freedom of expression in new communications and media services, but also included specific requirements, such as protecting the information privacy of children in these environments.[83] As the Committee declared in 2008, 'other than in the context of law enforcement, there should be no lasting or permanently accessible record of the content created by children on the Internet which challenges their dignity, security and privacy or otherwise renders them vulnerable now or at a later stage in their lives'.[84]

Data protection in international law

International public policy concerning transborder data flows first developed in the late Cold War era, when the core areas of consensus and the many areas of disagreement were first mapped out. While the importance of transatlantic policy making in world affairs has since declined, the positions taken by the United States and the western Europeans in that period continue to frame the evolving global debate over data protection. The United States government, concerned to secure the free flow of data essential to the growth and further integration of world markets, argued that commercial data use should be free as much as possible from legal and regulatory controls.[85] This reflected a domestic preference for private law based solutions worked out through contract obligations and property rights, supplemented with issue specific legislation. The American position also took full advantage of the rhetorical power of the combined liberal arguments for economic and political liberty, pursuing the goal of a 'free flow of information' as new communication and information technologies were opening up transborder financial and other commercial services.[86] In short, the United States wished to intervene as little as possible. For a majority of western European governments, however, liberalization of cross border data flows was only possible on the basis of comprehensive data protection rules, a view that had already prevailed in the Council of Europe's work on its own Data Protection Convention.[87] There was,

---

[83]   See, for example, Council of Europe, Committee of Ministers Recommendation for the Protection of Privacy on the Internet: Guidelines for the Protection of Individuals with Regard to the Collection and Processing of Personal Data on Information Highways, No. R (99) 5, Council of Europe, and Committee of Ministers, Declaration on human rights and the rule of law in the Information Society, CM (2005) 56 final (13 May 2005), 2. The right to respect for private life and correspondence.

[84]   Declaration of the Council of Europe Committee of Ministers on protecting the dignity, security and privacy of children on the Internet (February 2008).

[85]   Kirby, M., 'The History, Achievement and future of the 1980 OECD Guidelines on Privacy', *Round Table on the 30th Anniversary of the OECD Guidelines on Privacy, OECD* (10 March 2010).

[86]   Drake, W.,'Territoriality and Intangibility: Transborder Data Flows and National Sovereignty', in Nordenstreng, K. and Schiller, H. (eds), *Beyond National Sovereignty* (Greenwood Publishing Group, 1993), 259–313 at 279.

[87]   Council of Europe, 1981 Convention, n. 77 above. See also Bennett, C. and Raab, C., n. 16 above, and Kirby, M., n. 85 above.

consequently, considerable European support for a similar treaty based, multilateral solution.

During the 1970s, the Organisation for Economic Co-operation and Development (OECD) and the United Nations Commission on Human Rights separately initiated work on data protection standards. In comparison to the United Nations, the Paris based OECD, a closed membership club of democratic, market based economies, offered a relatively convenient forum for these states to work through differences regarding the transborder flow of data.[88] There were also few obvious alternatives in this pre-WTO era for negotiations restricted to market based economies. The GATT was limited to trade in goods, while transborder data flows were largely related to trade in services. The wider membership of the United Nations moreover risked the interjection of other policy agendas, which the then unfolding NWICO crisis in UNESCO aptly illustrated.[89] In 1980, the OECD negotiations led to the adoption of the OECD Guidelines on the Protection of Privacy and Transborder Flows of Personal Data.[90] The Guidelines contain a core area of consensus in the transatlantic debate over the regulation of transborder data flows, which is set out in eight principles of data protection regulation.[91] These principles are non-binding and leave member states considerable discretion in how they should be implemented, including the key issues of responsibility, accountability, and enforcement. This avoidance of specific rules was in effect an agreement to disagree on major underlying questions that included European assertions that the protection of personal data is grounded in a fundamental human right to privacy and that adequate data protection requires a legislative framework and an institutional authority with the power to enforce remedies. The Guidelines do however set out the principle that transborder personal data flows should only be restricted where the receiving country does not substantially observe the Guidelines or where domestic privacy legislation would be circumvented.[92]

While the Guidelines did not prevent a widening of the gulf between the American and European data protection policies, their generality also gave them flexibility to accommodate the ensuing revolution in information and communication technologies. The position within the OECD through the rise of the internet has continued to be that regulatory and self regulatory methods are equally valid, although it has also stressed the importance of integrating public and private sector

---

[88] Convention on the Organisation for Economic Co-operation and Development (adopted 14 December 1960), First recital: 'Considering that economic strength and prosperity are essential for the attainment of the purposes of the United Nations, the preservation of individual liberty and the increase of general well-being.'

[89] Drake, W., n. 86 above, 275. On the NWICO, see Chapter 6.

[90] 1980—OECD Recommendation concerning the Guidelines on the Protection of Privacy and Transborder Flows of Personal Data, adopted by the Council of the OECD on 23 September 1980, Annex: Guidelines on the Protection of Privacy and Transborder Flows of Personal Data.

[91] OECD Guidelines on the Protection of Privacy and Transborder Flows of Personal Data, Principles: 1) collection limitation, 2) data quality, 3) purpose specification, 4) use limitation, 5) security safeguards, 6) openness, 7) individual participation, and 8) accountability. See also Reidenberg, J and Gamet-Pol, F., n. 58 above, 118.

[92] OECD Guidelines, n. 91 above, para. 17.

methods of data protection and the achievement of effective enforcement.[93] More recently, the organization has emphasized the need for effective remedies for individuals who 'suffer harm from actions that violate laws protecting privacy wherever they may be located', but has not pursued the question of what an effective remedy entails.[94] While policy differences may have prevented the OECD from developing specific solutions to the protection of personal data, by charting the common ground the 1980 guidelines have remained an important reference point for data protection policies.

In 1990, the UN Human Rights Commission sponsored work on data protection finally culminated in the adoption of the United Nations Guidelines concerning Computerised Personal Data Files by the UN General Assembly.[95] Like the OECD Guidelines, the UN Guidelines also set out core principles that member states should take into account in their legislation and administrative regulations concerning data processing.[96] They are brief, general, and therefore open to widely different interpretation and make no specific mention of freedom of expression. They are at least applicable to all UN member states, unlike the OECD Guidelines, which are limited to its members. For proponents of a global standard setting agreement on the protection of personal data, the OECD and UN Guidelines were therefore important, but insufficient, steps towards that goal. Since their adoption, there have been several new initiatives aimed at the adoption of a multilateral convention or similar instrument to set comprehensive data processing standards. These efforts have faced several major difficulties, including not only the long running arguments over the proper balance between state and market based methods of protecting personal data, but also more recent governmental concerns about potential restrictions on the state's power to process personal data for national security and public order purposes.

---

[93] Member countries will take steps to 'ensure that effective enforcement mechanisms' are available both to address non-compliance with privacy principles and to ensure access to redress: OECD *Ministerial Declaration on the Protection of Privacy on Global Networks* DSTI/ICCP/REG(98)12/FINAL (October 1998). See also OECD Declaration on Transborder Data Flows (11 April 1985), which emphasizes an integrated approach combining regulation and self regulation as well as legal, technical and educational solutions to the problems or personal data processing, and see: 1998—OECD *Ministerial Declaration on the Protection of Privacy on Global Networks* DSTI/ICCP/REG(98) 12/FINAL, and also OECD Working Party on Information Security and Privacy, *Privacy Online: Policy And Practical Guidance*, DSTI/ICCP/REG(2002)3/FINAL, (4) which states that '[t]here is agreement, however, that there is no single uniform solution. A mix of regulatory and self-regulatory approaches blending legal, technical and educational solutions that suit the legal, cultural and societal context in which they operate holds the promise to provide effective solutions that, beyond the objective of building bridges, go to the actual integration of different elements into viable solutions.'

[94] 2007 OECD Recommendation on Cross-Border Co-operation in the Enforcement of Laws Protecting Privacy, Annex.

[95] Guidelines for the Regulation of Computerized Personal Data Files, Adopted by General Assembly Resolution 45/95 of 14 December 1990, A/RES/45/95, General Assembly, 68th plenary meeting, 14 December 1990.

[96] Ibid., 1. Principle of lawfulness and fairness, 2. Principle of accuracy, 3. Principle of the purpose-specification, 4. Principle of interested-person access, 5. Principle of non-discrimination, 6. Power to make exceptions, 7. Principle of security, 8. Supervision and sanctions, 9. Transborder data flows, 10. Field of application.

The pursuit of different solutions to data protection issues in different international fora has also limited progress towards a multilateral agreement. These have ranged from the International Law Commission,[97] through the International Conference of Data Protection and Privacy Commissioners (ICDPPC),[98] to the International Organization for Standardisation (ISO).[99] In May 1996, for example, the consumer policy working group of the ISO proposed the development of an international standard on privacy.[100] Recognizing the potential overlap with the work of the ICDPPC, the proposal called for cooperation in identifying 'mutual interests in the area of data protection and privacy within both organisations and the Working Group's goal to harmonise aspects for identity management, biometrics and privacy in the context of information technology with a set of international standards'.

The response of the International Conference of Data Protection and Privacy Commissioners to the ISO's work on data privacy was initially cautious, expressing concern that these plans were not consistent with internationally recognized privacy principles and that the proposed industry standard was intended as a replacement for legal and regulatory measures.[101] Its 2004 Resolution on a Draft ISO Privacy Framework Standard did however state that,

[a] global privacy standard could contribute to create and improve the guarantees on personal data protection particularly in those countries without any kind of adequate regulation. The standardisation of privacy technology could play an important role in assisting controllers to comply with existing national and international legal requirements on data protection.[102]

By 2007, Conference opposition had softened considerably. Its new resolution asked national data protection authorities to become actively involved in the work

---

[97] The United States government opposed International Law Commission work in this area. See State Department of the United States of America, Legal Adviser Bellinger's statement before UN 6th Committee (ILC report) re 'Diplomatic Protection' (25 October 2006), which states that, '[w]e see less utility for work by the Commission on the proposed topic of Protection of Personal Data in Transborder Flow of Information. This is a highly complex and technical subject, which is being considered in several other fora and about which there remain significant unresolved political and policy debates. We also question whether the topic meets the Commission's criteria for addition to the long-term agenda or active consideration in that it does not appear to be "sufficiently advanced in stage in terms of State practice to permit progressive development and codification."'

[98] From 1979 International Data Protection and Privacy Commissioners' Conferences have been held annually. The Conferences, which have no status in international law, work by consensus and function as both a cooperative network of national data protection authorities and an annual event, which includes the joint adoption of declarations and resolutions.

[99] The International Organization for Standardization (ISO) is not an intergovernmental organization. It is a worldwide federation of national standards bodies from around 130 different countries. The ISO's work results in international agreements which are published as International Standards.

[100] This consisted of three proposed standards including, ISO 29100—A Privacy Framework (defining privacy requirements for processing of personal information in any information system in any jurisdiction). ISO Working Group 5 (Identity Management and Privacy Technologies) within Sub-Committee 27 (Information Technology Security).

[101] Resolution on a Draft ISO Privacy Framework Standard, 26th International Data Protection and Privacy Commissioners' Conference (September 2004).

[102] Ibid.

of the ISO on international privacy standards affecting information technology.[103] The Conference has also moved forward with its own plans for a multilateral agreement on data protection standards. Following its 2005 Montreux Declaration, which called for a legally binding instrument which clearly sets out in detail the rights to data protection and privacy as enforceable human rights, the Conference took up this issue again at Madrid in 2009.[104] The resulting Madrid Resolution, also known as the Joint Proposal for International Standards on the Protection of Personal Data and Privacy, lays out the basic elements for a universal convention in terms that are wide enough to encompass American, European, and other approaches to data protection.[105]

If these efforts to create a binding agreement on the processing of personal data reach fruition, the relationship between the resulting convention rules and international trade law will require some clarification. Legal and other domestic measures intended to protect personal data clearly raise barriers to the cross border flow of data and obstruct international trade in goods and services. All international work, from the OECD Guidelines to the Madrid Resolution, envisions non-discriminatory domestic measures that provide general rules of conduct for public and private sector data processors regardless of base of operation. They therefore, in principle, fall outside the scope of the core GATT and GATS national treatment and MFN obligations and the equivalent provisions of preferential trade agreements.[106] Nonetheless, data protection regimes have grown increasingly complex, frequently involving national legislation and regulatory authorities working in combination with co regulatory frameworks and codes of conduct. There is consequently a considerable risk that these national measures are applied in discriminatory ways to foreign goods and services or their suppliers.[107] Having negotiated the Safe Harbour Arrangement with the United States, the European Union has, for example,

---

[103] Resolution on Development of International Standards, 29th International Data Protection and Privacy Commissioners' Conference (September 2007).

[104] Montreux Declaration: The Protection of Personal Data and Privacy in a Globalised World: A Universal Right Respecting Diversities, 27th International Conference of Data Protection and Privacy Commissioners (September 2005).

[105] Madrid Resolution: Joint Proposal for International Standards on the Protection of Personal Data and Privacy, 31st International Conference of Data Protection and Privacy Commissioners (November 2009). See also *Comments by the Department for Homeland Security Privacy Office and the Staff of the U.S. Federal Trade Commission on the Joint Proposal for International Standards in the Protection of Privacy with regard to the Processing of Personal Data*, Office of International Affairs at the US Federal Trade Commission (10 August 2010).

[106] General Agreement on Tariffs and Trade 1994 (incorporating GATT 1947), (15 April 1994), 33 ILM 1153 (1994), and General Agreement on Trade in Services, (15 April 1994), 33 ILM 1167 (1994). On the GATT and GATS national treatment and most favoured nation obligations, see Chapter 5. While electronic commerce provisions are now common in preferential trade agreements, few include specific data protection provisions. Wunsch-Vincent, S., 'Trade Rules for the Digital Age' in Panizzon, Pohl, and Sauvé (eds), *GATS and the Regulation of International Trade in Services* (Cambridge University Press, 2008) and Horn, H., Mavroidis, P.C., and Sapir, A., *Beyond the WTO? An Anatomy of EU and US Preferential Trade Agreements* (Bruegel Blueprint Series, vol. VII, 2009).

[107] Singleton, S., 'Privacy as a Trade Issue: Guidelines for U.S. Trade Negotiators', The Heritage Foundation, *Economic Freedom Project Report* No. 2-2002. See also Shaffer, G., 'Globalization and Social Protection: The Impact of EU and International Rules in the Ratcheting up of U.S. Data Privacy

laid itself open to the claim that the terms of the agreement are less demanding than those required of other trade partners.[108] Variations in treatment of this kind are potentially in conflict with multilateral as well as bilateral trade commitments.

While data processing controls now reach into all areas of commerce, including international trade in goods, their impact is greatest on trade in services, which in the media sector includes advertising, marketing, and subscription services as well as news and current affairs content services. To the extent that states have undertaken GATS obligations in media related sectors, the discriminatory application of data protection rules is a lurking issue for WTO law.[109] Data protection was an area of obvious difficulty for the negotiators during the Uruguay Round, who covered this field indirectly in the 'right to regulate' assurance in the Preamble to the GATS and directly in Article XIV general exceptions.[110] The legitimate grounds for derogation in that article include two grounds relevant to data protection. As discussed in Chapter 10, the Article XIV general exceptions include measures necessary to protect public morals, which include elements of personal privacy, whether protected by privacy laws or data protection rules. GATS XIV also includes measures 'necessary to secure compliance with laws or regulations which are not inconsistent with the provisions of this Agreement including those relating to . . . (ii) the protection of the privacy of individuals in relation to the processing and dissemination of personal data and the protection of confidentiality of individual records and accounts'. This legitimate ground is notably less extensive than other Article XIV grounds, such as public morals and public order, applying only to measures that secure compliance with laws or regulations that are themselves GATS consistent. Consequently, direct reference to data protection in this provision arguably reduces the extent that a privacy element within public morals includes data protection. On the other hand, the scope of public morals, which is a substantive ground, should not be significantly affected by this reference to a technical process.

There is, in addition, the question of whether a discriminatory data protection measure that falls within the scope of the GATS XIV grounds can also satisfy the necessity and chapeau conditions of Article XIV.[111] Gregory Shaffer has argued that, despite differences in the way the EU Data Protection Directive is applied to third countries as compared to the EU-US Safe Harbour Arrangement, it is likely to satisfy the GATS XIV conditions.

Standards', 25 *Yale Journal of International Law* (Winter 2000), 1–88 and Reidenberg, J., 'E-Commerce and Trans-Atlantic Privacy', 38 *Houston Law Review* (2001), 717.

[108] Shapiro, E., 'All is Not Fair in the Privacy Trade: The Safe Harbor Agreement and the World Trade Organization', 71(6) *Fordham Law Journal* (2002), 2781–2821.

[109] On audiovisual services commitments, see Chapter 5.

[110] The Preamble to the GATS refers not only to the need, when pursuing greater liberalization, to give 'due respect to national policy objectives', but also recognizes, 'the right of Member States to regulate, and to introduce new regulations, on the supply of services within their territories in order to meet national policy objectives [. . .]'.

[111] On the necessity and chapeaux conditions of GATT XX and GATS XIV, see Chapter 5.

The WTO Appellate Body would likely refrain from engaging in a close balancing of trade and privacy interests, and rather review the process by which the EC takes account of foreign privacy protections. In compliance with the WTO Appellate Body's approach in past jurisprudence, the EC has studiously assessed U.S. practices affecting the privacy of EC residents; U.S. authorities and companies have had access to EC officials to comment on the Directive and its applications; and the EC has engaged in prolonged, detailed discussions with U.S. representatives to examine 'adequate' (as opposed to identical) data privacy safeguards which could be applied. Thus, in the case of the EC data privacy enforcement, WTO rules should shield the EC from a U.S. retaliatory threat. WTO rules thereby have reinforced pressure on the United States to negotiate a set of more stringent, data privacy requirements in the form of the Safe Harbour Principles.[112]

Despite the many complexities of data protection policy in the international sphere, there is apparent momentum towards a binding multilateral agreement containing some prescriptive elements. Yet so far, the special data processing needs of the media, as part of their function of gathering and reporting information in democratic societies, have not featured as a special concern. The Madrid Resolution does contain several provisions that indirectly reflect the media's interest in the free flow of data and its underlying freedom of expression justifications for processing sensitive personal data without consent.[113] Principle 6 notably refers to the processing of data consistently with the purposes and principles of the Universal Declaration of Human Rights and the International Covenant on Civil and Political Rights. However, that reference is undoubtedly intended to invoke the Article 17 right to respect of privacy as much as the Article 19 right to freedom of expression. The Human Rights Committee of the International Covenant on Civil and Political Rights has interpreted that Article 17 right as including strong data protection elements, stating that,

[t]he gathering and holding of personal information on computers, data banks and other devices, whether by public authorities or private individuals or bodies, must be regulated by law. Effective measures have to be taken by States to ensure that information concerning a person's private life does not reach the hands of persons who are not authorized by law to receive, process and use it, and is never used for purposes incompatible with the Covenant. In order to have the most effective protection of his private life, every individual should have the right to ascertain in an intelligible form, whether, and if so, what personal data is stored in automatic data files, and for what purposes. Every individual should also be able to ascertain which public authorises or private individuals or bodies control or may control their files. If such files contain incorrect personal data or have been collected or processed contrary to the provisions of the law, every individual should have the right to request rectification or elimination.[114]

[112] Shaffer, G., 'Managing U.S. E.U. Trade Relations Through Mutual Recognition and Safe Harbor Agreements', EUI Working Papers, RSC No. 2002/28 (Robert Schuman Centre, 2002), 51–52.
[113] Madrid Resolution, n. 105 above, See 6. The Principle of Lawfulness and Fairness, and 12. The General Principle of Legitimacy.
[114] ICCPR Human Rights Committee, *General Comment 16, The right to respect of privacy, family, home and correspondence, and protection of honour and reputation (Article 17)*, (Thirty-second session, 1988).

Consequently, it appears likely that any future multilateral convention on data protection will be based on a majority view among participating states that fundamental rights to freedom of expression and privacy are of equal importance. It will therefore easily tolerate domestic rules that only permit the media to process sensitive personal data without consent where there is a compelling public interest and basic safeguards are retained.[115] On the other hand, a successful Convention will also need the tacit support of the United States, if not formal participation, and thus cannot include language that is directly incompatible with American constitutional doctrines concerning free speech and privacy.

[115] See, for example, the International Working Group on Data Protection in Telecommunications (the Berlin Group), within the International Conferences of Data Protection and Privacy Commissioners, Working Paper on Freedom of Expression and Right to Privacy regarding On-line Publications (15 April 2004), which states, 'If the information regarding private and family life, private correspondence, and dwelling relate to an identified or identifiable natural person, the main provisions concerning personal data protection must be applied and in balance. The right to freedom of expression should not prevail over the right to privacy.'

12

Pornography and Violence

For centuries, published words and images evoking sex and violence have flowed or filtered across national boundaries. What began with printed words and illustrations has been a driving force in the commercialization of new communications technologies, from photographs to mobile phone video downloads.[1] For just as long, state efforts to suppress or restrict these forms of public entertainment have also helped to define the relationship between the media and the state. Historically, the laws of the state regarding pornography, violence, and other harmful or offensive media content were often dictated by religious doctrine and ethics. The identity of the state was therefore frequently enmeshed with religious orthodoxy and it treated religious non-conformity as a form of political dissent. Despite the secularization of contemporary liberal democracy, few if any states have shed that historic responsibility for the policing of public moral conduct. The state's authority and legitimacy remains bound to public expectations that the state will use its powers to prevent or punish personal conduct that causes gross offence and few democratically elected governments feel entirely free to ignore that sentiment.

State restriction on the publication of sexual and violent content is consequently one of the great sources of public controversy for the liberal democratic state. Liberalism provides powerful economic and political arguments against state restrictions on the liberty to publish on grounds of obscenity or indecency. The publication of words and images evoking sex, violence, and other matters may cause general offence, but it is also sustained by a resilient market driven by strong demand and profitability. The state moreover can only suppress this form of entertainment media if it is prepared to use far reaching measures and unrelenting enforcement that is backed by a sustained public moral consensus. Liberal economic liberties, based on property rights and the freedom to engage in commerce, are in obvious tension with the suppression of this market and operate in tandem with liberal commitments to the political and social liberty of the individual to choose his or her own way of living and expression. For the media, liberalism therefore offers a broad argument for a liberty to publish that includes the right to offend and shock majority opinion in all aspects of life. Society in general, communities, and other individuals must tolerate these consequences of value pluralism. In short, if you do not like it, look away.

---

[1] 'Indeed, it is porn that has made the net into a viable medium for conducting electronic business, and continues to do so', Bradwell, D., 'Sex Drive', *Internet Magazine* (October 1998), 38.

That broad argument however has several weaknesses. The democratic argument, the mainstay of much liberal free speech theory, focuses on expression that is important to public participation in democratic life. That does not exclude depictions of sex or violence, which are obviously important to many political, social, and economic concerns. There are good reasons to allow the inclusions of sex and violence in dramatic as well as news programmes where it reflects important aspects of human life. Yet the democratic argument has little application to pornographic and violent content that is consumed for personal pleasure and has little or no connection with major public concerns. Similar considerations apply to the argument that sex and violence is an important subject for artistic expression, which can enrich personal and collective understanding of life.[2] Mass market pornography is however directed at stimulation rather than intellectual reflection.

Sexual or violent pornography fares better under the Millian argument for an open sphere of debate in which all ideas contend, even the self evidently bad.[3] In this market place of ideas, majority demands to suppress the publication of repugnant images and words are subject to close scrutiny, which in principle will expose superstition, ignorance, and misunderstanding.[4] The difficulty here is that the liberty to publish is intended to protect a sphere in which ideas of all kinds contend and pornography often does not express ideas. Its object is to gratify sexual lust and similar desires. To include pornography within this open sphere simply because it is a form of human expression reduces this to a market place that is simply a metaphor for indiscriminate consumption. There is nonetheless an alternative argument that the profits from pornography and other entertainment content of little intellectual value help to sustain the general flow of media goods and services. In contrast, liberal deontological arguments for personal autonomy provide a much stronger justification for the liberty to publish and distribute sexual and violent pornography. These arguments embrace personal exploration and fulfilment and give human sexual identity and desire a much higher value when it appears as a form of media content.

Liberal arguments that support the liberty to publish pornography rely heavily on the harm principle to define their limits. According to that idea, the liberty to speak and publish should not be restricted unless the expression at issue causes serious harm, or at least causes a significant risk of serious harm. The question of what forms of pornography are harmful is however one of the irresolvable controversies of contemporary liberal democratic life. It is certainly reasonable to think that the more extreme forms of sexual or violent pornography can influence at least some individuals to engage in physically or mentally harmful acts. Contemporary liberalism has however sought to contain that sphere of content, anxious that it will become an excuse to impose the illiberal moralist demands by democratic majo-

---

[2] On the importance of artistic expression within the framework of freedom of speech, Bezanson, R., *Art and Freedom of Speech* (University of Illinois Press, 2009).

[3] On Millian principles of freedom of expression, see Chapter 2.

[4] DeCew, J., 'Free Speech and Offensive Expression', 21(2) *Social Philosophy and Policy* (2004), 81–103 at 101.

rities.[5] Certainly the idea that pornography causes moral harm is often rejected because of its association with perfectionist views of human life that are inconsistent with a liberal society in which individuals are free to pursue their own form of a good life. There is nonetheless an intuitively influential view that extreme images of sex and violence need not result in observable harm to constitute a gross affront to human dignity.[6] On that basis, the harm principle arguably does not capture all forms of content that the state ought to restrict and should therefore be extended to include gross offence.[7]

In liberal democracies, acceptance of different values and the validity of individual choice have tended to transform the public policy problem of pornography from one of general public morality into one of specific harm. Here the focus has been overwhelmingly on the potential harm to children from exposure to images of sex and violence.[8] This focus on the protection of children is based on their mental immaturity and consequent susceptibility to harmful influences as well as the right of parents to determine the social and cultural environment in which their children live. While the extent to which children uncritically absorb or emulate what they see or the degree of control parents rather than the state ought to enjoy over their children's understanding of the world are debated in medical and social science, many liberal democracies enforce a public policy position that children require greater protection from sexually explicit or violent content.[9] Efforts to build a similar consensus around the argument that adult pornography should be restricted because it harms women have however been markedly less successful.[10]

---

[5] On moralism, see Chapter 2.

[6] See, for example, Koppelman, A., 'Does Obscenity Cause Moral Harm?', 105 *Columbia Law Review* (2005).

[7] Joel Feinberg argued that '[i]t is always a good reason in support of a proposed criminal prohibition that it would probably be an effective way of preventing serious offense (as opposed to injury or harm) to persons other than the actor, and that it is probably a necessary means to that end', Feinberg, J., *Offense to Others: The Moral Limits of the Criminal Law* (Oxford University Press, 1985), 1. Feinberg, however, also maintained that offence, as a justification for restricting expression, should be tightly limited (26).

[8] See, for example, Livingstone, S., *Children and the Internet: Great Expectations, Challenging Realities* (Polity Press, 2009), ch 6.

[9] On research issues, see United Kingdom, *Safer Children in a Digital World*, The report of the Byron Review for the Department for Children, Schools and Families (2008), paras 1.38–1.44. In Britain, it is a criminal offence to take, permit to be taken, make, possess, show, distribute, or advertise indecent images of children, which includes any images of children, apparently under 18 years of age, involved in sexual activity or posed to be sexually provocative. Section 1, Protection of Children Act 1978 (as amended).

[10] The feminist argument for severe restrictions on the publication or distribution of pornography is based on several kinds of apparent harm to women. The production of highly sexual images of women creates a repressive social environment, which limits the personal autonomy of women. This ultimately encourages violence against women. These arguments face several liberal concerns, including the basic objection that the contending desires and preferences of human beings make the world a hostile environment for many people in different ways. To attempt to restrict expression whenever it has those general negative effects would be ineffective and suffocate the liberty of every individual. See, for example, Feinberg, J., n. 7 above, 127–164; MacKinnon, C., *Feminism Unmodified* (Harvard University Press, 1987); Dworkin, A., *Pornography: Men Possessing Women*, (E.P. Dutton, 1989); Dworkin, R., 'Women and Pornography', 40 (17) *New York Review of Books* (21 October 1993);

Child pornography, meaning images of children intended to be sexually arousing, falls into an entirely different category. This form of pornography is suppressed not only because it may influence those who view it to molest children, but also because child pornography is often produced by harming children.[11] Efforts to suppress child pornography therefore stand out at one end of the spectrum for most liberal democracies, which typically prohibit the publication, distribution, or possession of such content. Few other categories of sexual or violent content are deemed as intolerable as child pornography and subjected to similar absolute prohibitions.[12] Yet, there are few forms of harmful content where it cannot be argued that, in an appropriate context, the content makes a valid contribution to public debate on a matter of general concern or, similarly, is a genuine artistic statement.[13] Aside from these public interest arguments, governments are also aware that efforts to suppress any form of pornography completely are usually ineffective. As efforts to suppress child pornography have shown, the demand for pornography remains high despite legal prohibitions and new communications technologies are quickly exploited to create new distribution networks.

In the face of very different perceptions of harm or gross offence and the difficulties of suppressing the commercial publication of sexual or violent images, liberal democracies have tended to favour rules that segregate rather than ban content. Ideally, segregation permits reasonable access for adults to content that is deemed to be harmful for children, but is judged to be an acceptable choice for informed adults. The sale or rental of film or video game DVDs can, for example, be controlled through age restrictions coded on the packaging and made legally enforceable against retail suppliers.[14] Children and adolescents can also be denied entry to cinemas showing adult rated films, while in the home adult content can be restricted to late evening television or to subscription channels.[15] Access to internet and mobile phone content services can also be limited to users who have access to a valid credit card, which operates as a surrogate age restriction.[16] These methods of segregation use typically mix state, provider, and end user control to prevent access

---

Strossen, N., *Defending Pornography: free speech, sex, and the fight for women's rights* (Scribner, 1995), 242–244; and Watson, L., 'Pornography', 5 *Philosophy Compass* (2010), 535–550.

[11] On the criminalization of child pornography, see O'Donnel, I. and Milner, C., *Child Pornography, Crime, Computers and Society* (Willan, 2007).

[12] See, for example, United Kingdom, Criminal Justice and Immigration Act 2008, section 63, which criminalizes possession of 'extreme pornographic images', which include images of acts involving or appearing to involve 'sexual interference with a human corpse'.

[13] See, for example, United Kingdom, Obscene Publications Act 1959, which makes it an offence to publish an obscene article, and also contains a defence that applies where the publication of the article in question is justified as being for the public good on the ground that it is in the interests of science, literature, art or learning, or of other objects of general concern (s. 4).

[14] See, for example, United Kingdom, Digital Economy Act 2010, ss. 40–41, which concern the regulation of children's access to potentially harmful video games through a combination of industry content rating and statutory offences.

[15] See, for example, United Kingdom, Office of Communications (OFCOM), Broadcasting Code, Section 1. Protecting the Under-Eighteens.

[16] See, for example, United Kingdom, Mobile Broadband Group, Code of Practice for the Self-Regulation of new Forms of Content on Mobiles (June 2009).

to potentially harmful or offensive content by children. They also provide methods of prior notice that adults can use to avoid content they also find distasteful or repugnant.

Many commonly used methods of controlling access to harmful or offensive content necessarily rely on the end user's judgement as to who should be allowed to view the content. Where a DVD is restricted to over 18 purchasers, or adult content is reserved for night-time broadcast or internet services require a valid credit card to gain access, the protection of children is plainly in the hands of the individual who is able to gain access. Indeed, in the internet era, there has been a marked shift towards greater consumer responsibility in liberal democratic states that have declined to apply broadcast era regulation to new media services.[17] Parents are therefore expected not only to understand a variety of content control methods, but also to use blocking and filtering software programmes in the home to control access to unsuitable content. These expectations can however exceed the capacity of individuals to understand new services and their specific access controls, which include content classification schemes as well as technical features.[18] Consequently, sexually explicit or violent content remains easily accessible for many children, not least in the form of user generated content made available through social networking services.

The highly regulated media environment of the analogue broadcast era cannot however be re-established without creating a comprehensive communications and media regulatory regime comparable to that operated in China, which is plainly incompatible with liberal democratic fundamental rights. Instead, many countries rely on an accumulation of regulatory standards and rules that carry different expectations of provider and user responsibility. Free-to-air radio and television may therefore restrict the use of language and images that are relatively unrestricted on competing new media services.[19] At the same time, other content restrictions are disappearing from public view as commercial providers block consumer access to websites and other content sources to avoid potential criminal or civil liability. As a result, national boundaries that appeared to be increasingly irrelevant in the borderless world of internet services are being rebuilt in the evolving architecture of new

---

[17] See Edwards, L., 'Pornography, Censorship and the Internet', in Edwards, L. (ed.), *Law and the Internet*. 3rd edn (Hart Publishing, 2009).

[18] In the United Kingdom, cinema and video films are classified according to the rating categories of the British Board of Film Classification and video games are classified according to the Pan European Game Information (PEGI) industry code, while content rules for television and radio programmes are set by OFCOM.

[19] In Britain, as the government debated the future of media regulation in the late 1990s, the BBC argued that '[b]roadcast media, particularly television, are such a powerful and pervasive influence in daily life that it is important that there are safeguards to protect children and other vulnerable groups against stumbling across unacceptable material at times when they might be watching or listening'. [BBC Presentation to the Culture, Media and Sport Committee Hearings, 1998, 18]. The Communications Act 2003, which underpins the current regulatory system, reflects that view. In the United States, restrictions on broadcast media were upheld under *Federal Communications Commission v. Pacifica Foundation*, 438 U.S. 726 (1978), but see *Fox Television Stations v. Federal Communications Commission* (2d Cir. 13 July 2010).

media services, in which access rules vary according to the user's location.[20] For liberal democracies, the obvious risk here is that these technologies of control not only sacrifice swathes of inoffensive content in order to achieve sufficient breadth to capture targeted harmful content, but also do so beyond public scrutiny.

Pornographic, violent, and offensive content in the European Union

In founding what was to become the European Union, the negotiators of the Treaty of Rome set out a framework that liberalized economic relations between the founding states, but also reserved their powers over the essential functions of the sovereign state. These permissive exceptions to the principles of free movement and market integration inevitably included the policing of public morals, a historic element of the European state. The protection of public morals is consequently both an express ground for legitimate discrimination against the goods and services of other member states under the Treaty on the Functioning of the European Union as well as an implied one under the principle of mandatory public policy exceptions, which covers generally applicable domestic measures.[21] National measures that restrict the publication or distribution of sexual or violent media content in most cases apply to all relevant content, whether published domestically or imported. Yet these measures vary considerably across Europe and, even where content standards are equivalent, the often complex regulatory rules and codes designed to protect the public from those images may be incompatible. Discriminatory effects are therefore common. European Union law nonetheless accepts that there is no common European standard in matters of public morals and that member states are entitled to a substantial margin of discretion when determining what content ought to be restricted on public morals grounds and what means should be used, especially where the object of the restrictions is the protection of children.[22]

That discretion is however subject to the requirements of proportionality, which has been highly effective in exposing major inconsistencies in domestic legislation, which is often directed at the satisfaction of influential public opinion as much as the rational restriction of a particular harm.[23] Once it has moved beyond basic

---

[20] See Maurushat, A. and Watt, R., 'Clean Feed: Australia's Internet Filtering Proposal' (19 March 2009), *Internet Law Bulletin*, 2009, UNSW Law Research Paper No. 2009-7.

[21] On express and implied exceptions to the rules of free movement, see Chapter 4.

[22] 'The principles of proportionality and subsidiarity must be applied and particular respect paid to the cultural diversity manifested in national and local perceptions of the protection of minors and human dignity', European Commission, *Protection of Minors and Human Dignity in Audiovisual and Information Services, Consultations on the Green Paper, Commission Working Document* SEC (97) 1203. On the special significance of the protection of children, see Case C-244/06, *Dynamic Medien Vertriebs GmbH v. Avides Media AG* (2008) 2 CMLR 23, para. 44.

[23] See, for example, Case 34/79, *Regina v. Henn and Derby* [1979] ECR 3795, Case 121/85, *Conegate Limited v. HM Customs & Excise* [1986] ECR 1007. See also *Green Paper on the Protection of Minors and Human Dignity in Audiovisual and Information Services* COM (96) 483 final (16 October 1996), which states, '[m]ember states are entitled to take non-discriminatory measures where justified

questions of rationality, proportionality analysis takes increasing account of competing public policy objectives, which brings European market and non-market public policy into the same legal framework. Here, European and international human rights law supply both context and weight to the problem of disciplining measures aimed at the protection of the public from pornography. The fundamental right to freedom of expression, consequently, works in tandem with the principles of free movement to limit the power of member states to restrict media content.[24] This however also raises the relatively unexplored issue for European media law of whether the economic and political justifications for greater liberty to publish should be given more weight when combined or whether they are instead incommensurable, belonging to different fields of moral thought and operating in different fields of law even when both are taken into consideration. What is certainly clear enough is that the European Court of Human Rights has made the protection of democracy the core purpose of the right to freedom of expression in European human rights law, which significantly limits its impact on domestic measures that restrict sexual and violent entertainment content.[25]

Those domestic measures are, on the other hand, more likely to prevail in the process of proportionality analysis when they convincingly place a competing fundamental human right into the balance. The chief difficulty however is that the European Convention on Human Rights does not refer directly to the most potent human rights obligation in this field: the protection of the rights of the child. The European Court of Justice has therefore turned to international human rights law to draw this obligation into consideration, finding that member states are required to take measures to protect children from material injurious to their well being under relevant United Nations human rights treaties, such as the Convention on the Rights of the Child.[26] Protection of the rights of the child is also enshrined in the objectives of the European Union in the Treaty on European Union and in the Charter of Fundamental Rights of the European Union.[27]

---

for overriding reasons of the public interest, provided that they are strictly proportional to the aim pursued and that there are no other less restrictive measures of equivalent effect available'.

[24] Case C-260/89, *Elliniki Radiophonia Tiléorassi AE v. Dimotiki Etairia Pliroforissis and others* [1991] ECR I-2925, para. 43. See also Chapter 4.

[25] On the core purposes of Article 10 of the European Convention on Human Rights, see Chapter 6.

[26] Case C-244/06, *Dynamic Medien Vertriebs GmbH v. Avides Media AG* [2008] ECR I-505, paras 39–40. See also Case C-540/03, *Parliament v. Council* [2006] ECR I-5769, para. 37. Note also the UN Optional Protocol to the Convention on the Rights of the Child on the sale of children, child prostitution, and child pornography, to which most European countries have already become, or have taken steps towards becoming, state parties. See below for further discussion of the Convention on the Rights of the Child.

[27] Treaty on European Union, Article 3(3) 'It shall combat social exclusion and discrimination, and shall promote social justice and protection, equality between women and men, solidarity between generations and protection of the rights of the child.' Article 24(1), 'Children shall have the right to such protection and care as is necessary for their well-being...' See also the Memorandum of Understanding between the Council of Europe and the European Union (2007), which includes 'the protection of the rights of the child' as a subject for cooperation between the two regional organizations.

In European law, restrictions on sexual, violent, and other harmful or offensive content are also associated with the umbrella concept of human dignity. While this concept is not expressly mentioned in the ECHR, it has become an important element in European human rights law and policy. Famously, the European Court of Justice found in its 2004 *Omega* judgment that the protection of human dignity is a general principle of European Union law and constitutes a legitimate interest capable of justifying a proportionate restriction on free movement.[28] That conclusion is now found in the Treaty on European Union, which declares that the EU is founded, *inter alia*, on respect for human dignity.[29] The EU Charter of Fundamental Rights also prominently states that human dignity is inviolable and must be respected and protected.[30] While the scope of the European right to the protection of human dignity is uncertain, it plainly encompasses protection from media content that a member state reasonably believes is harmful to children or to a wider part of society.[31] That does not however create an unlimited discretion. There will always be a strong EU counter interest in eliminating indefensible discrimination and disproportionate barriers to trade lurking in national controls over pornographic and violent content.

The Audiovisual Media Services Directive

Despite the firm principle of national autonomy in matters of harm and offence in media content, the decision to bring broadcast television services fully into the single market through sector specific legislation made it necessary to harmonize standards for content deemed harmful to children. No European media sector was more encumbered with domestic legal and regulatory restrictions affecting content than broadcast television. It was therefore impossible to achieve a common framework for free movement of television services based on the country of origin principle without addressing the problem of divergent national standards. The Television Without Frontiers Directive, now known as the Audiovisual Media Services Directive, therefore entailed assurances that member states would not be forced to receive television services under the jurisdiction of other member states that contained programme or advertising content falling well below national standards for the protection of children.[32] The solution lay in a mix of prescriptive common standards and rights of derogation. Accordingly, the Directive obliges member states to ensure that television broadcasts by broadcasters under their jurisdiction do not include any programmes 'which might seriously impair the

---

[28] Case C-36/02, *Omega Spielhallen- und Automatenaufstellungs-GmbH v. Oberburgermeisterin der Bundesstadt Bonn* [2004] ECR I-09609, 14.

[29] Article 2 TEU, 'The Union is founded on the values of respect for human dignity, freedom, democracy, equality, the rule of law and respect for human rights, including the rights of persons belonging to minorities. These values are common to the Member States in a society in which pluralism, non-discrimination, tolerance, justice, solidarity and equality between women and men prevail.'

[30] European Union, Charter of Fundamental Rights, Article 1.

[31] Case C-244/06, n. 26 above, para. 37.

[32] On the Audiovisual Media Services Directive generally, see Chapter 4.

physical, mental or moral development of minors, in particular programmes that involve pornography or gratuitous violence'.[33] The Directive also requires that they ensure that children are adequately protected from advertising content that causes physical or moral harm.[34]

These obligations were drafted in language compromised between the need to set out minimum European standards and national demands for autonomy in the field of public morals, which varied across the EU according to religious and cultural circumstances. It was, consequently, necessary to provide additional protection for states concerned that these loosely phrased obligations would force them to permit the reception of content well outside domestic standards for the protection of children. Member states therefore enjoy a right of derogation from the obligation to permit reception and retransmission where a television broadcast coming from another member state 'manifestly, seriously and gravely' breaches the Article 27(1) obligation to prevent the broadcast of content which might seriously impair the physical, mental, or moral development of minors.[35] While this right is subject to several conditions, which limit its use to extraordinary circumstances, the effect is to leave member states with a broad power to decide what content might harm children.[36]

Sexual and violent content in the new media

The European Union's initial policies regarding harmful and offensive content transmitted online were formed in the internet boom of the 1990s. To gain the economic rewards of an 'information society', European governments were urged not to apply the broadcast model of regulation to new internet content services. As the European Commission similarly stated in 1996 that, '. . . it is too early, at this stage of development of the new services, to make specific proposals, especially of a regulatory nature at the Community level'.[37] That year, the Commission also

---

[33] Directive 2010/13/EU of the European Parliament and of the Council of 10 March 2010 on the coordination of certain provisions laid down by law, regulation or administrative action in Member States concerning the provision of audiovisual media services (AVMS Directive), Article 27(1). Under Article 27(2), 'the measures provided for in paragraph 1 shall also extend to other programmes which are likely to impair the physical, mental or moral development of minors, except where it is ensured, by selecting the time of the broadcast or by any technical measure, that minors in the area of transmission will not normally hear or see such broadcasts'. On the AVMS Directive more generally, see Chapter 4.

[34] Ibid., Article 9(1)(g), 'Member States shall ensure that audiovisual commercial communications provided by media service providers under their jurisdiction comply with the following requirements: (g) audiovisual commercial communications shall not cause physical or moral detriment to minors.'

[35] Ibid., Article 3(2). See also Case C-14/96, *Proceedings against Paul Denuit* [1997] ECR I-2785 in which the ECJ determined that a member state cannot unilaterally adopt, on its own authority, corrective or protective measures, designed to obviate any breach by another Member State of rules of Community law, except for the Article 2a right of provisional derogation.

[36] Case E-8/97, *TV 1000 Sverige AB v. Norwegian Government* [1998] 3 CMLR 318 (EFTA Court). In the United Kingdom, the Article 2a right to provisional derogation is exercised under ss. 177 and 178 of the Broadcasting Act 1990. See also *Regina v. Independent Television Commission, ex parte TV Danmark 1 Limited* [2001] UKHL 42.

[37] *Green Paper on the Protection of Minors and Human Dignity in Audiovisual and Information Services* COM (96) 483 final (16 October 1996).

issued provisional guidance regarding illegal and harmful content on the internet that called for 'the right balance between ensuring the free flow of information and guaranteeing protection of the public interest' and rejected any systems of national censorship or control over internet access.[38] The early European policy consensus on internet content was therefore to intervene only where market mechanisms, including self regulation and consumer prudence, had demonstrably failed.

In European Union law, the basic principles were clear enough; newly developing commercial internet services were subject to EU rules on free movement and market integration. The Electronic Commerce Directive, adopted in 2000, built on that legal foundation, adding the principle of country of origin jurisdiction as well as general liability rules for content intermediaries.[39] These additional elements therefore extend across the broad field of information society services coordinated by the Directive, which effectively covers all commercial services that make content available to the public over electronic networks, including newspaper and magazine websites as well as video and blog hosting services, but excluding broadcast services and on-demand audiovisual services.[40] Unlike the AVMS Directive, however, the Electronic Commerce Directive does not contain prescriptive content rules harmonizing European content standards. Instead, it elaborates on the TFEU powers of member states to derogate conditionally from the obligation to permit free movement for reasons that notably include, 'public policy, in particular the prevention, investigation, detection and prosecution of criminal offences, including the protection of minors...'.[41]

The Directive's rules on intermediary liability include important provisions limiting the liability of information society services hosting third party content that violates national content rules. These stipulate that a hosting service should not be liable for third party content unless it possesses actual or constructive knowledge of its illegality.[42] Member states are nonetheless free to set legal and regulatory standards and consequences for harmful and offensive content delivered through information society services, subject of course to EU proportionality factors, including relevant human rights principles.[43] At the same time, the European

---

[38] Commission Communication on 'Illegal and Harmful Content on the Internet' COM (96) 487. See also EC Telecommunications Council Resolution on preventing the dissemination of illegal content on the Internet (27 September 1996), in which the Commission alluding to the model of internet control then developing in Singapore, stated: 'Such a restrictive regime is inconceivable for Europe as it would severely interfere with the freedom of the individual and its political traditions. Due to Europe's complex and open communications infrastructure the practical feasibility of such an approach also remains open to question.'

[39] Directive 2000/31/EC of the European Parliament and of the Council of 8 June 2000 on certain aspects of information society services, in particular electronic commerce, in the Internal Market (Directive on electronic commerce) [2000] OJ L178/1. On the Electronic Commerce Directive generally, see Chapter 4.

[40] On the definition of 'information society services', see Chapter 4.

[41] Directive 2000/31/EC, n. 39 above, Article 3(4). See also Recitals (24)–(26).

[42] Ibid., Article 14.

[43] 'Whereas the national laws in which Member States have laid down rules and principles on the protection of minors and human dignity reflect cultural diversity and national and local sensitivities; whereas, in this regard, particular attention must be paid to the application of the principle of subsidiarity.' Council Recommendation of 24 September 1998 on the development of the competi-

Union has adopted a series of instruments to dissuade member states from applying broadcast era content restrictions on harmful and offensive content to the internet. It has put forward instead an alternative model based on self or coregulatory regimes for service providers combined with greater responsibility or prudence on the part of consumers.[44] This model was certainly a pragmatic assessment of the difficulties of regulating the internet in any way similar to radio and television, but it also reflected the influence of market based policies on the introduction of internet services into Europe from the United States.[45]

The combined model of operator self or coregulation and consumer responsibility is set out in the 1998 Recommendation on the protection of minors and human dignity.[46] This Recommendation was the first EU legal instrument concerning internet based, content services. While its general principles on minors and human dignity apply to all electronic media, including the broadcasters, its Annex on self regulation only applies to information society services.[47] The Recommendation is addressed not only to the member state governments, but also to internet service and access providers, who are asked to develop and implement codes of conduct based on the requirements of applicable laws. In 2006, the EU adopted the supplementary Recommendation on Minors and Human Dignity to extend the range of matters covered by this initiative, including media literacy and media education.[48] These recommendations are also closely linked to a series of EU funded programmes that were initiated in 1998 along with the first recommendation.[49] The difficulty has been in developing both sides of the self

tiveness of the European audiovisual and information services industry by promoting national frameworks aimed at achieving a comparable and effective level of protection of minors and human dignity, Recital (18).

[44] Commission Communication, COM (96) 487, n. 38 above.

[45] 'For the moment, self-regulation seems the best way to promote good practice, possibly backed up by government measures.' European Commission, *Protection of Minors and Human Dignity in Audiovisual and Information Services, Consultations on the Green Paper*, Commission Working Document SEC (97) 1203. See also 1997: European Ministerial Conference at Bonn, 'Global Information Networks: Realising the Potential', 6–8 July 1997, Ministerial Declaration, which states: '19. Ministers stress the role which the private sector can play in protecting the interests of consumers and in promoting and respecting ethical standards, through properly functioning systems of self-regulation in compliance with and supported by the legal system.'

[46] Council Recommendation of 24 September 1998, n. 43 above, is a legal act under Article 249 (ex-A 189) of the EC Treaty.

[47] Annex: Indicative Guidelines for the Implementation, at National Levels, of a Self Regulation Framework for the Protection of Minors and Human Dignity in On-Line Audiovisual and Information Services. The Recommendation asks television broadcasters to try out new digital methods of parental control (such as personal codes, filtering software, or control chips), although it acknowledges the ultimate responsibility of broadcasters for programme content.

[48] Recommendation of the European Parliament and of the Council of 20 December 2006 on the protection of minors and human dignity and on the right of reply in relation to the competitiveness of the European audiovisual and on-line information services industry (2006/952/EC).

[49] The latest of these is the Safer Internet *plus* programme (IP/08/1571), which runs from 2009 to 2013. It follows on from the Safer Internet Action Plan (1999–2004) and its replacement the Safer Internet Plus programme (2005–08). See also Decision no. 276/1999/EC of the European Parliament and of the Council of 25 January 1999 adopting a Multiannual Community Action Plan on promoting safer use of the Internet and new online technologies by combating illegal and harmful content primarily in the area of the protection of children and minors. The aim of the Safer Internet *plus*

regulatory–consumer responsibility model. Governments have had some success in establishing national self or coregulatory regimes for service providers that cooperate to block consumer access to sites hosting harmful content.[50] Major internet content providers, such as YouTube or Facebook, have also established their own codes governing permissible content.[51] It has been far harder to equip the general public for its role in this regulatory network. The comprehensive systems of content classification and related filtering software the Commission called for in the mid-1990s, such as the once widely touted and now abandoned Platform for Internet Content Selection, have yet to be made effective.[52]

Over the past decade, European governments have also become increasingly prescriptive in their approach to new media services, classifying types of services and setting specific content standards. In European Union law, the changing public policy environment became evident it the 2007 amendments to the Audiovisual Media Services Directive. As discussed in Chapter 4, the Commission's initial proposals for a single instrument to govern all audiovisual content services aimed at the general public did not gain the support of a sufficient majority of member states. They did eventually agree, however, that on-demand audiovisual programme services, which compete directly with linear broadcast television services in broadband households, should be subject to equivalent content requirements. This was achieved by carving on-demand audiovisual media services out of the general category of 'information society services' and bringing them into the AVMS Directive under a new prescriptive content regime that included restrictions on harmful content affecting children.[53] The Directive nonetheless affirms the importance of self and coregulation for new media services.[54]

---

programme is to promote, as a supplement to the regulatory framework, the establishment on a voluntary basis of national frameworks for the protection of minors and human dignity in audiovisual and information services through: the encouragement, in accordance with national traditions and practices, of the participation of relevant parties (such as users, consumers, businesses, and public authorities) in the definition, implementation, and evaluation of national measures in the fields covered by this recommendation; the establishment of a national framework for self-regulation by operators of online services, taking into account the indicative principles and methodology described in the Annex; and cooperation at Community level in developing comparable assessment methodologies.

[50] See, for example, the Internet Watch Foundation, which was established in the United Kingdom to assist internet service providers in blocking access to child pornography and other specified illegal content (<http://www.iwf.org.uk>).

[51] See, for example, YouTube Community Guidelines (<http://www.youtube.com>), and Facebook Statement of Rights and Responsibilities (<http://www.facebook.com>).

[52] See Resnick, P. and Miller, J., 'PICS: Internet Access Controls Without Censorship', *Communications of the ACM* 39(10) (October 1996), 87–93. See also Commission Communication, COM (96) 487, n. 38 above, European Commission, *Protection of Minors and Human Dignity in Audiovisual and Information Services, Consultations on the Green Paper*, Commission Working Document SEC (97) 1203, and European Ministerial Conference at Bonn, Ministerial Declaration, n. 45 above, '19 . . . Ministers encourage industry to implement open, platform independent content rating systems, and to propose rating services which meet the needs of different users and take account of Europe's cultural and linguistic diversity.'

[53] Directive 2010/13/EU, n. 33 above, Article 12.

[54] Ibid., Article 4 (7), 'Member States shall encourage co- and/or self-regulatory regimes at national level in the fields coordinated by this Directive to the extent permitted by their legal systems. These

Child pornography

The treatment of child pornography in European media law is distinctively different from issues of general pornography or violent content, reflecting the simple fact
that European governments are all committed to suppressing the publication or
distribution of sexual images of children. In this policy field, European Union law
has gone beyond general and specific powers to derogate from the rules of free
movement to create common prescriptive rules concerning the criminalization of
child pornography. In 1997, under the then operating Justice and Home Affairs
Third Pillar, the member states agreed to criminalize 'the exploitative use of
children in pornographic performances and materials, including the production,
sale and distribution or other forms of trafficking in such materials, and the
possession of such materials'.[55] Another EU Framework Decision followed in
2004, concerning the sexual exploitation of children and child pornography. This
instrument broadened the definition of child pornography in EU law, requiring the
criminalization of the distribution, dissemination, transmission, supply, or making
available of child pornography, as well as its acquisition of possession by consumers.[56] Following the Treaty of Lisbon, the 2004 Framework Decision, which is
now the core EU instrument on child pornography, will become enforceable by the
European Court of Justice.

Council of Europe: offence, harm, and human rights

European human rights law has always shown considerable deference towards
national restrictions on the publication and distribution of sexual and violent
media content, which fall within a vaguely defined field of European public policy
traditionally known as the protection of morals. In this field, broad member state
autonomy is anchored in both principle and practicality. At a fundamental level,
European human rights law and institutions presume not only the existence of
effective states, but also their need to maintain authority and legitimacy. This
includes their ability to ensure that media outlets and forums do not make content
available in a manner that violates the general public's deeply held views about

---

regimes shall be such that they are broadly accepted by the main stakeholders in the Member States
concerned and provide for effective enforcement.' See also Recitals (44) and (58).

[55] Joint Action 97/154/JHA of 24 February 1997 adopted by the Council on the basis of Article
K.3 of the Treaty on European Union concerning action to combat trafficking in human beings and
sexual exploitation of children.

[56] Council of the European Union Framework Decision 2004/68/JHA on combating the sexual
exploitation of children and child pornography, See also the Council Decision of 29 May 2000 to
combat child pornography on the Internet. The Framework Decision defines 'child pornography' as
pornographic material that visually depicts or represents a real child involved or engaged in sexually
explicit conduct, including lascivious exhibition of the genitals or the pubic area of a child, or a real
person appearing to be a child involved or engaged in such conduct, or realistic images of a non-existent
child involved or engaged in such conduct.

harmful and grossly offensive content. While human rights law limits the impact of majority preferences where they may breach protected individual rights, it also accepts the legitimacy of those preferences, especially when they are expressed through democratic processes. Consequently, European member states are entitled to take into account the religious, social, and cultural traditions and beliefs of their citizens when imposing restrictions on media content. Indeed, the European Court of Human Rights accepts not only that moral standards vary significantly across Europe, but also that state parties to the European Convention on Human Rights are best placed to judge how local sensibilities should be protected, given 'their direct and continuous contact with the vital forces of their countries'.[57]

The protection of public morals also has its own foundations in European human rights principles, which potentially give measures that restrict the liberty to publish added weight when balanced against fundamental rights to liberty. These include the principle of human dignity, which underpins the protection of individuals and communities from gratuitous offence and harm, as well as the more specific rights of children to protection from physical and moral hazards.[58] As the Council of Ministers has stated,

Freedom of expression also includes, in principle, the right to impart and receive information and ideas which constitute portrayal of violence. However, certain forms of gratuitous portrayal of violence may lawfully be restricted, taking into account the duties and responsibilities which the exercise of freedom of expression carries with it, provided that such interferences with freedom of expression are prescribed by law and are necessary in a democratic society. More specifically, measures taken to counter gratuitous portrayal of violence in the electronic media may legitimately aim at upholding respect for human dignity and at the protection of vulnerable groups such as children and adolescents whose physical, mental or moral development may be impaired by exposure to such portrayal.[59]

Indeed, the Council of Europe Committee of Ministers has also stated that member states not only have a right but also an obligation to protect children from content which is unsuitable or inappropriate.[60] On the other hand, resort to these general principles highlights the flexibility of proportionality analysis and its openness to

---

[57] *Müller and Others v. Switzerland* (Application No. 10737/84) (24 May 1988), para. 35, *Wingrove v. The United Kingdom,* (Application No. 17419/90) (25 November 1996), para. 58.

[58] See, for example, the European Social Charter, (CETS No. 035), Part I, *Principle* 7: Children and young persons have the right to a special protection against the physical and moral hazards to which they are exposed. Article 7—The right of children and young persons to protection. See also European Social Charter (revised) (CETS No. 163), Part I: 17 Children and young persons have the right to appropriate social, legal and economic protection. Article 17, The right of children and young persons to social, legal and economic protection: With a view to ensuring the effective exercise of the right of children and young persons to grow up in an environment which encourages the full development of their personality and of their physical and mental capacities, the Parties undertake, either directly or in co-operation with public and private organisations, to take all appropriate and necessary measures designed: 1(b) to protect children and young persons against negligence, violence or exploitation.

[59] Council of Europe, Committee of Ministers, Recommendation on the portrayal of violence in the electronic media, R (97) 19, Guideline No. 1—General framework.

[60] Council of Europe, Committee of Ministers, Recommendation on measures to protect children against harmful content and behaviour and to promote their active participation in the new informa-

balancing of a wide array of values and interests against the constitutionalized rights of the individual to liberty.[61]

From a different perspective, all national measures concerning offensive and harmful media content fall within the framework of Article 10 of the ECHR.[62] This follows very clearly from the Court's expansive interpretation of Article 10 (1), which includes expression that offends, shocks, or disturbs the state or any sector of the population.[63] In the realm of explicitly sexual and violent expression, however, the Article 10 right to freedom of expression has played a remarkably muted role. As discussed in earlier chapters, the Court has identified the protection and fostering of democratic society as the core purpose of the right to freedom of expression under the Convention.[64] Consequently, Article 10 has its strongest impact on national measures that limit public access to information and ideas concerning matters of legitimate general interest, especially where they relate to democratic participation and decision making.[65] The Court has also determined that works of expression having an artistic value should also be protected under Article 10, although to a much lesser extent than democratically significant expression.[66]

In distinct contrast, the commercial value of trade in sexual or violent entertainment media has little weight under the ECHR when balanced against national interests in the protection of children from moral harm or the general public from gross offence, particularly where expression is likely to provoke public disorder.[67] These interests arise under Article 10(2), which includes the protection of morals as a named legitimate interest as well as the rights of others, which broadens this field to include offence to religious convictions.[68] On these grounds, the state enjoys a wide margin of appreciation and may, for example, restrict or even prohibit the exhibition or distribution of works of expression in public places.[69] That

tion and communications environment, CM/Rec (2009) 5, Guidelines: I. Providing safe and secure spaces for children on the Internet.

[61] On proportionality analysis, see Chapter 2.

[62] 'Article 10 of the European Convention on Human Rights, as interpreted in the case-law of the European Court of Human Rights, must constitute the general legal framework for addressing questions concerning the portrayal of violence in the electronic media.' Council of Europe, Committee of Ministers Recommendation no. R (97) 19 on the portrayal of violence in the electronic media, Guideline No. 1—General framework.

[63] *Handyside v. United Kingdom* (Application No. 5493/72) (7 December 1976), para. 49.

[64] See Chapters 6, 8, and 10.

[65] '. . . there is little scope under Article 10 para. 2 of the Convention (art. 10–2) for restrictions on political speech or on debate of questions of public interest', *Wingrove* n. 57 above, para. 58. See also *Vereinigung Bildender Künstler v. Austria* (Application No. 68354/01) (25 January 2007).

[66] *Müller and Others v. Switzerland*, n. 57 above, paras 35–36.

[67] On commercial expression under the ECHR, see *Markt Intern Verlag Gmbh and Klaus Beermann v. Germany* (Application No. 10572/83) (20 November 1989), para. 26. See *Otto Preminger Institut v. Austria* (Application No. 13470/87) (20 September 1994), in which the commercial elements of the film exhibition were virtually irrelevant.

[68] '[A] wider margin of appreciation is generally available to the Contracting States when regulating freedom of expression in relation to matters liable to offend intimate personal convictions within the sphere of morals or, especially, religion', *Wingrove*, n. 57 above, para. 58.

[69] *Müller and others v. Switzerland* n. 57 above.

margin is not unlimited, even when democratic interests are not engaged. Where children are adequately protected and no adult is confronted unintentionally or unwillingly with offensive content, there must be compelling reasons to justify an interference with the right to freedom of expression.[70]

In most cases concerning sexual or violent content, applications to the Court have concerned the proportionality of restricted access rather than absolute prohibitions on content. In these circumstances, the Court has taken a close interest in the methods of separation used to deal with potentially offensive or harmful content. It has found less ground for restrictions where plays, films, and exhibitions are made available in controlled environments, such as licensed sex shops or cinemas, rather than places freely accessible to an undefined audience.[71] In *Wingrove*, the Court noted that delivery of videos by post, for example, did not give adequate protection for children because 'once they become available on the market they can, in practice, be copied, lent, rented, sold and viewed in different homes, thereby easily escaping any form of control by the authorities'.[72]

The Court's Article 10 principles regarding the protection of morals have guided the Council of Europe in its efforts to coordinate national laws and policies concerning the broadcast media and later the arrival of internet based media. Throughout the broadcast era, the Court accepted the principle that the broadcast media are more intrusive into households and have greater influence on listeners and viewers than the print media or the cinema.[73] National measures aimed at the broadcast media are therefore not necessarily disproportionate even though they may place more restrictions on content than those applied to other forms of media.[74] The Council of Europe also created prescriptive content rules for satellite television services under the jurisdiction of member states. The 1989 Convention on Transfrontier Television obliges state parties to ensure that programmes on these services respect human dignity and the fundamental rights of others and, in particular, do not

---

[70] *Scherer v. Switzerland* (Application No. 17116/90) (14 January 1993) (E.Comm.H.R., Admissibility Decision), para. 65.

[71] Ibid., para. 62. Similarly, in *Müller v. Switzerland and others*, n. 57 above, at para. 36, the Court pointed out that the paintings at issue, '... were painted on the spot—in accordance with the aims of the exhibition, which was meant to be spontaneous—and the general public had free access to them, as the organisers had not imposed any admission charge or any age-limit. Indeed, the paintings were displayed in an exhibition which was unrestrictedly open to—and sought to attract—the public at large'. See also Council of Europe, Committee of Ministers, Recommendation concerning principles on the distribution of videograms having a violent, brutal or pornographic content, R (89)7, and, Council of Europe, Committee of Ministers, Recommendation on cinema for children and adolescents, R (90)10.

[72] See also *Handyside*, n. 63 above, which concerned the public sale of a book aimed at children that was therefore deemed likely to have a corrupting influence on a substantial proportion of the readers.

[73] *Jersild v. Denmark* (Application No. 15890/89), (Grand Chamber, 23 September 1994).

[74] See *Murphy v. Ireland* (Application No. 44179/98) (10 July 2003), which concerned a prohibition on religious advertising. See also Committee of Ministers Recommendation on the portrayal of violence in the electronic media, R (97) 19, which recommends that the licensing conditions for broadcasters include, 'certain obligations concerning the portrayal of violence, accompanied by dissuasive measures of an administrative nature, such as non-renewal of the licence when these obligations are not respected'.

contain pornography or give undue prominence to violence.[75] The Convention, which is the Council of Europe's most significant legislative initiative in the media sector, has however dwindled in importance as member states have joined the EU or otherwise agreed to accept the obligations of the EU Audiovisual Media Services Directive, which takes precedence over the Convention.[76]

The internet: new concepts of responsibility and liability

The arrival of public internet access in Europe brought an immediate surge in cross border communications, including a rising commercial and amateur trade in sexual and violent content. A decade later, the advent of broadband access to the internet created a vast new dimension to the European entertainment media sector, rapidly equalling or overtaking the influence of television in the home. The internet therefore also created an expansive new field for the application of European public policy regarding harmful and offensive content. As broadband access has become common across Europe, the perception of the internet as a place of potential harm for children has grown. In 2009, the CE Committee of Ministers stated that,

[t]he risk of harm may arise from content and behaviour, such as online pornography, the degrading and stereotyped portrayal of women, the portrayal and glorification of violence and self-harm, demeaning, discriminatory or racist expressions or apologia for such conduct, solicitation (grooming), the recruitment of child victims of trafficking in human beings, bullying, stalking and other forms of harassment, which are capable of adversely affecting the physical, emotional and psychological well-being of children.[77]

Six years earlier, the Committee of Ministers had already declared that, '[p]rovided that the safeguards of Article 10, paragraph 2, of the Convention for the Protection of Human Rights and Fundamental Freedoms are respected, measures may be taken to enforce the removal of clearly identifiable Internet content or, alternatively, the blockage of access to it, if the competent national authorities have taken a provisional or final decision on its illegality'.[78]

Here, however, the organization's initiatives to counter these risks of harm have been complicated by European policy commitments to ensure that the internet fosters economic growth and by differences in domestic standards and definitions for pornographic and violent content. The Council of Europe has consequently

---

[75] Council of Europe, European Transfrontier Television Convention (ETS No. 132), Article 7.

[76] On the failure of the 2009 amendments to the Convention, see Chapter 6.

[77] Council of Europe, Committee of Ministers, Recommendation on measures to protect children against harmful content and behaviour and to promote their active participation in the new information and communications environment, CM/Rec (2009) 5. See also Committee of Ministers Declaration on protecting the dignity, security and privacy of children on the Internet (2008), Committee of Minsters Recommendation on empowering children in the new information and communications environment, Rec (2006) 12, and Committee of Ministers Recommendation of the Committee of Ministers on self-regulation concerning cyber content (self-regulation and user protection against illegal or harmful content on new communications and information services), Rec (2001) 8.

[78] Council of Europe, Committee of Ministers, Declaration on Freedom of Communication on the Internet (Strasbourg, 28 May 2003).

adopted measures endorsing limited state regulation of internet based media services and greater autonomy for content providers and service operators.[79] It has also urged public authorities not to deny public access, through blocking or filtering measures, to information and other communication on the internet, regardless of frontiers. In the same vein, the Committee of Ministers has also declared that member states should not engage in systematic blocking or filtering that restricts public access to internet based information services or impose licence requirements on the operation of personal websites, although they may selectively remove or block illegal content.[80] It has however added the proviso that '[t]his does not prevent the installation of filters for the protection of minors, in particular in places accessible to them, such as schools or libraries'.[81]

The Council of Europe has also endorsed the principle that responsibility or liability for content should cascade down from primary content providers, through various intermediary services, to the ultimate consumer. Accordingly, the Committee of Ministers has urged member states not to impose liability on service providers that merely transmit information or provide access to the internet, or oblige them to monitor the content they carry.[82] In line with the EU Electronic Commerce Directive, the Committee has further recommended that service providers who host third party content should only be held co-responsible if they do not act expeditiously to remove or disable access to information or services after becoming aware of the illegal nature of content.[83] While setting out principles limiting the liability of service providers, the Council of Europe has promoted self or coregulation for internet content or service providers as well as the development of methods to enable greater user control over content.[84] This has included strong encouragement to provider companies to create codes of conduct as well as common standards regarding the rating and labelling of content that carries a risk of harm to children.[85] While supporting the shift in responsibility for content regulation

---

[79] Ibid.

[80] Ibid., Principle 3: Absence of prior state control; see also Council of Europe, Committee of Ministers Recommendation on measures to promote the public service value of the Internet, Rec (2007) 16E, Part III, Openness.

[81] Declaration on Freedom of Communication on the Internet, n. 78 above, Principle 3: Absence of prior state control.

[82] Ibid., Principle 6: Limited liability of service providers for Internet content.

[83] Recommendation on the portrayal of violence in the electronic media, n. 74 above. See also ibid., Principle 6: Limited liability of service providers for Internet content. On the provisions of the Electronic Commerce Directive concerning limits to the liability of internet intermediaries, see Chapter 4.

[84] See Committee of Ministers, Recommendation on self-regulation concerning cyber content, Rec (2001) 8, Declaration on Freedom of Communication on the Internet, n. 78 above, and, Committee of Ministers, Declaration on Human Rights and the Rule of Law in the Information Society, CM (2005) 56 final E (13 May 2005).

[85] Council of Europe, Committee of Ministers, Recommendation on measures to protect children against harmful content and behaviour and to promote their active participation in the new information and communications environment, CM/Rec (2009) 5: Guidelines: I. Providing safe and secure spaces for children on the Internet, II. Encouraging the development of a pan-European trustmark and labelling systems, III. Promoting Internet skills and literacy for children, parents and educators; see also Committee of Ministers, Recommendation on self-regulation concerning cyber content, Rec (2001) 8, and, Declaration on Human Rights and the Rule of Law in the Information Society, ibid., and Council

from the state towards private sector providers as well as consumers, the Council of Europe has nonetheless noted some of the problems lurking in that transfer. The Committee of Ministers has emphasized that the public cannot make informed decisions about content without greater transparency and access to information and guidance.[86] It has also recommended that content and service providers are encouraged to address the problem of private censorship where these companies block or remove content on their own initiative or on the request of a third party.[87]

Child pornography

Beyond the Council of Europe's general efforts to influence national public policy regarding sexual and violent content, the organization has sought to coordinate efforts to suppress access to child pornography. Although the organization began to address this issue well before the arrival of public internet access, as the flow of child pornography over the internet has become a pan-European public policy issue, the Council of Europe has become an important forum for the coordination of national measures.[88] Unlike other areas of sexual and violent media content, where there are often striking differences across Europe regarding what is deemed to be socially acceptable, child pornography has yielded a common European public policy, albeit one whose uniformity has been strengthened by European measures. It is also a form of expression that enjoys virtually no protection under Article 10 of the ECHR and therefore cannot be opposed by appeal to civil liberties. Indeed, the European Court of Human Rights has indicated that state parties are under a positive obligation to protect children from sexual harm.[89]

The Council of Europe's most significant work in this area has been the adoption of two major treaties that, among other things, seek to bring about a common standard of criminal responsibility and law enforcement in the field of child pornography.[90] The first of these is the 2001 Convention on Cybercrime, which was intended to strengthen international cooperation on crimes committed

---

of Europe, Committee of Ministers Recommendation on promoting freedom of expression and information in the new information and communications environment, CM/Rec (2007) 11.

[86] Recommendation on promoting freedom of expression and information in the new information and communications environment, ibid., and Committee of Ministers, Recommendation on measures to promote the respect for freedom of expression and information with regard to Internet filters, Rec (2008) 6.

[87] Declaration on Human Rights and the Rule of Law in the Information Society, n. 84 above.

[88] Committee of Ministers Recommendation concerning sexual exploitation, pornography and prostitution of, and trafficking in, children and young adults, R (91) 11.

[89] *K.U. v. Finland* (Application No. 2872/02) (2 December 2008), para. 46. '... Where the physical and moral welfare of a child is threatened such injunction assumes even greater importance. The Court recalls in this connection that sexual abuse is unquestionably an abhorrent type of wrongdoing, with debilitating effects on its victims. Children and other vulnerable individuals are entitled to State protection, in the form of effective deterrence, from such grave types of interference with essential aspects of their private lives.' See also *Stubbings and others v. The United Kingdom* (Application No. 22083/93), (22 October 1996).

[90] See also Declaration on Human Rights and the Rule of Law in the Information Society, n. 84 above, II. 3. '[P]rivate sector actors are urged to participate in the combat against virtual trafficking of child pornography images and virtual trafficking of human beings.'

through use of the internet and other computer networks and deals with child pornography amongst an assortment of internet related activities.[91] This treaty is also open to participation by selected non-European observer states.[92] These prominently included the United States, which took a leading role in the negotiation of the Cybercrime Convention and consequently had a major influence on its structure and content.[93] The treaty is therefore more than an instrument for European cooperation and is intended to be a model for global standards, offering a template for the development of further international agreements and domestic laws.

While the suppression of child pornography is grounded in the fundamental principle of human dignity and typically involves no major democratic concerns, the Cybercrime Convention does contain some protections against indiscriminate criminalization. Article 9 obliges state parties to criminalize the production, offering, making available, distribution, transmission, procuring, or possession of child pornography through use of a computer system.[94] This article however includes the proviso that these powers and procedures should be subject to 'conditions and safeguards provided for under its domestic law, which shall provide for the adequate protection of human rights and liberties, including rights arising pursuant to obligations it has undertaken under the 1950 Council of Europe Convention for the Protection of Human Rights and Fundamental Freedoms, the 1966 United Nations International Covenant on Civil and Political Rights . . . '. Aside from this resort to rights of freedom of expression where definitions of child pornography are overly broad, these treaties also guarantee rights to fair legal proceedings.[95]

The child pornography provisions of the Cybercrime Convention were however a somewhat opportunistic addition given space in a treaty primarily aimed at the problems of computer network security and intellectual property protection. They are, as a result, tied to internet based communication and isolated from the broader legal and policy context in which states more often deal with the protection of children. In 2007, the Council of Europe remedied that shortcoming when its introduced child pornography provisions into the new Convention on the

---

[91] Council of Europe, Convention on Cybercrime, (ETS No. 185), Articles 9, 15. The Cybercrime Convention came into force in 2004. It obliges state parties to establish and enforce laws concerning unauthorized access, interception, or interference with a computer or computer system as well as interference or misuse of devices, computer-related forgery, computer-related fraud, prohibited acts related to child pornography, or copyright and neighbouring rights.
[92] Aside from member states of the Council of Europe, the Cybercrime Convention is open to participation by Canada, Costa Rica, Dominican Republic, Japan, Mexico, Philippines, South Africa, and the United States, of which the United States alone has ratified the treaty. On participation by non-Council of Europe countries, see the Council of Europe, Committee of Ministers Recommendation on measures to promote the public service value of the Internet, Rec(2007)16.
[93] United States Department of Justice, Council of Europe Convention on Cybercrime: Frequently Asked Questions and Answers, <http://www.usdoj.gov>.
[94] Cybercrime Convention, n. 91 above, Article 9, which contains three possible elements: involvement of a child in sexually explicit conduct, involvement of a person appearing to be a child engaged in sexually explicit conduct, or realistic images representing a child engaged in sexually explicit conduct.
[95] See, for example, ECHR Article 6 and ICCPR Article 14.

Protection of Children Against Sexual Exploitation and Sexual Abuse. Article 20 of this treaty is adapted from Article 9 of the Cybercrime Convention, reasserting the obligation to criminalize the production, distribution, and possession of child pornography.[96] Here, however, the provision is closely related to other obligations and measures concerning the protection of children. It is moreover not limited to internet related activities and includes any form of child pornography.

The 2007 Convention also revisits the question of how child pornography should be defined. Article 20 of the treaty states that 'child pornography' means any material that visually depicts a child engaged in real or simulated sexually explicit conduct or any depiction of a child's sexual organs for primarily sexual purposes.[97] Photographs of naked children, which may incur liability under some domestic laws, are not sufficient to qualify as child pornography, which requires an explicitly sexual element. Article 20 also allows state parties the option of reservations in relation to computer generated pornographic images, except where such images appear to be images of real children.[98] These Council of Europe obligations to criminalize child pornography, although restricted to those states willing to become treaty parties, are a significant development in European law concerning freedom of expression and human dignity. They entrench key elements of the European model of freedom of expression into positive law, including the ease with which expression deemed to cause harm may be rendered a crime. American constitutional law, in comparison, possesses a stronger concept of personal liberty, which has placed the criminalization of child pornography under greater control.[99]

Pornography and violence in international law

National autonomy in the regulation of public morals has been a basic precept of international law since the Peace of Westphalia, which affirmed that statehood did not depend on the religious and moral convictions of a territory's ruler or its inhabitants. As discussed in preceding chapters, the drafters of the GATT and

---

[96] Council of Europe, Convention on the Protection of Children Against Sexual Exploitation and Sexual Abuse, (ETS No. 201). According to the Explanatory Report to the Convention on the Protection of Children Against Sexual Exploitation and Sexual Abuse, Article 20 on child pornography is inspired by the Council of Europe's Convention on Cybercrime (the Article 9—offences related to child pornography). It is also related to Article 3 of the Council of the European Union Framework Decision on Combating the Sexual Exploitation of Children and Child Pornography, and Article 2 of the Optional Protocol to the United Nations Convention on the Rights of the Child on the Sale of Children, Child Prostitution and Child Pornography.

[97] Convention on the Protection of Children, n. 96 above, Article 20(2). This definition is based on the Optional Protocol to the United Nations Convention on the Rights of the Child on the Sale of Children, Child Prostitution and Child Pornography. See also the Explanatory Report, ibid., para.143.

[98] Convention on the Protection of Children, n. 97 above, Article 20 and Explanatory Report, n. 97 above, para. 144. Article 20(4) also contains a further option for states to decline to criminalize the act of 'knowingly obtaining access, through information and communication technologies, to child pornography' as required by Article 20(1)(f).

[99] See *Ashcroft v. Free Speech Coalition*, 535 U.S. 234 (2002). See also Child Pornography Prevention Act 1996, 18 USC 2256 (8)(B).

the GATS put that autonomy in matters of public morals at the heart of international trade law.[100] Indeed, the protection of public morals is the first listed ground for permissible derogation from GATT obligations under Article XX and occupies a similar place in Article XIV of the GATS.[101] The public morals ground is also exceptionally broad, encompassing the protection of many threats to human well being, such as narcotics, alcohol, gambling, prostitution, child labour, and pornography.[102] On the other hand, there has certainly been a clear awareness amongst governments and international trade related organizations that national autonomy in the control of harmful and offensive content presents a major obstacle to the development of global markets for electronic commerce.[103]

In most cases, WTO member states need not resort to permitted GATT and GATS exceptions to secure their autonomy in matters falling within the scope of public morals as the main goal of trade law is to eliminate discriminatory treatment rather than trade barriers per se. In common with most other constraints on the liberty to publish, national restrictions on sexual and violent content are typically non-discriminatory in form. This reflects the fact that governments must include all media sources and outlets under their jurisdiction, regardless of their origins or chief places of business, when seeking effective control over public expression that engages the core concerns of the state. These laws or regulations restricting the publication or distribution of sexual or violent content can however be discriminatory in their application and thereby fall within the scope of the GATT or GATS. Aside from the use of public morals as a pretext for discrimination against foreign media goods and services or their suppliers, the sheer complexity of the contemporary media sector can also lead to inadvertent discrimination. The protection of children from harmful content, for example, frequently involves different legal and regulatory rules and enforcement methods based on qualitative standards spread across the print, broadcast, and internet based media. The risk of different

---

[100] General Agreement on Tariffs and Trade 1994 (incorporating GATT 1947), (15 April 1994), 33 ILM 1153 (1994), Article XX: General Exceptions, '(a) necessary to protect public morals', and General Agreement on Trade in Services, (15 April 1994), 33 ILM 1167 (1994), Article XIV: General Exceptions, '(a) necessary to protect public morals or to maintain public order'. On the general exception provisions of the GATT and the GATS, see Chapter 5.

[101] See Charnovitz, S., 'The Moral Exception in Trade Policy,' 38 *Virginia Journal of International Law* (Spring 1998), 689–745, 697, and see Voon, T., *Cultural Products and the World Trade Organization* (Cambridge University Press, 2007), 101–109.

[102] The WTO Appellate Body affirmed in the *US—Gambling* case that under GATS Article XIV(a), the term 'public morals' denotes standards of right and wrong conduct maintained by or on behalf of a community or nation. Appellate Body Report, *United States—Measures Affecting the Cross-Border Supply of Gambling and Betting Service*, WT/DS285/AB/R (7 April 2005), para. 296. See also Marwell, J.C., 'Trade and Morality: The WTO Public Morals Exception after Gambling', 81 *New York University Law Review* (2006), 802.

[103] See, for example, 'The issue of illegal and harmful content over global electronic networks needs to be addressed in a manner which is proportional to the problem and which recognises the importance of the principle of free speech. The identification and implementation of appropriate and effective global solutions requires international cooperation.' OECD Committee for Information, Computers and Communications Policy, 'Global Information infrastructure—Global information Society (GII-GIS) Policy Recommendations for Action' OECD 1997 [approved by OECD Council at Ministerial level, May 1997]. See also International Chamber of Commerce, *Policy Statement: The Impact of Internet Content Regulation*, doc no. 373–37/1 (18 November 2002).

consequences for domestic and foreign media is therefore high and those differences may amount to de facto discrimination under the rules of trade law, provided of course there is an applicable commitment to trade liberalization.[104]

Whether a discriminatory domestic measure is protected from the national treatment and MFN obligations of the GATT and the GATS under the public morals ground of GATT XX and GATS XIV has been considered by WTO panels and the Appellate Body in very few cases.[105] The first consideration in the application of these articles is that member states are free to determine what level of protection is necessary to achieve adequate protection of the public.[106] It is only the manner of achieving that level of protection that is subject to the necessity and chapeau conditions of the general exception articles. In the context of public morals, the application of the necessity condition is particularly sensitive as the decision whether the contested measure is the least restrictive one available may involve the 'weighing and balancing' of various factors that include the importance of the interests or values protected as compared to their restrictive effects on trade.[107]

While the Appellate Body largely found in favour of the United States on the question of necessity in the *US Gambling and Betting Services* case, in its December 2009 decision in the *China Publications and Audiovisual Entertainment Products* case, it found that China had not shown that its restrictive domestic measures were 'necessary' to protect public morals as required by Article XX of the GATT. The main reason for that conclusion was the Appellate Body's acceptance that the less trade-restrictive alternative proposed by the United States was 'reasonably available' to China.[108] For the Chinese government, these conclusions have threatened important elements of its comprehensive media regime, which has been under the exclusive control of the Communist Party since it came to power in 1949.[109] The Appellate Body's decision has also underscored the potential for using the necessity principle to strip away state controls on the media in non-democratic states. Yet, as Wu Xiaohui has argued, by focusing on 'necessity' and the potential for less trade restrictive measures, the Appellate Body shifted the basic issue away

---

[104] On the GATT screen quota exception and the limited application of the GATS to media services, see Chapter 5.

[105] The WTO Appellate Body decided its first GATS public morals case in 2005: *US—Measures Affecting the Cross-border Supply of Gambling and Betting Services*, Report of the Appellate Body, AB-2005–1, WT/DS285/AB/R (7 April 2005), and its first GATT public morals case in 2009: *China—Measures Affecting Trading Rights and Distribution Services for Certain Publications and Audiovisual Entertainment Products*, (WT/DS363/AB/R), Appellate Body (21 December 2009).

[106] *Korea—Measures Affecting Imports of Fresh, Chilled and Frozen Beef*, AB-2000–8, Appellate Body Report, para. 176.

[107] Ibid., para. 164, 'the contribution made by the compliance measure to the enforcement of the law or regulation at issue, the importance of the common interests or values protected by that law or regulation, and the accompanying impact of the law or regulation on imports or exports'. On the argument for a strict application of the GATT Article XX and GATS Article XIV tests, see Diebold, N.F., 'The Morals and Order Exceptions in WTO Law: Balancing the Toothless Tiger and the Undermining Mole', 11(1) *Journal of International Economic Law* (2008), 43–74.

[108] *China—Publications and Audiovisual Entertainment Products*, n. 105 above, para. 415(e).

[109] See Brady, A., *Marketing Dictatorship: Propaganda and Thought Work in Contemporary China*, (Rowman and Littlefield, 2008), ch 2, 'Guiding Hand: The Role of the Propaganda System'.

from non-discrimination and transparency to the acceptability of China's chosen methods of protecting public morals.[110] Wu's complaint, in essence, is that the WTO law is progressing through judicial decisions towards the elimination of trade barriers per se rather than the elimination of discriminatory barriers. A necessity test that demands greater rationality in domestic measures is a serious challenge to national autonomy in the broad sphere of public morals, where national restrictions on media content are often rooted in a jumble of political, social, cultural, and religious objectives and will struggle to satisfy that standard. Considerations of this kind are precisely why, as discussed in earlier chapters, the negotiation of a necessity based domestic regulation discipline in the Doha Round has been so difficult to achieve.[111]

Outside the WTO, the question of legitimate restrictions on pornographic or violent content has also arisen within the International Corporation for Assigned Names and Numbers (ICANN), which is the principal organization responsible for the orderly operation of the global internet.[112] Here, the main point of contention has been the development of a specialized domain name labelled .XXX for the voluntary use of websites featuring explicit sexual content. After initial rejections, the ICANN Board approved then rejected an agreement in 2007 to create the .XXX sponsored Top Level Domain (sTLD).[113] However, following an Independent Review Panel declaration that the Board's decision was not consistent with the application of neutral, objective, and fair documented policy, the Board voted to accept the Panel's declaration and initiate procedures to establish the proposed .XXX sTLD.[114] The creation of an sTLD for explicit sexual content has provoked intense interest from governments and social organizations since it was first proposed in 2004.[115] The opposition of governments, including the United States, has also brought the neutrality of ICANN decision making into question, in particular the potential for improper interference by major states.[116] Policy issues related to

[110] Wu, X., 'Case Note: China—Measures Affecting Trading Rights and Distribution Services for Certain Publications and Audiovisual Entertainment Products (WT/DS363/AB/R)', 9(2) *Chinese Journal of International Law* (2010) 415–432. See also Qin, J., 'Pushing the Limit of Global Governance: Trading Rights, Censorship, and WTO Jurisprudence—A Commentary on China-Audiovisual Services', (23 November 2010), Wayne State University Law School Research Paper, and Delimatsis, P., 'Protecting Public Morals in a Digital Era: Revisiting the WTO Rulings in US—Gambling and China—Publications and Audiovisual Products', TILEC Discussion Paper No. 2010-041.
[111] On the domestic regulation provisions of the GATS, see Chapter 5.
[112] ICANN is an independent, non-profit-making private corporation established and operated under the laws of California and entrusted with the coordination of technical administration of the global internet under the 2009 Affirmation of Commitments made between the United States Department of Commerce. See 'ICANN be independent: Regulating the internet', *The Economist* (25 September 2009).
[113] Adopted Resolutions from ICANN Board Meeting, 30 March 2007.
[114] Adopted ICANN Board Resolutions, 25 June 2010.
[115] Milton Mueller, 'Triple X, Internet Content Regulation and the ICANN Regime' (14 January 2007). Internet Governance Project, Paper IGP07-001.
[116] Mac Síthigh, D., 'More than words: the introduction of internationalised domain names and the reform of generic top-level domains at ICANN', 18(3) *International Journal of Law, Information and Technology*, Autumn 2010.

public morals will moreover continue to arise within ICANN as the internet domain name system develops. The body responsible for creating guidelines for new generic Top level Domains (gTLD), is for example, wrestling with the question of how to bar applications deemed to be contrary to 'generally accepted legal norms relating to morality and public order that are recognised under international principles of law'.[117]

International human rights law also recognizes the autonomy of states in the regulation of public morals. One of the great purposes of the liberal democratic project has therefore been to ensure that that autonomy is not only yoked to tolerance of social, cultural, and religious differences, but also constrained to prevent the regulation of public morals from being used as a pretext for the suppression of dissent. To achieve this second objective, liberal democracy depends on the right to freedom of expression, which takes precedence over state or popular demands for moral conformity where the expression at issue does not cause harm (or perhaps gross offence) or is a justifiable contribution to public affairs. For states outside the liberal democratic tradition, that set of principles is plainly incompatible with the foundations of an illiberal or non-democratic state. The opposition of these states has therefore helped to frustrate the entrenchment of those principles into international human rights law over the past half century. Major differences between American constitutional law and European human rights law on the proper limits of the liberty to speak and publish have also impeded the development of a clear relationship between the right to freedom of expression and the protection of public morals in human rights law. The extent to which the right to free speech protects expression that causes gross offence has been a particular point of disagreement.[118]

Article 19 of the International Covenant on Civil and Political Rights has rarely been used to mount a direct challenge to national restrictions concerning public morals before the ICCPR Human Rights Committee. The Article 19(3) public morals exception was left broadly stated to ensure that it remained flexible enough to cover a wide variety of national laws and regulations. Consequently, the leading example of a Committee decision on public morals in the media sector under Article 19(3) concerned restrictions on expression concerning homosexuality, which in many countries even at the time was no longer regarded as a matter self evidently requiring censorship.[119] In its 1982 communication on *Hertzberg v. Finland*, the Human Rights Committee found that Finland did not violate its obligations under Article 19 when prohibiting discussions in the broadcast media

---

[117] New gTLD Recommendation #6 Cross-Community Working Group ('Rec6 CWG'), Report on Implementation of GNSO New GTLD Recommendation #6, (21 September 2010).

[118] On the argument that the harm principle should be supplemented to include gross offence, see Chapter 2.

[119] Greater tolerance towards homosexuality in many countries, as well as legislative and judicial recognition in some countries that freedom to engage in homosexual acts is grounded in fundamental rights, has had a clear influence on interpretations of the right to privacy under Article 17 of the ICCPR. See, for example, *Toonen v. Australia*, Communication No. 488/1992. See also International Commission of Jurists, International Human Rights References to Human Rights Violations on the Grounds of Sexual Orientation and Gender Identity (October 2006).

that may encourage homosexual conduct.[120] In the view of the Committee, there is no universally applicable common standard in questions of public morals and consequently state parties enjoy a margin of discretion in determining what matters fall within this legitimate ground for interfering with the right to freedom of expression. It stated further that, '[a]ccording to Article 19(3), the exercise of the rights provided for in Article 19(2) carries with it special duties and responsibilities for those organs. As far as radio and TV programmes are concerned, the audience cannot be controlled. In particular, harmful effects on minors cannot be excluded.' The protection of children from ostensible moral harm was therefore a key element in the decision.

External efforts to inject explicitly liberal democratic elements into the interpretation of Article 19 and the right to freedom of expression generally in international human rights law have also attempted to address the scope and application of the public morals exception. The Siracusa Principles on the Limitation and Derogation of Provisions in the International Covenant on Civil and Political Rights state that, '[s]ince public morality varies over time and from one culture to another, a state which invokes public morality as a ground for restricting human rights, while enjoying a certain margin of discretion, shall demonstrate that the limitation in question is essential to the maintenance of respect for fundamental values of the community'.[121] The Principles also state that the 'necessity' condition in Article 19(3) should be interpreted as requiring not only that a restriction responds to a pressing public or social need, but that it must also be proportionate to its aim. The Siracusa Principles were not however intended to address the substantive purposes of the Article 19 right to freedom of expression. They therefore do not carry forward the liberal democratic principle that measures intended to protect public morals must be considered in light of their restrictive effects on democratic participation and decision making.

Divisions over the meaning of the public morals exception and its relationship with freedom of expression have also made it difficult to cooperate in areas of mutual concern regarding harm and offence in the new media. Nonetheless, child pornography emerged in the 1990s as a key area for intergovernmental cooperation as well as a limited harmonization of national standards. In the United Nations human rights system, the Convention on the Rights of the Child is the principal instrument creating obligations to protect children in relation to child pornography.[122] Article 34 of the Convention requires state parties to protect children from all forms of sexual exploitation and sexual abuse, including the exploitative use of children in pornographic performances and materials. These obligations have been substantially supplemented by the Optional Protocol to the Convention on the Rights of the Child on the sale of children, child prostitution, and child

---

[120] *Hertzberg v. Finland*, Communication No. 61/1979.
[121] Siracusa Principles on the Limitation and Derogation of Provisions in the International Covenant on Civil and Political Rights, Annex, UN Doc E/CN.4/1985/4 (1985), para. 27. On the role of the Siracusa Principles in international human rights law and policy, see Chapter 6.
[122] United Nations, Convention on the Rights of the Child, A/RES/44/25 (12 December 1989).

pornography.[123] Article 3 of the Protocol requires that state parties must prohibit, by the use of criminal or penal law, the production, distribution, dissemination, import, export, offer, sale, or possession of child pornography.[124] These obligations stand out in a legal field where universal obligations to restrict freedom of expression are exceedingly rare.

Efforts to create positive obligations requiring states to prohibit or restrict the publication of other forms of sexual and violent content have accordingly been far less successful. The Convention on the Elimination of All Forms of Discrimination Against Women (CEDAW) has, for example, been a focus for arguments that there is a legal duty to take positive action to prohibit or restrict the circulation of violent or degrading content concerning women. Article 5 of the Convention requires that state parties shall take all appropriate measures to modify the social and cultural patterns of conduct of men and women, with a view to achieving the elimination of prejudices and customary and all other practices which are based on the idea of the inferiority or the superiority of either of the sexes or on stereotyped roles for men and women. In 1992, the CEDAW Committee on the Elimination of Discrimination Against Women outlined the basis for such an obligation in its General Recommendation No. 19 concerning Violence Against Women.[125] In this recommendation, the Committee found that states parties have a duty to take positive measures to eliminate all forms of violence against women, including the portrayal of women in ways that encourage violence. In relation to Article 5 of the Convention, the Committee identified a connection between traditional attitudes in which women are regarded as subordinate to men and violence against women, asserting that, '[t]hese attitudes also contribute to the propagation of pornography and the depiction and other commercial exploitation of women as sexual objects, rather than as individuals. This in turn contributes to gender-based violence.'[126] Despite the rise of an enormous global trade in explicitly sexual and violent content since the arrival of the internet, these suggestions of a legal obligation have not led to further work on prescriptive obligations outside the area of child pornography.

---

[123] The United Nations, Optional Protocol to the Convention on the Rights of the Child on the sale of children, child prostitution and child pornography, A/RES/54/263 (25 May 2000) entered into force on 18 January 2002. It has attracted widespread support from many countries, including the United Kingdom, the United States, and China.

[124] Article 2 of the Optional Protocol, ibid., defines child pornography to mean any representation, by whatever means, of a child engaged in real or simulated explicit sexual activities or any representation of the sexual parts of a child for primarily sexual purposes. The Protocol also provides basic rules of jurisdiction based on nationality, residence, or presence of the offender or the nationality of the victim (Article 4) and establishes that the offences referred to in Article 3 are extraditable offences (Article 5). The Protocol also obliges state parties to afford one another the greatest measure of assistance in connection with investigations or criminal or extradition proceedings brought in respect of the offences (Article 6).

[125] CEDAW General Recommendation 19, A/47/38. (Violence against women) (29 January 1992). The CEDAW Committee monitors the implementation of the Women's Convention based on state parties' reports and also has the power to adopt suggestions and general recommendations.

[126] Ibid., Comments on Articles 2(f), 5, and 10(c), para. 12.

13

Incitement to Hatred

The suppression of incitement to hatred or 'hate speech' is one of the most divisive issues within the liberal democratic tradition.[1] It has come to epitomize deep running differences between American and European constitutional positions on the proper limits to the liberty to publish and the necessary risks and discomfort the state and public must endure to foster a healthy democracy. Beyond those transatlantic differences, the flourishing of incitement to hatred across national boundaries has also come to symbolize the redefinition of the power of the state in the internet era. As mass and personal communication have merged, the public sphere has expanded and thickened with networks of semi public communication and internet sites where ideas and opinions of any kind find an audience. From a liberal democratic perspective, the communications revolution has offered proof of technology's power to open new doors to liberty from the state as well as a searing demonstration of its capacity to enable harm.[2] The response has consequently been not only a celebration of greater freedom of expression, but also a scramble to use the full arsenal of legal, regulatory, and technological means to limit the dissemination of harmful and offensive content. Incitement to hatred has thus become, among other things, a test for the state in its struggle to re-assert authority in the media state relationship.

Despite its symbolic status, the treatment of incitement to hatred has much in common with other areas of liberal democratic media law, especially incitement to violence.[3] Indeed, where incitement to hatred against a particular community or group also involves a serious threat of violence, the relevant principles are indistinguishable. Even when that incitement to violence is not directed at institutions of the state, it is a threat to public safety that challenges the state's monopoly over coercive force and its authority as the protector of public order. Despite liberalism's

---

[1] The term 'incitement to hatred' or 'hate speech' refers to abusive spoken or published attacks on a community, group, or individual, typically directed at aspects of their identity or beliefs, such as race, ethnicity, or religion, which are also intended to incite feelings of hatred towards them amongst other groups or communities. On incitement to hatred, see Goodall, K., 'Incitement to Religious Hatred: All Talk and No Substance?', 70(1) *Modern Law Review* (2007), 89–113, Hare, I., 'Crosses, Crescents and Sacred Cows: Criminalising Incitement to Religious Hatred', *Public Law* (2006), 520–537, and Fisch, W., 'Hate Speech in the Constitutional Law of the United States', 50 *American Journal of Comparative Law Supplement* (2002), 463.

[2] See, for example, 'Cyber-nationalism: The brave new world of e-hatred', *The Economist* (24 July 2008).

[3] On incitement to violence, see Chapter 8.

misgivings about the abuse of state power, liberal democracies depend on the state to prevent or punish acts of unauthorized violence. Consequently, in the liberal democratic state, incitement of violence against a community or group is also an attack on the foundations of democracy, which rests on tolerance of difference as well as the right to enjoy equal protection from the state.

Incitement to hatred, like incitement to violence, also raises one of the major dilemmas of liberal free speech theory. According to the consequential argument that an expansive liberty to publish is essential to democratic self government, any restriction on the media is particularly damaging when it inhibits debate on a matter of general concern.[4] Public debates concerning virtually any aspect of race, ethnicity, religion, gender, sexuality, or other aspects of belief or identity are therefore normally within the most protected sphere of public expression. The right to argue one's point of view on such matters in intemperate and passionate language is moreover a well established hallmark of the liberal democratic state.[5] Even self evidently false views, as J.S. Mill famously argued, should be heard as they help to strengthen better understanding through the contest of vigorous public debate.[6] The problem has therefore been to fashion a workable distinction between legitimate comment on matters of public concern and expression that causes an excessive risk to public safety or state security. This is, in effect, an application of the principle that the liberty to speak and publish should be protected to the point it causes a significant risk of serious harm.[7] That intuitively appealing concept does however contain several problems of principle and application when applied to incitement to hatred. These include the identification of an unacceptable risk of harm and the manner in which that risk is identified. It would seem that no liberal democracy will regard an expression of hatred that results in individuals engaging in serious acts of violence as falling within the protection of the right to freedom of expression. Yet even here there is room for disagreement. An incitement of hatred towards a particular group may not directly advocate violence, but may instead inflame existing communal tensions and thereby indirectly but predictably contribute to violence. Plainly, there is no obvious boundary between incitement to hatred and incitement to violence.

The sharpest arguments have arisen over the question of whether expression should be restricted when it incites hatred but does not constitute an express or implicit threat of violence. In the social and cultural mix of contemporary life, where tensions easily arise between communities or groups thrust into close proximity, there is a strong argument that the liberal democratic state can best protect individual autonomy and equality in these circumstances by ensuring maximum liberty and demanding that communities and individuals accept a robust tolerance for difference.[8] On this view, the state should be prevented from creating

---

[4] On the democratic consequential argument for freedom of expression, see Chapter 2.

[5] Baker, C.E., 'Harm, Liberty, and Free Speech', 70 *Southern California Law Review* (1997), 979.

[6] On Millian arguments for greater liberty to speak and publish, see Chapter 2.

[7] On the harm principle, see Chapter 2.

[8] See, for example, Baker, E., 'Hate Speech', in Hare, I. and Weinstein, J. (eds), *Extreme Speech And Democracy*, (Oxford University Press, 2009); Greenawalt, K., *Fighting Words: Individuals, Communities,*

laws that restrict speech on matters of public concern where no serious risk of violence arises, as freedom of expression was hard won from the state and is always at risk.[9]

Contemporary challenges to that argument, while also emphasizing the need for individual liberty, have drawn on other notions of autonomy that have been drawn into liberalism's widening tradition, which importantly include the concept of human dignity. From this different perspective, autonomy encompasses a variety of physical and mental needs essential to a genuinely autonomous life, including the freedom from fear and oppression necessary for a life of dignity. This approach to autonomy leads to the crucial questions of when incitement to hatred, without any threat of violence, seriously diminishes the autonomy of people subject to this kind of abusive expression and how the state should respond. It is a matter of common sense that constant, vitriolic public abuse directed against a particular group can inflict mental harm on members of that group by, among other things, limiting their potential for personal development and participation in public affairs. This is, in effect, a denial of their moral equality and a refusal to accord them the basic tolerance demanded in a liberal democratic society. As Steven Heyman argues, '[p]ublic hate speech invades the rights of its targets, especially the right to recognition as a human being and a member of the community. And second, this form of speech violates the basic rules that should govern democratic debate, which depends on mutual respect among free and equal citizens.'[10]

These observations are not, in themselves, at the heart of the disagreement over hate speech, which concerns the question of whether the state has a duty to suppress serious public incitements to hatred.[11] Criminalization, the most heavy handed form of intervention, is likely to chill debate in matters of anxious public concern, such as the arrival of immigrants in local communities or the recognition of equal rights for gays and lesbians. That deliberate chilling effect will moreover be especially acute in the major domestic media, which are vulnerably exposed to the coercive powers of the state. But for advocates of criminal sanctions, whatever democratic discourse is lost by criminalization is more than regained by ensuring that minorities are not excluded from participation in public affairs by an abusive and degrading media environment. In the hard fought argument over the criminalization of incitement to hatred, context is hugely influential. In liberal democracies with a recent history of communal violence and authoritarian government,

---

and Liberties of Speech (Princeton University Press, 1995); and Volokh, E., 'Freedom of Speech and the Intentional Infliction of Emotional DistressTort', *Cardozo Law Review De Novo* (2010), 300. For relevant United States constitutional law, see *Brandenburg v. Ohio*, 395 U.S. 444 (1969), *National Socialist Party of America v. Village of Skokie*, 432 U.S. 43 (1977), and *R.A.V. v. St Paul*, 505 U.S. 377 (1992).

[9] Wilson, B., *What Price Liberty?* (Faber and Faber, 2009), ch 17.

[10] Heyman, S., 'Hate Speech, Public Discourse, and the First Amendment', in Hare I., and Weinstein, J. (eds), n. 8 above. See also Matsuda, M.J., Lawrence III, C.R., Delgado, R., and Crenshaw, K.W. (eds), *Words That Wound: Critical Race Theory, Assaultive Speech, and the First Amendment* (Westview Press, 1993).

[11] On the liberal arguments over the proper use of the coercive powers of the state, see, for example, Raz, J., *The Morality of Freedom* (Oxford University Press, 1996), 412 and 420.

intervention to preserve democratic participation and the openness of public debate to all groups is likely to have a much greater intuitive appeal than it does in countries where the liberal democratic foundations of public life seem deeply entrenched and beyond threat.[12] There is nonetheless a point of agreement for all sides in this debate. Whatever the chosen threshold for intervention, the liberal democratic state must use the least restrictive measures possible when limiting expression regarding matters of general concern. That does not necessarily eliminate the use criminal sanctions, but certainly does demand that they are narrowly focused when used.

Incitement to hatred in the European Union

Incitement to hatred has an exceptional character in European media law. Contemporary European public order was founded on the ruins of fascist dictatorship and in opposition to the Communist Party states installed to the east under Soviet power. The establishment of the Council of Europe and its human rights convention was the most important collective step towards the rejection of racial, ethnic, and religious killing, cleansing, and other violence as well as the incitement of hatred that has flourished with them. As European Union law has evolved, that formal rejection of incitement to hatred has become not only a recognized general principle of law, but also the object of major legislation.[13]

In principle, any domestic restriction on the publication or distribution of media content in a member state is open to challenge if it impedes free movement, regardless of whether that measure is intended to help secure the foundations of democracy in a member state. Conceptually at least, free movement remains the first principle of European media law. Yet the rules of free movement are framed around the unquestioned authority of member states to protect their populations from harm, which is established in the express and implied exceptions to the EU's rules of free movement and market competition. In this respect, incitement to hatred runs in close parallel to incitement to violence, which is discussed in Chapter 8. In determining the proper breadth of the applicable public policy and public security based exemptions from the rules of free movement, the European human rights law takes a similarly prominent role in the weighing of market and non-market public policy in relation to incitement to hatred.[14] Here, the democratic argument for greater liberty in the public discussion of matters of general

---

[12] Waldron, J., 'Free Speech & the Menace of Hysteria', 55 *New York Review of Books* (29 May 2008).

[13] Legislative competence for this non-market public policy goal rests in part on Article 19 of the Treaty on the Functioning of the European Union (TFEU), originally introduced in 1998 by the Treaty of Amsterdam, which empowers the EU to 'take appropriate action to combat discrimination based on sex, racial or ethnic origin, religion or belief, disability, age or sexual orientation'. See also Article 67, TFEU, discussed below.

[14] On express and implied public policy exceptions to the rules of free movement in European Union law, see Chapter 4.

interest provides a restraining influence on national measures, ensuring that legitimate restrictions on the media are no broader than necessary.[15] This argument, however, is also limited by its democratic concerns. In European human rights law, incitement to hatred is considered to be a grave risk to democracy and therefore falls outside the normal sphere of protection for robust commentary on public affairs.[16] Proportionate restrictions on incitement are thus comfortably sustained by the obligations of EU member states to protect democracy and human dignity.[17]

The same combination of market and non-market public policy principles, which permit national restrictions on the free movement of media goods and services to serve these fundamental aims, arise within the European Union's secondary legislation directed at media services. Yet more importantly, the EU has used this secondary legislation to introduce prescriptive rules compelling member states to criminalize and otherwise restrict publication that incites hatred. Article 6 of the Audiovisual Media Services Directive, first introduced in the original 1989 version, requires that member states, 'ensure by appropriate means that audiovisual media services provided by media service providers under their jurisdiction do not contain any incitement to hatred based on race, sex, religion or nationality'.[18] Member states may, in addition, derogate from the Directive's free movement obligations and impose proportionate restrictions on a television or on-demand audiovisual media service under the jurisdiction of another member state if that service has committed major breaches of this prohibition on incitement to hatred.[19]

The Directive's derogation provisions for on-demand audiovisual media services are also more extensive than those applying to television services. They allow proportionate derogation when an on-demand service presents a significant risk of prejudice to the goals of incitement to hatred laws and also extend this derogation power, which is expressly based on the wider ground of 'public policy', to other recognized forms of incitement to hatred. These provisions were copied from the Electronic Commerce Directive, which applies the same powers of proportionate derogation to its own free movement obligations to 'information society services'.[20]

---

[15] Case C-260/89, *Elliniki Radiophonia Tiléorassi AE v. Dimotiki Etairia Pliroforissis and others* [1991] ECR I-2925, para. 43. See also Chapter 4.

[16] See below for discussion of incitement to hatred in European human rights law.

[17] European Union Charter of Fundamental Rights, Article 1. See also Article 21 on the obligation of EU member states to prohibit discrimination.

[18] Directive 2010/13/EU of the European Parliament and of the Council of 10 March 2010 on the coordination of certain provisions laid down by law, regulation or administrative action in Member States concerning the provision of audiovisual media services (AVMS Directive), including Article 9 (1): Member States shall ensure that audiovisual commercial communications provided by media service providers under their jurisdiction comply with the following requirements: (c) audiovisual commercial communications shall not: (i) prejudice respect for human dignity; (ii) include or promote any discrimination based on sex, racial or ethnic origin, nationality, religion or belief, disability, age or sexual orientation. On the AVMS Directive generally, see Chapter 4.

[19] Ibid., Article 3 contains derogation provisions for television services and on-demand audiovisual services.

[20] Directive 2000/31/EC of the European Parliament and of the Council of 8 June 2000 on certain legal aspects of information society services, in particular electronic commerce, in the Internal Market (Electronic Commerce Directive), Article 3(4).

This Directive, unlike the AVMS Directive, does not however contain equivalent prescriptive obligations to ensure these services do not make available content that incites hatred. In addition, the Electronic Commerce Directive's internet liability rules, internet operators that host third party content that incites hatred are protected from liability unless they have actual or constructive knowledge.[21]

In 1997, when the member states agreed to include a prescriptive obligation in what is now the AVMS Directive to ensure that European television services do not contain incitements to hatred based on race, sex, religion, or nationality, the European Union had already proclaimed that year as the European Year against Racism.[22] In the aftermath of the Bosnian War, and the apparent failure of European institutions to act effectively during the Yugoslav crisis, the European Union launched several initiatives against racial, ethnic, religious, and other forms of collective hatred and violence. These included a new public policy obligation for the European Union, introduced through the Treaty of Amsterdam, which requires that the EU endeavours 'to ensure a high level of security through measures to prevent and combat crime, racism and xenophobia, and through measures for coordination and cooperation between police and judicial authorities and other competent authorities, as well as through the mutual recognition of judgements in criminal matters and, if necessary, through the approximation of criminal laws'.[23]

This new treaty provision followed the adoption of the 1996 Joint Action on combating racism and xenophobia by the EU Council.[24] The Joint Action called for judicial cooperation and criminalization where necessary for various forms of public incitement of discrimination, violence, or racial hatred. In 2008, the European Union introduced a Framework Directive to supersede the 1996 Joint Action and sharpen its prescriptive elements.[25] This instrument requires that member states make punishable all intentional acts 'publicly inciting violence or hatred directed against a group of persons or a member of such a group defined by reference to race, colour, religion, descent or national or ethnic origin, even by the dissemination or distribution of tracts, pictures or other material', or 'publicly condoning, denying or grossly trivializing crimes of genocide, crimes against humanity and war crimes'.[26]

The 2008 Framework Decision, which has been brought under the interpretation and enforcement powers of the European Court of Justice as a consequence of

---

[21] On the Electronic Commerce Directive generally, see Chapter 4.

[22] Resolution of the Council and the representatives of the governments of the Member States, meeting within the Council, (23 July 1996) designating 1997 as the European Year against Racism.

[23] This provision, previously contained in the Treaty on European Union, is now Article 67(3) of the Treaty on the Functioning of the European Union.

[24] Joint action/96/443/JHA of 15 July 1996 adopted by the Council on the basis of Article K.3 of the Treaty on European Union, concerning action to combat racism and xenophobia. See also Pech, L., 'The Law of Holocaust Denial in Europe: Towards a (qualified) EU-wide Criminal Prohibition', Jean Monnet Working Paper 10/09, (The Jean Monnet Center for International and Regional Economic Law and Justice, New York University, 2009).

[25] Council Framework Decision 2008/913/JHA of 28 November 2008 on combating certain forms and expressions of racism and xenophobia by means of criminal law, 28 November 2008.

[26] The Member States are obliged to make these acts punishable by a maximum sentence of at least one to three years' imprisonment.

the Treaty of Lisbon, has also sharpened important elements in the European model of the legitimate liberal democratic state. It has hardened a public policy preference, largely developed in the Council of Europe, into a common rule for EU member states, eliminating the possibility of adopting a different liberal democratic approach to the balance between freedom of expression and the harm caused by incitement to hatred. The Framework Decision is also part of the progressive integration of market and non-market public policy within the European Union, which has begun to displace the Council of Europe as the chief forum for the development of non-market based media policies.

Yet the extension of the EU's legislative competences, and its more assertive use of prescriptive rules to put national media law on a common basis in key areas, presents an image of growing regional order that must be seen in the context of the communications revolution. Even in the satellite television field, where the European Union has been favoured by national control of the major satellite systems used to broadcast television across Europe, the geographic limits of the European media space have been severely tested. The most important example of this in relation to incitement to hatred occurred when European authorities struggled to shut down reception of Al Manar, a television channel operated by the Lebanese political party Hezbollah, on the grounds that its programmes incited ethnic hatred and violence.[27] These bureaucratic difficulties led to technical changes in the AVMS Directive in 2007, which were intended to make it easier to impose European content rules on non-European broadcasters that use European satellite facilities.[28] Nonetheless, satellite broadcasters who operate entirely outside Europe, using non-European satellite facilities whose footprint includes Europe, can still broadcast incitements to hatred or other prohibited content beyond the legislative jurisdiction of the EU. Where these broadcasters, like Al Manar, are funded by political organizations based outside Europe, they may well be insulated from the usual methods of national control, which include restrictions on the flow of advertising or subscription revenue to proscribed broadcasters.[29] The internet, moreover, has given European residents access to a wealth of new content sources, including many that contain material prohibited under European law. In response, the EU has encouraged member states and European based internet operators that provide or host content or provide public internet access to develop 'effective means of fighting any incitement to discrimination in audiovisual and online information services.'[30] The European Union has, in short, committed itself to the global

---

[27] *EU Rules and Principles on Hate Broadcasts: Frequently Asked Questions*, MEMO/05/98 (17 March 2005).

[28] Following the 2007 amendments, Article 2(4) of the AVMS Directive now uses 'satellite up-link in a Member State' as the main ground for asserting jurisdiction where the broadcaster is not established in an EU member state.

[29] See, for example, United Kingdom, Broadcasting Act 1990, ss. 177–178.

[30] Recommendation of the European Parliament and of the Council of 20 December 2006 on the protection of minors and human dignity and on the right of reply in relation to the competitiveness of the European audiovisual and on-line information services industry (2006/952/EC). See also Safer Internet Programme 2005–2008, which contemplates the inclusion of incitement to discrimination in internet hotlines for the reporting of unlawful activities: Decision No. 854/2005/EC of the European

struggle of states to re-assert their historic power over the public information environment of their citizens.

Council of Europe, human rights, and incitement to hatred

The European Convention on Human Rights was created to set standards for liberal democracy in western Europe, which would help to ensure that Europe's disastrous turn to authoritarian dictatorship did not recur. The Convention thus necessarily embraced liberalism's basic principle that the individual should be as free as possible from the coercive powers of the state. Its Article 10 right to freedom of expression is one of the chief embodiments of that ideal. On the other hand, the failure of democratic institutions in Weimar Germany to prevent the rise of the National Socialists graphically illustrated the risk that democratic majorities may be swayed to abandon these freedoms and destroy the foundations of liberal democracy. The Convention therefore also embraces the idea that rights to liberty must be rigorously limited where they threaten to undermine the mutual tolerance on which European democracy is built. That idea, that tolerance of religious, ethnic, and other differences is essential to the European system of states, has been a recurring theme of European statecraft since the Thirty Years War. It is also an idea that has set European human rights law at odds with developments in American constitutional law, in which the principle of liberty is given a greater role in limiting the influence of intolerance on the exercise of state power.

The drafters of the Convention consequently included Article 17, which expresses the idea that the rights guaranteed by the Convention may not be used to attack the fundamental values of the treaty or European democracy.[31] In principle, Article 17 acts as a fetter on the scope of the right to freedom of expression protected by Article 10 as well as other Convention rights.[32] As the Council of Europe Committee of Ministers stated in 1997, '[n]ational law and practice should allow the courts to bear in mind that specific instances of hate speech may be so insulting to individuals or groups as not to enjoy the level of protection afforded by Article 10 of the European Convention on Human Rights to other forms of expression. This is the case where hate speech is aimed at the destruction of the rights and freedoms laid down in the Convention or at their limitation to a greater extent than provided therein.'[33] Yet, while the concept behind Article 17 is clear enough, it is also conceptually redundant in relation to Article 10 and interferes

---

Parliament and of the Council of 11 May 2005 establishing a multiannual Community Programme on promoting safer use of the Internet and new online technologies.

[31] European Convention on Human Rights, Article 17 states, 'Nothing in this Convention may be interpreted as implying for any State, group or person any right to engage in any activity or perform any act aimed at the destruction of any of the rights and freedoms set forth herein or at their limitation to a greater extent than is provided for in the Convention.'

[32] *Lehideux and Isorni v. France* (Application No. 24662/94) (23 September 1998).

[33] Council of Europe, Committee of Ministers Recommendation on 'Hate Speech', R (97) 20, Principle 4.

with the development of the Convention right to freedom of expression. Article 17 has taken over the doctrinal question of what kinds of expression are not included in the scope of Article 10(1), which the European Court of Human Rights has interpreted expansively without developing its potential to clarify the nature of freedom of expression in Europe.[34] As a result, where the Court has determined that a measure restricting an alleged incitement to hatred is not excluded by Article 17, its review moves almost directly to Article 10(2).

The Court has attempted to make a principled distinction between kinds of incitement to hatred that are categorically excluded under Article 17 and those that may be excluded through the operation of Article 10(2). It has, accordingly, decided that Article 17 excludes holocaust denial or other denials of historical fact relating to genocide in World War II from the protection of Article 10.[35] Given the historical context of the Council of Europe, founded in 1949, and the drafting of the Convention, the use of Article 17 in these cases is certainly reasonable. However, as the Court has discussed Article 17 in very few cases as compared to Article 10, the boundary between the two articles is far from clear. It is obvious from the Court's case law that the Convention will not protect expression that incites hatred, xenophobia, anti-Semitism, or other forms of intolerance towards particular communities and groups.[36] Yet the Court has faced several difficulties in working out the respective roles of Articles 17 and 10 in maintaining that position. In addition to the redundancy of Article 17 in relation to both Article 10(1) and 10(2), the Convention's other provisions that prohibit discrimination have added a further basis on which to review acts motivated by racial or other bias.[37] There is moreover the underlying question of whether the Court's intense focus on the rights of individuals in each case, whether as speakers or the subjects of comment, has prevented it dealing with instances of incitement to hatred in their more appropriate context as threats to democratic society as a whole.[38] Finally, the Court's fact specific method of analysis, which is especially fine grained when the words at issue in the case before the Court are political in nature, makes it difficult

---

[34] Schauer, F., 'The Exceptional First Amendment' in Ignatieff, M. (ed.), *American Exceptionalism and Human Rights* (Princeton University Press, 2005), 29–56.

[35] *Garaudy v. France* (Application No. 15814/02) (Admissibility Decision, 8 July 2003) and *Lehideux and Isorni v. France*, n. 32 above. See also Pech, L., n. 24 above.

[36] Council of Europe, Committee of Ministers, Declaration on Freedom of Political Debate in the Media, Decl-12 02 2004E.

[37] See ECHR, European Convention on Human Rights, Article 14 Prohibition of discrimination, Protocol No. 12 to the European Convention on Human Rights, (ETS No. 177), Article 1 of the Protocol provides that 'the enjoyment of any right set forth by law shall be secured without discrimination on any ground such as sex, race, colour, language, religion, political or other opinion, national or social origin, association with a national minority, property, birth or other status'.

[38] 'Funnelling the wider range of objectives legitimately pursued by such governmental action into the narrow channel of the protection of "the rights of others" mischaracterizes the case as involving a fundamental conflict between *the rights of distinct groups of individuals*, instead of primarily raising crucial questions of broader structural design *of relevance to all* in a democratic society', Bomhoff, J., The Rights and Freedoms of Others: The ECHR and its Peculiar Category of Conflicts between Individual Fundamental Rights' in Brems, E. (ed.), *Conflicts Between Fundamental Rights* (Intersentia, 2008), 21–22.

to discern the specific principles used to distinguish the boundary between Article 17 and Article 10.[39]

The Court has dealt with most cases involving allegations of incitement to hatred under Article 10(2), which has provided more than ample grounds for the Court to approve various national measures that restrict expression inciting contempt or hatred on racial and ethnic grounds, where the words convey a deep hostility towards or fundamental rejection of a community or group identified by race, ethnicity, or similar essential characteristics.[40] It has also found that Article 10 does not protect incitement to religious hatred or intolerance, including gratuitously offensive attacks on matters regarded as sacred by believers.[41] In *Otto Preminger Institut v. Austria*, the Court stated,

[T]hose who choose to exercise the freedom to manifest their religion, irrespective of whether they do so as members of a religious majority or a minority, cannot reasonably expect to be exempt from all criticism. They must tolerate and accept the denial by others of their religious beliefs and even the propagation by others of doctrines hostile to their faith. However, the manner in which religious beliefs and doctrines are opposed or denied is a matter which may engage the responsibility of the State, notably its responsibility to ensure the peaceful enjoyment of the right guaranteed under Article 9 (art. 9) to the holders of those beliefs and doctrines.[42]

As that quote suggests, the Court has sought to protect the right to comment critically on ethnic or religious traditions and beliefs, recognizing that these are matters of legitimate debate in any democratic society.[43] The Court has also set out a major distinction between legitimate restrictions on racist expression and the importance of informing the public about incitement to hatred, including explanation of specific instances.[44]

---

[39] Compare the decision of the European Commission on Human Rights in *Glimmerveen and Hagenbeek v. Netherlands* (Application Nos 8348/78; 8406/78) (Admissibility decision, 11 October 1979) with the more recent decisions of the Court in *Soulas and others v. France* (Application No. 15948/03) (7 October 2008) and *Féret v. Belgium* (Application No. 15615/07) (16 July 2009).

[40] See, for example, *Jean-Marie Le Pen v. France* (Application No. 18788/09) (20 April 2010), *Soulas and others v. France*, n. 39 above, and *Balsytè-Lideikienè v. Lithuania* (Application No. 72596/01) (4 November 2008).

[41] *Wingrove v. The United Kingdom* (Application No. 17419/90) (25 November 1996).

[42] *Otto-Preminger-Institut v. Austria* (Application No. 13470/87) (20 September 1994), para. 47.

[43] See, for example, *Gündüz v. Turkey* (Application No. 3507/97) (4 December 2004), in which the Court found that the statements at issue showed an intransigent attitude towards and profound dissatisfaction with contemporary institutions but did not incite violence or hatred. See also *Giniewski v. France* (Application No. 64016/00) (31 January 2006) and European Commission for Democracy through Law (Venice Commission), *Report on the relationship between freedom of expression and freedom of religion: the issue of regulation and prosecution of blasphemy, religious insult and incitement to religious hatred*, Doc. No. CDL-AD(2008)026, Conclusions, which state that 'it is neither necessary nor desirable to create an offence of religious insult (that is, insult to religious feelings) simpliciter, without the element of incitement to hatred as an essential component'. See also Sari, A., 'The Danish Cartoons Row: Re-Drawing the Limits of the Right to Freedom of Expression?' 16 *Finnish Yearbook of International Law* (2005), 365–398.

[44] *Jersild v. Denmark* (Application No. 15890/89) (23 September 1994). See also Council of Europe, Committee of Ministers Recommendation on 'Hate Speech', Rec (97) 20, Principle 6.

In the 1990s, incitement to hatred, which was in many respects a legacy issue for western European institutions, became an urgent public policy concern. Following the outbreak of war and ethnic atrocities in the Yugoslav successor states and severe ethnic tensions elsewhere in Europe, the Council of Europe became a major forum for efforts to build a set of common measures to contain the threat of ethnic and religious hatred. In these efforts, the European Convention on Human Rights provided core concepts and language to frame the major issues, but the Court itself had a limited institutional ability to coordinate European or domestic law and policy in this highly politicized field. The Council consequently put its authority behind a series of policy instruments intended to bring member states into a common position.

In 1993, the heads of state and government of the Council of Europe adopted the Vienna Declaration on Combating Racism, Xenophobia, Anti-Semitism and Intolerance. In this Declaration, the member states deplored the resurgence of racism in Europe and urged cooperation in suppressing racist activities as well as agreeing to other collective initiatives to support that goal.[45] These included the establishment of the European Commission against Racism and Intolerance (ECRI), which is now the Council's monitoring body on the effort to suppress racism, xenophobia, anti-Semitism, and intolerance.[46] The Vienna Declaration also directed the CE Committee of Ministers to draft the Framework Convention for the Protection of National Minorities, which the Council of Europe adopted in 1994. This treaty obliges parties to take appropriate measures to protect persons who may be subject to threats or acts of discrimination, hostility, or violence as a result of their ethnic, cultural, linguistic, or religious identity.[47]

The Council of Europe's work on incitement to hatred has repeatedly identified the media as the primary vehicle responsible for the spread of ethnic hatred as well as the most important positive influence in fostering greater tolerance. Its first prescriptive measure directed at the media's potential role in inciting hatred was the 1989 Convention on Transfrontier Television, which required state parties to ensure that television programmes provided by broadcasters under their jurisdiction did not contain incitements to racial hatred.[48] This obligation was noticeably

---

[45] The Vienna Declaration contains an undertaking to combat all ideologies, policies, and practices constituting an incitement to racial hatred, violence, and discrimination, as well as any action or language likely to strengthen fears and tensions between groups from different racial, ethnic, national, religious, or social backgrounds.

[46] The Council of Europe, Committee of Ministers granted ECRI its Statute on 13 June 2002. ECRI General Policy Recommendation No. 1: Combating racism, xenophobia, antisemitism and intolerance (1996) contains guidelines for the adoption of national measures concerning legal and policy aspects of the fight against racism and intolerance. See also General Policy Recommendation No. 6: Combating the dissemination of racist, xenophobic and antisemitic material via the internet (2000), which requests governments to take the necessary measures, at national and international levels, to act effectively against the use of the internet for racist, xenophobic, and anti-Semitic aims, and, ECRI: General Policy Recommendation No. 7 on National legislation to combat racism and racial discrimination (adopted on 13 December 2002).

[47] Council of Europe, Framework Convention for the Protection of National Minorities, (ETS No. 157), Article 6(2).

[48] Council of Europe, European Convention on Transfrontier Television (ETS No. 132), Article 7— Responsibilities of the broadcaster. See also the Explanatory Report on the Convention on Transfrontier

narrower than the parallel provisions of the EU Audiovisual Media Services Directive, which prohibits incitement to hatred on grounds of race, sex, religion, or nationality. This would have been remedied in the proposed 2009 amendments, but the failure of those proposals has left the future of the Convention uncertain.[49]

In 1997, which the EU had declared the European Year against Racism, the Committee of Ministers adopted two recommendations directed at the negative and positive influence of the media on the incitement of racial and other forms of hatred.[50] The first of these, Recommendation No. R (97) 20 on 'Hate Speech', has become a key point of reference for the European Court of Human Rights and the Council of Europe generally.[51] This Recommendation concerns the restraint of media born incitement to hatred, advising member states to 'establish or maintain a sound legal framework consisting of civil, criminal and administrative law provisions on hate speech which enable administrative and judicial authorities to reconcile in each case respect for freedom of expression with respect for human dignity and the protection of the reputation or the rights of others'.[52] The other recommendation, No. R(97) 21 on the media and the promotion of a culture of tolerance, concerns measures to encourage the media to promote between European cultural and ethnic communities. More recently, the Committee of Ministers has also urged the private sector media to take measures to deal decisively with 'hate speech, racism and xenophobia and incitation to violence in a digital environment such as the Internet' through self and coregulatory regimes.[53]

For the Council of Europe, the 2003 Cybercrime Convention provided a useful opportunity to apply the principles of its 1997 Hate Speech Recommendation, in the form of legally binding obligations, to the growing problem of internet based incitement to hatred. In the view of the United States, a major participant in the drafting of this treaty, those principles were blatantly contrary to US constitutional law concerning hate speech.[54] In response to these objections, the European negotiators proposing these obligations agreed to place them in a protocol treaty

---

Television, which states that Article 7 is grounded in International Convention on the Elimination of All Forms of Racial Discrimination (1965).

[49] Current amendments to the European Convention on Transfrontier Television (1989), Strasbourg, 17 November 2008; T-TT(2008)003Prov. On the failure of the 2009 amendments to the Convention, see Chapter 6.

[50] International Court of Justice, *The Application of the Convention on the Prevention and Punishment of the Crime of Genocide (Bosnia and Herzegovina v. Serbia and Montenegro)*, (26 February 2007), para. 297.

[51] See, for example, *Balsytė-Lideikienė v. Lithuania*, (Application No. 72596/01) (4 November 2008).

[52] Council of Europe, Explanatory Memorandum to Recommendation No. R (97) 20 on 'Hate Speech', Principle 2.

[53] Council of Europe, Committee of Ministers, Declaration on Human Rights and the Rule of Law in the Information Society, CM(2005)56.

[54] Council of Europe, Convention on Cybercrime, (ETS No. 185). On the Cybercrime Convention generally, see Chapter 12. See also United States Department of Justice, Council of Europe Convention on Cybercrime: Frequently Asked Questions and Answers, <http://www.justice.gov/criminal/cybercrime/COEFAQs.htm>.

attached to the Convention.[55] This Protocol requires that the state parties criminalize various computer based forms of incitement to hatred, including distribution or communication to the public of racist and xenophobic material, threats, or insults or making available to the public material that denies or approves of genocide or crimes against humanity.[56] The Protocol was also drafted to offer maximum flexibility to the state parties. They are, for example, allowed conditionally to make reservations to all the criminalization obligations, except the obligation to criminalize the making of racist or xenophobic threats in connection with the commission of a major criminal offence.[57] Yet even with these concessions, few states have become parties to the Protocol, despite Council of Europe efforts to promote the treaty amongst member and non-member states.[58] Nonetheless, European Union member states are now subject to the 2008 EU Framework Decision's much broader domestic legislation criminalizing incitement to hatred, which covers the main objectives of the Cybercrime Protocol.

Hate speech in international law

Since the adoption of Universal Declaration on Human Rights in 1948, the general problem of abuse of rights and the specific problem of incitement to hatred have been closely tied to the course of global politics. Prohibitions on incitement to hatred were initially embraced as a safeguard against a return to fascism. However, this created a model that was soon turned to other causes, including redress for the racist presumptions of colonialism and, more recently, the defence of religious faith. Through these decades of human rights diplomacy and law making, the western liberal democracies have been more often divided than united over the proper limits to public comment on race, ethnicity, religion, and other major social distinctions. The government of the United States has adamantly resisted the entrenchment of any principle, permissive or prescriptive, based on the idea that incitement to hatred, without direct threat of violence, should be prohibited by law. Yet European law has gradually moved over the same period in a different direction. While it began from a largely permissive position, allowing member states to impose proportionate criminal sanctions on expression that incites hatred, it now

---

[55] Additional Protocol to the Convention on Cybercrime concerning the criminalisation of acts of a racist and xenophobic nature committed through computer systems (ETS No. 189), adopted 28 January 2003 and now in force.

[56] Ibid., Articles 3 to 6. See also Article 8(1), which links Article 6 to denial of the Holocaust and other genocides recognized as such by the European Court of Human Rights and other international courts set up since 1945. Article 2 of the Protocol defines 'racist and xenophobic material' to mean 'any written material, image or any other representation of ideas or theories, which advocates, promotes or incites hatred, discrimination or violence, against any individual or group of individuals, based on race, colour, descent or national or ethnic origin, as well as religion if used as a pretext for any of these factors'. This definition draws on the UN International Convention on the Elimination of All Forms of Racial Discrimination as well as the CE Recommendation No. R (97) 20 on 'Hate Speech'.

[57] Ibid., Article 4.

[58] Committee of Ministers Recommendation on measures to promote the public service value of the Internet, Rec (2007)16.

insists that all EU member states establish criminal laws of that kind. This transatlantic divide has inevitably hampered efforts to oppose the use of incitement laws to attack particular groups or countries or to suppress peaceful domestic dissent.

International trade law has so far had little purchase on domestic measures that restrict media goods and services to prevent incitement to hatred. In this field, the rules of WTO law are applied in much the same way as they apply to measures intended to prevent incitement to violence or, to a lesser extent, to the publication and distribution of media content depicting violence.[59] Domestic measures prohibiting incitement to hatred will in most cases apply equally to domestic and foreign media goods and services and their suppliers and therefore presumptively lie beyond the reach of most WTO disciplines. There is nonetheless considerable potential for discriminatory application of these measures, which are narrowly focused on specific content issues that are often highly sensitive to particular states. Under Article XX of the GATT, the state concerned may however be able to demonstrate that the measure is necessary for the protection of public morals or human health, or where GATS XIV is applicable, that the measure is necessary for the protection of public order, provided that the discrimination is neither arbitrary or unjustifiable nor a disguised trade restriction.[60] There is no doubt that protection of the public from genuine incitement to hatred is a legitimate non-market policy objective under WTO law and any successful challenge would concern the necessity of discrimination and the manner it is achieved. More importantly, this is a highly politicized issue in international relations that also arises in a jealously guarded area of domestic autonomy, in which states expect a wide margin of discretion. The discriminatory application of national measures to combat incitement to racial, ethnic, or religious hatred moreover has a relatively small impact on cross border trade in media goods and services.

Incitement to hatred is consequently more often viewed as a human rights problem, having consumed years of argument in the United Nations human rights system. Here the developments have centred on two major multilateral conventions: the International Covenant on Civil and Political Rights (ICCPR) and the International Convention on the Elimination of all Forms of Racial Discrimination (ICERD). Like the European Convention on Human Rights, the ICCPR contains a general abuse of rights article, which in principle arguably also excludes expression that incites hatred from the protection of the Article 19 right to freedom of expression.[61] In the *Faurisson v. France* communication to the ICCPR Human

---

[59] On WTO trade law and the media generally, see Chapter 5. On trade law and incitement to violence, see Chapter 8. On trade law and restrictions on content depicting violence, see Chapter 12.

[60] Article XX, General Agreement on Tariffs and Trade 1994 (incorporating GATT 1947) (15 April 1994), 33 ILM 1153 (1994), and Article XIV, General Agreement on Trade in Services (15 April 1994), 33 ILM 1167 (1994). On the general exception provisions of the GATT and the GATS, see Chapter 5.

[61] International Covenant on Civil and Political Rights (ICCPR), GA Resolution 2200A (XXI), UN Doc. A/6316 (1966). Article 5: 1. 'Nothing in the present Covenant may be interpreted as implying for any State, group, or person any right to engage in any activity or perform any act aimed at the destruction of any of the rights and freedoms recognized herein or at their limitation to a greater

Rights Committee, France argued that Faurisson's conviction for Holocaust denial was legitimate as his published statement amounted to an abuse of rights under Article 5.[62] The Committee however rejected Faurisson's claim that France was in breach of its Article 19 obligations by applying the conditional exception provisions of Article 19(3), without referring to Article 5. Furthermore, the inclusion of an express obligation in Article 20 of the ICCPR requiring state parties to adopt laws prohibiting 'any advocacy of national, racial or religious hatred that constitutes incitement to discrimination, hostility or violence' has also limited the need for doctrinal development of Article 5.[63] In the view of the Human Rights Committee, the prohibitions required by Article 20, 'are fully compatible with the right of freedom of expression as contained in article 19, the exercise of which carries with it special duties and responsibilities'.[64] In the same General Comment, the Committee underscored the obligation on state parties under this Article to create 'a law making it clear that propaganda and advocacy as described therein are contrary to public policy and providing for an appropriate sanction in case of violation'.[65]

While drafted long after the major provisions of the ICCPR, the International Convention on the Elimination of all Forms of Racial Discrimination (ICERD) was adopted by the UN General Assembly in 1965, a year before the two Covenants.[66] Article 4 of this treaty requires state parties to make punishable by law any, 'dissemination of ideas based on racial superiority or hatred, incitement to racial discrimination, as well as all acts of violence or incitement to such acts against any race or group of persons of another colour or ethnic origin,' as well as participation in 'propaganda activities, which promote and incite racial

---

extent than is provided for in the present Covenant.' As yet, the ICCPR Human Rights Committee has not published a General Comment on Article 5. See also Articles 29 and 30 of the the Universal Declaration of Human Rights. Article 29(3) states that '[t]hese rights and freedoms may in no case be exercised contrary to the purposes and principles of the United Nations'. Article 30: 'Nothing in this Declaration may be interpreted as implying for any State, group or person any right to engage in any activity or to perform any act aimed at the destruction of any of the rights and freedoms set forth herein.'

[62] *Faurisson v. France*, Communication No. 550/1993, para. 7.4.

[63] On Article 20, see Coliver, S.W., *Striking a Balance: Hate Speech, Freedom of Expression and Non-Discrimination*, (ARTICLE 19, 1992).

[64] ICCPR Human Rights Committee General Comment No. 11: Prohibition of propaganda for war and inciting national, racial or religious hatred (Article 20) (Nineteenth session, 1983).

[65] See also *J.R.T. and the W. G. Party v. Canada*, Communication No. 104/1981, in which the applicant had been prosecuted for disseminating anti-Semitic views by playing recorded messages on a telephone service available to the public. In this Communication, the Human Rights Committee stated, '[t]he opinions which Mr T. seeks to disseminate through the telephone system clearly constitute the advocacy of racial or religious hatred which Canada has an obligation under Article 20(2) of the Covenant to prohibit'. See also *Ross v. Canada*, Communication No. 736/2000, in which the Committee stated, '[f]or instance, and as held in *Faurisson v. France*, restrictions may be permitted on statements which are of a nature as to raise or strengthen anti-Semitic feeling, in order to uphold the Jewish communities' right to be protected from religious hatred. Such restrictions also derive support from the principles reflected in Article 20(2) of the Covenant.'

[66] International Convention on the Elimination of all Forms of Racial Discrimination (ICERD), GA Resolution 2106 (XX), (21 December 1965), 660 UNTS 195.

discrimination'.[67] The CERD Committee on the Elimination of Racial Discrimination has underscored the importance of Article 4 and clarified its implications in its General Recommendations VII and XV.[68] In the first of these, the Committee confirmed the mandatory character of Article 4, stating in the second that, '[t]o satisfy these obligations, states parties have not only to enact appropriate legislation but also to ensure that it is effectively enforced'.[69] In General Recommendation XV, the Committee also stressed that, 'the prohibition of the dissemination of all ideas based upon racial superiority or hatred is compatible with the right to freedom of opinion and expression'.[70]

The United States government has refused to accept positive obligations to criminalize incitement to hatred under either the ICCPR or the ICERD. In its reservations to the ICCPR, made when it became a state party in 1992, the United States declared that, 'article 20 does not authorize or require legislation or other action by the United States that would restrict the right of free speech and association protected by the Constitution and laws of the United States'.[71] United States reservations to the ICERD also excluded the application of Article 4 to the extent that it is inconsistent with American constitutional law.[72] The American

---

[67] Ibid., Article 4: 'States Parties condemn all propaganda and all organizations which are based on ideas or theories of superiority of one race or group of persons of one colour or ethnic origin, or which attempt to justify or promote racial hatred and discrimination in any form, and undertake to adopt immediate and positive measures designed to eradicate all incitement to, or acts of, such discrimination and, to this end, with due regard to the principles embodied in the Universal Declaration of Human Rights and the rights expressly set forth in Article 5 of this Convention, inter alia: a. shall declare an offence punishable by law all dissemination of ideas based on racial superiority or hatred, incitement to racial discrimination, as well as all acts of violence or incitement to such acts against any race or group of persons of another colour or ethnic origin, and also the provision of any assistance to racist activities, including the financing thereof; b. shall declare illegal and prohibit organizations, and also organized and all other propaganda activities, which promote and incite racial discrimination, and shall recognize participation in such organizations or activities as an offence punishable by law; c. shall not permit public authorities or public institutions, national or local, to promote or incite racial discrimination.' See also Coliver, S., n. 63 above.

[68] ICERD Committee on the Elimination of Racial Discrimination, General Recommendation VII: Measures to eradicate incitement to or acts of discrimination, (1985), UN Doc. A/40/18. General Recommendation XV: Measures to eradicate incitement to or acts of discrimination, (1993), UN Doc. A/48/18.

[69] General Recommendation VII, n. 68 above, '3. Article 4 (a) requires States parties to penalize four categories of misconduct: (i) dissemination of ideas based upon racial superiority or hatred; (ii) incitement to racial hatred; (iii) acts of violence against any race or group of persons of another colour or ethnic origin; and (iv) incitement to such acts.'

[70] ICERD Committee on the Elimination of Racial Discrimination, *Gelle v. Denmark*, Communication No. 34/2004 (15 March 2006), para. 7.3. The Committee observes that it does not suffice, for purposes of Article 4 of the Convention, merely to declare acts of racial discrimination punishable on paper. Rather, criminal laws and other legal provisions prohibiting racial discrimination must also be effectively implemented by the competent national tribunals and other state institutions. See also *The Jewish Community of Oslo et al. v. Norway*, Communication No. 30/2003.

[71] Reservations of the United States of America to the International Convention on the Elimination of all Forms of Racial Discrimination, <http://treaties.un.org>.

[72] Ibid. 'The Constitution of the United States contains provisions for the protection of individual rights, such as the right of free speech, and nothing in the Convention shall be deemed to require or to authorize legislation or other action by the United States of America incompatible with the provisions of the Constitution of the United States of America', and, 'I. The Senate's advice and consent is subject to the following reservations: (1) That the Constitution and laws of the United States contain extensive

general rejection of incitement to hatred laws has the advantage of simplicity and clarity, yet even amongst liberal democratic countries it has not been a persuasive position, especially those with recent experiences of ethnic and religious conflict. Most western European governments, in contrast, supported the creation of UN treaty obligations prohibiting incitement to hatred, although insisting that these international commitments should be interpreted in conformity with the European Convention on Human Rights.[73] That objective has been achieved not only through reservations and declarations made by European states on becoming state parties to these treaties, but also through the work of European Court of Human Rights, whose case law assumes a general consistency between these UN obligations and the principles of the European Convention, including the Article 10 right to freedom of expression.[74] This has the strategic advantage of potentially exporting European standards into UN practice, but also requires constant vigilance as other states seek to take the issue of incitement to hatred in directions incompatible with European law. Converting the open language of international human rights treaties into explicitly liberal democratic obligations is however the unending task of the liberal democratic project.[75]

There are certainly strong counter pressures in international law and relations to adapt the ICCPR and ICERD incitement to hatred models to legitimize other restrictions on the media that would violate the free speech principles of any liberal democracy. In this decade, tensions between states on the question of incitement notably flared up during the World Conference against Racism, Racial Discrimination, Xenophobia and Related Intolerance held in Durban, South Africa, in 2001

---

protections of individual freedom of speech, expression and association. Accordingly, the United States does not accept any obligation under this Convention, in particular under articles 4 and 7, to restrict those rights, through the adoption of legislation or any other measures, to the extent that they are protected by the Constitution and laws of the United States.'

[73] Council of Europe, Committee of Ministers, Measures to be taken against incitement to racial, national and religious hatred Res(68)30E, 2. '[T]hat governments, when depositing their instruments of ratification with the United Nations, stress by an interpretative statement the importance which they attach, on the one hand, to the reference made in the Convention on the Elimination of all Forms of Racial Discrimination concluded under the auspices of the United Nations, to the safeguarding of all rights proclaimed in the Universal Declaration of Human Rights and, on the other hand, to the respect for the rights laid down in the European Convention for the Protection of Human Rights and Fundamental Freedoms.'

[74] France, Reservations to ICERD, <http://treaties.un.org>: 'With regard to article 4, France wishes to make it clear that it interprets the reference made therein to the principles of the Universal Declaration of Human Rights and to the rights set forth in article 5 of the Convention as releasing the States Parties from the obligation to enact anti-discrimination legislation which is incompatible with the freedoms of opinion and expression and of peaceful assembly and association guaranteed by those texts.' See also France, Reservations to the ICCPR, <http://treaties.un.org>, '(6) The Government of the Republic declares that articles 19, 21 and 22 of the Covenant will be implemented in accordance with articles 10, 11 and 16 of the European Convention for the Protection of Human Rights and Fundamental Freedoms of 4 November 1950.' See, for example, *Jersild v. Denmark* (Application No.15890/89) (23 September 1994), para 30.

[75] See, for example, the Camden Principles on Freedom of Expression and Equality, Principle 12: Incitement to hatred, which were sponsored by the ARTICLE 19 organisation (<http://www.article19.org>) and follow the model set by the Syracusa and Johannesburg principles (on these sets of principles, see Chapter 6).

and the follow up Durban Review Conference, held at Geneva in 2009.[76] While these conferences featured walkouts and boycotts by various western states, after intense negotiations their final documents did not seek major changes in the main principles of international law concerning racism and racial discrimination.[77] The Durban Review Outcome Document did not, in particular, include a declaration that defamation of religion is contrary to international law, although it did emphasize the importance of this issue for several states. The Document states that it, '[d]eplores the global rise and number of incidents of racial or religious intolerance and violence, including Islamophobia, anti-Semitism, Christianophobia and anti-Arabism manifested in particular by the derogatory stereotyping and stigmatization of persons based on their religion or belief'.[78]

The relationship between the right to freedom of expression and offence to religious beliefs has been a source of argument in the United Nations for half a century. After failing to agree on the content of a multilateral treaty, the UN General Assembly adopted the non-binding Declaration on the Elimination of all Forms of Intolerance and of Discrimination based on Religion or Belief in 1981. This instrument did not however contain an incitement to hatred on religious grounds in parallel to the ICERD as sought by some member states.[79] More recently, member states where Islam is the state religion have spearheaded efforts to initiate work on a UN multilateral instrument to create a binding obligation to prohibit defamation of religion. This has occurred not only through annual United Nations Human Rights Council resolutions on this subject, but also through changes to the mandate of the UN Special Rapporteur on the promotion and protection of the right to freedom of opinion and expression.[80] A large number of

---

[76] United Nations, World Conference against Racism, Racial Discrimination, Xenophobia and Related Intolerance (Durban, South Africa, 2001, <http://www.un.org/WCAR>). United Nations, Durban Review Conference, (Geneva, Switzerland, April 2009, <http://www.un.org/durbanreview2009>).

[77] World Conference against Racism, Racial Discrimination, Xenophobia and Related Intolerance, n. 76 above, Durban Declaration and Programme of Action (September 2001). See also Petrova, D., '"Smoke and Mirrors": The Durban Review Conference and Human Rights Politics at the United Nations', 10(1) *Human Rights Law Review* (2010), 129.

[78] Outcome Document of the Durban Review Conference, <http://www.un.org/durbanreview2009>.

[79] Declaration on the Elimination of all Forms of Intolerance and of Discrimination based on Religion or Belief, GA Resolution 36/55 (25 November 1981). See also Benito, E.O., Special Rapporteur of the Sub-Commission on Prevention of Discrimination and Protection of Minorities, *Elimination of all Forms of Intolerance and Discrimination Based on Religion or Belief* (UN Publication, 1989), and Taylor, P.M., *Freedom of Religion: UN and European human rights law and practice* (Cambridge University Press, 2005).

[80] See, for example, United Nations Human Rights Council, Resolution on Combating Defamation of Religions (11 March 2010), A/HRC/13/L.1, and, UN Human Rights Council, Resolution 7/36 of March 2008, which '[d]ecides to extend for a further three years the mandate of the Special Rapporteur whose tasks will be: (d) To report on instances in which the abuse of the right of freedom of expression constitutes an act of racial or religious discrimination, taking into account articles 19(3) and 20 of the International Covenant on Civil and Political Rights, and general comment No. 15 of the Committee on the Elimination of All Forms of Racial Discrimination, which stipulates that the prohibition of the dissemination of all ideas based upon racial superiority or hatred is compatible with the freedom of opinion and expression.' See also UN Secretary-General, *Combating Defamation of Religions*, A/65/263 (9 August 2010).

liberal democratic states have opposed these efforts, concerned that the concept of defamation of religion is incompatible with liberal principles of freedom of expression, not least because it confuses the protection of ideas, which must be open to robust challenge in a liberal democratic state, with the legitimate protection of specific individuals from harm.[81]

---

[81] See, for example, Joint Declaration on Defamation of Religions, and Anti-Terrorism and Anti-Extremism Legislation 2008 of the UN Special Rapporteur on Freedom of Opinion and Expression, the OSCE Representative on Freedom of the Media, the OAS Special Rapporteur on Freedom of Expression, and the ACHPR (African Commission on Human and Peoples' Rights) Special Rapporteur on Freedom of Expression and Access to Information (9 December 2008). See also the Joint Declaration *International Mechanisms for Promoting Freedom of Expression 2006*, Freedom of Expression and Cultural/Religious Tensions of the UN Special Rapporteur on Freedom of Opinion and Expression, the OSCE Representative on Freedom of the Media, the OAS Special Rapporteur on Freedom of Expression and the ACHPR (African Commission on Human and Peoples' Rights) Special Rapporteur on Freedom of Expression (19 December 2006).

PART IV

INTERVENTION IN
MEDIA MARKETS

14

Democracy, Pluralism, and the Media

It is an axiom of liberal democracy that citizens require reasonable access to a daily flow of diverse information and ideas regarding matters of public concern. Without that access, citizens cannot participate effectively in the many processes of collective self government.[1] In any large democracy this will require a significant degree of media pluralism. As the European Commission has put it,

[A] modern democratic society cannot exist without communication media which: are widely available and accessible; reflect the pluralistic nature of such a society and are not dominated by any one viewpoint or controlled by any one interest group; make available the information necessary for citizens to make informed choices about their lives and their communities; and provide the means whereby the public debate which underpins free and democratic society can take place, means that the market will not necessarily deliver on its own.[2]

While the importance of media pluralism to contemporary liberal democracy is broadly uncontested, there is no similar consensus on how that is best achieved. Indeed, the question of how media pluralism should be fostered and maintained immediately excites strong disagreement about the proper roles of the state and the market in ensuring democratic participation and choice.[3] It is certainly rare for democratic life to flourish on a large scale without the protection of an effective state. Yet the containment of that state is also one of the chief concerns of liberalism, which historically celebrates freedom of the press as primarily meaning emancipation from the arbitrary or excessive use of state power.[4] From this

---

[1] C. Edwin Baker describes this as the 'democratic distribution principle', which demands as wide as practical a dispersal of power within public discourse: Baker, C.E., *Media Concentration and Democracy* (Cambridge University Press, 2007), 7–9. See also Lichtenberg, J., 'Foundations and Limits of Freedom of the Press' in Lichtenberg, J., (ed.), *Democracy and the Mass Media* (Cambridge University Press, 1990), 102; Holmes, S., 'Liberal Constraints on Private Power: Reflections on the Origins and Rationale of Access Regulation' in Lichtenberg, J., (ed.), *Democracy and the Mass Media* (Cambridge University Press, 1990), 21.

[2] European Commission: European Audiovisual Policy, *Report from the High Level Group on Audiovisual Policy* (1998), ch I, 1.

[3] See, for example, Graham, A. and Davies, G., *Broadcasting, Society and Policy in the Multimedia Age* (John Libby Media, 1997); Islam, R., 'Into the Looking Glass' in Islam, R. (ed.), *The Right to Tell: The Role of Mass Media in Economic Development* (World Bank Institute, 2002). Understanding Speech Rights: Defensive and Empowering Approaches to the First Amendment, 26(1) *Media, Culture & Society* (2004), 103–120.

[4] That understanding of media freedom that remains highly potent today. See, for example, the 'European Charter on Freedom of the Press', adopted on 25 May 2009 by 48 editors-in-chief and

perspective, states are suspect and liable to use their formidable powers to limit or skew public debate even when attempting to counter specific evils or achieve particular public goods. It is for the media therefore not only to inform good citizens, but also to nurture a culture of democratic dissent.[5]

The entrenchment of constitutional rights to freedom of expression has become the anchor for that vision of liberty from the state. Indeed, the empowerment of courts to declare the unconstitutionality of laws and other measures that restrict the publication or distribution of information and ideas has become a cornerstone of contemporary liberal democracy. Beyond its obvious political dimensions, the idea of media pluralism as liberty from the state has a powerful economic element. This is, in other words, the twinned argument that the right to engage in commerce, when coupled with political and social liberty, jointly unleashes the full range of creative forces that sustain the market place of ideas. On this basis, a market economy is the best provider of the constant flow of rich, diverse information needed sustain effective democratic public life.

The liberty to speak and publish and also to receive information and ideas free from interference by the state is therefore the obvious starting place for liberal theories of pluralism. That concept of freedom has however been enriched and complicated by the broadening of the liberal tradition to include other ideas of personal autonomy and empowerment. The individual's right to receive information has thus become the conceptual and legal platform for more interventionist ideas of media pluralism. On this view, a person cannot live an autonomous life, including the opportunity to participate in public life, without adequate access to the information created by others.

Whether that conclusion leads to state intervention in media markets is however keenly debated. In any liberal democracy, the argument that media markets will satisfy the public's demand for information and ideas is bound to be highly influential. It promises to close the circle between the media's liberty to publish and the public's right to information without costly or burdensome intervention by the state. The argument for a market solution however begs several questions about the measurement of an adequate flow of information for democratic purposes. This could plausibly be no more than the sum of popular demand for news and current affairs content or, instead, could be based on some external assessment regarding effective democracy and informed public participation. Either view may lead to the conclusion that a particular media market is failing to deliver an adequate quantity or diversity of information content.[6]

In the broadcast era, most countries were reluctant or unable to allocate sufficient radiospectrum to support competitive markets for television and radio

---

leading journalists from 19 countries meeting in Hamburg, (<http://www.pressfreedom.eu/en/index. php>).

[5] Schudson, M., *Why Democracies Need an Unlovable Press* (Polity, 2008).

[6] See Graham, A. and Davies, G., n. 3 above; Alexander, P. and Brown, K., 'Policymaking and Policy Trade-offs: Broadcast Media Regulation in the United States', in Seabright, P., and von Hagen, J. (eds), *The Economic Regulation of Broadcasting Markets* (Cambridge University Press, 2007), 255.

services. For many, the more attractive option was to provide broadcast services directly or to impose content obligations on privately owned ones. Under state control, however, the achievement of pluralism in the broadcast media tended to be fashioned around the structure of national politics, serving in particular the needs of the established political parties. In Britain, for example, the BBC developed a principle of impartiality whose chief aim was to ensure proportionate coverage of the major political parties.[7] In the United States, the European example was rejected. The development of broadcasting was left to private interests, leading to both varied local ownership and national commercial networks. The new broadcast media were however deemed to be trustees of a public resource and made subject to special content obligations, which included a right of reply known as the 'fairness doctrine', until its abolition in the 1980s.[8] This limited regulatory obligation was intended to moderate the effects of partisan broadcasting, which was constitutionally protected.

By the 1990s, however, the communications revolution had begun to break down the technological arguments for state intervention.[9] Digitization was gradually resolving many of the problems of analogue transmission scarcity, bringing a rising flood of new forms of communication that have since redefined the nature of entertainment and information media. These changes also coincided with the strengthening influence of neoclassical economics over public policy in the western democracies. This political climate did not favour arguments to transform state supported broadcasters into multi-faceted bastions of the new media.[10] What emerged instead has been a greater reliance on market driven, internet based services to provide not only access to diverse content, but also opportunities for individuals or groups to communicate information and opinion to the wider public, albeit frequently buttressed by public service media that often remain predominantly anchored in the broadcast sector.

Nonetheless, while the communication revolution may have undercut technological arguments for the state provision of media services, it has yet to overcome scepticism about the capacity of market forces to guarantee social and political pluralism. In many countries, it remains questionable whether media markets can achieve the idealized state of openness and genuine competitiveness needed to

---

[7] *Seesaw to Wagon Wheel: Safeguarding impartiality in the 21st Century,* BBC trust report published 18 June 2007, (<http://www.bbc.co.uk/bbctrust/our_work/other/century21.shtml>).

[8] In its 1969 *Red Lion* decision, the United States Supreme Court upheld the 'fairness doctrine' imposed by federal regulations on the broadcast media, citing the constitutional right of the audience to hear conflicting views. In other First Amendment media cases, however, American courts have more often restricted governmental powers to intervene in media markets, even where its purpose is to foster greater pluralism. In addition, the Federal Communications Commission rescinded major parts of the fairness doctrine in 1987 and removed its remnants in 2000 after finding that changes in media markets had made them unnecessary. *Red Lion Broadcasting Co. v. Federal Communications Commission,* 395 U.S. 367. See also Baker, C.E., n. 1 above, 127–128 and Holmes, S., n. 1 above, 21, 45–52.

[9] See, for example, Chen, J., 'From Red Lion to Red List: The Dominance and Decline of the Broadcast Medium', 60 *Administrative Law Review* (2009).

[10] See Commission Decision regarding United Kingdom, BBC Digital Curriculum, N 37/2003, and, BBC Trust suspends BBC Jam, 14 March 2007 (BBC news report).

sustain a robust market place of ideas. Historically, media markets have been characterized by monopoly or oligopoly control of key technologies or forms of content, such as operating systems or sports rights that create significant barriers to entry and weak competition. Where these media businesses are also major information providers, the risks for media pluralism are obvious.[11] However much the media are identified as the foundation for a 'public sphere' of open debate and deliberation in democratic life,[12] media owners and editors are rarely passive or disinterested in the processes or outcomes of politics.[13] Their influence over the news may be overt or may occur through less obvious choices about what is deemed to be newsworthy and the manner in which events or issues are reported.[14] The communications revolution will therefore need to go a very long way to neutralize the influence of dominate news and current affairs providers through competitive market forces.

The communications revolution has plainly broadened media markets in much of the world, displacing the traditional media as the gatekeepers of public information and bringing a profusion of new information sources.[15] Blogs, tweeting, and other interactive forms of communication have also transformed journalism into a highly networked, relentless flow of information. On the other hand, increased competition and splintering markets have also severely reduced the funding available for journalism, thinning the depth and quality of news reporting in ways that an abundance of new media commentators are unlikely to remedy.[16] The control of key commercial bottlenecks, such as premium content rights or dominant distribution platforms or services has also led to new concentrations of corporate power over the flow of news and current affairs information.[17] The communications revolution has consequently changed the context and the focus for debates over media pluralism, but has certainly not resolved these arguments decisively in favour of market forces.[18]

---

[11] See Holmes, S., n. 1 above, 21, 50.

[12] Jürgen Habermas's idea of the public sphere, an idealized conception of the open sphere of public debate and engagement necessary for effective democracy, has become a core element in contemporary liberal democratic discussion of media pluralism. See, for example, Baker, C.E., n. 1 above, 7, Sunstein, C., *Democracy and the Problem of Free Speech* (Free Press, 1993), Craufurd Smith, R., *Broadcasting Law and Fundamental Rights* (Clarendon, 1997), 55–58, Hitchens, L., *Broadcasting Pluralism and Diversity* (Hart Publishing, 2006), 49–62, and Benkler, Y., *Wealth of Networks: How Social Production Transforms Markets and Freedom* (Yale University Press, 2006), ch. 7.

[13] Judith Lichtenberg, 'Introduction', in Lichtenberg, J. (ed.), *Democracy and the Mass Media* (Cambridge University Press, 1990), 1.

[14] See, for example, Lloyd, J., *What the Media Are Doing to Our Politics* (Constable & Robinson, 2004), 25.

[15] See Benkler, Y., n. 12 above.

[16] Bezanson, R. and Cranberg, G., 'Taking Stock of Newspapers and Their Future', 2(1) *Florida International Law Review* (2007); Alterman, E., 'Out of Print: The death and life of the American newspaper', *The New Yorker* (31 March 2008); Starr, P., 'Goodbye to the Age of Newspapers (Hello to a New Era of Corruption) Why American politics and society are about to be changed for the worse', *The New Republic* (4 March 2009).

[17] See Baker, C.E., n. 1 above, 120–121, and Hindman, M., *The Myth of Digital Democracy* (Princeton University Press, 2008), 13.

[18] See, for example, Balkin, J., 'Digital Speech and Democratic Culture, Digital Speech and Democratic Culture: A Theory of Freedom of Expression for the Information Society', 79(1) *New*

Nonetheless, the rise of neoclassical economic policy, neatly coinciding with the rise of the internet, has made competition law the preferred first line of defence for media pluralism amongst most major liberal democracies. Competition rules, when rigorously applied, can prevent or dismantle anti-competitive market structures and suppress commercial practices that block new entrants or innovation in media markets.[19] Yet, despite the global spread of competition law methods, consensus on the proper application of these rules in the media sector is limited. The economic rationales for particular remedies are not universally accepted and their application in fast changing communications and media markets is bound to be vigorously resisted by articulate, well resourced media companies.[20] Even where the methods are accepted in principle, subtle qualitative judgements are often required to determine when the exercise of property and commercial rights should be curtailed to promote the wider public good. In terms of media pluralism, not only are national and local media markets uniquely structured, but the influence of particular media companies on public knowledge is often a matter of qualitative rather than quantitative judgement.

Beyond these controversies, there is a more profound objection to the pursuit of media pluralism through market forces. Even accepting that new communication technologies and media services, subject to effective competition law, can achieve a well funded highly competitive media market, there is still the question of whether the satisfaction of consumer demand is the same as satisfying the diverse information needs of a democratic society. If media pluralism is no more nor less than the news and other information sought by the public, then vigorous, well funded market competition will probably suffice. There is however an argument that the collective demands of media consumers, even in a highly competitive and well funded media market, cannot deliver adequate pluralism because of the exceptional diversity of content, as well as low cost accessibility, that is necessary if all citizens are to have a reasonable opportunity for informed participation in public life. In economic terms, this is sometimes described as a merit goods argument.[21] Simply put, the breadth of information needed by citizens in a democracy is unlikely to be fully satisfied by consumer preferences as these tend towards entertainment rather than in depth news and current affairs information.

On this view, the production and distribution of content diversity is only a chance by product of media markets and not their central purpose. Intervention

York University Law Review (2004), Sunstein, C., *Republic.com 2.0* (Princeton University Press, 2007); Krotoszynski, Jr, R.J., 'The Irrelevant Wasteland: An Exploration of Why Red Lion Doesn't Matter (Much) in 2008', 60 *Administrative Law Review* (2008).

[19] See Polo, M., 'Regulation for Pluralism in Media Markets', in Seabright, P. and von Hagen, J. (eds), n. 6 above, 150; Hope, E., 'Competition Policy and Sector Specific Media Regulation: And Never the Twain Shall Meet?', in Seabright, P. and von Hagen, J. (eds), n. 6 above, 310.

[20] See, for example, in Britain, *BSkyB Plc, Virgin Media Inc v. Competition Commission, Secretary of State for Business Enterprise and Regulatory Reform* [2010] EWCA Civ 2, in which the Court of Appeal (in the fourth ruling in this matter) dismissed BSkyB's appeal from an order that it sell a large part of the shares it had acquired in the rival ITV broadcaster because of fair competition objections.

[21] Merit goods are discussed at greater length in Chapter 15.

beyond competition law is therefore often required.[22] In the broadcasting sector, intervention for purposes that ostensibly include pluralism can be seen in state funding or direct provision of news and current affairs content as well as the imposition of licence obligations on commercial broadcasters to provide similar content. The nature of that content is also frequently controlled through regulatory or licence obligations that reporting and commentary be impartial or balanced.[23] While this kind of intervention is still common, the digitization of broadcasting and the growing availability of internet based, audiovisual news sources has significantly undermined the technical justifications and economic viability of this model. It is, for example, no longer self evident that broadcasting should be treated differently than other platforms delivering media content. Nor are commercial broadcasters as willing to accept positive content obligations or restrictions on bias that their print and online operations or competitors do not share.[24] There is as well often bitter resentment that public service media, which enjoy public funding or other support, are now competing directly with private commercial media across a range of information, entertainment, and educational services.[25] Yet, despite long running tensions between public and private information providers, there is still as much argument as agreement over the principles that govern the state provision of these services in a rapidly changing and expanding media sector.[26]

Debates over the proper role of the state and market forces in fostering media pluralism are further complicated by changing ideas about democracy itself. Through much of its history, liberal democracy has been synonymous with representative forms of government and latterly organized political parties. Pluralism, as a matter of public policy, has consequently tended to mean public access to plentiful information about the policies and activities of these parties, including their candidates and elected representatives. While there are obvious justifications for this heavy emphasis on organized politics of this kind, this is also arguably a narrow view of democracy and political participation that can slide into censorship of alternatives to these established parties and forums of public debate. Quite apart from the dense relationship between the media and the state, political parties have always depended on the media for access to the public and therefore have strong incentives not only to cultivate media allies, but also to use the powers of government, when possible, to foster a stable, cooperative media sector. In these circumstances, it is often a matter of anxious concern for smaller parties, activist groups, and independent candidates that the rules promoting media pluralism appear

---

[22] Doyle, G., *Media Ownership* (Sage, 2002); *Review of Media Ownership Rules*, OFCOM: (2006), Section 2 'Introduction'.

[23] In Britain, see Office of Communications (OFCOM), Broadcasting Code, Section 5: Due Impartiality and Due Accuracy and Undue Prominence of Views and Opinions.

[24] In Britain, see Sweney, M., 'Ofcom slashes cost of ITV and Channel 5 regional broadcasting licences: Price cut to almost zero in recognition of cost of delivering public service obligations', *The Guardian* (1 October 2010).

[25] See, for example, European Publishers Council, *State Aid and Public Service Broadcasters*, (<http://www.epceurope.org>).

[26] See below for discussion of state aid to the media under European Union law.

skewed to the advantage of the major parties.[27] It is certainly true that regulatory concepts of balance or impartiality in news reporting have traditionally been measured in terms of neutrality between political parties with coverage often dictated by records of electoral success.[28]

Aside from the marginalization of non-mainstream candidates and parties, these rules can also work against alternative forms of democracy. If citizens are viewed as participants in diverse politically significant activities, rather than simply as potential voters, their information needs will be more diverse and less party oriented. Plainly, the growth of new interactive forms of social communication and organization have already changed the character of political participation and organization in many countries, stimulating debate over the role of the citizen in contemporary politics.[29] Yet, once the focus for media pluralism moves away from political parties, it becomes increasingly difficult to assess the effectiveness or adequacy of regulatory rules or other measures. Rules intended to ensure balanced exposure for major parties, for example, at least provide a basic framework for measuring media pluralism, which is much more difficult to achieve once the goal is a simply a diversity of politically and socially important information.[30]

Concerns about the diversity media content have gone hand in hand with other concerns about inequalities in public access to the communications infrastructure that sustains the public information environment. One of the great advances of broadcast radio, and later television, was their potential capacity to overcome the effects of low income and education, which had historically limited access to the print media. But that capacity depended on access to a radio or television set able to receive a sufficient diversity of programme content, which meant that national transmission systems frequently required subsidies to reach remote areas and poorer households had to wait for the retail price of these appliances to fall. The arrival of dial up internet access in the 1990s brought these questions of fair access back on a global scale. As Jean Seaton observed at the time,

[t]here is a growing voluntary apartheid here which did not previously exist, and one with alarming implications for our democracy: the gap between the richest and the poorest, employed and unemployed, educated and uneducated, may come to be measured not just in differences in health and opportunities, but by an increasing polarisation of increasing degrees of knowledge and understanding of current issues and political debates.[31]

While basic internet access has improved enormously in much of the world since then, the liberal democratic debate over access has also evolved. In wealthier states, the policy argument is now whether an individual can participate fully in demo-

---

[27] See, for example, *TV Vest As & Rogaland Pensjonistparti v. Norway* (Application No. 21132/05) (11 December 2008).

[28] See, in Britain, OFCOM Broadcasting Code: Section 6, Elections and Referendums.

[29] Sunstein, C., *Republic.com 2.0* (Princeton University Press, 2007); Coleman, S. and Blumler, J.G. *The Internet and Democratic Citizenship* (Cambridge University Press, 2009).

[30] See, for example, *From Seesaw to Wagon Wheel*, n. 7 above.

[31] Seaton, J., 'A Fresh look at Freedom of Speech' in Jean Seaton (ed.), *Politics and the Media* (Blackwell, 1998), 119.

cratic public life without reasonable broadband access to the internet. As Jack Balkin argues,

Freedom of speech depends not only on the mere absence of state censorship, but also on an infrastructure of free expression. Properly designed, it gives people opportunities to create and build technologies and institutions that other people can use for communication and association. Hence policies that promote innovation and protect the freedom to create new technologies and applications are increasingly central to free speech values.[32]

Media pluralism in European public order

European media law is marked by a deep commitment to media pluralism in the service of democracy. This commitment in both the European Union and the Council of Europe has sustained a formidable drive to entrench principles and rules that promote the pluralist, democratic character of Europe's media and thus its member states. As the Committee of Ministers of the Council of Europe stated in 1982, 'states have the duty to guard against infringements of the freedom of expression and information and should adopt policies designed to foster as much as possible a variety of media and a plurality of information sources, thereby allowing a plurality of ideas and opinions'.[33] Similarly, the European Court of Human Rights has repeatedly declared that member states must respect 'the demands of pluralism, tolerance and broadmindedness, without which there is no "democratic society"'.[34]

While the European Union was first established to create a common European market for goods, services, investment, and employment, the liberal democratic character of the participating states was also essential to the design of these new obligations and their permitted exceptions. Inevitably, this brought the enormous tensions between the roles of the market and the state in achieving public policy goals into the heart of European Union law. On the one hand, the basic obligations of free movement and fair competition support arguments for market based growth of content diversity in the media. In Europe, however, market forces have traditionally been regarded as defective suppliers of media pluralism. Pluralism instead required intervention by the state to restrain commercial interests. European Union

---

[32] Balkin, J., 'The Future of Free Expression in a Digital Age', 36 *Pepperdine Law Review* (2009). See also Balkin, J., 'Media Access: A Question of Design', 76(4) *George Washington Law Review* (2008).

[33] Recital (6) of the Committee of Ministers, Declaration on the Freedom on Expression and Information (April 1982), which also urges member states to seek to achieve 'the existence of a wide variety of independent and autonomous media, permitting the reflection of diversity of ideas and opinions'. See also Committee of Ministers, Declaration on the freedom of expression and information (1982), Part II objectives include, '*d.* the existence of a wide variety of independent and autonomous media, permitting the reflection of diversity of ideas and opinions.'

[34] See Nieuwenhuis, A., 'The Concept of Pluralism in the Case-Law of the European Court of Human Rights', 3 *European Constitutional Law Review* (2007), 367. See also Komorek, E., 'Is Media Pluralism a Human Right? The European Court of Human Rights, the Council of Europe and the Issue of Media Pluralism', 3 *European Human Rights Law Review* (2009).

law has moreover fully accepted that its principles of free movement and fair competition were never intended to hinder the member states when pursuing necessary democratic public policy goals. The European Court of Justice has accordingly determined that member states may legitimately introduce proportionate measures to maintain or foster media pluralism despite obstructing the free movement of media goods and services.[35] Beyond its importance as a major public policy exception in relation to the treaty principles of free movement, the right of member states to take measures to foster media pluralism is also prominently featured in EU secondary legislation.[36]

In 2007, Advocate General Poiares Maduro underscored the importance of media pluralism in his *Centro Europa 7* opinion, stating that

the part often played by the media as editors of the public sphere is vital to the promotion and protection of an open and inclusive society in which different ideas of the common good are presented and discussed. In this regard, the European Court of Human Rights has stressed that the fundamental role of freedom of expression in a democratic society, in particular where it serves to impart information and ideas to the public, 'cannot be successfully accomplished unless it is grounded in the principle of pluralism, of which the State is the ultimate guarantor'. Accordingly, the application of EU law in the area of national broadcasting services is guided by the principle of pluralism and, moreover, assumes special significance where it strengthens the protection of that principle.[37]

That ringing endorsement of media pluralism reflects the commitment to freedom and pluralism proclaimed in the EU Charter of Fundamental Rights.[38] The difficulty here is that European human rights law is no better equipped than European economic law to resolve conflicts over the proper role of the market and the state in achieving media pluralism. The right to freedom of expression, as set out in the Charter or in the European Convention on Human Rights, can be used to justify both approaches and, consequently, the proportionality arguments must be made between freedom of expression as the liberty to publish and freedom of expression as empowered autonomy.

---

[35] Case C-368/95, *Vereinigte Familiapress Zeitungsverlags und-vertriebs GmbH v. Heinrich Bauer Verlag* [1997] ECR I-3689. See also Case C-250/06, *United Pan-Europe Communications Belgium SA and others v. Belgium* [2007] ECR I-11135.

[36] See, for example, Directive 2000/31/EC of the European Parliament and of the Council of 8 June 2000 on certain legal aspects of information society services, in particular electronic commerce, in the Internal Market (Electronic Commerce Directive), Article 1:6. This Directive does not affect measures taken at Community or national level, in the respect of Community law, in order to promote cultural and linguistic diversity and to ensure the defence of pluralism. On the Electronic Commerce Directive generally, see Chapter 4.

[37] Case C-380/05, *Centro Europa 7 Srl v. Ministero delle Comunicazioni e Autorità per le garanzie nelle comunicazioni* (Opinion of the Advocate General: 12 September 2007, Decision of the ECJ: 31 January 2008). But see Case C-540/08, Reference for a Preliminary Ruling, *Mediaprint Zeitungs- und Zeitschriftenverlag GmbH & Co. KG* (9 November 2010), in which the ECJ Grand Chamber found that Directive 2005/29, which harmonizes rules on unfair commercial practices, does not permit member states to prohibit commercial practices because of their adverse effects on media pluralism. Note that, in this pre-Treaty of Lisbon case, the Charter of Fundamental Rights was not at issue.

[38] European Union, Charter of Fundamental Rights, Article 11:2.

Historically, the broadcasting sector has been at the heart of European legal and policy disagreements over media pluralism.[39] When creating, or later joining, the Council of Europe and the predecessors of the European Union, the states of western Europe brought with them well established, state owned, or supported broadcasters, which were subject to content mandates reflecting national political, social, and cultural policy priorities. The basic rights and obligations of the member states in both organizations were therefore based on the presumption that this intervention in media markets and the accompanying restrictive effects on the liberty to publish were essentially legitimate. Consequently, major disputes in European economic and human rights law regarding public service media regimes have concerned the proportionality of their design or operation and not their existence. Yet, despite this pervasive commitment, European rules aimed as safeguarding pluralism in the media sector are neither comprehensive nor well planned. They are instead a patchwork of judicial and legislative responses to member state laws and regulations that are at best a rough compromise between European economic and political principles supporting the liberty to publish free from state controls and the interventionist methods of media pluralism. Having made media pluralism one of the fundamental goals of the legitimate member state, European institutions have struggled to create a clear vision of what that goal specifically entails. This is in part due to the great variety of media regimes across Europe that must be accommodated within any pan-European concept of pluralism, many of which mix commercial and state funded provision of news and other information content. It also reflects the sensitivity of media sector regulation for member states generally and their major political parties in particular. Major media content providers are not only public sources of information and ideas, but are also the main forums in which matters of political concern are debated. In a liberal democracy, the stability of the media structure is consequently a key concern for dominant political parties.

At the same time, the destruction of democracy through state control of the media is a deep historic and present concern for European public policy. The European Union and the Council of Europe were both not only founded on the ruins of fascism, but also built in conscious opposition to the Soviet model of state and society to the east. Consequently, if European media law has any anchoring principle it must surely be that all forms of media ought to be as free as possible

---

[39] European Commission, *Communication on Audiovisual Policy* COM (90) 78 final, which stated the importance of ensuring 'that the audiovisual sector is not developed at the expense of pluralism, but on the contrary, it helps to strengthen it by encouraging, in particular, the diversity of the programmes offered to the public'. As one expert group advised the European Commission, '[I]t has never been assumed in Europe that the broadcasting and audiovisual sector should be treated as an economic subject only or that the market would per se guarantee a pluralistic service... this is not to say that American regulators have not intervened decisively in the market when they have considered it necessary for industrial and other policy objectives... However, in Europe the approach to the audiovisual sector has systematically encompassed more than a simple need to ensure the operation of the market: the specific nature of the sector and its crucial social function have always been clearly recognised by European governments.' *Digital Age: European Audiovisual Policy*, Report from the High Level Group on Audiovisual Policy, Directorate General X. ch 1, 3.

from interference by the state in the production as well as the distribution of information and ideas. If that is so, all other considerations, including the adequacy of public access to a diversity of information, are enclosed within that anchoring principle. European institutions and the member states have however often failed to agree on the weight of the liberty principle in determining the proper boundaries between excessive and beneficial state intervention in European media markets. Indeed, with the collapse of the Soviet Union, the European regional order expanded eastward, amplifying tensions in European media law between the state and the economic and political liberty to publish. Applicant and new member states have thus been strongly urged to copy the western European public service broadcasting model, yet also anxiously exhorted to protect the independence of the media.[40]

The end of the Cold War also coincided with the rapid spread of cross border satellite television services in Europe. This development, unlike the expansion of European public order eastwards, overwhelmingly favoured the growth of new private sector, cross border broadcasting enterprises. For these commercial broadcasters, the dual liberal economic and political arguments for greater liberty from the state could be used to great effect against national barriers to foreign entry into domestic media systems.[41] The communications revolution has carried that shift in media public policy further. The digitization of radio and television services undermined the scarcity argument for public service broadcasting, leaving it more narrowly dependent on the argument that impact or influence of television on the public was qualitatively different than any other medium. The strength of that argument, however, began to fade quickly with the arrival of broadband internet access. For many households, new audiovisual media services have as much influence as traditional linear television services. As News Corporation argued in 2001,

[t]he variety of ways in which consumers receive news, views, entertainments and advertising messages is increasing almost daily. And no one group dominates, or can hope to dominate all the pathways to the public. To continue to bar a participant in one segment of the industry from making its skills and capital available to the others would be to no purpose and would be contrary to what consumers want.[42]

Arguments of this kind were often well received in a changing international public policy environment that, against considerable resistance, had become more receptive to market based solutions to media policy goals.[43] Governments were

---

[40] See, for example, Council of Europe, Committee of Ministers, Recommendation on measures to promote media pluralism, Rec (99) 1, and Committee of Ministers Recommendation on the independence and functions of regulatory authorities for the broadcasting sector, Rec (2000) 23.

[41] On the role of EU litigation brought by commercial broadcasters in developing European media law, see Chapter 4.

[42] News International response to the United Kingdom, Communications White Paper, *A New Future for Communications,* Cm 5010, (December 2000), which preceded the Communications Act 2003.

[43] In its key recommendations in 1997, for example, the OECD Council approved recommendations that underscored the importance of a global free market to the development of the GII-GIS. OECD Committee for Information, Computers and Communications Policy, 'Global Information

anxious not to slow the growth of new communications services by imposing unnecessary regulatory burdens. In this climate, European governments broadly accepted the American government's view that the private sector should take the lead in developing internet facilities and services.[44] That preference was, moreover, important to both European and American expectations that the internet would develop into a unified global communications platform based on liberal economic and political values.[45]

These radical changes did not however overwhelm the public policy argument in Europe for extensive state intervention to maintain media pluralism. The terrain may have changed, but the view that market forces alone will not guarantee sufficient media pluralism remains highly influential in European institutions. In the European Union, the General Court has for example firmly rejected the argument that EU law only permits subsidized public service broadcasters to offer programme content in genres not provided by their commercial competitors.[46] The Council of Europe has similarly recommended that,

in view of the fact that digital convergence favours the process of concentration in the broadcasting sector, member states should maintain regulation which limits the concentration of media ownership and/or any complementary measures which they may decide to choose to enhance pluralism, while strengthening public service broadcasting as a crucial counter-balance to concentration in the private media sector.[47]

The Council of Europe had moreover maintained a sweepingly broad definition of pluralism that includes a diversity of views on local as well as national political and social matters of general interest.[48]

Structural solutions for the protection of media pluralism

European governments use an extraordinarily diverse range of measures to pursue their media policy goals, many of which are related directly or indirectly to the protection of pluralism. In principle, all of these assorted measures are subject to the disciplines of European Union economic law, at least where they breach its rules concerning free movement and fair competition in the single market. This simply

infrastructure—Global information Society (GII-GIS) Policy Recommendations for Action' OECD 1997 [approved by OECD Council at Ministerial level, May 1997] [6].

[44] See, for example, European Ministerial Conference at Bonn 'Global Information Networks: Realising the Potential' (6–8 July 1997), which declared that, 'the expansion of Global Information Networks must essentially be market-led and left to private initiative'.

[45] See, for example, Council of Europe, Committee of Ministers, *Declaration on freedom of communication on the Internet* (28 May 2003), Principle 3.

[46] Cases T-309/04, T-317/04, T-329/04, and T-336/04, *TV2 Danmark et al. v. Commission*, Court of First Instance, paras 122–123.

[47] Committee of Ministers, Recommendation on Measures to Promote the Democratic and Social Contribution of Digital Broadcasting, Rec (2003) 9, Appendix: Basic principles for digital broadcasting, Principle 18.

[48] See, for example, Council of Europe, Committee of Ministers, Recommendation on media pluralism and diversity of media content, Rec (2007) 2.

reflects the fundamental assumption that, in spite of significant state participation, Europe's media sector should operate on market principles. While state intervention in media markets may therefore be a distinctive contribution to the European media model, these forms of intervention are nonetheless only legitimate when they conform to the conditional exceptions permitted under EU law. As a result, the EU's primary goals of fair competition and open borders are aligned with market based principles of media pluralism as they support the liberty to publish and distribute information and ideas across Europe.

On this basis, European Union competition law provides some of the most important methods for sustaining media pluralism in European law, even though that is not its primary purpose. That purpose is instead to ensure that firms operating in the same market do not engage in practices that significantly reduce competition or create serious barriers to new entrants.[49] Very often, the most significant contribution competition law makes to media pluralism is through its rules concerning the creation or abuse of dominant positions in media markets. Here, for example, competition rules can be used to block the acquisition of a dominant position in media markets that not only disadvantage consumers, but also reduce the number of independent sources of news information available to the general public. In this regard, EU competition law is especially important to media pluralism as there is no parallel development in European human rights law that obliges member states to force changes in the ownership or control of media firms in a comparable manner.

The growth of excessively dominant content providers and distributors is a long standing problem for competition across the media sector. From the earliest hand operated presses through industrial printing to radiospectrum broadcasting facilities, the media has relied on layers of production and communications technologies that are often relatively expensive and also in short supply. The individuals or companies controlling these assets are therefore often gatekeepers in particular media markets, sometimes achieving greater dominance where these technologies lead to economies of scale that competitors without similar access to these technologies cannot match. This also reflects the plunging marginal cost curve that typically occurs in media markets. Initial outlays for the production or acquisition of popular content, such as major films or drama series, in combination with the capital and operation costs of distribution systems, such as satellite television broadcasting, are in most cases very high. Once these costs have been absorbed, however, the marginal cost of increased distribution is often low, especially in the electronic media, and revenue from additional readers, listeners, or viewers is therefore highly profitable. Control of some premium content, such as major sports events that have a unique appeal for many consumers, can also provide enormous advantages in building a dominant position. Live broadcasts of league football games, for example, have a mass appeal and very limited substitutability, even for

---

[49] Whish, R., *Competition Law*, 6th edn (Oxford University Press, 2008), ch 1. See also Nietsche, I., *Broadcasting in the European Union: The Role of the Public Interest in Competition Analysis* (T.M.C. Asser Press, 2001).

similar sports.[50] Where this occurs, media competitors are either unable to offer this premium content or must buy it from the rights holder at a high price. Digitization of content has also made it possible for premium content rights holders to leverage their market power in existing media markets, such as broadcasting, to acquire a leading position in new media markets, such as on-demand audiovisual services. In these circumstances, large media companies, especially those that control content production as well as distribution, are typically in a better position to cover high initial costs and later reap the benefits of increasing economies of scale. The problem for media pluralism is that commercial dominance tends to reduce the number of independent media firms capable of funding and producing news and current affairs information.

Over the past two decades, the European Commission has attempted to loosen the grip of dominant companies over media markets, particularly in relation to exclusive broadcast rights to live sports events. In several instances, it has demanded that major European sports leagues sell their games for shorter periods of time and find ways to structure the sale of rights to allow more media providers access to rights.[51] Yet intervention by European competition authorities to protect competition in EU media markets is very often an interference with lawfully acquired property rights and commercial agreements, which rest on fundamental claims to economic and political liberty from the state. It is also difficult to show that dominance in a particular media sector has a serious effect on existing or potential competition in the mid course of a communications revolution, where the boundaries between different communications and media markets are rapidly changing and the barriers to entry into those markets are transient. Moreover, under EU competition law, ostensibly anti-competitive agreements are acceptable where the benefits to consumers outweigh the detrimental effects.[52] The supply of live sports games and events from a well established media company can, for example, provide consumers with a stable source of supply and secure source of major funding for the sports concerned.[53] For the European Commission, which has no direct responsibility for media pluralism when pursuing its competition objectives, these economic considerations may well weigh more heavily than the possible effects of market dominance on democracy.

---

[50] Seabright, P. and Weeds, H., 'Competition and Market Power in Broadcasting: where are the rents?' in Seabright, P. and von Hagen, J. (eds), *The Regulation of Broadcasting Markets*, (Cambridge University Press, 2007), 47. See also Rumphorst, W., *Sports Broadcasting Rights and EC Competition Law* (25 July 2001) (<http://www.ebu.ch>).

[51] UEFA Champions League Decision: Commission Decision of 23 July 2003 relating to a proceeding pursuant to Article 81 of the EC Treaty and Article 53 of the EEA Agreement (notified under document number C (2003) 2627). See also Commission Decision COMP/C.2/38.173, joint selling of the media rights of the FA Premier League on an exclusive basis (March 2006).

[52] Treaty on the Functioning of the European Union, Article 101(3).

[53] European Commission, White Paper on Sport COM (2007) 391 final, Annex I: Sport and EU competition rules.

Structural pluralism beyond competition law

Where competition law is applied rigorously and helps to maintain competitive media markets, it also fosters, albeit in a generic way, a plurality of suppliers of news and current affairs information. Yet, the fact that media pluralism is a by product rather than a principal aim of competition law has meant that, in certain circumstances, it is arguably incapable of resolving the problem of structural pluralism.[54] For example, a large, vertically integrated business that has grown to be dominant across several media markets may well crowd other sources of news and current affairs information out of the market, even when no abuse of dominance occurs in competition law terms. Consequently, European Union member states routinely impose additional measures limiting concentrations of ownership or other controlling interests in media providers that are not caught by competition law rules. These measures include market share or other quantitative limits directed at specific sectors, such as the broadcast media, or similar rules that restrict concentrations across specific media sectors, such as newspaper and broadcast media holdings.[55]

Given the importance of liberal democracy to European public order, European Union law has always been broadly tolerant of these interventions, even when they obstruct the right of establishment in the single market. As noted above, pluralism is a well accepted legitimate ground for member states to derogate from their primary economic obligations, provided that these derogations also satisfy the requirements of proportionality. Secondary EU legislation also contains express provisions that allow member states to intervene in media markets. These notably include Article 21(4) of the Merger Regulation, which allows member states to impose tighter restrictions on company acquisitions and mergers than ordinarily permitted by EU competition law rules where necessary for the protection of the 'plurality of the media'.[56] In addition, while EU law prohibits discriminatory restrictions on foreign ownership between member states, limits on non-European ownership of media providers are permitted as these are not regarded as impeding trade between member states.

During the 1990s, the Commission proposed a harmonization of national controls on media ownership directed at structural pluralism, creating instead a common EU model for limits on the ownership or control of media companies.[57] The concern here is not simply that differences between national rules create barriers to free movement, in particular the right of establishment, but also that

[54] Commission Staff Working Document: *Media pluralism in the Member States of the European Union* (SEC (2007) 32).
[55] See, for example, in Britain, Communications Act 2003, Chapter 5 Media ownership and control.
[56] Council Regulation 139/2004 of 20 January 2004 on the control of concentrations between undertakings.
[57] 1992 *Green Paper on Pluralism and Media Concentration in the Internal Market: an assessment of the need for Community action*, COM (92) 480, 1995 draft Directive on Concentrations and Pluralism, and 1997 draft Directive on Media Ownership in the Internal Market.

there is no consensus on the principles that underpin these measures. Unlike competition law, where the working principles may be contested but are at least based in economic theory, there is no agreed framework for structural pluralism. The larger objective of protecting the plurality of independent sources of news and current affairs information is based on highly qualitative judgements about the influence of particular forms of media and content genres on the public. Certainly, economic analysis, relying on the concepts of 'public goods' and 'merit goods', plays an important role in demonstrating that media markets may fail to produce or distribute an adequate supply of socially or culturally diverse content.[58] However, while these arguments are useful in showing the potential for market failure, they lead back to difficult to assess, qualitative judgements by the state on the need for intervention. Nonetheless, in the view of most member states, aside from the EU's lack of legislative competence in this non-market public policy area, the structure of each national media market is unique and consequently structural pluralism needs to be designed and implemented locally.[59] As a result, and as the Commission conceded in its 2003 Green Paper on Services of General Interest, the protection of media pluralism is primarily a responsibility of the member states as a matter of subsidiarity.[60] The Commission moreover has shown little interest in resurrecting the idea of harmonizing national measures concerning structural pluralism in the foreseeable future, despite pressure from the European Parliament, which has directed strong criticism at particular member states, such as Italy, for significant concentrations of media ownership that influence electoral politics.[61]

The European Commission has thus limited its work to ensuring the transparency and proportionality of domestic measures so that member state derogations from single market obligations are no greater than necessary.[62] Under its 'Three Step Plan' announced in 2007, it has pushed this work forward, drawing on the work of the Council of Europe on media pluralism to establish basic principles and

[58] On the concepts of 'public goods' and 'merit goods', see Chapter 15.

[59] Hitchens, L., 'Identifying European Audiovisual Policy in the Dawn of the Information Society', *Yearbook of Media and Entertainment Law* 1996 (Clarendon Press, 1996), 44 at 46. See also Craufurd Smith, R., 'Rethinking European Union competence in the field of media ownership: The internal market, fundamental rights and European citizenship', 29(5) *European Law Review* (2004), 652–673.

[60] *Commission Green Paper on Services of General Interest*, 21 May 2003. See also *Communication from the Commission on the Future of European Regulatory Audiovisual Policy* Com (2003) 784 Final.

[61] Commission Staff Working Document: *Media pluralism in the Member States of the European Union*, n. 54 above. See also Boogerd-Quaak, J., Resolution on the risks of violation, in the EU and especially in Italy, of freedom of expression and information (Article 11(2) of the Charter of Fundamental Rights), 22 April 2004, report A5-0230/2004. European Parliament Committee on Citizens Rights, Justice and Home Affairs, European Parliament (2004): Report on the risks of violation, in the EU and especially in Italy, of freedom of expression and information (Article 11(2) of the Charter of Fundamental Rights)2003/2237(INI)). Committee on Citizens' Freedoms and Rights, Justice and Home Affairs Rapporteur, Boogerd-Quaak, J.L.A. and Blatman, S., 'A Media Conflict of Interest: Anomaly in Italy'. *Reporters sans frontières* (April 2003).

[62] European Commission, *Media pluralism: Commission stresses need for transparency, freedom and diversity in Europe's media landscape* (16 January 2007) (IP/07/52).

common reference points.[63] Under the plan, the Commission sponsored an independent study on media pluralism in EU member states, which attempts to provide a universal set of indicators for risks to media pluralism from a range of perspectives.[64] Yet even this study has sparked concerns that it will provide justifications for further EU or even national intervention into media markets.[65] The Commission also has plans to issue a Communication on the subject of common indicators for media pluralism in the member states.

These arguments over common indicators for media pluralism are, to some extent, merely a resurfacing of the debates of the 1990s about the need for European measures to safeguard structural pluralism in the media, while also eliminating barriers to free movement in the Single Market. Since then, however, the communications and media context for that debate has been radically transformed. As the European Publishers Council argued, in criticizing the independent study on media pluralism,

[t]he introduction of such complex measurement tools at the very moment when we are seeing burgeoning freedom of expression and diversity of opinion through the rapid expansion of new forms of communication and media outlets, as well as through new forms of distribution which fall outside traditional patterns of media ownership, seems unnecessarily complex and disproportionately burdensome on traditional media companies. There is no barrier to entry any more, not even in broadcast media.[66]

On this view, the spread of broadband access to new media services has created close to ideal conditions for realization of an efficient market place of ideas in which the state has minimal justifications for intervention. The relevance of print and broadcast era measures developed to remedy weaknesses in structural pluralism is therefore fading fast. That view is plainly not universally accepted. While few would dispute that the media landscape is now utterly changed, it is not obvious that the result is close to the idealized 'public sphere', in which fully informed and inclusive democratic deliberation and decision making spontaneously occurs. In many European households, newspapers, radio, and traditional television channels are still the most important sources of information on current affairs, especially in relation to politics and the democratic process. That is self evidently changing as new forms of media provide alternative ways not only to be informed, but also to participate in public comment and debate. Nonetheless, the new media has its own powerful gatekeepers and power brokers, including the old media companies that

---

[63] European Commission: Three step plan—Task Force for Co-ordination of Media Affairs, January 2007. Commission Staff Working Document: Media pluralism in the Member States of the European Union (SEC (2007) 32).

[64] K.U. Leuven—ICRI, Jönköping International Business School, Central European University, Ernst & Young Consultancy Belgium, *Independent Study on Indicators for Media Pluralism in the Member States—Towards a Risk-Based Approach*. See also Angelopoulos, C., 'European Commission Independent Study on Indicators for Media Pluralism in the Member States', *IRIS*, 2009–10.

[65] K.U. Leuven, et al., ibid., 8.2.1 Concerns about Use of the Media Pluralism Monitor.

[66] Comments on the Media Pluralism Monitor on behalf of the European Publishers Council, June 2009 (<http://www.epceurope.org>).

have extended their presence online, as well as new information controllers, such as search engines that effectively determine what information exists and what does not.[67]

European law and public policy will inevitably continue to reflect these uncertainties and divergent views. While EU law imposes proportionality requirements on domestic measures aimed at safeguarding structural pluralism, it certainly does not oblige member states to intervene in media markets for that purpose. The Audiovisual Media Services Directive for example only fleetingly addresses the issue of medial pluralism. In a recital, largely carried forward from the original 1989 version of the Directive, it only reminds member states that it is essential that they ensure the prevention of any acts which 'promote the creation of dominant positions which would lead to restrictions on pluralism and freedom of televised information and of the information sector as a whole'.

The Council of Europe institutions have been similarly cautious in creating binding obligations to intervene in media markets. While the European Court of Human Rights is committed to the principle that pluralism is essential to European democracy, it has not found a positive obligation under Article 10 compelling state parties to intervene to safeguard structural pluralism. Its case law on pluralism is concerned instead to ensure, on the one hand, that state interventions in the media sector do not restrict pluralism, and on the other that state interventions for the legitimate purpose of fostering pluralism do not disproportionately affect the liberty to speak and publish.[68] The CE Committee of Ministers has also tended to stress the legitimacy of intervention for pluralist purposes, while leaving it to member states to determine if such intervention is necessary.[69] Even the legally binding CE Transfrontier Television Convention, which contains provisions on pluralism not present in the parallel EU Directive, only states that the state parties 'shall endeavour to avoid' that broadcasting services transmitted or retransmitted within their jurisdiction endanger media pluralism.[70] In contrast, the Council of Europe has declared that member states should put regulatory measures in place to guarantee full transparency of media ownership.[71]

---

[67] See Balkin, J., 'The Future of Free Expression in a Digital Age', 36 *Pepperdine Law Review* (2008), 427–444.

[68] See, for example, *Informationsverein Lentia and others v. Austria* (Application No. 13914/88 et al.) (24 November 1993).

[69] Council of Europe: Declaration of the Committee of Ministers on protecting the role of the media in democracy in the context of media concentration (January 2007), Committee of Ministers, Recommendation on media pluralism and diversity of media content, CM/Rec (2007) 2, Part I, Measures promoting structural pluralism of the media, and, Committee of Ministers, *Declaration on freedom of communication on the Internet*, n. 45 above, Principle 3. See also Council of Europe, Committee of Ministers Recommendation on media pluralism and diversity of media content, n. 48 above, General principle II.1: 'Pluralism of information and diversity of media content will not be automatically guaranteed by the multiplication of the means of communication offered to the public. Therefore, member states should define and implement an active policy in this field, including monitoring procedures, and adopt any necessary measures in order to ensure that a sufficient variety of information, opinions and programmes is disseminated by the media and is available to the public.'

[70] European Convention on Transfrontier Television (ETS No. 132), Article 10*bis*.

[71] Council of Europe, Committee of Ministers, Declaration on protecting the role of the media in democracy in the context of media concentration, n. 69 above, Part II.

State monopolies and broadcast licensing

One of the most distinctive features of European media law is its accommodation of state owned or supported media within a liberal, market based, media sector. For the past century, this has been in contrast to the United States, where the broadcast media developed almost entirely in private hands even when subject to public interest content obligations.[72] The European accommodation of state media has consequently also required a careful articulation of the liberal democratic character of these media organizations and the proper limits for their activities. Yet, that necessary imprint of liberal democratic values has been developed in a legal framework that was firstly committed, in principle, to the legitimacy of not state intervention but also broad state monopolies in the media sector. For the drafters of the Treaty of Rome, the state provision of radio and television was simply another of the many services commonly carried out by the state at that time, including postal services and telecommunications. Accordingly, the European Court of Justice had little choice but to hold subsequently that 'nothing in the Treaty prevents Member States, for considerations of a non-economic nature relating to the public interest, from removing radio and television broadcasts from the field of competition by conferring on one or more establishments an exclusive right to carry them out'.[73] The Court has instead insisted that so long as a broadcast monopoly is in place, the 'manner in which the monopoly is organized or exercised may infringe the rules of the Treaty, in particular those relating to the free movement of goods, the freedom to provide services and the rules on competition'.[74]

For several decades, it also appeared that broadcast monopolies were equally secure under the third sentence of Article 10(1) of the European Convention on Human Rights, which makes the state's power to license cinemas as well as radio and television a special exception to the right to freedom of expression.[75] The founding parties of the European Convention on Human Rights, concerned that the right to freedom of expression declared in Article 10 might be used to challenge the legality of monopolies and licensing restrictions, had included this sentence to underscore the unique importance of media licensing.[76] However, in the 1993 *Informationsverein Lentia v. Austria* decision, the European Court of Human Rights sharply limited the legitimate scope of a monopoly media service. By the late 1980s, most member states had abandoned their monopolies in favour of mixed state and private broadcasting regimes, leaving only a few countries, including Austria, barring

---

[72] See n. 8 above.

[73] Case C-155/73, *Sacchi* [1974] ECR 409, para. 14.

[74] Case C-260/89, *Elliniki Radiophonia Tiléorassi AE and Panellinia Omospondia Syllogon Prossopikou v. Dimotiki Etairia Pliroforissis and Sotirios Kouvelas and Nicolaos Avdellas and others* [1991] ECR I-2925, para. 11.

[75] Article 10(1): 'This article shall not prevent States from requiring the licensing of broadcasting (*i.e. radio*), television or cinema enterprises.'

[76] European Commission of Human Rights, Preparatory Work on Article 10 of the European Convention on Human Rights (17 August 1956).

private participation in domestic broadcasting.[77] In *Informationsverein Lentia*, the Court found that the domestic broadcasting monopoly enjoyed by the ORF, Austria's public service broadcaster, constituted a breach of Article 10. While the Court accepted that Austria's purpose, the protection of pluralism and diversity, was a legitimate reason to grant the monopoly, it also concluded that that purpose could be achieved by means that were less restrictive and less burdensome to the rights of others to freedom of expression.[78] This decision confirmed that the total state monopoly over broadcast services, which once epitomized European radio and television, was no longer lawful. Admittedly, this was not an example of the Court using the idea of liberty to push back the swelling frontiers of the state as much as it was the more pedestrian one of taking the law forward into an area already vacated by most state parties in the face of irresistible technological, commercial, and political pressures.[79] The Court moreover did not rule that every state monopoly in the media sector will violate Article 10, later upholding the legality of a much narrower residual monopoly in Austria over analogue, terrestrial broadcasting.[80]

European broadcasting monopolies were largely secured through restrictive licensing of access to essential communications resources or facilities, most importantly including the use of allocated radiospectrum. While these monopolies have largely disappeared, the licensing of broadcasting remains a central feature of state regulation of the media. In fact, licensing is a near universal feature of broadcasting because of its necessary reliance on radiospectrum, which is rationed between multiple users who must also be prevented from causing radio interference between various users. The persistence of broadcast licensing is however also an exception in the broad trend of liberal democratic history, in which the removal of licensing controls on the print media has an iconic status.[81] The licensing of broadcasting is therefore often a suspect exercise of state power, in which the state acts as gatekeeper to this media sector and is potentially able to deny entry or eject any media content provider for illegitimate reasons. These concerns have been particularly acute where broadcast licensing has tied the privilege of access to broadcast spectrum to the fulfilment of restrictive and positive content obligations.

In Europe, coordination of communications and media law by the EU has pushed states to make a basic regulatory distinction between licensing content providers and licensing the use of communications infrastructure, including the radiospectrum, satellite facilities, and cable systems. In 2002, the European Union extended the scope of harmonization across the electronic communications field through a regulatory framework for electronic communications networks and services governing access, interconnection, and other user issues.[82] The object of

---

[77] *Informationsverein Lentia and others v. Austria*, n. 68 above.

[78] Ibid.

[79] In Britain private commercial television was first permitted in 1954 and private commercial radio in 1973. See Crissell, A., *An Introductory History of British Broadcasting* (Routledge, 1997).

[80] *Tele 1 Privatfernsehgesellschaft mbH v. Austria* (Application No. 32240/96) (21 September 2000).

[81] Curran, J. and Seaton, J., *Power Without Responsibility: Press, Broadcasting and the Internet in Britain* (Routledge, 2010), chs 1 and 2.

[82] On the Communications Framework Directives, see Chapter 4.

these reforms was to remove regulatory barriers to the Single Market by fostering competitive market conditions in which, as far as possible, all electronic communications platforms are treated equally, including radiospectrum. Platform neutrality has therefore become a basic principle of European communications regulation. While the principles of EU electronic communications regulation are primarily economic, they do have important secondary consequences for the protection of media pluralism in broadcast and new media services. It is, for example, a fundamental principle of the main Framework Directive that member states award rights of access to communications infrastructure on objective, transparent, non-discriminatory, and proportionate criteria.[83] In the *Centro Europa 7* reference to the European Court of Justice, the Court found, in effect, a failure to respect those essential criteria when awarding radiospectrum access.[84] In this case, the Italian authorities had granted the Centro Europa 7 company terrestrial broadcasting rights, but had failed to award the necessary radiospectrum frequencies, while also allowing incumbent competitors to broadcast on frequencies previously awarded on an ad hoc basis.

Member states have however rebuffed proposals for positive EU measures in this area. In the 2007 amendment process for the Audiovisual Media Services Directive, the Commission had, for example, proposed including an obligation that member states guarantee the independence of national media regulatory authorities and ensure that they exercise their powers impartially and transparently.[85] Those proposals were rejected in favour of a weaker interpretive statement on the independence of regulators and the promotion of pluralism contained in the recitals to the amending Directive.[86] In contrast to its comprehensive treatment of electronic communications infrastructure licensing, the European Union has taken an entirely different approach to content licensing, recognizing on the one hand its historical importance for member states in the broadcast sector and, on the other, the policy arguments against extending broadcasting content regulations to the new media. While the Audiovisual Media Services Directive does impose common standards for harmful or offensive content on broadcast television or on-demand audiovisual services, it does not oblige member states to create or maintain licence or authorization requirements.[87] Whereas the Electronic Commerce Directive states that 'Member States shall ensure that the taking up and pursuit of the activity of an

[83] Directive 2002/21/EC of the European Parliament and of the Council of 7 March 2002 on a common regulatory framework for electronic communications networks and services ('Framework Directive'), Article 9(1), and Directive 2002/77/EC of 16 September 2002 on competition in the markets for electronic communications networks and services, Article 4(2).

[84] Case C-380/05, *Centro Europa 7 Srl v. Ministero delle Comunicazioni e Autorità per le garanzie nelle comunicazioni* (ECJ, 31 January 2008).

[85] European Commission, Proposal for a Directive of the European Parliament and of The Council amending Council Directive 89/552/EEC on the Coordination of Certain Provisions Laid Down By Law, Regulation or Administrative Action in Member States concerning the Pursuit of Television Broadcasting Activities (13 December 2005), Com (2005) 646 Final, Article 23 B.

[86] Directive 2010/13/EU of the European Parliament and of the Council of 10 March 2010 on the coordination of certain provisions laid down by law, regulation or administrative action in Member States concerning the provision of audiovisual media services, Recital (94).

[87] Ibid., Recitals (19) and (20).

information society service provider may not be made subject to prior authorisation or any other requirement having equivalent effect'.[88]

In European human rights law, the relationship between broadcast licensing and the right to freedom of expression has developed under similarly strong conflicting pressures. The European Court of Human Rights has identified the third sentence of Article 10(1) as the key provision protecting the legality of European public service broadcasting under the Convention. It has accordingly given the sentence an expansive interpretation. As the Court stated in its decision in *Demuth*,

> The Court reiterates that the object and purpose of the third sentence of Article 10(1) is to make it clear that States are permitted to regulate by means of a licensing system the way in which broadcasting is organised in their territories, particularly in its technical aspects. The latter are undeniably important, but the grant or refusal of a licence may also be made conditional on other considerations, including such matters as the nature and objectives of a proposed station, its potential audience at national, regional or local level, the rights and needs of a specific audience and the obligations deriving from international legal instruments.[89]

Nonetheless, in the Court's view, the placement of this sentence in the first rather than the second paragraph of Article 10 does not take it outside the core purposes of that article or the constraints imposed on legitimate exceptions to freedom of expression. As the Court made plain in *Informationsverein Lentia*, the third sentence of Article 10(1) is subject to all the conditions arising under Article 10(2).[90] The tools of proportionality analysis can therefore be used to force state parties to justify media licensing requirements and practices where these interfere with the liberty to publish. The question is therefore whether the benefits for media pluralism of positive state intervention through licensing restrictions and obligations demonstrably outweigh the restrictive effects. In *Informationsverein Lentia*, the Court found that the ORF's complete domestic monopoly was a disproportionate restriction on freedom of expression, despite its pluralist intentions and elements.

While the Court has moved cautiously in trimming back the legitimate scope of public service broadcast monopolies, it has been more confident in addressing arbitrary or discriminatory licensing practices. It has long accepted that, in conditions of radiospectrum scarcity, there is no right of access to this public resource and therefore no right to a broadcast licence. Article 10 nonetheless also obliges state parties to act impartially when determining the award of licences according to legitimate criteria in a transparent process.[91] As the Court has also pointed out in different circumstances, prior restraints on publication or other forms of expression by the state are only exceptionally permissible, which underscores the exceptional

---

[88] Electronic Commerce Directive, n. 36 above, Article 4.

[89] *Demuth v. Switzerland* (Application No. 38743/97) (5 November 2002), para. 33.

[90] *Informationsverein Lentia and others v. Austria*, n. 68 above, para. 29.

[91] *Meltex Ltd and Mesrop Movsesyan v. Armenia* (Application No. 32283/04) (17 June 2008), see also *Glas Nadezhda Eood and Elenkov v. Bulgaria,* (Application No. 14134/02) (11 October 2007).

nature of restrictions on access to broadcast spectrum.[92] Yet the Court has a limited ability to assess the complex mix of technical, economic, political, and social issues that underpin broadcast licensing regimes, let alone develop comprehensive principles to govern media ownership, the independence of media regulators or public service media, and the many other regulatory issues affecting media pluralism. As a supranational supervisory body, equipped primarily to determine whether the actions or omissions of a state party amount to a violation of fundamental rights, the Court's focus is inevitably quite narrow. As Jacco Bomhoff has argued, its institutional purposes have 'directed the Court's gaze away from questions of *power and structure*, and placed it firmly on issues of *rights*'.[93] Despite its often skilful use of proportionality reasoning, the Court therefore has particular difficulty where the rights of the applicant must be weighed against the public interest served by the general objectives of a regulatory regime.[94] Against this, it can be argued that the very purpose of constitutionalized rights is to punch holes in legal regimes that, however beneficial in general terms, disproportionately restrict the freedom or dignity of particular individuals. On that basis, the Court is fulfilling its limited but essential purpose.

Given its modest ability to fashion comprehensive principles for media regulation, the Court has turned to the work of the CE Committee of Ministers to provide a general framework of principles, which it can then use to locate the issues in specific cases concerning broadcast licensing.[95] In this area, the Committee of Ministers has promoted a model of independent and impartial media regulation for newer democracies in Eastern Europe as well as long established member states. In its 2000 Recommendation on the independence and functions of regulatory authorities for the broadcasting sector, the Committee urged that, 'the rules governing regulatory authorities... should be defined so as to protect them against any interference, in particular by political forces or economic interests' and that they are not 'under the influence of political power'.[96] It returned to this topic in 2008, when the Committee adopted a further declaration underscoring the need

[92] *Gaweda v. Poland* (Application No. 26229/95) (14 March 2002), para. 35. Lastly, the Court reiterates that Article 10 of the Convention does not in terms prohibit the imposition of prior restraints on publications. However, the dangers inherent in prior restraints are such that they call for the most careful scrutiny.
[93] Bomhoff, J., '"The Rights and Freedoms of Others": The ECHR and its Peculiar Category of Conflicts Between Individual Fundamental Rights', in Brems, E. (ed.), *Conflicts Between Fundamental Rights* (Intersentia, 2008).
[94] See, for example, *Verein Gegen Tierfabriken Schweiz (Vgt) v. Switzerland (No. 2)* (Grand Chamber) (Application No. 32772/02) (30 June 2009), and *TV Vest As & Rogaland Pensjonistparti v. Norway* (Application No. 21132/05) (11 December 2008).
[95] See, for example, *Meltex Ltd and Mesrop Movsesyan v. Armenia*, n. 91 above. See also Council of Europe, Committee of Ministers, Recommendation on the independence and functions of regulatory authorities for the broadcasting sector, n. 40 above, and Committee of Ministers, Declaration on the independence and functions of regulatory authorities for the broadcasting sector (26 March 2008).
[96] Recommendation on the independence and functions of regulatory authorities for the broadcasting sector, n. 40 above, Appendix, Guidelines: II.3 and II.4.

for a 'culture of independence' in broadcasting regulation and failure to achieve that standard in some member states.[97]

Impartiality and elections

For European states, the highly sensitive relationship between the domestic politics and the media is a critically important aspect of national autonomy, where European regional intervention is often unwelcome. European institutions have also been reluctant to interfere with that autonomy except where national measures create clear conflicts with fundamental European principles of economic and political freedom. Member states are therefore required to structure and apply these measures in ways that satisfy the conditions required by European law for exceptional treatment, including the various elements of proportionality. There is consequently a strong tension between the tendency of European law to work towards common solutions informed by a consensus view of the nature of European public order and member state demands for broad autonomy in the operation of domestic politics. The achievement of democratic pluralism is after all a matter of qualitative judgement, which will vary according to local conditions and ideas about democracy itself.

Questions of ownership and control related to structural pluralism resonate in both European economic and human rights law. With some specific exceptions, the field of internal pluralism, which largely concerns the regulation of the news and current affairs output of broadcasters, tends however to fall outside the reach of most EU economic obligations, which permit proportionate measures that advance media pluralism. These exceptions come in the form of content source obligations. The Audiovisual Media Services Directive, for example, obliges member states to maintain a minimum proportion of European works and works by independent producers, which not only have cultural justification, but also have a role in democratic media policy, arguably increasing public access to a greater diversity of content.[98] The other major exception to the EU's general silence on matters relating to internal pluralism is the EU obligation to create rights of reply in the broadcast and new media, which is discussed in Chapter 10.

In the institutions of the Council of Europe, however, the problems of internal pluralism have arisen both generally and in cases before the European Court of Human Rights. As a general matter, internal pluralism implies that news and

---

[97] Declaration on the independence and functions of regulatory authorities for the broadcasting sector, n. 95 above, Recital: 'Concerned, however, that the guidelines of Recommendation Rec (2000) 23 and the main principles underlining it are not fully respected in law and/or in practice in other Council of Europe member states due to a situation in which the legal framework on broadcasting regulation is unclear, contradictory or in conflict with the principles of Recommendation Rec (2000) 23, the political and financial independence of regulatory authorities and its members is not properly ensured, licences are allocated and monitoring decisions are made without due regard to national legislation or Council of Europe standards, and broadcasting regulatory decisions are not made available to the public or are not open to review.'
[98] On the minimum European content requirement, see Chapter 15.

current affairs programmes include most significant information and opinion in a reasonably balanced or impartial manner. Obligations of this kind reflect the historic importance of the broadcast media to national politics and the anxious concern amongst political parties and elsewhere that their influence could come under the control of a particular party or interest. They also open up the tension between negative and positive freedom contained within Article 10 of the ECHR. The Court has made clear that state parties to the Convention have a positive duty under Article 10 to guarantee media pluralism, but has left open whether that is accomplished through market forces or state intervention.[99] The Committee of Ministers has however encouraged states to adopt impartiality or fairness obligations not only in the broadcast sector, but also potentially for some new media services. In its important 2007 Recommendation on media coverage of election campaigns, the Committee of Ministers stated,

With due respect for the editorial independence of broadcasters, regulatory frameworks should also provide for the obligation to cover election campaigns in a fair, balanced and impartial manner in the overall programme services of broadcasters. Such an obligation should apply to both public service media and private broadcasters in their relevant transmission areas.[100]

This Recommendation also contains specific guidance regarding news and current affairs programmes and proposes that internet based and other non-linear audiovisual services offered by public service media be subject to similar obligations.[101] Indeed, in a significant divergence from the EU Audiovisual Media Services Directive, state parties to the CE Convention on Transfrontier Television are required to ensure that broadcasters under their jurisdiction present facts and events fairly and encourage the free formation of opinions.[102]

For the European Court of Human Rights impartiality obligations are, in principle, acceptable because they compel broadcasters to include sources of information and ideas that might otherwise not easily reach the wider public, thereby enhancing the right to receive information protected under Article 10. National measures that attempt to safeguard pluralism by excluding sources that might otherwise be too dominant are much more problematic. Content obligations of any kind interfere with the liberty of the broadcaster to choose the nature of its programme or advertising content, but restrictions on sources of supply potentially restrict the liberty of a much wider range of individuals and organizations. On this basis, the Court has found that complete prohibitions on political advertising are likely to violate Article 10. In *Verein Gegen Tierfabriken v. Switzerland* (*VGT*), the

---

[99] '[F]or freedom of expression to fulfil its mission of informing public debate/opinion, pluralism must be guaranteed by State' (*Verein Alternatives Lokalradio Bern v. Switzerland* (Application No. 10746/84) (Admissibility Decision, 16 October 1986).

[100] Council of Europe, Committee of Ministers Recommendation on measures concerning media coverage of election campaigns, Rec (2007) 15, Part II. Measures concerning broadcast media, 1. General framework.

[101] Ibid., Part II. Measures concerning broadcast media: 2. News and current affairs programmes; 3. Non-linear audiovisual services of public service media.

[102] European Convention on Transfrontier Television, n. 70 above, Article 7(3).

Court determined that a prohibition of this kind, while imposed for a legitimate and potentially justifiable purpose, was a disproportionate interference with freedom of speech.[103] In the Court's view, the small activist group concerned, which was denied permission to advertise, should not have been caught by controls aimed at powerful financial interests.[104] It disregarded the argument that a total ban was necessary to create an effective barrier to financially powerful groups.[105] In a subsequent Grand Chamber decision, the Court confirmed the earlier *VGT* decision without change in its reasoning or scope.[106]

On one view, *VGT* and similar decisions have demonstrated the effectiveness of European human rights supervision, which brings into sharp focus the disproportionate burden national law, even when well intentioned, can impose on an applicant. In the *TV Vest As & Rogaland Pensjonistparti v. Norway* case, the Court was clearly impressed by the plight of the small Pensioners Party, which was hardly mentioned in the television election coverage. Consequently, as the Court stated,

[P]aid advertising on television became the only way for the Pensioners Party to get its message across to the public through that type of medium. By being denied this possibility under the law, the Pensioners Party's position was at a disadvantage, compared to that of major parties which had obtained edited broadcasting coverage that could not be offset by the possibility available to it to use other but less potent media.[107]

The injustice in the *TV Vest* case was particularly acute because the prohibition on political advertising restricted the party's ability to campaign during an election. In that situation, it has no Article 10 based right of access to the broadcasting time generally or even under any scheme of allocation of free broadcast time.[108] In these important cases on political advertising, the Court has once again cut back the legitimate scope for state intervention in media markets when ostensibly seeking to enhance media pluralism. It has turned instead to the underlying principle that

---

[103] *VGT Verein Gegen Tierfabriken v. Switzerland*, n. 94 above.
[104] Ibid., para. 75.
[105] See criticism of the VGT judgment made or referred to in *R. (Animal Defenders International) v. Secretary of State for Culture, Media and Sport* [2008] UKHL 15 (12 March 2008).
[106] *Verein Gegen Tierfabriken Schweiz (VGT) v. Switzerland (No. 2)* (Application No. 32772/02) Grand Chamber. In the Grand Chamber *VGT* decision, the Court distinguished the case of *Murphy v. Ireland* (Application No. 44179/98) [2004] 38 EHRR 13, which concerned a prohibition on religious advertising. See also *TV Vest As & Rogaland Pensjonistparti v. Norway*, n. 94 above.
[107] *Verein Gregen Tierfabriken (VGT) v. Switzerland (No. 2)* ibid., paras 72–73.
[108] Where a state party chooses to offer free broadcast time to political parties or candidates it is entitled to ration that air time in a fair and proportionate manner. *Huggett v. United Kingdom* (Application No. 24744/94) (Admissibility Decision, 28 June 1995). See also Committee of Ministers Recommendation on measures concerning media coverage of election campaigns, n. 100 above, in which the Committee encourages states to consider introducing provisions in their regulatory frameworks 'whereby public service media may make available free airtime on their broadcast and other linear audiovisual media services and/or an equivalent presence on their non-linear audiovisual media services to political parties/candidates during the election period'; Part II. Measures concerning broadcast media, 4. Free airtime and equivalent presence for political parties/candidates on public service media.

democratic elections require the maximum liberty to speak and publish. As the Court stated in *Bowman v. United Kingdom,*

Free elections and freedom of expression, particularly freedom of political debate, together form the bedrock of any democratic system. The two rights are interrelated and operate to reinforce each other: for example, as the Court has observed in the past, freedom of expression is one of the 'conditions' necessary to 'ensure the free expression of the opinion of the people in the choice of the legislature'. For this reason, it is particularly important in the period preceding an election that opinions and information of all kinds are permitted to circulate freely.[109]

Nonetheless, this move towards greater liberty in the broadcasting of partisan political appeals has created potentially insurmountable problems for the state parties. As a consequence of the election advertising cases, regulatory schemes intended to protect media pluralism and democratic processes from imbalances of wealth and funding must become more finely tuned. State parties must therefore only restrict, in a proportionate manner, the expression of those individuals or organizations whose financial and other resources give them the capacity to over-whelm or at least skew public debate. In these cases, the Court has not however engaged in any serious discussion of whether that fine tuned distinction can realistically be achieved. Nor has the Committee of Minsters ventured far in this sensitive area, merely advising that, '[m]ember states may consider introducing a provision in their regulatory frameworks to limit the amount of political advertising space and time which a given party or candidate can purchase'.[110] Yet despite the Court's apparent lack of concern for the wider effects of these decisions, it has at least forced a reconsideration of the restrictive effects of broadcast regimes as well as their close ties to dominant political parties and emphasis on the needs of representative democracy. The difficulty for state parties remains to find less restrictive ways to address funding imbalances between political parties, groups, and causes that translate into imbalances in media exposure, especially in relation to elections and other aspects of public participation in democratic political life.

Public service media

In Europe, state owned or supported public service media are the most visible form of state intervention aimed at enriching the supply of information and ideas to enhance democratic pluralism. Their remits to enhance pluralism frequently in-clude specific obligations to provide news and current affairs programmes.[111] Within the European Union, the obvious economic concern is that state financial support and other privileges granted to public service media will distort competi-

---

[109] *Bowman v. United Kingdom* (Application No. 24839/94) (19 February 1998), para. 42.
[110] Committee of Ministers Recommendation on measures concerning media coverage of election campaigns, n. 100 above, Part II. Measures concerning broadcast media, 5. Paid political advertising.
[111] See, for example, in Britain, Agreement Between Her Majesty's Secretary of State for Culture, Media and Sport and the British Broadcasting Corporation, Cm 6872 (July 2006), Clause 47.

tion in the Single Market and create barriers to free movement. In principle, national funding of public service media is a violation of the prohibition on state aid set out in the TFEU.[112] Yet, as discussed in greater detail in Chapter 15, member states have forced the development of a broad safe harbour in EU law for subsidized public service media under the concept of 'services of a general economic interest'. As the Commission acknowledged in 1996, '[I]n most member states, television and radio have a general interest dimension... The general interest considerations basically concern the content of broadcasts, being linked to moral and democratic values, such as pluralism, information ethics and protection of the individual.'[113] That concession led to the Amsterdam Protocol, which affirmed the place of media pluralism in the public service broadcasting remit and recognized the primary competence of the member states in conferring, defining, and organizing that remit.[114] Nonetheless, the Commission has used transparency and financial disciplines to force reforms in the operation of domestic public service media regimes.[115]

The Council of Europe, in comparison to the European Union, has warmly promoted the cause of public service media. The Committee of Ministers has stressed that, 'adequately equipped and financed public service media, in particular public service broadcasting, enjoying genuine editorial independence and institutional autonomy, can contribute to counterbalancing the risk of misuse of the power of the media in a situation of strong media concentration'.[116] More generally, the Committee has described public service media as providing,

> a) a reference point for all members of the public, offering universal access; b) a factor for social cohesion and integration of all individuals, groups and communities; c) a source of impartial and independent information and comment, and of innovatory and varied content which complies with high ethical and quality standards; d) a forum for pluralistic public discussion and a means of promoting broader democratic participation of individuals.[117]

The communications revolution has plainly failed to diminish the Council of Europe's enthusiasm for the benefits of public service media, despite its equally strong support for a comparatively open internet.[118] Indeed, several Committee of

---

[112] On the rules governing state aid under European Union law, see Chapter 15.
[113] European Commission, Communication on services of general interest in Europe, COM (1996) 443 final.
[114] Protocol on the System of Public Broadcasting in the Member States, Treaty of Amsterdam amending the Treaty on European Union, the Treaties establishing the European Communities and certain related Acts, 2 October 1997.
[115] On European Commission state aid decisions, see Chapter 15.
[116] Council of Europe, Committee of Ministers, Declaration on protecting the role of the media in democracy in the context of media concentration (January 2007).
[117] Council of Europe, Committee of Ministers Recommendation on the remit of public service media in the information society, CM/Rec (2007) 3, *Guiding principles concerning the remit of public service media in the information society.*
[118] See, for example, Committee of Ministers, Recommendation on measures to promote media pluralism, n. 40 above, Appendix to Recommendation, Committee of Ministers Recommendation on media pluralism and diversity of media content, n. 48 above, Part 4. Support Measures, and Recommendation on the remit of public service media in the information society, n. 117 above.

Ministers recommendations point out that there are still fundamental problems of access and diversity in European media markets. In the broadcasting sector, for example, the Committee has raised concerns about adequate public access to new digital services.[119] It has accordingly supported the argument that public service media should be available through the internet and other new media platforms. In 2007, the Committee of Ministers recommended that,

[m]ember states should ensure that existing public service media organisations occupy a visible place in the new media landscape. They should allow public service media organisations to develop in order to make their content accessible on a variety of platforms, notably in order to ensure the provision of high-quality and innovative content in the digital environment and to develop a whole range of new services including interactive facilities.[120]

Support for public service media in the Council of Europe however has its firm limits. In a liberal democracy, state owned or supported media are always a potential vehicle for partisan political interests and public policy blunders. Consequently, the Committee of Ministers recommended in the mid 1990s that member states not impose *a priori* controls on public service broadcasters and also ensure that their boards of management are not at risk of political or other interference.[121] More recently, the Committee has called for sweeping improvements in the regulatory regimes and management of state supported broadcasters in member states.[122] In its 2006 Declaration, it identified weaknesses in several national public service broadcasting regimes, ranging from inadequate legislation and poor implementation to undue influence from governmental and other public bodies as well as politicians, political parties, and commercial interests over public service broadcasters.[123] The Declaration also lamented that, in some member states, there is little understanding within media, politicians, or the public of the relationship between public service broadcasting and democracy.[124] The European Court of Human Rights has moreover found that the abuse of government powers over public service media can amount to a breach of a state party's Article 10 obligations. In *Manole A.O. v. Moldova*, the Court concluded that the Moldovan ruling party's interference with decision making and the functioning of TRM, the national public service media organization, had violated the freedom of expression rights of the journalists,

---

[119] Committee of Ministers Recommendation on Measures to Promote the Democratic and Social Contribution of Digital Broadcasting, n. 47 above, which discusses, 'the responsibility of member states to ensure plurality of voice in new digital broadcasting services' and 'public access to an enlarged choice and variety of quality programmes, including the maintenance and, where possible, extension of the availability of transfrontier services'.

[120] Committee of Ministers Recommendation on media pluralism and diversity of media content, n. 69 above, Part 3. Public service media. See also Recommendation on the remit of public service media in the information society, n. 117 above, Guiding Principles.

[121] Council of Europe, Committee of Ministers, Recommendation on the Guarantee of the Independence of Public Service Broadcasting, Rec (96) 10, Appendix, Guidelines: I and II.

[122] Council of Europe, Committee of Ministers, Declaration on the guarantee of the independence of public service broadcasting in the member states (September 2006).

[123] Ibid.

[124] Ibid.

editors, and producers working for the organization.[125] As TRM had a virtual monopoly over audiovisual broadcasting in Moldova, the court also decided that, 'it had been of vital importance for the functioning of democracy in the country for TRM to transmit accurate and balanced information reflecting the full range of political opinion and debate'.[126]

Media pluralism and intellectual property rights

In Europe, state owned or supported public service media are the most visible form of state intervention in media markets to enrich the supply of information and ideas to enhance democratic pluralism. Other less obvious forms of direct intervention include special exceptions to the normal rules governing intellectual property rights.[127] While these exceptions are broadly enough stated to apply to a variety of content genres, in practice they are most often used to secure free public access to live and recorded sports events through the audiovisual media.[128] There is an obvious political incentive for governments to provide the public with free access via television to premium sports content; these measures also arguably support social cohesion, which is essential to democratic political communities. In the 1990s, new subscription television services began to acquire exclusive rights to the live broadcasts of major sports events, taking these events away from more widely available free-to-air television services. European governments responded with rules dictating the terms for the purchase and licensing of exclusive broadcast rights, which were intended to ensure that the most popular events, such as football league championships, remained on free-to-air television.[129] For sports bodies and commercial broadcasters, these measures were a direct interference with commercial transactions involving highly valuable content rights and were, in effect, a barely disguised subsidy for the public service media who tended to be the major beneficiaries.[130]

In 1997 the European Commission was nonetheless persuaded that the public benefits of these national measures outweighed their anti-competitive effects on media markets and agreed that their position under EU should be secured in revisions to the then titled Television Without Frontiers Directive.[131] In short,

---

[125] *Manole A.O. v. Moldova* (Application No. 13936/02) (17 September 2009).

[126] Ibid., para 100.

[127] Directive 2001/29/EC of the European Parliament and of the Council of 22 May 2001 on the Harmonisation of Certain Aspects of Copyright and Related Rights in the Information Society, Article 5: Exceptions and Limitations.

[128] Recital (49) of Directive 2010/13/EU, n. 86 above, refers to 'the Olympic games, the football World Cup and European football championship' as examples of 'events of major importance for society'.

[129] See European Commission, Consolidated list of national measures taken pursuant to Article 14(1) of the Audiovisual Media Services Directive, OJ C17 of 24 January 2008, 7–10.

[130] European Publishers Council, *State Aid and Public Service Broadcasters*, n. 25 above.

[131] Communication from Mr Oreja to the Commission, *Exclusive Rights for TV Broadcasting of Major (Sports) Events* (Brussels, 3 February 1997), (*internal*) (author's copy).

they could 'be justified for overriding reasons of public interest as long as the measures are proportionate to the objectives pursued and non-discriminatory'.[132] The resulting rules not only protect national listed event schemes from EU competition law constraints, but also address their vulnerability to avoidance by foreign based, satellite broadcasters. The Directive requires member states not to allow broadcasters under their jurisdiction to acquire or exercise exclusive rights to an event listed by another member state in a manner that prevents a substantial proportion of the population of that state from viewing the event.[133] While thus forced to accept the validity of national listed events rules, commercial broadcasters have challenged their application, determined not to lose control of some of the world's most lucrative audiovisual content.[134]

In the more recent amendments to the Directive, the EU has also included measures that permit the use in news programmes of short extracts, or short reports, from broadcasts of sports events that are subject to exclusive rights.[135] As early as 1991, the Council of Europe's Committee of Ministers had adopted a recommendation urging member states to implement domestic short reporting schemes.[136] Commercial broadcasters and rights holders however argued strongly against any parallel EU legislation creating enforceable rights to short reports.[137] In their view, this right would not only interfere with complex commercial agreements between organizers of events, owners of premises, and broadcasters, but also wreck existing cooperative arrangements between broadcasters that were working well. The Commission however was concerned that these agreements and practices were potentially in breach of EU law.[138] The short reporting practices of many broadcasters, for example, appeared to exceed the rights of fair use protected under copyright law.[139] Consequently, the 2007 amendments to the Audiovisual Media Services Directive introduced a right of access for the broadcast media to 'short reporting'. These provisions, in effect, oblige member states to ensure that holders of exclusive rights to an event of high public interest (typically a major sports event) grant broadcasters and their intermediaries a licence or right to use short extracts for the

---

[132] Ibid.
[133] See also Article 14(1) and Recitals (48)–(52), Directive 2010/13/EU, n. 86 above, and Article 9 *bis*, European Convention on Transfrontier Television, n. 70 above.
[134] See, for example, Case T-33/01, *Infront. WM AG v. Commission of the European Community* of 15 December 2005.
[135] Directive 2010/13/EU, n. 86 above, Article 15(1). Member States shall ensure that for the purpose of short news reports, any broadcaster established in the Community has access on a fair, reasonable, and non-discriminatory basis to events of high interest to the public which are transmitted on an exclusive basis by a broadcaster under their jurisdiction. See also Recitals (55)–(57).
[136] Council of Europe, Committee Of Ministers, Recommendation on the right to Short Reporting on Major Events where Exclusive Rights of their Television Broadcast have been Acquired in a Transfrontier Context, No. R (91) 5.
[137] European Commission, Communication on the future of European regulatory audiovisual policy (COM (2003) 784 final), para. 3.3.
[138] Ibid.
[139] Directive 2001/29/EC of the European Parliament and of the Council of 22 May 2001 on the harmonization of certain aspects of copyright and related rights in the information society (1) and the relevant international conventions in the field of copyright and neighbouring rights.

purpose of general news programmes. In the Council of Europe, the Committee of Ministers has also debated whether to extend its 1991 recommendation to other media such as the press, radio, and the new services. But that proposal stumbled on the complexity of national arrangements that address this issue and the opposition of many rights holders.[140]

Must carry, universal service, and network neutrality

Media pluralism is primarily seen as a problem of adequate supply, which may be addressed by increasing the number of independent news media sources or using other methods, such as public service media, to enrich the supply of information and ideas available to the public. Yet without sufficient public access to those media sources, the diversity of information and ideas they may provide will not yield an informed public capable of participating effectively in democratic processes. Ensuring convenient public access is consequently a key element in the concept of public service media.[141] The root public policy issue here is clearly inequalities of access, which in most cases is a question of income and the ability to afford access to the major media, but can also be a matter of location. Distribution networks, such as terrestrial television transmitters, may not reach residents in remote areas without public subsidies of some kind. Adequate access to the media is consequently an issue that combines demands for public expenditure and the imposition of service obligations on private parties.

In terms of remedies, the problem of sufficient access breaks down into two distinct elements. The first of these is the problem of ensuring that a reasonable diversity of content is available on the most common distribution systems for media content, which has historically meant the imposition of 'must carry' obligations that compel cable or other distribution networks to carry the principal national television channels.[142] Must carry obligations of this kind have been a significant barrier to the free movement of media services, particularly for areas still dependent on analogue transmission where the number of available cable channels is quite limited. In European Union law, they are also protected, in principle, from free movement and competition rules as measures intended to achieve greater pluralism.[143] While accepting that fundamental legitimacy, the EU Universal

---

[140] Council of Europe, Steering Committee on the Media and New Communication Services Meeting Report, CDMC (2005) 028.

[141] Committee of Ministers, Recommendation on the remit of public service media in the information society, n. 117 above, Guiding Principles.

[142] See OVUM and Squire Sander and Dempsey, 'An inventory of EU "must-carry" regulations', Report to the European Commission, February 2001. See also European Commission, Working Document: 'Must-carry' obligations under the 2003 regulatory framework for electronic communications networks and services, 22 July 2002.

[143] Case C-336/07, *Kabel Deutschland Vertrieb und Service GmbH v. Niedersächsische Landesmedienanstalt für privaten Rundfunk*, para. 37.

Service Directive nonetheless attempts to harmonize some of their basic features.[144] The recitals of the Directive therefore state that, '[m]ust carry obligations imposed by Member States should be reasonable, that is they should be proportionate and transparent in the light of clearly defined general interest objectives, and could, where appropriate, entail a provision for proportionate remuneration'.[145] Cable network operators in countries where must carry obligations are heavily used, such as Germany, have however turned to the courts in efforts to limit what can be an unprofitable regulatory burden. In response, the ECJ has affirmed that the Directive, and EU law more generally, leave member states a wide discretion in determining domestic must carry obligations.[146] Yet however reassuring this judgment is to member states, the importance of must carry obligations in a digital, multi-platform media environment is open to strong doubts.[147]

The second element concerns the problem of ensuring that the public has reasonable access to those delivery systems. This involves both the construction of sufficient infrastructure and the price of access to the services they carry, which may be guaranteed by the state at minimum level of service at a particular price level. In telecommunications regulation, that is often referred to as a 'universal service' requirement. The EU Universal Service Directive requires that all member states ensure that members of the public within their jurisdiction, regardless of location, have fixed point access at an affordable price to the public communications network.[148] This obligation is intended to represent the minimum level of public access necessary for effective economic and social well being and reflects fundamental European rights to dignity and autonomy.[149] However, the concept of universal service under the Directive, while well beyond simple voice telephony, lags well behind the cutting edge of popular communications technologies and services, only providing for simple data transmission at speeds fast enough for basic internet access.[150] This reflects the fact that universal service is also a compromise between European ideals and what is affordable for governments, communications operators, and the general public.

While the concept of universal service developed in the regulated telecommunications sector, it now has important implications for public access to internet based media, in effect combining with the public access principle of public service media.

---

[144] Directive 2002/22/EC of the European Parliament and of the Council of 7 March 2002 on universal service and users' rights relating to electronic communications networks and services, Recitals (43) and (44) and Article 31.

[145] Ibid.

[146] Case C-336/07, n. 143 above. See also Case C-250/06, *United Pan-Europe Communications and others v. Belgium.*

[147] See 'To Have or Not To Have—Must Carry Rules', *IRIS Special 2005*, European Audiovisual Observatory. See also Commission Staff Working Document: *Media pluralism in the Member States of the European Union*, (SEC (2007) 32), 62.

[148] Directive 2002/22/EC, n. 144 above.

[149] European Commission, Communication accompanying the Communication on 'A single market for 21st century Europe' Services of general interest, including social services of general interest: a new European commitment, COM (2007) 725 final, Brussels, 20 November 2007.

[150] Directive 2002/22/EC, n. 144 above. See also van Eijk, N., 'New European Rules for the Communications Sector' (*IRIS Plus*, 2003–2).

As public access to the internet arrived in Europe, it was readily apparent that without internet access individuals and households would be cut off from rapidly growing opportunities for education and employment, popular culture, and participation in democratic politics and public affairs.[151] This problem of 'digital divide' has also evolved with the development of new communications technologies and services, most importantly including the arrival of broadband internet access in the home. Since the late 1990s, the Council of Europe has urged member states to extend the obligation of public access to new media services. The Committee of Ministers recommended in 1999 that, 'the continued development of new communication and information services should serve to further the right of everyone to express, to seek, to receive and to impart information and ideas, for the benefit of every individual and the democratic culture of any society'.[152] More specifically, it has urged that public service broadcasters should be available on new digital television platforms and that where necessary must carry obligations be used to accomplish this.[153] Beyond television services, the Committee has stressed the importance of public access to new information and communication technologies, especially the internet, to enable participation in public life and democratic processes.[154]

The difficulty for European governments is to determine what threshold of universal service is essential when services are changing so quickly. It is at least clear that broadband access has become the obvious target for an expanded universal service obligation. At present, the Universal Service Directive sets a reasonably flexible standard for internet access, requiring connection to public networks 'at data rates that are sufficient to permit functional Internet access, taking into account prevailing technologies used by the majority of subscribers and technological feasibility'.[155] This has, in short, meant internet connection at dial up speeds. There is however an EU commitment to the revision of universal service standards as communications technologies, services, and user demand

---

[151] See European Ministerial Conference at Bonn 'Global Information Networks: Realising the Potential', 6–8 July 1997, Ministerial Declaration: '45. Ministers stress the importance of wide accessibility of information . . . including those in remote regions and disadvantaged groups, e.g. the long term unemployed, people with disabilities and elderly people.' See also Final Policy Report of the High Level Expert Group, *Building the European Information Society for us all* (April 1997): section G, entitled 'Including everyone: the cohesion challenges' addresses the problem of social exclusion in the Information Society.

[152] Council of Europe, Committee Of Ministers Recommendation on Universal Community Service concerning New Communication and Information Services, Rec (99) 14.

[153] Committee of Ministers, Recommendation on Measures to Promote the Democratic and Social Contribution of Digital Broadcasting, n. 47 above, Appendix to Recommendation Rec (2003) 9, Principles 20 and 21. See also Recommendation on media pluralism and diversity of media content, n. 69 above, para.3.3.

[154] Council of Europe, Committee of Ministers, Recommendation on promoting freedom of expression and information in the new information and communications environment, CM/Rec (2007)11, Guidelines, IV. See also Recommendation on Measures to Promote the Democratic and Social Contribution of Digital Broadcasting, n. 47 above, Appendix to Recommendation Rec (2003) 9, and, Committee of Ministers, Declaration on human rights and the rule of law in the Information Society (13 May 2005).

[155] Directive 2002/22/EC, n. 144 above, Article 4(2).

change.[156] The Commission has moreover suggested that 'the focus of universal service may evolve towards providing an affordable broadband access link for all'.[157] Policy makers have however generally stopped short of that commitment, which would impose a considerable burden on the state and internet service providers. There is moreover little pressure so far from European human rights law to raise the universal service standard. Its strong positive obligation on states to ensure media pluralism has rarely been used to formulate an individual right to receive specific media services.[158]

The problem of whether and how to mandate universal broadband access is considerably complicated by more recent communications policy controversies over network neutrality. While almost everything about network neutrality invites dispute, including its definition, in simple terms it means that public communications network operators do not discriminate when granting access to internet content providers and users and, thus, provide open access to all content, services, and applications throughout end-to-end delivery.[159] One of the main public policy concerns in this area is that commercially driven differences in levels of service are beginning to emerge, creating different classes of internet users and content, which will arguably destroy the basic architecture that has made the internet a common economic, social, and political space.[160] This has obvious negative implications for democratic pluralism. In the worst case, parts of the population will be unable to afford access to services and information sources that have become essential to understanding and participating in contemporary democracy.

The policy argument in many countries is whether trends towards service level differences should be blocked by the creation of a right to network neutrality.[161] The European Commission has moved cautiously, wishing to avoid regulatory intervention that might create unnecessary barriers to the development of internet communications.

The Commission attaches high importance to preserving the open and neutral character of the Internet, taking full account of the will of the co-legislators now to enshrine net neutrality as a policy objective and regulatory principle to be promoted by national regulatory authorities, alongside the strengthening of related transparency requirements

---

[156] Ibid., Recital (1). See also European Commission, Communication on the second periodic review of the scope of universal service in electronic communications networks and services in accordance with Article 15 of Directive 2002/22/EC, and European Commission March, 2010 consultation Telecoms: consultation on future universal service in digital era, IP/10/218.

[157] Communication on the Report regarding the outcome of the Review of the Scope of Universal Service in accordance with Article 15(2) of Directive 2002/22/EC, COM (2006) 163 final.

[158] See, for example, *Khurshid Mustafa and Tarzibachi v. Sweden* (Application No. 23883/06) (16 December 2008), where the Court determined, in unusual circumstances, that state parties are under a positive duty to ensure that individuals are not prevented from gaining access to significant media sources.

[159] Marsden, C., *Net Neutrality Towards a Co-Regulatory Solution* (Bloomsbury, 2010). See also Valcke, P., Hou, L., Stevens, D., and Kosta, E., 'Guardian Knight or Hands Off: The European Response to Network Neutrality', 72 *Communications & Strategies* (4th Quarter 2008), 89.

[160] van Schewick, B., *Internet Architecture and Innovation* (MIT Press, 2010), 57.

[161] See, for example, Council of Europe, Committee of Ministers, Declaration on Network Neutrality (29 September 2010).

and the creation of safeguard powers for national regulatory authorities to prevent the degradation of services and the hindering or slowing down of traffic over public networks.[162]

At present, network neutrality rests on a set of provisions contained in the amended EU electronic communications regulatory framework. These require that national regulatory authorities, 'promote the interests of European citizens by . . . promoting the ability of end-users to access and distribute information or run applications and services of their choice'.[163] The protection of network neutrality is otherwise secured by transparency obligations placed on operators as well as the reserve power of national regulatory authorities to set minimum quality of service requirements.[164] There is however no fundamental right to network neutrality in European Union law.

International trade, democracy, and the media

The gradual integration of European economic and human rights law has made the principle of media pluralism a core feature of European media law. It is secured first by the parallel market based objectives of free movement and fair competition and the liberty oriented elements of freedom of expression and, second, by the protective aspects of freedom of expression, which justify state intervention in property rights and commercial agreements in the media sector. The relationship between international economic law and democratic pluralism is much more tenuous. Whatever the aspirations of the architects of the WTO, world trade law has no necessary relationship with liberal democracy. The international sphere moreover lacks a policy forum comparable to the Council of Europe, which is able to articulate common principles to govern political and social law and policy. The United Nations human rights system, in comparison, remains deeply divided by the conflicting aims of its member states. It is, as a result, incapable of penetrating the core issues that define the relationship between the media and the state and has not developed effective institutional arrangements to bring human rights principles to bear on law or policy making in the WTO. By default, justifying and protecting democratic pluralism in the trade law field falls to liberal democratic member states acting singly or collectively.

For these states, the conceptional relationship between their domestic protection of media pluralism and WTO law is obvious enough. To the extent that the WTO's principles of national treatment and most favoured nation (MFN) principles liberalize the flow of media goods and services, they support media pluralism

---

[162] European Commission, Declaration on Net Neutrality (March 2010). See also European Commission, *Report on the Public Consultation on 'The Open Internet and Net Neutrality in Europe'* (9 November 2010).

[163] Directive 2009/140/EC of the European Parliament and of the Council of 25 November 2009 amending Directives 2002/21/EC on a common regulatory framework for electronic communications networks and services, 2002/19/EC on access to, and interconnection of, electronic communications networks and associated facilities, and 2002/20/EC on the authorisation of electronic communications networks and services. See also Article 8.4(g) of the Framework Directive.

[164] Directive 2002/22/EC, n. 144 above, Articles 20 and 21.

by increasing the sources of supply. The WTO transparency discipline, which requires the publication of laws, regulations, and the mode of administration in tradable services, also supports openness in public affairs, which can contribute to democratic pluralism.[165] However, unlike European Union law, the WTO does not impose significant competition law obligations on member states, which means that international trade law does not underpin structural pluralism in media markets in a similar manner.[166]

Where domestic measures violate trade in services disciplines, the GATS Article XIV general exception includes public order, which covers measures aimed at securing the fundamental interests of society.[167] Media pluralism is clearly a fundamental interest for any liberal democratic member state. At present, of course, the Uruguay Round compromise, which left the audiovisual sector largely free from WTO disciplines in most states, has meant that discriminatory measures intended to enhance media pluralism are not yet within the scope of the GATS.[168] In a similar manner, Article XX of the GATT also permits general exceptions from the disciplines applicable to trade in goods, which includes printed works and the entertainment media content traded in the form of CDs or DVDs. Article XX does not however mention 'public order' or any similar public policy goal broad enough to cover media pluralism.[169] Yet this is a narrow vulnerability. As the GATT concerns domestic rules affecting trade rather than investment, any discriminatory rules concerning foreign investment in the production or distributors of media goods would fall outside the GATT. What is more, the GATT's trade obligations cover only a small part of international trade in media content, most of which is deemed to be trade in services and therefore governed by the GATS. Finally, many domestic measures intended to protect media pluralism that affect trade in goods or services do not violate the GATT or GATS national treatment or MFN provisions. These measures are either equally applicable or impose burdens on the domestic

---

[165] Julia Qin, for example, has argued that the special transparency provisions included in China's Protocol of Accession to the WTO were intended in part to further the development of democracy and the rule of law in China. Qin, J., '"WTO-Plus" Obligations and Their Implications for the World Trade Organization Legal System: An Appraisal of the China Accession Protocol', 37(3) *Journal of World Trade* (2003), 483–522, 495.

[166] The WTO has undertaken limited work on trade and competition policy in the Doha Round. Fourth WTO Ministerial Conference (Doha, November 2001): Ministerial Declaration, (20 November 2001), Wt/Min(01)/Dec/1, 'negotiations will take place after the Fifth Session of the Ministerial Conference on the basis of the decision to be taken, by explicit consensus, at that session on modalities of negotiation'. A Working Group on this subject was subsequently set up by the 1996 Singapore WTO Ministerial Conference, which identified the core principles of competition law should include transparency, non-discrimination, and procedural fairness.

[167] General Agreement on Trade in Services, (15 April 1994), 33 ILM 1167 (1994). Article XIV and Footnote 5. On the general exception provisions of the GATS, see Chapter 5.

[168] On the Uruguay Round compromises regarding audiovisual services, see Chapter 5.

[169] OECD, *Media Mergers*, DAFFE/COMP(2003)16, which identifies quality and diversity of content as legitimate public policy concerns: 'Pluralism presents a number of difficult and highly important questions for media merger review, but there is no consensus about how to answer them. Although competition authorities can make a positive contribution to pluralism even when not explicitly trying to do so, it is unlikely that review focused only on economic efficiency will adequately address pluralism concerns.'

media that do not negatively affect foreign media goods or services, such as impartiality or fairness obligations imposed on domestic broadcasters.

While WTO trade disciplines may currently leave media pluralism measures relatively unscathed, non-democratic states have other concerns about the impact of those disciplines on their domestic media rules, which safeguard different forms of political and social order. For non-democratic states, any liberalization of cross border trade in media goods and services has the unwelcome potential of increasing plurality in the supply of news and current affairs. Certainly, the general exceptions to the GATT and the GATS offer some defence against arguments that national treatment and MFN obligations require the removal or modification of domestic controls on the media. The public order ground for invoking Article XIV of the GATS is just as apt for non-democratic fundamental public policy as it is for democratic pluralism. Domestic measures essential to maintaining the fundamental nature of the state fall within 'public order' even if they are illiberal in nature. Undoubtedly, such measures are likely to be assessed strictly under the necessity and other conditions of GATS Article XIV.[170] Moreover, the lack of a parallel public order exception in GATT Article XX has forced states onto the narrower 'public morals' ground, which is less likely to justify aggressive state controls over the media.[171]

WTO law has some potential use to force changes in non-democratic media regimes where national laws or regulatory measures are discriminatory and cannot satisfy the GATT or GATS exemption conditions. This can be seen in the WTO dispute case initiated by the European Union, the United States, and Canada against China in 2008.[172] The complainants alleged, *inter alia*, that China had violated its GATS Article XVII national treatment obligations when it introduced regulations requiring foreign financial information suppliers to provide their services through an entity designated by China's regulatory authority. In their view, that entity, the Xinhua News Agency, could not act impartially because it was also a major market competitor to the foreign financial information suppliers concerned. China settled this dispute later that year, conceding the major points at issue to its trade partners.[173]

The most obvious politically motivated, discriminatory measures that ostensibly protect pluralism tend to involve preferential subsidies and restrictions on foreign ownership. Domestic subsidies are of course the essential foundation for state owned or supported media, which often have enormously important political purposes in liberal democracies and non-democratic states. As discussed in Chapter 5, WTO subsidy disciplines concern trade in goods and are principally intended to curb the

---

[170] n. 166 above.
[171] See, for example, China—Measures Affecting Trading Rights and Distribution Services for Certain Publications and Audiovisual Entertainment Products (WT/DS363/AB/R), Appellate Body (December 2009).
[172] China—Measures Affecting Financial Information Services and Foreign Financial Information Suppliers, DS 272, 273, and 278 (request for consultations 3 March 2008).
[173] Hille, K. and Dickie, M., 'Beijing Opens to Financial News Providers', *Financial Times*, (14 November 2008).

use of export subsidies. If a new subsidies discipline for services is eventually agreed in the Doha Round, it seems certain that discriminatory subsidies used to support the national media will be exempted, given the sensitivity of this issue for many member states. Similarly, rules affecting foreign investment are largely outside the scope of the WTO. Yet if a state were to make a commitment to liberalize trade in audiovisual services under the GATS that included a mode 3 right to establish a commercial presence, this would potentially subject its discriminatory investment rules to GATS market access disciplines.

GATS Article VI on domestic regulation also poses a present and future challenge for domestic regulations aimed at securing greater media pluralism. As also discussed in Chapter 5, Article VI states that generally applicable or non-discriminatory domestic regulations must be 'administered in a reasonable, objective and impartial manner'.[174] This would, for example, include restrictions on the purchase of broadcast advertising by political parties or interest groups. The GATS Working Party on Domestic Regulation is however working towards a wider set of disciplines that, while currently open to change, could be applied in the future to curb the use of pluralism related regulations.[175] While the Working Party has drawn back from including a full 'necessity' discipline, some form of necessity element may be included in the final instrument.[176] This discipline has already appeared in a WTO subsidiary instrument that affects an aspect of contemporary media pluralism. The 1996 WTO Telecommunications Services Reference Paper, which binds most parties to the Basic Telecommunications Agreement (the GATS Fourth Protocol), states that '[a]ny Member has the right to define the kind of universal service obligation it wishes to maintain. Such obligations will not be regarded as anti-competitive per se, provided they are administered in a transparent, non-discriminatory and competitively neutral manner and are not more burdensome than necessary for the kind of universal service defined by the Member'. The creation of even an indirect necessity test under Article VI could see a discipline of this kind applied not only to internet access, universal service obligations but across the full range of regulatory requirements relating to media pluralism.[177]

As bilateral and other preferential trade treaties have come to dominate the development of international trade relations, the status of audiovisual services, including new electronic media services, has progressed beyond the dated compromises of the Uruguay Round. In agreements that do encompass traditional and new media services, it is however discriminatory cultural policy measures that remain

[174] On the GATS Article VI Domestic Regulation Working Party negotiations, see Chapter 5.
[175] Disciplines On Domestic Regulation Pursuant To GATS Article VI:4—Annotated Text, 14 March 2010 'pre-established, based on objective and transparent criteria and relevant to the supply of the services to which they apply'.
[176] GATS, n. 167 above, Article VI.
[177] Adlung has commented on the uncertainties in this area, '[w]hat is the status of typical universal service obligations stipulating, for example, minimum capacity and service requirements for social, regional and similar policy objectives? Apart from Article VI:1, would Articles VI:4 and VI:5 apply as well? If so, to what effect?' Adlung, R., 'Public Services and the GATS', 9(2) *Journal of International Economic Law* (2006), 455–485.

the source of greatest difficulty in the media services sector.[178] As noted above, national measures intended to foster or to restrict media pluralism are often non-discriminatory and are therefore outside the reach of standard trade disciplines. However, where these agreements include investment rules, they can require the opening of the domestic media to greater foreign investment and the removal of any domestic rules that discriminate against foreign media.[179] Bilateral investment agreements may also offer some scope for challenging arbitrary regulatory practices affecting foreign invested media.[180]

The media, democracy, and international human rights law

State intervention in media markets for democratic purposes presents a serious problem for any liberal democratic vision of the global future. In relation to freedom of expression, the effort to entrench liberal democratic values in international law has stressed the idea that the right to free speech is held against the state and it is protected by limiting government intervention in the media. This emphasis on restraint of the state has much to do with the Cold War circumstances in which international human rights law first developed and the special importance given to the meaning of freedom of speech in that long struggle. For the United States and its democratic allies, breaking the grip of the socialist and other targeted non-liberal states on their national public information environments was essential to the destruction of their non-democratic forms of government.

Not surprisingly, in this conflict the historic imagery of liberalism, in particular the idea that the essence of personal freedom is liberty from the state, was omnipresent. In American foreign policy, this strategy was often captured by the simple expression, 'the free flow of information'.[181] This is not to argue that the western democracies shared a unified position on the meaning of freedom of expression. The open language of Articles 19 of the UDHR and the ICCPR was not only a contested field between these liberal democracies and their socialist antagonists, but was also a grey area that concealed their differences. Yet during the Cold War those differences did not often become a source of public transatlantic tension. Certainly, there was little effort to promote the issue of legitimate intervention in media markets for democratic purposes.[182]

---

[178] On cultural policy measures and trade obligations, see Chapter 15.

[179] *Joseph C. Lemire v. Ukraine*, ICSID Case No. ARB/06/18, See, generally, Peterson, L., 'International Investment Law and Media Disputes: a complement to WTO law', 17 *Columbia FDI Perspectives* (27 January 2010).

[180] Wälde, T., 'CME/Lauder v. Czech Republic: Case Comment', *Transnational Dispute Management* (June 2003).

[181] On the UNESCO New World Information and Communication Order (NWICO) crisis, see Chapter 6.

[182] See, however, the brief mention in ICCPR General Comment No. 10: Freedom of expression (Article 19) (Nineteenth session, 1983), 1. Not all States parties have provided information concerning all aspects of the freedom of expression. For instance, little attention has so far been given to the fact that, because of the development of modern mass media, effective measures are necessary to prevent such control of the media as would interfere with the right of everyone to freedom of expression in a way that is not provided for in paragraph 3.

In the post Cold War era, the dual liberal argument for economic and political liberty from the state achieved a brief but powerful ascendency. The growing international influence of neoclassical economic policies coincided with the advent of the internet, a communications platform that appeared to embody the libertarian dream of freedom from the state. The internet, it seemed, would usher in a networked global society based on liberal economic and political principles in which the state would respect market forces.[183] During this period, an emboldened ICCPR Human Rights Committee issued its General Comment No. 25 on the right to participate in public affairs, voting rights, and the right of equal access to public service. Here, the Committee declared that, 'the free communication of information and ideas about public and political issues between citizens, candidates and elected representatives is essential. This implies a free press and other media able to comment on public issues without censorship or restraint and to inform public opinion.'[184] In its decisions on individual applications under Article 19, the Committee also began to make a cautious connection between the textual requirement of 'necessity' and the concept of proportionality.[185]

Media pluralism also gained a foothold in international policy discussions. In UNESCO, previously the setting for the NWICO debacle, new programmes and declarations began to touch on the problems of media pluralism, including the threat of non-governmental power to the diversity of public information. The significant 1991 UNESCO sponsored Windhoek Declaration declared support for 'an independent, pluralistic and free press . . . independent from governmental, political or economic control' and 'the greatest possible number of newspapers, magazines and periodicals reflecting the widest possible range of opinion'.[186] Although media pluralism did not become a central issue in UN freedom of expression initiatives, it was at least a recognized element in the debate. Even the much criticized UN Commission on Human Rights took up the question of undue concentrations of private ownership of the media in 2006, the last year of its existence.[187]

In the lengthy preparation process for the UN sponsored World Summit on the Information Society (WSIS), arguments over the significance of liberal democratic principles to global internet policy arose continually. At Geneva in 2003, the state parties eventually adopted a Declaration of Principles that reiterated the main

---

[183] OECD Committee for Information, Computers and Communications Policy, 'Global Information infrastructure—Global information Society (GII-GIS) Policy Recommendations for Action' OECD 1997 [approved by OECD Council at Ministerial level, May 1997].
[184] ICCPR Human Rights Committee, General Comment No. 25, para. 26.
[185] *Kim Jong-Cheol v. Republic of Korea*, Communication No. 968/2001, UN Doc. CCPR/C/84/D/968/2001 (2005).
[186] UNESCO, Declaration of Windhoek on Promoting an Independent and Pluralistic African Press, Namibia, 3 May 1991. See other UNESCO sponsored regional declarations adopting the Windhoek principles, including the 1992 Declaration of Alma-Ata and the 1994 Declaration of Santiago.
[187] UN Commission on Human Rights, *The Right to Freedom of Opinion and Expression*, Resolution 2005/38, Part 4.

principles of global freedom of expression.[188] These did not however break any new ground on the critical question of how 'necessary' restrictions on freedom of expression should be contained. The Declaration did mention the importance of pluralism and diversity, stating in broad language, '[d]iversity of media ownership should be encouraged, in conformity with national law, and taking into account relevant international conventions'.[189] Yet it did not reflect in any depth the arguments made by participating civil society organizations that market forces were inadequate to create a genuinely open and participatory international communications system. Their arguments for the recognition of a new umbrella 'right to communicate' drew on the legacy of NWICO and drew a sharp rebuke from advocates of a more classically liberal concept of freedom of expression.[190]

While international human rights law left the question of state intervention to protect media pluralism largely to state parties, the question of reasonable public access to communication and media services has become a fertile area for global initiatives. In 1990s, as the communications revolution gathered pace, the question of equitable access to internet services quickly became a practical and symbolic development issue. While the developed world was enjoying an internet and mobile phone fed communications boom, many households in the developing world had no access to a telephone service, let alone a personal computer. As the ITU stated in 1997, 'The information and technology gap and related inequities between industrialised and developing nations are widening: a new type of poverty—information poverty—looms.'[191] This emerging digital divide created immense challenges across the social, educational and cultural public policy fields in democratic and non-democratic states alike. It was consequently relatively easy to build support in international organizations for the principle of better public access to basic internet services.[192]

---

[188] World Summit on the Information Society (WSIS) 2003 Declaration of Principles, Part A: Our Common Vision of the Information Society.

[189] Ibid., Part B9: Media.

[190] Drake, W. and Jørgensen, R.F., *Human Rights in the Global Information Society* (MIT Press, 2006), 1–51. 'The campaign for Communication Rights in the Information Society, commonly known as the *CRIS Campaign*, was initiated in 2001 by the Platform for Communication Rights, a transnational group of NGOs and individuals involved in policy advocacy around global media and communication issues. The *right to communicate* is a general norm based on ideals of participatory democracy. It asserts that all citizens must have a say, a communication right, in any and every governance process that affects them. It believes that a "right to hear and be heard, to inform and be informed," and "to participate in public communication" [MacBride Commission] should be the touchstone of communication policy.' See, however, ARTICLE 19, *Statement on the Right to Communicate*, Document WSIS/PC-2/CONTR/95-E (London, February 2003), and, Bullen, D.,'What's Wrong with a "Right to Communicate"', in *New Code Words for Censorship* (World Press Freedom Committee, 2002).

[191] ITU, ACC Statement on Universal Access to Basic Communication and Information Services', Inter-Agency Project on Universal Access to Basic Communication and Information Services (11 April 1997).

[192] 1995 G-7 Ministerial Conference on the Information Society adopted 8 core principles, including 'ensuring universal provision of and access to services': Chair's Conclusions: G-7 partners commit themselves to '[p]romote universal service to ensure opportunities for all to participate. By establishing universal service frameworks that are adaptable, they will ensure that all citizens will have

In the preparations for the Geneva and Tunis WSIS meetings, which were charged with finding ways to overcome digital divide problems, the extent of a positive obligation on the state to provide communication services was a major point of contention.[193] In this, as in other matters, the WSIS Declaration of Principles was cast in general language that skirted the many unresolved questions of methods and objectives. The Declaration did however suggest that every individual is entitled to internet access. 'Communication is a fundamental social process, a basic human need and the foundation of all social organization. It is central to the Information Society. Everyone, everywhere should have the opportunity to participate and no one should be excluded from the benefits the Information Society offers.'[194] That idea of an entitlement to access is grounded in the international right to freedom of expression and its constituent right to receive information.[195] It is also closely connected to concepts of just global governance, in particular the idea of knowledge as a public good.[196]

A commitment to universal internet access not only leads back to the contested issue of content pluralism, but also immediately confronts the problem of how that access should be provided and what responsibilities the state should bear in the process.[197] The provision of less than universal broadband access has required enormous investments in national and local communications infrastructure and the eventual cost of global, universal broadband access will be extraordinary. Yet in a policy climate that has hitherto favoured market solutions, there has been considerable opposition to any state intervention that may distort the operation of communications and media markets. In the preparations for the WSIS, an alliance of organizations representing media organizations issued a collective statement emphasizing the dangers of state intervention: '[t]hose who seek answers to the so-called "digital divide" neglect to recall that previous communication technologies such as printing, radio and television also started in advanced, more developed countries and spread virtually throughout the world, largely thanks to

---

access to new information services and thus be able to benefit from new opportunities. . . . Strategies to prevent marginalisation and to avoid isolation will be developed.'

[193] See, for example, International Federation of Journalists, *Quality Journalism for the Information Age: Policy Statement to The United Nations World Summit on the Information Society* (January 2003), Document WSIS/PC-2/CONTR/75-E.

[194] WSIS Declaration of Principles, Part A: Our Common Vision of the Information Society, 4.

[195] UN Commission on Human Rights, *The Right to Freedom of Opinion and Expression*, Resolution 2005/38, part 4 (m): 'To facilitate equal participation in, access to and use of, information and communications technology such as the Internet.'

[196] See Kaul, I., and Mendoza, R., 'Advancing the Concept of Public Goods' in Kaul, I., Gonceicao, P., Le Goulven, K., and Mendoza, R., *Providing Global Public Goods* (Oxford University Press, 2003), 95 and 105. See also Spar, D.L., 'The Public Face of Cyberspace: The Internet as a Public Good' in Kaul, I., Grunberg, I., and Stern, M.A. (eds), *Global Public Goods: International Cooperation in the 21st Century* (Oxford University Press, 1999); Stiglitz, J., 'Knowledge as a Public Good', ibid., and Spar, D.L., 'The Public Face of Cyberspace: The Internet as a Public Good', ibid.

[197] See OECD, Working Party on Telecommunication and Information Services Policies, *Policy Considerations for Audio-Visual Content Distribution in a Multiplatform. Environment*, DSTI/ICCP/TISP(2006)3/FINAL.

natural market processes'.[198] More recently, the influence of market led solutions on public policy has faded in light of the failures of international financial markets. The collapse of those markets has however also limited the sources of funding for major infrastructure projects.

[198] Coordinating Committee of Press Freedom Organisations, *Statement of Vienna: Press Freedom on the Internet* (21 November 2002). [Committee to Protect Journalists, Commonwealth Press Union, Inter American Press Association, International Association of Broadcasting, International Federation of the Periodical Press, International Press Institute, North American Broadcasters Association, World Association of Newspapers, World Press Freedom Committee.]

15

Cultural Policy and the Entertainment Media

Culture policy has always been a difficult and even suspect basis for liberal democratic law or policy making. Whatever clarity the idea of culture once had, it has become increasingly incoherent as it has expanded and shifted in meaning over time.[1] Once used to describe the high culture of European civilization, the word culture is now regularly used to encompass language, ethical beliefs, music, drama, and art, as well as food, dress, manners, and other shared practices. This wider, near boundless, idea of culture has also become a way to express anxieties about the loss of individual and collective identities through globalization, and with them, the loss of vital bonds of social cohesion.[2]

Resistance to these changes, often voiced through opposition to the influx of foreign entertainment media, has tended to rest on a particular understanding of human identity. In that understanding, cultural identity provides an essential framework in which each person is embedded and also uses to make sense of the world.[3] These identities, which have evolved through the relative separation of communities and peoples, are also distinctively different. The erosion of that distinctiveness through the effects of globalization is thus an irreplaceable loss for human society generally as well as harm felt by individuals and communities.[4] This claim that a secure cultural identity is vitally important to human well being is also frequently expressed in terms of rights of access to and participation in culture. These entitlements concern the cultural contexts in which individuals and communities are embedded, requiring that they are preserved and developed in ways that protect their distinctiveness. This may involve positive assistance from the state

---

[1] Eagleton, T., *The Idea of Culture* (Blackstone, 2000), ch 1.

[2] See, for example, Lear, J., *Radical Hope: Ethics in the Face of Cultural Devastation* (Harvard University Press, 2006). See also 1999 UNDP Human Development Report 'Globalization with a Human Face', which stated that, '[t]oday's flow of culture is unbalanced, heavily weighted in one direction, from rich countries to poor. Weightless goods—with high knowledge content rather than material content—now make for some of the most dynamic sectors in today's most advanced economies ... Such onslaughts of foreign culture can put cultural diversity at risk, and make people fear losing their cultural identity' (4).

[3] See Appiah, K.A., *Ethics of Identity* (Princeton University Press, 2005); Taylor, C., *Philosophical Arguments* (Harvard University Press, 1995); and Margalit, A. and Halbertal, M., 'Liberalism and the Right to Culture', 61(3) *Liberalism* (Fall 1994), 491.

[4] 'As Europeans we strongly believe that it does matter and that we do need to care whether we watch programmes that reflect our own cultural identity, values and experiences, or whether we feed our minds on the images of the lives of people of foreign cultures, with different attitudes and value systems': Fritz Pleitgen, *Cultural Diversity and Pluralism: the European Audiovisual Model*, speech to the Audiovisual Industry Seminar, WTO, Geneva, 4 July 2001.

where ways of life are in danger of being swamped by more dominant cultural influences that benefit disproportionately from market forces.

Cultural policy of this kind has provoked fierce concerns about the arbitrary or unwarranted use of state power. From this perspective, the defence of national or local culture translates too easily into mandatory rules on preferred forms of information or entertainment media and discrimination against foreign sourced content. Rejection of the idea of cultural entitlement does not however necessarily trivialize or underestimate the extent of global social and cultural change. A cosmopolitan position, for example, simply holds a more positive perspective on the consequences of those changes and the adaptability of individuals and communities.[5] It celebrates the creativity of change and emphasizes freedom of choice in a time of globalization and uncertainty. These arguments also rest on traditional liberal freedoms of individual conscience, expression, and association. From this view, cultural needs are best satisfied through access to a wide, diverse range of information and ideas, including images. State support that privileges a particular national or local cultural tradition over others is accordingly a fetter on that access and the individual rights on which it rests. It is an illegitimate preference granted to one idea of the good life over others.

Plainly, the entertainment media occupy a central place in these debates over cultural policy and the underlying arguments about the proper purposes and limits of the contemporary state and the significance of market driven choices for public policy making. Over the past century, the entertainment media have become the principal providers of the information, images, and ideas that sustain national cultural life.[6] In much of the world, the broadcast media, both public and private, grew to become national institutions charged with the delivery of major public policy goals. Indeed, in western Europe, the public policy mission of national broadcasters became the basis for a deeply entrenched, continent wide, media

---

[5] See, for example, Franck, T., 'Community Based on Autonomy', 36 *Columbia Journal of Transnational Law* (1997), 41; Appiah, K.A., n. 3 above; Waldron, J., 'What is Cosmopolitan?', 8(2) *Journal of Political Philosophy* (2000), 227–243; and Waldron, J., 'Minority Cultures and the Cosmopolitan Alternative', 25 *University of Michigan Journal of Law Reform* (1992), 751.

[6] As the European Commission has observed, 'the audiovisual media play a fundamental role in the development and transmission of social values. This is not simply because they influence to a large degree which facts about and which images of the world we encounter, but also because they provide concepts and categories—political, social, ethnic, geographical, psychological and so on—which we use to render these facts and images intelligible. They therefore help to determine not only what we see of the world but also how we see it.' EU Commission, Principles and Guidelines for the Community's Audiovisual Policy in the Digital Age, COM (1999) 657 final. See also Report from the High Level Group on Audiovisual Policy, *Digital Age: European Audiovisual Policy* (the Oreja Report), Directorate General X, (26 October 1998), ch 1, 1, which states that the '. . . communication media also play a formative role in society. That is, they are largely responsible for forming (not just informing) the concepts, belief systems, and even the languages—visual and symbolic as well as verbal—which citizens use to make sense of and interpret the world in which they live . . . in other words, the media also play a major role in forming our cultural identity', and see Cultural Industries Sectoral Advisory Group on International Trade (SAGIT), *New Strategies for Culture and Trade: Canadian Culture in a Global World* (February 1999).

model.[7] Even as the current communications revolution has torn apart long established, mass media models, new forms of media, from on-demand programme and film services to video games and social networking sites, have assumed a central role in cultural change.

State efforts to control cultural life are as old as the state itself. In China, the first emperor of the Qin not only militarily united the warring kingdoms of ancient China, but also ordered the use of a standardized written script throughout his new territories and the burning of the historical, philosophical, and literary works of these defeated states.[8] His methods were famously ruthless, but his desire to mould language, traditions, and beliefs was also elemental to the creation of a more cohesive, state centred society. As an influential report to the Canadian government more recently stated 'Culture is the heart of a nation. As countries become more economically integrated nations need strong domestic cultures and cultural expression to maintain their sovereignty and sense of identity. Indeed some have argued that the worldwide impact of globalisation is manifesting itself in the reaffirmation of local cultures.'[9]

For liberal democracies, the media's powerful influence over social cohesion and national identity is particularly important.[10] As discussed in Chapter 14, the media holds a special place in liberal arguments for freedom of speech because of its apparent capacity to maintain an informed, democratic society.[11] But beyond access to information, sustainable democratic politics also requires a sense of

---

[7] 'Radio and television have traditionally played a major role in public opinion forming, the functioning of democratic systems, safeguarding and shaping national and regional cultural identities, promoting exchanges between different cultures, respecting linguistic diversity and developing the creative potential, and making a significant contribution to education and social inclusion. They thus play a special role in fostering the core values which lay at the heart of the European construction: freedom of expression, freedom and pluralism of the media, respect for and promotion of the diversity of national and regional cultures, equality and solidarity, the provision of public services to all citizens, etc. These values have also been taken up in the European model for the information society': EBU, *Audiovisual Services and GATS: EBU Comments on US Negotiating Proposals of December 2000*, [12 April 2001]).

[8] Bodde, D., 'The State and Empire of Ch'in', in Twitchett, D. and Loewe, M. (eds), *The Cambridge History of China: Volume I: the Ch'in and Han Empires, 221 B.C.–A.D. 220.* (Cambridge University Press, 1986).

[9] Cultural Industries Sectoral Advisory Group on International Trade (SAGIT), *New Strategies for Culture and Trade: Canadian Culture in a Global World* (February 1999). See also European Commission, Communication on the Community framework programme in support of Culture (2000–2004), which argues that, 'culture is able to strengthen social cohesion, especially in vulnerable areas or among marginalized groups of the population', and Graham, A. and Davies, G., *Broadcasting, Society and Policy in the Multimedia Age* (John Libbey Media, 1997), Chapter V, 'Citizenship, Culture and Community'.

[10] Regulation of the media for cultural purposes is certainly not limited to democratic states. China is well known for its controls over the treatment of political issues in the media, but it media policies also include extensive cultural objectives. See, for example, Several Opinions of the Ministry of Culture, State Administration of Radio, Film and Television, General Administration of Press and Publication, National Development and Reform Commission and the Ministry of Commerce on Introducing Foreign Investment into the Cultural Sector, Order [2005] No. 19 of the Ministry of Culture (6 July 2005). See also Niu, Z., 'The Door Is Wedged Open: China's Regulation on Foreign Access to Audiovisual Markets', 18(8) *Entertainment Law Review* (2007), 265.

[11] See also European Commission, Principles and Guidelines for the Community's Audiovisual Policy in the Digital Age, COM (1999) 657 final.

community, in which a commitment to collective bonds outweighs particular interests. Liberalism is therefore not inevitably hostile to government measures that use the media to develop national culture and thereby protect the fundamental stability of the democratic political system.[12] Nonetheless, even where broadly accepted, state intervention in the media for cultural purposes is subject to the various constitutional limitations liberal democracies now place on the state.

Yet liberal democracies often disagree vehemently on the legitimacy of cultural policy aims and methods. In the broadcast era, Europeans developed an interventionist media model that was characterized by dominant state owned or supported radio and television broadcasters entrusted with positive programme remits.[13] While commercial competition and technological change have reduced their audience share, public service media remain a key element in European cultural policies. Their content obligations are sustained by a variety of state support mechanisms, including annual subsidies, tax privileges, and special access to communications infrastructure.[14] Foreign competition is moreover restrained by quotas on the domestic distribution of foreign films and other audiovisual content.[15]

In liberal democracies, like the United States, that are wary of any state involvement in the media, this combination of subsidies, privileges, and quotas is doubly objectionable. The protection of domestic media content production and distribution breaches the market based principle of equality of competitive opportunity.[16] A properly functioning market, according to this perspective, will provide culturally significant goods and services through consumer demand. As the OECD has argued, 'open competitive markets must not be viewed as antagonistic to concepts of cultural and linguistic diversity. On the contrary, in these markets where there is vibrant competition, low prices and rapid service diffusion, domestic industries have an incentive to produce content at a much more rapid rate, and of higher quality, than in closed markets which tend to be limited in size.'[17] Accordingly, an efficient market will produce culturally significant goods and services in sufficient

[12] See, for example, Nissen, C., *Public Service Media in the Information Society*, Report prepared for the Council of Europe's Group of Specialists on Public Service Broadcasting in the Information Society (MC-S-PSB), Media Division, Directorate General of Human Rights, Council of Europe, February 2006, 22.

[13] See Crisell, A., *An Introductory History of British Broadcasting* (Routledge, 1997), ch 2; Humphreys, P., *Media and Media Policy in Germany*, 2nd edn (Berg, 1994), chs 3–4; Kuhn, R., *The Media in France* (Routledge, 1995), chs 4–5.

[14] On the funding of public service media in Europe, see European Audiovisual Observatory, 'Public Service Media: Money for Content', *IRIS Plus*, 2010–4: (2010). On the future funding of public service media in Britain, see House of Lords Communications Committee Report, *Public Service Broadcasting: Short-Term Crisis, Long-Term Future?* (HL 61), Session 2008–09.

[15] On European content quotas under the Audiovisual Media Services Directive, see below.

[16] Sauvé, P., and Steinfatt, K., 'Towards Multilateral Rules on Trade and Culture: protective regulation of efficient protection?' in Productivity Commission and Australian National University (ed.), *Achieving Better Regulation of Services*, (The Australian National University Canberra, 2000), 322–352.

[17] OECD Committee for Information, Computers and Communications Policy, 'Global Information infrastructure—Global information Society (GII-GIS) Policy Recommendations for Action' OECD 1997 [approved by OECD Council at Ministerial level, May 1997] 16.

quality and diversity to safeguard the richness of both national and local cultures, provided there is sufficient consumer demand.[18]

Secondly, these interventions violate liberal arguments for greater political and social liberty as much as they do economic ones. Consumer driven market solutions have an obvious affinity with cosmopolitan contentions about the importance of personal autonomy.[19] On this ground, the state should not prejudge the value or benefits of expression, which is a matter for personal choice, provided no harm is done to others. The catchphrase 'market place of ideas' thus neatly combines these economic and political arguments for market based solutions to the supply of diverse media content.

In an era dominated by market based economics, supporters of interventionist cultural policy have looked for economic counter-arguments, questioning whether consumer demand alone, even in a well functioning market, can deliver an adequate range of culturally rich media content needed for collective well being. The 'public goods' argument, for example, posits that individuals are reluctant to pay the full cost of goods where they do not enjoy an exclusive right to consume them.[20] In these circumstances public goods include high quality, diverse, or challenging media content. Nor are individuals inclined to pay for 'merit goods', because their distinctive cultural or social value is greater than the valuation consumers commonly place on them.[21] According to this argument, the capacity of the information and entertainment media to expand human knowledge and experience vastly exceeds the knowledge and tastes of individuals. They are therefore likely to refuse to invest in that expansion as the benefits are difficult to quantify or to compare to other forms of consumption.[22]

---

[18] Even supporters of state intervention to protect cultural diversity acknowledge the importance of local demand for local culture. The *Digital Age: European Audiovisual Policy*, Report from the High Level Group on Audiovisual Policy, n. 6 above, for example conceded that, '... in Europe, the phenomenon of network globalisation is counterbalanced by cultural and linguistic diversity in content. Demand for domestic, regional or local material will remain a strong feature of the content market, alongside demand for certain "global" products (e.g. blockbusters).'

[19] 'Deviations from free trade are seen as particularly harmful for consumers in countries imposing import restrictions, as they deprive them of the cultural products that they want as sovereign individuals': Sauvé, P. and Steinfatt, K., n. 16 above, 323–352 at 327.

[20] 'A good is "public" if providing the good to *anyone* makes it possible, without additional cost, to provide it to *everyone*. A public good has two distinguishing features—non-rivalry and non-exclusivity. The essential problem with public goods is that it is difficult to get people to pay for goods where they do not have exclusive rights to consume the good in question (non-exclusivity) and when their consumption of the good does not affect the good itself (non-rivalry)'; Graham, A., 'Market Failure in the Broadcasting Industry', Department of Culture, Media and Sport, *The Future Funding of the BBC* (1999). Annex 8. See also Samuelson, P., 'The Pure Theory of Public Expenditure', 36(4) *The Review of Economics and Statistics* (November 1954) 387–389, and Olson. M., *The Logic of Collective Action*, 2nd edn (Harvard University Press, 1971).

[21] 'A merit good is a good whose value exceeds the valuation an individual would place upon it. Merit goods are deemed intrinsically desirable and provide one rationale for the government providing access to health care, museums and libraries, etc.' Davies Report, *Future Funding of the BBC*, Annex 8 'Market Failure in Broadcasting'. See also Graham, A. and Davies, G., *Broadcasting, Society and Policy in the Multimedia Age* (John Libby Media, 1997), and Peacock, A., 'Market failure and government failure in broadcasting', 20(4) *Economic Affairs* (2000), 2.

[22] *Future Funding of the BBC*, Annex 8, n. 20 above.

Despite these ambitious economic counter-arguments, the chief justifications for interventionist cultural policy remain essentially social and political. As the European Commission argued in response to pressure to liberalize access to the European audiovisual sector during the WTO Uruguay Round, '[c]ultural goods, especially cinema and television programmes, cannot be treated like other products: they are privileged mediums of identity pluralism and integration'.[23] In 1999, in setting out the principles underlying European audiovisual policy, it restated this position.

> The audiovisual industry is not an industry like any other and does not simply produce goods to be sold on the market like other goods. It is in fact a cultural industry par excellence, whose 'product' is unique and specific in nature. It has a major influence on what citizens know, believe and feel and plays a crucial role in the transmission, development and even construction of cultural identities.[24]

This position is moreover reasonably consistent with Europe's hierarchical approach to freedom of expression, which places greatest weight on the protection of politically significant speech.[25] State intervention in general entertainment content, particularly when its purpose is to preserve or expand content diversity, is in general not subject to the narrower margin of appreciation and stronger protections accorded to the discussion of political and social affairs. Where foreign news and public affairs commentary is readily available, moderate quotas on the broadcast of foreign drama and comedy programmes are arguably an acceptable infringement of freedom of expression under the European Convention on Human Rights.

The arrival of the global internet has radically changed the context of this debate. As early as the internet boom of the 1990s, long before the impact of mass public broadband access, communications and media convergence had begun to show its potential for a market driven explosion of socially and culturally diverse content.[26] The communications revolution had accelerated the production and distribution of culturally significant media content. Most importantly, digitization had begun to ease the congestion of analogue radiospectrum and cable transmission, enabling national media markets to work more efficiently and to improve cross border access to information and entertainment content, lowering costs and other barriers to participation in online media and significantly improving the commercial viability of specialist niches.[27]

---

[23] *Europe's way to the Information Society*—An Action Plan Communication from the European Commission to the Council and the European Parliament COM (94) 347 (19 July 1994).

[24] *Principles and Guidelines for the Community's Audiovisual Policy in the Digital Age* (COM (1999) 657 final), 7.

[25] On the core purposes of ECHR, Article 10, see Chapter 6.

[26] See, for example, *OECD Webcasting and Convergence: Policy Implications,* ECD/GD(97)221 (OECD, 1997), which argued that, 'the initial indications are that webcasting holds the potential for greater pluralism and cultural diversity—two of the traditional goals of broadcasting policy' (6.). See also European Ministerial Conference, *Global Information Networks: Realising the Potential,* Bonn, 6th–8th July 1997, Ministerial Declaration: 'Building on Europe's strengths'.

[27] According to MAVISE: Database on television channels and TV companies in the European Union (<http://mavise.obs.coe.int>), in September 2010, there were, for example, 832 television channels broadcasting using English language in Europe.

Yet the rise of a content rich, globalized media has transformed but not ended arguments over the ability of market forces to deliver deep cultural diversity. The world may be awash in content, but high quality, audiovisual content is still a premium product. Spectrum scarcity is no longer a major problem for developed economies, but other bottlenecks in the supply chain remain, including limited access to production funding and to revenue producing distribution channels. In a globalized, entertainment environment dominated by multinational content producers and aggregators, there is still a risk that local content production will lose its vibrancy and distinctiveness. Local cultures may slip from the mainstream to backwaters, sustained and altered by tourism.

Cultural protection in the European media sector

The European Union has pursued the integration of its own national media markets with some vigour. To achieve that result, however, European law has accumulated a thicket of compromises that balance protectionist national cultural policies and market access objectives. These compromises, hammered out over decades of negotiation between the member states and the Commission, were often achieved at the expense of Europe's trade partners, particularly the United States. Indeed, the European Union, the home of America's most powerful allies in creating the WTO, has been a key centre of resistance to American entertainment media export policies.

The biggest stumbling block for integration of media services into the European Single Market was the need to accommodate protectionist national broadcasting policies while also applying the EU's principles of free movement and fair competition.[28] For much of the past century, western European governments have relied on state owned or supported broadcasters to deliver a diverse range of cultural policy objectives.[29] Their national broadcasting regimes typically involved restrictions and privileges that blocked unauthorized access to domestic broadcast audiences and revenue streams. These included controls on advertising revenue, access to cable networks, and the domestic rebroadcast of foreign programmes as well as generous subsidies to national broadcasters. By the 1980s, with the arrival of satellite broadcasting, the tension between these national policies and European economic obligations had become acute. New commercial broadcasters demanded access to protected national markets. As one commentator noted,

The articulation, range and intensity of public service obligations imposed on, or adhered to, by European broadcasters varies markedly, as does the success of their realisation. It is

---

[28] As the Oreja report stated in 1998, 'there are two main principles: the first is that public television plays a vital role in most member states of the European Community . . . the second is that European economic integration is rooted in competition and the free market.' *Digital Age: European Audiovisual Policy*, Report from the High Level Group on Audiovisual Policy, n. 6 above.
[29] See Kelly, M., Mazzoleni G. and McQuail, D. (eds), *The Media in Europe: The Euromedia Handbook* (Sage, 2004).

precisely this relativity and lack of clarity with which public service obligations have tended to be expressed which now presents problems for a sector called upon to justify its privileges not only at the national but also at the European level.[30]

Any accommodation between domestic cultural policy in the media field and the removal of barriers to the European single market had to come to terms with the primary concerns of European governments. These included a deep concern that European popular culture was becoming subordinated to American popular culture, with a consequent loss of national identity and social cohesion. This anxiety can be traced back to the early rise of Hollywood to become the centre of the world's nascent cinema industry. European governments responded to this apparent cultural and economic threat by limiting American film imports, followed later by restrictions on television programme imports.[31]

The European argument for quotas and other defensive measures against American audiovisual entertainment goods and services has ultimately rested on the claim that the United States has permanent cost advantages. As one European study stated,

[t]he USA's television market—which is eight times the size of Europe's largest national markets of Germany and the UK—has the scale to fund large volumes of high-value drama and comedy. Although this output does not necessarily appeal directly to the various national cultures in Europe, high production values, plus the fact that most of the production cost has been recouped in the USA, means that such programming can prove extremely cost effective for commercially driven national European broadcasters . . . Once such an advantage is established, it can reinforce itself. The US industry becomes commercially vibrant and actively seeks overseas appeal, while foreign markets struggle to find a business model that works—capital, quality commercial management and creative talent flow into the US industry and out of the domestic sectors, helping to reinforce the US advantage. Global centres of creative excellence quickly develop in such knowledge-based industries, concentrating resources and investment in specific cities and regions such as Hollywood.[32]

In comparison, European authorities have argued that audiovisual production and distribution in Europe has historically been fragmented and under-capitalized.[33]

---

[30] Craufurd Smith, R., 'Getting the Measure of Public Services: Community Competition Rules and Public Service Broadcasting', *The Yearbook of Media and Entertainment Law* (1997/98), 147–175 at [148].

[31] See, for example, the United Kingdom's Cinematograph Films Act 1927, which introduced domestic film quotas for distributors and cinemas. See also Voon, T., *Cultural Products and the World Trade Organization* (Cambridge University Press, 2007), 44–50.

[32] Impact Study of Measures (Community and National) Concerning the Promotion of Distribution and Production of TV Programmes Provided for Under Article 25(a) of the TV Without Frontiers Directive, Final Report, May 2005. Similar arguments were put forward in *Digital Age: European Audiovisual Policy*, Report from the High Level Group on Audiovisual Policy, n. 6 above, [ch 2,1 and 2]; and, *Broadcasting Public Notice* Canadian Radio-television and Telecommunications Commission, CRTC *1999–84*, para. 61.

[33] See, for example, the Green Paper *Strategy Options to Strengthen the European Programme Industry in the Context of the Audiovisual Policy of the European Union* COM (94) 96 final, which argued that, 'the industry is increasingly characterised by a disjunction between a small number of well capitalised companies which control the electronic delivery systems, and are moving towards European

At the same time, European governments were facing the destabilization of revenue sources for national media as their once comparatively isolated media markets have been broken open by the commercial use of new communications technologies. The advent of satellite television broadcasting, in particular, opened a host of opportunities for commercial broadcasters to use favourable regulatory rules in one EU member state to create services for listeners and viewers in others. These inroads threatened to destabilize national providers as their advertising and sub-scription revenue began to drain away.[34] That cross border commercialization of Europe's electronic media services has continued at an even greater pace with the spread of broadband internet access.

The communications revolution has not only transformed broadcast era media laws and regulatory regimes, but also the character of the European liberal demo-cratic state. State intervention in the media for cultural and social policy purposes undoubtedly remains a core principle for many national media regimes. Their public service media have a protected status under EU law and enjoy long standing support in the Council of Europe.[35] Nonetheless, the European audiovisual sector has shifted decisively away from state provision towards the private, commercial sector, which has left the once unchallenged legitimacy of state intervention no longer secure. Under EU law, the conditions placed on state involvement in the media have steadily tightened, requiring greater transparency and clearer justifica-tions in the operation of public service media regimes.[36]

Content quotas in European media law

Cultural measures in the European media sector have predominantly taken the form of quotas that favour domestic content in culturally significant forms of entertainment media as well as subsidies that support public service media and domestic film industries. These quotas and subsidies create obvious and sometimes

integration, and on the other hand' (6). See also European Commission Communication, *The Future of European Regulatory Audiovisual Policy*, 15.12.2003 COM (2003) 784 final.

[34] Mowes, B., *A Media Policy for Tomorrow*, historical document prepared for the 6th European Ministerial Conference on Mass Media Policy (Cracow, June 2000).

[35] In the European Union, Article 22 of the Charter of Fundamental Rights of the European Union declares that, 'The Union shall respect cultural, religious and linguistic diversity.' The European Commission has moreover argued that, '[p]reservation and promotion of cultural diversity are among the founding principles of the European model.' Commission Communication, *Towards an international instrument on cultural diversity*, Brussels, 27.8.2003 COM (2003) 520 final. In the Council of Europe, the Committee of Ministers has repeatedly declared the importance of intervention in media markets to achieve cultural and social policy goals. See, for example, Committee of Ministers Recommendation on the promotion of audio-visual production in Europe, R (86) 3, Committee of Ministers Recommendation containing principles aimed at promoting the distribution and broadcast-ing of audio-visual works originated in countries or regions with a low audio-visual output or a limited geographic or linguistic coverage on the European television markets, Rec (93) 5, Committee of Ministers Declaration on Cultural Diversity (7 December 2000), and Committee of Ministers Recommendation on media pluralism and diversity of media content, Rec (2007) 2.

[36] On state aid and public service media, see below.

severe clashes with the market based principles of European economic law. The
European Union has consequently taken the lead in shaping European cultural
policy in the media sphere, despite its limited legislative competence in this field.
Conversely, close involvement in cultural and social policy has had a formative
effect on European Union law. It has forced the European Commission and the
European Court of Justice not only to recognize, but also to develop significant
non-market aspects of media law and policy.

During the 1980s, commercial conflicts between new satellite television broadcasters and EU member states brought a spate of broadcasting services cases before
the European Court of Justice. The Court moved cautiously in applying the
principles of free movement to these services, mindful of the importance of
the broadcast sector to national public policy.[37] The general thrust of its decisions
were clear enough: the rules of market integration could accommodate the discriminatory effects of social and cultural policies, provided safeguard provisions
were satisfied.[38] However, the specific application of the Court's position to the
diverse media regimes of the member states was not as self evident. In the wake of
these decisions, neither governments nor commercial broadcasters could be sure of
the legality of various national measures.

Faced with these conflicting uncertainties, the member states were willing to
compromise their differences and agree on the basic principles to govern cross
border television broadcasting in the Single Market.[39] The drafters of the resulting
directive, renamed the Audiovisual Media Services Directive in 2007, attempted to
maintain a balance between the economic objectives of European market integration and national social and cultural policies.[40] In pursuit of the former, the

---

[37] On free movement and cross border broadcasting, see Chapter 4.

[38] As the European Court of Justice affirmed in Case C-250/06, *United Pan-Europe Communications and others v. Belgium* [2007] ECR I-11135, 'first, that a cultural policy may constitute an
overriding requirement relating to the general interest which justifies a restriction on the freedom to
provide services ... Consequently, it must be accepted that the national legislation at issue pursues an
aim in the general interest, since it seeks to preserve the pluralist nature of the range of television
programmes and thus forms part of a cultural policy the aim of which is to safeguard, in the audiovisual
sector, the freedom of expression of the different social, cultural, religious, philosophical or linguistic
components which exist in that region.'

[39] See Hitchens, L.P., 'Identifying European Audiovisual Policy in the Dawn of the Information
Society', *The Yearbook of Media and Entertainment Law* (Oxford University Press, 1996), 45–73. See
also Green Paper *Strategy Options to Strengthen the European Programme Industry in the Context of the
Audiovisual Policy of the European Union* COM (94) 96 final, 'The European market and cultural
diversity' (450), and Schlesinger, P. and Doyle, G., 'Contradictions of Economy and Culture: the
European Union and the Information Society' 2(1) *Cultural Policy* (1995), which points out 'the
contradictory pull between industrial policy and cultural policy. We are being offered two distinct
images: one of a society of consumers founded in notions of economic choice, the other—increasingly
marginalised now at least in respect of media and communications policy—of a society of complexity
rooted in persistent cultural difference' (25).

[40] See Council Conclusions of December 2002 on the 'Television without Frontiers' Directive, OJ
C 13, 18.1.2003, which states that, '[t]he Council of the European Union ... recalls the underlying
principles on which the Directive is based, some of which can be summarized as follows:—to ensure
the free movement of television broadcasting services in the Community, on the basis of the country of
origin principle,—to promote cultural and linguistic diversity and the strengthening of the European
audiovisual industry,—to reinforce the indispensable role of television broadcasting in the democratic,
social, and cultural life of society.'

Directive imposes an obligation to permit the reception and retransmission of television broadcasts from other EU member states, based on the country of origin principle.[41]

To balance this powerful market integration element, the Directive contains other provisions to assist member states in safeguarding their major audiovisual content policies. Those provisions include the right of member states to impose stricter content obligations on domestic broadcasters than those required by the minimum standards of the Directive.[42] Member states can thus take advantage of the linguistic and cultural barriers that fragment Europe's media markets to impose local language and production obligations on domestic broadcasters, as 'much European audiovisual material reflects and addresses the tastes, interests and events, cultural preferences and languages of viewers in individual countries'.[43] Certainly, broadcasters can avoid these potentially burdensome domestic rules by re-establishing themselves in other member states. Major broadcasters, however, who are often the primary producers of culturally significant programme content, are often too closely wedded to their home markets to consider moving sufficient staff and facilities to qualify for the jurisdiction of a less demanding member state. The ECJ has moreover given this provision an emphatically broad interpretation, rejecting the demand that local language requirements need to be linked to specific cultural content objectives.[44]

In addition to this reserved right, Article 16 (previously Article 4) of the Directive famously requires that member states ensure that television broadcasters under their jurisdiction broadcast work to achieve at least 50 per cent European content in films, dramas, and other targeted programme genres.[45] The purpose of this obligation is to protect domestic programme production and distribution from American and other non-European competition.[46] Without a minimum European

---

[41] Directive 2010/13/EU of the European Parliament and of the Council of 10 March 2010 on the coordination of certain provisions laid down by law, regulation or administrative action in Member States concerning the provision of audiovisual media services (AVMS Directive), Recital (33), The country of origin principle should be regarded as the core of this Directive, as it is essential for the creation of an internal market. This principle should be applied to all audiovisual media services in order to ensure legal certainty for media service providers as the necessary basis for new business models and the deployment of such services. It is also essential in order to ensure the free flow of information and audiovisual programmes in the internal market.

[42] Ibid., Article 4(1).

[43] *Digital Age: European Audiovisual Policy*, Report from the High Level Group on Audiovisual Policy, n. 6 above.

[44] Case C-222/07, *Unión de Televisiones Comerciales Asociadas* (UTECA) *v. Administración General del Estado* [2009] 3 CMLR 2.

[45] Directive 2010/13/EU, n. 41 above, Article 16: 'Member States shall ensure where practicable and by appropriate means, that broadcasters reserve for European works, within the meaning of Article 6, a majority proportion of their transmission time, excluding the time appointed to news, sports events, games, advertising, teletext services and teleshopping. This proportion, having regard to the broadcaster's informational, educational, cultural and entertainment responsibilities to its viewing public, should be achieved progressively, on the basis of suitable criteria.'

[46] On the origins and early application of the European content requirement, see Salvatore, V., 'Quotas on TV Programmes and EEC Law', 29 *Common Market Law Review* (1992), 967–990; Drijvers, J., 'Community Broadcasting: A Manifesto for the Media Policy of Small European Countries', 14(2) *Media, Culture and Society* (1992); Collins, R., 'The Screening of Jacques Tati:

content requirement, a broadcaster could use a compliant member state as a base to transmit 100 per cent American content across Europe, relying on the country of origin principle.[47] This provision is also supported by a second quota requirement. Member states must ensure that television broadcasters aim to devote 10 per cent of their transmission time or programming budget to European works by independent producers.[48]

For several years, it was not clear that the European Union even possessed the legislative competence to adopt these obligations, whose justification is almost wholly cultural. The EU's limited competence to act in the cultural field was only convincingly secured by the 1993 Maastricht Treaty, whose provisions on competence in cultural matters are now contained in Article 167 of the Treaty on the Functioning of the European Union (TFEU).[49] While this may have secured the legislative basis for the Directive's content quotas, these provisions were drafted with deliberate ambiguity. According to Article 16, member states are only obliged to act 'where practicable and by appropriate means'. This cautious language is the result of strong differences between the negotiating governments on the appropriate methods for state intervention in media markets. Britain, for example, preferred to rely on subsidized domestic programme production through the BBC and other public service broadcasters and opposed the use of quotas, which were well established in France and other member states.[50]

The ambiguous language of the Directive's content quota provisions has given rise to serious compliance problems. Member states have used different interpretations to determine when these content obligations should apply and how they should be enforced.[51] The Commission has however taken a positive view of the evidence submitted by member states and reports a generally acceptable level of

---

Broadcasting and Cultural identity in the European Community', 11 *Cardozo Arts and Entertainment Law Journal* (1993), 361, De Witte, B., 'The European Content Requirement in the EC Television Directive', 1 *Yearbook of Media and Entertainment Law* (1995), 101; and Harrison, J. and Woods, L., 'Television Quotas: Protecting European Culture', 12(1) *Entertainment Law Review* (2001), 5–14.

[47] This in fact occurred for a period of years when the United Kingdom not applying Article 4 to 'non-domestic satellite services' established in the UK, Case C-222/94, *Commission of the European Communities v. United Kingdom* [1996] ECR I-4025. See also Case C-14/96, *Paul Denuit v. Kingdom of Belgium* [1997] ECR-2785.

[48] Directive 2010/13/EU, n. 41 above, Article 17. There is no European Union level definition of independent producer or independent production, but see Recital (31), which sets out general criteria to be taken into account.

[49] TFEU, Article 151(4), The Community shall take cultural aspects into account in its action under other provisions of this Treaty. See also Council Resolution of 21 January 2002 on the role of culture in the development of the European Union, (2002/C 32/02).

[50] Collins, R., 'The European Union Audiovisual Policies of the U.K. and France' in Scriven, M. and Lecomte, M. (eds), *Television Broadcasting in Contemporary France and Britain*, (Berghahn Books, 1999), 200.

[51] See Key Findings and Conclusions, *Final Report: Impact Study of Measures (Community and National) Concerning the Promotion of Distribution and Production of TV Programmes Provided for Under Article 25(a) of the TV Without Frontiers Directive*, David Graham and Associates Limited for the Audiovisual, Media and Internet Unit, Directorate-General Information Society and Media, European Commission, May 2005.

national enforcement.[52] Its willingness to accept reasonable efforts rather than strict compliance also has some justification. It is arguable that the breadth and flexibility of these provisions is necessary for obligations that apply to an expanding number of diverse television channels across the EU. New, financially vulnerable channels as well as thematic and other specialized channels will often have greater difficulty in achieving the content thresholds required by the Directive. The audiovisual markets for Europe's smaller language populations have historically also been hard pressed to fund substantial local production and, in these markets, American imports have tended to compete well against content from other European programme exporters.[53]

Beyond these problems of legislative intent, the Directive's positive content obligations are open to criticism for their crude cultural and economic protectionism. They shelter European production from international competition, which protects the market share and profitability of European broadcasters, but raises costs for consumers. These effects are moreover spread unevenly across member states. While the Directive's content obligations, in principle, aim to protect generic European programme production, in practice they primarily benefit the major production centres for each European language market.[54] Thus, from a market economic perspective, benign consumer choice is being frustrated by these barriers to access to non-European content.

The rise of broadband internet services has taken the debate over the Directive's cultural content obligations in new directions. On one view, protective national quotas should be adapted to all new forms of media that are culturally significant.[55] During the negotiations leading to the 2007 amendment of the Directive, the focus was on those on-demand programme services that had begun to compete directly with traditional broadcast television channels. Opponents of state intervention have however argued for well over a decade that market forces are the most effective means of providing diverse range of content in convergent, digitized forms of media.[56] Until the 2007 amendments, this argument carried enough weight within the EU to block the introduction of common cultural obligations relating to new media services.[57] The Electronic Commerce Directive, which previously governed on-demand as well as other new media services, merely recognized the right of

[52] See European Commission, Ninth Communication on the Application of Articles 4 and 5 of Directive 89/552/EEC, as amended by Directive 97/36/EC and Directive 2007/65/EC for the period 2007–2008, (6).

[53] European Commission, Third Communication on the Application of Directive 89/552/EEC, 'Television without Frontiers' COM (2001) 9 final.

[54] Harrison, J. and Woods, L., n. 46 above, 5–14.

[55] The merits of extending the AVMS Directive content quotas has been discussed since the rise of the new media in Europe, See, for example, *Building the European Information Society for us all*, Final policy report of the high-level expert group on the Information Society, for the European Commission, (15 April 1997), p. 57.

[56] Hitchens, L., 'Identifying European Audiovisual Policy in the Dawn of the Information Society', *Yearbook of Media and Entertainment Law* (Clarendon Press, 1996), pp. 44–73, at 61.

[57] Nenova, B., 'The New Audiovisual Media Services Directive: Television *Without* Frontiers, Television *Without* Cultural Diversity', 44 *Common Market Law Review* (2007), 1689.

member states to derogate from single market rules where necessary to promote cultural and linguistic diversity.[58] The amended AVMS Directive now obliges member states to ensure that on-demand audiovisual media services under their jurisdiction 'promote, where practicable and by appropriate means, the production of and access to European works'.[59] Looking forward, as other new entertainment media develop, such as online games having a major dramatic context, the debate over cultural dominance and protective measures is sure to follow.

Changes in technologies and services have also made it increasingly difficult to determine the definitional boundaries for content that satisfies the European quota obligation. The drafters defined 'European works' according to the geographical ties of programme production, as no sensible legal distinction could be made between European and foreign cultural influences.[60] Yet this definition strengthened the claim that the quotas are essentially economic protectionism as the categorization of a work as European turns on how investors and producers choose to structure programme production. The arbitrariness of the European works definition has moreover increased with the globalization of film and programme production.

Despite nearly two decades of criticism, the AVMS Directive's content obligations survived the 2007 amendment process without change. While unmistakably protectionist, they have nonetheless been judged moderately successful in pushing member states to promote European audiovisual programme production and distribution.[61] Leaving the major burden on linear television broadcasters also has a certain logic, despite the growing importance of competing new audiovisual entertainment services. Through the rise of new media services, the major national broadcasters have continued to be important producers of dramas and other high cost, culturally significant forms of audiovisual content, regardless of whether that content is broadcast or made available through the internet.[62]

Cultural policy is a stepchild in the European Union, where it was first only recognized as a legitimate ground for derogation from the primary EU goals of free movement and fair competition in the single market. The broad competence of the

---

[58] Directive 2000/31/EC of the European Parliament and of the Council of 8 June 2000 on certain legal aspects of information society services, in particular electronic commerce, in the Internal Market (Electronic Commerce Directive). Article 1(6) On the Electronic Commerce Directive generally, see Chapter 4.

[59] Directive 2010/13/EU, n. 41 above, Article 13 and Recital (70).

[60] Ibid., Article 1(1)(n).

[61] Eighth Communication from the Commission to the European Parliament, the Council, the European Economic and Social Committee and the Committee of the Regions on the application of Articles 4 and 5 of Directive 89/552/EEC 'Television without Frontiers', as amended by Directive 97/36/EC, for the period 2005–2006, COM (2008) 481 final, 'The above results show a generally positive picture as regards the objectives of Article 4. Overall, the majority proportion required by Article 4 has largely been achieved by the Member States, including the new Member States, the average proportion having stabilised at a relatively high level of over 63%, well above the 50% minimum set by the Directive, with continuously rising compliance rates' (9).

[62] See, for example, United Kingdom Office of Communications, (OFCOM), *Communications Market Report* (19 August 2010), Section 1.6.6 Spending by public service broadcasters on television and radio content across the UK's nations.

Council of Europe in social matters therefore makes it the more obvious forum for the development of common principles in the cultural field.[63] Indeed, the CE Committee of Ministers has adopted several instruments regarding the validity of national and European measures to protect cultural diversity. As its Declaration on Cultural Diversity states, '[C]ultural diversity has always been a dominant European characteristic and a fundamental political objective in the process of European construction, and that it assumes particular importance in the building of an information and knowledge based society in the 21st Century'.[64] In the media sector, the Committee of Ministers has emphasized the importance of public service media to the achievement of cultural policy goals.[65]

Despite this broad competence and purposeful rhetoric in cultural matters, the Council of Europe's efforts to define cultural policy in the media field have been largely hortatory, with the major exception of the Transfrontier Television Convention. This treaty obliges state parties to maintain protective content quotas for European works in culturally significant programmes.[66] These provisions are modelled on the content quota rules of the EU Audiovisual Media Service Directive, although the definition of European works is different.[67] Their major purpose is to extend the Directive's rules to European states outside the EU, provided of course they can be persuaded to become parties to this treaty. As the European Union has expanded or concluded cooperation agreements with non-members, the Convention has however declined in importance.

The European Court of Human Rights, which usually leads the development of CE legal principles affecting the media, has had comparatively little to say about cultural policy in this area. In several important cases, the Court has given an

---

[63] The 1989 European Convention on Transfrontier Television (ETS No. 132), the Council of Europe's parallel instrument to the Directive, contains similar content obligations. See Article 10 Cultural objectives. See also Council of Europe, Warsaw Declaration 2005: '6. We shall foster European identity and unity, based on shared fundamental values, respect for our common heritage and cultural diversity. We are resolved to ensure that our diversity becomes a source of mutual enrichment, inter alia, by fostering political, inter-cultural and inter-religious dialogue. We will continue our work on national minorities, thus contributing to the development of democratic stability. In order to develop understanding and trust among Europeans, we will promote human contacts and exchange good practices regarding free movement of persons on the continent, with the aim of building a Europe without dividing lines.' See also Council of Europe Treaties: European Cultural Convention 1954 (ETS No. 018), European Agreement concerning Programme Exchanges by means of Television Films (1958), Framework Convention for the protection of national minorities (1995).

[64] Committee of Ministers, Declaration on Cultural Diversity (7 December 2000).

[65] See, for example, Council of Europe, Committee of Ministers Recommendation on media pluralism and diversity of media content CM/Rec (2007) 2, Committee of Ministers Recommendation to member states on the remit of public service media in the information society Rec (2007) 3, and, Committee of Ministers, Declaration on Cultural Diversity (7 December 2000).

[66] European Convention on Transfrontier Television, n. 63 above, Article 10.

[67] Under the Convention, ibid., 'European audiovisual works' means creative works, the production or co-production of which is controlled by European natural or legal persons (Article 2), which is considerably less precise than the Directive. The 2008 proposed amendments to the Convention would not have eliminated this difference. See Secretariat note on the amendments to the European Convention on Transfrontier Television as proposed by the Drafting Group of the Standing Committee on Transfrontier Television, September, 2008. On the failure of the amendments, see Chapter 6.

expansive interpretation to the third sentence of Article 10(1) of the ECHR, which recognizes the right of state parties to license the broadcast media.[68] According to the Court, the legitimate objectives of broadcast licensing include 'such matters as the nature and objectives of a proposed station, its potential audience at national, regional or local level, the rights and needs of a specific audience'.[69] State parties may therefore take linguistic and cultural factors into account when awarding licences or imposing licence obligations. From a more market oriented conception of free speech, these state restrictions on freedom of speech are illegitimate as they prefer one kind of content over another.

European content quotas do not however close media markets to foreign sourced content. Their effect is to reduce market opportunities, which translates poorly into a claim of an infringement of a specific person's Article 10 right to freedom of expression. These quotas are moreover directed at the protection of domestic drama and other fiction genres rather than news and current affairs content. They are therefore less likely to restrict public access to foreign supplied information concerning matters of political and social importance, which is the most strongly protected form of expression under the ECHR. Yet, changes in communications and media services continue to reshape the circumstances in which Article 10 operates. As digitization increases the audiovisual transmission capacity of radio-spectrum or cable, the rejection of licence applicants on cultural or social content grounds has become much more difficult to justify. Nevertheless, while extensive state media monopolies are no longer acceptable, the principle of state involvement in the production and supply of media content is still celebrated in European human rights law.[70]

Subsidies, state aid, and public service media

The Audiovisual Media Services Directive solution to the problem of content quotas has been a relative success. The Article 16 European content rule created a significant barrier to non-European works and reserved the right to impose stricter domestic obligations, which gave member states further leeway to impose language or production obligations on television providers under their jurisdiction. The Directive does not however address the problem of national media subsidies and their effects on competition in the European Single Market. This issue has

---

[68] See *Demuth v. Switzerland* (Application No. 38743/97) (5 November 2002), para. 33. See also, on the third sentence of ECHR, Article 10(1) and pluralism, Chapter 14.

[69] Ibid.

[70] On public monopolies in the broadcast sector, see *Informationsverein Lentia and Others v. Austria,* (Application No. 37093/97) (24 November 1993), and *Tele 1 Privatfernsegesellschaft v. Austria* (Application No. 32240/96) (21 September 2000). See also Council of Europe, Committee of Ministers, Recommendation on measures to promote the public service value of the Internet, Rec (2007) 16.

fallen to EU competition law, where special rules have been developed to protect subsidized public service media from the EU prohibition on state aid.[71]

For the member states, targeted subsidies are often an effective way to achieve social and cultural public policy goals in the media. Given the highly qualitative nature of these goals, governments have frequently combined state funding with state ownership of the principal public service media.[72] Qualitative, positive obligations, which are difficult to impose on private, commercial providers, can thus be built into both the mandate and institutional culture of a public broadcaster. European Union law also broadly accepts the legitimacy of this model, provided that the distorting effects on trade and competition in the Single Market are properly contained.[73] As the European Commission declared in 1999, 'Public service television plays an important role in the member states of the European Community: this is true with regard to cultural and linguistic diversity, educational programming, in objectively informing public opinion, in guaranteeing pluralism and in supplying, on a free to air basis, quality programming.'[74] The European Union, moreover, has injected its own subsidy programmes into the audiovisual media sector.[75]

These state funded or supported media, however, enjoy obvious advantages over Europe's commercially funded television providers. In many programme genres, public service providers offer free or subsidized content that competes directly with privately held media businesses.[76] For over a decade, the European Union has struggled to create a clear, principled method of limiting the impact of public service media on competitive media markets. The key difficulty has been to settle on the conditions that restrict the use state resources to support media services. In a market based system, the provision of goods and services by the state is an

[71] Bron, C., 'Financing and Supervision of Public Service Broadcasting', in *Public Service Media: Money for Content, IRIS Plus*, 2010–4 (Strasbourg, June 2010). See also Craufurd Smith, R., n. 30 above.

[72] Gripsrud, J., 50 years of European television: an essay', in Gripsrud, J. and Weibull, L., *Media, Markets & Public Spheres: European Media at the Crossroads* (Intellect, 2010).

[73] On Services of a General Economic Interst (SGEI) see also Chapter 4, and see Szyszczak, E., *The Regulation of the State in Competitive Markets in the European Union* (Hart Publishing, 2007), ch 7.

[74] European Commission, *Principles and Guidelines for the Community's Audiovisual Policy in the Digital Age* (COM (1999) 657 final), See also Communication from the Commission on the application of State aid rules to public service broadcasting, (2009/C 257/01), 2. The Role of Public Service Broadcasting.

[75] Decision No. 1718/2006/EC of the European Parliament and of the Council of 15 November 2006 concerning the implementation of a programme of support for the European audiovisual sector (MEDIA 2007), which is a single programme with a budget of (€755 million over seven years (2007–2013) focusing on pre and post-production activities (distribution and promotion). The previous MEDIA support programmes include MEDIA I (1990–1995), MEDIA II (1996–2000), and MEDIA Plus (2001–2005). On the policy background, see European Commission, Green Paper *Strategy Options to Strengthen the European Programme Industry in the Context of the Audiovisual Policy of the European Union* COM (94) 96 final, which argued that, 'the safeguarding of the diversity of national and regional cultures, often expressed in terms of maintaining the choice available to the public, is now clearly linked to the development of a predominantly European programme industry which must ultimately be profitable' (4).

[76] See, for example, in the United Kingdom, Richard Lambert, *Independent Review of BBC News 24*, for the Department of Culture, Media and Sport, (December 2002).

466

unavoidably controversial issue, raising core questions about the legitimate purposes and limits of the state.[77] In the European broadcasting sector, these issues have been acutely sensitive. Radio and television services were introduced directly or indirectly by the state and the legacy of that state provision of broadcasting remains practically and symbolically influential. Moreover, the basic concept of public service media is extraordinarily broad and uncertain. Originally confined to the broadcast sector, it has evolved to include new communications platforms, such as the internet, and new interactive media genres and services.[78]

It has fallen to European Union competition law to provide the major conceptual devices and rules that determine the proper limits for public service media in the member states. Where a public broadcaster, for example, occupies a dominant position in the national market, it is constrained by European competition law from abusing that dominance.[79] This includes unfairly entering markets outside its public service remit or unfairly excluding external suppliers from its own services.[80] More importantly, European Union disciplines controlling the grant of state aid apply to the transfer of public resources to media providers for cultural and social policy objectives. In principle, Article 107(1) of the TFEU prohibits state aid that distorts competition in cross border markets by favouring particular undertakings.[81] This key provision is however limited by exceptions that protect the right of member states to use selective subsidies for important domestic public policy purposes. The legality of public service media rests on a dynamic balance between these opposing provisions.

The scope of the Article 107(1) prohibition, firstly, does not necessarily capture all national measures used to support public service media, even when they distort markets. State aid must involve a transfer of state resources that favours particular undertakings. A state mandated benefit, such as preferential access to cable or satellite television distribution systems, may therefore fall outside that definition if no state resource is transferred, despite the obvious commercial advantage bestowed.[82] Public service media providers in several European states also enjoy preferential access to broadcast rights for major sports events.[83] These schemes are

---

77   See Szyszczak, E., n. 73 above.

[78]   On this transition, see Ferrell Lowe, G. and Bardoel, J. (eds), *From Public Service Broadcasting to Public Service Media* (Nordicom, 2007).

[79]   Case 155/73, *Sacchi* [1974] ECR 409, para. 15.

[80]   See Case 311/84, *Centre belge d'études de marché—Télémarketing v. SA Compagnie luxembourgeoise de télédiffusion (CLT) and Information publicité Benelux* [1985] ECR 3261, and, Case C-260/89, *Elliniki Radiophonia Tiléorassi AE v. Dimotiki Etairia Pliroforissis and others* [1991] ECR I-2925.

[81]   TFEU, Article 107(1). Save as otherwise provided in this Treaty, any aid granted by a Member State or through State resources in any form whatsoever which distorts or threatens to distort competition by favouring certain undertakings or the production of certain goods shall, insofar as it affects trade between Member States, be incompatible with the common market.

[82]   See, for example, the Commission Decision concerning the complaint of *Verband Privater Rundfunk und Telekommunikation (VPRT)* against *Arbeitsgemeinschaft der Öffentlich-rechlichen Landesrundfunkanstalten der Bundesrepublik Deutschland (ARD)* and *Zweites Deutsches Fernsehen (ZDF)*, OJ C238, 21.8.1999, 3. On 'must carry' obligations, see Chapter 14.

[83]   Schoenthal, M., 'Major Events and Reporting Rights', *IRIS Plus: Legal Observations of the European Audiovisual Observatory*, April 2006. On 'listed events', see Chapter 14.

intended to ensure that most national residents have the opportunity to view these socially important events live. They also typically and disproportionately benefit the public service media, whose main channels are usually amongst those universally available free to air and are therefore the preferred delivery platform for listed events. Yet, as no state resources are transferred, these listed events schemes do not amount to state aid. European law also excuses any resulting obstacles to the free movement of services.[84]

Nor is it always the case that a transfer of funds or other resources by a member state to a particular undertaking will amount to prohibited state aid. Article 107(1) is not intended to prevent governments from, in effect, purchasing the supply of public services from public or private providers under market conditions. The European Court of Justice affirmed this principle in its important *Altmark* decision in 2003.[85] In that case, the Court also determined that state funding of this kind must satisfy rigorous conditions to avoid classification as state aid, which remarkably few public service media funding schemes have satisfied.[86] National public service broadcasting regimes typically developed over decades and, when instituted, were neither awarded through public tender nor tested against market equivalent conditions. Although the Court of First Instance has obliquely suggested that some public service broadcasters might satisfy the *Altmark* criteria, the concept of services purchased under market conditions has had little impact on the development of EU rules for state aid to public service media.[87]

In most cases, state media funding therefore needs be sheltered in some other way from the Article 107(1) prohibition on state aid. The vast range of public service media objectives do not however fit easily into the Article 107 permitted exceptions. The Article 107(3) exception for the promotion of culture and heritage is, for example, too narrow to include the educational and democratic purposes that are normally a major element in European public service media remits.[88] This

[84] Directive 2010/13/EU, n. 41 above, Article 14.

[85] Case C-280/00, *Altmark Trans GmbH v. Regierungspräsidium Magdeburg*. See also Case C-53/00, *Ferring SA v. Agence centrale des organismes de securite sociale* [2001] ECR I-9067. See also Louis, F. and Vallery, A., '*Ferring* Revisited: the *Altmark* Case and State Financing of Public Services Obligations', 57 *World Competition* (2004), 53.

[86] *Altmark*, n. 85 above. 'First, the recipient undertaking must actually have public service obligations to discharge, and the obligations must be clearly defined. Second, the parameters on which the compensation is calculated must be established beforehand in an objective and transparent manner. Third, the compensation does not exceed what is necessary to cover all or part of the costs incurred in discharging the public service obligations. Fourth, if the undertaking discharging the public service obligations is not chosen in a public procurement procedure, the level of compensation needed must be determined according to the costs that a typical undertaking, well run and adequately provided with means, would incur to fulfill those obligations.' See also Communication (2009/C 257/01), n. 74 above, para. 23.

[87] Cases T-309/04, T-317/04, T-329/04, and T-336/04, *TV2 Danmark et al. v. Commission*, para. 203, See also Case T-442/03, *SIC—Sociedade Independente de Comunicação, SA v. Commission of the European Communities*, para. 159.

[88] TFEU, Article 107(3). The following may be considered to be compatible with the common market: '(d) aid to promote culture and heritage conservation where such aid does not affect trading conditions and competition in the Community to an extent that is contrary to the common interest.' See also Commission Decision concerning the complaint of *Verband Privater Rundfunk und Telekommunikation (VPRT)*, n. 82 above, 3.

exception has, nonetheless, provided a sufficient legal basis to justify national subsidies and other forms of state aid to domestic film industries.[89]

Consequently, the defence of subsidized media rests primarily on Article 106(2) of the TFEU, which concerns 'services of general economic interest' (SGEI).[90] Given the substantial, if conditional, shelter the SGEI principle offers from both free movement and competition rules, it has an obvious attraction for member states that fund public service media. Under European Union law, these media undertakings are engaged in public purposes that the Commission has expressly recognized as being services of general economic interest.[91] The problem, as ever, has been to determine proper limits for those services as well as the conditions under which they enjoy an exemption from the state aid prohibition, which has required compromises of political principle as well as economic interest. Public service media providers, often influential domestic institutions in their own right, have been anxious to protect not only their funding, but also their freedom to provide a broad range of content and to expand into new media services.[92] Commercial media companies, on the other hand, have pressed hard for the development of effective restrictions on all these fronts.[93]

---

[89] See Council Resolution on national aid to the film and audiovisual industries (2001/C73/02), Commission communication on certain legal aspects relating to cinematographic and other audiovisual works, COM (2001) 534 final, Commission Communication of 28 January 2009 concerning the State aid assessment criteria of the Commission communication on certain legal aspects relating to cinematographic and other audiovisual works (Cinema Communication) of 26 September 2001, OJ C31, 7.2.2009, Communication, (2009/C 257/01), n. 74 above, 5. Assessment of the Compatibility of State Aid under Article 87(3). See also Council of Europe, Committee of Ministers, Recommendation on national film policies and the diversity of cultural expressions, Rec (2009) 7E, and, Broche, J., Chatterjee, O., Orssich, I., and Tosics, N., 'State aid for films—a policy in motion?' *Competition Policy Newsletter*, No. 1 (2007), 44.

[90] See also Article 36, Charter of Fundamental Rights of the European Union; TFEU, Article 14, and, Protocol on Services of General Interest (Treaty of Lisbon). On 'services of general interest' and 'services of a general economic interest', see Chapter 4.

[91] 'The broadcast media play a central role in the functioning of modern democratic societies, in particular in the development and transmission of social values. Therefore, the broadcasting sector has, since its inception, been subject to specific regulation in the general interest. This regulation has been based on common values, such as freedom of expression and the right of reply, pluralism, protection of copyright, promotion of cultural and linguistic diversity, protection of minors and of human dignity, consumer protection': Communication from the Commission—*Services of general interest in Europe* (2001/C 17/04). No similar statement appears in the 2007 European Commission Communication on 'Services of general interest, including social services of general interest: a new European commitment', COM (2007) 725, which does nonetheless refer to public service broadcasting.

[92] See, for example, European Broadcasting Union (EBU) contributions to the Review of the Communication from the Commission on the application of State aid rules to public service broadcasting, including EBU Reply to the Commission's questionnaire (March 2008), EBU Contribution to the Commission's second public consultation (January 2009), and, EBU Comments on the second draft revised Broadcasting Communication of 8 April 2009 (May 2009) (<http://www.ebu.ch>).

[93] Association of Commercial Television in Europe (ACT), *Comments on the second draft Communication on State Aid and Public Broadcasting* (<http://www.acte.be>) (May 2009). See also Association of Commercial Television in Europe, International Communications Round Table, European Newspapers Association, European Publishers Council, and Association of European Radios, *Broadcasting and Competition Rules in the Future EU Constitution: A View from the Private Media Sector*, May 2003, and Association of Commercial Television in Europe, Association Européenne des Radios, European

In 1997, the EU member states adopted the Amsterdam Protocol on public service broadcasting, a short, subsidiary treaty to what is now the TFEU.[94] This instrument set out a basic formula for the treatment of public service broadcasting under Article 106(2).[95] The Protocol, by implication, rejects the argument that state aid can only be justified in programme genres where a competitive market clearly fails to provide adequate supply of content.[96] Instead, it affirms a broader purpose, declaring that public service broadcasting is directly related to a society's democratic, social, and cultural needs as well as its need to preserve media pluralism. The Protocol also declares the right of member states to confer, define, and organize those services, effectively pushing back the demand for a rigorous, restrictive definition. State funded broadcasters may therefore validly transmit sports programmes, game shows, and popular dramas as well as content for niche audiences.

Despite these important concessions, the Protocol is an application of Article 106(2) and is therefore subject to the general rules on SGEI developed by the General Court, the ECJ, and the Commission.[97] And while the Courts have generally supported a broad discretion for member states in setting the remit for public service media, they have also indicated that operation purely as a commercial provider is beyond the limits of Article 106(2).[98] The Commission's interest is to ensure not only that the remits of national public service media are clearly defined and entrusted, but also that the exemption claimed from the EU's free movement and competition rules is no more than necessary for the performance of the service.[99] In addition, the Commission has demanded that the funding arrangements meet Community transparency standards.[100]

Spurred by the complaints of commercial broadcasters, the Commission has investigated numerous national, subsidized public service media regimes.[101] In

---

Publishers Council, *Safeguarding the Future of the European Audiovisual Market: A White Paper on the Financing and Regulation of Publicly Funded Broadcasters*, March 2004.

[94] Protocol on the System of Public Broadcasting in the Member States, Treaty of Amsterdam amending the Treaty on European Union, the Treaties establishing the European Communities and certain related Acts, 2 October 1997. See also Council Resolution concerning public service broadcasting, (1999/C 30/01).

[95] Important groundwork for the Amsterdam Protocol occurred at the Council of Europe, Prague Conference of European Ministers responsible for the media, which adopted a Resolution on The Future of Public Service Broadcasting.

[96] Communication (2009/C 257/01), n. 74 above, 6.1. Definition of public service remit; see also Cases T-309/04 etc., *TV2/Danmark*, n. 87 above, para. 123. 'As TV2 A/S rightly submits, when the Member States define the remit of public service broadcasting, they cannot be constrained by the activities of the commercial television channels.'

[97] 2007 European Commission Communication on 'Services of general interest, including social services of general interest: a new European commitment', COM (2007) 725.

[98] Cases T-309/04 etc., *TV2/Danmark*, n. 87 above, regarding purely commercial services, see also Case T-442/03, *SIC v. Commission*, n. 87 above.

[99] Communication (2009/C 257/01), n. 74 above, 6.2. Entrustment and supervision.

[100] Ibid., 6.4. Transparency requirements for the State aid assessment. On the transparency obligations of European Union law more generally, see Chapter 9.

[101] See for example, Commission Decision on the ad hoc financing of Dutch public service broadcasters, C2/2004/ (ex NN 170/2003).

many cases, the Commission has found that they comply with the generous terms applied to public service broadcasting under Article 106(2), or at least can do so with modifications.[102] The Commission has however shown greater concern regarding the expanding range of online activities pursued by state supported media.[103] In Britain, for example, Commission concerns, voiced following complaints from commercial competitors, brought about the closure of a major BBC project to provide online educational resources.[104] This move into new media has become a defining issue for the future of the European public service media model. There is certainly a good argument for the transformation of traditional public service broadcasting into a multi-platform public service provider that meets changing public needs and expectations.[105] Yet that transformation is bringing state subsidies into areas not previously part of the broadcasting sector, arguably disadvantaging commercial competitors and deterring private investment.

In principle, Article 106(2) can be used to protect state funding for the internet based public service media. As early as 1999, the EU Council asserted that 'public service broadcasting is not limited to traditional services and includes the development and diversification of activities in the digital age and that it is legitimate for public service broadcasting to seek to reach wide audiences'.[106] Given the instability of commercial funding models for the media, it is also plain that subsidised media providers will continue to be key vehicles for national cultural policy. But the terms on which the public service media provide new media services are still very much in debate.[107] The Commission, for its part, has opposed any expansion beyond the conceptual boundaries approved under the Protocol.[108] The underlying problem is to distinguish legitimate moves into new methods of content

---

[102] Commission decisions on State aid to public service broadcasting (1999–2010), (<http://ec.europa.eu/competition/sectors/media/decisions_psb.pdf>).

[103] See, for example, Commission Decision on measures implemented by Denmark for TV2/Danmark No C 2/2003 (ex NN 22/02), 19 May 2004.

[104] See Commission Decision regarding United Kingdom, BBC Digital Curriculum, N 37/2003, and, BBC Trust suspends BBC Jam, 14 March 2007 (BBC news report).

[105] See OFCOM, *A New Approach to Public Service Content in the Digital Media Age: The Potential Role of the Public Service Broadcaster*, January 2007. See also Widemann, V., 'Public Service Broadcasting, State aid, and the Internet: Emerging EU Law' in *Diffusion online* 2004/47. The European Commission has also conceded that public service broadcasters can legitimately move into new forms of media. See Commission, 2008 Review of the Communication from the Commission on the Application of State Aid Rules to Public Service Broadcasting, in which it stated, 'The Commission's overall objective is to design an appropriate legal framework for the future financing of public service broadcasting in a new media environment.'

[106] Resolution of the Council and of the Representatives of the Governments of the Member States concerning Public Service Broadcasting (1999/C 30/01). See also Council of Europe, Committee of Ministers, Recommendation to promote the democratic and social contribution of digital broadcasting, Rec (2003) 9, 2.2 Principles applicable to public service broadcasting, a. Remit of public service broadcasting, Clause 19, and Committee of Ministers, Recommendation on the remit of public service media in the information society, Rec (2007) 3, Clause 19.

[107] See, for example, Graber, C., 'State Aid for Digital Games and Cultural Diversity: A Critical Reflection in the Light of EU and WTO Law', NCCR Trade Regulation Working Paper No. 08 (2009).

[108] See Depypere, S. and Tigchelaar, N., The Commission's state aid policy on activities of public service broadcasters in neighbouring markets, *Competition Policy Newsletter*, No. 2 (2004), 19.

distribution from new activities that are outside the established purposes of public service media. The communications revolution has brought new media services, such as social networking media, where the interactive method of communication is both an aspect of distribution and the media form itself.

Trade and culture in the Uruguay Round

In contrast to the European Union, work in the WTO on the issue of trade liberalization and domestic cultural policies has progressed little over the past two decades. The issue was a major stumbling block for the Uruguay Round and has not seen significant progress in the Doha Round. Instead, the focus of debate has moved outside the WTO to the negotiation of bilateral and other free trade agreements and to the recent UNESCO Convention on Cultural Diversity. Disagreements over trade and culture in the WTO over the past two decades have, in large measure, been a consequence of Europe's success in finding its own regional solutions to this issue. These were built on compromises between European states that could not be transferred to the international sphere because of their protectionist nature and, for the same reason, could not be reconciled with the disciplines of global trade liberalization. The United States has, in particular, objected to any special exceptions for cultural policy measures in the media sector, having been for decades the chief target for the protectionist cultural policies of its trade partners.

In the long centuries of the print media era, governments regularly banned or restricted the import of foreign publications because of their language or cultural content. Their motivations however were more often political or religious than economic. It was only with the growth of the cinema film industry that the question of economic protectionism became inseparable from national claims of cultural preservation. Films were not only hugely popular and influential, but they could also be produced abroad without local financial or creative participation. This was unprecedented in popular entertainment. The United States quickly emerged in the 1920s as the leading producer and exporter of films for this new international market. But just as quickly, European governments sought to limit the impact on their own fledgling film industries by imposing screen quotas and other import restrictions.[109] Two decades later, when the United States and its market economy allies drafted the original General Agreement on Trade and Tariffs, the right to maintain film import quotas was preserved.[110] Under Article IV, state parties enjoy a conditional right to impose screen quotas that are exempt from the GATT's MFN and national treatment principles.[111]

---

[109] See Sauvé, P. and Steinfatt, K., n. 16 above, 323.

[110] Voon, T., *Cultural Products and the World Trade* (Cambridge University Press, 2007), 92–96. The Havana Charter of 1948 establishing the International Trade Organisation, which was abandoned for lack of American support, also recognized the right of state parties to retain screen quotas (Article 19, Chapter IV).

[111] General Agreement on Tariffs and Trade 1994 (incorporating GATT 1947), (15 April 1994), 33 ILM 1153 (1994), Article III(10). The provisions of this Article shall not prevent any contracting

GATT Article IV provided valuable protection for domestic film industries from foreign competition. The question therefore soon arose whether its terms could also be applied to television programme videotapes sold for broadcast in other countries. In 1961 the United States pressed its trading partners to accept that, while this was also a trade in goods subject to the GATT, it fell outside the Article IV derogation.[112] Despite the logic of that argument, it left state parties wishing to protect domestic television content production in a near defenceless position, as the GATT offered no general exception for domestic cultural policies.[113] This issue was, however, never definitively resolved under the GATT. It simply festered until the larger question of liberalizing international trade in audiovisual content broke open during the Uruguay Round trade negotiations.

Once the United States and the western Europeans agreed to include a new instrument to govern the liberalization of trade in services in the Uruguay Round objectives it was plain that a confrontation over media services was looming.[114] The application of non-discrimination disciplines and prohibitions on quantitative restrictions under the proposed GATS treaty could potentially force the removal of many discriminatory barriers to the cross border transmission of foreign films and television programmes.[115] Given its formidable comparative advantage in the production and distribution of audiovisual entertainment, the United States government made a determined effort to achieve liberalization commitments in this sector. It argued that trade liberalization in media services would not only advance the general economic interest, but would also increase the international flow of information and ideas, advancing the cause of freedom of speech.[116] At the time, these arguments seemed resonant with the force of historical change. Not only was the Soviet Union in decline, but global communications services, including satellite television, were developing at an extraordinary pace.

The European view was mixed. While Britain was generally receptive to American arguments, France and other European governments had deep reservations. An international agreement on trade in services threatened the difficult compromises reached in the recently concluded Television Without Frontiers Directive (now the

---

party from establishing or maintaining internal quantitative regulations relating to exposed cinematograph films and meeting the requirements of Article IV. Any exemption claimed under Article IV may not be increased at a later date, WTO document MTN.GNS/AUD/W/1, 4, 10, 1990. On the GATT generally, see Chapter 5.

[112] See Voon, T., n. 110 above, 94.

[113] GATT, Article XIX only provides emergency protection against the import of particular goods. Article XX(f) allows member states to adopt measures, 'imposed for the protection of national treasures of artistic, historic or archaeological value'. That limited exception is moreover subject to further conditions contained in the 'chapeau' to Article XX.

[114] Graber, C., 'Audio-visual policy: the stumbling block of trade liberalisation', in Geradin, D. and Luff, D. (eds), *The WTO and Global Convergence in Telecommunications and Audio-visual Services* (Cambridge University Press, 2004).

[115] See Sauvé, P. and Steinfatt, K., n. 16 above, 326. General Agreement on Trade in Services, (15 April 1994), 33 ILM 1167 (1994). On the GATS generally, see Chapter 5.

[116] Ibid. See also Wunsch-Vincent, S., *The WTO, The Internet and Trade in Digital Products*, (Hart Publishing, 2006), 122, and Braithwaite, J. and Drahos, P., *Global Business Regulation* (Cambridge University Press, 2000), 523.

Audiovisual Media Services Directive). The decision to include a minimum European content requirement in the Directive was, for example, a deliberate quantitative barrier erected against US and other non-European audiovisual imports. These concerns prevailed, shaping the European Union's position on audiovisual services during the Uruguay Round.[117]

While the architecture of the GATS offered great flexibility to the negotiating states in deciding how far any services sector should be subject to trade disciplines, that flexibility was also designed to wane over time.[118] GATS sectoral commitments are not only subject to obligations to accord national treatment and remove restrictive quotas, but are also subject to the GATS general obligation to pursue further liberalization in subsequent negotiations.[119] These commitments are, moreover, difficult and costly to retract.[120] European negotiators therefore focused on the creation of a special provision to shelter audiovisual services permanently from GATS trade disciplines.[121] This would need to be more than an express exception for national measures necessary to protect domestic cultural interests. According to the rules of interpretation that were likely to apply to the GATS, any exception to the main purposes of the treaty would be read restrictively.[122] Consequently, a cultural exception could easily be whittled away by WTO dispute resolution panels applying rigorous necessity tests to the imprecise, qualitative goals of cultural policy.[123]

The Canadian government proposed the radical alternative of a wholesale exclusion of the audiovisual sector from the GATS.[124] This followed the precedent of the 1987 Canada-United States Free Trade Agreement, concluded just as the Uruguay Round was getting underway.[125] It was however readily apparent that the

[117] de Witte, B., 'Trade in Culture: International Legal Regimes and EU Constitutional Values' in de Burca, F. and Scott, J. (eds), *The EU and the WTO* (Hart Publishing, 2001).

[118] On the architecture of the GATS, see Chapter 5.

[119] GATS, Article XIX.

[120] On New Zealand's abandonment of local content quotas because of GATS obligations, see Kelsey, J., *Serving whose interests?: the political economy of trade in services agreements*, (Routledge, 2008), 232.

[121] See Sauvé, P. and Steinfatt, K., n. 16 above, 326.

[122] On GATS Article XIV general exceptions, see Chapter 5. See also Voon, T., n. 110 above, 100–109 and 156–159, and European Broadcasting Union, *Audiovisual Services and GATS: EBU Comments on US Negotiating Proposals of December 2000* (12 April 2001).

[123] Falkenberg, K., 'The Audiovisual Sector', in Bourgeois, J., Berrod, F., and Fournier, E. (eds), *The Uruguay Round Results* (European University Press, 1995), 431.

[124] Ibid. The Canadian government had previously secured a cultural exemption from the obligations of the North America Free Trade Agreement (NAFTA) with the United States. However, the broad language of NAFTA's Article 2005 cultural exemption is restricted by the narrow language of Article 2012, which defines the particular culturally relevant industries that potentially benefit from 2005. NAFTA also gives Canada's trade partners the right to take equivalent discriminatory measures in other sectors in compensation for any measures Canada takes under Article 2005. See Cahn., S. and Schimmel, D., 'The Cultural Exception: Does it Exist in GATT and GATS Framework?', 15 *Cardozo Arts & Entertainment Law Journal* (1997), 281.

[125] Canada–United States Free Trade Agreement, Article 2005: Cultural Industries. A similar exemption was later incorporated into the North American Free Trade Agreement (NAFTA) Annex 2106 Cultural Industries. This exclusion also carried the condition that where one state party relies on it to establish measures that are otherwise inconsistent with the Agreement, the other party is entitled to take measures having equivalent commercial effect.

withdrawal of the audiovisual sector was likely to provoke other states to demand the withdrawal of other sectors from the GATS, killing or crippling the treaty.[126] The European Union proposed instead that the GATS treaty should include a special annex setting out key principles regarding the 'cultural specificity' of audiovisual services.[127] This would ensure that the future liberalization of trade in audiovisual services would be protected by principles that were themselves safe from the restrictive reading normally given to exceptions.[128] This proposal was however unacceptable to the United States.[129]

The resolution of the dispute over audiovisual services, which by the early 1990s had severely delayed the conclusion of the Uruguay Round, was essentially an agreement to disagree. Under the final agreement, audiovisual services are subject to the normal rules of the GATS. However, under those rules, the treaty's national treatment discipline only applies when a country has made a positive commitment in a services sector in relation to one or more modes of supply.[130] By refusing to make any commitments in the audiovisual sector, the European Union avoided those disciplines. It also blocked the application of the treaty's generally applicable 'most favoured nation' obligations by invoking the exceptional right to claim exemptions from the MFN provisions when becoming a party.[131]

Trade and culture in the Doha Round

The Uruguay Round compromise on audiovisual services was a moderate success for European negotiators. Refusal to make any commitments in relation to audiovisual services protected current European cultural measures, which could potentially be extended to the new internet media services that were beginning to be imagined.[132] Yet this pragmatic compromise had its obvious weaknesses. The incorporation of the audiovisual sector into the GATS, even without European commitments, created a presumption that audiovisual services are subject to the

---

[126] See Falkenberg, K., n. 123 above.

[127] World Trade Organization, Council for Trade in Services, *Audiovisual Services: Background Note by the Secretariat* (S/C/W/40) 15 June 1998. See also Stewart, T., *The GATT Uruguay Round: A Negotiating History (1986–1992)* (Kluwer, 1993).

[128] Communication from the European Communities to the Working Group on Audiovisual Services: *Draft Sectoral Annex on Audiovisual Services*, (MTN.GNS/AUD/W/2, 4 October 1990). The proposed annex also required a supporting clause in Article XX of the GATS granting parties a conditional right to resist progressive liberalization.

[129] See Falkenberg, K., n. 123 above.

[130] On the sectoral structure of the GATS, see Chapter 5.

[131] The European Union claimed broad MFN exemptions covering the right to impose redressive import duties and import quotas on film products, community subsidy programmes, bilateral and plurilateral preferential cultural cooperation agreements as well as protection for the definition of European origin for parties to the Council of Europe Convention on Transfrontier Television. Spain, Italy, and Denmark also claimed further MFN exemptions for specific national concerns. See Voon, T., n. 110 above, 113–117 on culture related MFN exemptions.

[132] Commission of the European Communities, *Communication on the Future of European Regulatory Audiovisual Policy*, Brussels, 15.12.2003 COM (2003) 784 final.

treaty's underlying principle of progressive liberalization. In addition, the communications revolution was already injecting a wealth of new uncertainties into the scope and application of WTO trade rules.[133]

On entering the Doha Round negotiations, the European Union insisted that audiovisual services, at least as far as the EU was concerned, would remain outside GATS disciplines indefinitely.[134] The concept of audiovisual services moreover should evolve to encompass new electronic services delivering audiovisual content to the public, which has become the crucial argument as the broadcast era has given way to the internet.[135] The EU's strenuous efforts to preserve its right to use protective cultural measures would rapidly dwindle in importance if these measures were treated as an exceptional public policy legacy confined to broadcast era services.[136]

The European long term strategy has therefore been to maintain flexibility or room to manoeuvre in the application of WTO rules to new communications services.[137] This approach is also consistent with the EU's internal regulatory framework for electronic communications, which is in principle based on technological neutrality and makes a clear distinction between content and infrastructure regulation.[138] Even before the Doha Round commenced, the European Commission proposed that the same principles should be applied within the WTO.

With regard to electronic commerce . . . it is important to stress that, in view of the position taken by the EU and its Member States on technological neutrality, any commitment or lack of commitment for an activity involving the supply of services is valid both when the services are supplied in the traditional way and when supplied electronically—unless otherwise specified. This means that cultural services that fall into the category of "electronic commerce" do not form a separate sub-category and should be considered to be part of the specific activity concerned.[139]

The United States pursued a radically different approach to electronic commerce and trade law.[140] It pushed for the development of rules to liberalize market access

---

[133] Peng, S.,'Trade in Telecommunications Services: Doha and Beyond', 41(3) *Journal of World Trade* (2007), 289–314.

[134] WTO Trade in Services, Conditional offer from the EC and its members states (29 April 2003), (<http://ec.europa.eu/trade/creating-opportunities/eu-and-wto/doha/submissions>). See also Pauwels, C. and Loisen, J., 'The WTO and the Audiovisual Sector. Economic Free Trade vs Cultural Horse Trading', 18(3) *European Journal of Communication* (2003), 291–313.

[135] European Commission, Directorate-General X, Consultation on GATS 2000 (February 1999). See also European Broadcasting Union, Audiovisual services and GATS negotiations. EBU contribution to the public consultation on requests for access to the EU market (January 2003).

[136] See Wunsch-Vincent, S., *The WTO, The Internet and Trade in Digital Products: EC-US Perspectives*, n. 116 above, 101–164, and Wunsch-Vincent, S., 'Trade Rules for the Digital Age' in Panizzon, M., Pohl, N., and Sauvé, P., *GATS and the Regulation of International Trade in Services* (Cambridge University Press, 2008).

[137] European Commission, Communication on the Future of European Regulatory Audiovisual Policy (15 December 2003) COM (2003) 784 final. See also Freedman, D., 'GATS and the audiovisual sector. An update', 1(1) *Global Media and Communication* (2005), 124–128.

[138] European Commission, 1999 Communications Review, COM (1999) 539 final (10 November 1999).

[139] Consultation on GATS 2000, n. 135 above.

[140] On the negotiation of rules for trade in electronic commerce, see Chapter 5.

for internet based services offering films, television programmes, music, games, and other digitized products. To do so, the American government argued that products downloaded from the internet should be treated as goods and therefore subject to the more demanding rules of the GATT.[141] Interactive audiovisual services, including on-demand audiovisual services, should moreover not be subsumed into existing services categories or subject to their regulatory regimes. At the same time, the United States offered a new compromise on traditional broadcast television services.[142] It dropped its insistence on the removal of discriminatory measures, but has demanded a commitment to maintain existing degrees of market openness for these services.[143] This would arguably increase transparency and predictability in the audiovisual sector, while also preserving the inbuilt flexibility of the GATS for state parties to protect cultural diversity.[144]

Quite separate from the issue of quotas and other discriminatory restrictions on trade in media services, the funding for public service media is potentially open to WTO disciplines, particularly where foreign competitors are directly disadvantaged.[145] For its part, the United States has expressed an intention to use the WTO to attack discriminatory subsidies affecting its audiovisual exports.[146] Provided the impasse over the audiovisual services sector is broken, it will certainly have the grounds to do so as subsidies are 'measures by Members affecting trade in services' and are thus subject to GATS disciplines. They are moreover unlikely to be fully protected by the major GATS exceptions.[147] The exemption for services 'supplied in the exercise of governmental authority' only applies to services that are supplied neither on a commercial basis nor in competition with other service suppliers.[148] This plainly does not include most public service media providers.

It is also unclear whether discriminatory cultural subsidies can be fully protected under the GATS Article XIV exception for measures necessary to maintain public order, which clearly has some application to public service media content that is directed at social cohesion and democratic pluralism. A member state would however have to show that its discriminatory subsidies were necessary to protect a 'fundamental interest of society' from a 'genuine and sufficiently serious threat'.[149] That is a high hurdle for purely cultural subsidies for films and dramas.

---

[141] Wunsch-Vincent, S., n. 116 above.

[142] Wheeler, M., 'Globalization of the Communications Marketplace', 5(3) *Harvard International Journal of Press and Politics* (2000), 27–44, [36].

[143] Office of the United States Trade Representative, United States Proposals for Liberalizing Trade in Services, Executive Summary (1 July 2002). See also European Broadcasting Union, Audiovisual services and GATS. EBU Comments on US negotiating proposals of December 2000, 12 April 2001.

[144] WTO, Council for Trade in Services, Communication from the United States—Audiovisual and Related Services, S/CSS/W/21 (18 December 2000). See also United States Proposals for Liberalizing Trade in Services, n. 143 above.

[145] Herold, A., 'European Public Film Support within the WTO Framework'. *IRIS Plus, Legal Observations of the European Audiovisual Observatory*, Issue 2003–6.

[146] Wunsch-Vincent, S., n. 116 above, 123.

[147] GATS, Article, I(1).   [148] GATS, Article 1(3).   [149] GATS, Article XIV, Footnote 5.

On the other hand, Doha Round negotiators have shown little appetite for creating strict disciplines for non-discriminatory subsidies under the GATS, preferring instead to aim for transparency and non-arbitrary application.[150]

Ironically, WTO efforts to impose disciplines on the domestic regulation of services pose a less important challenge to national cultural policy measures, despite the ferocious anxiety and criticism aroused by this element in the GATS.[151] Certainly, Doha Round negotiations to develop those rules, as mandated by GATS Article VI, are potentially far reaching, even though current proposals are comparatively weak.[152] Nonetheless, Article VI concerns non-discriminatory measures that are not already caught by GATS national treatment obligations or prohibitions on quantitative restrictions. It is aimed at apparently non-discriminatory measures that create unjustifiable obstacles to foreign competitors and their services. Protectionist cultural policy measures however by their nature usually discriminate against foreign media content. Where they are subject to a GATS sectoral commitment, they will face a serious challenge because of that discriminatory nature.

Trade and culture outside the WTO

The conflict between discriminatory cultural policies and international trade disciplines has remained an irresolvable issue for the WTO since the Uruguay Round. At present, there is no prospect that a cultural exception will be introduced into the WTO treaties. In launching the Doha Round, the state parties chose not to include the protection of culture in its key objectives, which focused instead on the Round's trade and development theme.[153] The United States, moreover, has not relaxed its determination to improve access to foreign media markets for its audiovisual and other entertainment exports.[154] States attempting to retain autonomy in cultural matters therefore have few advantages available within the WTO instruments, aside from the built-in flexibility of the GATS.[155] Consequently, they shifted their

[150] On the Article XV commitment to enter negotiations on subsidies, see Chapter 5. See also Adlung, R., 'Negotiations on Safeguards and Subsidies: A Never-Ending Story', 10(2) *Journal of International Economic Law* (2010), 235.
[151] See Bernier, I., 'Content Regulation in the Audio-Visual Sector and the WTO' in Géradin, D. and Luff, D. (eds), *The WTO and Global Convergence in Telecommunications and Audiovisual Services* (Cambridge University Press, 2004), 215–242.
[152] On the GATS VI negotiations on domestic regulation, see Chapter 5. See also Delimatsis, P., 'Due Process and 'Good' Regulation Embedded in the GATS—Disciplining Regulatory Behaviour in Services through Article VI of the GATS', 10(1) *Journal of International Economic Law* (2006), 13–50.
[153] Fourth WTO Ministerial Conference (Doha, November 2001): Ministerial Declaration, (WT/MIN(01)DEC/W/1). See also Neil, G., 'WTO's New Round of Trade Negotiations: Doha Development Agenda Threatens Cultural Diversity', *Report to International Network on Cultural Diversity*, 20 November 2001 (<http://www.incd.net>).
[154] See, for example, *China—Measures Affecting Trading Rights and Distribution Services for Certain Publications and Audiovisual Entertainment Products*, (WT/DS363/AB/R), (Appellate Body Report, December 2009).
[155] Roy, M., 'Audiovisual Services in the Doha Round: '*Dialogue de Sourds*, the Sequel?' 6(6) *Journal of World Investment & Trade* (2005), 923–952.

efforts to the creation of a new multilateral instrument outside the WTO, but with potential effects on the future development of global trade law.

While this initiative had many goals, its chief one was to provide a core statement of legal rights and obligations concerning cultural diversity capable of blunting the impact of multilateral trade rules on domestic cultural policies. It was, in short, an attempt to remedy the failure of these states to secure a cultural exception during the Uruguay Round. That failure did not immediately lead to a multilateral treaty initiative. In 1995, the G-7 Ministerial Conference on the Information Society adopted Core Principles for the development of national information societies, one of which declared the importance of cultural and linguistic diversity.[156] But this non-legally binding declaration merely captured the outlines of a vague consensus and did not begin to address the critical differences between states over the methods used to promote that diversity.[157] For states determined to retain autonomy in this field, an effective way forward needed specific rights declared in a legally binding form. In doing so, they would also engage one of the central issues of contemporary international law and politics: the relationship of WTO law with the broader field of public international law and its other specialized fields.[158]

On 18 March 2007, their efforts were finally rewarded with the coming into force of the UNESCO Convention on the Protection and Promotion of the Diversity of Expressions.[159] In the statemented Doha Round, this treaty was a signal event in the development of international law concerning trade in culturally sensitive goods and services. Its drafters sought to strengthen the position of culture in international law by emphasizing its human rights foundations and its special importance in the public policy interests of sovereign states. The Cultural Diversity Convention was thus aimed at transforming the patchwork of international declarations and obligations regarding the culture into a coherent set of legal rights that can be brought to bear on the treatment of trade in goods and services.

While the UNESCO Convention could not have been adopted without substantial European support, Canada is widely credited with initiating the treaty project. In 1997, Canada had lost the *Periodicals* case before the WTO Appellate Body, which had demonstrated the vulnerability of Canadian cultural measures to

---

[156] G-7 Ministerial Conference on the Information Society (February 1995), A Shared Vision of Human Enrichment, Principle 3: Serve cultural enrichment for all citizens through diversity of content: Citizens should be provided with access to all content, including a strong presence for indigenous cultural products and services. Diversity of content, including cultural and linguistic diversity, should be promoted.

[157] See, similarly, *Our Creative Diversity: The Report of the World Commission on Culture and Development* (UNESCO, 1995).

[158] On the relationship between the WTO treaties and public international law, see Chapter 5.

[159] UNESCO, Convention on the Protection and Promotion of the Diversity of Cultural Expressions (2005) entered into force 18 March 2007. The Intergovernmental Committee for the Protection and the Promotion of the Diversity of the Cultural Expressions, created under Article 23 of the Convention, first met in Ottawa, Canada, from 10 to 13 December 2007. See also Graber, C.B., 'Substantive Rights and Obligations Under the UNESCO Convention on Cultural Diversity' in Schneider, H., and van den Bossche, P. (eds), *Protection of Cultural Diversity from an International and European Perspective* (Antwerp, 2008).

its GATT obligations.[160] In that case, the United States had brought a complaint regarding discriminatory measures directed at American 'split run' magazines exported to Canada. The Canadian government had argued that these measures were necessary to protect the domestic periodical sector, which carried important benefits for Canadian culture. However, without a cultural exception in the GATT treaty, that argument could not be made directly in the WTO proceedings, in which Canada was found to be in violation of its national treatment obligations.[161] After the loss of the *Periodicals* case, the Canadian government looked for other ways to change the balance between trade obligations and domestic cultural policies.[162] In 1998, it organized the International Network on Cultural Policy, an intergovernmental association created to increase cooperation between countries wishing to safeguard national autonomy in cultural matters.[163]

During this period, sympathetic governments worked on a series of regional and international declarations stressing the importance of cultural diversity in international relations and the right to domestic autonomy in the cultural field.[164] These

---

[160] *Canadian Periodicals: Canada—Certain Measures Concerning Periodicals*, AB-1997–2, WT/DS31/AB/R, (WTO Appellate Body) (30 July 1997). See also Carmody, C.C., 'When Cultural Identity was not at Issue; Thinking about Canada: Certain Measures concerning Periodicals', 30 *Law and Policy in International Business* (1999), 231, and Voon, T., n. 110 above, 81–84. In May 1999 the Canadian and American governments reached a negotiated settlement following the decision of the WTO Appellate Body in which the principle of majority Canadian content was recognized but the discriminatory tax rules favouring publications based in Canada were substantially weakened.

[161] The WTO Appellate Body affirmed that 'imported split-run periodicals and domestic non-split-run periodicals are directly competitive or substitutable products in so far as they are part of the same segment of the Canadian market for periodicals', *Canada—Certain Measures Concerning Periodicals*, n. 160 above, 29. Any distinctively domestic cultural content in the Canadian publications did not affect that market based issue.

[162] See Voon, T., n. 110 above, 175–178. See also Cultural Industries Sectoral Advisory Group on International Trade (SAGIT), *New Strategies for Culture and Trade: Canadian Culture in a Global World* (February 1999).

[163] See Voon, T., n. 110 above, 178–180. At the same time, Canadian domestic organisations active in national cultural policy helped to found a parallel international body, the International Network on Cultural Diversity, to champion the domestic and international importance of cultural diversity and cultural rights. According to the INCD, its membership is 'open to organizations and individuals in the arts and culture communities who support our principles and our work' (<http://www.incd.net>).

[164] See, for example, the *Action Plan on Cultural Policies for Development* adopted by the 1998 UNESCO World Conference on 'Cultural Policies for Development', which emphasized the responsibility of governments to protect and develop culture; the 1999 UNDP Human Development Report '*Globalisation with a Human Face*', which also affirmed the right of states to protect cultural diversity while also encouraging cultural exchange (103); the Communiqué of the July 2000 Summit of the G-8, which endorsed the importance of cultural diversity; the Council of Europe *Declaration on Cultural Diversity*, adopted in December 2000, which set out key principles supporting cultural diversity and declared that '[c]ultural and audiovisual policies, which promote and respect cultural diversity, are a necessary complement to trade policies' (Clause 2.1); the 2001 *Cotonou Declaration* of the Cultural Ministers of the Francophonie, which affirmed that cultural goods and services should be given special treatment; the 2001 *Quebec Declaration* of the Summit of the Americas, which declared that 'respect for and value of our diversity must be a cohesive factor that strengthens the social fabric and the development of our nations'; the 2001 UNESCO *Universal Declaration on Cultural Diversity*, which declared in Article 11 that '[m]arket forces alone cannot guarantee the preservation and promotion of cultural diversity, which is the key to sustainable human development. From this perspective, the pre-eminence of public policy, in partnership with the private sector and civil society, must be reaffirmed'; the 2002 *Brixen/Bressanone Declaration on Cultural Diversity and the GATS* (adopted by the European

non-binding instruments, including the watershed 2001 UNESCO *Universal Declaration on Cultural Diversity*, created useful groundwork and momentum for a multilateral treaty.[165] By early 2003, the major states leading these efforts had agreed to use UNESCO as the forum in which to negotiate and adopt a binding, global agreement.[166] UNESCO was a difficult choice for this endeavour, given its troubled history in the media field.[167] But despite the NWICO debacle and the organization's poor relations with the United States, it had done much during the 1990s to reform its internal affairs and cultivate better relations with the major democratic states. Britain had returned to the organization in 1997, followed by the United States in 2003. In addition, American non-membership during the preparatory work on the UNESCO Declaration and the subsequent Convention made the organization better suited to the creation of a treaty vehemently opposed by the United States government. Even following re-admission, US representatives were likely to be less experienced in UNESCO's decision making processes.

Culture was also clearly within UNESCO's proper sphere of responsibility. The organization had moreover previously addressed several issues in the overlapping sphere of trade and culture. Shortly after its creation, the organization had sponsored the 1950 'Florence Agreement' on the import of objects of an educational, scientific, or cultural nature and its important 1976 Nairobi Protocol.[168] On the other hand, UNESCO's competence in cultural matters was not unlimited and, in particular, it had no authority to set rules for trade in goods and services. Any multilateral treaty negotiated under its authority would carry those limitations.

A UNESCO convention on the rights and obligations of states in the cultural field nonetheless had apparent potential to influence the development of trade law. The WTO Appellate Body's willingness to consider, albeit cautiously, the relationship between trade and external fields of law had opened new points of possible access.[169] The changing relationship between international trade and environmental law, in particular, created an attractive, albeit somewhat deceptive, precedent. International environmental obligations are not only well established in several

---

Regional Ministers for Culture and Education); and the 2003 *Declaration of Principles* of the World Summit on the Information Society, which affirmed the importance of cultural diversity to the growth of a global information society.

[165] See European Commission Communication, *Towards an International Instrument on Cultural Diversity*, COM (2003) 520 final.

[166] The Executive Board of UNESCO, during its 166th Session, decided to put the Convention on Cultural Diversity on the agenda of the General Conference in October 2003. See UNESCO, Executive Board, *Preliminary Study on the Technical and Legal Aspects relating to the Desirability of a Standard setting Instrument on Cultural Diversity*, 166 EX/28 (12 March 2003).

[167] On the UNESCO New World Information and Communication Order (NWICO) crisis, see Chapter 6.

[168] See UNESCO, Executive Board, *Preliminary Study*, n. 166 above.

[169] Perez, Oren, 'Multiple Regimes, Issue Linkage and International Cooperation: Exploring the Role of the WTO', *University of Pennsylvania Journal of International Economic Law* (Spring 2006). See also *United States—Import Prohibition of Certain Shrimp and Shrimp Products*, WT/DS58/AB/R, Report of the Appellate Body (12 October 1998), para. 129, and *Mexico—Tax Measures on Soft Drinks and Other Beverages*, Report of the Appellate Body, WT/DS308/AB/R (6 March 2006), paras 56 and 78.

major multilateral treaties, but it is a field of overriding international concern. Culture is, in comparison, a weak and fragmented field of international law and policy. While the UNESCO Convention is a significant step towards a more coherent concept of cultural sovereignty in international law, its influence on trade law is not assured.[170]

Culture, as an international legal concern, does have its obvious strengths. Although cultural issues arise in many areas of international law, the concept of a right to a cultural identity sits squarely within the field of human rights.[171] All three of the foundational instruments of international human rights law expressly include some form of cultural rights.[172] That strong association with human rights has advantages when governments assert that the cultural significance of trade in goods and services must be taken into account. Although international human rights law lacks the coherence and institutional strengths of trade law, a recognized human right widely accepted by WTO member states can nonetheless strengthen a public morals or public order based claim under GATT XX and GATS XIV.[173]

In other respects, this association between cultural diversity and human rights is less advantageous. Cultural rights, such as the right to a cultural identity or to participation in cultural life, are broad, ill defined ideas that stretch across all three generations of international human rights.[174] They are both individual and communal rights and even the rights of peoples. Yet these various cultural rights are not usually regarded as primary rights comparable to rights to freedom of conscience, expression, and association. They protect an essential dimension of human life, an outgrowth of human dignity, but also depend on the protection of those primary rights.

The role of primary rights in the protection of cultural diversity is, however, a critical and divisive problem. In the liberal tradition, primary rights are held by individuals and are, in large measure, intended to protect the individual from state interference with personal freedom. Thus, on one view, restrictions on access to foreign content through screen or broadcast quotas or discriminatory subsidies are unjustifiable restrictions on that freedom. Alternatively, where those restrictions are

---

[170] On the aims of the sponsoring states, see European Commission, Communication to the Council and European Parliament, *Towards an international instrument on cultural diversity* COM (2003) 520 final.

[171] UNESCO Declaration on Cultural Diversity, Article 5: 'Cultural rights are an integral part of human rights, which are universal, indivisible and interdependent.' See also Almqvist, J., *Human Rights, Culture and the Rule of Law* (Hart Publishing, 2005); Stamatopoulou, E., *Cultural Rights in International Law: Article 27 of the Universal Declaration of Human Rights and Beyond* (Brill, 2007); and Francioni, F., and Scheinin, M. (eds), *Cultural Human Right* (Leiden, 2008).

[172] Universal Declaration of Human Rights, Articles 22 and 27, International Covenant on Civil and Political Rights, Article 27, and International Covenant on Economic, Social and Cultural Rights, Article 15.

[173] On the general exception provisions of the GATT and GATS, see Chapter 5.

[174] UNESCO, Executive Board, *Preliminary Study*, n. 166 above, 'International law still does not clearly define cultural rights; nor does it determine exactly which rights fall into that category. What is more, provisions pertaining to cultural rights are scattered about in various international instruments, which impairs consistency and understanding of cultural rights as a whole.' See also Almqvist, J., n. 171 above.

proportionate, these are justifiable measures for ensuring that distinctive national and local cultural traditions continue to enrich individual freedom of choice. From that perspective, cultural diversity is not only enjoyed through the exercise of primary rights, but is also a precondition to the effective exercise of those rights.[175]

The UNESCO Convention draws heavily on the human rights associations of culture. Its preamble, for example, celebrates, 'the importance of cultural diversity for the full realisation of human rights and fundamental freedoms proclaimed in the Universal Declaration of Human Rights and other universally recognized instruments'.[176] The treaty also affirms the right of states to adopt an exceptional range of measures to protect or promote the diversity of domestic cultural expression.[177] It therefore embraces the idea that liberal democratic values are consistent with state intervention to ensure that individual choice occurs within a culturally diverse context, including a strong representation of local languages and traditions. Nevertheless, the drafters included other provisions that limit the scope and purposes of any national measures taken to advance cultural policy goals. Article 2:1 states that

[c]ultural diversity can be protected and promoted only if human rights and fundamental freedoms, such as freedom of expression, information and communication, as well as the ability of individuals to choose cultural expressions, are guaranteed. No one may invoke the provisions of this Convention in order to infringe human rights and fundamental freedoms as enshrined in the Universal Declaration of Human Rights or guaranteed by international law, or to limit the scope thereof.[178]

Article 2:8 also introduces a principle of 'openness and balance', which obliges states to seek to promote, in an appropriate manner, openness to other cultures of the world.

Regardless of its close association with human rights, the UNESCO Convention was not constructed in the mould of a human rights treaty, which typically sets out the specific rights of individuals and the corresponding duties of states. The Convention is more concerned with the autonomy of states in cultural matters. As Article 2(2) states, 'States have, in accordance with the Charter of the United Nations and the principles of international law, the sovereign right to adopt measures and policies to protect and promote the diversity of cultural expressions within their territory.'[179] Those measures are then spelled out in Article 6 in broad, unconditional terms.

---

[175] See, for example, Article 27, ICCPR: UN Human Rights Committee, General Comment 23, Article 27, The Rights of Minorities, UN Doc. HRI\GEN\1\Rev.1 at 38 (1994). See also European Framework Convention for the Protection of National Minorities, ETS No. 157.

[176] See also UNESCO Convention on Cultural Diversity, Article 1.

[177] Ibid., Article 6.

[178] The UNESCO General Conference was clear on this matter in 32C/Resolution 34 endorsing plans for a convention, explicitly: 'Emphasizing the importance of Article 19 of the Universal Declaration of Human Rights, which declares that everyone has the right to freedom of information and expression, including the freedom to seek receive and impart information and ideas through any media and regardless of frontiers.'

[179] See also UNESCO Convention on Cultural Diversity, Article 5(1): 'The Parties, in conformity with the Charter of the United Nations, the principles of international law and universally recognized human rights instruments, reaffirm their sovereign right to formulate and implement their cultural

This invocation of sovereignty is critical to the UNESCO Convention's relationship with WTO trade law. The autonomy of sovereign states in essential domestic matters is the basis on which the GATT and GATS treaties recognize specific, express exceptions to trade disciplines. The Convention, while plainly outside the sphere of trade law, uses that model, claiming a similar right to autonomy in cultural matters.[180] Whether the boundary between trade law and the developing field of cultural law is permeable enough to make this parallel claim effective has been widely debated.[181] A strong association with sovereignty moreover clouds the human rights foundations of the right to cultural diversity argument. In international law, human rights are typically claimed by individuals, who possess rights against the state or, less often, rights to compel the state to take action. The Convention instead primarily sets out the rights of states. If cultural diversity is truly grounded in human rights, under this treaty it is the state that acts on behalf of individuals and communities to realize those rights.

In choosing to address the relationship between trade and culture in a non-trade law forum, the states sponsoring the UNESCO Convention were faced with the limitations as well as the advantages of that forum shifting strategy.[182] There was an obvious risk that instead of engineering a productive coincidence of obligations, the Convention would instead create conflict or confusion.[183] In adopting the final text, however, the negotiating states drew back from that possibility, deciding that the Convention should not give even the impression that its obligations were intended to supersede those of the GATT and GATS.[184] The final version of Article 20 of the Convention therefore makes a direct clash of UNESCO Convention and WTO treaty obligations reasonably unlikely. That Article states that, '[n]othing in this Convention shall be interpreted as modifying rights and obligations of the Parties under any other treaties to which they are parties'. If taken literally, this will mean that the Convention will not modify the rights or obligations of the parties under both existing and future WTO agreements. The dispute

---

policies and to adopt measures to protect and promote the diversity of cultural expressions and to strengthen international cooperation to achieve the purposes of this Convention.'

[180] UNESCO, Executive Board, *Preliminary Study*, n. 166 above: 'Such an instrument should also ensure that each State is free to define its cultural policies, its cooperation agreements and its partnership initiatives in a global world.'

[181] See, for example, Voon, T., 'UNESCO and the WTO: A Clash of Cultures?' 55(3) *International and Comparative Law Quarterly* (2006), 635. Craufurd Smith, R., 'The UNESCO Convention on the Protection and Promotion of the Diversity of Cultural Expressions: Building a New World Information and Communication Order?' 1 *International Journal of Communication* (2007), 24–55; Graber, C., 'The New UNESCO Convention on Cultural Diversity: A Counterbalance to the WTO?' 9 *Journal of International Economic Law* (2006), 553–574; and Hahn, M., 'A Clash of Cultures? The UNESCO Diversity Convention and international trade law, 9 *Journal of International Economic Law* (2006), 515–552.

[182] On forum shifting, see Chapter 3.

[183] Vienna Convention on the Law of Treaties, 1155 UNTS 331, Article 30.

[184] Craufurd Smith, R., n. 181 above, 45–46.

resolution provisions of the Convention are also largely consensual and effectively non-binding. There is consequently little risk of parallel, enforceable proceedings.[185]

On the other hand, Article 20 also asserts that the Convention is not subordinate to any other treaty. This assertion supports the argument that the Convention should be taken into account when its provisions are relevant to the interpretation of rights and obligations stemming from WTO treaties.[186] This could occur where the Convention is treated as a special agreement applicable to relations between those states that are party to both the Convention and the WTO treaties. That issue, however, would almost certainly take place within the WTO dispute resolution processes. In its previous decision, the Appellate Body has generally looked at the WTO agreement at issue for a convincing reason to rely on a principle or rule of law from a non-WTO source.[187] In many cases, there will be no 'textual anchor' that will justify a reference to the rules of the Convention.[188]

The Convention may also have an important role in guiding, or at least influencing, the future conduct of its parties. Article 20(1)(b) states that, 'when interpreting and applying the other treaties to which they are parties or when entering into other international obligations, parties shall take into account the relevant provisions of this Convention'. This provision could affect how state parties individually manage the relationship of Convention and WTO rights and obligations. A state may, for example, accept that it is bound, as a party to the Convention, to permit a proportionate use of the cultural policy measures listed in Article 6 to the full extent possible under a favourable interpretation of the GATT or GATS. The Convention may also be used as a point of reference in future WTO or bilateral negotiations, potentially binding the negotiating positions of its parties.[189]

While the European Union and other regional bodies and state parties have proclaimed the global importance of the UNESCO Convention, the United States has refused to become a party.[190] It voted almost alone against the adoption of the text in the UNESCO General Conference in 2005 and has objected that the treaty will not only interfere with WTO law but also provide a pretext for illegitimate

---

[185] See Voon, T., n. 110 above, 195–198 on the possibility of using the Convention procedures in circumstances where a state has used its rights under WTO agreements in a manner that is inconsistent with its obligations under the UNESCO Convention.

[186] See Voon, T., n. 110 above, 202–215.

[187] Under the Dispute Settlement Understanding, the Appellate Body or the Panels are not permitted, in their recommendations or rulings, to add to or diminish the rights and obligations provided in the WTO covered agreements: *WTO Understanding on Rules and Procedures governing the Settlement of Disputes*, Article 3.2.

[188] Graber, C., 'The New UNESCO Convention on Cultural Diversity: A Counterbalance to the WTO?' 9 *Journal of International Economic Law* (2006), 553–574.

[189] See ibid. See also Neuwirth, R., 'The "Culture and Trade Debate" Continues: The UNESCO Convention in Light of the WTO Reports in China—Publications and Audiovisual Products: Between Amnesia or Déjà-Vu?', 44 *Journal of World Trade* (2010), 1333.

[190] See, for example, Council of Europe, Committee of Ministers, Recommendation on the remit of public service media in the information society, Rec (2007)3 , Committee of Ministers Recommendation on measures to promote the public service value of the Internet, CM/Rec (2007) 16, Part IV diversity). See also Case C-222/07, *Unión de Televisiones Comerciales Asociadas* (UTECA), n. 44 above, para. 33.

restrictions on the free flow of information.[191] The American government has also vigorously pursued its trade interests through the negotiation of bilateral agreements on trade and investment. In these agreements, the United States has secured greater access to foreign information and entertainment markets as well as favourable treatment of internet delivered, digital content.[192] In bilateral agreements with the United States, several WTO member states that had refused to make commitments concerning audiovisual services during the Uruguay Round have accepted major obligations in this sector.[193] In relation to the traditional media, such as broadcast radio and television, the American negotiators have conceded rights to retain existing discriminatory measures, such as local content quotas in exchange for increased market access for US providers.[194] In exchange, the United States has obtained greater access for its new media services and secured favourable ground rules for trade in electronic commerce, thus achieving some of its key negotiating objectives for the Doha Round.[195]

Bilateral and regional trade and investment treaties are likely to have a major influence on future WTO negotiations on global trade in media content. Having committed themselves to these bilateral trade relationships with the United States, the states concerned have effectively accepted many of its arguments for liberalizing trade in media services and internet based services more generally. The United States is not however alone in taking advantage of the Doha Round stalemate to advance its trade interests through bilateral agreements. Bilateral and regional preferential trade and investment agreements have proliferated, containing a diverse range of economic interests and policy positions.[196] In its agreements with non-member states, the European Union has, for example, pursued managed cooperation in a broadly defined audiovisual sector, including joint production agreements.[197]

---

[191] Riding, A., 'U.S. Stands Alone on UNESCO Cultural Issue', *New York Times*, 13 October 2005.

[192] Wunsch-Vincent, S., *The WTO, The Internet and Trade in Digital Products: EC-US Perspectives* (Hart Publishing, 2006), 126. See also Wunsch-Vincent, S., 'The Digital Trade Agenda of the U.S.: Parallel Tracks of Bilateral, Regional and Multilateral Liberalization', 58(1) *Aussenwirtschaft* (March 2003).

[193] Roy, M., Marchetti, J., and Lim, H., *Services Liberalization in the New Generation of Preferential Trade Agreements (PTAs): How Much Further than the GATS?* Staff Working Paper ERSD-2006–07 September 2006, World Trade Organization, Economic Research and Statistics Division. See also the 2004 Australia—United States Free Trade Agreement and the (as yet unratified) 2007 United States—Korea Free Trade Agreement, and see Breen, M., 'Digital determinism: culture industries in the USA-Australia Free Trade Agreement', 12(4) *New Media Society* (June 2010), 657–676.

[194] Roy, M., Marchetti, J., and Lim, H., n. 193 above.

[195] Ibid. See also Wunsch-Vincent, S., 'Treatment of electronic commerce in bilateral PTA's: Trade Rules for the Digital Age' in Panizzon, Pohl, and Sauvé (eds), *GATS and the Regulation of International Trade in Services* (Cambridge University Press, 2008), who comments that, '[t]he PTA e-commerce chapters appear next to the chapter on trade in goods and the chapter on cross-border trade in services without addressing the question of the classification of digital products', 657.

[196] The website <http://www.bilaterals.org> maintains a comprehensive resource of text and commentary on preferential trade and investment treaties.

[197] European Commission, Communication *Towards an international instrument on cultural diversity*, (27 August 2003) COM (2003) 520 final, Article 151.3: 'The Community and the Member States shall foster co-operation with third countries and the competent international organisations in

Disputes about culture and trade have always been closely related to changes in media technologies and services. In the 1930s, European governments responded to the popularity of American cinema films with screen quotas and later applied similar measures to restrict the import of American television programmes. For the time being, import restrictions remain an important trade barrier where cinemas and linear television channels are still the primary outlets for the first release of culturally significant, major audiovisual products. Some forms of new media, such as domestic on-demand audiovisual services, are moreover susceptible to content quotas.[198] Broadband internet connections have however now given many households in liberal democracies direct access to foreign based, online audiovisual services. Viewed from this perspective, the cultural policy argument has reached its end game as linguistic and cultural goods and services wash ceaselessly across porous borders through a multitude of connections, from film downloads to social network blog posts. Yet, collective identity and social cohesion remain the essential glue for territorially based states, in particular liberal democratic ones, and their governments will continue to pursue cultural policies that engender that sense of identity and cohesion. For the foreseeable future, quotas will enjoy a declining but strategic role, while subsidies for domestic production and distribution will undoubtedly flourish where national finances permit.

the sphere of culture, in particular the Council of Europe.' See also Article 27 on 'Cultural development' of the Cotonou Agreement, Chapter III on 'Partnership in social, cultural and human affairs: developing human resources, promoting understanding between cultures and exchanges between civil societies' of the 1995 Barcelona Declaration founding the new Euro-Mediterranean Partnership, and Article 5 of Protocol 3 on Cultural Co-operation of the 2009 EU-Korea Free Trade Agreement, (signed October 2010), granting conditional entitlement for co-produced audiovisual works to benefit from EU and South Korean local or regional cultural content promotion schemes.

[198] See, for example, Directive 2010/13/EU, Article 13 and Recital (70), n. 59 above.

Index